Lecture Notes in Computer Science   11585

Commenced Publication in 1973
Founding and Former Series Editors:
Gerhard Goos, Juris Hartmanis, and Jan van Leeuwen

More information about this series at http://www.springer.com/series/7409

Aaron Marcus · Wentao Wang (Eds.)

Design, User Experience, and Usability

Application Domains

8th International Conference, DUXU 2019
Held as Part of the 21st HCI International Conference, HCII 2019
Orlando, FL, USA, July 26–31, 2019
Proceedings, Part III

 Springer

Editors
Aaron Marcus
Aaron Marcus and Associates
Berkeley, CA, USA

Wentao Wang
Zuoyebang, K12 education
Beijing, China

ISSN 0302-9743   ISSN 1611-3349   (electronic)
Lecture Notes in Computer Science
ISBN 978-3-030-23537-6   ISBN 978-3-030-23538-3   (eBook)
https://doi.org/10.1007/978-3-030-23538-3

LNCS Sublibrary: SL3 – Information Systems and Applications, incl. Internet/Web, and HCI

This Springer imprint is published by the registered company Springer Nature Switzerland AG
The registered company address is: Gewerbestrasse 11, 6330 Cham, Switzerland

Foreword

The 21st International Conference on Human-Computer Interaction, HCI International 2019, was held in Orlando, FL, USA, during July 26–31, 2019. The event incorporated the 18 thematic areas and affiliated conferences listed on the following page.

A total of 5,029 individuals from academia, research institutes, industry, and governmental agencies from 73 countries submitted contributions, and 1,274 papers and 209 posters were included in the pre-conference proceedings. These contributions address the latest research and development efforts and highlight the human aspects of design and use of computing systems. The contributions thoroughly cover the entire field of human-computer interaction, addressing major advances in knowledge and effective use of computers in a variety of application areas. The volumes constituting the full set of the pre-conference proceedings are listed in the following pages.

This year the HCI International (HCII) conference introduced the new option of "late-breaking work." This applies both for papers and posters and the corresponding volume(s) of the proceedings will be published just after the conference. Full papers will be included in the *HCII 2019 Late-Breaking Work Papers Proceedings* volume of the proceedings to be published in the Springer LNCS series, while poster extended abstracts will be included as short papers in the HCII 2019 *Late-Breaking Work Poster Extended Abstracts* volume to be published in the Springer CCIS series.

I would like to thank the program board chairs and the members of the program boards of all thematic areas and affiliated conferences for their contribution to the highest scientific quality and the overall success of the HCI International 2019 conference.

This conference would not have been possible without the continuous and unwavering support and advice of the founder, Conference General Chair Emeritus and Conference Scientific Advisor Prof. Gavriel Salvendy. For his outstanding efforts, I would like to express my appreciation to the communications chair and editor of *HCI International News,* Dr. Abbas Moallem.

July 2019   Constantine Stephanidis

HCI International 2019 Thematic Areas and Affiliated Conferences

Thematic areas:

- HCI 2019: Human-Computer Interaction
- HIMI 2019: Human Interface and the Management of Information

Affiliated conferences:

- EPCE 2019: 16th International Conference on Engineering Psychology and Cognitive Ergonomics
- UAHCI 2019: 13th International Conference on Universal Access in Human-Computer Interaction
- VAMR 2019: 11th International Conference on Virtual, Augmented and Mixed Reality
- CCD 2019: 11th International Conference on Cross-Cultural Design
- SCSM 2019: 11th International Conference on Social Computing and Social Media
- AC 2019: 13th International Conference on Augmented Cognition
- DHM 2019: 10th International Conference on Digital Human Modeling and Applications in Health, Safety, Ergonomics and Risk Management
- DUXU 2019: 8th International Conference on Design, User Experience, and Usability
- DAPI 2019: 7th International Conference on Distributed, Ambient and Pervasive Interactions
- HCIBGO 2019: 6th International Conference on HCI in Business, Government and Organizations
- LCT 2019: 6th International Conference on Learning and Collaboration Technologies
- ITAP 2019: 5th International Conference on Human Aspects of IT for the Aged Population
- HCI-CPT 2019: First International Conference on HCI for Cybersecurity, Privacy and Trust
- HCI-Games 2019: First International Conference on HCI in Games
- MobiTAS 2019: First International Conference on HCI in Mobility, Transport, and Automotive Systems
- AIS 2019: First International Conference on Adaptive Instructional Systems

Pre-conference Proceedings Volumes Full List

34. CCIS 1033, HCI International 2019 - Posters (Part II), edited by Constantine Stephanidis
35. CCIS 1034, HCI International 2019 - Posters (Part III), edited by Constantine Stephanidis

http://2019.hci.international/proceedings

8th International Conference on Design, User Experience, and Usability (DUXU 2019)

Program Board Chair(s): **Aaron Marcus, *USA*, and Wentao Wang, *P.R. China***

- Sisira Adikari, Australia
- Claire Ancient, UK
- Jan Brejcha, Czech Republic
- Silvia De los Rios, Spain
- Marc Fabri, UK
- Josh Halstead, USA
- Wei Liu, P.R. China
- Yang Meng, P.R. China
- Judith Moldenhauer, USA
- Jingyan Qin, P.R. China
- Francisco Rebelo, Portugal
- Christine Riedmann-Streitz, Germany
- Elizabeth Rosenzweig, USA
- Patricia Search, USA
- Marcelo Soares, P.R. China
- Carla G. Spinillo, Brazil

The full list with the Program Board Chairs and the members of the Program Boards of all thematic areas and affiliated conferences is available online at:

http://www.hci.international/board-members-2019.php

HCI International 2020

The 22nd International Conference on Human-Computer Interaction, HCI International 2020, will be held jointly with the affiliated conferences in Copenhagen, Denmark, at the Bella Center Copenhagen, July 19–24, 2020. It will cover a broad spectrum of themes related to HCI, including theoretical issues, methods, tools, processes, and case studies in HCI design, as well as novel interaction techniques, interfaces, and applications. The proceedings will be published by Springer. More information will be available on the conference website: http://2020.hci.international/.

General Chair
Prof. Constantine Stephanidis
University of Crete and ICS-FORTH
Heraklion, Crete, Greece
E-mail: general_chair@hcii2020.org

http://2020.hci.international/

Contents – Part III

DUXU for Well-Being

DUXU for Learning

DUXU for Automated Driving, Transport, Sustainability and Smart Cities

Designing the Way We Move: From Navigating the Users to Users of Navigation Devices

Carlos Alberto Barbosa[(✉)]

School of Communication, Arts, Design, and Fashion,
Anhembi Morumbi University, Rua Jaceru 247, 04705000 São Paulo, Brazil
carlosalberto.barbosa@gmail.com

Abstract. This article discusses the relationship between information generated by GPS navigation applications and the appropriation and significance of urban spaces by these applications' users in large urban areas such as the city of São Paulo, Brazil. Although applications such as *Waze* make life easier for drivers in cities with dense road networks and daily commutes riddled with heavy traffic jams, they also promote a change in the perception and significance of cities' physical spaces. Hanssen [9] recalls that "what Benjamin teaches us is how sensation gets repeatedly transformed in ways that necessarily tighten the circuit binding human perception with its technical supplementation" [9, p. 63]. In this text, ubiquitous technology is interpreted as what may promote not only a transformation in human perception of territory but also a change of what Milton Santos named as used territory [16].

Keywords: Design · Philosophy · Cities

1 Introduction

The metropolitan region of São Paulo (Brazil) is one of the world's most populous areas and has a considerably large fleet of vehicles moving daily through its street-and-road network. In 2018 the Traffic Department – DETRAN [4] reported the existence of over 8.6 million vehicles in the city of São Paulo. In addition to the sum of other cars from the neighboring cities, the metropolitan area of São Paulo presented a daily average of 300 km of congestion in 2013 and the estimation of hitting around 350 km of daily congestion by 2020 [8]. In this scenario, navigation apps with geolocation systems have become almost mandatory onboard items. These devices guide "disoriented" drivers, facilitate the choice of routes and help to avoid the city's heaviest traffic areas and most congested points. Such applications are the driver's "eyes" foreseeing the way to go.

All this technological advantage offered by navigator apps can also charge a price: the perceived territory is modified. The application-mediated driver no longer needs to set waypoints along the route he travels. His attention to the cardinal points is restricted to the north on a digital map interface, and gradually he is shifted from the concreteness of the city to the virtual interaction with a screen. The resulting perceived city by the

A. Marcus and W. Wang (Eds.): HCII 2019, LNCS 11585, pp. 3–13, 2019.
https://doi.org/10.1007/978-3-030-23538-3_1

driver became transformed as the city itself occupies another territory, which has distinct characteristics from the one that preceded the existence of such applications. Are these changes positive or negative? Is the technology that operates on the city territory harmful to the signification of urban space? In fact, such judgment derives from a false point, since technology *per se* does not contain enough elements to re-signify the territory, as it will be discussed throughout this text.

This work assumes that new forms of interaction with the city introduce new possibilities of re-signifying the territory. Therefore, this paper does not discuss the positive or negative aspects of relations with urban space. It purely proposes a reflection concerning technology, as Bull [3] pointed out "the impact that these technologies have on the fabric of everyday urban life is complex and multifaceted both structurally and individually". From the structural point of view, as it is discussed below, a relation between systems of which the human agent is a fundamental part, not only as an observer but and mainly as the organizer and operator of these systems, must be considered. What this work proposes, therefore, is to relate navigation devices and apps to the new ways of perceiving, operating and organizing the territory and discussing the possibility to propose new meanings for used territories, considering the resources derived from navigation apps.

For that purpose, this text first presents the notion of used territories as a result of an interrelation of different systems [15–17]. In the sequence, the text presents the relation of means and purpose of technology as pointed by Feenberg [5, 6], and finally, the guiding concepts of two final projects developed by undergraduate students of a Digital Design Bachelor Program are presented, which proposes experiences of re-signifying the used territory from navigation apps.

2   Territory, Technical Systems, and Used Territory

According to Santos and Silveira [15], geographic space is the result of a set of interrelated systems. They are the systems of objects, of actions, and their hybrid forms, which are the techniques. Technical systems "include, on one hand, materiality and, on the other, its ways of organization and regulation" [15, p. 20]. Therefore, technique is understood as a set of forces that result not only in objects in which technology is embodied, but also implies the dynamics of using such technology. In other words, it implicates the purpose of the use as well as the conditions of the environment where it affects. This environment upon which technical system operates is the geographical environment, which is only constituted by means of technique operating over the geographic space. Consequently, "there is no such thing as a geographical environment on one side and a technical environment on the other. What has always been created from their fusion is a geographical environment" [16, p. 24]. Furthermore, for the authors, such techniques, or hybrid systems, are indicators of the territory's use and through them, one can reconstitute the historical context of the territory itself.

This geographic space, generated by the interaction of systems, consists the used territory which "points out to the necessity of an effort meant to systematically analyze the constitution of a territory" [15, p. 20]. If in the past the constitution of used territory was related to the production of concrete objects which physical materiality was capable of transforming the territory itself, nowadays used territories are reconfigured and constituted not only from physical objects, but also from informational devices that affect the relationship between the territory occupant and the occupied territory itself. That is the case of GPS navigator apps, which can reconfigure the use of territory by directing a greater or lesser flow of vehicles to a particular area. Thus, used territory is seen dialectically as a whole. It is the synthesis of the simultaneous different actions and technical systems that operate upon it, just as it is a fundamental element for defining the type and quality of the actions undertaken, as "a territory conditions the location of actors, since the actions that operate upon it depend on its own constitution" [15, p. 22]. Therefore, this text follows the authors' conclusion that "territory, seen as unity and diversity, is a central issue in human history" [15, p. 20].

City's inhabitant constitutes and repositions new places on the territory whenever geolocation and navigation technologies mediate the covered territory. Besides, when making use of navigation devices for traveling, a driver, this provisional occupant of a particular urban space, is not ruled just by the materiality of the covered territory or by the information available in the mobile interface, since individually neither the informational technology nor the physical territory are able to determine and configure such places. That also implies the conclusion that, if both of them are individually unable to determine and signify places, neither are they able to impose and dictate what kind of use should be made of each territorial space.

3 Authoritarianism, Territory, and Technology

In this sense, Feenberg [6] also points out that technologies are usually seen as repositories of authoritarianism and alienation, but this is a naive vision if political intentions and government actions hidden technological developments, are not taken into account. For the author, "What human beings are and will become is decided in the shape of our tools not less than in the action of statesmen and political movements. The design of technologies is thus an ontological decision fraught with political consequences" [6, p. 03]. To those who attribute to the subject the ability to impose his will, regardless of any technological mediation, Feenberg [6, p. 63] recalls that "subjects and means are dialectically intertwined [...] The army is not merely accidentally related to their weapons, but is structured around the activities they support". Santos [17, p. 59] points to the same direction when asserting that "it is evident that technique alone does not explain anything" as well as the technique linked to "organizational forms of labor, be it in space, in time, or in the domain of relations among agents" [17, p. 59] do not stand the domination relations. According to Santos [17], in addition to these two factors, it must be considered the capacity of these agents to influence the political environment outside their organization of labor and action. As they manage to influence politically in a wider environment that contains their ways of production and transformation. Thus, the author concluded, "the study of techniques goes far beyond, this way, purely technical data and demands a much deeper incursion into its social relation area" [17].

The deeper incursion in social relations was a central concern of Jacobs' [11] when she wrote in 1961 her classic The Death and Life of Great American Cities, and also of

Henri Lefebvre's in 1968, in his work The Right to The City (Le Droit à La Ville) [12], heir to the discussions engaged by the Situationists [10].

In the introduction to her work, Jacobs [11] points out a methodological concern which reflects the understanding of the city as a dynamic and clashed space. The author intends to analyze "how cities work in real life, because this is the only way to learn what principles of planning and what practices in rebuilding can promote social and economic vitality in cities, and what practices and principles will deaden these attributes" [11, p. 4]. Therefore, Jacobs does not want to discuss aspects related to the difference between planned and accomplished, but why, for example, certain public spaces change with use, while other similar spaces do not have the same destination. These dynamics of differences "are not a form of chaos. On the contrary, they represent a complex and highly developed form of order" [11, p. 222], which assists in the spatial location and identity construction of city dwellers. For Jacobs, "scenes of thorough-going sameness lack these natural announcements of direction and movement or are scantily furnished with them, and they are deeply confusing. This is a kind of chaos" [11, p. 224].

In an article published in Le Monde Diplomatique, in 1989, Lefebvre [13] points out that the modern city corresponds to the deterioration of social relations, and that "since the end of the 19th century, cities in most developed countries have experienced an extraordinary growth, kindling considerable hopes. But, in reality, city life has not produced entirely new social relations" [13, p. 203]. This concern was present on Lefebvre's critical horizon in 1968, when he published Le Droit à la Ville. What is new in the 1989 text is the concern with new outlines of social relations scattered in the city due to new technologies that had already been presented in a dramatic and accelerated way, and whose emergence "leads simultaneously to new ways of organizing production and new ways of organizing urban space. The latter interact in ways that are mutually detrimental rather than beneficial" [13, p. 203]. It should be remembered that Lefebvre died in 1991, about two years after the original publication of the article. So, the author did not experience the advent and popularization of the Internet, and even less the Internet of Things – IoT ubiquity.

Digital technologies, ubiquity and IoT have changed the experience of territory occupation. But were they in fact totally and *per se* prejudicial to the urban experience and the territory's occupation? Would not Lefebvre be aligned with what Feenberg [5] called technological determinism? Maybe technologies have widened the possibilities of appropriation and significance of urban space by the inhabitants of large cities? Even further, do such technologies also embody the political elements which determine and exert authoritarian power over the meaning of urban space? In cities like São Paulo, strongly marked by individual motorized transportation [14], how do navigation applications interfere with and signify (or not) urban spaces?

When we take a look at the cities and at the way their inhabitants deal with the formation of these small and large agglomerations of people on a piece of land, it is inevitable to remember that urban agglomerations have been the subject of most varied authors and have been present in texts since the classical period [7]. But two periods of time call attention to the impact of these changes on recent history. The first one comprises the time that ranges from the mid-nineteenth century to the mid-twentieth century, after the two World Wars. Throughout this period, new technologies have directly interfered with urban life and the skyline of big metropolises. The liberal city of the nineteenth century, as Benevolo [2] named it, was well marked for the numerous infrastructure works, such as gas, electricity and mass transportation, apart from the new technologies and building materials that made it possible to erect buildings much faster and reaching heights that had never been seen before. On the other hand, the period between wars was marked by rationality in the architectural and urbanistic projects, which resulted in large functional urban spots as an expression of the modern city [2].

To all this technological domain as well as to the policies of territory occupation during that period – which set the conformation upon urban space and promoted new arrangements of its use - corresponded a series of counter-movements warning to a curtailment of the individual before the collective. An imposition of private desires disguised as universality [6, p. 33]. The period after World War II had the role of discussing the consequences of technology that operated on urban territory, thus, evidencing the conflict between the individual and the collective, the totality and its parts. From the Situationist texts to Jacobs' and Lefebvre's classics [10–12], urban life and city conformation were marked not only by technology but also by the clash between planned area and inhabited area, built space and experienced space, domination and freedom. This clash of forces reveals not only the struggles within the built-up cityscape but a dynamic system that reacts to imprisonment. Opposed to what a simplistic view suggests, leading to technological determinism, it is through the dynamism of conflict that the city reacts and shapes itself. Used territories, as seen before, is built by clashes, as a living body that reacts to being stimulated. A body as alive as the society that inhabits it, dismantling, renovating and rebuilding the territory and its meanings.

4 Navigating the Used Territory: Navigation Devices and Their Modes of Organization and Regulation of Territory

If there is an authoritarian and hegemonic sense in used territories, it must and can also be perceived in its condition of transience, which is the constitution of a totality condition. Harvey points out that it is not necessary to wait for "great revolutions" to constitute new spaces [10, p. 22]. They are in everyday life, in the fabric of the perceived, observed and reflected life. Such spaces must be recognized in a city where not only the inhabitants are moving, but also where there is intense mobility of information [20] that constitutes new types of occupations and relations with used territory. The mobility of information draws to a possible autonomy in the face of the city physical structure. The information circulates over the built city dimensions, determining routes, establishing parameters of consumption and delivering goods. The city dweller, stand and still, physically gains in space and mobility through his connectivity with social networks which then bring in new experiences of territorial occupations and which, in their turn, were generated by technical informational environment [16]. These environments, as previously explained in this text, are hybrid, once they are constituted both by the materiality and by the organization and regulation modes [15]. Today we follow the impacts that the hybrid environments' updates cause in the fluidity of used territories. Santos [15–17], who died in 2001, did not fully experience the organization and regulation modes of hybrid environments associated with their ubiquitous condition and their materiality associated with information networks through IoT. These new technical informational territories are hybrid in a double sense. First, because the organization and regulation mode is not detached from the system of objects, but embodied in the object itself. The geographic space is miniaturized in the very object that is organized and regulated by algorithms. Second, because the other agent of transformation involved in changes that reconfigure the territory - the human agent - became part of the variables operated by software algorithms embodied in the objects.

Supported by satellite geo-referencing (GPS) systems, and on mobile data hubs loaded into the system by users themselves, navigation devices have the potential to constantly reconfigure used territories. One *Waze* user, for example, establishes navigation parameters for many others whose route, designed by the application, passes by the same point that is occupied by him. Data, which remain available in the geolocation coordinates and act on the algorithm system variables, constitute an used territory, even in an ephemeral way, and allow "to think of territory as an actor and not only as scenario, that is, territory in its active role" [15, p. 11].

Ideally, this condition provides data so that the involvement in occupying the territory through these applications becomes a rich experience in transience since data is continually changing. However, it is possible to observe that the system eventually establishes a recurrence of information generated by the user's routine, which, in a way, is addicted and interdicts significant changes in the algorithm calculations of these routes. It is also possible to observe that the human agent, who relates itself with the system's interface, experiences time and space through the new scenario of used territory formed from the hybridization of the physical object, the physical environment, and data available in the navigated coordinates. This new experience may abandon the physical territory as the primary geographic space. In this case, with the eyes stuck in the navigator app interface, the user risks approaching the experimentation of city space as the chaos of a "thoroughgoing sameness", using Jacobs' words [11]. Navigating through the cell phone interface makes building facades, shops, and corners differences vanish away. Gradually the cardinal points and the spatial references are reduced to the verticality or horizontality of the application interface. Routes are determined by algorithms that guide the user through the paths that have already been contemplated by others or by his own routine. There are no longer discoveries, surprises or even curious looks towards the urban landscape. The inhabitant displaces himself from the city as he dominates it in a touch of fingers on the screen. Thus, the constitution of new used territories and the idea of territorial fluidity become jeopardized.

5 *Waze* and the Used Territory

The occupation of metropolitan space by vehicles in a city like São Paulo is not only mediated by technology but also produced by the interaction link comprising users, physical territory and technology. Another element to consider remains in the fact that systems such as *Waze* are powered by mobile hubs of information that are generated and distributed amongst users as they travel throughout the city. This information network that overruns the physical space of the metropolitan territory would shape the way that city is occupied, significantly changing the flows and concentration of automobiles in different city areas.

According to data released by *Waze* [19], there are now more than 90 million active users of the app in the world, spread across 185 countries. Data sent to and collected from the system make the application much more than a navigation aid interface. *Waze* is a social network based on information flow that spreads from physical space to digital interface, through geolocation points provided by the users themselves, along with data of speed, direction and time of movement. The interrelationship of these different "spaces" forms a peculiar hybrid territory, with its specificities and own mode of territorial occupation. With the proposal of facilitating the movement through the road-and-street network of large urban centers, the application quickly established also a strategy of selling advertising space by using travel data collected from users. Information ranging from traffic situations to data that increases traffic in certain areas may support the expansion of local commerce [1]. As an example, in Brazil, between May and June 2015, Adidas took about 7,000 customers to their stores through ads on *Waze*. Remarkably, the increase of ad recall for the brand during the same period hit 295% [18].

Once the navigation app has its monetary income tied to demands of advertisers' interests, it would come as no surprise if at least in part, the routes suggested by the algorithms would consider stores' location data linked to advertisers, or some other element strange to the objective of merely avoiding traffic and quickly taking the user to a particular destination. Thus, the indicated routes might not be precisely the result of hybridization in which the user is conscious of his own routes' options. Again, the user can easily be exposed to the "sameness" observed by Jacobs [11] or, as Feenberg pointed out "technologies is thus an ontological decision fraught with political consequences" [6, p. 3] or economic consequences.

6 Overcoming Sameness and the New Used Territories

Within the context, of opposing users to the sameness or to the heteronomy which determines the routes and occupations of territories, two final undergraduate projects from Digital Design students at Anhembi Morumbi University (São Paulo, Brazil) were proposed. The idea behind the projects was to destabilize the navigation apps users' looks, launching them into a proposal of resignification and new territorial occupations enabled by geolocation data. Without losing the goal of the user's territorial movement from one point to another. What the projects propose, therefore, is a re-conquest of the urban territory.

The first of these projects, produced in 2015, is called Tangled (*Emaranhado*) (see Fig. 1). In this project, from the moment a user establishes its starting point and intended destination, the application searches for previous record of the same origin and destination pair selected by the same user. If there is a previous record, the application calculates and suggests a new route within a certain perimeter, but different from that one previously traveled by the same user. Thus, a routine journey, such as moving from home to work or study, would be systematically altered without compromising the starting and finishing points. The user would move through different routes within a given area, both consuming and generating data for different occupations of territories, thereby promoting discoveries and occupations of the environment.

Fig. 1. User of the app "Tangled" (*Emaranhado*), image composite made from material provided to the examining board of group thesis available on *Behance*. https://www.behance.net/gallery/32001331/Emaranhado-(TCC)

The second project named Revisit (*Revisite*), was produced in 2018 and proposed a reorganization of the boundaries and limits of neighborhoods, having as starting point the experiences of city dwellers with their own visited and reconsidered spaces. Once again, the origin and destination intended by the user are respected, but what is intended is to establish a geographic division of the city based on the areas of interest and of territory's re-significances proposed by the user. The boundaries established by the political-administrative divisions of districts are used as a reference in order to match the searching criteria of destination intended by users (see Fig. 2). The user profile will display a specific city map, resulting from places the user has passed by and occupied. Records of such occupations remain as data available to new users, from the moment they also get to these territories, and become able to collaborate with images and readings about that environment too, whereas constituting, over the same space, their own territory.

Fig. 2. Composite of images made from material provided to the examining board of group thesis available on *Behance*. https://www.behance.net/gallery/72784683/REVISITE

Both projects end up responding to concerns that are held dear in a democratic society, once they oppose the perpetuation of a dominant model which allow little space for different forms of organizing the territory.

In the specific case of navigation applications, the discourse that legitimates the indications for routes is sheltered in the logic "the faster, the better". That is the same rationality of capital and markets that justify modes of control and organization of territory according to what is good for markets and production modes. However, are lives and the most private interests of individuals actually considered by the logic and pace imposed by markets? After all, as Feenberg [6, p. 163] points out, "The question is not just who profits but what way of life is determined by the markets". If the logic coming from the markets and the rhythm of a hallucinating timing perpetuate a dominant model of space occupation and experience, a critical design "must undermine the standard of rationality that defines it" [6, p. 163].

By proposing trips that are not determined by the dynamics of an accelerated time, or by the pre-established boundaries of the dominating territory occupation, these projects collaborate to undermine the standard of rationality that defines such dominant occupations transcending dominant interests. They also promote different individual views in the collective space, providing new experiences and new used territories.

7   Final Considerations

From what was discussed so far, two aspects of the relationship between GPS navigation applications and territory can be considered from the concepts of technique as a hybrid system and used territories. The first one concerns the relationship between the navigation applications and their circumstances regarding the setting of territorial occupations. Devices such as *Waze*, which receives a massive flow of information in areas where the app is frequently used, have the effect of determining "flows" to certain regions of the city, establishing routine routes which lead the user to focus on the instructions from the application interface, transforming what could be an experience of diversity and attention to the physical plan of the city in an experience of a relationship with a digital interface, and in so doing, it is close to the "sameness" pointed out by Jacobs [11].

The second aspect to be considered calls attention to the possibilities that the same technology, able to withdraw the user from the navigation experience around the city, can also be an experience of re-signification and occupation of territories. According to the final undergraduate projects presented, it is possible to establish contact with the city by using information streams that help in the process of territory re-signification. As it was seen, technology *per se* does not submit or free users from heteronomy experiences. Technology may leverage territory re-signification exercise and even stimulate new appropriations, once it is part of a hybrid technical system that evokes the materiality of objects, information streams, and space transformed into used territory. Not only is human perception broadened with technical systems, but new territories are created. Therefore, it is possible that technical systems also play a pivotal role in the expression and exercise of criticism on used territories.

References

1. Ask, J.: Google acquires waze: what it means. Forrester research, 11 de 06 de 2013 (2013). https://go.forrester.com/blogs/13-06-11-google_acquires_waze_what_it_means/. Accessed 22 Dec 2018
2. Benevolo, L.: História da cidade, 5th edn. Perspectiva, São Paulo (2012)
3. Bull, M.: The end of flânerie: ipods, aesthetics, and urban experience. In: Ekman, U. (ed.) Troughout: Art and Culture Emerging with Ubiquitous Computing, pp. 151–162. Michigan Institute of Technology Press, Cambridge (2013)
4. Departamento de Trânsito DETRAN (2018). Frota de Veículos em SP - por tipo de veículo. Detran.sp. https://www.detran.sp.gov.br/wps/wcm/connect/portaldetran/detran/detran/Estatis ticasTransito/sa-frotaVeiculos/d28760f7-8f21-429f-b039-0547c8c46ed1?presentationtemplate= portaldetran%2FAT-detranPaginaODetranImpressao. Accessed 12 Jan 2019
5. Feenberg, A.: Democratic rationalization: technology, power, and freedom. In: Scharff, R.C., Dusek, V. (eds.) Philosophy of Technology: the Technological Condition - An Antology, pp. 652–665. Blackwell Publishing, Malden (2003)
6. Feenberg, A.: Transforming Technology. Oxford University Press, New York (2002)
7. Fernandes, J.A.R., Meirinho, J.F.: Cidades ideais, ideias de cidade, cidades reais. In: Pereira, P.C. (ed.) Filosofia e a cidade, pp. 127–157. Campo das Letras, Porto (2008)
8. Gandra, A.: Custo de congestionamentos no Rio e em São Paulo atinge R$ 98 bilhões. Empresa Brasil de Comunicação EBC, July 2014. http://agenciabrasil.ebc.com.br/economia/noticia/2014-07/custo-de-congestionamentos-no-rio-e-sao-paulo-atinge-r-98-bilhoes. Accessed 01 Jan 2019

9. Hansen, M.B.N.: Ubiquitous sensation: towards an atmospheric, collective, and microtemporal model of media. In: Ekman, U. (ed.) Throughout: Art and Culture Emerging with Ubiquitous Computing. Massachusetts Institute of Technology Press Book, Cambridge (2013)
10. Harvey, D.: Cidades rebeldes: do direito à cidade à revolução urbana. Martins Fontes, São Paulo (2014)
11. Jacobs, J.: The Death and Life of Great American Cities. Vintage Books, New York (1992)
12. Lefebvre, H.: O direito à cidade. Centauro, São Paulo (2001)
13. Lefebvre, H.: Dissolving city, planetary metamorphosis. Environ. Plann. D: Soc. Space **32** (2), 203–205 (2014). https://doi.org/10.1068/d3202tra
14. Menezes, C.: Cidade de São Paulo tem 7,4 veículos para cada 10 habitantes, aponta levantamento da CET, August 2018. https://g1.globo.com/sp/sao-paulo/noticia/cidade-de-sp-tem-74-veiculos-para-cada-10-habitantes-aponta-levantamento-da-cet.ghtml. Accessed 22 Dec 2018
15. Santos, M., Silveira, M.L.: O Brasil: território e sociedade no início do século XXI, 9th edn. Record, Rio de Janeiro (2006)
16. Santos, M.: A natureza do espaço, 4th edn. Editora da Universidade de São Paulo, São Paulo (2006)
17. Santos, M.: Técnica, espaço, tempo, 5th edn. Edusp, São Paulo (2013)
18. Waze: Waze for brands - Adidas. https://www.waze.com/brands/success/adidas/. Accessed 23 Dec 2018
19. Waze: Waze for brands: data driven. https://www.waze.com/brands/drivers/. Accessed 22 Dec 2018
20. Wisnik, G.: Estado crítico: à deriva nas cidades. Publifolha, São Paulo (2009)

Study on the Usability of Residential Buildings in Traditional Villages in Southern China from the Perspective of Human Settlements

Yali Chen[1(✉)], Jiongjiong Yuan[2], and Qi Lu[3]

[1] School of Design, South China University of Technology, Guangzhou, China
chenyali@scut.edu.cn
[2] School of Architecture, Huaqiao University, Quanzhou, China
[3] School of Architecture, South China University of Technology,
Guangzhou, China

Abstract. The paper explored the building renewal technology and the wisdom in the constructions of traditional villages in southern China through the quantitative analysis of the statistical data. The eco-environment deterioration has gradually become a serious and innegligible problem in China. The paper explored the ecological energy-saving technology and the wisdom in the constructions of traditional villages in southern China through the quantitative analysis of the statistical data. It revealed that modern technology has been integrated into traditional energy-saving technology for further development and it proposed to strengthen the systematic instruction and management for better development of ecological system and human settlement environment. It provides the usability of residential buildings in traditional villages in southern China from the perspective of human settlements.

Keywords: Traditional villages · Living environment ·
Ecological development

1 Introduction

Energy-saving, environmental protection and sustainable development have become the theme of the world. Traditional houses contain rich and simple green design concept, the overall design reflects the natural, energy saving and environmental protection design guiding ideology, covering the human and natural low consumption goals, advocate the use of renewable resources, pay attention to the use of geographical and local technology, Protect the ecological environment, to achieve the sustainable development of the building. Traditional residential construction technology focuses on technical suitability and nature, and seeks to update and develop the traditional architecture technology. It emphasizes the combination of construction technology and regional climate, natural resources and ecological environment, and explores the sustainable development of buildings in the natural ecological sense Technical design ideas. Thus, it is important to explore and understand the eco-energy-saving technologies and construction technologies in traditional villages, which may help us better to achieve sustainable development in traditional villages.

© Springer Nature Switzerland AG 2019
A. Marcus and W. Wang (Eds.): HCII 2019, LNCS 11585, pp. 14–28, 2019.
https://doi.org/10.1007/978-3-030-23538-3_2

The coupling research of ecosystem and practical life has become a hot topic in the fields of human settlements and been successively carried out by governments and scholars. In this paper, we analyzed the literatures published in the past 20 years in this field, and summarized the results. The research may help to provide instruction and reference for the development of ecosystem in traditional villages in Southern China. There are more than 1,600 related publications on the ecological development in domestic environment of human settlements from 1995 to 2016 through survey and statistics from the CNKI database. These researches involved in urban planning, landscape, ecology, geography, sociology and many other disciplines, which have been mainly distributed in 10 research directions (Fig. 1). Environmental Science and resources utilization is the most concentrated one.

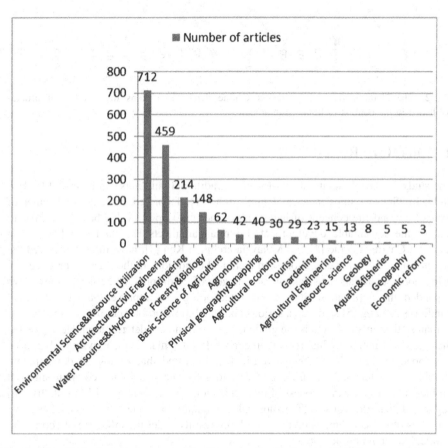

Fig. 1. The field of ecological coupling literature distribution in CNKI's view of human settlements.

From 1995 to 2017, more than 140 articles on ecological development in the context of human settlements have been collected in the Netherlands Science Direct Online database. The annual publications have kept increasing since 2003 as shown in Fig. 2.

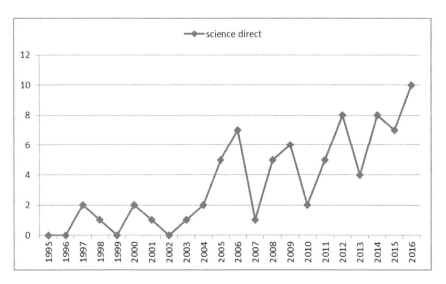

Fig. 2. The Netherlands Science Direct Online database contains the number of articles published in the context of human settlements.

2   Literature Review

The study on energy-saving technologies in traditional buildings can be traced back to 1894. In "Seven Lamps in Architecture", John [1] elaborated the natural attributes of technology and the concept of handicrafts. The philosophy in this book is similar to that of the sustainable development. Egyptian architects Hassna Fathy [2], Indian architect Charles Corrae [3] and Malaysia architect Ken [4], have fully considered the architectural economic conditions and technical conditions in their design practice. By using local materials and taking advantages of traditional technology, they have expanded the application of traditional technology to improve the environmental conditions. Zhang [5] said that a serious and inneligible problem in the construction of human settlements in China is the gradual eco-environment deterioration. He suggested that the construction of human settlements and better management system should be developed together. Yu, Wang and Lin [6] suggested that ecological development should be considered as an important way to solve the social and eco-environmental problems t caused by the process of modernization. Turnar et al. [7], ELD-Initiative [8] suggested that the causes of ecological degradation include the direct destructive activities of human beings and the underlying results under the influence of economic, political and cultural activities.

The wisdom for the adaptation of Chinese traditional houses to the climate could be seen everywhere. Wang [9] proposed and discussed the two main aspects in construction, including climatic factors and the adaptation to climate. Zhao [10] refined the climate regulation technology of the traditional buildings through the prototype analysis of the development of traditional building's architectural form. Bai and Liu [11] analyzed the mechanism of adapting to dry and heat, and the big temperature difference between day and night as well as other climate characteristics of houses in Xinjiang province. The subtropical area of the Xia Linqi [12] systematically expressed the modern theory that the building heat protection should conform to the local climate in the subtropical area. Professor Tang [13] of Guangzhou university combined the method of classification summary, formula derivation and local measurement to quantitatively analyze the elements of Chinese traditional architecture in the south to adapt to the hot and humid climate. On the basis of the summary of the traditional ventilation wisdom, Zeng [14] has applied the effective ventilation experience of the traditional houses to the modern engineering design. Vitiello [15] proposed to integrate multidisciplinary (architecture, landscape science, natural environment, demography and anthropology) into the framework of the ecological research framework, emphasizing the need to develop the idea of ecological development in the View of Human Settlements within a broader framework of environmental compatibility. Vemuri et al. [16] emphasized that the study of the theory and method of ecological development in the context of human settlements must be a consideration of economic factors, social factors and ecological factors, dependent on population resources, building resources, natural resources and the co-ordination of social resources. Costanza [17] argued that the ecological service performance of human settlements ecosystem is the ability to derive benefits (social, economic, and human health) from human ecosystems; MEA [18] has identified ecosystems The ecological service performance can be qualitatively and quantitatively analyzed from multiple levels. Boumans [19] constructed the GUMBO model to quantitatively explore the ecological service performance of the ecosystem and provide a scientific and rational basis for the ecosystem assessment. Quantitative analysis means. Robert, Pastorok et al. [20] in their framework for the construction of ecological decision-making clearly put forward the ecological development project requires a professional, full planning and monitoring system, pointed out that the living environment should involve policy and institutional research. Matthias [21] emphasized that public management in ecological coupling should involve professionals with different subject backgrounds throughout.

3 Research Method

It is a typical hot and humid climate in Southern China. The summer is long and hot. The winter is cold and short. When people are in a certain environment will have a corresponding heat adaptation, then the hot and humid areas of rural residents how to adapt to heat, we conducted a thermal comfort-related survey and residential samples of the test analysis.

According to the types of rural residential areas in southern China, combined with their distribution characteristics and climatic conditions, the experimental subjects selected several typical farmers in Houtian Village, Heshan Village, Houxi Village and Army camp Village in southern China to carry out indoor thermal environment. Basic characteristics as shown in the following Table 1: Houtian village villagers to the traditional fishery, close to the beach life, the climate has typical coastal climate characteristics, residential use mainly to self-occupied, residential building structure is mainly mixed structure, reinforced concrete structure Combined with brick or mixed in the bottom of the case for the stone houses in the case of the upper combination of mixed structure; against the village of the villagers to pay salaries and rental mainly to the traditional village homestead building form, its building density, climate and environment Similar to the characteristics of urban inland climate, residential building structure is mainly reinforced concrete structure combined brick-based; Houxi village villagers to pay the main, new village building density, climate similar to the characteristics of urban inland climate, residential The structure is mainly based on reinforced concrete structure combined brick-based; Army camp village living on the hillock above the highest elevation, the majority of the villagers to traditional agriculture for a living, residential self-occupied and production activities of the regional functions, new residential The building structure is mainly mixed structure, reinforced concrete structure combined with brick-based. Army camp village measured the object has two farm houses, but in order to better and lower altitude of the farm to compare, the main choice of which the highest elevation of 160 farm house for comparative analysis. It is shown in Fig. 3 that the test sample house layout and measurement control points.

Table 1. Samples of rural residential survey in southern China

Location of farmhouse	Altitude (m)	Building density	Building materials	Structure form	Test place
Houtian Village (Cui Heng Village) No. 467 (object 1)	20	High	Brick and reinforced concrete	Hybrid structure	Living room, bedroom
City Village No. 24 (object 2)	9.5	High	Brick, wood and stone	Hybrid structure	Living room
Pan Tu community No. 44 (object 3)	14	High	Stone and reinforced concrete	Hybrid structure	Living room, bedroom
Army camp village (Gu pai village) 160 (object 4)	300	High	Stone and brick	Hybrid structure	Living room

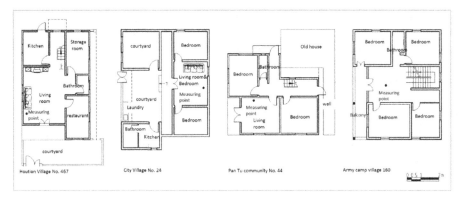

Fig. 3. Test sample house layout and measurement control points

4 Data Collection and Analysis

4.1 Basic Characteristics of Indoor Thermal Environment and Analysis of Air Temperature in South China

China's rural areas in southern China are widely distributed. In the context of the summer heat and warm (southern) climate of the large area, the local climate and environment are different due to the different geographical environment of the rural residential areas. The environment has obvious characteristics. Take the altitude of the different conditions for the classification, the altitude from low to high followed by the seaside village one after another Tamura, inland villages one by one against the village and after the village, mountain village one armor village. According to the finishing of the research data, the basic characteristics of the indoor thermal environment of rural residential areas in southern China are shown in following Fig. 4.

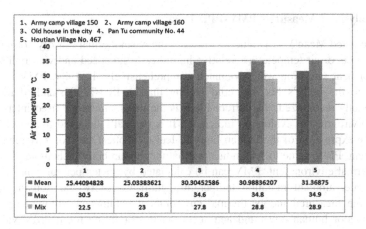

Fig. 4. Comparison of average temperature, maximum and minimum values of indoor temperature in summer in 2015

Comparison of the air temperature between the different measured objects The maximum, minimum, average and change trend of the air temperature of the measured objects 1, 2, 3 and 4 are shown in Fig. 4. The average temperature of the farmhouse in the barracks village is the lowest, and the temperature of the farmhouse in the city is the highest. The temperature change of the farmhouse and the barracks in the city is more intense. House temperature changes are more stable. Summer farmhouse indoor temperature in 2015 is shown in Fig. 5.

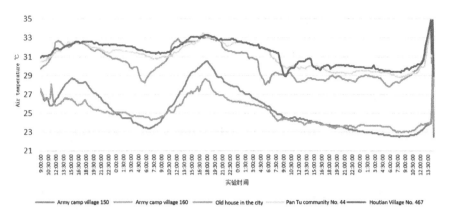

Fig. 5. Comparison of indoor temperature of rural households in 2015

4.2   Analysis of Measured PMV-PPD Data

PMV (Predicted Mean Vote) value was used as the mean thermal sensory voting index, and the effects of air temperature, relative humidity, wind speed and wall radiation on the indoor heat sensation were evaluated comprehensively. In 1984, PMV-PPD corresponds to the body's hot and cold feeling that as ISO-7730 standard has been internationally recognized, the current PMV is the most commonly used international thermal environmental evaluation indicators. It is generally believed that −0.15 PMV 0.15 is the expression of the human body to feel the hottest and comfortable thermal environment, PMV value to 1.6, indicating that the human body feels more discomfort to this thermal environment. PMV can be calculated by air temperature, air humidity, air flow rate, ambient radiation temperature, human activity and human clothing. Through the measured indoor thermal environment parameters, combined with the summer indoor human dress and activities, the indoor living room PMV value, the results shown in Fig. 6. The results showed that the PMV average was the most close to the thermal comfort interval, and the comfortable time period was longer than that of the rest of the experimental subjects. The experimental results were similar to those of the experimental subjects 1 and 3, and the measured data showed that the PMV of the experimental object 1. The PMV of the experimental object 2 was similar to that of the experimental object 4, and the PMV of object 2 was lower than that of the experimental subjects 1 and 3, but the thermal stability of the experimental subjects 2 and 4 were worse than that of other experimental subjects. It is shown in Fig. 6.

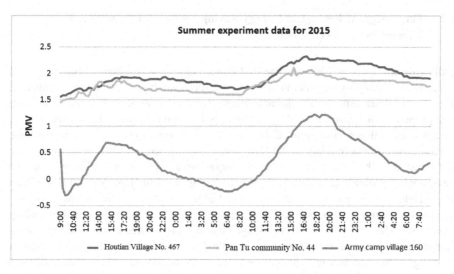

Fig. 6. Summer measured data PMV calculated value

5   Discussion

5.1   The Characteristics of Indoor Thermal Conditions in Traditional Villages in Southern China

(1) The change trend of the indoor temperature of the typical Chinese rural house is similar to that of the external environment, but the change of the terrain and the environment has the greatest influence on the thermal environment of the farmhouse. The highest temperature of the farmhouse has the highest temperature, the maximum change range, the indoor thermal environment The worst stability.

(2) For the buildings with similar orientation and material structure and similar structure, the indoor temperature convergence and the changing relationship are also convergent. The stability of the indoor thermal environment is similar to that of the modern concrete frame mixed structure. The use of the main building materials for the stone and red brick of the traditional rural house temperature is lower, but the magnitude of change.

(3) The layout of the village has a large influence on the thermal environment of the farmhouse, the high terrain height and the layout of the village are in line with the dominant temperature, and the thermal comfort is high, that is, the layout of the villages conforming to the climatic characteristics of the dominant wind direction is favorable The formation of a more comfortable indoor greenhouse thermal environment.

(4) The trend of the design of the experimental object is different, and the data show that the trend of temperature changes has nothing to do with the basic, the terrain is very close, different towards the temperature difference between the farm house is not large, we can see the building towards the rural areas of southern China's indoor heat The environment is a decisive factor.

5.2   The Design of Ecological Energy-Saving System for Traditional Villages in Southern China

Following the Law of Nature. The traditional villages in southern China have been planned reasonably by consideration of the site selection, layout, ventilation, sunshine, climate and other aspects. Traditional village living environment emphasizes the natural properties of houses, according to geographical conditions and terrain relations to organize the village environment. In the case of harmonious coexistence with the natural environment to adapt to the local life, the residence to follow here, rather than the other, and thus the formation of a unique humanities, geomorphology and the environment. China's Guangdong Province, Zhongshan Cui Heng Village is the Pearl River Delta alluvial plains into the sea typical of the traditional villages, the village on three sides around the mountains, east to the sea, just in the mountains of water holding the central. The vast majority of the village buildings are located in west, facing to east, leaning against the three sides of the Castle Peak, facing the Pearl River estuary blowing to the sea breeze. The village's location and layout reflects the traditional Chinese nature fully respect the concept, in line with possession of the wind together, yin and yang in the feng shui theory, and the surrounding terrain and landscape natural landscape to achieve harmony and unity. Its spatial pattern in the landscape shape, feng shui forest, feng shui tree, wind reservoir is formed under the sign of the pattern of settlement, and it is formed that the "mountain - farm - village - water - road" space corridor between the plow head of the mountain and the golden champagne hill. By emphasizing the traditional living environment combined with geographical conditions, relying on the mountain and river, homeopathic construction, a natural energy saving design idea is expressed. Figure 7 showing the settlement pattern of Zhongshan Cuiheng village which reflect law of nature "mountain - farm - village - water - road".

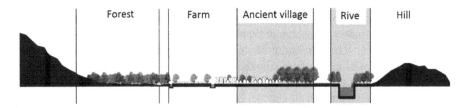

Fig. 7. Zhongshan Cuiheng Village "mountain - Farm - village - water - road" Road law natural settlement pattern

Adapting to Local Climate. The traditional living environment in southern China has been adapted to the regional ecological and climatic conditions and architectural functions, shape and space and other elements, through the appropriate architectural forms and appropriate technical measures, control of natural conditions and favorable climate resources to obtain the thermal environment of the building environment, Creating a low-energy and comfortable living environment. Residential sites to avoid the wind speed of the top of the mountain and pass, as well as valleys and depression, and choose back to ying and facing to yang, back to mountain facing to water, screening winter cold at the same time to meet the summer cool breeze, settling near river to facilitate living water, to avoid flooding, while regulating the village micro-climate. Because of the design wisdom of the climate is also reflected in the traditional layout of the traditional residential space, to show the unique natural terrain and climate blend of group spatial characteristics. As shown in Fig. 8, the south of the village is designed to face the water. While in Fig. 9, the layout of the village is planned according to the shape of watery region.

Fig. 8. Planned design: the south of the village is facing to the water (Nanshe Village, Dongguan)

Fig. 9. Freestyle: the layout is according to the shape of watery region (Songtang Village, Foshan)

5.3   The Construction Technology for Ecological Energy-Saving in Traditional Villages in Southern China

The construction technology of traditional villages in southern China is a kind of construction method which is homogeneous with the local natural environment, and has simple ecological thoughts. It is based on local conditions for the characteristics of the technical system. This simple eco-technology is based on the analysis of the ecological environment and climate in the area where the building is located, and selects the most suitable type of building technology, including building type, tectonic technology, ventilation cooling and climate change.

Modeling Design. The traditional villages in southern China, which focus on the overall layout, are simple in size and have fewer bumps, so the building body size is smaller, thus reducing the heat transfer area. China's southern region has both warm and hot summer weather, and thus the traditional houses from the space layout, form of treatment and structural material design on the ground. Winter architectural space convergence closed in order to facilitate insulation, summer expansion and open to facilitate ventilation and cool air. The difference of thermal conductivity between the outer surface of the same volume under different volume is very different, so the pursuit of the same volume of the lower body surface area of the smallest residential building space form is the preferred way of traditional Chinese houses in southern China, the building size coefficient is the smallest, Low, less energy consumption. Residential buildings are mostly regular rectangle or square form and its combination, bump changes are relatively small, to achieve ecological energy and economic principles. As shown in Fig. 10, the traditional design of the new houses in the traditional houses in southern China.

Fig. 10. The graphic design of the newly built residence in the traditional village homestead in South China

Adjusting the Ecological Environment Through Natural Ventilation Technology.
China Southern residential building space natural ventilation technology using the patio, the atrium and the combination of the layout of the organization of ventilation. The interior of the building is open space, circulation, the room into the deep, hall wide and high, doors and windows, windows and windows formed to wear the wind, so that the air convection and heat. This patio is both an air outlet and an outlet. The wind in the summer, the patio in the sun exposure under the hot air transpiration, hot air rising, patio or side courtyard wind to form negative pressure area, cool breeze from the courtyard around the room into the courtyard, or both sides of the street cooling air Through the channel, to the patio continue to add the formation of hot and cold air temperature convection, hall, high windows and doors between the air flow, forming a

good wind, constitute a natural energy-saving natural ventilation system to achieve the purpose of summer natural cooling. Traditional houses in the many natural ventilation measures, adapt to the climate and automatically adjust. In addition, some houses in the courtyard set the water, because the water in the air there is the temperature difference, will form a wind cycle, take the indoor hot air, which play a role in indoor ventilation, lower room temperature, with cooling effect. China Southern traditional village houses through reasonable design, relying on the construction itself to form a wind cycle, which significantly adjust the indoor temperature, saving energy while regulating the environment microclimate. Figure 11 Ventilation design of the new houses in the traditional village house in southern China.

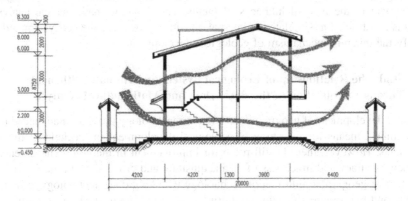

Fig. 11. Sectional ventilation design of new folk house in traditional Chinese village homes in South China

6 Conclusion

Traditional houses contain rich and simple green design concept, the overall design reflects the natural, energy saving and environmental protection design guiding ideology, covering the human and natural low consumption goals, advocate the use of renewable resources, pay attention to the use of geographical and local technology, Protect the ecological environment, to achieve the sustainable development of the building.

China's traditional ecological energy design in the south of the island is due to natural, mountain on the potential of the natural terrain to achieve the greatest degree of fit; the overall layout of the space to consider the winter wind and summer natural ventilation, and strive to the summer ventilation, winter wind unity; Reduce the building shape coefficient, increase the green planting surface and water to effectively solve the building in summer heat insulation and winter heating needs; in the residential space design in the use of courtyard, patio and stairs and other adjustable space technology strategy to achieve energy saving design purpose.

The layout of the village has a large influence on the thermal environment of the farmhouse, the high terrain height and the layout of the village are in line with the dominant temperature, and the thermal comfort is high, that is, the layout of the villages conforming to the climatic characteristics of the dominant wind direction is favorable The formation of a more comfortable indoor greenhouse thermal environment. In the building environment, the local people feel very comfortable user experience.

6.1 Strengthening the Study on the Internal Relationship of Ecological System and Human Settlements

In the future research process, we should strengthen the study of the internal mechanism of ecological development in the field of human settlements, strengthen the application of complex system theory and computer simulation technology in the field of ecological development, combined with the theoretical framework of ecological development in the field of human settlements. The dynamic mathematical analysis model is constructed to simulate the internal operation process of the ecosystem and to identify the inherent mechanism of ecological development.

6.2 Study the Relationship of Ecological System and Human Settlements Through Acquisition of the Basic Data and Mathematical Analysis

The rapid development of geographic information technology provides a advanced and rich technical means for the study of ecological development in the field of human settlements. However, there is still room for improvement in the comprehensiveness, accuracy, accuracy and timeliness of data acquisition and processing. In the future, we can integrate geographic information technology with "big data" technology, establish accurate and real-time ecosystem monitoring system in data acquisition, improve the acquisition technology and method of basic data, and establish the whole people in data storage and processing Participation, dynamic and long-term ecological development information network platform for scholars to study, government decision-making, public supervision to provide help and reference.

6.3 Establishing a Systematic Management and Instruction for Better Ecological System and Human Settlement Environments

The process of ecological development is a dynamic process that is ongoing over a long period of time. Therefore, ecosystem monitoring should be strengthened as a factor to consider the construction of human settlements, especially in areas such as regional planning, urban planning and rural planning. Standards, the development of ecological development project guidelines, and further develop regionalized, type of engineering and technical standards to improve the ecological development of the project technical guidance; in the regulation, should strengthen the ecological development project implementation process and after the implementation of the ecological effect of continuous testing and management.

Absorbing traditional building energy-saving technology, and into modern technology, not only can improve the contemporary high-tech, so that it has ecological suitability, and can promote the development of traditional residential building technology. The ecological spirit and energy-saving technology embodied in the traditional architectural technology still shine the wisdom of light, so that architects can jump out of modern high energy consumption and high pollution design thinking for the future of China's traditional villages in the ecological development of the coupling relationship with the environment Provide some effective measures and strategies.

Acknowledgements. We thank the National Natural Science Foundation of China (51278194) for the financial support. We also thank the School of Architecture Huaqiao University for the support.

References

1. John, R.J.: The seven lamps of architecture. J. Southeast Univ. (Philos. Soc. Sci., Nanjing) (2009)
2. Frampton, K.: Modern Architecture: A Critical History of European Oriental Rientalism, Beijing (2005)
3. Rao, X.: Review of the works of Charles Correa. Arch. Worlds **27**(1), 5–9 (1996)
4. Ken, Y.: Shell Energy-Saving Plan. Zhan's Bookstore, Taibei (1997)
5. Zhang, W., Chen, L., Yang, Y.: Research progress on human settlement evolution. Progross Geogr. **32**(5), 710–721 (2013)
6. Yu, K., Wang, X., Lin, S.: Urban design needs a "Big Foot Revolution" - practice of "Shuangxiu" in Sanya City. Urban Constr. **9**, 56–59 (2016)
7. Turnar, K.G., Anderson, S., Gonzles-Chang, M.: A review of methods, data, and models to assess changes in the value of ecosystem services from land degradation and restoration. Ecol. Model. **319**, 190–207 (2016)
8. ELD-Initiative: The rewards of investing in sustainability land management. In: Interim Report for the Economics of Land Degradation Initiative: A Global Strategy for Sustainable Land Management (2013)
9. Wang, P.: Climate Oriented Architecture with a Critic on Vernacular Architecture and Its Climatic Strategy. Qsinghua University, Beijing (2001)
10. Zhao, Q.: Research on the Ecological Experiences and Pattern Language of Traditional Residential Buildings. Xi'an University of Architecture and Technology, Xian (2005)
11. Bai, H., Liu, J.P., Jiang, S.G.: Study on climate adaptability of traditional houses with earth-envelopment wall in Turpan. Key Eng. Mater. **517**, 274–280 (2012)
12. Lin, Q.: Subtropical Buildings: Climate, Environment, and Architecture. Guangdong Science and Technology Press, Guangzhou (1997)
13. Tang, G.: Lingnan Hot and Humid Climate and Traditional Architecture. China Architecture & Building Press, Guangzhou (2005)
14. Zeng, Z.: Ventilation Method and Its Application in Modern Architecture of Traditional Residential Buildings in Guangzhou. South China University of Technology, Guangzhou (2010)
15. Vitiello, M.: Ecoperspectives restoration second. In: International Study Forum on Life of Traders, Less More Architecture Design Landscape, pp. 185–194 (2012)
16. Vemuri, A.W., Costanza, R.: The role of human, social, built, and natural capital in explaining life satisfaction at the country level: toward a national well-being index (NWI). Ecol. Econ. **58**, 119–133 (2006)
17. Costanza, R., Argem, E.: The value of the world's ecosystem services and natural capital. Nature **387**, 253–260 (1997)
18. MEA: Ecosystems and Human Well-Being: Synthesis. Island Press, Washing DC (2005)

19. Boumans, R., Costanza, E.: Modeling the dynamics of the integrated earth system and the value of global ecosystem services using the GUMBO model. Ecol. Econ. **41**, 529–560 (2002)
20. Robert, A., Pastorok, A., Anne, M.: An ecological decision environmental restoration projects. Ecol. Eng. **9**(1–2), 89–107 (1997)
21. Junker, B., Buchecker, M.: Aesthetic preferences versus ecological objectives in river restorations. Landsc. Urban Plan. **85**(3–4), 141–154 (2007)

A Literature Review of the Research on Interaction Mode of Self-driving Cars

Zhongshi Hu[1]([✉]), Xin Xin[1], Wanting Xu[1], Yuwei Sun[1],
Zhenyu Jiang[1], Xiangyu Wang[1], Yishan Liu[1], Siyao Lu[1],
and Min Zhao[2]

[1] Beijing Normal University, 19 Xinjiekouwai Street, Beijing, China
HZS13546325555@outlook.com, xin.xin@bnu.edu.cn,
15856911002@163.com, 1216198339@qq.com,
710922793@qq.com, miya_hi@163.com,
liuyishan1313@126.com, Lynn6917@163.com
[2] Baidu. com, Inc., No. 10 Xibeiwang East Road, Beijing, China
zhaomin04@baidu.com

Abstract. With the developing of the technology on self-driving, more and more L3 driverless vehicles are launched in market, people get opportunities to experience the self-driving cars in their daily life. As a result, there is a growing demand for the autopilot experience. Natural and efficient human-computer interaction can not only improve the driving experience, but also accelerate the process of self-driving commercialization. This paper discusses eye-movement interaction, voice interaction and gesture interaction in self-driving car, and analyzes the technology, advantages and disadvantages of the existing interaction modes, and prospect the future development trend of self-driving human-computer interaction.

Keywords: Self-driving · Human-computer interaction · Voice interaction · Eye-movement interaction · Gesture interaction

1 Introduction

With the progress of artificial intelligence research and the rapid development of sensor technology, the research field of self-driving cars is also expanding. In recent years, the research and development of self-driving technology is mainly divided into two camps: Tesla, Audi mainly car companies and Google, Baidu led by the Internet enterprises. At present, the research in the field of self-driving is more related to the application of self-driving vehicle obstacle avoidance algorithm and self-driving vehicle sensor, but the research on the internal human-computer interaction of self-driving car is not very in-depth [1]. The human-computer interaction system of self-driving cars is the last threshold for the commercialization of self-driving cars. With the development of eye tracking technology, speech recognition technology and gesture interaction technology, based on these technologies, the human-computer interaction of autonomous cars must be the focus of the next research [1]. Starting from three kinds of human-computer interaction technologies, this paper discusses the application and development of the three technologies at the present stage,and analyzes the advantages and disadvantages

© Springer Nature Switzerland AG 2019
A. Marcus and W. Wang (Eds.): HCII 2019, LNCS 11585, pp. 29–40, 2019.
https://doi.org/10.1007/978-3-030-23538-3_3

of each technology at the present stage, and prospect the development trend of human-computer interaction in autopilot situation in the future.

2 Eye-Tracking Based Human-Computer Interaction

2.1 Technical Background

In recent years, many universities and research institutes in Chinese and abroad began to carry out eye-movement based human-computer interaction related research. Professor Zhu Xichan of Tongji University once proposed that the human eye can be used as a sensor in the driving process, which is equivalent to a part of human-computer interaction media. The eye's line of sight changes in the driving process and the region of interest can reflect the driver's intention to some extent [2].

2.2 Technical Principle

The fixation point of the human eye is determined by two factors: the head position and the eye position. The orientation of the head determines the range of gaze, while the precise direction of gaze is determined by the orientation of the eye, but it is limited by the orientation of the head. Stiefelhagen et al. classified visual tracking technology, mainly divided into hardware-based and software-based [3].

The basic principle of hardware-based visual tracking technology is image processing technology, which mainly records the change of line of sight by locking special cameras of both eyes, so as to achieve the purpose of the line of sight tracking. Nowadays most eye trackers are implemented in this way. This method requires the user to wear a specific helmet or fixture, which has great influence and interference. Software-based visual tracking technology mainly captures faces through cameras and then locates faces and eyes respectively. Through the algorithm, the head and eye trajectories are analyzed, and the gaze position is estimated. To track the line of sight.

2.3 Application of Eye-Movement Technology

The Application of Eye-Movement Technology in Psychology. Eye-tracking technology has been widely used in psychology and other fields. For example, Yan Guoli and others have used eye-tracking technology to study driving behavior under different road conditions and the psychological and physiological factors affecting their behavior [4].

The Application of Eye-Movement Technology in Interaction Design. In the early days, eye-movement interaction was used to assist people with disabilities in operating and interacting with computer devices, such as patients with ALS (Amyotrophic Lateral Sclerosis) disease. And Stephen Hawking's "talking eyes" and so on [5].

The Human-Computer Interaction Technology and Intelligent Information Processing Laboratory of the Chinese Academy of Sciences have carried out a number of national-level "multi-channel human-computer interaction interface" research projects.

Professor Tan Hao's team has carried out research on eye-movement interaction in-vehicle music player, used eye-movement interaction to control the car music, designed a set of interactive mode, and achieved good results [6, 7].

2.4   Application of Eye-Movement Technology in Self-driving

Eye-movement technology is mainly used in automatic driving from two aspects. One is to detect drivers' visual perception and driving behavior, and the other is to improve existing vehicle interaction through eye-movement technology.

Eye-Movement Technology Analysis of Driving Behavior. Most of the research focuses on psychology. The visual tracking technology of eye-movement is used to analyze driver's response and eye-movement law in different scenes. The aim is to reduce a driver's cognitive load and distraction in order to improve a driver's driving safety. Yan Guoli et al. used eye-tracking technology to study driving behavior under different road conditions [4]. Zhou Yang et al. constructed a cognitive distraction recognition model by simulating driving and eye-tracking technology and using the random forest method to study driver's distraction behavior [8]. Yuan Wei of Chang'an University studied three typical urban traffic environment characteristics, namely, channel width, running speed and traffic sign height, through the simulation test in the test site, and analyzed the changing rule of driver's dynamic vision under each characteristic condition in order to reduce the probability of traffic accidents in urban environment [9]. Guo Yingshi used the high-speed eye-tracking system to record the driver's dynamic eye-movement data such as gaze time, gaze target, scan time and scan speed during driving and analyzed the influence of traffic environment and driving experience on driver's eye-movement and workload [10]. Yang Meng et al. used eye-tracking technology to study the effects of different background music rhythm and lyric language familiarity on driving behavior and eye-movement. The results show that music rhythm has a significant impact on driving speed, eye jump and vertical search breadth. Compared with slow rhythm, fast rhythm has faster driving speed, shorter average eye jump distance and shorter vertical search breadth. The familiarity of lyric language has a significant effect on driving speed, error number and average gaze time. Compared with unfamiliar language, familiar language has a slower driving speed, more errors, longer average gaze time for novices and no influence for veterans. The experiment suggests that drivers choose music with unfamiliar language lyrics when choosing music, and the rhythm of music depends on the situation [11].

Eye-Movement Technology Interaction. Nowadays eye-movement technology can realize text input and control by human-computer interaction with the device through the user's gaze, eye jump, and smooth tracking. Gao Jun of Southeast University improved the vehicle navigation system by using eye-movement interaction and on-board head-up display. Li Ting of Hunan University redesigned the vehicle music application through eye-movement interaction, which greatly reduced the distraction of drivers [2].

2.5   Defects of Eye-Movement Interaction in Self-driving

Accuracy. According to the foregoing, line-of-sight tracking technology is divided into hardware-based and software-based. When hardware-based, the accuracy will be relatively high. At present, most laboratories use hardware-based eye tracker, but in practical application scenarios, the comfort and convenience of hardware wearing are low, which affects the experience. While software-based, although there is no physical device, comfort and convenience are very high, but the existing technology has low recognition accuracy, it is very difficult to get accurate focus [12].

Midas Touch. Midas contact means that if the cursor always follows the user's implementation, it will make the user feel bored, because the user may want to see anything at will, not necessarily "mean" anything, let alone start a computer command every time he changes his sight. Therefore, how to avoid Midas contact is a challenge in the future [13].

2.6   Prospects of Eye-Movement Interaction in Self-driving

Self-driving has developed rapidly in recent years. According to the standard of SAE (SAE J3016), the role of the driver will no longer exist in the L5 stage, and the traditional way of human-vehicle interaction will no longer exist. In the vehicle control, the car entertainment music function, navigation function and so on. Eye-movement interaction has broad prospects for development.

3   Voice Interaction in Self-driving

3.1   Technical Principle

The process of voice interaction includes automatic speech recognition (ASR), intelligent dialogue system and speech synthesis. Automatic speech recognition converts vocabulary content in human speech into computer-readable input, such as buttons, binary codes, or sequences of characters [15]. The intelligent dialogue system first understands the information conveyed by human beings, regards it as an internal state, then adopts a series of corresponding behaviors according to the strategy of dialogue state, and finally transforms the action into the expression of natural language [16]. Speech synthesis is a technique for producing artificial speech by mechanical and electronic methods. TTS technology (also known as text-to-speech technology) is a part of speech synthesis. It is a technology that converts computer-generated or externally-entered text information into an audible and fluent Chinese spoken language output [17].

3.2   Application of Voice Interaction in Self-driving

In addition to the visual channel, hearing is also one of the important sensory channels, which can obtain outside information without taking up the main channel of the driving operation - the visual channel [17]. Because of this feature, voice interaction has become the mainstream in the automatic driving interaction mode.

Dong Changqing divides the voice interaction in automatic driving into two types. The voice system is placed in the smartphone and the voice system is configured in the vehicle terminal [1]. The voice system is placed in the smartphone, which uses the mobile phone as the carrier for voice interaction. Ford, Hyundai, General Motors, BMW and other car companies use this as a solution for in-vehicle voice interaction. Tesla, Audi, GM, Geely, and Changan have adopted the solution of the car terminal voice system. Representatives of the existing automotive voice interaction systems include Nuance's Dragon Drive voice assistant, the Cloudrive 2.0 system jointly developed by Chery and HKUST.

At present, the applications of voice interaction in automatic driving mainly include car navigation system, fatigue driving analysis, in-vehicle infotainment system, and emotional voice interaction system.

Car Navigation System. Liu Wang divides the car navigation voice interaction system into several steps: dialogue mode, keyword recognition, voice control command, name recognition, and speech synthesis. Liu Wang's experimental results prove that the system can meet the requirements of car navigation human-machine voice interaction [18].

The practical application of the in-vehicle voice navigation system is mainly embodied in: (1) Operation command input: control various instructions of the interface of each layer of the car navigation system, as long as the car navigation device starts menu, navigation, game, music and enters the speech recognition library and the navigation device can be operated freely with a simple input command. (2) Destination input: The building name and main traffic road of a specific city can be entered into the speech recognition library if the system allows. (3) Auxiliary Facilities Query: Find out the auxiliary facilities in the service stations, hospitals, restaurants, etc.

Fatigue Driving Analysis. Li Xiang believes that the current mainstream human fatigue detection method is based on facial performance characteristics and eye, but it still has limitations that are inconvenient to measure [19]. The driver's voice signal covers a large amount of human physiological or psychological state information, and its collection means is simpler and more convenient than other indicators, and the voice processing system has real-time, non-contact, strong environmental adaptability, and the noise reduction technology is mature.

Li Xiang proposed a method to detect driving fatigue using speech psychoacoustic analysis [20]. By processing the psychoacoustic model of the speech signal, the method can highlight the frequency components which are susceptible to fatigue and give more critical band descriptions, so that more detailed and intuitive fatigue information expression can be obtained.

In-Vehicle Infotainment. The voice interaction system is also applied to an in-vehicle infotainment system. In-Vehicle Infotainment is an in-vehicle information processing system based on body bus system and Internet service, which can realize car information, navigation, entertainment and other services [21]. Peng Yuyuan believes that voice interaction can help drivers put visual attention on road driving and help drive safety.

Emotional Voice Interaction System. Emotional speech interaction system refers to the ability to give emotional recognition and expression to interactive systems, making human-computer interaction more humane [22]. In recent years, this field has received great attention.

In the 2000 study, V. Kostov and S. Fukuda developed VIS (Emotional Information Voice Interaction System), the ability to perceive users by investing in acoustic similarities in eight states of emotion (neutrality, anger, sadness, happiness, disgust, surprise, nervousness, distress, and fear). VIS and its research methods have laid the foundation for contemporary emotional voice interaction systems.

The experimental results of Won-Joong Yoon in 2007 show that using k-NN and SVM with probability estimation to estimate the degree of emotion, the accuracy rate in the five basic emotions (neutral, happy, sad, angry and troubled) is 72.5% [23]. It is possible to use the voice interaction to estimate the emotional level in the automatic driving in the later stage. In 2018, Li Zhenzhen studied the emotional design of voice assistants from the instinct, behavioral and reflective layers, and combined the speech interaction design with emotional design to provide new ideas and methods for the promotion of voice assistant experience.

3.3 The Challenge of Voice Interaction in Self-driving

According to the US J.D. Power agency released 2016 new car quality survey shows that among the many interaction problems, the voice interaction failure rate is as high as 23%. It can be seen that the voice interactive application in autonomous driving still has certain challenges. Dong Changqing believes that the main challenges are: (1) The low naturalness of voice interaction: the current voice commands have low recognition of local accents, proper nouns and flexible collocations, which limits the recognition of voice interaction. (2) Insufficient flexibility: Even if the accuracy of system identification is improved, the driver's spoof will affect the correct interaction. (3) Poor noise resistance [1].

Wang Haifeng believes that the challenge may also include (1) The sound environment in driving is difficult to be compatible: different acoustic signals are easy to cover each other. (2) The sound signal is time-sensitive: unlike visual information, if the auditory information cannot be accepted by the listener when it is generated, it will lose its usefulness [23]. Yezi analyze the problems of voice interaction from three levels of product design (operational layer, functional layer, and emotional layer) [24]. He believes that at this stage, the voice interaction does not liberate the hands well in the operation layer, and the recognition accuracy is not high in the functional layer. The emotional layer does not satisfy the user's perceptual psychological needs well.

At the same time, the results of 2001 John D. Lee, David L. Straye in 2014 and Douglas Getty in 2018 can prove that some voice-based interactions in the car may increase the driver's cognitive load, which is not good for traffic safety [25–27]. How to avoid this negative impact is also a research issue in the future of voice interaction in autonomous driving.

3.4 Prospects for Voice Interaction in Self-driving

Li Zhiyong believes that the future development of voice interaction is divided into three phases. The first phase should aim to improve the accuracy of speech recognition in order to accurately respond to the user's voice input in a typical environment. This is also the focus of existing voice interaction research. The second stage reflects the personalization of voice interaction, which realizes the initial anthropomorphism and enhances the naturalness of voice interaction [28]. The third stage reflects the borderless nature of back-end content expansion. In essence, the future development of voice interaction is the process of digitization and intelligence, and the process of materialization in the form of ideals.

4   Gesture Interaction in Self-driving

Gesture interaction is an interactive way to complete human-computer interaction by recognizing human gestures through mathematical algorithms.

4.1   Technical Background

In recent years, with the development of gesture detection and recognition technology, a new way of interaction has emerged in the field of human-computer interaction, called gesture interaction. At present, gesture interaction is mainly used in the control of navigation and music playing interface. In a specific area of the car, the content of the interface is manipulated by specific gestures. Gesture interaction is a new interactive mode of human and vehicle, which is different from the traditional interaction mode of button operation and touch screen operation.

4.2   Technical Principles

The realization of gesture interaction technology is mainly determined by two parts, one is the capture and tracking of gesture action, the other is the recognition and conjecture of gesture action.

The capture and tracking of gesture action is mainly realized by hardware foundation. According to the different hardware implementation, there are about three kinds of gesture recognition technology used in the industry at present. The first is structure light technology, through laser refraction and algorithm to calculate the position and depth information of the object, and then restore the whole three-dimensional space. The second is time of flight technology. A luminous element is loaded in the hardware, and the flight time of photons is captured and calculated by CMOS sensor. According to the flight time of photons, the flight distance of photons is calculated, and the depth information of objects is obtained. The third is Multi-camera, which uses two or more cameras to capture images at the same time. By comparing the differences between the images obtained by these different cameras at the same time, an algorithm is used to calculate the depth information. It can restore the entire three-dimensional space. The recognition and conjecture of gesture action is mainly realized by software. According to the development of gesture recognition technology, there are template matching technology, neural network technology of statistical sample features and neural network technology of deep learning. The template matching method is mainly used in two-dimensional gesture recognition, and the recognition method based on neural network technology is mainly used to recognize three-dimensional gestures.

4.3   Application of Gesture Interaction Technology

Application of Gesture Interaction in Non-driving Field. Interaction for virtual environments. It is mainly used in virtual manufacturing, virtual assembly and game fields. Virtual manufacturing and assembly is the integration of design and manufacturing processes under a unified model. It integrates all kinds of processes and technologies related to product manufacturing into the solid digital model of three-dimensional, dynamic simulation process. As a result, the production is simulated more effectively and economically. The backtracking changes brought by the pre-design to the later manufacturing are effectively reduced. The production cycle and cost of the product are minimized, and the design quality of the product is optimized. Virtual manufacturing and assembly directly carry out the assembly of parts in the virtual environment through the movement of the hand. On the other hand, gesture interaction is also used in the field of somatosensory games. Microsoft, for example, released Kinect, a somatosensory device for use with XBOX360, in 2010. Kinect can recognize human movements, including gestures [29].

For sign language recognition. Sign language is the language of deaf and mute people. it is a relatively stable expression system composed of hand movements supplemented by expression postures. The goal of sign language recognition is to make the machine understand the language of the deaf, so that the machine is a sign language translation machine, which is convenient for deaf people to communicate with the surrounding environment. The process of deaf people communicating with the machine is the process of sign language recognition. It is also the process of gesture interaction [29].

Application of Gesture Interaction in Self-driving. The somatosensory interaction in the self-driving interaction mainly focuses on gesture interaction. Different from other traditional interaction methods (such as physical interaction and touch-screen interaction), gesture interaction is considered to be a more natural and more in line with people's own cognitive style way of human-vehicle interaction [30]. Gesture interaction has become the focus of automotive human-computer interaction interface design, because gesture interaction can reduce the visual distraction and cognitive burden of drivers [31]. At present, gesture interaction is mainly used in the interaction of vehicle navigation system, video and audio system, and the interaction of light and air conditioning system. Fang Yinan of Donghua University has designed and developed a set of map and music programs for on-board tablets, which use Leap Motion to capture and recognize gestures and complete the driver's control of maps and music through gesture movements, with a success rate of 90.5%. Nie Xin of Beijing University of Technology obtained the degree of driving distraction and driving load of each gesture by testing the brain power, vision and pressure of gesture operation, observing the lane, speed and distance, and designed a set of operation gestures [31]. Li Moyang of Hunan University has studied and designed a vehicle-borne system based on gesture interaction, which can answer phone calls, play music, change radio stations and operate navigation maps through hand movements [32]. Yang of Hunan University applied situation awareness to the study of human-computer interaction in self-driving cars, and designed and produced HMI system, which proved the feasibility of gesture interaction as a natural interaction for secondary driving tasks in the car [33].

4.4   Advantages of Gesture Interaction in Self-driving

In Alpen's study, they explored on-board systems based on gesture control by comparing gesture-operated entertainment tasks with traditional radio tuning tasks. It is found that gesture operation can make drivers make fewer mistakes in driving tasks than traditional radio adjustments. By comparing the control mode of the gesture operation interface with the touch screen operation interface to the music player, Pirhonen found that the gesture operation interface significantly reduces the user's workload and task operation time. Li Moyang of Hunan University believed that gestures provide a new space for human-computer interaction in the car. It can alleviate the contradiction between the growing functions and the limited space in the car. Gestures provide the possibility for the realization of these functions, especially the operation of the secondary driving task function.

4.5   Challenges of Gesture Interaction in Self-driving

Dong Changqing of the China Automobile Research Center summarizes the shortcomings of gesture interaction: (1) The current gesture recognition technology is not mature enough. It is difficult to accurately complete gesture control; (2) The similarity between different gestures and the fuzziness of gesture range are easy to lead to systematic misjudgment; (3) The content that gesture can convey is limited. Compared with speech interaction, gesture interaction is difficult to express the specific task content. In addition to solving the above difficulties, the design of gesture interaction in the future should also be in line with people's cognitive habits. Because gesture interaction requires users to invest more learning cost than speech interaction and eye movement interaction, gesture interaction in accordance with users' cognitive habits can greatly reduce its learning cost and make the interaction process more natural. It can also save users' cognitive resources. At the same time, with the gesture design on the basis of simple and easy understanding, designer need to consider the cultural customs of different regions and design the gesture which is close to the daily natural communication posture of local users [1].

4.6   Development Prospect of Gesture Interaction in Self-driving

Jing Chunhui of Sichuan University believes that with the rapid development of self-driving technology and the upgrading of in-vehicle electronic equipment, the traditional interaction mode will account for a smaller and smaller proportion in the future self-driving interaction mode. On the other hand, with the saturation of visual channel interaction design, the design of other sensory channels will be paid attention to. In this trend, gesture interaction will become one of the main stream of interaction design [34]. At the same time, with the application of gesture interaction on other mobile devices, desktop devices and object-linked devices, users will naturally apply gestures learned on one device to another platform, which will lead to the emergence of gesture standards. Although the research on gesture interaction of self-driving cars is in the development stage, there is no unified standard in the industry. But in the near future, there will certainly be similar organizations to produce and develop the corresponding gesture standards.

In the era when self-driving cars liberate drivers' hands from the steering wheel, gesture interaction will play a great role in how to complete the operation of audio-visual system, navigation system and light air conditioning system more efficiently and comfortably.

5 Conclusion

In the future, the main task of human-computer interaction in the self-driving is to integrate eye movement, voice, gestures and other interaction technologies to achieve efficient human-car interaction. A better human-computer interaction will lay a foundation for the commercial use of self-driving car. The final form of the development of human-computer interaction in the self-driving is that there is no interaction. The existing human-computer interaction technology is still a long way to get 100% natural interaction. The interactions are issued by human and executed by cars. If user makes a mistake in the interactive process, the car would not correctly complete the tasks, which is a big hidden danger to the safety of the whole driving environment. Li Deyi, an academician of the Chinese Academy of Engineering, said in a speech in November 2016 that "interactive cognition is very important for smart cars to become interactive wheeled robots." If the unmanned car lacks of effective interaction, passengers will think it is a ghost and afraid to ride. After the further developing of human-computer interaction in the self-driving situation, the natural human-computer interaction is mainly based on situational recognition. Cars automatic recognize the driving environment to predict the needs of users. Such a system can further reduce the operation of users and more intelligently meet the needs of users.

In a word, the trend of the development of human-computer interaction of autopilot situation is to achieve intelligent and humanized user needs safely and stably. Industry needs to apply vehicle engineering, industrial design, artificial intelligence, psychology and other fields of knowledge and skills to achieve this goal.

References

1. Dong, C., Din, T., Huang, X., et al.: A survey of research on unmanned human-computer interaction. Times Car, 11–12 (2017)
2. Gao, J.: Research on human-computer interaction of electric vehicle navigation system based on eye-movement information. (Doctoral dissertation) (2017)

3. Stiefelhagen, R., Yang, J.: Gaze tracking for multimodal human-computer interaction. In: IEEE International Conference on Acoustics (1997)
4. Yan, G., Tian, H., Zhang, X.: Eye-movement study of automobile driving behavior. Psychol. Sci. **28**(5), 1211–1212 (2005)
5. Vidal, M., Bulling, A., Gellersen, H.: Pursuits: spontaneous interaction with displays based on smooth pursuit eye movement and moving targets. In: ACM International Joint Conference on Pervasive & Ubiquitous Computing (2013)
6. Feng, F., He, R., Tan, H.: Research on eye-movement interaction in vehicle oriented to information entertainment system. J. Automot. Eng. **5**(2), 108–115 (2015)
7. Feng, F.: Design and research of eye-movement interaction in vehicle music application. (Doctoral dissertation, Hunan University) (2014)
8. Zhou, Y., Fu, R., Yuan, W., Wang, D., Zhang, R.: Study on random forest model for driver cognitive distraction recognition. J. China Saf. Sci. (1) (2018)
9. Yuan, W., Guo, Y., Fu, R., Chen, Y.: Effects of urban road types on drivers' workload. J. Chang'an Univ. (Nat. Sci.) **34**(5), 95–100 (2014)
10. Guo, Y.: Study on the effects of traffic environment and driving experience on drivers' eye movement and workload. (Doctoral dissertation, Chang'an University) (2009)
11. Yang, M., Wang, J., Xia, Y., Yang, F., Zhang, X.: The influence of background music rhythm and lyric language familiarity on driving behavior and eye-movement. Psychol. Sci. (5), 1056–1061 (2011)
12. Zhang, L., Li, H., Ge, L.: Application of tobii eye tracker in human-computer interaction. Chin. J. Ergon. **15**(2), 67–69 (2009)
13. Feng, C., Shen, M.: Application of eye-tracking in human computer interaction. J. Zhejiang Univ. (Sci. Ed.) **29**(2), 225 (2002)
14. Li, T.: Eye-movement interaction interface design and case development. (Doctoral dissertation, Zhejiang University) (2012)
15. Harris, R.A.: Voice Interaction Design: Crafting the New Conversational Speech Systems. Elsevier, Amsterdam (2004)
16. Basir, O.A., Miners, W.B.: Multi-participant, mixed-initiative voice interaction system: U.S. Patent (2014)
17. Lee, K.J., Joo, Y.K., Nass, C.: Partially intelligent automobiles and driving experience at the moment of system transition, pp. 3631–3634. ACM (2014)
18. Liu, W., Yang, D., Lian, X.: Implementation of vehicle navigation human-computer voice interaction system. Electron. Prod. World, 127–130 (2007)
19. Li, X., Li, G., Shi, J., et al.: Driving fatigue detection based on speech psychoacoustic analysis. J. Instrum. **10** (2018)
20. Car Infotainment System: CN201115295[P] (2008)
21. Zhang, S., Li, L., Zhao, Z.: Research progress on speech emotion recognition in human-computer interaction. J. Circuits Syst. 440–451 (2013)
22. Yoon, W.J., Cho, Y.H., Park, K.S.: A study of speech emotion recognition and its application to mobile services. In: Indulska, J., Ma, J., Yang, L.T., Ungerer, T., Cao, J. (eds.) UIC 2007. LNCS, vol. 4611, pp. 758–766. Springer, Heidelberg (2007). https://doi.org/10.1007/978-3-540-73549-6_74
23. Wang, H.: Human-computer interaction interface design in the cab of driverless electric vehicle (2017)
24. Ye, Z.: Research on the problems existing in human-computer voice interaction. Technol. Commun. **9** (2017)
25. Lee, J.D., Caven, B., Haake, S., et al.: Speech-based interaction with in-vehicle computers: the effect of speech-based e-mail on drivers' attention to the roadway. Hum. Factors **43**, 631–640 (2001)

26. Strayer, D.L., Turrill, J., Coleman, J.R., et al.: Measuring cognitive distraction in the automobile ii: assessing in-vehicle voice-based. Accid. Anal. Prev. **379** (2014)

27. Getty, D., Biondi, F., Morgan, S.D., et al.: The effects of voice system design components on driver workload. Transp. Res. Rec. (2018). https://doi.org/10.1177/0361198118777382

28. Li, Z.: Anatomy of the hierarchy behind the voice interaction. China Acad. J. Electron. Publ. House, 14–15 (2019)

29. Li, Q., Fang, Z., Shen, M., Chen, Y.: Gesture recognition technology and its application in human-computer interaction. Chin. Ergon. **01** (2002)

30. Tan, H.: Research on automotive human machine interface design based on complex interaction context. Packag. Eng. **18** (2012)

31. Nie, X.: Research on the gesture operation of BMW in the user experience mode. (Master dissertation, Beijing University of Technology) (2015)

32. Li, M.: Research and application of user-defined gesture design for automobile human machine interface. (Master dissertation, Hunan University) (2015)

33. Yang, W.: Research of intelligent automobile human-machine interaction design based on situational awareness. (Master dissertation, Hunan University) (2017)

34. Jing, C., Zhang, J., Deng, C.: Vehicle gesture interaction design. Packag. Eng. **8** (2018)

Research on Design Model of Human-Machine Interface of Automatic Driving Takeover System Based on User Experience

Lijun Jiang[1,2(✉)], Xiu Wang[1], Zhelin Li[1,2], and Yu Zhang[1]

[1] South China University of Technology, Guangzhou 510041, China
ljjiang@scut.eud.cn
[2] Human-Computer Interaction Design Engineering Technology Research Center of Guangdong, Guangzhou, Guangdong, China

Abstract. The human-machine interaction interface of the cockpits of autonomous vehicles need to be redesigned to ensure safety and improve the user experience. Aiming at the interaction requirements in the takeover scenarios of the L3 level automatic driving, the human-machine interface design model of automatic-driving takeover system based on the user experience is obtained through the specific study on the human-vehicle-environment relationship of the automatic-driving takeover system, combined with the design knowledge of the human-machine interface of the vehicle. The model provides design guidance for the designer of human-machine interface of the automatic-driving takeover system to optimize the design strategy, and create better driving experience for the users.

Keywords: User experience · Automatic driving · Takeover system · Interface design

1 User Experience Theory in Human-Vehicle Interaction

1.1 User Experience Needs in Human-Vehicle Interaction

Based on Maslow's hierarchy of needs [1], Ren divides the user experience into five levels of needs, which are sensory experience, interactive experience, emotional experience, social experience and personalized experience, from the lowest level to the highest [2]. According to this classification, the following five levels of needs are necessarily to be considered to plan the blueprint of the user experience in the driving process.

Sensory Experience Needs. When interacting with cars, the most intuitive and perceptible information is expected by the drivers, including visual information, auditory information, tactile information, and even olfactory and taste information through multiple channels.

Interactive Experience Needs. High availability, ease of use, learnability, fault tolerance and other properties of driving system is expected, because it is related to whether the functions and contents of the system can be correctly transmitted to the driver.

A. Marcus and W. Wang (Eds.): HCII 2019, LNCS 11585, pp. 41–60, 2019.
https://doi.org/10.1007/978-3-030-23538-3_4

Emotional Experience Needs. When interacting with cars, more driving pleasure are needed by the drivers, and emotional comfort are needed by the drivers when frightened during driving process.

Social Experience Needs. When the driver interacts with the car, they hope to gain recognition and respect from others for his driving performance and car brand.

Personalized Experience Needs. Driving system is expected to meet the individual needs by the drivers.

1.2   User Experience Elements of Human-Vehicle Interaction

The user experience element mainly refers to the factors that affect the driver's experience during the interaction between the car and the driver. Garrett [3] divided the user experience of information products into five levels in the "Elements of User Experience": strategic layer, scope layer, structure layer, framework layer and presentation layer. The above five user experience elements are applied in the process of interaction between people and cars.

Huanle Zhang, Tianqiu Huang and others, divide design knowledge into three categories: user, design object and situation, according to the characteristics of automotive user research data [4]. The design process is in fact the process by which the designer transforms the design knowledge into specific and external product-related attributes through design behavior. Therefore, the new research results of the human-computer interaction interface are proposed based on the existing research results related to the three elements.

1.3   Users

Different users have different user information, which can be divided into three categories: basic information, life form information and personal situation information, covering economic status, living environment, living habits, personality hobbies and consumption concepts. The differences of these user information reflect the difference in user experience requirements of various users [5].

1.4   Design Object

The design object is essentially the product, interface, interaction and other objects in the design of the human-vehicle interaction interface. There are concrete parts and visual interfaces, as well as abstract interaction and interaction strategies. The design object contains design factors, design carriers and design concepts, and the organizational relationship is shown in Fig. 1.

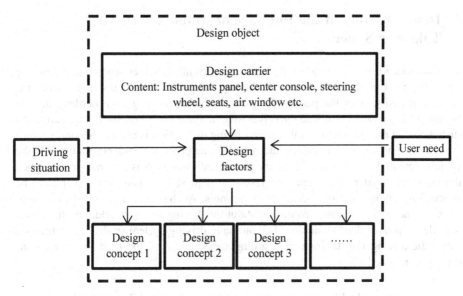

Fig. 1. The organizational relationship of design object

1.5 Situation

The situation is the bridge connecting users and design objects. Each situation has corresponding users behind it. Each user has different performances in the same situation. The situation is important for studying user behavior and psychology [1]. There are N situation categories in each driving situation, and multiple sub-contexts in each context. Each sub-context has its own situational features. The key points in the design goals are the situational problems that users encounter under contextual characteristics. The framework for the classification of situations is shown in Table 1.

Table 1. The framework for the classification of situations

Classification	Content	Classification	Content
S1. Normal driving situation	S1.1 Local commute S1.2 Travel S1.3 Commercial use S1.4 To pick up friends	S2. Micro situations of driving	S2.1 Inspection and start S2.2 Parking S2.3 Traffic jam S2.4 Overtake ......
S3. Driving aids in progress	S3.1 Fixed speed cruise S3.2 Adaptive cruise S3.3 Navigation S3.4 Head up display	S4. Information consumption and entertainment	S4.1 Telephone call/answer S4.2 Online social S4.3 Music S4.4 Broadcast ......
S5. Cooperating with occupants		S6. Special situation	

2 Design Factors of the Interface of Automatic-Driving Takeover System

The interaction design strategy in the automatic-driving takeover process can affect the safety [6]. First of all, in the automatic driving state, if the driving task is too easy, the driver can easily enter the passive fatigue due to the low cognitive burden, and the boring driving process also lead the driver to participate more in non-driving main tasks such as social entertainment. In this way, driving distraction is caused. Secondly, since the main attention resources in the automatic driving process are not concentrated in the vehicle state and the road condition, the situational awareness is lowered, so that when the automatic system exits and the takeover request is issued, the driver may be shocked by unexpected state changes or prompts. At the same time, insufficient situational awareness may cause confusion about the driving mode. In addition, the driver may develop over dependence on the automatic driving system or decreased trust on automatic-driving due to frequent warning messages. And the trust in autonomous driving is reduced [7].

2.1 Interaction Problem of Takeover Switching in Level 3 Automatic Driving

For HAD (Highly Automated Driving) vehicles, the interactive interface design of the automatic-driving takeover system based on user experience is very important for driving safety. The design of the takeover system should plan a better way for the driver to be more involved in the driving mission, paying attention to the vehicle status and traffic situation in order to maintain a good situational awareness [8]; At the same time, it is necessary to plan a better warning mode, indicating the current automatic driving status and its restrictions, transmitting information appropriately, clearly and efficiently, and makes it easily accessible by the driver, avoiding the driver's detachment beyond the human-vehicle-environment system. Therefore, the takeover request method conveyed by the automatic-driving takeover system should balance the workload and urgency well, neither too early (may be interpreted by the driver as a false positive) nor too late (may result in loss of access to the artificially driven vehicle). At the same time, in the context of connected driving, the interactive interface design of the automatic-driving takeover system should also help the driver to get certain economic and entertainment experience, that is, the balance between safety and experience [9].

2.2 User Research of Automatic-Driving System

Norman [10] proposed user-centered design principles, and advocated design to focus on the needs and interests of users to ensure the comprehensibility and usability of the product. In the process of automatic driving, a car will face unexpected situation that various systems can't solve or can't completely solve, which is random. Therefore, when conducting user research, it is necessary to select typical users according to certain conditions and obtain different types and degrees of user information in order to discover differences between different users.

The scope of this study is defined in all driving operations performed by the automatic-driving system of L3 driving. Human need to respond to certain request. And the main body of the operation is humans and systems, that is, the automatic driving background with restrictions. The research subjects of this study are not universal, so they can not be classified according to the conventional driving proficiency, but according to the user's proficiency and understanding of the automatic-driving system, the users are divided into three categories: novice users, intermediate users and expert users.

Novice Users. Users who have certain driving experience and have used automatic-driving or assisted driving functions. The automatic driving here is not limited to L3 driving and above. Such users have weak auto-driving experience and less knowledge of takeover system.

Intermediate Users. Users who have rich driving experience and have more auto-driving experience, including automatic driving experience of L3 or above. Such users are more familiar with the knowledge of automatic driving, their functions and operation methods.

Expert Users. Users who have rich driving experience and have a deep understanding and experience of L3 automatic-driving cars. Such users are very familiar with the automatic vehicle human-vehicle interaction system, and study more on applications of various new technology inside the car.

Three typical users are interviewed in this article, who represent their respective groups. Let the user describe the situation in which the automatic driving system is used, especially in the situation of takeover operations. Three user-specific individual situational issues and needs are documented and analyzed, and the situational characteristics are summarized based on the research of integrated relevant document. The user information is divided into three dimensions: basic information, life form information, and personal situation information of users. The basic information of and life form information of users are shown in Tables 2 and 3.

The specific personal situation problems and needs of the three users are recorded and analyzed, through Interview and survey, allowing users to describe the situation of using the autopilot system, especially the situation relevant to takeover operation. Personal situational interviews provide designers with an overview of the user, help to find problems and discover needs. However, it should be noticed that during the interview process, the users describe the personal situation without much thought. The information obtained by the interview is usually incomplete, which may include the

Table 2. Basic information of users

Type	User	Age	Driving years	Present address	Occupation
Novice user	Mrs. Zhang	25	2 years	Guangzhou, Guangdong	Fashion designer
Intermediate user	Mr. Yu	30	9 years	Jinhua, Zhejiang	Car styling designer
Expert user	Mr. He	31	11 years	Guangzhou, Guangdong	Intelligent driving vehicle technology researcher

Table 3. Life form information

Type	User	Automatic driving system	Frequency of use	Take over habit	Non-driving activity
Novice user	Mrs. Zhang	Tesla	Occasionally for outing	Helding the wheel	Chatting
Intermediate user	Mr. Yu	Tesla, Baidu	Generally Usually in downtown	Helding the wheel	Playing games, and social contact
Expert user	Mr. He	Independent developed and non-commercial	Frequently Usually in depopulated zone	Helding the wheel with foot on the brake	Watching mobile phone and distraction task

users' personal emotion color or even error. It is the best way to find more missing content and error information to interview multiple objects, but for the limit of conditions, the author will integrate relevant literature research and summarize the situational features.

2.3   Study of Auto-driving Takeover Situation Study

The above personal situation of three typical users, combined with the results of the existing auto-driving situation-related literature research [11–15], the features of the auto-driving takeover situation include:

Diversity of Takeover Situations. Due to the cars are constantly moving objects in the driving process, and the complexity of the traffic situation in real world traffic, the ADAS (Advanced Driver Assistant System) of the self-driving car will receive the situation information from different directions, including roads, environment, pedestrians, signs, equipment and other information. The system makes a takeover request when ADAS can't recognize the current situation information or the situational information exceeds the auto-driving condition. Secondly, when the driver controls the car, the state is also uncertain, they would do sub-tasks such as listening to songs, playing mobile phones, reading newspapers, and so on. Therefore, the takeover situation is also diverse. This requires that the interface design of the takeover system should be adapted to different situations.

Dynamics of the Takeover Situation. Because the car is constantly moving during the driving process, the surrounding situation is in the process of changing, including location, weather, time and so on. When the auto-driving function is activated, the driver also has more time and space to do non-driving tasks. At this time, the driver is in a distraction state, affecting the perception of the changing situation, and resulting in a decline in situational awareness. This requires that when the situation changes significantly, the driver should be informed immediately that the driver cannot be completely separated from the driving situation.

The Randomness of the Takeover Situation. During the driving process, the driving environment is constantly changing, and the content of the takeover situation changes with time and place, showing the characteristics of randomness. The driver cannot predict when the system will make a takeover request, and the sudden appearance of the request may cause the driver's psychological panic, affecting the efficiency and quality of the takeover. Taking the randomness of the situation, the timing and method of requiring the takeover system to make a warning should balance the urgency well, neither too early (may be interpreted by the driver as a false positive) nor too late (may lead to loss of access to the artificially driven vehicle). The human factors that affect the time of auto-driving takeover include:

Driving Distraction. Driving distraction is a problem of attention resource allocation during driving. During the automatic driving process, the boring feeling result in low workload. So the driver wants to participate in more interesting tasks instead of monitoring and supervising autonomous driving. Although the system has a warning function, such long-term distraction still poses a threat to the safety of automatic driving.

Passive Fatigue. In the process of automatic driving, the driver's workload is too small. Lacking of direct control of the task in hand, the driver will fall into passive fatigue because the cognitive load is too low. Passive fatigue can reduce overall performance of the driver.

Situational Awareness. When the major task is handed over to the system, the driver's attention is diverted from the driving task, and less attention resources are used to maintain an understanding of the vehicle state and road conditions, the level of attention to the situation is reduced at the same time. When the situation changes significantly but doesn't need to be taken over, the driver also needs the system to mainly inform the change of situation, or to improve the driver's takeover motivation through some mechanism to ensure the maintenance of good situational awareness.

Excessive Trust. Because the automatic driving system takes over most of the driving tasks, after a period of time, the driver overestimates and relies too much on the autopilot function, and doesn't doubt whether the auto-driving system can really detect all the dangers. The problem with over-reliance and trust in auto-driving systems is that the driver may mistakenly believe that the technology can accurately warn them every time when necessary. These consequences of over-reliance on autonomous driving are known as negative behavioral adaptation effects and may be detrimental to safe driving.

Skills Degradation. Drivers who rely heavily on highly automated driving systems may not be able to use their manual driving skills for long periods of time. Conversely, ignoring manual driving skills may reduce the flexibility and driving cognitive skills required to manually complete the task successfully and safely. Therefore, in an automatic driving system, it is necessary to encourage the use of a manual driving mechanism.

In the real driving process, the human factor affects the driver's autopilot takeover performance, and the factors also affect each other. To reduce the impact of human factors on driving efficiency and quality, a good human-vehicle interface design for auto-driving takeover systems is indispensable.

3 Human-Machine Interface Design Model of Automatic Driving Takeover System Based on User Experience

Through the research on user experience and automobile human-vehicle interface, the user and the situation are analyzed separately, and the situational characteristics of the auto-driving takeover situation and the human factors affecting the takeover process are summarized. Based on the above conclusions, the user needs under the takeover scenario are listed, as shown in Table 4 below:

Table 4. The specific contents of each level that affect the driver experience

Need	Content
Sensory experience need	Intuitive multi-channel communication with visual, auditory, and even tactile sensations
Interactive experience need	The information is presented in an accurate and intuitive way to reflect current situational information and doesn't affect the identification of other information. The situational information here is not only the information that takes over the moment, but also when the situation changes
Emotional experience need	There can be more interesting tasks to improve takeover motivation, reduce distraction time and increase driving load and enhance situational awareness
Social experience need	When the driving task is completed, the driver can get more recognition and respect
Personalized experience need	Users and their' cars can have their own unique attributes and be different

The design of human-vehicle interaction interface should regard safety as the first principle and then meet the needs of users at all levels as much as possible. When multiple needs are not met, low-level needs are more important. The needs of each level are interdependent and overlapping. During the same period, people may have multiple needs, and designers need to think comprehensively to propose specific solutions. Therefore, the design goal is to design an interactive interface that assists the driver to safely complete the takeover of driving control and improve the user experience in the automatic driving mode.

Through the research on the background of the subject, the selected design carrier is the car window and AR-FWSD technology. The characteristics of the large display area and the use of the peripheral field of view can effectively help the driver to understand the situation [15]. The above design factors are introduced into the design model, and the human-vehicle interface design model of the automatic driving takeover system based on the user experience is obtained, as shown in Fig. 2.

In the human-vehicle interface design of the automatic driving takeover system based on user experience, safety is the first design principle. In general, non-high-frequency operations or non-professional functions often regard visual effects as a priority, within the acceptable range of interactive experience. But for the car, the interactive experience is definitely more important than the visual effect. If there was a problem with car interaction, the cost may be a car crash [16], so in this design model, all design factors must also be designed with safety as the first criterion. In addition, the hum an-vehicle interaction interface needs to be repeatedly verified in the design process, and the emergency plan should be prepared in advance.

User experience elements include strategy layer, scope layer, structure layer, framework layer, and presentation layer. Design factors include design goals, design vectors, and multiple user needs. According to the design model guidance, the design factors of the auto-driving takeover system are introduced into the strategic layer, and the design is layer by layer according to the bottom-up construction principle. Finally, presentation layer expresses the whole design concept through the prototype, interface and story version.

3.1 Strategy Layer Design

The strategic layer consists of "design goals" and "user needs", so that design factors can be imported directly. The goal is to design an automatic driving takeover system interface that assists the driver in safely completing the control switching and improves the driver's user experience. Quantifying this design goal into three specific metrics of design success: through the interaction strategy design of the takeover system. ① When the takeover warning is issued, the driver successfully takes over the vehicle in a safe time, or takes over faster, which improve the efficiency of takeover and quality; ② The driver's distraction is reduced, the situational awareness is improved; ③ Improves the driver's user experience in the automatic driving mode. In the design process, the specific user needs are placed in the dominant position to dominate the design direction.

3.2 Scope Layer Design

The scope layer design of the automatic driving takeover system is to design appropriate strategies and functions for the user according to the needs and objectives of the

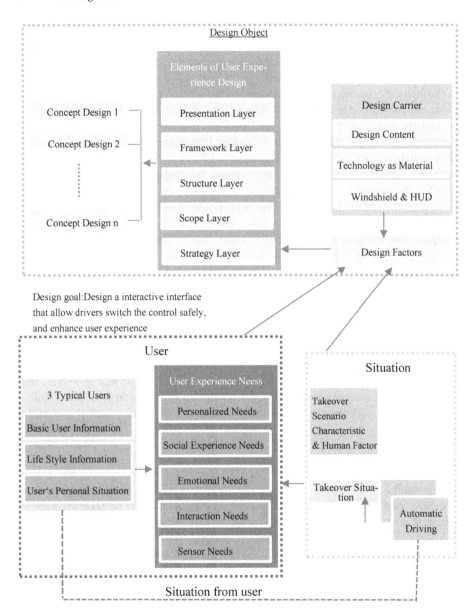

Fig. 2. Interface design model

strategic layer. There are two kinds of strategies according to the functional attributes, situation information notification strategy and game incentive strategy.

The Situation Information Notification Strategy. It is the main function of the takeover system, which is mainly used to improve the driver's situational awareness, reduce distraction, and enhance driving load. The user experience mainly meets the user's sensory experience needs and interactive experience needs.

The Game Incentive Strategy. It is a secondary function of the takeover system. It is mainly used to improve the driver's takeover motivation and increase the driving load to improve the situational awareness. At the same time, the game incentive can also meet the high level of user experience. The user experience mainly meets the user's emotional experience needs, social experience needs and personality experience needs.

After determining the two strategies, combined with the highly automatic driver's takeover process model [16], as shown in Fig. 3, the autopilot takeover is divided into two sections: the waiting time and the takeover time, and the functional scope is separately set for the two processes.

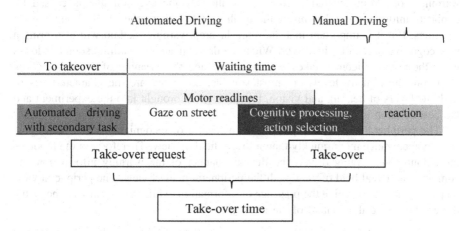

Fig. 3. Highly automatic driver's takeover process model

Notification Strategy of Situational Information

Waiting Time to Takeover. In the waiting time, the driver's situational awareness is low, and the system recognizes the change of the external situation. In highly automatic driving, most of the changes do not meet the takeover conditions, such as parallel cars, following cars or entering the tunnel. In order for the driver to maintain a certain situational awareness, the system needs to actively inform the driver of these situational information. The system informs the driver of the information visually and audibly, and the driver needs to look up and understand the information. This process increases the driving load during the autonomous driving process and reduces driving distraction. At the same time, maintaining a certain level of situational awareness is more conducive to responding to takeover requests more quickly.

Takeover Time. When the takeover condition is triggered, the automatic driving takeover system issues a visual and audible alert request to the pilot to take over. The situation is constantly changing and the road load is not the same. For the driver, it may be necessary to know more quickly the criticality and information of the current takeover situation in order to make the appropriate response faster. This requires that the risk of the takeover warning message be consistent with the takeover scenario. Lerner proposes a multi-level alert, in the highest level of warning, criticality is very important to ensure full warnings are achieved [17]. Road load degree refers to the ratio of the actual traffic flow of the road section to the traffic capacity of the road section, which can be used for dynamic analysis of traffic operation status [17]. The high-risk takeover scenarios are more likely to occur when using automatic driving in high-load roads. Therefore, in the automatic driving takeover system, it is necessary to classify the urgency of the takeover according to the road load, and convey the information to the driver through a multi-level warning method.

The layered warning method can predict the importance of the event in advance and make a takeover warning when the driver hears the warning sound or looks up the warning icon. Multi-layered warnings can alleviate the aversion that is caused by duplicate information and improve the quality of takeovers compared to single-level warnings. But it is important that the multi-layered warning method will also bring a new cognitive burden to the driver. When the driver hears the warning sound or looks up at the warning icon, it takes time to understand the meaning of the information. Therefore, how many levels are most suitable, and what are the characteristics of multiple layers of hearing and vision, this problem is brought into the experiment and the best solution is got.

The peripheral vision of a person has a feature of recognizing a fast moving or sudden appearance more quickly than a foveal field of view. Therefore, in the mood of the autonomous driving driver, the display manner of the warning information can combine the foveal field of view with the peripheral field of view. The peripheral view helps the driver to perceive the presence of information, while the foveal view helps the driver understand the content of the message.

Game Incentive Strategy. In the process of automatic driving, the driver's situational awareness is low, and the essential reason is the lack of motivation to look up the road. Motivation refers to behavior characterized by intention and will. It affects whether humans decide to take action and whether it is internal or external. Intrinsic motivation stems from the desire to engage in specific behaviors for their own benefit, with internal rewards such as enjoyment or satisfaction. Extrinsic motivation stems from the desire for specific behaviors caused by external reward commitments or threatened external rewards. These motivations affect the driver's active acquisition of situational awareness and willingness to take over. Although traffic laws and regulations require each driver to take over, individual factors such as mood, time pressure or social status often lead to disregard and non-cooperation. The concept of gamification, in the background of connected driving, is considered to have the potential to be applied to the driving process and to solve more problems. The table below summarizes some of the game elements that are suitable for an automatic driving takeover system, as shown in Table 5.

Table 5. The specific contents of each level that affect the driver experience

Game elements	Description
Scoring system	Measures for success or failure, representing the driver's takeover efficiency
Grade growth	Cumulative experience can keep users challenging
Feedback and progress	Feedback is the most basic of interaction, allowing users to clearly understand the progress of the task
Trophy and badge	To encourage, and symbolize the completion of the goal
Communication	It is important to form an interconnected communication system for the automatic driving system
Time pressure	Time limits can make drivers more motivated
Continuity	Successful continuity of tasks that users do not want to interrupt

Waiting Time to Takeover. During the waiting time, the driver's driving load is low, and it is necessary to encourage the driver to use artificial driving. On the one hand, it prevents the driver from over-trusting the automatic driving system, and on the other hand, prevents the driver's driving skills from deteriorating. Second, it can also motivate drivers to participate more in social tasks on the windshield. When the driver interacts with other drivers, cars or the environment on the wind window, he can passively obtain situational awareness, which is benefit for the takeover. Other than that, Social activities themselves can also meet the user's social experience needs, even personalized needs.

Takeover Time. At the takeover time, the entire process of taking over the action is "gamed", so that the takeover task is considered to be "want to take over" rather than "must take over", which is "interesting" rather than "responsibility." Adding game factors to the takeover task and setting up a "takeover behavior scoring mechanism", the fun of which improves the takeover motivation and satisfies the user's emotional experience needs.

In the true HAD situation, the "game rewards" of the system for the driver may be fulfilled as actual economic benefits. For example, if the driver takes over the score, the corresponding ones may receive real rewards such as free car wash, refueling discount, and free toll. However, if the driver scores poorly, there will be certain penalties, such as limiting the speed of self-driving and the length of use. The game incentive strategy may involve more advanced business strategies in the development of connected driving.

The design of the interface layer of the automatic driving takeover system interactive interface is shown in Table 6.

Table 6. The design of the interface layer of the automatic driving takeover system interactive interface

Type	User needs layer	Strategy	Time	Function
Low level	sensory experience needs	The situation information notification strategy	Waiting time to take over	Notification of situational change information without reaching the takeover condition, including visual and auditory.
	interactive experience needs.		Takeover time	Multi-level requests take over warning notices, including visual and auditory
	Emotional needs	Game incentive strategy	Waiting time to take over	Encourage manual driving
	Respect needs			Social mechanism on the windshield
High level	Personalized needs		Takeover time	Takeover behavior scoring

3.3   Design of Structure Layer

The structural layer design of the automatic driving takeover system is to refine the functional contents of the takeover system, tease out the structure and hierarchical relationship between the interfaces, etc. The design can according to two strategies, which are the situation information classification strategy and the game incentive strategy. Although the function of the takeover system is simple, reasonable content planning, classification, and subdivision can ensure the integrity of the final output, which is very important for the notification strategy of situational information and driving safety. Classification strategy of situation information as follows:

Divide the Situation into the Waiting Time and Takeover Time. Both time periods need to provide the user with the situation, especially the takeover time.

Notification Policy for Change of the Takeover Time (The Situation Where the Takeover Condition Is Not Reached). The information of situation change is divided into four categories: road change information (multiple corners, front tunnel), dynamic vehicle change information (with car following, with cars in parallel), traffic congestion information and target distance information, and so on.

Takeover Time (In the Situation of the Takeover Condition) Using the Stratification Strategy of Takeover Warning. The current situational load is conveyed through multiple levels of warnings. The specific warning information includes visual warning information and audible warning information. The warning layer is divided into three levels, and more than three layers would have significant cognitive. Game incentive strategy as follows:

Scoring Mechanism of Takeover Behavior. The scoring mechanism takeover behavior is divided into five information elements, including the current takeover status, the current takeover time, the current takeover score, the comprehensive takeover score, and the number of consecutive successful takeovers. The current takeover status represents the success or failure of this takeover, the time from the issuance of the warning message to the successful control of the driver and the score for the efficiency and quality of this takeover. The grade of comprehensive takeover is to calculate the average score of each takeover and give the driver a badge. The badge is graded according to the game routine, and is divided into five colors: gray, green, blue, and purple. The higher the level, the more privilege the driver can have. Permissions, such as unlocking patterns, phrases, etc. available for social features. The number of consecutive successful takeovers is represented by the number of combo times. The higher the number of Combo, the more "achievement" is obtained.

The badges in the comprehensive takeover score have different powers according to the badge level. When the score level is higher than the blue badge, the higher the level, the more real world economic rewards, such as free car wash, free toll, fuel discount, etc. When the rating is lower than the blue badge, the lower the level, the restrictions will be imposed, such as limiting the cruising speed limit or even disabling the autopilot function.

Social Mechanism of Windshield. The social mechanism of windshield refers to simple interaction with other cars, drivers, environments, etc. on the car window directly through gestures or touch screens. The mechanism is divided into "nearby riders" and "personalization". "Nearby riders" can identify nearby vehicles and issue daily phrases and patterns. "Personalization" means that the driver can choose and set his or her favorite personality. Icons and titles represent the attributes of yourself and the car. These icons and titles can be obtained by increasing the overall takeover score, or by unlocking achievements by completing the incentive task.

Mission Achievement Mechanism. There are "Today's Mission" and "Task Achievement". "Today's mission" includes "completed missions" and "unfinished missions". The mission here is to encourage more drivers to use manual driving and windowing, etc. Completion of tasks can improve the overall score. "Task Achievements" also includes "Achieved Achievements" and "Unfulfilled Achievements". Achievements can unlock icons and titles in "Personalization".

3.4 Design of Framework Structure

The windshield may become a new display carrier, and the Augment Reality Full Windshield Display (AR-FWSD) may also play an important role in the future of HAD cars. Unlike ARDs, AR-FWSD can use a large area of windshield as the display area, while a typical HUD is usually only three to five inches. The small display area imposes significant restrictions on driving and safety-related information, because its instrument area is more crowded, giving the driver a cognitive load when performing driving tasks. At the same time, the information prompts are spatially separated from the real world, and the driver needs to distract attention to find the location of the event, such as a pedestrian warning, and the driver still needs time to search for the specific location of the pedestrian.

At the same time, most AR-HUDs currently put information in the driver's visual center (i.e., the foveal view) because the visual resolution in the center of the field of view is much higher than elsewhere, and the spatial resolution of the human field of view declines sharply from the center to the edge. So the peripheral area except the fovea area (i.e., the peripheral field of view) is considered unsuitable for putting important information. However, the peripheral vision of a person has a feature of recognizing a fast moving or sudden appearance more quickly than a foveal field of view. Therefore, in the automatic driving mode, the driver is distracted and when the system detects a burst of non-fixed information, it won't work if it is displayed in the peripheral area. AR-FWSD not only provides opportunities for new information presentations and visual experiences, but also integrates automatic driving, car networking and social entertainment applications. AR-FWSD will be the most appropriate interactive window for driving sub-tasks.

Based on AR-FWSD, in the human-computer interaction interface design model based on user experience, design factors include design goals, user experience needs and design carriers. Among them, the design carrier is the front windshield of the car, and the design goals and user experience needs are related to the user information and the current user driving situation.

The main content of the frame layer design is the layout and planning of the information on the AR-FWSD, that is, how to clearly and properly present the contents and functions of the takeover system to the driver. The visual resolution of a person's central field of view is much higher than elsewhere, and the spatial resolution of a person's field of view is sharply reduced from the center to the edge [18]. The human peripheral field of view has a feature that can identifies things that move quickly or suddenly more quickly when compared to the foveal field of view. It is necessary to arrange the information in a reasonable position of the AR-FWSD based on the visual characteristics of these two points.

Each layer of the warning information includes auditory information and visual information, and the visual information is simultaneously displayed on different areas of the AR-FWSD through two presentation modes. The first type is a peripheral area for peripheral visual field information display along the edge of the wind window. The flashing information appears in a more favorable manner for the driver to recognize the presence of the warning information in the distracting state. In a highly automated driving situation, the driver's behavior is uncertain and does not necessarily have to sit in a regular driving position. At the same time, in recent years, more and more autonomous car interior concept design allows the driver to have more space for activities, so the driver's most central view on the wind window is uncertain. Therefore, the intermediate area except the edge area of the wind window can be used to display specific warning information.

In addition, the information visualization feature in the AR system can solve the user's attention-guided problem [19]. The dynamic display method the information is superimposed on the road or tracking the target's activity (world-Fixed) helps the driver find the exact location where the risk exists [20]. Better tracking performance allows the driver to get better driving performance in the right lane. AR information design should aim at enhance tracking of activity symbols [21].

3.5 Design of Presentation Layer

The presentation layer visualizes the strategic layer, the scope layer, the structural layer and the framework layer. It is a direct expression of the mechanism of the driver's takeover system and a carrier that reflects the usability of the interaction strategy design.

To ensure that the symbols of the car's functions and functions can be (uniquely) identified and their functions are easy to use, ISO 2575 (ISO 2010a) defines symbols and colors that describe the state of the system (e.g., correct operation or failure). DIN EN ISO 15005 (DIN 2012) provides principles for dialogue management and sets standards for compliance. The principles of this standard complement the previous guidelines and address the requirements and compliance procedures for using dialogue while driving. The visual presentation of the IVIS ergonomics direction is covered in EN ISO 15008 (DIN 2011c), for example with regard to the image content and readability of (dynamic) content. To display alphanumeric messages in IVIS, SAE J2831 (SAE n.d.) provides information and design recommendations for OEM and aftermarket systems.

For the use of AR-HUD, Yang [22] and others summarized the existing theoretical results and conclusions of experimental research, and intensively study from the four aspects: road safety prompt information interface layout, information type compatibility, color and quantity. The research proposed the design principle of road safety prompt information interface of the vehicle AR-HUD.

Regarding the design of the voice user interface, the SAE J2988 is a standard being developed that will provide principles and guidance on how to safely use the voice user interface to control the vehicle's selection functions and functions. The audible output DIN EN ISO 15006 (DIN 2012) provides ergonomic specifications for the design and integration of IVIS using sound and speech output. For example, details regarding sound frequency and loudness, information encoding, and enhancement of information (e.g., additional synchronized visual output).

Based on the above specifications and principles, the author designs the presentation layer of the automatic driving takeover system prototype. The design of situational information notification interface is shown in Figs. 4 and 5, and the design list is shown in Table 7.

Fig. 4. Interface design of layering strategy of takeover warning (Color figure online)

Fig. 5. Interface design of notification of situational change information

Table 7. Design list of situational information notification interface

Situational information	Visual warning symbol Peripheral area of the windshield.	Central area of the windshield	Auditory warning spectrum
Situational change		△	
First level warning		!	
Secondary level warning	⌐⌐	! 注意	
Third level warning	⌐⌐	! 危険	

Identification symbols of obstacles

𝅸 𝅷 𝅺 𝅻 𝅼 𝅽 𝅾

Identification symbols of situational change

⚠ ⚠ ⚠ ⚠ ⚠ ⚠ ⚠

In the design of warning information, when designing a logo element, its edges can be enhanced. Use a contrasting color or white that has a high contrast with the environment to set the color edges and increase the contrast between the target color and the background to make it easier to recognize. At the same time, the color principle of importance information is observed, and red is the highest warning color. The warning information is displayed on the wind window in the form of AR. The warning icon would block the driver's sight to some degree, so it is allowed to reduce the transparency of a certain icon, and the recognition of the warning icon does not completely affect the identification of the real environment information.

Add game elements to the interface design of the game motivation strategy to match the policy function settings. The relevant interface information of the game incentive strategy does not belong to the warning information. In order to avoid excessive occupation of the driver's attention resources, no enhanced edge processing is performed. The selected color is technology blue, which represents intelligence, technology and security. The interface design of the takeover behavior scoring mechanism is shown in Fig. 7, and the design list is shown in Table 7. The interface design of the interconnection social mechanism is shown in Fig. 6. The interface design of task achievement mechanism is shown in Fig. 7.

Fig. 6. Interface design interconnected social mechanism achievement mechanism (Color figure online)

Fig. 7. Interface design of task (Color figure online)

The simulated automatic driving system developed based on this experimental research can realize the main functions of manual driving, automatic driving and driving control right switching, and can also synchronously record data related to tests, such as the times of collision, takeover time and takeover score. In the simulator, The automatic driving function is implemented by setting a default path in the map. When the car enters the range of collision module, a takeover warning is issued to simulate the takeover situation of the automatic driving, and the simulated road driving is as shown in Fig. 8.

Fig. 8. Simulated automatic driving system developed by Unity 3D

4 Conclusion

Based on the user experience, the human-machine interface design of the automatic driving takeover system must always be user-centered, and deeply analyze user needs and situational features to perform function and content design in order to obtain a perfect user experience. The model is effective for the automatic driving takeover system, and explains the intrinsic connection between the user, the situation and the design object in the human-machine interface design of the system, which is conducive to understanding and integrating the survey information. The model will provide design guidance for the human-vehicle interface designer of the automatic driving takeover system to provide a better driving experience for drivers in an automatic driving situation. At the same time, the human-vehicle interface design model of the automatic driving takeover system based on user experience enriches the theoretical system of interaction design methodology and contributes to the design method of human-vehicle interface for the automatic driving takeover system.

References

1. Sha, Q., Han, Y.: The study of human behavior vehicle driving process. Art Des. (z1), 104–106 (2015)
2. Ren, Z.: The Studies about Interface Design of Smart TV Based on Use Experience. Hefei Univ. of Technology (2015)
3. Garrett, J.J.: User Experience, 2nd edn. China Machine Press, China (2011)
4. Zhang, H.L.: The Context-based Research and Applications of Automotive User Interface Design Knowledge System. Hunan Univ. (2014)
5. Huang, T.Q.: Interaction Design of a Segment Car for Family in the Future. Beijing Institute of Technology (2015)
6. Tan, H., Tan, Z.Y., Jing, C.H.: Automotive Human Machine Interface Design, 1st edn. Publishing House of Electronics Industry, China (2015)
7. Regan, M.A., Lee, J.D., Young, K., et al.: Driver distraction: theory, effects and mitigation. Automobile Drivers (2008)
8. Gold, C., Körber, M., Hohenberger, C., et al.: Trust in automation – before and after the experience of take-over scenarios in a highly automated vehicle. Procedia Manufact. 3, 3025–3032 (2015)
9. Cunningham, M., Regan, M.A.: Autonomous vehicles: human factors issues and future research. In: Australasian College of Road Safety Conference, Australia, p. 11 (2015)
10. Norman, D.A.: Emotional Design, 2nd edn. China CITIC Press, China (2012)
11. Noy, Y.I., Lemoine, T.L., Klachan, C., et al.: Task interrupt ability and duration as measures of visual distraction. Appl. Ergon. 35(3), 207–213 (2004)
12. Feldhütter, A., Gold, C., Schneider, S., Bengler, K.: How the duration of automated driving influences take-over performance and gaze behavior. In: Schlick, C.M., et al. (eds.) Advances in Ergonomic Design of Systems, Products and Processes, pp. 309–318. Springer, Heidelberg (2017). https://doi.org/10.1007/978-3-662-53305-5_22
13. Underwood, P.: Driver acceptance of new technology: theory, measurement and optimisation. Ergonomics 19(10), 1–3 (2015)
14. Rauch, N., Kaussner, A., Krüger, H.P., et al.: The importance of driver state assessment within highly automated vehicles. In: 16th ITS World Congress and Exhibition on Intelligent Transport Systems and Services, Sweden, p. 8 (2009)
15. Rane, P., Kim, H., Marcano, J.L., et al.: Virtual road signs: augmented reality driving aid for novice drivers. 60(1), 1750–1754 (2016)
16. Zeeb, K., Buchner, A., Schrauf, M.: What determines the take-over time? An integrated model approach of driver take-over after automated driving. Accid. Anal. Preve. 78, 212 (2015)
17. Lerner, N.D.: Preliminary human factors guidelines for crash avoidance warning devices. Interim Report NHTSA (1996)
18. Park, H., Kim, K.H.: Efficient information representation method for driver-centered AR-HUD system. In: Marcus, A. (ed.) DUXU 2013. LNCS, vol. 8014, pp. 393–400. Springer, Heidelberg (2013). https://doi.org/10.1007/978-3-642-39238-2_43
19. Tönnis, M.: Towards automotive augmented reality (2008)
20. Dan, C., Mizell, D., Gruenbaum, P., et al.: Several devils in the details: making an AR app work in the airplane factory. Am. J. Epidemiol. 96(4), 263–269 (1999)
21. Mainak, B., Xu, S.: 47.3: invited paper: world fixed augmented-reality HUD for smart notifications. In: SID Symposium Digest of Technical Papers, pp. 708–711 (2015)
22. Yang, X.: Research of Driving Environment Safety Information Interface Design Principles for In-Vehicle AR-HUD. South China Univ. of Technology (2017)

A Study of Lingnan Garden's Adaptability to Hot and Humid Climate

Mingjie Liang and Li Li[✉]

School of Design, South China University of Technology, Guangzhou 510006,
People's Republic of China
563188440@qq.com

Abstract. Lingnan garden is one of the three major styles of Chinese classical garden. This paper is intended to analyze the construction methods used in the building of Lingnan gardens to minimize the influences of hot and humid climate, including ventilation, sunshade, heat insulation, temperature reduction, damp proofing, wind proofing and rain proofing, and to discuss its adaptability to climate. To conclude, in the context of ecology, sustainability and green construction, the 'passive ecology' strategy stated above has important implications to the building of public modern urban landscape and green spaces.

Keywords: Lingnan garden · Climate adaptability · Passive ecology

1 Introduction

Lingnan garden is one of the three major styles of Chinese classical garden. Having gone through the Nanyue reign in Western Han Dynasty and Southern Han period, it emerged unexpectedly since Qing Dynasty, centering on Pearl River Delta and covering Guangdong, Guangxi, Fujian, Taiwan and other provinces. Chinese private garden has experienced a long-term development, and resulted in a situation with three dominating styles: Northern garden, Jiangnan garden, and Lingnan garden. Lingnan garden is designed to fit in daily life activities, and the garden environment is a part of the architectural space; therefore, Lingnan garden is also called 'Lingnan courtyard' [1].

The adaptation of gardens to nature is specifically reflected in their adaptation to climate, to geography, to environment and to construction materials. Among all the elements, climate is very important in creating local characteristics, and different climates lead to different garden styles to a large extent. What is called 'passive ecology' is different from the current 'active ecology', which is accomplished by modern techniques; the passive ecology strategy aims to create relatively adaptable and healthy space at a very low cost. Undoubtedly, the 'natural' passive ecology model is the concept that should be referential to modern green construction modes. In the context of ecological sustainability and green construction, it has become an important subject to inherit and innovate the climate adaption and 'passive ecology' strategy of Lingnan garden, to master the regionalism of green construction, and furthermore to build a living environment adaptive to Lingnan climate.

© Springer Nature Switzerland AG 2019
A. Marcus and W. Wang (Eds.): HCII 2019, LNCS 11585, pp. 61–73, 2019.
https://doi.org/10.1007/978-3-030-23538-3_5

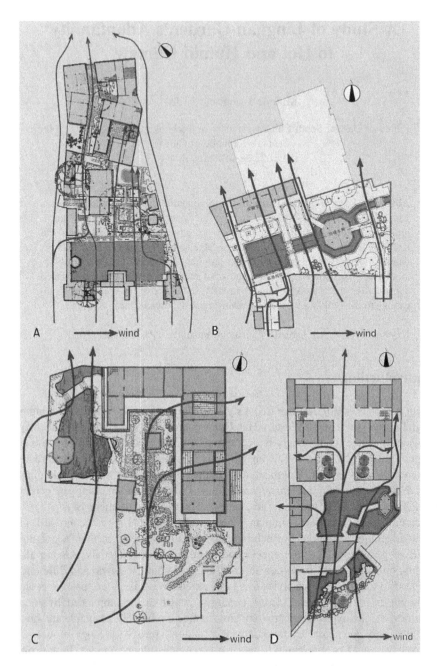

Fig. 1. Temperature reduction by water surface in Lingnan garden: A. pond dug in front courtyard B. pond dug in back courtyard C. pond dug in side courtyard D. ponds dug in both front and back courtyards.

Lingnan is located in the south of the East Asian monsoon region, and has characteristics of tropical and subtropical monsoon and oceanic climates, with the Tropic of Cancer running through its middle part. Most parts of Lingnan have a humid subtropical monsoon climate, while Leizhou Peninsula, Hainan Island and South China Islands have a tropical climate. With a relatively large solar zenith angle, the summer can be longer than half a year in most parts, and stays all year around on South China Islands. Meanwhile, the climate is also characterized by distinct dry and wet seasons: the summer rainfall contributes 80% of the total annual precipitation, while it seldom rains in winter and spring; the distribution of precipitation reflects the monsoon climate features. Apart from northerly-wind cold waves, typhoons and strong storms, the region also has long wet seasons and flood periods. Thus, the Lingnan climate is mainly hot and humid with high temperature and rainfall. Climate conditions have two major influences on the building of gardens in Lingnan. On one hand, the solution to hot and humid climate mainly consists of ventilation, sunshade, heat insulation, temperature reduction, damp proofing, wind proofing and rain proofing. During the construction of a Lingnan garden, it is both important and necessary to consider the influences of hot and humid climate. On the other hand, with rich heat and waterfall, long summers and warm winters, and distinct dry and wet seasons, the evergreen plants reach growth spurt twice a year, and blossom twice or throughout the year. Rich plant resources lay a groundwork for the construction of Lingnan gardens. In the long history, the Lingnan people have followed the nature and improved the environment; they have learned lessons of climate adaptation and integrated gardens into architecture. Thus, a large number of gardens, which are proved to be successful in life and have great research values, have been created [2].

2 Temperature Reduction

In Lingnan gardens, the water surface is one of the important environmental factors to lower temperature, as well as a very effective measure to adjust the microclimate in the garden environment. People dug a pond as the 'water courtyard', or brought water into the garden: both measures help the exchange of hot and cool air and convection, thus resulting in natural ventilation and temperature reduction [3]. As shown in Fig. 1, the ponds are classified by their locations in the garden: they can be built in front courtyard, middle courtyard, back courtyard or side courtyard; some gardens have ponds in both front and back courtyards. For example, the building of Qinghui Garden in Shunde is characterized by its adaptability. In order to adapt to hot climate in the south, the garden was designed to be sparse and lower in the front and dense and higher in the back. The front yard faces south while the residential zone is in the north. A large water surface covers the front yard; the specific heat capacity of water is high, so when water evaporates it can take away a lot of heat. The houses in the back yard have a compact layout, which is sparse but not empty, dense but not crowded. Most of the buildings were built against the prevailing wind in summer for good ventilation. In summer, the cool winds flow upon the large water surface in the front yard and blow endlessly to the residential zone in the back, making people feel fresh and relaxed.

3   Ventilation

The effect of thermal pressure, also called 'stack effect', is often applied in the building of Lingnan gardens for ventilation and heat radiating. Since buildings are different in sizes and shapes, temperature differences in architectural spaces cause air infiltration between interior and exterior under the drive of thermal pressure. Therefore, the temperature differences in different spaces is necessary for thermal pressure effect. As shown in Fig. 2, the Ke Garden in Dongguan adopts an ordered layout, which is common in Lingnan, and its building complex of 'connected houses and high mansions' stands around the courtyard. There are totally one building, six towers, five pavilions, six terraces, five ponds, three bridges, nineteen halls and fifteen houses in the garden, including two staggered flat courtyard structure; high belvederes, slender but quiet buildings and open forecastles make up the main body of the whole garden. Courtyards, patios, doors, windows and halls are used as major vents, and various spaces are used as air passages, such as compound stairs, staired paths, walk stops and stair houses. As shown in Fig. 3, after the ground in courtyards or patios absorb solar radiation heat, its temperature increases, and long-wave radiation heat is emitted and the near-ground air is heated. Therefore, the hot air rises to the top opening of the courtyard or the patio and spreads in the sky. The air pressure at the bottom of courtyards or patios is low, while the pressure at the bottom of halls is high. Resulting from such a pressure difference, the air at the bottom of halls will flow to courtyards or patios to fill the empty space left by the rising air from bottom of courtyards or patios to top. Meanwhile, the temperature at the top of courtyards or patios is relatively low, which allows a large amount of fresh air flowing from under the eaves into halls. The fresh air can fill the empty space left by the original bottom air, thus the 'thermal pressure ventilation' effect is caused: the relatively hot air in the halls flows out at the bottom, and the relatively cold air flows in at the top, resulting in a heat convection.

Fig. 2. The stairwell vent, the courtyard vent and the patio vent of the Ke Building in Ke Garden.

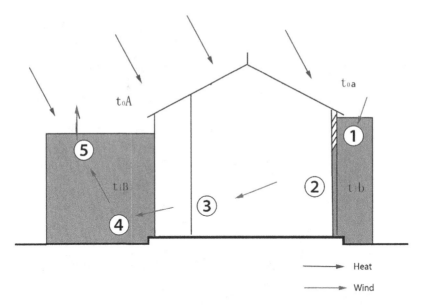

Fig. 3. The thermal pressure ventilation of courtyards and patios in summer

Note:

toA = air temperature in the upper portion of the big patio
tiB = air temperature in the lower portion of the big patio
toa = air temperature in the upper portion of the small patio
tob = air temperature in the lower portion of the small patio

In summer daytime: tiB > toa, tiB > tib, tib < toa, toA ≈ toa. Measured airflow: sky→①→②→③→④→sky

In summer nighttime: tiB < toA, tib > tiB, tib > toa, toa ≈ toA. Measured airflow: sky→④→③→②→①→sky

As shown in Fig. 4, the wind driven ventilation effect is that according to the fundamental of fluid mechanics, when a wind blows towards a building, the air flow against the wind is blocked, so the wind is forced to decelerate. The kinetic energy of the wind transforms into static pressure, and the pressure on the windward side becomes higher than atmospheric pressure, resulting in a positive pressure area [4]. When the wind is blocked by the windward side, it is forced to take a circular route quickly upon the building roof or around the building. The circle flow adds to wind speed, and the pressure on the top, the sides and the leeward side of the building is lower than atmospheric pressure, resulting in a negative pressure area. The so-called 'draught' refers to cross ventilation: when the positive pressure on the windward side and the negative pressure on the leeward side appear, and both sides have openings, a short, straight and unobstructed air passage between the two openings can allow wind go through with little volume loss. The wind enters via the opening on the windward side, and leaves via the opening on the leeward side: such a wind driven ventilation is called 'draught'.

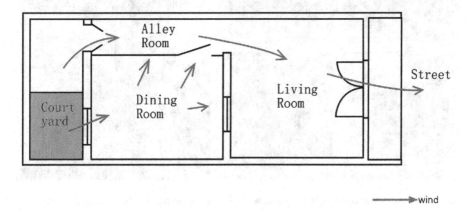

Fig. 4. A diagram of the wind driven ventilation of draughts.

The design of gates and windows in Lingnan gardens has a great influence on the cross-ventilation effect. In terms of gates, most entrances have a ventilated batten door outside, as well as a short batten door, which is commonly known as 'Tanglong'. The main functions of batten doors are ventilation, safeguard and privacy protection. Doors are often designed as mobile partition boards, and indoor screens are also mobile. Some doors have separate upper parts and lower parts; some are mobile at top half and a big gap at the bottom from the ground, allowing air flow freely from bottom to top; some are equipped with hollowed-out partition boards at top half and with ventilated short-wall partitions. All these varied styles of doors are beneficial for convection and ventilation [4]. As shown in Fig. 5, Manchuria window is also a common kind of window used in Lingnan gardens, and has various styles, including open will window, Manchuria window, side-axis window, center-axis window, removable window and wooden window. The windows can open by up-and-down sliding and upwards pushing, and both aim to form a larger windward surface, to create a larger windward angle and to accelerate air convection. On the second floor, the windows are replaced by ground partitions, whose lower half is equipped with ventilated and fixed wooden railings. Such a design can guarantee safety as well as double the wind volume.

Fig. 5. The center-axis Manchuria window designed by author in the expansion project of Qinghui Garden; the side-axis window in the Ke Garden.

4 Sunshade

Sunshade is one of the important measures to protect from heat and to lower temperature. Apart from cutting out direct sunlight and lowering temperature, sunshade can also increase shading surface and reduce radiant heat. Shading the opening parts on the wall can cause pressure difference and accelerate air flow to enhance ventilation. It is common for Lingnan gardens to adopt balcony sunshade, colonnade sunshade and overhanging eaves sunshade above doors and windows. An overhanging balcony can be used for sunshade, rain proofing and keeping cool; while the colonnade is available for passers-by, its sunshade can also help protect people from sun and raindrops, which can be found in the Yu Garden in Panyu. Besides, various kinds of overhanging eaves are common above doors and windows, including zig-zag brick eaves, corrugated brick eaves, polygonal brick eaves and overhanging brick eaves-bracket; in the Ke Garden of Dongguan and Li Garden of Kaiping, there were even wooden board overhanging shades and clamshell overhanging shades. In late Qing Dynasty and Minguo Period, under the influence of western architecture, gardens like Yuyin Hill House in Panyu began to adopt blinds. Meanwhile, the ground temperature will rise with the long-time sunshine casting on the ground, then the hot air will rise and pass into interior spaces easily. Therefore, preventing the ground's heat reflection caused by sunshine is a very important measure. It is common that Lingnan gardens adopt a dense layout. When the patio is big or the alleys are narrow and long, lattice walls or openwork windows are used to separate the big space, and the shades of lattice walls can decrease direct sunlight on the ground. The grounds in Lingnan gardens are usually laid by granites or mosaic bricks. The granites are hard and smooth, and not prone to absorb radiant heat; they can absorb less heat and lose heat quickly, which helps reduce temperature. The mosaic bricks are hard with patterns in one-centimeter relief. The patterns in relief can not only help with skid proofing, prevent moss from growing high, and make the environment more delicate, but also add to shades effectively and reduce dazzling light reflection caused by direct sunlight. As presented in Fig. 6, in the Yuyin Hill House Garden, the Ke Garden in Dongguan and the new expansion of Qinghui Garden, the outdoor grounds are all laid by mosaic bricks. Besides, neat and crowded flower bases and flower stands are also common in Lingnan gardens, which can not only enrich the shading levels in space, but also help with sunshade. The flower bases and flower stands divide the surface into small squares to reduce the ground area exposing to sunlight. At the same time, the shadows cast by flower bases and flower stands can keep most parts of the garden stay in shade for most time of a day, which is also an important feature of Lingnan garden.

Fig. 6. The mosaic bricks adding to shades in the Ke Garden of Dongguan; the flower base and flower stand presented in a dense layout.

5   Rain Proofing

As there is no lagoon in Lingnan area, the rivers flow into sea directly, and tides will hold up river water or even enter into riverways. Such happens a lot especially in springs and summers, when intensive storms cause water puddles and fill pools and rivers, and floods may outbreak. Therefore, the layout of riverside towns in Lingnan is principally based on water directions, and the 'comb layout' has become an important feature of Lingnan residences. The structure of comb layout is characterized by neat and ordered buildings, which align in north-south lines just like combs, and the alleys between two lines of buildings are named 'Li' and work as major traffic passages. Most of the Lingnan riverside towns have a small square, a semicircular pond or an elliptical pond in the front, and ancestral shrines are mostly located by water; almost all the houses were designed based on the principles that buildings should face waterbody directly, and alleys should be normal to the waterbody. Such a design is beneficial to quick rainwater drainage, and thus most of the Lingnan gardens follow this usual practice. For example, as shown in Fig. 7, the layout of Yuyin Hill House Garden in Panyu is very ordered: the Wugong Shrine Alley is normal to both the pond and the riverway outside the gate, and the pond is used for water storage, fish farming, drainage and flood control; the Hall of Deep Willows, the Cottage of Laid Ladle, the Waterside Pavilion and other main buildings, as well as alleys, are all normal to the square water surface, which, to the east, connects to the water network outside the garden by circular riverways. In the Liang Garden in Foshan, the Ancestral Shrine of Liang Family and alleys are all normal to the original Chen's Pond, and the Fenjiang Thatched Cottage, the Wuxiaduo House, the Qunxing Thatched Cottage, the Twelve-Stone House and other main buildings are also normal to the curled lake surface: the stagnant water are altogether drained into the urban river on the west.

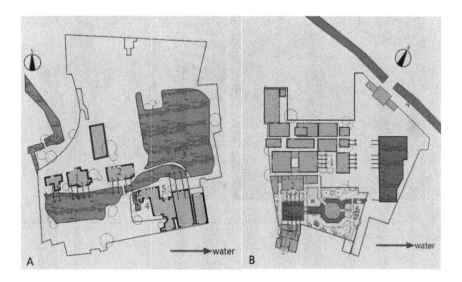

Fig. 7. The drainage normal to waterbody:

A. Liang Garden 1. Fenjiang Thatched Cottage 2. Wuxiaduo House 3. Ancestral Shrine 4. Qunxing Thatched Cottage 5. Sewer at the garden gate

B. Yuyin Hill House in Panyu 1. Wugong Shrine of Good Words 2. Hall of Deep Willows and the Cottage of Laid Ladle 3. Waterside Pavilion

6 Damp Proofing

The humidity is high in most of the buildings in Lingnan area, and will cause great harm to people who live for long periods. Ji Kang of Jin Dynasty had recorded in his Essay on Nourishing Life: 'A residence should be built on dry and cool high grounds to prevent the harm of dampness and miasma.' His essay indicates the importance of damp proof when building gardens. The humidity in buildings has three main sources. First, the water vapor in the air may pass into interior spaces, especially in springs when the relative humidity outdoors can be higher than 95% or even reach 100%. When water vapor comes indoors, the humidity and pressure will rise, making people feeling unfit. Second, when the construction quality is low, there can be leaks on the exterior protection, and the interior spaces will be humid. Third, the groundwater can also rise and permeate, which increases indoor humidity. Therefore, most of the Lingnan gardens use rock foundations. One choice is to build up firm dados, which can be as high as 1.5 m, as the groundwater can also rise for approximately 1.5 m. The dados can be built by laying bricks or stones. Another choice is to build stone pillars and pillar bases, which can prevent groundwater from permeating along bases and pillars. The stone pillar base is usually as high as the diameter of the pillar, and the biggest one can be 1 m high. The interior grounds and galleries are built by big red step bricks without any decoration, which are commonly known as 'termite bricks'. As shown in Fig. 8, the termite brick was a common kind of flooring material in Lingnan and was still in use until 1960s. The termite brick is square, and its size is 33 cm × 33 cm × 7 cm. The ground needs to be leveled with dry sands by 3 to 5 cm, then the bricks are laid, after which the joints should be filled by cement plaster. Such a practice is cheap and labor-saving; the bricks can absorb water, reduce dampness and prevent termite infestations. In the open air in Lingnan gardens, the grounds are often laid by mosaic bricks of Shiwan and local red sandstones, and grass belts are planted along the brick gaps. The mosaic brick is ivory with patterns cut in relief; it is not enameled and can absorb much humidity. The big step bricks, mosaic bricks and grass belts are all permeable materials, and are also very fit for the current 'sponge city' conception. The permeable materials, as stated above, are quite 'elastic' when adapting to environment changes and different natural conditions. When the weather is rainy or damp, the mosaic brick can absorb and permeate water, which is suitable for natural precipitation, surface water and groundwater. When it turns sunny, the brick, which is also hard and wear resistant, will turn dry and pale again.

Fig. 8. The permeable materials of Ke Garden in Dongguan: big step bricks indoors and mosaic bricks, red sandstones and grass belts outdoors. (Color figure online)

7 Wind Proofing

Lingnan is a typhoon-prone area. In summers and autumns, 50% of the typhoons in south China make their landfall in Lingnan, which makes the most serious natural disaster in the area. Therefore, in addition to good ventilation, the typhoon-proof measures were also taken into consideration when building Lingnan gardens [2]. Most of the Lingnan gardens are relatively small-sized and connected with residential buildings. Dense layout and multi-layer layout are very common. A garden with dense layout depends on closeness of buildings to enhance its wind resistant capability, and one with multi-layer layout always faces directly against the prevailing wind or typhoon around the year. It is measured that in a garden compound with four or five layers, the courtyard in the last layer will only receive less than 20% of the wind force. In terms of garden plants, those with deep roots and strong trunks were preferable for their wind resistant capability; local species such as camphor trees, Chinese banyan, palm trees, mango trees, longan trees and lychee trees are also common, while shallow-rooted plants like poplars, paulownia trees and southern magnolia are relatively rare. From the perspective of species, diverse kinds of plants grow in dots and clusters in Lingnan gardens. Trees with different forms and structures are chosen according to different environments or planting areas. Large arbors and small trees are planted together, with bushes and grass growing under them. From the perspective of arrangement, the designs often aim to enrich shadings and enlarge vertical greening area, in order to reach the whole contour's free flowing. A proper proportion of tall trees and density can help the plants' beauty as well as their wind resistant capability.

8 Conclusion

To conclude, in order to deal with hot and humid climate, measures such as ventilation, sunshade, heat insulation, temperature reduction, damp proofing, wind proofing and rain proofing were often used in the building of Lingnan gardens for their climate adaptability. Making rational use of sunshine, wind, temperature, humidity and other natural resources can help reduce our dependence on conventional energy; such a strategy is named 'passive ecology' by academy, which is different from 'active ecology'. Therefore, the study of Lingnan garden's climate adaption has become a global focus in the field of ecology and sustainability design. In the context that Chinese local features are gradually disappearing, the study has important implications to the building of public modern urban landscape and green spaces, as well as the guarantee of urban health and sustainable development.

Acknowledgements. This research is supported by China National Social Science Fund Project - 'Lingnan Garden Art Research' (project number 5BG085).

References

1. Lu, Q.: The Building of Lingnan Garden and Its Aesthetics, 1st edn. China Architecture & Building Press, Beijing (2005)
2. Zeng, Z.: Collected Works of Mo Bozhi, 1st edn. Guangdong Science & Technology Press, Guangzhou (2003)
3. Lu, Y., Yanjun, W.: Guangdong Residences, 2nd edn. China Architecture & Building Press, Beijing (2005)
4. Tang, G.: The Hot and Humid Climate in Lingnan and Its Traditional Buildings, 1st edn. China Architecture & Building Press, Beijing (2005)

Extracting Contour Shape of Passenger Car Form in Front View Based on Form Similarity Judgement by Young Chinese Consumers

Chunrong Liu[(⊠)] and Qing Xu

School of Design, Shanghai Jiao Tong University, Shanghai 200240, China
cheeronliu@sjtu.edu.cn

Abstract. It explores how a reduced contour shape is extracted to reveal the underlying vital parts of passenger car form in front view based on young Chinese consumers' form similarity judgement. Young Chinese consumers as subjects are invited to estimate the similarity of 130 form samples of triple-compartment passenger car form in front view from main brands in Chinese auto market, and 76 form samples are selected as representative ones by cluster analysis. By defining 20 character lines of form in front view and segmenting points on each character line, coordinate value data on all points are recorded and slope values of all 76 segments are calculated. Furthermore, factor analysis is completed and 15 common factors is extracted. The result shows that (1) the passenger car form in front view can be extracted and presented as a reduced but recognizable contour shape with about forty-one percent loss of information on the form in front view; and (2) the contour shape is mainly consisted of character lines defining such basic design parts as side windows, side doors, the upper boundary and the transitional edges of engine hood, the upper and the lower boundaries across Y0 section of grille, almost entire contour of fog light, most of the upper contour of headlight, and the entire contour of intake and almost entire skirt line of front bumper.

Keywords: Passenger car form in front view · Reduced contour shape · Consumer research

1 Introduction

Many researchers have studied and analyzed passenger car form's styling and design and related consumer perception, showing that passenger car form in front view has a stronger influence on the aesthetic perception of passenger car than form in side view as well as form in rear view [1]. The typical and iconic features of passenger car form in front view is an important recognition and guidance for consumers to establish visual information channels between working memory and long-term memory [2]. The form of passenger car in front view is a shaping direction that consumers pay more attention to [3].

In ergonomics field, it is found that different types of visual appearance of passenger car form in front view will bring different emotional experiences to consumers [4]. There has a mapping relationship in customers' potential cognition between lexical semantics of passenger car form in front view and its styling elements [5], and the

© Springer Nature Switzerland AG 2019
A. Marcus and W. Wang (Eds.): HCII 2019, LNCS 11585, pp. 74–84, 2019.
https://doi.org/10.1007/978-3-030-23538-3_6

organizational relationship between the various partial elements has an important impact on the consumer's evaluation on the 'overall aesthetics' of passenger car form in front view [6]. In the cognition of automobile brands, there are several methods that can help satisfy consumers' perceptions and emotional appeals to the brand: by means of machine vision to establish the image training library for passenger car form in front view [7], encoding the styling elements of passenger car form in front view by the theory of Cognitive Psychology [8], and developing sustainable styling language which can be used as shape grammars in articulating brand identity [9]. In terms of consumers' perception of the passenger car form in front view, Liu [10] studied the cognitive characteristics of young consumers' judgement on similarity as well as the differentials presented in consumers' perceptional space when they are exposed to different passenger car forms in front view.

These studies show that the visual appearance of passenger car form in front view has an important impact on consumers' understanding of forms and brands and helps generate differentiated cognition. In view of the facts that passenger car form in front view is composed of complicated line-surface structure and that, in passenger car market background, the Chinese consumer group tends to be younger and is paying more and more attention to the styling and brand characteristics [11], analyzing and extracting the vital parts of the passenger car form in front view as a reduced but recognizable contour shape is conducted in this study based on young Chinese consumers' judgement on similarities between passenger car forms in front view. It will not only help designers to precisely target the young consumer group so as to understand their styling cognitions and consumption choices, but enable designers to carry out innovative design based on specific brand and visual identity targeted at young consumers.

2 Methods

2.1 Cluster Analysis and Sample Screening

Experimental Preparation. In the early stage of the experiment, pictures of 130 triple-compartment passenger car forms in front view with engine exhaust capacity of 1.5 L to 2.4 L in current Chinese mainland market are collected from the Internet and selected as stimuli, involving in the following 31 brands: Beijing Benz, Beijing-Hyundai, BYD, Dongfeng, Dongfeng-Honda, Dongfeng-Peugeot, Dongfeng-Renault, Dongfeng-Yueda-Kia, Dongfeng-Nissan, Dongfeng-Citroen, Qoros, GAC, GAC-Honda, GAC-Toyota, BMW-Brilliance, Chery, SAIC MG, SAIC Volkswagen, SAIC Roewe, SAIC-GM Buick, SAIC-GM Chevrolet, SAIC-GM-Wuling, FAW, FAW Audi, FAW-VW, FAW-Toyota, FAW-Mazda, Changan, Changan Ford,Changan-Mazda and Great Wall.

In order to avoid the distraction of car body color, material, internal structure and environment on subjects' judgement in the coming experiment, all pictures of 130 samples are preprocessed: car bodies in the pictures are reorientated to a unified angle of view and size and are put in white background; the influencing elements such as brand logo, vehicle license plate and sticker are removed; the messy light and shadow are also adjusted; all pictures are transformed to grayscale images. The pictures of all samples are randomly numbered in the order of V1 to V130, respectively.

Similarity Judgement Experiment. 10 professionals in car styling and design are invited to divide passenger car form in front view into basic design elements by their professional knowledge and experience. The passenger car form in front view is initially divided into six parts, namely overall contour of passenger car form in front view, engine hood, headlights, grille, front bumper and front fog lights. 30 young consumers aged 18 to 28 are invited as subjects to estimate on the similarity between passenger car forms in front view by a grouping task tool where samples in pictures are divided into two groups in each turn until all 130 samples fall into eight groups. After the similarity judgement experiment is completed, 30 valid data are obtained and they are processed to export an averaged similarity matrix data. Next, the averaged matrix data is analyzed by hierarchical cluster analysis. By observing the resulted dendrogram, it is reasonable to divide all 130 samples into six cluster groups according to the relevant principle [12].

Then K-means cluster analysis is performed with K value set to 6, and distance of each sample in every cluster group is calculated to the center of cluster group where it belongs to. In each cluster group, the closer a sample is to the group center, the more it can represent the form characteristics of its cluster group, and it is then selected as representative sample. In this way, a total of 76 samples are selected from 130 passenger car forms in front view approximately at a screening rate of 60%.

2.2   Character Line Definition

The styling characteristics have a great impact on consumers' perception of the overall appearance of a passenger car [13]. People can often deepen their cognition and memory of things through the prominent features of complex things. In this way, features help people to build awareness and differentiation of a complete form of things. Moreover, it can be seen in car styling and design practice from sketching to 3D modeling, that lines are the first and the most important expression carrier to convey styling language [14].

Because passenger car form in front view has the characteristics of symmetry from the left to the right, the pictures of the selected 76 samples are divided along the center line so as to define character lines and to perform data acquisition only on half of passenger car form in front view. As mentioned above, passenger car form in front view can be divided into six basic design elements: the overall contour of passenger car form in front view, the engine hood, the headlights, the grille, the front bumper and the front fog lights. Therefore, when defining character lines, it should be considered that all character lines need to be combined together to express both the overall shape in front view and the relationship between the parts while being able to describe shape features of each part. At the same time, the versatility of the configuration of character lines is considered, ensuring all 76 forms can be outlined in front view by the configuration of character lines in brief and to the point way. Based on considerations mentioned above, a total of 20 character lines are defined and labeled (as shown in Fig. 1 and listed in Table 1).

Fig. 1. Character line definition on a half of passenger car form in front view.

In order to facilitate the quantitative description of passenger car form in front view, the appropriate number of edit points are defined for every character line with consideration of appropriate spacing according to the different characteristics of the partial shape so that a character line can fit and represent the corresponding contour and partial shape. To put it in another way, the least number of edit points and the segments connected by the two adjacent edit points are used to describe each character line.

Table 1. Character line definition.

Parts character lines	
The contour in front view:	
The roof contour	a
The side window contour	b
The body shoulder contour	c
The side body contour	d
Bottom of the front bumper	e
The engine hood	g; i; j
The headlight	l; m; n; o
The grille	p; q; r
The front bumper	f; h; k
The front fog light	s; t

Finally, 20 character lines are defined to describe and to fit different contours and shapes in six parts. For example, in view of that, for headlight, the difference in the shape among samples is obvious and great, the character lines describing the shape of the headlights are divided into more segments. Finally, 76 segments are defined to form a configuration of 20 character lines and are named after the labelling letter of the corresponding character line together with its staring and ending points' serial numbers. For example, as shown in Fig. 2, the segment 'a12' is one of segments of 'character line a' with starting and ending points with serial number '1' and '2', respectively.

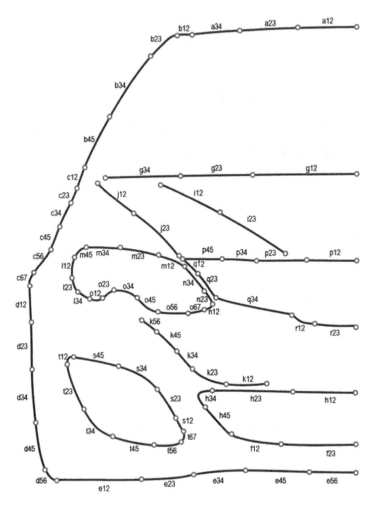

Fig. 2. 76 segments on 20 character lines.

2.3   Edit Points' Coordinate Value Extraction

The slope of each segment on a character line defines its own direction and has influence on the local flow of that character line. To calculate the slope of a segment, the coordinate values of its starting point and ending point need to be acquired as follows.

First of all, the preprocessed picture of a sample is imported into the top viewport of the CAD software, aligned with it height at a fixed value, and moved to coincide the intersecting point of left and right symmetry line and horizontal line across the bottom of the tires with the origin of coordinate system. Nextly, all character lines are figured out according to the defined configuration of character lines and the corresponding segments, and then adjusted, if necessary, by moving edit points to fit the contour and partial shapes in passenger car form of that sample. Since there are 96 edit points used to define all 76 segments for a sample, 96 pairs of coordinate values of edit points on character lines for that sample are acquired and recorded. In this way, all coordinate values of edit points in all form samples are acquired and recorded respectively.

2.4   Slope Calculation

An edit point's coordinate value data is composed of a pair of x-coordinate and y-coordinate values. The slope of a segment can be calculated from the coordinate value data of its starting point and ending point, more specifically, the ratio of the difference between its ending and starting points' y-coordinate values divided by that between its ending and starting points' x-coordinate values. In this way, 76 segments' slope values of character lines for all samples are calculated and recorded respectively.

2.5   Factor Analysis and Result

In this phase, factor analysis is employed to analyze the data on slope values for all samples. When conducting factor analysis, the principal components method is used, and the extraction is based on setting the eigenvalue and varimax rotation method is selected for extracting common factors. Three trials of setting the eigenvalue to 'greater than 1', 'greater than 2', and 'greater than 3' are carried out, respectively. When the eigenvalue is set to 'greater than 1', the total variance explained is 82.848%, while the total variance explained is 30.062% if the eigenvalue is set to 'greater than 3'. Both trials are not ideal as the contour shape extracted is not concise enough by the former trial and by the latter trial, the contour shape extracted has too much loss to be recognized.

After three attempts, it is found that when the eigenvalue is set to 'greater than 2', the contour shape is reduced but recognizable with the total variance explained of 58.816% and 15 common factors are determined and extracted by 51 segments, which have absolute value of loading greater than 0.5 on one common factor but relatively small value on the other common factors. They are retained for outlining the contour shape with about 41% of character lines erased. The partial rotated component matrix is shown in Table 2 and the retained 51 segments are listed in Table 3.

Table 2. Result of factor analysis.

Rotated component matrix[a]

	Component														
	1	2	3	4	5	6	7	8	9	10	11	12	13	14	15
a23	−0.15	0.01	0.15	0.06	−0.18	−0.02	−0.23	−0.21	0.33	−0.01	**0.57**	0.04	0.23	−0.08	−0.08
b12	−0.03	−0.10	**0.60**	0.00	0.23	−0.08	0.17	−0.09	−0.12	0.02	−0.04	0.04	0.30	−0.05	−0.01
b23	0.12	0.06	**0.78**	0.15	0.13	0.07	-0.02	−0.07	−0.05	0.06	−0.01	−0.11	0.06	0.20	0.07
b34	0.07	0.18	**0.80**	0.10	−0.13	0.04	−0.03	−0.08	−0.04	0.04	−0.03	0.01	−0.04	0.17	0.02
b45	0.13	0.05	**0.68**	−0.01	−0.24	0.08	−0.08	−0.10	−0.02	0.02	0.06	−0.09	−0.17	0.02	−0.03
c12	0.11	0.11	0.08	−0.09	0.01	0.09	−0.30	−0.05	0.07	−0.04	0.19	0.03	0.20	**0.55**	−0.02
c23	0.18	−0.08	0.06	0.06	−0.22	−0.01	−0.05	0.16	−0.14	−0.12	0.02	0.16	0.03	**0.63**	0.00
c56	0.04	−0.02	0.08	0.03	0.02	−0.04	−0.12	0.04	0.13	0.03	**−0.66**	0.03	0.14	−0.01	0.03
c67	−0.05	0.00	0.07	**0.66**	0.11	−0.02	0.04	0.01	−0.06	0.00	0.01	0.01	0.01	−0.12	−0.03
d12	−0.02	0.02	−0.12	−0.19	−0.14	−0.04	−0.05	−0.04	−0.01	**0.71**	−0.05	0.04	0.00	0.11	−0.03
d23	−0.01	0.01	−0.07	−0.01	0.01	0.03	**0.72**	−0.06	−0.02	−0.04	−0.06	0.04	0.01	−0.09	−0.19
d56	0.09	0.02	−0.13	0.10	0.01	0.18	0.14	−0.08	0.00	**−0.67**	−0.06	−0.09	−0.01	0.18	0.18
e12	0.33	−0.15	−0.07	−0.06	−0.02	0.63	−0.02	−0.08	0.10	0.11	0.08	0.01	0.01	0.14	−0.17
e45	0.18	−0.01	−0.01	0.05	0.14	0.11	0.09	−0.07	−0.09	0.19	0.26	**0.69**	−0.30	0.12	−0.07
e56	0.08	0.09	−0.12	0.11	0.00	0.11	0.15	0.03	0.03	0.10	0.14	**0.62**	0.10	0.08	−0.09
f12	0.05	−0.03	0.02	0.22	0.11	0.02	0.08	0.18	0.06	0.27	0.13	0.14	0.07	0.18	**−0.70**
f23	−0.09	−0.02	0.00	0.17	0.10	0.07	−0.32	0.02	−0.01	0.12	0.11	0.00	0.05	0.06	**−0.77**
g12	0.00	−0.03	−0.20	**−0.72**	−0.04	0.05	0.04	-0.02	0.01	0.15	−0.04	−0.03	0.10	0.10	0.17
g23	−0.01	0.12	−0.04	**−0.56**	0.25	0.12	−0.12	−0.21	0.00	0.14	−0.03	0.10	0.05	−0.08	0.16
h12	−0.02	0.00	0.02	−0.02	0.06	−0.02	**0.71**	0.01	−0.05	0.02	0.58	0.08	0.02	0.05	0.17
h23	0.09	0.10	−0.01	−0.06	0.11	0.03	0.17	0.13	−0.04	−0.02	**0.74**	0.02	−0.04	0.02	−0.05
h34	−0.03	−0.01	0.19	0.20	0.10	0.01	0.08	0.18	−0.04	**0.53**	0.00	0.07	−0.18	0.07	−0.02
h45	0.26	**−0.50**	−0.11	0.03	−0.03	−0.01	0.02	0.09	−0.09	−0.08	−0.02	0.05	0.05	−0.35	−0.02
i12	**0.89**	−0.03	0.08	0.04	−0.01	0.10	−0.06	0.02	0.05	0.04	0.01	0.03	0.12	−0.06	0.12
j12	**0.86**	−0.02	0.03	0.12	−0.03	0.16	−0.07	−0.04	0.06	0.07	−0.01	−0.07	0.12	0.00	0.13
k23	0.01	**−0.87**	−0.05	0.10	0.07	0.08	0.05	−0.05	−0.05	0.05	0.00	−0.07	0.08	0.09	−0.08
k34	0.01	**0.90**	−0.01	0.01	−0.01	0.08	0.01	−0.03	0.05	0.05	0.05	0.01	0.08	−0.01	−0.06
k45	−0.01	0.03	0.05	0.01	0.03	−0.07	**0.80**	0.01	0.03	−0.01	0.22	0.12	0.08	0.06	0.22
k56	−0.08	0.00	0.25	−0.01	**0.64**	−0.12	0.47	0.12	0.10	0.03	0.14	0.14	−0.02	0.05	0.12
l34	−0.02	0.05	0.12	−0.07	−0.03	**0.81**	0.01	−0.04	0.02	−0.22	−0.02	0.02	−0.02	−0.08	0.04
m12	0.25	0.03	−0.08	0.06	−0.08	−0.01	0.16	−0.07	**−0.53**	0.08	0.38	−0.13	−0.05	−0.22	−0.25
m23	0.26	0.01	−0.11	−0.01	0.08	−0.03	−0.01	−0.01	−0.23	0.02	0.10	0.01	−0.07	**−0.57**	0.11
m45	−0.07	0.01	0.15	0.01	0.02	0.00	−0.04	**−0.75**	0.08	0.13	0.03	−0.05	0.12	−0.18	0.19
n23	−0.08	0.07	0.15	−0.09	−0.02	**0.80**	0.02	0.14	0.02	−0.07	−0.03	−0.01	−0.10	−0.05	−0.04
o23	−0.03	0.03	−0.09	−0.02	**0.84**	−0.02	−0.05	0.00	−0.01	0.03	−0.01	−0.04	−0.01	−0.03	−0.01
o34	0.01	−0.05	0.04	0.03	**−0.86**	0.05	0.06	−0.02	−0.03	−0.01	−0.03	−0.01	0.05	0.05	0.05
o67	0.04	0.12	−0.05	−0.14	0.00	0.04	0.04	−0.03	**0.81**	0.05	0.00	0.01	−0.08	−0.02	0.01
p12	0.05	0.00	−0.01	0.08	0.02	0.08	0.02	0.07	0.00	0.09	0.16	**−0.82**	0.06	−0.04	0.05
p34	0.04	−0.02	0.09	0.02	0.05	−0.37	−0.01	−0.07	**−0.65**	0.01	−0.04	0.03	0.13	−0.06	0.05
q12	0.00	0.07	−0.03	0.06	**−0.53**	−0.22	−0.06	−0.11	0.19	0.23	0.19	0.16	−0.09	0.03	0.25
q23	0.11	0.13	−0.06	0.12	0.07	−0.18	−0.14	**0.69**	0.21	0.05	0.09	0.11	−0.06	−0.02	0.23
r12	−0.02	−0.24	0.04	**−0.76**	0.13	−0.04	0.17	0.09	0.09	0.06	0.11	−0.17	0.15	−0.01	0.00
r23	0.04	**−0.80**	0.03	−0.39	0.04	0.03	0.09	0.03	0.02	0.05	0.05	−0.24	0.06	0.06	0.01
s23	**0.82**	0.05	0.17	−0.01	0.00	−0.04	0.06	0.04	0.04	0.04	−0.01	−0.02	0.02	0.04	−0.08
s34	0.14	**0.68**	0.10	0.00	0.15	0.00	0.14	0.01	−0.02	0.13	0.21	−0.10	0.29	0.05	−0.06
s45	0.00	0.28	0.09	−0.02	0.06	0.03	0.04	−0.06	−0.05	0.06	0.12	−0.17	**0.53**	−0.06	0.10
t12	0.10	−0.04	0.02	−0.06	0.00	0.01	−0.03	0.04	**0.70**	−0.02	0.03	0.06	0.08	−0.03	0.07
t23	0.02	0.10	0.13	0.09	−0.03	−0.16	0.00	**−0.57**	0.02	−0.10	0.08	0.13	0.06	−0.08	0.08
t34	**−0.61**	−0.02	0.09	0.11	0.04	0.07	−0.01	−0.42	0.04	0.11	0.01	−0.08	−0.02	0.18	0.21
t45	−0.10	−0.03	0.07	0.20	0.11	0.09	0.04	0.07	−0.03	0.17	0.10	−0.02	**−0.65**	−0.07	0.08
t56	0.15	−0.02	0.02	−0.05	0.02	−0.01	0.06	−0.06	−0.11	0.00	−0.07	0.10	**0.71**	0.15	−0.07

Rotation Method: Varimax with Kaiser Normalization.

[a] Rotation converged in 17 iterations.

Table 3. Common factors and the corresponding segments.

Common factors	Remained segments
Loading value > 0.5	
Common factor 1	i12, j12, s23, t34
Common factor 2	h45, k23, k34, r23, s34
Common factor 3	b12, b23, b34, b45
Common factor 4	c67, g12, g23, r12
Common factor 5	k56, o23, o34, q12
Common factor 6	e12, l34, n23
Common factor 7	d23, h12, k45
Common factor 8	m45, q23, t23
Common factor 9	m12, o67, p34, t12
Common factor 10	d12, d56, h34
Common factor 11	a23, c56, h23
Common factor 12	e45, e56, p12
Common factor 13	s45, t45, t56
Common factor 14	c12, c23, m23
Common factor 15	f12, f23

The retained 51 segments are then drawn to rebuild the reduced passenger car form in front view. The retained character lines are plotted as shown as the left figure in Fig. 3 and the extracted contour shape is shown as the right figure in Fig. 3. The contour shape reflects underlying vital parts in passenger car form in front view selected by consumer's perception of and judgement on similarity between passenger car forms.

The contour shape is mainly composed of 51 retained segments related to the shape of six parts of passenger car form in front view. By mirroring the contour shape, a complete contour shape is generated and shown in Fig. 4. As listed in Table 1, each part is outlined by at least one character line, but significant differences in contribution of six parts to the contour shape are observed in the contour shape. The more segments retained in the contour shape a character line has, the more important it is to the entire form. As for the whole contour of passenger car form in front view, side window contour and bottom of the front bumper are more vital than roof contour, body shoulder contour and side body contour while, as for the partial shapes, front fog lights and front bumper are more important to the styling and design and have carried more basic design elements of the passenger car form in front view.

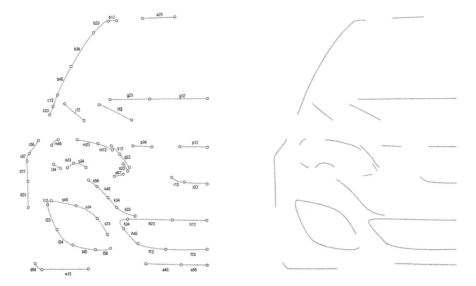

Fig. 3. Underlying vital parts of passenger car form in front view expressed in retained character lines and extracted contour shape.

Fig. 4. A reduced but recognizable contour shape of passenger car form in front view.

3 Conclusions and Discussion

Based on young Chinese consumers' perception of and similarity judgement on triple-compartment passenger car forms in front view in the mainstream brands in the Chinese market, an approach to extract the contour shape of passenger car form in front view is completed with quantitative analysis methods.

By cluster analysis method, 76 form samples of triple-compartment passenger car form in front view are selected as representative ones in a total of 130 form samples from 31 main brands in the Chinese passenger car market. With the acquired coordinate values of edit points segmenting 20 character lines, factor analysis is conducted, and the contour shape with about 41% loss of information on passenger car form in front view is extracted and illustrated.

The extracted contour shape is mainly related to and reflected by the following parts and their shapes: side windows, the upper side doors, the upper boundary and the transitional edges of engine hood, the upper and the lower boundaries across Y0 section and vertical boundary of grille, almost entire contour of fog light, most of the upper boundary of headlight, and the entire contour of intake, almost entire skirt line of the front bumper and the transitional edge of the upper area on front bumper. Among these parts, it is noticeable that frog lights and air intake seem to play more influential role in defining the contour shape than headlights and grille.

These findings imply the key areas for the front-view shape of the form in front view in the context of similarity judgement on passenger car form in front view by young consumers, suggesting to certain extent what basic design elements designer may focus on to highlight innovative car styling and design for the targeted consumer population.

Acknowledgment. The authors would like to extend thanks to Xiaoguo Ding for participating in part of the work in this study.

References

1. Ranscombe, C., Hicks, B., Mullineux, G., Singh, B.: Visually decomposing vehicle images: exploring the influence of different aesthetic features on consumer perception of brand. Des. Stud. **33**, 319–341 (2012)
2. Lu, Z., Zhang, Y., Cheng, B., Li, S., Fritz, F.: A study on the cognitive mechanism of car styling based on style feature. Automot. Eng. **38**(3), 280–287 (2016). (in Chinese)
3. Liu, G., Huang, D., Liu, C.: Preference of car form feature based on DEMATEL method. China Packag. Ind. (24), 34–36 (2014). (in Chinese)
4. Li, S., Zhang, H., Qin, Z.: Optimization design of the shape of automobile front face based on inference Kansei Engineering. Pack. Eng. **38**(18), 82–84 (2017). (in Chinese)
5. Li, B., Dong, Y., Zhao, D., Wang, B.: A computational method for car family analysis based on fine-grained classification. Chinese J. Automot. Eng. (4), 250–258 (2018). (in Chinese)
6. Xu, Z., Huang, M., Yuan, Q.: Research on family design theory of vehicle styling based on cognitive psychology. Automobile Appl. Technol. (7), 121–123 (2016). (in Chinese)
7. McCormack, J.P., Cagan, J.: Speaking the buick language: capturing, understanding, and exploring brand identity with shape grammars. Des. Stud. **25**, 1–29 (2004)

8. Guo, R., Yin, H., Peng, J.: Analysis of visual force in automobile front face modeling design. Pack. Eng. **38**(16), 152–157 (2017). (in Chinese)

9. Chen, L.: Research on front face modeling of cars based on gestalt theory. Master's thesis, Hunan University, Changsha (2007). (in Chinese)

10. Liu, C., Ding, X., Xie, Y., Jin, Y.: Young consumers' perception of the similarity between the passenger car forms in front view. Pack. Eng. **39**(24), 158–162 (2018). (in Chinese)

11. IRESEARCH: 2017 China automotive digital marketing case study report. http://report.iresearch.cn/report/201801/3120.shtml. Accessed 1 Nov 2018. (in Chinese)

12. Zhang, W.: Advanced Course of Statistical Analysis in SPSS, pp. 235–251. Higher Education Press, Beijing (2004). (in Chinese)

13. Jing, C.: The car design method based on evolutionary thinking. Doctoral dissertation, Hunan University, Changsha (2015). (in Chinese)

14. Zhao, D., Zhao, J.: Automobile form feature and feature line. Pack. Eng. **28**(3), 115–117 (2007). (in Chinese)

Based on Usability Experience-Enhanced Potential Community Transportation Design Study in China: A Case of Kindergarten Bus Stop Design

Zhen Liu[1](✉) and Wang Kin Ng[2]

[1] School of Design, South China University of Technology, Guangzhou 510006,
People's Republic of China
liuzjames@scut.edu.cn
[2] The British School of Guangzhou, Guangzhou 510000,
People's Republic of China

Abstract. With the development of China's economy and the improvement of urban living standards, the design and study of urban bus stations has become an emerging topic in recent years. The current study on the design of urban bus stops in China is distributed in the following six areas: aesthetics and culture, informatization, built, way of use, place of use, and user experience design. With the advent of the service design and experience economy era, study on bus stations with user experience design as the core has become a hot topic in recent years, which includes interaction and service system, integrated application, platform design, and experience of waiting for the bus. The design of community transportation bus stops based on university campuses, has gradually received attention. However, little attention has been paid to the experience and design of bus stop associated with school transfers close to kindergartens, which is the most important issue to the community transportation. Hence, this emphasizes the need for exploring potential user experience design factors for community transportation design in a case of bus stop design to kindergarten in China, which is this paper aimed at. Based on the result of the study, a bus stop design potential framework for children is proposed in terms of experience design, where the nine factors need to be considered when designing bus stop to help with safety and comfort for children in line with problems and factors: the four problems when waiting for the bus with children at the bus stop, the three inappropriate factors of the current bus stop, and the six inappropriate factors for protection of children safety in the current bus stop design.

Keywords: Community transportation · Kindergarten bus stop design ·
Usability · Transportation experience

1 Introduction

With the development of China's economy and the improvement of urban living standards, the design and study of urban bus stations has become an emerging topic in recent years. As shown in Fig. 1, the current study on the design of urban bus stops in

A. Marcus and W. Wang (Eds.): HCII 2019, LNCS 11585, pp. 85–100, 2019.
https://doi.org/10.1007/978-3-030-23538-3_7

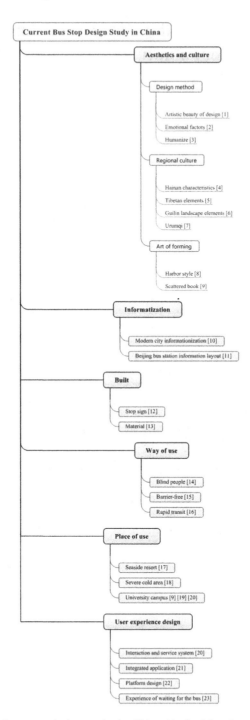

Fig. 1. The current bus stop design study in China (devised by the authors based on the literature).

China is distributed in the following six areas: aesthetics and culture [1–9], informatization [10, 11], built [12, 13], way of use [14–16], place of use [9, 17–20], and user experience design [20–23]. Among them, the study mainly focuses on the aesthetics and culture of the station, which involves: design method [1–3], regional culture [4–7], and art of forming [8, 9]. Moreover, with the advent of the service design and experience economy era, research on bus stations with user experience design as the core has become a hot topic in recent years. These studies include: interaction and service system [20], integrated application [21], platform design [22], and experience of waiting for the bus [23]. Furthermore, the design of community transportation bus stops based on university campuses [9, 19, 20], has gradually received attention. However, little attention has been paid to the experience and design of bus stop associated with school transfers close to kindergartens, which is the most important issue to the community transportation. Hence, this emphasizes the need for exploring potential user experience design factors for community transportation design in a case of bus stop design to kindergarten in China, which is this paper aimed at.

2   Research Methods

A semi-structure online questionnaire was adopted to explore the user (parents and children) experience to the current bus stop and design, based on parents' views. As shown in Fig. 2, the structure and questions are designed for the questionnaire that has been upload to asking.wenjoy.com. The semi-structure online questionnaire has been sent to parents' groups of a kindergarten in Guangzhou, China, via WeChat that is the most popular social media platform in China. 93 completed questionnaires have been received within a week. SPSS (Statistical Product and Service Solutions) software is used for the quantitative data analysis and content analysis is implemented for qualitative answer.

3   Results

3.1   The Most Frequently Used Means of Transportation for Kindergarten

The questionnaire respondents were asked to select the most frequently used means of transportation for taking their children to go to and back from kindergarten. The results in Fig. 3 show that more than half of (54.8%) responding parents most used their own cars for sending to and taking back their children from kindergarten than using public transportation bus (15.1%). Interestingly, there is no one selected the subway as the transportation for their kids. However, nearly one third of (30.1%) responding parents reported that their employed other methods, which were bicycle and electric bicycle.

Asking https://asking.wenjoy.com/s/fYCKiGo

Λ Asking

- Home

About Kindergarten Bus Stop Design

* Mandatory

* 1. The most frequently used means of transportation for your children to and back from kindergarten is:
○Bus
○Drive
○The subway
○Other

* 2. How long do you usually wait for a bus :
○Less than 5 minutes
○5-10 minutes
○More than 10 minutes

* 3. Do you often take your children on the bus?
○Yes
○No

* 4. What do you do when you wait for the bus?
○Reacing/mobile phone
○Chatting with children
○Concentrate on waiting for the bus
○Other

* 5. What does your child do while waiting for the bus?
○Reacing/mobile phone
○Play

Asking https://asking.wenjoy.com/s/fYCKiGo

○Concentrate on waiting for the bus
○Other

* 6. Do you think the current bus stop is appropriate?
○Appropriate
○Inappropriate

* 7. Why ?

* 8. Do you think the current bus stop design can protect your child's safety?
○Yes
○No

* 9. Why ?

* 10. Would you like to have a bus stop specially designed for children?
○ Yes
○ No

* 11. What problems do you have with your children waiting for the bus? Why is that?

* 12. What do you think needs to be added to children's bus stops to help with safety and comfort?

Submit

© 2014-2019 Powered by Wenjoy Technology Inc. All rights reserved.

Fig. 2. The structure and questions of a semi-structure questionnaire for exploring the user experience to the current bus stop and design, based on parents' views (devised by the authors).

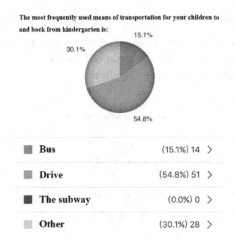

Fig. 3. The most frequently used means of transportation for children go to and back from kindergarten (responding parents' view).

3.2 Parents' Waiting Time for Their Buses

The questionnaire respondents were asked to select their waiting time for their buses at bus stops. The results are shown in Fig. 4, which suggests that overwhelming (88.2%) responding parents spent more than five minutes on waiting for their buses. It even cost more than 10 min of nearly one third of (30.1%) responding parents for it.

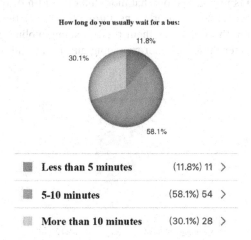

Fig. 4. Parents' waiting time for their buses at bus stops for taking their children to go to and back from kindergarten (responding parents' view).

3.3   Parents with Their Children for Their Buses

The questionnaire respondents were asked whether they usually take their children with them for their buses. As shown in Fig. 5, about one fourth of (28%) responding parents use to bring their children with them on the buses.

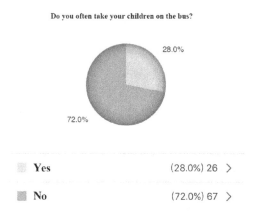

Do you often take your children on the bus?

Yes	(28.0%) 26 >
No	(72.0%) 67 >

Fig. 5. Parents with their children for their buses (responding parents' view).

3.4   What Parents Do When They Wait for Their Buses

The questionnaire respondents were asked to select what they do when they wait for their buses. The results in Fig. 6 show that more than two fifth of (41.9%) responding parents chat with their children, nearly one third of (31.2%) them do nothing but waiting, about one fourth of (23.7%) them prefer reading/mobile phone, and few of (3.2%) them prefer other things without providing any further information.

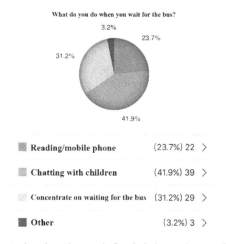

What do you do when you wait for the bus?

Reading/mobile phone	(23.7%) 22 >
Chatting with children	(41.9%) 39 >
Concentrate on waiting for the bus	(31.2%) 29 >
Other	(3.2%) 3 >

Fig. 6. What parents do when they wait for their buses (responding parents' view).

3.5   What Children Do When They Wait for Their Buses

The questionnaire respondents were asked to select what their children do when they wait for their buses. The results in Fig. 7 show that more than two fifth of (41.9%) responding parents reported that their children do nothing but waiting. More than one fourth of (26.9%) the parents saw their children playing. About one fifth of (22.6%) the parents stated that their children prefer reading or using mobile phone instead doing nothing. Nearly one tenth of (8.6%) them revealed that their children are doing other things without providing any further information.

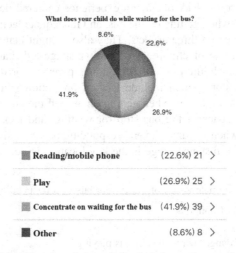

▇ Reading/mobile phone	(22.6%) 21 >
▇ Play	(26.9%) 25 >
▇ Concentrate on waiting for the bus	(41.9%) 39 >
▇ Other	(8.6%) 8 >

Fig. 7. What children do when they wait for their buses (responding parents' view).

3.6   Appropriateness of Current Bus Stop

The questionnaire respondents were asked whether they think the current bus stop is appropriate. As shown in Fig. 8, nearly half of (45.2%) responding parents thought that the current bus stop is inappropriate.

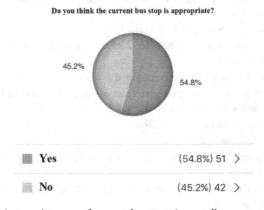

▇ Yes	(54.8%) 51 >
▇ No	(45.2%) 42 >

Fig. 8. Appropriateness of current bus stop (responding parents' view).

The questionnaire respondents were further asked to provide their qualitative opinion to the reasons of their answers to the current bus stop appropriateness. Most of the responding parents believed that the current design of bus stop is appropriate, since the location of the stop, frequency of the bus, and the distance between bus stops are acceptable.

However, there are 36 of the responding parents provide their views on inappropriate issues of the current bus stop. As shown in Table 1, there are three main inappropriate issues of the current bus stop according to the responding parents' perspective, which are experience design issue, safety issue, and location issue. 19 of responding parents stated that the experience design causes inappropriateness of the current bus stop, where the lack of human experience centered design, easily getting crowded and confused when getting on the bus, and inadequate facilities for waiting the bus, are the most concerned three aspects. They also thought that the bus stop design did not consider the issue of children, and further suggested that there should be a dedicated bus stop for children. 12 of responding parents worried about the safety issues of current bus stop, which include lack of protection when children playing within the stop, lack of protection when getting on and off the bus, waiting on the road caused by inadequate space of the bus stop for waiting, and lack of caution lines to warm danger area of when waiting. Several responding parents indicate the lack of bus stop in their convenient distance range is the key location issue.

Table 1. The inappropriate issues of the current bus stop (responding parents' view).

Issues	Aspects of opinions	Number of mentions
Safety	Fear of danger while the child is playing	1
	There are always electric bikes and shuttles when getting on and off the bus	1
	Some places where the station is set up are unreasonable. The platform should be set up in a relatively empty place to avoid the danger of traffic accidents caused by people waiting for the car to stand on the road	1
	There is no yellow line or red line in the danger area for warning	1
	Other potential dangers for children (without any further information)	8
Location	There is no bus stop close to my home	4
	The distances between bus stops are not equal and lack of unified planning	1
Experience design	Lack of human experience centered design	7
	When the bus stops, passengers can easily get crowded and confused when they get on the bus	7
	Inadequate facilities for waiting	2
	Not clean and comfortable	1
	Too many ads are boring, which can be interesting content or bus messages	1
	Most of the city has station kiosks, and other areas have not been equipped	1

3.7 Current Bus Stop Design for Protection of Children Safety

The questionnaire respondents were asked whether they think the current bus stop can protect their children. As shown in Fig. 9, two third of (66.7%) responding parents thought that the current bus stop design can not protect their children when they waiting for the bus.

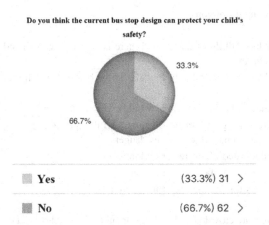

Do you think the current bus stop design can protect your child's safety?

▨ Yes	(33.3%) 31 >
▨ No	(66.7%) 62 >

Fig. 9. Current bus stop design for protection of children safety (responding parents' view).

The questionnaire respondents were further asked to provide their qualitative opinion to the reasons of their answers to the current bus stop design for protection of children safety. Most of the responding parents believed that the current design of bus stop works for their children protection, because the stop platform embankment is higher than the road; and every bus stop is carefully designed (without any further information). Interestingly, a responding parents stated that child safety awareness requires parental guidance and role models to the bus stop.

However, 47 of the responding parents provide their views on the inappropriate issues for protection of children safety in the current bus stop design. As shown in Table 2, there are six main inappropriate issues of the current bus stop design according to the responding parents' perspective, which are related to experience design, fence, departure area, a dedicated way, platform, and waiting area. 14 of the responding parents stated that inadequate facilities for safety of children, and lack of dedicated design for children to use are the most concerned experience design aspects. As one responding parent made it clear that the function of the current bus stop is small, but there is a place for people waiting for the bus to shelter from the rain. 15 of the responding parents concern fence issue, because, without a barrier, the child would run into the road easily, and could cause danger without guardrail for queuing since the queuing order is poor in China. There are two issues indicated by seven of the responding parents: people are crowded and children are not safe to get on and off; and there are always electric bikes and shuttles when getting on and off the bus. Five of the responding parents thought that a dedicated way for children should be considered as children fall down easily and more likely to walk on the bus path when they get on the bus. Some responding parents pointed out that the platform of the bus stop is too close and facing to the road and without dedicated waiting area for children.

Table 2. The inappropriate issues for protection of children safety in the current bus stop design (responding parents' view).

Issues	Aspects of opinions	Number of mentions
A dedicated way	Children fall down easily, and there is no passage designed for children	3
	Children are more likely to walk on the bus path when they get on	2
Fence	Without a barrier, the child would run into the road	14
	There is no guardrail for queuing, and the queuing order is poor in China, which causes danger	1
Platform	No dedicated platform for children	2
	Too close and facing to the road	2
Waiting area	There is no waiting area for children	2
Departure area	People are crowded and children are not safe to get on and off	5
	There are always electric bikes and shuttles when getting on and off the bus	2
Experience design	Inadequate facilities for safety of children	10
	Lack of dedicated design for children to use	4

3.8   A Bus Stop Specially Designed for Children

The questionnaire respondents were asked whether they would like to have a bus stop specially designed for children. As shown in Fig. 10, a vast majority of (92.5%) responding parents said YES to the question.

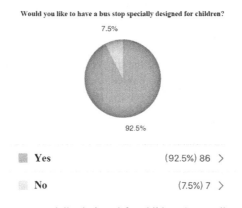

Fig. 10. A bus stop specially designed for children (responding parents' view).

3.9   Problems When Waiting for the Bus with Children at the Bus Stop

The questionnaire respondents were asked to provide qualitative views for what problems they had with your children when waiting for the bus at the bus stop. 66 of the responding parents provided their perspectives. As shown in Table 3, there are six key related issues elected by responding parents to the problems when waiting for the bus with children at the bus stop, which are parent, children, other passengers, bus stop, bus, and environment. There are 33 responding parents highlighted that passengers are crowded without lined up, resulting in getting on the bus disorderly, which could potentially hurt children. This could be blamed for inadequate guardrail in bust stop, as one responding parent emphasized that, because there is no order to get on the bus, if there is no guardrail, children will be squeezed and collision. The bus stop related problems are associated with waiting seat, guardrail, on-stop information board, platform space and roof, and form outlook design. Interestingly, one responding parent raised a issue of environment, which the bus exhaust emission could be harmful to children when waiting in a open space.

Table 3. The problems when waiting for the bus with children at the bus stop (responding parents' view).

Issues	Aspects of opinions	Number of mentions
Parent	Need to hold the child's hand tightly, fearing that the child will be unsafe for naughty, or child will rush out when the bus is approaching the station	3
	Keep an eye on the children for fear of danger	2
	Boring	1
Children	Children will run around, which will not be safe enough	4
	Easy to walk into the driveway	1
Other passengers	Crowded and not lined up	30
	Get on the bus disorderly	3
Bus stop	Inadequate waiting seat, such as special seat for child, comfortable seat, dirty seat, and without seat at all	5
	Inadequate guardrail	2
	Ineffective user friendly on-stop information board for children	2
	Insufficient platform space	1
	Insufficient platform roof in the case of rain	1
	Inadequate bus stop form outlook design	1
Bus	Long waiting time	4
	Irregular approach and departure, such as dangerous parking method, stopped before arriving at the station, and too short to stay	4
	Delay	1
Environment	Bus exhaust emission could be harmful to children	1

3.10   Things Need to Be Added into Bus Stop to Help with Safety and Comfort for Children

The questionnaire respondents were asked to provide qualitative views for what kind of things need to be added into bus stop to help with safety and comfort for children. 84 of the responding parents provided their suggestions. As shown in Table 4, there are night key related issues suggested by responding parents to the things need to be added into bus stop to help with safety and comfort for children, which include platform, roof, seat, guardrail, information board, waiting area, boarding area, experience, and dedicated bus station. Safety related issues, such as guardrail, and boarding area, are caught more attention of the responding parents. In addition, the responding parents more concerned seat number, safety and comfort, and even special seat for children. Further, the responding parents suggested following aspects to improve user experience of parents and children: to add devices that interest children so they don't get bored waiting for a bus, such as toy, and showing short animation film, to range a staff to maintain order at the stop and look after the children, to put a water machine at the stop, and to keep clean environment. They even went further for calling for design dedicated bus station for parents and children, which is close to kindergarten.

Table 4. The things need to be added into bus stop to help with safety and comfort for children (responding parents' view).

Issues	Aspects of opinions	Number of mentions
Platform	Spacious docking station	1
	Access to the sidewalk requires precautions	1
Roof	Children's taste can partly shelter from wind and rain	1
Seat	More seats	11
	Safe and comfortable seat	7
	Special seat for children	7
Guardrail	Add guardrails so passengers can get on the train in an orderly way	13
Information board	Add bus arrival information prompts	3
	User friendly for children	1
Waiting area	Set up a waiting area for children	5
	Reading area	4
Boarding area	Children express boarding path	6
	Add guardrail to set up safe boarding path	3
	Need staff to guide the safety of getting on and off the bus	3

(continued)

Table 4. (*continued*)

Issues	Aspects of opinions	Number of mentions
Experience	Add devices that interest children so they don't get bored waiting for a bus, such as toy, and showing short animation film	7
	Need a staff to maintain order at the stop and look after the children	5
	Need a water machine at the stop	2
	Clean environment	2
Dedicated bus station	For parents and children	2

4   Discussion and Conclusion

Based on the results of the research, currently in China, parents who have children attending kindergartens, usually spend more than five minutes waiting for the bus. When waiting for a bus with their children, most parents and children will do other things, such as playing, using mobile phones and reading, chatting with their children instead of concentrating on waiting for the bus. Most parents of children prefer to use private cars and other means they can control, such as bicycles and e-bikes, to transport their children to kindergarten. According to the mutual verification of question 1 and question 3, only a small number of people choose public transportation when they are with their children. This could explain why less than half of parents think the current bus stops are inappropriate. They believe that inappropriate issues cover three issues: safety, location and experience design. Most parents don't think the current bus station design can protect their children. They argue that unreasonable factors for protecting children's safety in current bus station design, including a dedicated way, fence, platform, waiting area, departure area and experience design. They mentioned the problem of waiting at bus stops with their children. These problems are about parent, children, other passengers, bus stop, bus, environment. Most parents would like to have bus stops specially designed for their children. They further gave the things that are need to be added into bus stop to help with safety and comfort for children, such as platform, roof, seat, guardrail, information board, waiting area, boarding area, experience, and dedicated bus station. Hence, based on the result of the study, a usability experience bus stop design potential framework for children close to kindergarten in community transportation design is proposed as shown in Fig. 11, in terms of experience design, where the nine factors need to be considered when designing bus stop to help with safety and comfort for children in line with problems and factors: the four problems when waiting for the bus with children at the bus stop, the three inappropriate factors of the current bus stop, and the six inappropriate factors for protection of children safety in the current bus stop design. Further study will look into design in line with results of this study and validate a bus stop for a kindergarten.

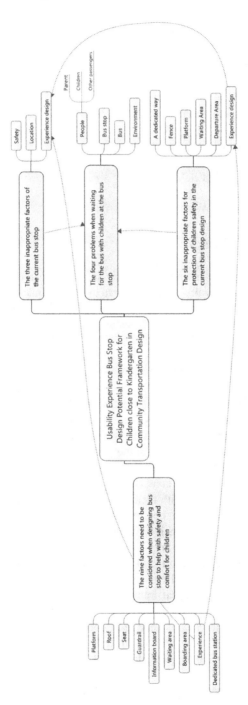

Fig. 11. The usability experience bus stop design potential framework for children close to kindergarten in community transportation design (devised by the authors).

Acknowledgements. The authors wish to thank all the people who provided their time and efforts for the investigation.

References

1. Bai, K., Wen, S.: From the design art beauty of wuhan city bus station design. Shanxi Architect. **38**(12), 4–6 (2012)
2. Wu, C., Li, L.: Analysis of emotional factors in the design of urban bus stations. Art Des. (Theory) (z1), 102–103 (2012)
3. Zhao, Q., Wang, L.: Discussion on the humanized design of bus shelters. Shanxi Architect. **33**(19), 12–13 (2007)
4. Hua, D.: Discussion on the application of Hainan characteristic elements in the design of bus stations. China High-tech Zone (10), 7+117 (2017)
5. Hao, L.: Application of tibetan elements in the design of bus stations in Lhasa tourist area. J. Tibet Natl. Univ. (Philos. Soc. Sci. Ed.) **34**(1), 102–104 (2013)
6. Rao, J.: Research on the integration of landscape cultural elements and Guilin bus station design under the background of "One Belt And One Road". Beauty Times (part 1) (2) (2018)
7. Sun, X.: Design of Urumqi bus station under the concept of regional culture. Ind. Des. (6), 78–79 (2017)
8. Han, B., Ma, J., Shao, G.: Design analysis of bus stop in harbor style. J. Nanjing Forest. Univ. (Nat. Sci. Ed.) **27**(5), 69–71 (2003)
9. Zhao, T., Liu, Y.: The conceptual design of "Scattered Book"—design of bus station of new campus of Hebei University of Technology. Popular Lit. (8), 129 (2014)
10. Chen, D.: Research on the design of modern city bus station under the background of information. Art Technol. **29**(11) (2016)
11. Zhang, Z.: Preliminary study on information layout design of Beijing bus station. Decoration (5), 8–9 (2005)
12. Zhang, S., Hou, X., Ding, C.: Based on the innovative bus stop sign research and design. Technol. Commun. (15) (2014)
13. Wang, X., Wang, H.: Product semantic expression of materials in bus station design. Beauty Times (City Ed.) (11), 73–74 (2017)
14. Xia, Y., Zhao, Y.: Research on the accessibility of bus station space guidance based on the needs of the blind—taking the design practice of bus stations in Xi'an as an example. Decoration (8), 68–69 (2014)
15. Feng, X.: Research on Design and Use Behavior of Barrier-Free Bus Stations in Chinese Cities. Tianjin Academy of Fine Arts (2008)
16. Ding, Q.: Analysis of the design of bus rapid transit station—taking Hangzhou and Changzhou bus rapid transit design as an example. Transp. Res. (20), 156–160 (2011)
17. Wang, D., Gao, Y., Zhang, S.: Design of bus station in seaside tourism resort. Mech. Des. (1) (2015)
18. Zeng, X., Cheng, W.: Study on Design Optimization of Bus Stations in Big Cities in Severe Cold Region–Taking Harbin as an Example. China Urban Planning Annual Meeting (2014)
19. Kang, X.: Research on landscape facilities design in universities – a case study of campus bus station design. Popular Lit. (16), 73–74 (2013)
20. Xing, Y.: Design of Campus Bus Station Service System Based on Interaction Theory. Shandong Jianzhu University (2015)

21. Hu, F.: Urban Bus Platform Experience Design and Application Research. Wuhan University of Technology (2012)
22. Jin, X.: Detail design and experience of Wuhan bus station site from multi-dimensional perspective. Build. Mater. Decoration (5), 118–119 (2018)
23. Dong, X.: Research on the design of optimizing the waiting experience of bus users. Ind. Des. (7), 60–61 (2017)

Transition to Automated: The Interaction of Activating the In-vehicle Automated Driving System

Weiyi Ning$^{(\boxtimes)}$, Xuning Wang, and Yingzhu Qian

Baidu IDG Intelligent Driving Experience Center, Beijing, China
{ningweiyi,wangxuning}@baidu.com

Abstract. Automated driving system (ADS) becomes more popularized in recent years, and the level 2 and level 3 ADS have already been equipped on several production car models in the market. The activating interaction of the ADS is very important since it is the very first step for users to manipulate and understand the system. However, most existing studies are focusing on the process of transition to manual—drivers taking over of the vehicles. We collected 21 different activating interactions that have already been equipped or proposed in production or concept cars, and explored their usability in a simulated driving environment with 30 recruited participants via a subjective evaluation. An experimenter measurement of the steering wheel turning angle was also included in order to compare the driving safety level between different activating interactions. With the ANOVAs of the usability score and steering wheel turning angle done, the result shows that six interactions "press the button on the right part of the steering wheel", "press the button on the left part of the steering wheel", "press the button on the center console", "pull the paddle behind the steering wheel on the right once", "pull the left and right paddles behind the steering wheel together once" and "keep pulling the left and right paddles behind the steering wheel for 1 s" are recommended for the ADS in terms of offering great usability and ensuring basic driving safety.

Keywords: Automated driving system · Activating interaction · Usability · Driving safety

1 Introduction

"The automated driving technology has the potential to fundamentally change road transportation and improve quality of life. Automated vehicles (AVs) are anticipated to reduce the number of accidents caused by human errors, increase traffic flow efficiency, increase comfort by allowing the driver to perform alternative tasks, and ensure mobility for all, including old and impaired individuals" [1, 2]. In recent year, this technology has become more and more popular and widely discussed. We could see some production car models that are already equipped with different levels of automated driving system in the market such as Tesla Model S and 2019 Audi A8.

Automated driving systems (ADS) are leveled in different ways. In this paper the NTHSA driving automation taxonomy (see Fig. 1) is adopted [3].

© Springer Nature Switzerland AG 2019
A. Marcus and W. Wang (Eds.): HCII 2019, LNCS 11585, pp. 101–113, 2019.
https://doi.org/10.1007/978-3-030-23538-3_8

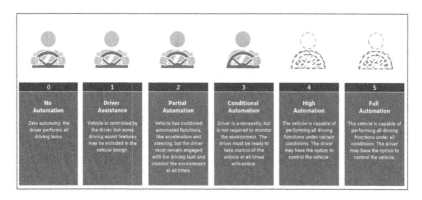

Fig. 1. The NHTSA driving automation taxonomy

Most existing product vehicles that are equipped with ADS have level 2 or level 3 automation capabilities. For example, Tesla's Autopilot with Hardware version 1 can be classified as somewhere between levels 2 and 3 [4], and the 2019 Audi A8's Audi AI system supports level 3 autonomous driving [5]. In Fig. 1, we could see that the level 2 automation is defined as "partial automation" which it requires that "the driver must remain engaged with the driving task and monitor the environment at all times", and the level 3 automation is called "conditional automation", the driver does not need to monitor the environment all the time, but has to take control of the vehicle when the system cannot keep working under certain circumstances. During a driving journey for a car that's equipped with level 2 or level 3 ADS, the automation is usually activated by the driver when it is available, and requires a takeover of the vehicle when the environment or the vehicle's condition no longer supports the automation. The driver must take over the vehicle with a certain manipulation, e.g. pressing the brake pedal immediately. So, for the whole process, activating and taking over are the two nodes that the human control and ADS intersect. Any mistake that happens in these nodes could incur potential road safety hazards. For example, in March 2018, a Tesla Model X fatal crash happened in California, U.S. because the driver didn't notice the takeover warning message that lasted for six seconds prior the crash [6]. This crash caused the car on fire and the death of the driver (see Fig. 2).

Fig. 2. Tesla Model X fatal crash site, March 2018, California

This accident raised a huge public debate, should the level 2 or level 3 ADS be equipped on product vehicles? How quickly can a distracted human turn to take control of the vehicle in what might be a sudden emergency [7]? We could see many scholars are researching on the safety issue of transition from automation to manual in the ADS. Such as the proper lead time of the takeover request [8] and the driver's driving stabilizing time after resuming control of the vehicle [9], etc.

However, with the plentiful and diverse existing research on the taking over side, we cannot see enough work on the activating side. When a driver initiates the ADS, the necessary interaction between the driver and the interior HMI (Human-machine-interface) could create potential accident risk e.g. driver distraction when the system is not yet turned automated [10]. So, it is important to provide the driver easy-to-use and un-distracting manual-to-automation (activating) interaction in the whole automated driving experience, and this needs a lot professional and systematic research.

In different L2 & L3-automated-driving-supported vehicles, the ADS is usually named in different ways such as Tesla's "Autopilot" [4], Audi A8 2019's "Audi AI Traffic Jam Pilot" [5], Volvo XC90's "Pilot Assist" [11] and Cadillac CT6 2018's "Super Cruise" [12]. Those vehicles are equipped with different hardware units that provide different activating interactions such as pulling a stalk behind the steering wheel, pressing a physical button on the steering wheel or a pressing physical button on the interior center console, etc. Different types of interactions have their pros and cons in terms of usability. We decided to investigate that through an experiment study among different existing activating interactions we collected via desk research.

We collected different activating hardware units from the existing production or concept cars models that are equipped with ADS including Tesla Model S, Audi A8 2019, Volvo XC90 2018, Cadillac CT6 2018, Volvo Concept Cockpit 26, Nissan Leaf 2018. Mainly there are three types of hardware units: button, stalk and paddle. These hardware units can be located in the following places: steering wheel front, steering wheel back and the center console (see Fig. 3).

Fig. 3. A pile of images of the existing ADS activating hardware units from production or concept cars

We listed all the possible locations & hardware unit types and there are totally 10 different variations: (1) a paddle behind the steering wheel on the left; (2) a paddle behind the steering wheel on the right; (3) a button on the left part of the steering wheel; (4) a button on the top part of the steering wheel; (5) a button on the right part of the steering wheel; (6) a button on the bottom part of the steering wheel; (7) a button on the left console; (8) a button on the center console; (9) a stalk behind the steering wheel on the left; (10) a stalk behind the steering wheel on the right.

For each type of hardware unit, based on the current common setups in modern production cars that we researched on there could be one or several interactions for each hardware: *(1) Button*: press once. *(2) Stalk*: pull downward once; pull upward once; pull forward once; pull backward once; pull backward twice. *(3) Paddle*: pull one paddle twice; pull two paddles once; keep pulling two paddles together for 1 s; keep pulling two paddles together.

So, considering about all 10 different hardware unit location variations, the number of the total activating interactions is 21, which is shown in the Fig. 4 below.

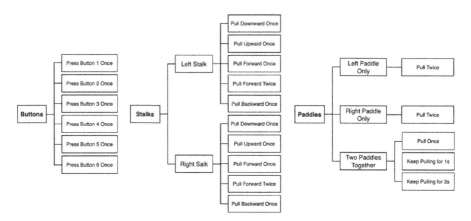

Fig. 4. Total 21 different activating interactions based on the collected hardware unit variations

According to the research of distraction in driving activities that was done by Tang, Wang, Shan and Zhu [16], the steering wheel turning angle is a key parameter to judge whether a certain in-vehicle manipulation or interaction could distract the driver and generate potential hazard and it was involved in this research to evaluate the driving safety level of different activating interactions.

The objective of this research was to figure out which one or several of those 21 interactions could offer great usability and ensure the basic safety of driving. Results could help and provide strong theoretical basis for the interior design of our own autonomous-driving demo car and offer recommendations of selecting ADS activating hardware units for those automotive OEMs we will cooperate with in the future.

2 Experiment Design

2.1 Participants

Thirty participants (21 males, 9 females, according to the Chinese driver gender ratio which is approximately 7:3 in 2017 [13]) ranging from age 18 to 44 (M = 29.57, SD = 2.67) years of age took part in this laboratory experiment. Their reported years of driving experience ranged from 0.5 year to 10 years (M = 3.6, SD = 2.81). All of them had normal or corrected-to-normal vision, valid driver licenses, and had driven within the past month. Participants were compensated with 100 RMB/hour. Written informed consent was obtained prior to the experiment.

2.2   The Simulated Driving Environment

We set up the simulated in-cockpit environment in our research laboratory in Beijing (see Fig. 5) in order to investigate how users would react and behave to the ADS activating scenarios. This simulated environment was built using the Pinguanfeida driving simulator. This simulator includes a steering wheel with embedded buttons, stalks and paddles, an accelerator & brake pedal set, a monitor that's placed on a table could display a virtual driving track and people could actually drive a car on that track with controlling the accelerator and brake. All 10 activating hardware units were embedded in this simulated environment: (1) a paddle behind the steering wheel on the left (left paddle); (2) a paddle behind the steering wheel on the right (right paddle); (3) a button on the left part of the steering wheel (button 1); (4) a button on the top part of the steering wheel (button 2); (5) a button on the right part of the steering wheel (button 3); (6) a button on the bottom part of the steering wheel (button 4); (7) a button on the left console (button 5); (8) a button on the center console (button 6); (9) a stalk behind the steering wheel on the left (left stalk); (10) a stalk behind the steering wheel on the right (right stalk).

Fig. 5. The simulated environment

2.3   Usability Evaluation Criteria

Prior to the experiment, we did an expert discussion that includes four in-vehicle experience design professionals trying to discover what principles could be adopted for evaluating the usability of activating the ADS based on the key factors from several existing in-vehicle or in-aircraft user experience studies, such as "user could learn from previous experience" [14], "the system should prevent manipulating errors" and "the manipulation could be reached within a short distance" [15], etc. We collected the key findings and summarized, generally there are five key principles could be worth considering and adopted as the usability test criteria: (1) *Error prevention.* How a certain interaction or experience process in the HMI system could be done with a low chance of accidentally making an error; (2) *Co-existing with other manipulations.* How a

certain interaction or experience process could be done without affecting other interaction or experience process; (3) *Easy to reach physically*. How a certain interaction or
experience process could be easily initiated by moving any body part for a short
distance; (4) *Comfortable to manipulate*. How a certain interaction or experience
process could be done in a comfortable way; (5) *Easy to learn from previous experience*. How a certain interaction or experience process could be easily learnt from
previous experience of using the same type of products.

All participants were asked to marked the above five criteria from 1–5 (1 stands for
not important at all, 5 stands for very important), and we got the mean value of each
criteria's score (x) and a clear importance ranking. This result would help us to evaluate
the general score for each activating interaction finally (will be explained later). The
marking result is shown in Fig. 6 below.

Criteria	Error prevention	Co-existing with other manipulation	Easy to reach physically	Comfortable to manipulate	Easy to learn from previous experience
Score (x)	4. 58	3. 08	2. 73	2. 5	2. 12
Importance	★★★★★	★★★★	★★★	★★	★

Fig. 6. Usability test criteria marking and the importance ranking result

We could clearly see a ranking order: The "error prevention" is considered as the
most important usability criteria. And the "easy to learn from previous experience" is
considered as the least important one.

2.4   Experiment Design and Procedure

The experiment was conducted as a within-subjects design. The independent variables
were the 21 ADS activating interactions, the dependent variables were the usability
evaluation score of each interaction from the participant evaluation result and the
steering wheel turning angle from the experimenter measurement result.

The usability score of each ADS activating interaction from the participant evaluation was considered as the mainly-considered result because the main goal of this
experiment is comparing the usability between different ADS activating interactions.
The steering wheel turning angle from the experimenter measurement was only used to
filtrate the good-usability activating interactions to ensure the basic driving safety.

Participant Evaluation. Firstly, each participant was asked to understand the background of this experiment and get familiar with all the software and hardware in the
simulated environment in five minutes. Secondly, each participant was asked to
manipulated all 21 activating interactions in a completely random order. For each
round, the driving will drive the "car" in virtual track. When it went on the straight road
(the virtual car is hard to control on curved road), the experimenter would send a
message "automated driving is available now" to the monitor, and the participant needs
to activate the ADS via a certain interaction immediately. When the activation is
successfully done, the screen message is turned to "automated driving successfully

activated" and the screenshot of the monitor at that moment will be taken automatically. All participants were asked to activate the ADS via all 21 types of functions in a completely random order (Fig. 7). After each round, the participant is required to evaluation the certain activating interaction based on the five usability criteria by marking from 1–5 (1 stands for not matched at all, 5 stands for very well matched) and filling out a form.

Fig. 7. The experiment in process

Experimenter Measurement. During each round of the experiment for each participant, the steering wheel turning angle is measured from the monitor screenshot of the successful activating moment, it is 100% matched with the physical steering wheel's turning angle. We leveled the turning angle for 5 levels based on the maximum turning angle and the minimum turning angle we observed during the whole experiment: "1" represents very subtle turning (0°–5°); "2" represents subtle turning (5°–10°); "3" represents normal turning (10°–15°); "4" represents obvious turning (15°–20°); "5" represents very obvious turning (20°–25°).

3   Result

3.1   Participant Evaluation Result

Under each usability criteria there are 21 mean value score of the 21 activating interactions from 30 participants' evaluation result (see Figs. 8, 9, 10, 11 and 12). Hence, each activating interaction has 5 usability criteria scores (f). If we use this 5 usability-criteria scores to multiply its importance score (x) that has been mentioned above, we would get a total usability score (T) for each interaction (Table 1).

$$T = x1f1 + x2f2 + x3f3 + x4f4 + x5f5 \qquad (1)$$

Repeated measures ANOVA revealed that the total usability scores of 21 activating interactions were significantly different from each other (F [6.24, 181.08] = 7.65, p = 0.001). Bonferroni post hoc analyses indicated that there was no significant

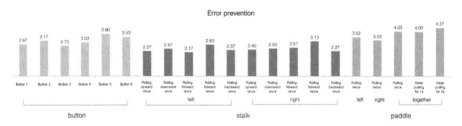

Fig. 8. Usability score of the 21 activating interactions under "Error prevention" criteria

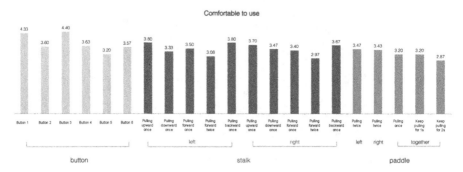

Fig. 9. Usability score of the 21 activating interactions under "Comfortable to use" criteria

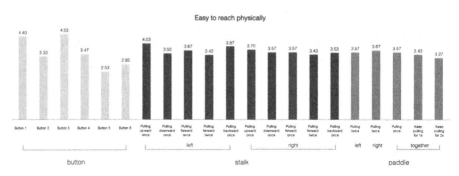

Fig. 10. Usability score of the 21 activating interactions under "Easy to reach physically" criteria

difference between the top-eight usability interactions "press the left button on the steering wheel once", "press the right button on the steering wheel", "press the button on the center console once", "pull the left paddle twice", "pull the right paddle twice", "Pull left and right paddles together once", "keep pulling left and right paddles for 1 s" and "keep pulling left and right paddles for 2 s". This means that from the participants' perspective these interactions have no difference in terms of usability.

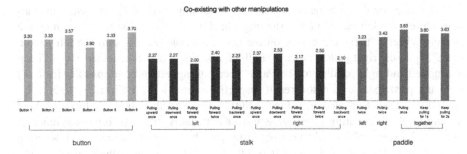

Fig. 11. Usability score of the 21 activating interactions under "Co-existing with other manipulations" criteria

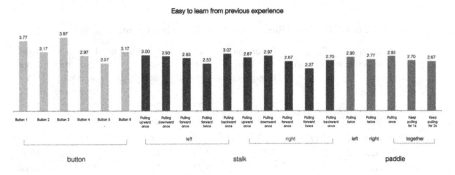

Fig. 12. Usability score of the 21 activating interactions under "Easy to learn from previous experience" criteria

3.2   Experimenter Measurement Result

We collected the data of the steering wheel turning angles of all 21 interactions for each participant, and matched those angles with different levels that has been mentioned in the "experimenter measurement" section. Then we calculated the mean value of all 30 participants' steering wheel turning level for each interaction. The result is shown in Fig. 13 below.

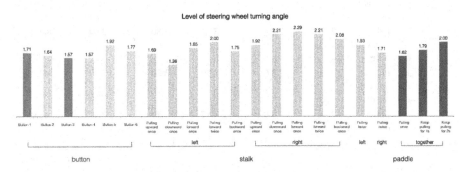

Fig. 13. Mean steering wheel turning level of 21 activating interactions

We could see that the mean steering wheel turning level of the top-eight interactions ("press the left button on the steering wheel once", "press the right button on the steering wheel", "press the button on the center console once", "pull the left paddle twice", "pull the right paddle twice", "Pull left and right paddles together once", "keep pulling left and right paddles for 1 s" and "keep pulling left and right paddles for 2 s") from the participant evaluation result respectively are: 1.71, 1.57, 1.77, 1.93, 1.71, 1.62, 1.79, 2.00. Repeated measures ANOVA revealed that these 8 steering wheel turning level of activating interactions were significantly different from each other (F [4.56, 132.24] = 2.62, p < 0.05). Bonferroni post hoc analyses indicate that steering wheel turning level of "pull the left paddle twice" and "keep pulling left and right paddles for 2 s" were significantly greater than other 6 activating interactions (ps > 0.05).

Table 1. Total usability score (T) for 21 activating interactions

			Criteria importance	Error prevention	Co-existing with other manipulations	Easy to reach physically	Comfortable to manipulate	Easy to learn from previous experience	Total score (T)
				4.58	3.08	2.73	2.50	2.12	
Button	Press button	Button 1		2.87	3.30	4.40	4.33	3.77	54.12
		Button 2		3.17	3.33	3.33	3.60	3.17	49.58
		Button 3		2.73	3.57	4.53	4.40	3.97	55.29
		Button 4		3.03	2.90	3.47	3.63	2.97	47.66
		Button 5		3.80	3.33	2.53	3.20	2.57	48.03
		Button 6		3.53	3.70	2.93	3.57	3.17	51.22
Stalk	Left	Pull upward once		2.27	2.27	4.03	3.80	3.00	44.23
		Pull downward once		2.47	2.27	3.50	3.33	2.93	42.39
		Pull forward once		2.17	2.00	3.67	3.50	2.83	40.85
		Pull forward twice		2.83	2.40	3.42	3.08	2.53	42.78
		Pull backward once		2.37	2.23	3.87	3.80	3.07	44.28
	Right	Pull upward once		2.40	2.37	3.70	3.70	2.87	43.71
		Pull downward once		2.50	2.53	3.57	3.47	2.97	43.95

(*continued*)

Table 1. (*continued*)

		Criteria importance	Error prevention	Co-existing with other manipulations	Easy to reach physically	Comfortable to manipulate	Easy to learn from previous experience	Total score (T)
			4.58	3.08	2.73	2.50	2.12	
		Pull forward once	2.57	2.17	3.57	3.40	2.67	42.32
		Pull forward twice	3.13	2.50	3.43	2.97	2.27	43.65
		Pull backward twice	2.27	2.10	3.53	3.67	2.70	41.39
Paddle	Left	Pull twice	3.52	3.23	3.57	3.47	2.90	50.62
	Right	Pull twice	3.23	3.43	3.67	3.43	2.77	49.84
	Both	Pull once	4.03	3.83	3.57	3.20	2.93	54.24
		Keep pulling for 1s	4.00	3.60	3.43	3.20	2.70	52.51
		Keep pulling for 2s	4.37	3.63	3.27	2.87	2.67	52.93

4 Conclusion

The participant evaluation result provided eight activating interactions that could offer great usability, and the experimenter measurement result of the steering wheel turning angle helped us narrow down the number to six in terms of ensuring the basic driving safety. Generally, six activating interactions: "press the left button on the steering wheel once", "press the right button on the steering wheel", "press the button on the center console once", "pull the right paddle twice", "Pull left and right paddles together once" and "keep pulling left and right paddles for 1 s" obviously exceed other fifteen interactions in terms of offering great usability and ensuring the basic driving safety.

5 Discussion

This research could help us establish a systematic usability evaluation method for the ADS activating interaction including the five key evaluation criteria. It also has important reference value for other ADS user experience research, e.g. driver take-over the control of a vehicle from ADS. The experiment result allowed us to narrow down the total twenty-one activating interactions to six with regard to providing great usability and ensuring driving safety, it generated great tips of the autonomous vehicle interior design for OEMs and our demo car in the future.

There were some limitations in our project that we did not consider or could not improve when we conducted this research. (1) the simulated environment we built could not 100% simulate the real on-road environment. For example, when placing the buttons on the table we did not consider enough ergonomic issues, so in a real cockpit these buttons could be easier or harder to reach and manipulate and that might influence the result of the experiment. (2) The steering wheel we used in the simulated environment did not offer the same level of resistance that a real steering wheel could offer. And the turning angle data we collected is not realistic enough. In a real driving scenario, pressing a button on the steering wheel may only cause a 2° turning. And different interactions may not show obvious differences in steering wheel turning angle. (3) We did not consider that the participants could be left-handed or right-handed, that this would influence usability evaluation results of the left-hand side interactions (e.g. press the button on the left part of the steering wheel) and the right-hand side interactions (e.g. press the button on the left part of the steering wheel).

In the future, first of all, we will keep investigating this topic by doing more experiments with the existing problems revised in an improved simulated driving environment based on the findings of our project, e.g. investigating the ergonomics of the ADS activating paddle design. Secondly, other types of activating interactions would be focused on such as voice control, hand gesture control and multi-touch control. Lastly, other user experience attributes will be investigated. According to Marc Hassenzahl's UX theory of pragmatic and hedonic attributes of products, from the user perspective, the pragmatic attribute could provide the functionality and ways to access functionality, to fulfill externally given or internally generated behavioral goals. And the hedonic attributes emphasize individuals' psychological well-being [17]. For the activating interaction of ADS, the hedonic attribute could possibly make ADS – a relatively new thing in people's life more appealing and interesting. It would be icing on the cake for the ADS when the basic pragmatic needs are fulfilled, and that is worth researching on.

References

1. Fagnant, D.J., Kockelman, K.: Preparing a nation for autonomous vehicles: opportunities, barriers and policy recommendations. Transp. Res. Part A: Policy Pract. **77**, 167–181 (2015)
2. Mui, C., Carroll, P.B.: Driverless Cars – Trillions Are up for Grabs. Cornerloft Press, Seattle (2013)
3. National Highway Traffic Safety Administration.: Automated Vehicles for Safety. https://www.nhtsa.gov/technology-innovation/automated-vehicles-safety. Accessed 20 Nov 2018
4. Jordan, G.: Volvo autonomous car engineer calls Tesla's Autopilot a "wannabe". The Verge. https://www.theverge.com/2016/4/27/11518826/volvo-tesla-autopilot-autonomous-self-driving-car. Accessed 30 Nov 2018
5. Wasef, B.: 2019 Audi A8 L Review—Brilliant engineering in an unassuming wrapper. Autoblog. https://www.autoblog.com/2018/10/16/2019-audi-a8-l-review-first-drive. Accessed 15 Dec 2018

6. Matousek, M.: The Tesla Model X that crashed into a barrier while in Autopilot sped up right before the accident. Business Insider. https://www.businessinsider.com/tesla-model-x-in-fatal-autopilot-crash-sped-up-right-before-accident-2018-6. Accessed 19 Oct 2018

7. Rosevear, J.: How Far Along Is Self-Driving Car Technology, Really? The Motly Fool. https://www.fool.com/investing/2017/10/22/how-far-along-is-self-driving-car-technology-reall.aspx. Accessed 20 Nov 2018

8. Wan, J., Wu, C.: The effects of lead time of take-over request and non-driving tasks on taking-over control of automated vehicles. IEEE Trans. Hum. Mach. Syst. **48**(6), 1–10 (2017)

9. Merat, N., Jamson, A.H., Lai, F., Daly, M., Carsten, O.: Transition to manual: driver behaviour when resuming control from a highly automated vehicle. Transp. Res. Part F: Traffic Psychol. Behav. **27**, 274–282 (2014)

10. Lua, Z., Happeea, R., Cabralla, C., Kyriakidisa, M., Winter, J.: Human factors of transitions in automated driving: a general framework and literature survey. Transp. Res. Part F: Traffic Psychol. Behav. **43**, 183–198 (2016)

11. Volvo Cars: Tips for using Pilot Assist. https://www.volvocars.com/uk/support/article/262a8effb8f7b055c0a801512d0e05b8. Accessed 18 Nov 2018

12. Cadillac: Introducing Cadillac Super Cruise: Giving You the Freedom to Go Hands-free. https://www.cadillac.com/world-of-cadillac/innovation/super-cruise. Accessed 30 Oct 2018

13. Sina Kandian: The "post-80s" illegal record is the most, male and female driver ratio is 7/3. http://k.sina.com.cn/article_2208160981_839ddcd5020007fpl.html

14. Wang, C., Jiang, T.: Study on ergonomic design of display-control system in manual-control rendezvous and docking. Manned Spacefl. **17**, 2 (2011)

15. Annie, W.Y., Alan, H.S.: Tactile symbol matching of different shape patterns: implications for shape coding of control devices. In: IMECS 2014, vol. 2 (2014)

16. Tang, Z., Wang, Z., Shan, D., Zhu, C., Detection of distracted-driving due to smartphone taxi-hailing. J. Transp. Eng. Inf. **16**, 1 (2018)

17. Hassenzahl, M.: The thing and I: understanding the relationship between user and product. In: Blythe, M.A., Overbeeke, K., Monk, A.F., Wright, P.C. (eds.) Funology: From Usability to Enjoyment. Human-Computer Interaction Series, pp. 31–42. Springer, Dordrecht (2015). https://doi.org/10.1007/1-4020-2967-5_4

Usability Experiment of Waste Materials in Pulp Design

Yan Wang$^{(\boxtimes)}$, Xuanxuan Zhou, Zhenan Li, and Feiran Zhu

School of Design, South China University of Technology, Guangzhou 510006,
People's Republic of China
yanw@scut.edu.cn

Abstract. Pulp is a fibrous material made from plant fiber and processed by different processing methods. It is widely used in various fields such as paper making, chemical industry, building materials, household and daily use. Pulp also favored by artists in recent years, as a new art materials, in the two aspects of theory and form the recognition of academia, since artists use the waste paper and other fibrous materials that are relatively easy to get started when creating pulp works, the pulp art has great environmental and regeneration features from its birth. This paper mainly explores the usability experience of art design with waste paper and waste clothes after the fiber decomposition, through the experimental cases of paper clothes, paper lampshade and paper engraving.

Keywords: Usability experiment · Waste material · Pulp design · Paper cloth · Paper design · Handmade paper · Sustainability

1 Introduction

Pulp is a fibrous material made from plant fiber and processed by different processing methods. It is widely used in various fields such as paper making, chemical industry, building materials, household and daily use. In recent years, pulp has also been favored by artists. In the 1970s, the pulp-plastic art activity initiated by American curator Taylor has been responded to by contemporary artists Rauschenberg and David Hockney. A batch of pulp paintings that produced the earliest influences created the first peak of modern pulp plastic art. In 1983, the "International Paper Conference" held in Kyoto, Japan, discussed the current status of the traditional hand-made paper industry, the exploration of pulp plastic art, and the traditions and innovations, art and technology. At the same time, sponsored by the American Art Foundation, the "New Ideas of Paper Art · America" exhibition was held, showing 60 pulp works of 20 avant-garde artists in the United States. As a new art creation material, pulp has gained recognition in both the theory and the form. From the use of original pulp materials to directly make art works, to the use of various processed paper and paper materials for artistic creation, which extends and expands the application field of pulp, and also brings infinite space for artistic creation. Since artists use the waste paper and other fibrous materials that are relatively easy to get started when creating pulp works, the pulp art has great environmental benefit features from its birth.

© Springer Nature Switzerland AG 2019
A. Marcus and W. Wang (Eds.): HCII 2019, LNCS 11585, pp. 114–129, 2019.
https://doi.org/10.1007/978-3-030-23538-3_9

The art of pulp plastic in China started late. In the past ten years, some artists have used pulp directly for artistic creation. The experimental cases of this study are mainly aimed at paper cloth, paper lampshade and paper engraving. It explores the usability experience of creating works of art by fibrillating and decomposing waste paper and waste clothes.

2 Case of Paper Clothes

"Paper clothes", as the name implies, are clothes made of paper materials. Early in the Wei Jin Southern and Northern dynasties period in China there are records about paper clothing supplies, such as paper shoes, paper clothes, paper hats, etc., mostly used for funeral supplies [1]. By the Song dynasty, the paper industry was gradually developed, the output of paper increased, and the price decreased accordingly. Paper garments with practical function began to prevail among monks and literati. Entering the modern era with the development of mechanized production and science and technology, various textile fabrics emerged in an endless stream, and paper garments gradually faded out of people's horizons. Until the 1980s and 1990s, paper, as a new fashion material, reignited a boom in paper clothing production in the fashion industry. However, this craze is like a flash in the pan, and has not really made paper clothes enter the daily life of contemporary people. The experiment of this paper aims to explore the possibility of recycling paper and fiber materials in daily life to realize its regeneration.

In this experiment, the most easily found waste t-shirts, jeans and hemp rope are used to make paper cloth, among which the t-shirts were made of 100% cotton material. The experiment was carried out in the pulp art studio of South China University of Technology. Instruments and equipment used are beating machine, press machine, rinsing machine, electric cooking pot, pattern copying machine, and pattern drying machine.

2.1 Experiment of Making Paper Cloth

Fibrillation of Waste Clothes and Hemp Rope Fiber Materials. First of all, the waste cloth should be cleaned with washing liquid to remove all stains as much as possible. Then, the pattern parts and buttons should be removed. These cleaned fabrics are then cut into blocks, in which the T-shirt is 1 cm square, the denim is 2 cm square, and the twine is 1 cm long. After soaking and cooking the shredded denim, hemp, cotton and denim fiber paper materials with baking soda powder respectively, and washing them in cold water after cooling, the fiber for paper copying can be obtained.

Papermaking for Paper Cloth. The processed materials are separately placed in the beater, and the paddles are used for evacuation, until the fibers are dispersed into the slurry, and the pulverized pulp is filtered and dried with a sieve to obtain a pulp which can be used as a cloth paper. Prepare a sink suitable for papermaking. This experiment used a 80 cm by 100 cm size paper box and an 80 mesh screen. The water tank is poured into the water to two-thirds position, and an appropriate amount of pulp dispersant is added, and after uniformly stirring, it becomes a paper-making slurry. Insert the paper frame into the water tank, lift it up and shake the paper frame hard for a moment, which can shake out the excess water and pulp, at the same time make the fibers interweave with each other. After the water is filtered out of the screen frame, it can be inverted on the operating table covered with cotton cloth for water absorption treatment. After completely drying, the paper that can make paper clothes can be obtained, as shown in Fig. 1.

Fig. 1. Pulp and paper made by mixing waste cloth and hemp.

Waterproof and Reinforced Treatment of Cloth Paper. The paper used as a paper garment should be processed to increase the softness and adhesion of the paper, but also with a certain degree of toughness and water resistance. In this experiment, we used konjac paste as a waterproof material, and the round stick was used as a rolling tool. The konjac solution with a concentration of 2% was evenly coated on the paper. After drying, the paper was rolled up with a stick, according to the longitudinal direction of the paper. The horizontal, frontal, and reverse sides are repeatedly smashed and pressed, and this process needs to be repeated several times until the desired flexibility is achieved.

2.2 Performance Test of Cloth Paper

The paper prepared in this experiment was cut into three pieces with a width of 1.5 cm and a piece with a width of 6.3 cm. Carry out weighing, tear resistance test, breaking test and tensile test successively. The parameters in the table below can be obtained after completing these tests, as shown in Table 1.

Table 1. Test paper strength composite index.

Test item\Sample name		Cotton	Denim	50% cotton + 50% denim	30% cotton + 30% denim + 40% hemp	Plain paper	95% cotton + 5% white latex
Quantitative	Paper weight/g	5.07	1.42	3.51	1.58	2.39	1.67
	Length/cm	17	17.1	16.8	17	16.7	6.3
	Width/cm	11.6	11	11.5	12.4	6.3	6.3
	Paper area/m^2	1.97%	1.88%	1.93%	2.11%	1.05%	0.40%
	Quantitative (absolutely dry)/ (g/m^2)	257.1	75.5	181.7	75.0	227.2	420.8
Tear resistance	Tear resistance/mN 1	5823	2610	3211	2759	2318	2080
	2	5353	2064	2915	3350	2468	1480
	3	5258	1985	5542	3932	2389	
	Average tear/mN	5478.00	2219.67	3889.33	3347.00	2391.67	1780.00
	Tear index/ (mN * m^2/g)	21.31	29.40	21.41	44.65	10.53	4.23
Burst resistance	Burst resistance/kPa 1	169	149	240	287	295	336
	Burst index/ (kPa * m^2/g)	0.66	1.97	1.32	3.83	1.30	0.80
Tensile strength	Tensile strength/ (kN/m) 1	2.61	2.17	1.64	1.85	3.48	2.43
	2	3.37	3	2.44	1.56	6.56	2.34
	3	3.78	2.63	2.47		3.6	2.55
	Average tensile/ (kN/m)	3.25	2.60	2.18	1.71	4.55	2.44
	Break length/km	1.29	3.51	1.23	2.32	2.04	0.59
	Tensile index/ (N * m/g)	12.65	34.44	12.02	22.75	20.01	5.80
Elongation	Elongation/% 1	1.95	3.26	2.83	1.25	1.54	4.47
	2	3.02	3.53	3.04	1.09	3.18	4.46
	3	3.88	3.53	3.06		1.21	3.97
	Average elongation/%	2.95	3.44	2.98	1.17	1.98	4.30

Tear resistance test: 30% cotton + 30% denim + 40% hemp - denim - 50% cotton + 50% denim - cotton - plain paper - 95% paper + 5% white latex
Burst resistance test: 30% cotton + 30% denim + 40% hemp - denim - 50% cotton + 50% denim - plain paper - 95% paper + 5% white latex - cotton
Tensile strength: denim -30% cotton + 30% denim + 40% hemp - plain paper - cotton - 50% cotton + 50% denim - 95% paper + 5% white latex

2.3 Creative Design of Paper Clothes

The experimental results show that the paper can be made into the paper clothes, although the paper has a certain degree of softness after continuous processing, the paper material is significantly different from the general fiber cloth. It can't be combined with the human body like a normal cloth to reflect the curve of the body. Therefore, in the design, the garment shape can be formed in a straight line, or the form of the multi-layer stitching is more suitable for the forming of the paper garment. Since the cloth of the paper material has no difference in the warp and weft, the cutting is relatively free without considering the direction.

3   Case of Light Transmission of Handmade Paper

The paper that was born as a writing carrier not only opened the process of human civilization history, but also penetrated into people's daily life [2]. The transparency of paper was well known in ancient times, and it is widely used in the door windproof and lamp lighting. The Kongming Lantern reflects the wisdom of the Chinese people in the military [3]. The paper has an inseparable relationship with light. Modern interior lighting often uses the soft effect of paper on the light source to create an indoor atmosphere. The experiment to be introduced below is the experimental analysis on the light transmittance of hand-made paper based on the daily recycled paper fiber materials, and then discusses the feasibility of lamp shade design with this kind of handmade paper.

3.1   Recycling Waste Paper Fibers for the Production of Handmade Paper

A variety of fiber materials were selected for testing to explore the comparative study of light presentation of different materials. The materials are: printing paper, newspaper, rice paper, raw paper, denim, hemp rope, cotton T-shirt, etc. The experimental steps are the same as 1.1 and 1.2 above, and finally the paper to be tested - denim fiber paper, hemp rope fiber paper, blue cotton fiber paper, as shown in Fig. 2.

Fig. 2. Paper making process – take the treatment of hemp rope as an example. (Color figure online)

3.2   Color Temperature Test of Light Source Through Paper

The test of the color temperature of the light source through the paper was carried out at the State Key Laboratory of Luminescent Materials and Devices of the School of

Materials Science, South China University of Technology. The experimental equipment used was: Ocean Optical Fiber Spectrometer (USB2000+, Ocean Optics); white light source (color temperature 5600 K, blue light with wavelength of 450 nm and yellow light with wavelength of 560 nm). The experimental steps are shown below.

Lighting Adjustment. White light source spectrum, color temperature measurement, the fiber optic probe of the fiber optic spectrometer is directly opposite the white light source, collect data and read the color temperature data.

Equipment Construction. The white light source is wrapped in foil paper, and a hole of 3 mm in diameter is reserved for measuring the spectrum and color temperature of the white light after passing through the sample.

Spectral and Color Temperature Measurements of White Light Passing through the Paper. The samples were placed between the optical fiber probe and the light source hole. Data of 5 different positions were measured for each sample successively and recorded.

Data Processing. Origin was used to normalize the spectral data.

Experimental Results. The color temperature of the white light source used in the experiment was 5600 K. After the white light passed through the rice paper, the yellow light component in the spectrum increased and the color temperature decreased. With the increase of rice paper thickness, the color temperature becomes lower. For rice paper samples with a weight of 2 g, the color temperature decreases from 5600 K to 5212 K after the white light passes through. When the weight increases to 5 g, the color temperature decreases to 4500 K.

For newspapers and hemp paper, white light through the color temperature are reduced. In terms of spectrum, due to the absorption of different degrees of blue light components, the color temperature decreases, and the standard white light turns into warm white light. For newspapers and hemp paper of 2 g weight, the color temperature decreased from 5600 K to 3900 K and 4300 K, respectively. With the increase of paper thickness, blue light absorption enhancement, color temperature low to about 2500 K.

Standard white light through the denim paper, mainly blue. The color temperature is above 10000 K. The long - wave yellow light in the spectrum is absorbed and its intensity is reduced. Because the blue paper is blue, white light only leaves short-wave blue light after passing through, and the color coordinates (0.23, 0.2).

Paper, rice paper, newspaper and hemp paper of the same quality absorb blue light more strongly, the color temperature decreases, and the standard white light becomes warm white light. For denim paper and blue cloth paper, due to its strong absorption of long-wave yellow light, color temperature rise, and yellow light is most of the absorption. The test results are shown in Figs. 3 and 4.

Spectral normalization: Dividing the spectral data by the maximum value in the data (origin has a normalization function), and then putting together the same type of sample spectrum, you can compare the blue light part reduction or the yellow light part reduction, so as to correspond to the change of color temperature.

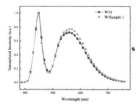

W/O: No sample is added for filtering, which is the spectrum of the original source.

W/Sample1: Adding sample 1, the spectrum changes slightly, the yellow part increases, and the color temperature increases.

Fig. 3. Paper test result. (Color figure online)

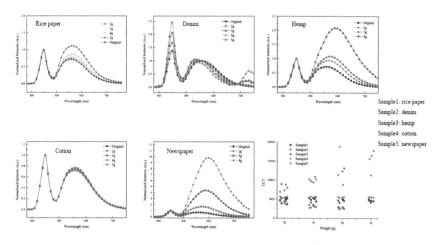

Fig. 4. Paper making material test result. (Color figure online)

Data Processing. Origin was used to normalize the spectral data.

3.3   Case Conclusion

Made of the same raw material, the paper prepared by different weight samples increases in thickness as the weight increases, and the light absorption at a specific wavelength is enhanced, and the color temperature change is more obvious. Paper of the same weight, due to the nature of the material, has different absorption characteristics for light. Rice paper, hemp paper and newspapers absorb blue light more strongly, and the color temperature decreases after white light is transmitted. The blue denim paper and blue cloth paper itself appear blue, and the long-wave light absorption is strong, and the color temperature rises after white light is transmitted.

The color temperature can adjust the space atmosphere, the high color temperature light gives a bright and refreshing feeling, while the low color temperature light gives a warm and relaxed feeling. In addition, the cooperation between the color temperature and the basic color tone of the environment is also considered [3]. For example, low color temperature light can enhance the warmth of the space in the warm color space. Therefore, taking several materials in the experiment as an example, using a rice paper, newspaper or hemp paper to make a lampshade, the light color is warmer, which can enhance the warmth of the space. The lampshade made of denim paper and blue cloth paper has a colder color after light transmission, which can create a fresh and calm feeling. A good coordination in space allows the material to fully exploit its own characteristics and aesthetics.

3.4 Creative Design of Pulp Lampshade

Through experiments, the characteristics of the above materials are implemented to make a pulp lampshade, and the production method is as follows:

1. Use the balloon mould method, that is, blow the balloon up, hang or frame it up, then put the semi-dry paper paste on the surface of the balloon, at the same time paste the edge with a sponge to ensure that the surface of the lampshade is flat. The surface is brushed with a layer of water paste to make it firm;
2. While the surface is still wet, pour some denim paper pulp on the pasted paper layer to enrich the surface effect;
3. With the balloon perimeter length of the rope dipped in some yellow and pink pulp, from all angles wrapped in the paper layer, and then paste a layer of rice paper and cloth pulp mixed pulp, reinforce the lamp shade and play a color gradient effect; and
4. After the balloon is punctured after drying, a hand-made lampshade can be obtained, as shown in the colorful effect of the lampshade on the yellow light bulb, as shown in Fig. 5.

Fig. 5. A process example of making a pulp lampshade. (Color figure online)

4   From Pulp to Paper Carving Works

The two-dimensional form of paper-carving art is commonly known as "paper-cutting". The prototype of paper-cutting can be traced back to the Xihan Dynasty when paper was born. The earliest type of paper-cutting was the human-shaped paper used for funeral. With the development of paper production technology, the paper output increased. The variety of paper products has become more and more abundant. The paper-cutting art in the Tang and Song Dynasties has entered a period of great development. Paper-cut window blossoms and paper-leaked plates have become popular decorative forms, reaching the peak stage in the Ming and Qing Dynasties. It took a long time for papermaking technology to spread to the west. Papermaking appeared in Europe before the Renaissance. Therefore, the use of paper in the West for the development of modeling was late, but once it appeared, it developed rapidly [4]. After the French Revolution, handicrafts made of origami and paper-cuts began to flourish in European villages. Then Poland and the United Kingdom began to popularize the three-dimensional shape of the paper. The complexity and superb skill of the modeling skills reached a very high standard. At the beginning of the 20th century, the use of paper for the shaping of geometric shapes was carried out at Bauhaus College in Germany [5]. With the rise of the modern Western industrial revolution, machine papermaking technology has replaced traditional manual papermaking. The publishing and printing industry has developed rapidly in the West. The 3D and semi-3D paper art works carved with paper have begun to be used in book binding and window display, etc. to carry on the popularization and application, and penetrate into people's daily life, forming a unique artistic expression.

The main purpose of this experiment is to test the strength of paper by adjusting the formula of pulp raw materials from the self-made paper, and to design paper engraving on the paper with suitable strength. In order to get the experimental results more quickly, the experimental paper is made by Rapid-Koethen paper sheet former, which is used to produce handwritten paper sheets for testing physical properties. The finished paper can be made from raw materials in a short time, which is convenient for timely testing the performance of the paper.

4.1   Papermaking Experiment

Experimental Materials. Several kinds of pulp materials were selected - nanocellulose (ultrafine fiber with diameter less than 1000 nm), eucalyptus (hardwood pulp fiber, fiber generally about 1 mm in length, lignin content generally between 20–24%), larch (original coniferous wood pulp fiber), silver star (bleached softwood fiber, fiber generally between 2.56–4.08 mm, high lignin content, between 25–35%). The papermaking test was carried out by chemical instruments, and the experiment was carried out at the State Key Laboratory of Pulp and Paper Engineering of South China University of Technology.

Experimental Instruments. BSA623S-CW electronic precision balance scale, RK3AKWT Rapid-Koethen paper sheet former, and LW slurry fluffer.

Paper Production. The materials were pretreated, and four different materials were placed in a dry place for several hours. When the materials reached a relatively balanced drying degree, different slurry of the same weight was placed in the cup. Soak the slurry in a mixing cup for several hours to allow the slurry to spread out. The slurry fluffer is used for beating, mainly to disperse the dispersing fiber and produce moderate fibrillation. The beating time and the speed cycle selection are different depending on the raw materials. Therefore, it is necessary to observe the fiber length and observe the change of fiber length. From pulp board to decomposition into fibrous slurry, sometimes the selected beating speed cycle should be 30,000 to 50,000 rpm.

The slurry is poured into a container of a fully automatic Rapid-Koethen paper sheet former, and the papermaking machine automatically performs steps of water injection, bubbling separation slurry, gravity pumping, and water filtration. The pulp is made into a circular shape with a diameter of about 20 cm and cut off from the filter screen by using absorbent paper or cloth. It is placed on the Rapid-Koethen paper sheet former integrated with automatic Rapid-Koethen papermaking machine to dry, and the drying time depends on the situation. In this experiment, 10–20 min is selected.

The entire process of papermaking is accomplished by removing the completely dry paper. Taking all the above steps as an example, papermaking is performed on different materials. Figure 6 shows the papermaking process and the completion effect.

Fig. 6. The papermaking process.

4.2   Paper Performance Test and Comparison

The finished paper was tested for performance test, and the main test was the tear resistance and burst resistance index. Paper tear and burst strength are important technical indicators for evaluating paper shear resistance and compression resistance.

Paper Tear Resistance Measurement. The machine used is a tear resistance tester. The force required to tear the pre-cut paper to a certain length is mN.

Experimental principle: raise the pendulum to a certain height so that it has a certain potential energy. When the pendulum is swinging freely, it will tear the sample with its stored energy, and the energy consumed when tearing the sample will be calculated by the computer control system, so as to obtain the force required for tearing the sample.

Experimental steps: cut the paper into the same 3–4 strip shapes, place them on the instrument, make the pendulum swing freely after pre-cutting, record the force used to tear the paper calculated by the instrument, and take the average value of 3–4 data.

Test Method for Paper Bursting Resistance. The machine used is a burst tester. Burst resistance refers to the maximum uniformly increased pressure that paper or board can bear per unit area, in kPa.

Experimental principle: The basic principle of the burst strength test is to place the sample on the film, clamp the sample, and then apply pressure evenly to make the sample bulge under the top pressure of the film until the sample breaks. At this time, the instrument displays the maximum value of the hydraulic pressure as the sample resistance value.

Experimental procedure: Take the paper sample and place it on the film, apply pressure until the paper breaks. Place the position 3–4 points and take the average of 3–4 pressure data.

4.3   Laser Engraving of Paper

On the basis of the experiment and the consideration of paper properties, the author selected broad-leaved wood fiber materials and original needle wood fiber materials as raw materials to make paper, and tried to produce a variety of paper carving works. There are many kinds of paper carving methods, including carving. Knives, scissors, etc., the author uses the method of laser engraving.

2D and Semi-3D Paper Carving Effect Production. First, draw the pattern on the computer with the 2D software ADOBE ILLUSTRATOR and then transfer it to the line drawing in CAD format, and use the laser engraving machine to engrave the paper. The point to note is that you need to close off the lines where the cutting is needed. In order to make the paper embossed better, you need to add several layers with different patterns.

3D Paper Carving Effect Production Process. Still use the software to draw the pattern on the computer, and then use the laser engraving machine to engrave the paper. The 3D paper carving should pay attention to the fact that the gap between the structure and the structure should not be too large, and the joint between the surface and the surface needs to be aligned.

3D Paper Carving Lamp Production Process. First, use the software to draw the pattern on the computer, and then use the laser engraving machine to engrave the paper. The forming principle of the 3D paper carving lamp is that multiple patterns of different plane sizes are arranged before and after, and form a visual 3D effect. When drawing graphics, you need to consider the position of the front and rear graphics to avoid important patterns being covered. Since the paper needs to be buckled at a later stage, the position of the buckle should be considered when drawing the pattern.

4.4   Experimental Results and Discussion

As shown in Fig. 7, for the same kind of paper, with the quantitative increase of materials, the thickness of the paper will increase, tear resistance and burst resistance will also increase, and the transmittance will also become weaker; And the same weight of paper, due to the different properties of the material itself, its tear resistance and burst resistance is also different, its thickness and light transmission is not the same; The paper thickness of broad-leaved wood pulp, original needle wood pulp and bleached needle wood pulp prepared under the same weight is relatively thick, and the value difference is not large, while the paper thickness of nanocellulose is relatively thin.

Fig. 7. Comparison of paper thickness (mm) under quantitative conditions of 5 g and 10 g respectively.

As shown in Figs. 8 and 9, the nanofibers have the lowest tear resistance and burst resistance and the thinnest thickness at 5 g. The tear resistance of broad-leaved wood pulp is lower than that of needle wood pulp, but the bursting resistance is not much different from that of needle wood pulp. The tear resistance of needle wood pulp is higher than that of broad-leaved wood pulp and nanofiber. Under the quantitative measurement of 10 g, the nanofiber has the lowest tear resistance and the lowest

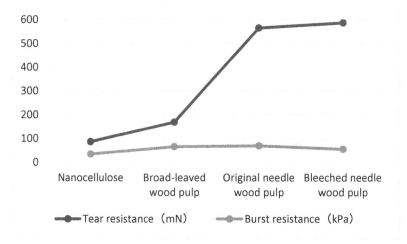

Fig. 8. Paper performance test of each material under the quantitative condition of 5 g.

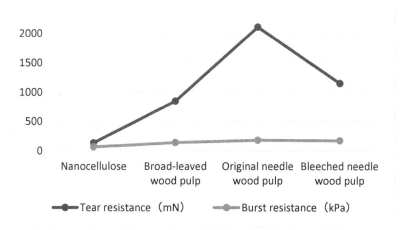

Fig. 9. Paper performance test of each material under the quantitative condition of 10 g.

bursting resistance, and the thinnest thickness. The tear resistance and bursting resistance of the broad-leaved wood pulp are higher than that of the nanofiber, but lower than that of the needle wood pulp. The thickness of broad-leaved wood pulp and needle wood pulp is not much different in thickness. The tear resistance and bursting resistance of needle wood pulp are the highest among several materials, and the tear resistance of original needle wood pulp and bleached needle wood pulp is much different, but the bursting resistance and thickness is similar.

Combining several performance comparisons, we also comprehensively consider the effects of the products that need to be produced. The production of 2D and semi-3D laser engraving works does not require paper with too strong strength, and only needs to meet the conditions that can be engraved by the laser engraving machine. Broad-leaved wood pulp and needle wood pulp are selected with a quantitative value of about 5 g, which is most suitable for making planar and semi-3D laser engraving works. Hand-made collage paper carving products will do harm to the paper in the later stage, so it is necessary to choose paper with better performance. The quantitative selection of needle wood pulp is about 10 g, which is the most suitable for the production of 3D collage paper carving products. However, the tearing and bursting resistance of nanofiber materials are generally low, and they were burned by sparks in the later laser engraving experiment, so they are not suitable as raw materials for laser engraving experiment.

Figure 10 shows the preparation of computer graphics in the early stage of 2D and semi-3D paper carving, the laser engraving process and the final rendering effect. The selected material is broad-leaved wood fiber (the raw material is selected to be 10 g). Since the 2D and semi-3D paper carvings on the paper requirements are not high, the material selected here does not need to be too high tear resistance and bursting resistance, but it is necessary to avoid paper materials which are thin and easy to be burned by sparks.

Fig. 10. 2D and semi-3D paper carving effect.

Figure 11 shows the preparation of the computer drawing in the early stage of the 3D paper carving, the laser engraving process and the final rendering effect. The 3D

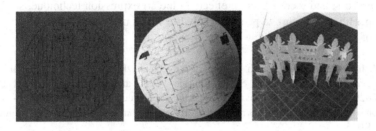

Fig. 11. 3D paper carving effect.

128   Y. Wang et al.

paper carving will cause more or less damage to the material during the cutting and post-hand stitching process, so the 3D effect paper carving requires a material with high strength and hardness. The materials used here are broad-leaved wood fibers with high tear resistance and bursting resistance (the raw material is selected to be 20 g).

Fig. 12. 3D paper carving light effect.

Figure 12 is the computer drawing preparation in the early stage of making the 3D paper carving lamp effect and the presentation of the 3D paper carving works manually collaged after laser carving. Here, due to the need for good light transmission effect, there is no need to choose materials that are too thick or too hard. The strength and toughness of the original needle wood fiber are strong, and when the raw material is 2 g, the thickness of the paper will not be too thick to block the light. Therefore, the author chooses to use the original needle wood fiber (the raw material is 2 g).

5   Conclusion

Through the above experiments, it can be seen that the waste cotton and linen fiber materials and waste paper in daily life have been recycled and processed, and then processed into paper pulp by hand processing, thereby conducting experiment and exploration of art design. The aim is to explore more possibilities for the recycling of pulp materials, especially for used paper. Waste paper materials such as newspapers, magazines, cartons, used cotton and linen materials, can be reused by recycling and hand-pulping paper, and then use a variety of processing forms, so that it becomes the creative materials of designers and artists. There are more ways to choose the production process, and there are more effects in the art expression technique, so that the waste paper fiber can return to people's daily life with a new look, and truly realizes the concept of green and sustainable design.

Acknowledgements. This research is supported by Guangzhou 13th Five-Year Plan for the Development of Philosophy and Social Science "2016 annual planning project funding 2016GZGJ29", and Guangdong Provincial Department of Education Research Project - Featured Innovation Project (educational research) "Research on pulp plastic art education" 2016GXJK006.

References

1. Liu, R.: Chinese Ancient Paper Spectrum, p. 260. Intellectual Property Publishing House (2009)
2. Zhang, K.: I am with printmaking and pulp molding art. Chinese Arts (2009)
3. Mende, K.: Paper optics. Sun and paper, Japan Pingfan Publishing, Japan (1982)
4. Zhang, K.: Preliminary Study on the Art of Pulp. Fine art research (2014)
5. Okura, Y.: Paper Sculpture in Basic Design (II): on the Bending, p. 3, 10. Oita Prefectural College Art and Culture (1973)

A Method to Automatic Measuring Riding Comfort of Autonomous Vehicles: Based on Passenger Subjective Rating and Vehicle Parameters

Ya Wang[1]([⊠]), Qiuyu Zhang[1], Lizhi Zhang[2], and Yunyan Hu[2]

[1] Baidu Intelligent Driving Experience Design Center, Beijing, China
wangya02@baidu.com
[2] Baidu Autonomous Driving Technology Department, Beijing, China

Abstract. As a milestone product of the AI era, the autonomous vehicle has attracted tremendous attention from the whole society. When autonomous vehicles (AV) provide transportation services as passenger vehicles in the future, a comfortable riding experience will be the fundamental element of usability. In such a case, it is necessary to establish an objective and sound evaluation system to evaluate the comfort level of autonomous vehicles. We hereby develop the comfort level model of autonomous vehicles with the following three steps: (a) Explore subjective evaluation indicators: Invite passengers to test autonomous vehicles and collect their ratings of the comfort level; (b) Establish the subjective comfort evaluation model: classify the evaluation indicators, continuously collect the evaluation data of the comfort level from the passengers during the testing process, and then use the structural modelling method to form a subjective evaluation model of the comfort level; (c) Develop the automatic scoring tool: collect subjective and objective data through data collection apps, form a calculation function with machine learning algorithm that fits the subjective and objective data, and develop an automatic scoring tool based on it. This precisely developed evaluation system and the empirical data-based scoring tool can be used to guide technological development, optimize algorithms, and improve strategies within the AV corporate. On the other hand, it can help to unify evaluation standard for AV industry, improving the experience of autonomous vehicle rides.

Keywords: Autonomous vehicles · Riding comfort · User research · Machine learning · Pioneer users

1 Introduction

As a milestone product of the AI era, the development of autonomous vehicles has attracted tremendous attention from the whole society. The future of autonomous transport service should be a seamless, on-demand, all-weather service with no restrictions on age, gender, physical function or any other aspect, and thereby freeing the public from driving tasks. From the city and government levels, a transportation network of autonomous vehicles can provide a safer traffic environment, improve

A. Marcus and W. Wang (Eds.): HCII 2019, LNCS 11585, pp. 130–145, 2019.
https://doi.org/10.1007/978-3-030-23538-3_10

vehicle utilization, reduce fuel consumption, and lower the traffic volume. However, being able to be accepted by the public is a prerequisite for the success of autonomous transport service.

In the initial stages of technological penetration, the passenger's primary need for autonomous vehicles is to ensure safety. Once this need is sufficed, the next focus is on the comfort level of the ride. Ride comfort is a continuous variable for evaluating ride experience, which can be perceived by users and also be measured (e.g. evaluation standards such as Sperling Method and UIC513). Ride comfort of passengers should also be taken as an important consideration for autonomous vehicles. However, the measurement scheme for conventional vehicles is not entirely suitable for driverless areas where scenarios are complex, scoring is required to be more precise, and users' psychological experience of the security and intelligence of the system is involved. Comfort is an important experience for passengers as they ride on the vehicle. As such, comfort level should be considered as an important evaluation indicator in developing autonomous vehicles, and it is therefore particularly important to establish an evaluation model for ride comfort of autonomous vehicles.

Many scholars have defined the perceptual comfort of human beings. Hertzberg [1] believes that comfort is a state of human perception, and comfort means that people do not have uncomfortable experiences. Coreltt [2] points out that human comfort is the feeling of balancing all parts of the human body, when the balance of external disturbing factors is broken, the human body will feel uncomfortable. Slater [3] points out that comfort is a state of physical and psychological pleasure and harmony in the environment. De Looze [4] recognizes that comfort is a state of physical and psychological pleasure and harmony in the environment. To be comfortable would be affected by physiological, psychological and material factors, which are the subjective response of human beings to the environment. To sum up, comfort is first of all a subjective response of the human body to the stimulation of the external environment, and the condition for human body to feel comfortable is that the external physical conditions are suitable; comfort contains two meanings: one is that the physiological mechanism of human beings is in a relaxed state, the other is that human beings feel happy psychologically.

There have been many studies on ride comfort both in China and abroad for conventional transportation vehicles such as cars, trains, buses, etc., involving influencing factors, evaluation indicators, and evaluation methods. We summarized the current research status based on the influencing factors, evaluation indicators and evaluation methods of ride comfort, and according to this, we considered the contents and methods of the differentiated research on ride comfort for autonomous vehicles.

1.1 Influencing Factors and Evaluation Indicators

There are many studies on the ride comfort of conventional vehicles, and it is found that the ride comfort of passengers is mainly affected by two factors: "ride environment" and "vehicle driving characteristics".

The riding environment is one of the factors influencing riding comfort, which can be divided into internal environment and external environment. In evaluating the internal driving environment, Liu et al. [5] and Zhu et al. [6] adopted the concept of environmental factors, including specific indicators such as space size, noise intensity, temperature level, and seat performance. Wang [7] used noise and pressure, air quality, vehicle decoration environment, etc. to evaluate the internal driving environment; in evaluating the external driving environment, Taghirad [8] built the function model of ride comfort, including indicators such as road roughness. A recent study by Telpaz et al. [9] also found that the distance between pedestrians, buses and other objects close to the vehicle will also affect ride comfort. Richards [10] and others collected the physical characteristics of bus and train environments and subjective scores of passengers on the interior environment to determine vehicle comfort. Suzuki et al. [11] defined comfort degree, and studied the influence of vibration and noise factor, olfactory factor, seating factor, visual environment, skin factor on human riding comfort. Masakazu [12] et al. developed a facial expression-based evaluation method to evaluate the quality of in-car ride. The comprehensive psychological feelings of users in-car can be judged by facial factors such as eyes and mouth. Sivilevičius [13] et al. established various factors describing users' satisfaction with trains, such as comfort, safety, travel time and price, and established a multi-objective optimization mathematical model to calculate the comprehensive quality index of trains.

Vehicle driving characteristics is another important factor affecting ride comfort. Ni, Wang [14] and Ma [15] pointed out that the two indicators widely used by Chinese and foreign railway transport agencies are stationarity and comfort. With regard to stationarity, some more classical evaluation standards, such as Sperling Method, are used to evaluate the running quality of vehicles by calculating stationarity using amplitude, vibration frequency, and acceleration, etc. Nastac and Picu [16] have adopted this method. As for comfort, many researchers such as Ma et al. [15] mentioned UIC513 comfort index, in which the acceleration in the transverse, longitudinal and vertical directions of the measured points is comprehensively weighted to evaluate comfort. In addition to Sperling Method and UIC513, there are many different indicators/combinations of indicators for evaluating vehicle driving characteristics. Earlier studies by Smith et al. [17] predicted passengers' feelings based on vehicle acceleration. Strandemar [18] also evaluated ride comfort by acceleration parameters; Sun et al. [19] directly measured vehicle vibration; Taghirad [8] evaluated ride comfort by the passengers' movement (left and right sway, upward and downward bounces), tire deflection, etc.

1.2   Evaluation Methods

After determining the influencing factors of ride comfort and specific evaluation indicators, it is necessary to evaluate the comfort of riding a certain vehicle through specific evaluation methods. The academia mainly uses subjective feedback of passengers and objective data collection.

Subjective feedback from passengers. Data were collected through questionnaires and interviews. For example, Liu et al. [5] asked passengers to report their subjective feelings and built a subjective evaluation model for riding comfort. Yang and Zhang [20] used the passengers' subjective evaluation table on ride comfort to collect user feedback on vehicle noise, ride vibration, up and down jolt, left and right sway, front and back sway, ride comfort, discomfort during the ride, etc.

Objective data collection, such as Sperling Method, UIC513 and other standards calculate the stationarity or comfort index by collecting the amplitude, vibration frequency and acceleration data of the vehicle in the lateral, longitudinal and vertical directions, thus rating the stationarity and comfort level of the vehicle during a ride.

Most of the existing studies on conventional vehicles will be mainly carried out based on one of two above methods, aiming at building a ride comfort model system. However, the study of this paper combines subjective and objective methods to build a more efficient evaluation system that can automatically rate the comfort level of autonomous vehicles.

1.3 Summary

The purpose of this study is to establish an evaluation method for ride comfort of autonomous vehicles. Currently, there are few studies specifically for autonomous vehicles. The influencing factors and evaluation indicator mentioned in conventional studies can be referenced but cannot be directly applied. As for the "riding environment", the influence of the external environment on riding autonomous vehicles such as surrounding vehicles and pedestrians needs to be considered. However, the internal environment of autonomous vehicles will remain in a stable state for most of the time, and through regular cleaning and maintenance, passengers' feelings will not change greatly. Therefore, the internal environment is not the focus of this study. Regarding the "vehicle driving characteristics", there are differences in driving characteristics between different types of vehicles and different products of the same type of vehicles. In this area, autonomous vehicles also need to be paid close attention to. In addition to these two factors, because driverless technology is closely related to safety, intelligence, etc., the "system intelligence" factor should also be considered in evaluating ride comfort. Specifically, "system intelligence" can be regarded as the ability to handle special situations, the ability of the system to maintain accurate and stable, etc. This study will also split specific evaluation indicators based on this factor.

When summarizing the existing research on conventional vehicles, we found that most of the researches only adopted either subjective evaluation or objective data, which could not directly guide the update of autonomous driving technology and had certain difficulties in converting results. In addition, a subjective evaluation model can be established through subjective scoring, but the cost of purely manual scoring is relatively high. With the increase of autonomous vehicles, running scenarios and locations, manual scoring will no longer be feasible and more efficient scoring methods are needed. Therefore, we need to consider how the subjective evaluation corresponds to the objective behavioral data of the vehicles, so as to combine both the subjective and objective methods, and finally form an automatic scoring tool.

The structure of this paper is as follows. In the second part, we will roughly describe the overall research ideas and methods. In the following third part, we will discuss the details of the research steps and how to obtain the research results through derivation. In the fourth part, the results are summarized. And through discussion, there is a reflection on the achievements and experience gained from this work.

2   Research Overview

2.1   Research Steps

A long-term user research is conducted based on the prototype of autonomous vehicles (see Fig. 1). Nearly one thousand users were invited, known as the "Test-riding Pioneers", to experience autonomous vehicles.

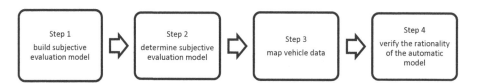

Fig. 1. Research process

In the process of inviting users to test, influencing factors of ride comfort on autonomous vehicles have been identified, and the subjective evaluation model is gradually built and verified. Based on this, the vehicle's driving data were simultaneously collected, such as acceleration/deceleration, steering angle, etc. Also, a one-to-one correspondence between the driving data and the passenger's real-time feedbacks was made. Finally, an automatic evaluation tool for ride comfort on autonomous vehicles was formed.

2.2   Tools

The autonomous vehicle used by the research institute was a modified Lincoln MKZ (shown in Fig. 2);

Fig. 2. The prototype of an autonomous vehicle used by passengers for the trial ride (a modified Lincoln MKZ)

The Lincoln MKZ vehicle used for the test has been modified with a driverless system on it and has the capability of Level 4 automatic driving on open roads. Each test vehicle has an automatic driving test license issued by the Beijing municipal government, and a safety officer will be assigned to supervise the safe driving at all times during the test. The subjects all sat in the back seat.

In addition, a data collection app for instant comfort evaluation is developed to evaluate passengers' subjective experience.

The subjects were asked to evaluate the ride experience in real time through a data acquisition APP on mobile phones (shown in Fig. 3) during the ride of the autonomous vehicle, and the APP would timestamp each evaluation.

Fig. 3. The comfort evaluation and data acquisition app

2.3   Test Scenario

The study has set up a driving test route for an autonomous vehicle in Beijing's Daoxianghu road section (as shown in Fig. 4). The road was in good condition (traffic density was not high, traffic was slow, and obstacles were few). After traveling 16.2 km from the intersection of Beiqing Road and Daoxianghu Road, the car would return to the starting point.

The average speed of the autonomous vehicle is 48 km/h, and it takes about 20 min for it to complete a full round. In the autonomous vehicle, two safety officers were arranged to take over the car under special circumstances. In addition, an instructor was arranged to guide the tasks to be performed by the subjects and give explanations when the subjects ask questions.

Fig. 4. The test route in Beijing Daoxianghu road section

3 Procedure and Results

In this part, we will illustrate in detail the procedure and results obtained through the above methods and steps. The part can be mainly included into four parts as below.

3.1 Set up Subjective Evaluation System

At the beginning of the study, we first need to build a subjective evaluation system for the ride comfort of autonomous vehicles. In the first part, we listed the factors that affect the comfort of vehicles in reality and believed that the dimensions that are more relevant to autonomous vehicles are driving factors and external environmental factors. Then based on the analysis in the first part, we will analyze and sort out the influencing dimensions of the ride comfort on autonomous vehicles in this part.

Research Set

We firstly invited 30 test-riding pioneers in the early tests of unmanned vehicles. The gender, age, driving experience, and other attributes were evenly distributed, thus reducing the impact of sampling.

They had a complete experience of the nearly 17 km driverless journey on the Daoxianghu section. During the test, there was a safety officer in the front row, and the passengers were seated in the back row. At the same time, there was a tester in the back row who followed them all the way.

The study would invite the subjects to take the vehicle, ask them to think aloud their evaluation of riding comfort. Their comments had been recorded during the whole test with passengers' consent.

Semantic Analysis

We conducted semantic analysis on the evaluation from 30 passengers. We analyzed the collected information according to different types of driving scenes. And we filled the subjective evaluation in each scene. In the end, we sort out the words related to comfort by word segmentation (Table 1).

Table 1. The analysis of the passenger's evaluation on testing experience

Scenes	Subjective evaluation of the experience	Semantic analysis
Start	The feeling of starting is strong. Unless driving a sports car, or I would not have this strong feeling of starting a car	Start/The acceleration feeling/Unsafe
Driving straight forward	Is it braking all the time?	Brake/Performance/Unsafe
Stop	Not very strong. When driving in low speed, it feels like I pushed the brake all the way to the end	Hard brake/Low speed/Unsafe
Avoid pedestrians and obstacles	Normally I don't have to avoid obstacles intentionally when I drive. This is too intentional	Pedestrian/Avoid/Sudden turn/Unsafe
Driving straight forward, falling leaves detected	I don't know why suddenly it brakes, and the brake was hard	Sudden brake/Unsafe
Stop	Not very strong. When driving in low speed, it feels like I pushed the brake all the way to the end	Hard brake/Low speed/Unsafe
Avoid pedestrians and obstacles	Normally I don't have to avoid obstacles intentionally when I drive. This is too intentional	Pedestrian/Avoid/Sudden turn/Unsafe
Switching lanes with no other vehicle in front	I don't know why it changes lane	In explicable lane-switching/Unsafe
Switching lanes with other vehicles in front	It doesn't feel like a hard brake, and the lane-switching was smooth	Brake/Smooth/Safe
...	...	...

By sorting out the interview records of all 30 passengers, we found out some main factors that affect passenger comfort and then further cluster these factors.

Finally, three types of comfort evaluation dimensions are sorted out: driving factors (the feeling of leaning forward, the feeling of braking, the feeling of swaying, the feeling of shaking, the feeling of bumping, the feeling of being pushed back), external environment factors (the sense of safety related to speed, the sense of safety related to distance), and specific factors (accurate driving, flexible driving, and stable driving). Among them, the specific factors are the special influencing factors of ride comfort of autonomous vehicles, which mainly reflect the degree of intelligence of autonomous vehicles. The passengers repeatedly mention that the degree of intelligence of autonomous vehicles will directly affect the psychological comfort of the passengers, which is also the reason why we include it into the subjective model.

After naming all the factors and confirming the corresponding meaning, a preliminary subjective comfort evaluation model was formed (Table 2).

Table 2. The subjective evaluation model framework of AV's riding comfort

Overall	Main factors	Detail factors
AV's riding comfort	Somatosensory	Lean forward
		The feeling of swaying
		The feeling of repetitive jerks
		The feeling of being pushed back
		The feeling of bumping
	Sense of safety	The sense related to speed
		The sense related to distance
	Sense of intelligence	Driving accuracy
		Driving flexibility
		Driving stability

3.2 Verify and Determine Subjective Evaluation Model

Based on the preliminary subjective evaluation model, we will confirm the validity of the model through quantitative verification, modify the evaluation dimension and finally determine the model.

Research Set

We have continuously invited 377 test users to experience autonomous vehicles in nearly half a year, and these users would fill in the ride comfort chart through the data recording app after a complete experience of autonomous vehicles. We used a 5-point system to measure the comfort level of each type of ride. We set one item to match each layer of subjective model. No. 2–6 fit detail factors of somatosensory. No. 8–9 were for sense of safety and No. 11–13 were for sense of intelligence. No. 2, 7, 10 were set to measure general feeling of 3 main factors. The whole feeling of riding comfort can be measured by the first item. Please refer to Table 3 for specific items.

In order to reduce the differences in each individual's understanding, we defined each scoring dimension, taking the feeling of leaning forward as an example (Table 4).

Verify Through Model.

Based on the above definitions, we collected 377 questionnaires.

The validity of the model was verified by the structural equation model, and finally a complete subjective evaluation model was formed (as shown in Fig. 5).

When verifying through the model, we removed two dimensions: the feeling of being pushed back and the feeling of bumping, both of which had little influence on ride comfort. We found that somatosensory perception is an important factor that

Table 3. Questionnaire of AV's riding comfort

No.	Questionnaire items	Score				
1	Overall comfort level of this autonomous ride	1	2	3	4	5
2	During the ride, I feel the brakes caused by constant deceleration	1	2	3	4	5
3	When turning, I felt thrown out	1	2	3	4	5
4	The ride is not very smooth, I can feel my body swings a bit from side to side	1	2	3	4	5
5	During the ride, my body suddenly leans forward at times	1	2	3	4	5
6	I feel being pushed back when the car accelerates	1	2	3	4	5
7	My body feels very comfortable during the whole ride (e.g. no carsickness, discomfort, etc.)	1	2	3	4	5
8	The speed of the whole car and the speed relative to external objects make me feel safe	1	2	3	4	5
9	During the ride, I kept a proper distance from objects in the external environment, which made me feel safe	1	2	3	4	5
10	Generally speaking, I feel safe during the ride	1	2	3	4	5
11	During the ride, the autonomous vehicle can judge and identify road conditions accurately	1	2	3	4	5
12	The autonomous vehicle can deal with different road conditions in a very flexible manner	1	2	3	4	5
13	The autonomous vehicle can handle same situations in the same way	1	2	3	4	5
14	I think the autonomous vehicle is intelligent during my ride	1	2	3	4	5

Table 4. Scoring criteria for riding comfort-the feeling of leaning forward

Score	Feeling intensity	Corresponding driving behavior
1 point	Basically, I don't feel the braking	Careful and attentive driving
2 points	There is some feeling of braking	Normal driving
3 points	I clearly know the car is braking	Casual driving; driving under tiredness; driving habits are not so good
4 points	The braking is relatively obvious	The car is driven by a novice driver who cannot brake smoothly
5 points	The braking is very obvious	Emergency brake

affects ride comfort. Secondly, the sense of security also directly affects ride comfort, while the sense of intelligence affects overall comfort by affecting the sense of security.

The model fitted well, Chi-square = 22.00 (p = 0.341), CFI = 0.999, RMR = 0.005, RMSEA = 0.017.

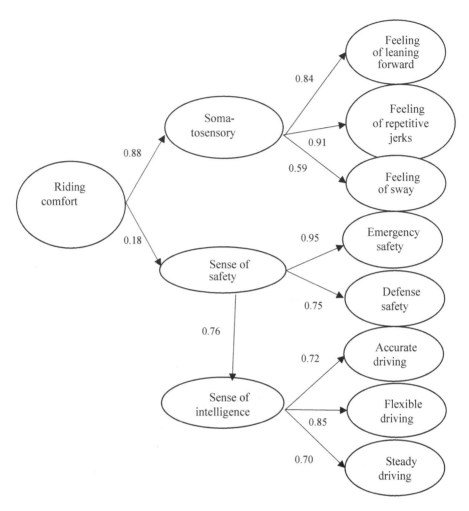

Fig. 5. Structural equation model for riding comfort (subjective evaluation) of autonomous vehicles

3.3 Mapping Vehicle Data Based on Subjective Models

In the third step, vehicle data are mapped to the third dimension of the subjective model, and through machine learning, a subjective-objective automatic model is established, so that an automatic score of the third dimension can be obtained. Then the overall comfort score can be deduced based on the influencing weight of the dimensions in the subjective model.

Acquiring Subjective-Objective Corresponding Data Sets
Based on the subjective model established above, we need to collect vehicle data under different comfort scores for each third-level dimension. Taking the feeling of leaning forward as an example, we need to obtain the vehicle data sets under 1–5 scores

respectively, and in order to suffice machine learning, the number of data sets under each score needs to reach 1000.

We continued to invite nearly 400 passengers to experience the autonomous vehicles and used data app to collect data. The data app provides such a function that whenever a passenger feels uncomfortable with certain behaviors of the vehicle, the data app will record the timestamp of the current evaluation. For example, if passengers feel that leaning forward is relatively uncomfortable, they click the button of "the feeling of leaning forward" and give corresponding scores, and the app will record the timestamp of the rating. Using this timestamp, we can extract the current data set of the test vehicle from the automatic driving system, including transverse acceleration and deceleration, lateral acceleration and deceleration, steering angle, etc., thus forming a data packet with the subjective data corresponding to the objective ones. With this process, nearly 8,000 data packets from 8 experience dimensions were collected.

Develop the Automatic Scoring Tool

Based on the data packets for each evaluation dimension, we used the following methods for data training. Taking the feeling of leaning forward as an example, we found out the vehicle data that really affects the change of the score of the feeling of leaning forward through machine learning from the data packets with scores of 1–5, thus forming a function that calculates the score of the feeling of leaning forward according to the vehicle data.

We adopted two major types of calculation models commonly used in 6 industries to train the data. One is depth learning models such as MLP and TCN; The other is integrated learning models such as Decision Tree, Random Forest, GBDT, GBRT. Finally, we would calculate the average score based on the model data included in the overall tool to obtain the score of the dimensions of the evaluation, and the formula is as follows:

$$S_{avg} = \frac{1}{M} \sum\nolimits_{M=1}^{M} f_m(x) \tag{1}$$

By analogy to the other 7 three-level evaluation indicators, the function of the vehicle data for calculating the scores of the 8 indicators is finally obtained.

Based on this, we can automatically calculate the scores of eight three-level latitude indicators according to the data of any autonomous driving segment, and finally write the weights of all levels of indicators in the subjective model into the calculation system to automatically calculate the final total score of ride comfort.

3.4   Validation of the Automatic Scoring Tool

When we finish developing the automatic tool, we will continue to verify the validity of the model in the next step.

Research Set

We verified it by comparing manual scoring with machine scoring. We will continue to invite users to take a test ride in the following time. After users complete the test ride, they will fill in an optimized questionnaire. At the same time, the machine will also score the same journey. Finally, we will examine the difference between manual scoring and machine scoring.

Validation Results

We used the Mean Score Error method to verify the consistency between manual scoring and machine scoring. As shown in the following Table 5, the comprehensive accuracy rate of the models of the three somatosensory indicators is close to 0.8, which we believe has reached the usable level.

Table 5. Verification of accuracy of the models of the three somatosensory indicators

Model name	MSE	Accuracy
The feeling of leaning forward	0.196	0.80
The feeling of braking	0.374	0.78
The feeling of shaking	0.270	0.75

Because inviting users to take a test ride and the data processing take a long time, we have currently completed the validation of the secondary dimension somatosensory indicators, and the validation of other dimensions is still in progress.

4   Model Application

After the somatosensory model passed the validation, we applied it in two directions:

4.1   Verify Change of Capability

We used the model of the somatosensory data to backtrack the road test data of autonomous vehicles in the past year, and calculated the somatosensory score of the daily road test data. In order to facilitate the monitoring of abnormal data, we cut the vehicle data into 10-min segments, and the somatosensory score of the day was the average of all segments. As shown in Fig. 6, the horizontal axis represents the date, and the vertical axis is the distribution of mean, maximum and minimum scores of the somatosensory score for the day.

In the whole scope, we can find that the change trend of somatosensory scores in the past year shows an overall upward trend, representing that passengers' somatosensory perception on autonomous vehicles is also gradually optimizing.

4.2   Real-Time Monitoring Experience

On the other hand, we applied the model to the current daily road test data monitoring. When the autonomous vehicle completed a day's road test, the technician uploaded the day's data to the data platform. The automatic scoring tool will trigger the automatic scoring mechanism in the early morning of each day to query and download the data of Daoxianghu road section in the past day and perform automatic scoring.

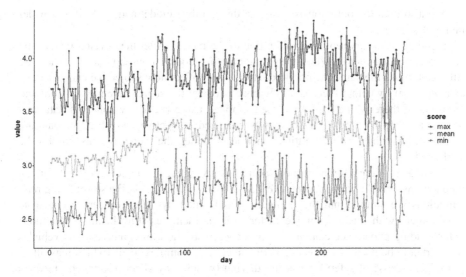

Fig. 6. Structural equation model for riding comfort (subjective evaluation) of autonomous vehicles

For the scoring results, on the one hand, we can use it as a measure to monitor the somatosensory change curve; On the other hand, it can help technicians locate the abnormal scores of the day. If abnormal low scores are found, it can quickly locate the low score data packet, check the video playback of the road test to locate the problem, and solve the technical problems instantly and efficiently.

5 Conclusion

Through this study, we have formed a set of scientific and universal evaluation criteria and scoring tools for the riding comfort of autonomous vehicles. This model can conveniently, quickly, and stably measure the riding comfort of autonomous vehicles, and can play its role and bring value both internally and externally.

Internally, based on this model, we can continuously observe the riding comfort changes of our own autonomous vehicles. Such changes can guide the technological R&D team to continuously optimize their technological algorithms to create products with better ride experience. Compared with the past methods of technicians randomly extracting data for playback and testers recording somatosensory problems on cars, it not only saves manpower, but also can locate problems more quickly and improve unmanned driving technology.

Externally we hope that this model can become a unified evaluation standard, which can be used to conduct horizontal comparison and evaluation of different autonomous vehicles. Also, we hope to cut in from the perspective of riding comfort to promote the autonomous vehicle industry.

We also plan to continuously optimize this comfort model and apply it to a wider range of scenarios.

Continuous observation and calibration of the model: After the development of the automatic scoring tool based on the riding comfort model of autonomous vehicles, we still need to use the same method to continuously collect new subjective and objective data and verify whether there is a difference between the scores given by the tool and the users. If there is, the model will be calibrated using the newly collected data, and will iterate step by step, until the newly collected subjective and objective data are completely matched with the fitting function, and then the model is considered to be calibrated.

Testing and application in more scenarios: At present, the scenarios set for the autonomous vehicle riding are relatively loose: the speed is slow, the surrounding road conditions are simple, and the riding is accompanied by safety officers. In such an environment with many favorable factors, the problems existing in the autonomous vehicle riding experience cannot be fully exposed. In the future, autonomous vehicles will certainly be used in various scenarios, including complex roads (which may affect passengers' sense of safety) and faster driving (which may affect passengers' feelings of being pushed back and centrifuged), etc. We will consider more testing scenarios and apply and verify this riding comfort model.

Acknowledgments. The authors would to thank IDX group for help in the user tests and data collection involved. We acknowledge the contribution of ADT group in the scoping of the machine learning analysis.

References

1. Hertzberg, H.T.E.: The human buttock in sitting: pressures, patterns and palliatives. Am. Automob. Trans. **12**(2) (1976)
2. Corlett, E.N.: Human factors in the design of manufacturing systems. Hum. Factors **25**(6), 701–711 (1983)
3. Slater, K.: Human Comfort. Thomas, Springfield (1985)
4. De Looze, M.P., Kujit-Evers, L.F.M., Van Dieen, J.: Sitting comfort and discomfort and the relationships with objective measures. Ergonomics **46**(10), 985–997 (2003)
5. Liu, J.Z., Ling, M.J.: Establish subjective assessment model for automobile riding comfort. Automob. Technol. (9), 11–20 (1994)
6. Zhu, T.J., Zong, C.F., Yang, D.J., Li, W., Xiang, H.: Subjective evaluating methods on car ride comfort. Automob. Technol. (3), 8–11 (2008)
7. Wang, G.: The data-based appraisal method of riding environment comfort. Doctoral dissertation of Beijing Jiaotong University (2013)
8. Taghirad, H.D., Esmailzadeh, E.: Automobile passenger comfort assured through LQG/LQR active suspension. J. Vib. Control **4**(5), 603–618 (1998)
9. Telpaz, A., Baltaxe, M., Hecht, R.M., Cohen-Lazry, G., Degani, A., Kamhi, G.: An approach for measurement of passenger comfort: real-time classification based on in-cabin and exterior data. In: 2018 21st International Conference on Intelligent Transportation Systems (ITSC), pp. 223–229. IEEE, November 2018

10. Richards, L.G., Jacobson, I.D., Barber, R.W., et al.: Ride quality evaluation in ground based vehicles: passenger comfort models for buses and trains. Ergonomics **21**(6), 63–72 (1978)
11. Ling, M., Hao, M.: Ride Comfort Evaluation in Trains (02), 28–34 (1999)
12. Masakazu, A., Kazuto, I.: Fuzzy modeling of facial-expression analysis for evaluating ride comfort. J. Jpn. Soc. Nav. Arch. Ocean. Eng. **25**(1), 145–150 (2005)
13. Sivilevičius, H., Maskeliūnaitė, L., Petkevičienė, B., et al.: The model of evaluating the criteria, describing the quality of organization and technology of travel by international train. Transport **27**(3), 307–319 (2012)
14. Ni, C.S., Wang, Y.M.: A brief discussion for ride index and comfort. Railw. Locomot. Car **23**(6), 1–3 (2003)
15. Ma, S.Q., Wang, M., Wang, X.J., Wang, C.Q., Deng, H.: Evaluation and measurement of high speed train by ride comfort and ride index. J. Dalian Jiaotong Univ. (S1), 66–68 (2015)
16. Nastac, S., Picu, M.: Evaluating methods of whole-body-vibration exposure in trains. Ann. "Dunarea De Jos" Univ. Galati, Fasc. XIV Mech. Eng. **2**, 55–60 (2010)
17. Smith, C.C., McGehee, D.Y., Healey, A.J.: The prediction of passenger riding comfort from acceleration data. J. Dyn. Syst. Meas. Control **100**(1), 34–41 (1978)
18. Strandemar, K.: On objective measures for ride comfort evaluation. Doctoral dissertation, KTH (2005)
19. Sun, H., Zuo, S.G., Yang, Z.C., Hu, Z.Z., Wei, H.: Subjective feeling estimate and experience on the car riding comfortability. J. Tongji Univ. **29**(2), 239–241 (2001)
20. Yang, C.P., Zhang, Y.F.: Using fuzzy mathematics to evaluate the effect of every factor on ride comfort. J. Xi'an Highw. Univ. **17**(1), 68–74 (1997)

A Study on the User Interaction Information System Design of a City Park Planning

Xuchao Wu[1]([✉]) and Qing Fang[2]

[1] Academy of Arts and Design College, Fuzhou University,
Xiamen, Fujian, China
wu.xuchao@gmail.com
[2] Xiamen Road & Bridge Landscape Art Co., LTD., Xiamen, Fujian, China

Abstract. The concept of landscape design was born in the 19th century. The design criterion has undergone changes for nearly a hundred years, and the form is constantly changing, but there is always a problem that makes people wonder. What kind of design is a good landscape design? Based on the landscape design criterion summarized in the existing literature, this study uses fuzzy Delphi, analytic hierarchy process (AHP) and technology for order preference by similarity to ideal solution (TOPSIS) to evaluate landscape design criterion. Using above methods, we can deal with the contradictions which arising from the disagreement of the design concept are emphasized in the landscape design, and forming a more uniform design evaluation method. First, use Fuzzy Delphi to evaluate the design concept and determine that the selected design criterion is consistent. And then use the AHP plus TOPSIS to determine the primary and secondary relationships of the landscape design principles by the weight values of the criteria. The research results show that using the above method can quickly and effectively determine the primary and secondary relationship of landscape design criterion, and can achieve better results.

Keywords: Landscape design criterion · Evaluation · Fuzzy Delphi · AHP · TOPSIS

1 Introduction

1.1 The Relationship Between Park and Human

Birkenhead Park, Liverpool, is the first true urban park in the world, the early parks are mostly royal parks or private gardens. When it represented to the city, it improved the urban environment, and the living standards of residents. More importantly, Birkenhead Park provides a reference for people in other regions. We can identify that, park is an urban installation produced in the 19th century. It is a "product of civilization" bred by the unique ideas and systems of West. Nowadays, the most basic function of the park is providing a place where resident visit. With the continuous development of the city, the number of urban parks is also increasing. In the Mainland China, park is responsible for the spiritual civilization education and the popularization of scientific knowledge to the citizens. It is also an important resource for the government to promote social harmony and cultivate urban culture. At some levels, urban cultural experiences and even urban

© Springer Nature Switzerland AG 2019
A. Marcus and W. Wang (Eds.): HCII 2019, LNCS 11585, pp. 146–159, 2019.
https://doi.org/10.1007/978-3-030-23538-3_11

cultural symbols tend to be concentrated or hidden in urban parks, so urban parks are the best place to experience local culture. The city is like a hot island, and the park is like a plant on a hot island. The park is rich in plant configuration, and the large water area not only beautifies the city's space, but also regulates the urban environment, improves the city's air quality, and maintains the urban ecological balance. Sometimes when a disaster occurs, the park is responsible for the emergency shelter. As such, the scales of human life in cities will generate different feelings as the surrounding environment changes. Usually, parks can potentially be the center of the region that afford the all kinds of natural elements and provide a place to let people participate and enjoy.

City parks are no longer a luxury for citizens, but an important part for the city growth. In the park, people are both designers and users, and each part has different preferences for the park, which creates different needs. Gehl [1] insisted that the different behavior of people in parks or squares will have more than 10 different directions in the social life of small urban spaces. Usually, people decide their behavior based on the influence of the external environment. In the various behaviors in the park, it is worth exploring on which one is necessary or unnecessary as well as how to define their priorities. According to those priorities, we can examine which aspects of the park/landscape design should be strengthened and others should shorten. But no matter which one all worth us to explore.

There is always a problem in people's minds, what kind of park design is a good park design?

1.2 Literature Review

Nowadays, evaluation studies focus on two areas: qualitative research and quantitative research. Qualitative research accounts for a large proportion of park evaluation research, focusing on the use patterns, functions, ecosystem characteristics and management models of the park. McHarg [2] expanded the scope of traditional "rules" and "design", and raises it to the height of ecological science, making landscape design develop in the direction of multiple comprehensive disciplines [1]. Ahern [3] said that landscape functions can be quantified and measured, they represent our best criteria for such a determination. Francis [4] framed a conceptual framework for understanding the social context of parks versus gardens in cities.

Quantitative research is reflected in the evaluation of ecological benefits, the evaluation of ecological functions and the sustainability of landscapes. Turner [5], suggests that different landscape indexes may reflect processes operating at different scales. Spatial pattern has been shown to influence many processes that are ecologically important. The long-term maintenance of biological diversity may require a management strategy that places regional biogeography and landscape patterns above local concerns. Urban et al. [6] suggested that landscape is a mosaic of patches, the components of pattern, it can help scientists understand spatial patterns.

According to previous literature review, six criteria for park/landscape design can be summarized, which is the basis of this questionnaire. These six criteria cover all aspects of park/landscape design, reflecting the economic and social benefits of the park, the user/visitor experience in the park, the details of the park/landscape design, and the park/landscape level and a series of problems in plant.

1.3 Study Area and Information

Jiageng Park is located in the southeast coast of Jimei District, Xiamen, Fujian Province, it around the sea and connecting the land on the west. The park consists by two parts, the south side is Ji Mei Ao Yuan, a square for the Tan Kah Kee (also known as Chen Jiageng was a Chinese businessman, community leader, communist and philanthropist. He was born in Xiamen, Fujian Province China.) Memorial and the north side is Jiageng Park that was completed in 1994 and remedy in 2016. The park covers an area of 30,000 square meters and the building area is 5,500 square meters. It is a national 4A level scenic spot in China. Entering the garden, you can find that on the top of the pavilions it was Chinese-style and support by western-style pillars, which is the embodiment the Chinese and Western cultural integration. Among them, the most representative ones are "Ao pavilion" and "Mingshi pavilion", they were built at the 1950s and 1960s, and all has a long history. It can be regard as the extension of the architectural style of Ao Yuan.

In 2012, Xiamen City, Fujian Province revised the Park Management Regulations for Xiamen, is the revision of the 1998 and 2002 version, which consists of five chapters and twenty-nine rules [7]. The regulations stipulate many regulations for the construction, management and use of parks. With the improvement of living standards, people's aesthetic level and requirements for material culture are also increasing, and the corresponding requirements for providing people's daily leisure and entertainment parks will increase. The design, construction, management and rational use of the park depend on a complete and scientific evaluation index system to facilitate better improvement and development. Therefore, the establishment of a set of practical evaluation index system suitable for the characteristics of the park is crucial for the construction of park in Xiamen.

2 Method and Result

2.1 Fuzzy Delphi

Delphi can be characterized as a method for structuring a group communication process so that the process is effective in allowing a group of individuals, as a whole, to deal with a complex problem. In order to accomplish this "communication process", Delphi method provide "some feedback of individual contributions of information and knowledge; some assessment of the group judgment or' view; some opportunity for individuals to revise views" [8].

Delphi usually goes through the following four steps. In the first step, the relevant views from different sources (or experts) are collected. In the second step, the respondents verify if they have a broad consensus or a big disagreement about the goals. If there is a big disagreement, this part will be reviewed in the third step to find out the root cause and evaluate it. The fourth step combines the above collected data for sorting and feedback. During the experiment, according to the previous literature review, first we developed a basic survey scope, it including the 6 categories (the questionnaire can be seen below), and then sent to the interviewed group, waiting for their feedback. Six elements of landscape design are economic factors (the following refers to (a), aesthetic criterion (b), Spatial pattern (c), design elements (d), construction factors (e) and ecological factors (f), which serve as the basic criteria for this study (Table 1). Subsequently, a number of experts related to the field were invited to conduct a Delphi questionnaire survey.

The Delphi questionnaire design is shown in Tables 2 and 3 and the analysis steps are detailed as follows.

First, ask each expert to rate A, B, and C aspects for the seven design elements we used. The values range from 0 to 10, and negative > median > positive.

Second, calculate the standard deviation and the average value for each design element separately, first exclude the extreme values outside the "two standard deviations", and then calculate the minimum value C_L of the remaining values, the average value C_M and the maximum value C_U. Then continue to calculate O_L, O_M and O_U according to the above method (see Fig. 1).

Third, according to the Negative Value and Positive Value, create a triangular fuzzy function, as shown in the Tables 4 and 5.

It can be seen from Table 5 that all the final results are greater than 0, indicating that all the experts have a common consensus on the above six criterions. However, it can still be found that the lowest value is the Aesthetic criterion (*b*), is 3.30, far away from the other value. In order to facilitate subsequent research and calculations, this element will be excluded.

Although Delphi has its own advantages, it still has drawbacks. First of all, it is more difficult to select the right expert, and the consultation or collection period is tedious, which is not suitable for the quick judgment and prediction. Secondly, the collection of consensuses is judged by the collective consciousness of experts, usually them has strong personal will. At the same time, Delphi needs to go through multiple rounds of operation, it takes time and effort and easy to make a sloppy response.

2.2 Analytic Hierarchy Process

The Analytic Hierarchy Process (AHP), introduced by Saaty [9], is an effective tool for dealing with complex decision making, and may aid the decision maker to set priorities and make the best decision. By reducing complex decisions to a series of pairwise comparisons, and then synthesizing the results, the AHP helps to capture both subjective and objective aspects of a decision. In addition, the AHP incorporates a useful technique for checking the consistency of the decision maker's evaluations, thus reducing the bias in the decision making process.

Table 1. Evaluation criteria

Explanation	Degree (0–10)		
	N	M	P
a Can earn money through tickets? (a1)			
Generate revenue by tourists? (a2)			
Can generate cultural benefits? (a3)			
Whether the park is endemic? (a4)			
Improve the quality of life of residents? (a5)			

(*continued*)

Table 1. (*continued*)

	Explanation	Degree (0–10)		
		N	M	P
b	Reflect the local aesthetic tendency? (b1)			
	Is the aesthetic element reasonably used? (b2)			
	Is the aesthetic element combined with artistry? (b3)			
c	Difference between the main entrance and the secondary entrance? (c1)			
	Does the park have convenient parking? (c2)			
	Does the park have a complete road system? (c3)			
	Are there enough rest facilities? (c4)			
	Is there a complete lighting system? (c5)			
d	Does design reflect sustainable development? (d1)			
	Does the park have a reasonable layout? (d2)			
	Does the design reflect the artistry? (d3)			
	Does the park have old and famous trees? (d4)			
e	Does the park use local materials? (e1)			
	Does the park reflect the local characteristics? (e2)			
	Are the details of the park reasonable? (e3)			
	Is the facility used in the park safe? (e4)			
f	Is planting suitable for local conditions? (f1)			
	Are plants fit for the architectural style? (f2)			
	Does plant have multiple levels of diversity? (f3)			

The respondents compared the criteria provided in the questionnaire based on their own perceptions (the ratio between the two criteria is shown in the table below). The result is the value for each evaluation criterion, the higher the value represents approximately important and vice versa. Next, for a fixed criterion, assigning scores to each evaluation criterion. A higher score means better performance of the standard represented. Ultimately, the results are integrated and ranked. Because the final ranking and scores are based on the comparison between the offered options and the standard, and the decision maker's knowledge system is embedded in the process, no expert advice is required, making AHP extremely flexible. The calculations are based on a large number of respondents' assessments, which translate many qualitative and quantitative criteria into multi-criteria rankings.

Table 2. 10 experts Delphi questionnaire results 1

	a			b			c		
	N	M	P	N	M	P	N	M	P
Expert 1	7	8	9	3	4	6	5	6	7
Expert 2	5	7	9	2	3	5	3	6	8
Expert 3	4	7	10	3	4	6	6	8	10
Expert 4	7	9	10	2	3	4	5	9	10
Expert 5	5	7	8	3	4	5	7	9	10
Expert 6	4	6	8	2	3	4	7	8	9

(continued)

Table 2. (*continued*)

	a			b			c		
	N	M	P	N	M	P	N	M	P
Expert 7	5	7	8	3	4	6	5	6	7
Expert 8	7	8	9	3	5	6	7	9	10
Expert 9	6	7	8	3	4	5	5	6	7
Expert 10	5	6	7	2	3	4	7	9	10
SD	1.18	0.92	0.97	0.52	0.67	0.88	1.34	1.43	1.40
MV	5.50	7.20	8.60	2.60	3.70	5.10	5.70	7.60	8.80
Min	4	6	7	2	3	4	3	6	7
Max	7	9	10	3	5	6	7	9	10

Table 3. 10 experts Delphi questionnaire results 2

	d			e			f		
	N	M	P	N	M	P	N	M	P
Expert 1	4	6	7	6	7	8	5	7	8
Expert 2	5	6	7	5	6	7	2	4	5
Expert 3	3	6	8	5	6	8	5	7	8
Expert 4	4	7	9	7	8	10	6	8	9
Expert 5	6	8	10	7	9	10	4	8	9
Expert 6	5	7	8	6	7	8	6	7	9
Expert 7	7	8	9	4	6	9	3	4	6
Expert 8	7	8	9	4	6	8	2	4	6
Expert 9	6	7	8	4	7	9	3	5	7
Expert 10	7	9	10	5	7	9	3	5	6
SD	1.43	1.03	1.08	1.16	0.99	0.97	1.52	1.66	1.49
MV	5.40	7.20	8.50	5.30	6.90	8.60	3.90	5.90	7.30
Min	3	6	7	4	6	7	2	4	5
Max	7	9	10	7	9	10	6	8	9

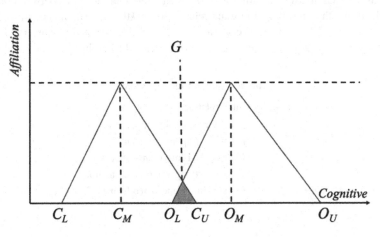

Fig. 1. Triangular fuzzy function

Table 4. Landscape design guidelines statistical analysis results 1

	Negative		Median		Positive		Mean value		
	L	U	L	U	L	U	C	O	S
a	4.00	7.00	6.00	9.00	7.00	10.00	5.50	7.20	8.60
b	2.00	3.00	3.00	5.00	4.00	6.00	2.60	3.70	5.10
c	3.00	7.00	6.00	9.00	7.00	10.00	5.70	7.60	8.80
d	3.00	7.00	6.00	9.00	7.00	10.00	5.40	7.20	8.50
e	4.00	7.00	6.00	9.00	7.00	10.00	5.30	6.90	8.60
f	2.00	6.00	4.00	8.00	5.00	9.00	3.90	5.90	7.30

Table 5. Landscape design guidelines statistical analysis results 2

	O_M-C_M	C_U-O_L	Verification	C_U-C_M	O_M-O_L	Result
a	1.70	1.00	0.70	1.50	1.20	6.10
b	1.10	0.00	1.10	0.40	0.70	3.30
c	1.90	1.00	0.90	1.30	1.60	6.70
d	1.80	1.00	0.80	1.60	1.20	6.40
e	1.60	1.00	0.60	1.70	0.90	5.80
f	2.00	2.00	0.00	2.10	1.90	8.00

First, computing the vector of criteria weight.

In order to calculate the weights of different standards, an n * n real Matrix is created, where n is the quantity to be evaluated. In the matrix, a_{jk} represents the importance of the jth criterion relative to the kth criterion.

If $a_{jk} > 1$, it means that the jth criterion is more important than the kth criterion, and vice versa.

If $a_{jk} = 1$, it means that the jth criterion is as important as the kth criterion.

The entries a_{jk} and a_{kj} satisfy the following constraint: $a_{jk} \cdot a_{kj} = 1$

The same can be proved, $a_{jj} = 1$.

Usually we will use a metric of 1 to 9 to indicate the relative scores between the two standards. If the jth criterion is important relative to the kth criterion, it is displayed as j: k = 9:1 (7:1, 5:1, 3:1), and vice versa (as shown in Table 6). In this way, the importance between two standards can be easily converted into numbers.

Table 6. Table of relative scores

Value of a_{jk}	Interpretation
1	j and k are equally importance
3	j is weak importance than k
5	j is essential importance than k
7	j is very strong importance than k
9	j is absolute importance than k

If matrix A is built, we can derive from A the normalized pairwise comparison matrix by making equal to 1, the sum of the entries on each column each entry a_{jk} matrix A is computed as:

The criteria weight w is built by averaging the entries on each row of A:

Second, computing the matrix of option scores. The matrix of option scores is a n * m real matrix S. Each entry s_{ij} of S represents the score of the ith option with respect to the jth criterion. In order to derive such scores, a pairwise comparison matrix $B^{(j)}$ is first built for each of the m criteria, $j = 1, \ldots, m$. The matrix $B^{(j)}$ is a n * n real matrix, where n is the number of options evaluated. Each entry $B^{(j)}$ of the matrix $B^{(j)}$ represents the evaluation of ith the ith option compared to the hth option with respect to the jth criterion.

If $b_{ih}^{(j)} > 1$, then the ith option is better than the hth option, while if $b_{ih}^{(j)} < 1$, then the ith option is worse than the hth option.

If two options are evaluated as equivalent with respect to the jth criterion, then the entry $b_{ih}^{(j)} = 1$.

The entries $b_{ih}^{(j)}$ and $b_{hi}^{(j)}$ are satisfy the following constraint:

Finally, ranking the options. However, in the process, we should try to avoid inconsistencies between standards and evaluation. The consistency of the calculation matrix is usually used to test the standard of mutual comparison, and will be described only for the matrix A. The Consistency Index (CI) is obtained by first computing the scalar x as the average of the elements of the vector whose jth element is the ratio of the jth element of the vector $A \cdot w$ to the corresponding element of the vector w. Between decision maker should always obtain CI = 0. Inconsistencies within the margin of error are tolerable, which ensures that the AHP is expected to be reliable. RI is the Random Index, the consistency index when the entries of A are completely random. The values of RI are illustrated in Table 7.

Table 7. Values of the Random Index (RI) for inconsistencies

m	2	3	4	5	6	7	8	9	10
RI	0	0.58	0.90	1.12	1.24	1.32	1.41	1.45	1.51

In the course of the survey, 20 questionnaires were distributed and recovered.

Firstly, the consistency of the five-landscape design criterion was tested. 14 valid questionnaires were selected, and the Consistency Ratio was 0.0349 < 0.1, within the confidence interval, which proves that 14 questionnaires have high consistency and can be adopted, used as a basis for research. The AHP assignment and weight of each principle are illustrated in Tables 8 and 9.

Table 8. Values of the AHP assignment of five design principle

	a	c	d	e	f
a	1.000	0.322	1.095	0.697	2.356
d	3.103	1.000	2.802	2.020	5.824
c	0.913	0.357	1.000	0.704	2.552
e	1.434	0.495	1.419	1.000	2.688
f	0.424	0.172	0.392	0.372	1.000
Sum	6.874	2.346	6.708	4.794	14.421

Table 9. Weight of the five-design principle

	a	c	d	e	f	Weight
a	0.145	0.137	0.163	0.145	0.163	0.151
d	0.451	0.426	0.418	0.421	0.404	0.424
c	0.133	0.152	0.149	0.147	0.177	0.152
e	0.209	0.211	0.212	0.209	0.186	0.205
f	0.062	0.073	0.058	0.078	0.069	0.068

It can be found that the park's Spatial pattern (c) impressed the respondents, and the park did not impress too much on the ecological factors (f).

Then, continue to calculate the weights occupied by each factor, and multiply the weight of each factor by the weight of the associated section to obtain the weight of each factor in the overall evaluation. The first one is the evaluation of the Economic factor (a), it's value and factor weight and overall weight are shown in the Table 10.

The second is Usage principle, shown in the Table 11.

The third is design elements, shown in the Table 12.

The fourth is construction factors, shown in the Table 13.

The last one is the ecological factors, its detail shown in the Table 14. All details are displayed in subsequent content.

Table 10. Values of the economic factor and weight

	a1	a2	a3	a4	a5	Factor weight	Overall weight
a1	1.000	0.299	1.190	0.249	0.334	0.082	0.0125
a2	3.343	1.000	3.005	1.088	1.586	0.297	0.0037
a3	0.841	0.333	1.000	0.247	0.233	0.075	0.0003
a4	4.012	0.919	4.046	1.000	1.482	0.309	0.0001
a5	2.997	0.630	4.298	0.675	1.000	0.237	0.0000
Sum	12.193	3.182	13.539	3.259	4.634		

Table 11. Values of the usage principle and weight

	c1	c2	c3	c4	c5	Factor weight	Overall weight
c1	1.000	0.364	0.328	0.303	1.083	0.092	0.0389
c2	2.749	1.000	1.069	1.053	2.051	0.256	0.1086
c3	3.045	0.935	1.000	0.823	3.429	0.267	0.1132
c4	3.298	0.950	1.214	1.000	3.145	0.288	0.1222
c5	1.050	0.488	0.292	0.318	1.000	0.097	0.0410
Sum	11.142	3.737	3.904	3.497	10.708		

Table 12. Values of the design elements and weight

	d1	d2	d3	d4	Factor weight	Overall weight
d1	1.000	0.480	0.634	3.337	0.830	0.1262
d2	2.083	1.000	1.837	5.088	1.734	0.2636
d3	1.577	0.544	1.000	4.435	1.154	0.1753
d4	0.300	0.197	0.225	1.000	0.282	0.0429
Sum	4.960	2.221	3.697	13.860		

Table 13. Values of the construction factors and weight

	e1	e2	e3	e4	Factor weight	Overall weight
e1	1.000	1.594	1.150	0.225	0.150	0.0307
e2	0.627	1.000	0.604	0.166	0.094	0.0192
e3	0.897	1.655	0.855	0.214	0.136	0.0278
e4	4.440	5.844	4.679	1.000	0.620	0.1272
Sum	6.965	10.093	7.289	1.605		

Table 14. Values of the construction factors and weight

	e1	e2	e3	Factor weight	Overall weight
e1	1.000	0.729	1.010	0.293	0.0199
e2	1.371	1.000	1.927	0.447	0.0304
e3	0.990	0.519	1.000	0.260	0.0177
Sum	3.361	2.248	3.937		

2.3 Technique for Order of Preference by Similarity to Ideal Solution

The Technique for Order of Preference by Similarity to Ideal Solution (TOPSIS) is a multi-criteria decision analysis method [10]. According to the closeness of the evaluation and the idealized target, then ranking. Find out the optimal solution and the negative solution in the scheme through the normalized matrix. Calculate the distance from the evaluation to the optimal solution and the negative solution, respectively. The relative proximity of each evaluation object to the optimal solution is obtained as a basis for evaluating the merits and demerits.

When encountering multi-objective optimization problems, there are usually m targets $D_1, D_2, \dots, D_m$, and each target has n indicators $X_1, X_2, \dots, X_n$. First, experts are invited to score the indicators, and then the score results are expressed in the form of mathematical matrix, and the following characteristic matrix is established:

$$D = \begin{bmatrix} x_{11} & \cdots & x_{1j} & \cdots & x_{1jn} \\ \vdots & & \vdots & & \vdots \\ x_{i1} & \cdots & x_{ij} & \cdots & x_{in} \\ \vdots & & \vdots & & \vdots \\ x_{m1} & \cdots & x_{mj} & \cdots & x_{mn} \end{bmatrix} = \begin{bmatrix} D_1(x_1) \\ \vdots \\ D_i(x_j) \\ \vdots \\ D_m(x_n) \end{bmatrix} = \begin{bmatrix} X_1(x_1) \cdots X_i(x_j) \cdots X_n(x_m) \end{bmatrix}$$

(1)

Normalize the feature matrix to obtain the normalized vector r_{ij} and build the matrix:

$$r_{ij} = \frac{x_{ij}}{\sqrt{\sum_{i=1}^{m} x_{ij}^2}} (i = 1, 2, \ldots, m, j = 1, 2, \ldots, n)$$

(2)

Then normalize the value v_{ij} by calculating the weight and build the matrix:

$$v_{ij} = w_j r_{ij}, i = 1, 2, \ldots, m, j = 1, 2, \ldots, n$$

(3)

Here, w_j refers to the weight of the jth indicator. Determine optimal solution (A^+) and negative solution (A^-) according to the weight normalization value v_{ij}.

$$A^+ = \left(max_i v_{ij} | j \in J_1\right), \left(min_i v_{ij} | j \in J_2\right), |i = 1, 2, \ldots, m = v_1^+, v_2^+, \ldots, v_j^+, \ldots, v_n^+$$

(4)

$$A^- = \left(min_i v_{ij} | j \in J_1\right), \left(max_i v_{ij} | j \in J_2\right), |i = 1, 2, \ldots, m = v_1^+, v_2^+, \ldots, v_j^+, \ldots, v_n^+$$

(5)

J_1 is a set of profitability indicators, indicating the optimal value on the ith indicator; J_2 is the loss-disaggregation indicator set, indicating the worst value on the ith indicator. The greater the profitability indicator, the better the evaluation result; the smaller the loss index, the better the evaluation result, and vice versa.

Calculate the distance from target to the positive idea solution and the negative ideal solution. The distance from the target to the positive idea solution A^+ is S^+, and the distance from the negative ideal solution A^- is S^-:

$$S^+ = \sqrt{\sum_{j=1}^{n} \left(V_{ij} - V_j^+\right)^2}$$

(6)

$$S^- = \sqrt{\sum_{j=1}^{n} \left(V_{ij} - V_j^-\right)^2}$$

(7)

v_j^* and v_j^- are the distances from the jth target to the optimal target and the worst target, respectively, and v_{ij} is the weight normalized value of the jth evaluation index of the ith target. S^* is the proximity of each evaluation target to the optimal target. The smaller the S* value, the closer the evaluation is the ideal target, and the better the solution. When $C_i^* = 0$, $A_i = A^-$ indicates that the target is the worst target; when $C_i^* = 1$, $A_i = A^*$, indicating that the target is the optimal target.

In actual multi-objective decision making, the optimal target and the worst target are less likely to exist.

$$C_i^* = \frac{S_i^-}{(S_i^* + S_i^-)}, \ i = 1, 2, \ldots, m \tag{8}$$

Finally, each target is arranged from small to large according to the value of C*. The result more closely to C* value, means the better target is, and the largest C* value is the optimal target. For this evaluation, the largest weight is the optimal solution, and the smallest weight is the negative ideal solution. Because the content contained in the questionnaire is inconsistent, the vacant part is replaced by 0. All weights are listed in Table 15, and the maximum and minimum values in the matrix are found to be the optimal solution and the negative ideal solution. The optimal solution will be labeled as red and negative as grey.

Table 15. Weighted matrix of 5 criteria

	1	2	3	4	5
a	0.0825	0.2973	0.0747	0.3087	0.2369
c	0.0918	0.2562	0.2671	0.2882	0.0967
d	0.1499	0.0938	0.1358	0.6204	0.0000
e	0.1499	0.0938	0.1358	0.6204	0.0000
f	0.2929	0.4474	0.2598	0.0000	0.0000
Max	0.2929	0.4474	0.2671	0.6204	0.2369
Min	0.0825	0.0938	0.0747	0.2882	0.0967

The optimal solution is:

$$A_i^* = (0.2929, 0.4474, 0.2671, 0.6204, 0.2369)$$

The negative solution is:

$$A_i^- = (0.0825, 0.0938, 0.0747, 0.2882, 0.0967)$$

Calculate the distance between 5 principles and optimal solution and negative solution, get D_i^+ and D_i^-, and proximity value (C_i) and ranking as illustrated in Table 16. Based on the proximity value, the order of the Ao yuan landscape design criterion is: Construction factors, Economic factors, Spatial pattern, Design elements, Ecological factors. If based on the weight of the design principle, the order is: Spatial pattern, Construction factors, Economic factors, Design elements, Ecological factors. There has been a change in ordering.

Table 16. D_i^+, D_i^-, and C_i value

	D_i^+	D_i^-	C_i	Ranking	Ranking in weighted
a	0.4579	0.3878	0.4586	2	3
c	0.4555	0.3560	0.4387	3	1
d	0.6050	0.4233	0.4117	4	4
e	0.4741	0.5861	0.5528	1	2
f	0.6647	0.4550	0.4064	5	5

3   Conclusion

This study uses Fuzzy Delphi, AHP, TOPSIS, etc., and selects the landscape design of Jimei Ao yuan as the research object. Through research, it can be found that Fuzzy Delphi can quickly obtain the consensus of experts when confirming the relevant criteria. The evaluation of landscape design by AHP collection TOPSIS can achieve more reasonable results than the traditional public perception of landscape design. The traditional methods of landscape design evaluation have different standards and diverse concepts, and can only be used to give ambiguous evaluations of impressions.

When using traditional evaluation methods, Spatial pattern and Construction factors usually at the center of the core. Using AHP and TOPSIS, we can find that in the evaluation of Ao yuan landscape design, Construction factor and Economic factor played an important role.

According to this process, in the future, landscape architects or park managers and maintainers can quickly meet the different needs of people, and can accurately discover the deficiencies in the park and improve them. The park development and construction will enable the park to continue to present a good state of environmental quality, enabling Jimei Ao yuan to achieve high-speed, healthy and stable sustainable development.

References

1. Gehl, J.: Life between Buildings: Using Public Space, 6th edn. Island Press, USA (2011)
2. McHarg, I.L., Mumford, L.: Design with Nature, 2nd edn. Wiley-Blackwell, USA (1995)
3. Ahern, J.: Planning for an extensive open space system. Landsc. Urban Plan. **21**, 131–145 (1991)
4. Francis, M.: Some different meanings attached to a city park and community gardens. Landsc. J. **6**(2), 101–112 (1987)
5. Tunner, M.G.: Landscape ecology: the effect of pattern on process. Ann. Rev. Ecol. Syst. **20**(1), 171–197 (1989)
6. Urban, D.L., et al.: A hierarchical perspective can help scientists understand spatial patterns. BioScience **37**(2), 119–127 (1987)
7. Xiamen Municipal Bureau of Justice Homepage. http://www.xmpf.gov.cn/fzdt/xmfg/2002/201612/t20161203_1785790.htm

8. Linstone, H.A., Turoff, M.: The Delphi Method Techniques and Applications, 1st edn. Wiley-Blackwell, USA (2011)
9. Saaty, T.L.: How to make a decision: the analytic hierarchy process. Eur. J. Oper. Res. **48**(1), 9–26 (1990)
10. Lai, Y.J., Liu, T.Y., Hwang, C.L.: TOPSIS for MODM. Eur. J. Oper. Res. **76**(3), 486–500 (1994)

A Literature Review of the Research on Take-Over Situation in Autonomous Driving

Xin Xin[1(✉)], Min Zhao[2], Moli Zhou[2], Siyao Lu[1], Yishan Liu[1],
Daisong Guan[2], Qianyi Wang[1], and Yuezhou Zhang[1]

[1] Beijing Normal University, 19 Xinjiekouwai Street, Beijing, China
xin.xin@bnu.edu.cn, Lynn6917@163.com,
liuyishan1313@126.com, {allen.w,
yuezhou.zhang}@mail.bnu.edu.cn
[2] Baidu.com, Inc., NO. 10 Xibeiwang East Road, Beijing, China
{zhaomin04,zhoumoli,guandaisong}@baidu.com

Abstract. In order to understand driver's response time from automatic driving to manual driving and driving behavior after taking over in the complex traffic environment, and influencing factors of driver's driving switching process, this paper systematically combs the common experimental situations in the research of the take-over situation in autonomous driving, and analyzes the characteristics of the take-over situation, driver's behavior characteristic, take-over time and driving performance. We hope in the future, autonomous driving take-over procedure could balance safety and experience for drivers.

Keywords: Autonomous driving · Take-over · Situational awareness · Driving behavior · Driving workload

1 Introduction

In recent years, information technology is playing an important role in traditional automobile industry. Artificial intelligence, control algorithms and sensors is continuously developing, autonomous driving achieved rapid development, autonomous driving cars improved driving safety, comfort and efficiency. Various driving assistance systems are constantly developing and come into use. The increasing of intelligence has become a trend in automobile industry. Chris Urmson, director of the Google's former autonomous driving car business unit, believes that "when people enjoy themselves in the car, they couldn't always get the driving done safely." According to statistics, 75% of traffic accidents were caused by human, while autonomous driving technology is a technology designed to release human from the traffic system [1]. With the continuous development and improvement of technology, autonomous driving technology would come to be applied in practice, people could travel freely without worrying about accidents made by human.

According to the classification standard established by the American Society of Automotive Engineers (SAE) [2]. Autonomous driving is divided into 6 levels: No Automation (L0); Driver Assistance (L1); Partial Automation (L2); Conditional Automation (L3); Highly automation (L4); Fully automation (L5). At present, Chinese

A. Marcus and W. Wang (Eds.): HCII 2019, LNCS 11585, pp. 160–169, 2019.
https://doi.org/10.1007/978-3-030-23538-3_12

legal [3] provisions only L1 self-driving vehicles with automatic steering or automatic acceleration and braking functions, as well as L2 self-driving vehicles with automatic steering and automatic acceleration and braking functions could be driven on public roads. Autonomous driving system of L3 and above requires human intervention, and it will be a difficult problem to define clearly who should take the responsibility for driving by vehicle or driver [4].

July 2017, Audi released Audi A8, which is the first vehicle with an L3-class autopilot system, and it had the highest level of autonomous driving capability in production models all over the world. In L3 autonomous driving, driver does not need to pay attention to the driving environment at all times, and perform non-driving tasks (music, games, etc.). Meanwhile the autonomous driving system cannot handle all driving tasks, when system recognizes that the current situation could not be processed, it would present the driver demand with visual or audible information, to prompt driver to take over the vehicle again. The principal of main driving task is transferred from the autonomous driving vehicle to driver, this is called the take-over technique in autonomous driving. According to the definition of Bundesanstalt fur StraBenwesen, highly automated driving constitutes a system that takes over a complete driving task for a specific time. Driver doesn't need to monitor the system, but if the system requires, driver should take over the driving task. During the take-over process, driver must have hands and feet back the controlling to state, restore the situation awareness, and make decisions and reactions after taking over [5].

During the process of switching from autonomous driving to manual driving, driver needs a certain period of time to re-enter the driving state and resume driving ability, and this adaptation period is much likely to cause an accident [6]. In 2012, during the road test of Google Unmanned Vehicles, people promised to keep an eye on the road conditions during the test so that they can take over the driving in time when an emergency occurs, but in fact many people are distracted to do all sorts of things in the road test. In the study of autonomous driving, this classic problem is called the "hands-off problem" [7]. It can be seen that non-driving tasks have a great impact on the take-over process and quality. In addition, when studying the take-over problem in autonomous driving, traffic conditions, user's situational awareness, etc. are closely related to driving take-over [8]. Many scholars have carried out a series of studies on the behavior of drivers during the take-over process, mainly in terms of take-over time and driving performance after take-over. For example, when explored the appropriate time point for guiding driver's attention back to the driving task, Gold et al. found the shorter the take-over request time, the shorter the time taken by the driver take over the vehicle, and the faster the driver's reaction and decision, the worse the driver's take-over quality [9]. After conducting experiments, Strand et al. found that the intelligent level of the vehicle and the degree of system failure have an impact on the driving performance of driver after taking over. The higher the level of automation, the greater the reduction in driving performance [10].

The process of taking over affects the subsequent driving safety, and many factors influence this process. Take-over situation is very important as an objective condition, and it is also an important experimental condition for many scholars to conduct driving take-over research. This paper will analyze the driving take-over problem in autonomous driving from the perspective of take-over situation, specifically by the take-over situational characteristics, the driver's behavioral characteristics, take-over time and driving performance. Combined with user's psychological and behavioral characteristics, this paper hope to provide a theoretical reference for the future interaction design for take-over of highly autonomous driving.

2 Take-Over Situation

2.1 Capability Limits of ADAS

When people drive, the ADAS (Advanced Driver Assistant System) of the autonomous driving car receives various types of information from roads, environments, pedestrians, signs, and equipment. The autonomous driving system analyzes and makes decisions based on the received situational information, and ultimately controls the vehicle. However, the road surface, road conditions, weather and other factors are complex and changeable. In some scenarios, ADAS cannot identify the situation information accurately, or the ability of the automatic driving system is insufficient to deal with the situation, then the system is difficult to make accurate operational decisions. The take-over system of vehicle is triggered, and driving authority is handed over to the driver, driver starts to respond to the situation.

Taking Audi A8 as an example, driver can perform other tasks besides the main driving task in the car, and even can remove the hands and feet from the steering wheel, the brake and the accelerator pedal. However, in some situations, driver still needs to respond to the control switch request from autonomous driving system at any time. For example, the vehicle is close to the high-speed exit and needs to change lanes to drive off the highway, the front vehicle with a slow speed, the vehicle needs to give way for an ambulance at the rear, temporary construction of road and the lane suddenly becomes less, and there is a traffic accident in front.

Lu explored the driving take-over response characteristics of young drivers, and the impact of take-over request time and visual tasks on the take-over time. The study set a driving take-over situation: when the subject is doing the visual tasks during the autonomous driving process, an anchored vehicle suddenly appears in front of the lane. The autonomous driving system will send a prompt message to the driver "autonomous driving is about to expire, please take over!", and display a text prompt icon on the central display screen. After hearing the tone, driver needs to quickly press the toggle button to switch the vehicle from the autonomous driving mode to the manual mode. The study considers the collision avoidance time between the driving vehicle and the front anchored vehicle as the take-over request time. The experimental results show that the take-over time with secondary tasks increase significantly compared to that without secondary tasks. When handle the take-over scenarios with an obstacle in the front, the participants tended to apply the operation of combined brake and swerve [11].

2.2   Common Situations of Autonomous Driving Take-Over

There are four common situations in the experimental research related to autonomous take-over [12–15]. First, the travel planning changes, the driver should choose a specific route; Second, the road markings can't be recognized, such as the lane line or the turning mark is ambiguous; third, the vehicle itself doesn't work, the sensor fails, the software is wrong, etc.; Fourth, the road construction and road conditions become complicated and it is difficult for vehicles to ensure safe driving. Based on the consideration of the current automatic driving system restrictions, Kuehn et al. set these four scenarios [16]. In scenario 1, the driver is required to take over control of the vehicle to select a particular route or leave the highway. There are no other vehicles within 5–5.25 s after the take-over request is issued, and the navigation arrow appears on the head up display, prompting the driver to change lanes. In scenario 2, the vehicle is no longer able to turn safely enough because the system can't recognize the lane markings clearly, so the system transfers control to the driver. There is a car 250-m - far in front of the driver's vehicle. The car initially maintains a speed of 120 km/h. After 5–5.25 s, the vehicle in front is braked until it reaches a speed of 80 km/h and maintains the speed. In scenario 3, the vehicle is no longer able to turn safely enough due to sensor failure or software error, thus transferring control to the driver. The only difference between scenario 3 and scenario 2 is that there is no absence of lane markings (Fig. 1).

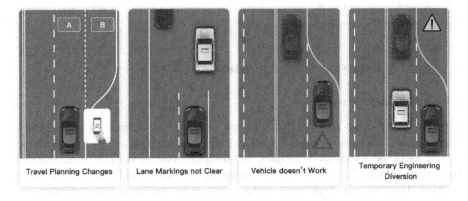

| Travel Planning Changes | Lane Markings not Clear | Vehicle doesn't Work | Temporary Engineering Diversion |

Fig. 1. Four common situations in the experimental research related to autonomous take-over.

In the scenario 4, due to road works, the vehicle can no longer be turned safely enough, so control is transferred to the driver. The autonomous system issues a high traffic density alert while decelerating the driver's vehicle based on the speed limit shown on the road sign, from 120 km/h to 60 km/h. In addition to setting up road works 300 km away from the point of take-over request, at the same time, the experiment simulate stationary vehicle in driving, and the stationary vehicle was 175 m away from the take-over request point. From the literature, it was found that multi-lane highways were used as the basis context for experimental simulation in many take-over scenarios. As in the four scenarios mentioned above, the take-over situations are all on the highway. During autonomous driving, the automation system keeps 60 m away from the vehicle in front. Once the distance is less than 60 m, the autonomous system is activated with an audible warning signal. The results of the study indicate that the automation system should provide the current road conditions to the driver as early and clear as possible, and if 90% of drivers are required to respond correctly, the take-over time should over 8 s. During the take-over process, the automation system should always control the vehicle safely until the driver takes over explicitly.

A summary of the above scenarios reveals that the situation in which the take-over takes place has two characteristics. First, the complexity of the situation is high, such as lane change, complicated road conditions of so many vehicles, unpredictable trajectory of pedestrian or non-motorized vehicles, and irregular driving behavior from other vehicles. Second, situational urgency is in high level, such as the situation of serious rear-end collisions when the vehicle ahead has emergency brakes, and the general conflict situation in which other vehicle suddenly cut the line. In the future, we could start from these scenarios and define the situation that requires driving take-over more clearly. This also helps to balance the safety and experience when driver is in autonomous driving context.

In addition, above context are take-over scenarios which will be adopted in the current research, all of them belong to the case when the automatic driving system initiative proposes to take over the request. While in the actual driving process, driver could also take the initiative for a take-over request, for getting fun in driving, or not satisfied with the speed of the automatic driving system, and soon in the future, we can start a research base on the analysis above.

3   Driver's Behavior Characteristics

3.1   Situation Awareness

Different drivers have different behavior and responses in different road conditions, especially in dangerous situations, such as traffic flow density, relative speed of the vehicle itself and surrounding vehicles, and distance between vehicles, these external factors and internal factors like driver's attention state can greatly influence driver's decision. Therefore, the perception of the environment, the intent recognition of surrounding vehicles and the prediction of vehicle track are important for driver to make decisions and corresponding behavior. It needs driver to maintain a good situation awareness. Situation awareness in the context of autonomous refers to the driver's perception and understanding of all environmental factors including time and space during the autonomous driving process, and the prediction of what's happening around [17].

Zhang Yu's interviews with three autopilot users (novice users, intermediate users and expert users), and found that during driving autonomous vehicles, drivers are prone to have four characteristics, driving distraction, passive fatigue, over-trust of autonomous driving system, and driving skill degradation [18]. Driving distraction is expressed by the driver's attention and cognitive resources shifting from basic driving tasks such as controlling the car, maintaining the lane, and monitoring the road conditions to non-driving tasks. Passive fatigue is manifested by a drastic reduction in driving workload, resulting in a cognitive load that is too low to fall into passive fatigue. Excessive trust is manifested by the driver's over-estimation and over-reliance on the auto-driving function after using the autonomous system for a period of time, which also further increases the tendency to drive distraction. Degradation of driving skills is manifested by the reduced flexibility and driving cognitive skills required to manually complete mission success and safety after prolonged use of the autonomous driving function. All of these four features are extremely detrimental to the driver's safe driving (Fig. 2).

Fig. 2. Four characteristics of driving degradation.

When driving main task is handed over to the system, driver's attention will be diverted from driving task, and only a small amount of attention resources will be used to maintain an understanding of the vehicle's state and road conditions, and the attention to the situation will be reduced. So the "hands-off problem" of the Google testers mentioned above has arisen. At this point, driver receives a take-over prompt, driver will be very surprised and need more time to come back to the driving state, and the increase in reaction time and transfer of the attention object lead to the risk in driving. Jamson et al. found that vehicles with higher levels of autonomous driving ability can better reduce accidents and human brain load, but driver's situational awareness will be lower [19]. There is no doubt that it is very dangerous in the event of an emergency.

3.2 Driver's Switching Mode

In the study of the driving behavior during the take-over of autonomous driving vehicles in dangerous traffic situation, Niu used the driving speed, headway distance, vehicle lateral control and vehicle steering behavior as the driver's driving performance assessment. It was found that after receiving the danger warning, driver would have two different switching modes, driver switched immediately and regained the control of the vehicle quickly, the other is to monitor the road and vehicle information for a period of time [20]. This situation of monitoring the situation after receiving the take-over prompt mainly occurs when driver is in a relaxed state at present, and the "person" in charge of the main driving task is an automatic driving system. At this time, it is necessary to switch its own alert/wake level before the take-over, identify and analyze the driving situation in which it is located.

Human factors in the autonomous take-over process will have an impact on driving safety. First of all, in the automatic driving state, if the driving task is too easy, driver can easily enter the passive fatigue due to the low cognitive burden, and the boring driving process will cause the driver to participate in non-driving tasks more, such as social entertainment. Then it leads to driving distraction. Secondly, because driver's main attention resources in the automatic driving process are not concentrated on the vehicle and the road situation, the situation awareness is reduced, and when the automatic system exits and the switching control request is issued, the driver may be frightened by unexpected state changes or prompts. At the same time, insufficient level of situation awareness may cause confusion about the driving mode. In addition, driver may also be overly dependent on the autonomous driving system, reduce the trust in automatic driving by frequent warning messages.

4   Take-Over Time and Driving Performance

4.1   Take-Over Time

After receiving the take-over request from the vehicle, the driver needs to take over the vehicle again, and driver's decision on the situation and the control of the vehicle will be affected. Happee et al. studied the autopilot take-over by using Time to Collision (TCC) and the distance from the obstacle as an evaluation indicator of the emergency take-over operation. It was found that the autopilot would make the driver more likely delay in steering and brake intervention than the manual driving behavior [21].

The workload during driving is an important factor affecting the driver's take-over response time and driving performance. According to Yed's rule, too high or too low workload will both affect driving performance [22]. Merat et al. compared the driving performance between the driver experience on autonomous driving switch to manual driving and purely manual driving, found that drivers who have experienced autonomous driving have worse driving performance. This is because driver is in low workload during autonomous driving [23].

In studying the impact of non-driving tasks on driving take-over performance, it was found that the driver's distraction and tension can affect the reaction time and further affect the time taken by the driver to take over the vehicle. The reaction time required by driver to play the game is significantly greater than listening to music. Eriksson et al.'s research also shows that the driver's take-over reaction time is longer under the influence of the sub-tasks [24]. Zeeb et al.'s research has drawn different conclusions. The experiment has studied the effects of different real sub-tasks (writing e-mails, reading news, watching videos) on the take-over operation, and the results show that the sub-tasks have no effect on driver's take-over time [25]. Comparing these above studies, it can be found that the conclusions of the two studies may be caused by factors such as the driver's own characteristics, the state before the take-over operation, and the urgency of the take-over situation. At the same time, the impact of the non-driving task on the driving take-over, take-over time and driving performance is difficult to strip, as Zeeb et al.'s research also shows that driving take-over will deteriorate the driving quality after taking over.

4.2 Driving Performance

In addition, traffic conditions can also have an impact on driving performance. Radlmayr et al. study the influence of different traffic situations and non-driving tasks on the take-over process during highly autonomous driving. The standardized visual Surrogate Reference Task (SuRT) and the cognitive n-back Task are used to simulate the non-driving related tasks, results show that take-over quality does not seem to significantly depend on varying the chosen non-driving related tasks prior to the take-over. On the other hand, it indicates a strong influence of the traffic situation on take-over time and quality. A higher criticality of driver behavior can clearly be observed in the situation which features a high traffic density [8].

At present, researchers have carried out a series of studies on the driving take-over behavior in autonomous driving, which focus on workload and traffic conditions. However, the research on driving operation characteristics under specific situation and driving sub-tasks on driving take-over time and driving performance are not deep enough. Researchers can do more comparison of the driver's operation data under different take-over situations, it will provide a more comprehensive theoretical basis for the study of driving take-over behavior.

5 Meaning of Driving Take-Over

Since the excessive or low workload during the autonomous driving process will both affect the take-over time and driving performance, which will affect the driving safety, the take-over system should design a better way for the driver to participate more in the driving task, pay attention to vehicle status and road traffic scenarios in order to maintain a good situation awareness. At the same time, it is necessary to design a better warning mode, indicating the current automatic driving status and its limitations, clearly and efficiently transmitting information, which is easy to be obtained by driver, avoid driver separating from the human-car-environment system. A study by Seppelt et al. found that giving driver a continuous message is more effective than a generic failure hazard warning [26].

The manner in which driver take-over system issues a switching request to the driver should balance the workload and urgency, not too early for the driver to interpret it as a false positive, but also not too late to catch the opportunity to switch the manually driven vehicle. The operation and reaction time during the process of taking over the vehicle affects driver's subsequent driving safety, based on the diver's behavior characteristics under different take-over situations and take-over conditions, scholars can do further study on the way of request driver to take over the vehicle.

6 Conclusion

With the developing of various active safety technologies, highly autonomous driving cars will gradually become popular in the next decade, bringing significant social and economic benefits. While the higher the level of automation, the more important the human operator is. The existing research has found that the ADAS will lower driver's situational awareness and decreased control skills, workload and traffic conditions during the take-over process will also influence the take-over time and driving performance. In the context of the continuous development of autonomous driving, how to ensure the driving safety in the take-over situation while driver's participation in the driving main task is continuously reduced is a major difficulty in the future.

At present, research on the autonomous driving take-over does not involve the study of the stability of the vehicle under different take-over conditions. However, this is very important for the driving experience. In the future, scholars can carry out these researches, provides a richer theoretical basis for the rational design in driving take-over system, realize reliable, safe and interesting driving maneuver switching.

References

1. Salmon, P.M., Regan, M.A., Johnston, I.: Human Error and Road Transport: Phase One – Literature Review. Highway Safety (2005)
2. SAE On-road Automated Vehicle Standards Committee: Taxonomy and Definitions for Terms Related to On-road Motor Vehicle Automated Driving Systems. SAE, Warrendale (2014)
3. 《Road Traffic Safety Law of the People's Republic of China》, Chap. II Sect. 2 Motor Vehicle Drivers (2011)
4. Editorial Department of China Journal of Highway and Transport: Review on China's Automotive Engineering Research Progress: 2017. China J. Highw. Transp. **30**(6), 1–197 (2017)
5. Radlmayr, J., Gold, C., Lorenz, L., Farid, M., Bengler, K.: How traffic situations and non-driving related tasks affect the take-over quality in highly automated driving. In: Proceedings of the Human Factors and Ergonomics Society Annual Meeting, vol. 58, no. 1, pp. 2063–2067 (2014)
6. Russell, H.E.B., Harbott, L.K., Nisky, I., Pan, S., Okamura, A.M., Gerdes, J.C.: Motor learning affects car-to-driver handover in automated vehicles. Sci. Robot. **1**(1), 1–10 (2016)
7. Wang, Y.: Audi new A8 defining the future—analyzing Audi's new generation A8 autopilot technology. World Automob. **09**, 30–37 (2017)
8. Radlmayr, J., Gold, C., Lorenz, L., Farid, M., Bengler, K.: How traffic situations and non-driving related tasks affect the take-over quality in highly automated driving. In: Proceedings of the Human Factors and Ergonomics Society 58th Annual Meeting, pp. 2063–2067. SAGE Publications (2014)

9. Gold, C., Dambock, D., Lorenz, L., Bengler, K.: "Take Over!" How long does it take to get the driver back into the loop?. In: Proceedings of the Human Factors & Ergonomics Society Annual Meeting, pp. 1938–1942. SAGE Publications (2013)

10. Strand, N., Nilsson, J., Karlsson, M.A., Nilsson, L.: Semi-automated versus highly automated driving in critical situations caused by automation failures. Transp. Res. Part F: Traffic Psychol. Behav. **27**, 218–228 (2014)

11. Lu, G., Zhao, P., Wang, Z., Lin, Q.: Impact of visual secondary task on young drivers' take-over time in automated driving. China J. High. Transp. **31**(04), 165–171 (2018)

12. Maurer, M., Gerdes, J.C., Lenz, B., Winner, H.: Autonomes Fahren: Technische, rechtliche und gesellschaftliche Aspekte. Springer Vieweg, Heidelberg (2015). https://doi.org/10.1007/978-3-662-45854-9

13. Hillel, A.B., Lerner, R., Levi, D., Raz, G.: Recent progress in road and lane detection: a survey. Mach. Vis. Appl. **25**(3), 727–745 (2014)

14. Meyer, G., Beiker, S.: [HRSG]: Road Vehicle Automation. Springer, Cham (2014). https://doi.org/10.1007/978-3-319-05990-7

15. Ziegler, J., et al.: Making Bertha drive—an autonomous journey on a historic route. IEEE Intell. Transp. Syst. Mag. **6**(2), 8–20 (2014). https://doi.org/10.1109/mits.2014.2306552

16. Kuehn, M., Vogelpohl, T., Vollrath, M.: Takeover times in highly automated driving (level 3). In: 25th International Technical Conference on the Enhanced Safety of Vehicles (ESV) (2017)

17. Feng, C., Wanyan, X., Chen, H., Zhuang, D.: Situation awareness model based on multi-resource load theory and its application. J. Beijing Univ. Aeronaut. Astronaut. **44**(07), 1438–1446 (2018)

18. Zhang, Y.: Research on Human-Machine Interaction Strategy Design of Automated Driving Take-over System Based on User Experience, pp. 21–30. South China University of Technology (2018)

19. Jamson, A., Meratn, N., Carsten, O., et al.: Behavioural changes in drivers experiencing highly-automated vehicle control in varying traffic conditions. J. Transp. Res. Part C **30**(5), 116–125 (2013)

20. Niu, J., Zhang, X., Sun, Y., Qin, H.: Analysis of the driving behavior during the takeover of automatic driving vehicles in dangerous traffic situations. China J. High. Transp. **31**(06), 272–280 (2018)

21. Happee, R., Gold, C., Radlmayr, J., et al.: Take-over performance in evasive manoeuvres. J. Accid. Anal. Prev. **106**, 211–222 (2017)

22. Coughlin, J., Reimer, B., Mehler, B.: Driver Wellness, Safety & the Development of an Aware Car. AgeLab, Boston (2009)

23. Merat, N., Jamson, A., Lai, F., et al.: Highly automated driving, secondary task performance, and driver state. J. Hum. Factors **54**(5), 762–771 (2012)

24. Eriksson, A., Stanton, N., Davis, K.: Takeover time in highly automated vehicles: noncritical transitions to and from manual control. Hum. Factors: J. Hum. Factors Ergon. Soc. **59**(4), 689–705 (2017)

25. Zeeb, K., Buchner, A., Schrauf, M.: Is take over time all that maters? The impact of visual-cognitive load on driver take-over quality after conditionally automated driving. J. Accid. Anal. Prev. **92**, 230–239 (2016)

26. Seppelt, B., Lee, J.: Making Adaptive Cruise Control (ACC) limits visible. J. Int. J. Hum.-Comput. Stud. **65**(3), 192–205 (2007)

Research on Interactive Strategy for Boosting Novice Drivers' Confidence Based on Internet of Vehicles

Yan-cong Zhu and Di Zhu[✉]

Beijing Normal University, Beijing 100875, China
{Yancong.zhu,di.zhu}@bnu.edu.cn

Abstract. With the economic growth and the realization of technology, the development of Internet of Vehicles (IoV) further facilitates People's Daily traffic. But numerous problems in driving are also gradually emerging, especially for novice drivers. In the IOV system composed of people, vehicles and the environment, people are one of the factors causing system instability as a core of controlling and balancing the whole interaction process. The driver of different human-car interaction stages has different behavioral characteristics. Interactive strategies connect novices and experienced drivers in an effective way. Experienced drivers can be purposeful and effective in guiding novices. It also provides intelligent guidance for novice drivers to drive independently. At the evaluation stage, three experts were invited to give comments and suggestions on the interactive strategies. This purpose of this paper is to explore the driving style, pain points and requirements of novices, and propose interactive strategies specifically, to help novice drivers improve interactive experience, improve driving confidence, and effectively practice driving.

Keywords: Internet of Vehicles (IOV) · Novice drivers ·
Interactive strategies · Interactive experience · Driving confidence

1 Background

1.1 A Subsection Sample

With developing of economy technology, automobile industry is also improving. According to the China National Bureau of Statistics, China's automobile production in 2016 was 28.119 million, an increase of 14.8% over the previous year. By the end of 2016, the national civil vehicle ownership. The number reached 194.4 million, of which 165.59 million were private cars, an increase of 15% [1]. The increase in car ownership in the country has brought a great convenience to people, but it also brought waste gas pollution. So, the automotive industry, especially in the field of Internet of vehicles, is booming.

© Springer Nature Switzerland AG 2019
A. Marcus and W. Wang (Eds.): HCII 2019, LNCS 11585, pp. 170–180, 2019.
https://doi.org/10.1007/978-3-030-23538-3_13

Internet of Vehicles is a branch of the Internet of Things. That refers to the integration of vehicles, pedestrians, roads and infrastructures into an organic information system using advanced information and network technologies to provide a variety of services for vehicles, for instance, driving safety, traffic control, road maintenance, life entertainment, and comprehensive Information and Internet access [2], so as to achieve the purpose of reducing traffic accidents and improving traffic efficiency [3]. At present, USA, Canada, UK, etc. has basically realized vehicle location sharing, traffic situation perception, intelligent navigation system and intelligent parking management system. Chinese research of vehicle network starts later than these contrived but in fast speed. The researchers learned how to address low transportation efficiency and poor driving safety, unbalanced driving resources [4]. Nevertheless, popularity of Internet of Vehicles also brought new problems, for instance, information systems of vehicles are more and more complicated, drivers have new approaches to interact with vehicles.

So how to adapt vehicles to Internet of Vehicles context? In this context, drivers, vehicles combined with the environment into an interactive system. Drivers drive vehicles. Meanwhile receive information from the road system. They control and balance the system. research shows that human behaviors took a large proportion in traffic accidents. Based on traffic accident liability data analysis from 2006 to 2014, researchers found that 70%–80%'s responsibility lay with drivers [5]. Driver's accident factors show that driver's experience and confidence have an important impact on the driving process. As a result, there has been research and system design aimed at enhancing the potential hazard prediction ability of drivers. For instance, automatic driving assistance system is developed for expressway context, including many assistant systems, such as emergency braking, automatic cruise, lane detection, etc. [6]. A novel technology to increase the control mode of adaptive system that aiming at the defects of automobile adaptive system [7]. Although driving assistance systems can help drivers avoid certain dangers, most of researches are focusing on how to acquire new features in auxiliary systems, while ignoring the psychological factors of drivers in the driving.

Based on this, this paper makes an in-depth study on Chinese novice drivers from the perspective of psychological factors, aiming at putting forward reasonable interaction schemes and strategies to help novice drivers improve their driving self-confidence.

2   Research Contents and Process

2.1   A Subsection Sample

The key research questions in this paper are shown in Fig. 1. By exploring the driving behavior and driving style of novice drivers, analyzing the mental model, pain points and user needs of novice drivers. Finally, it will put forward new interactive strategies that increase the driving confidence of novice drivers.

This research process is divided into four stages and progressively. In the first stage, this paper will do desk research, literature review and quantitative researches. After analyzing, it will determine the driving style of novice drivers in the Chinese context. In the second stage, it will do qualitative analysis and translate results into design languages that can provide a theoretical basis for the interactive scheme. In the third stage, it will put forward interactive scheme by visualizing approaches, and iterate the scheme based on user test outcomes. And in the fourth stage, it will discuss and reflect the scheme based on evaluation outcomes, as showed in Fig. 2.

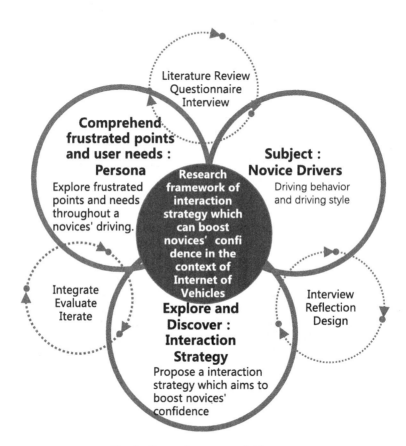

Fig. 1. Research contents of this paper.

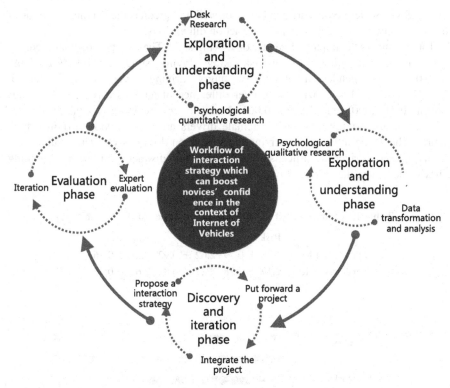

Fig. 2. Research process of this paper.

3 Interactive Strategies Research

3.1 Quantitative Research

In this research stage, it mainly through the questionnaire method to explore Chinese drivers' driving styles, possibly driving behavior of novice drivers, influencing factors, and collected 365 questionnaires through network tools, of which 302 were valid. Then compiles an interview outline according to the influencing factors and behavioral tendencies. Questionnaire contents are based on literature review outcomes. The purpose of the questionnaire is to screen participants, record the basic information, investigate the driving style and find out the reasons for the driving influence factors. The questionnaire contains the Chinese version of the Multidimensional Driving Style Scale, which can well confirm the driving style of Chinese drivers, and its multiple dimensions have a good predictive function for the possible actions of drivers [8, 9].

Based on the analysis of variance and cross-correlation of the valid data collected, it is concluded that the driving styles of Chinese drivers are mainly divided into three types: risk-taking, anger and anxiety. Gender and driving experience has a significant impact on the driving style of Chinese drivers. The driving style of novices and less experienced drivers is mainly anxious type style. The Chinese version of the Multidimensional

Driving Style Scale predicts driving behavior well and predicts the driving behavior of novices mainly in anger, anxiety and distraction dimensions.

Table 1 shows the impact of gender on driving style. The results show that there are significant gender differences in risk-taking driving style, F $(1,3.494)$ = 5.69, P = 0.018. The gender difference of angry driving style is significant, F $(1,9.381)$ = 12.37, P = 0.001. The gender difference of anxious driving style is significant, F $(1,7.070)$ = 12.49, P < 0.001. Male drivers are more risk-taking driving style and angry driving style, while female drivers are more anxious driving style. Figure 3 shows the influence of driving experience on driving style. The results show that the longer a driver has a license, the less anxious, distracted and sensory seeking behavior he or she has during driving.

Table 1. Comparison of mean values in the scale (M ± SD) tables.

	Risk-taking	Anger	Anxious
Male (N = 146)	2.38 ± 0.79	2.62 ± 0.92	2.31 ± 0.76
Female (N = 156)	2.17 ± 0.78	2.27 ± 0.82	2.62 ± 0.74

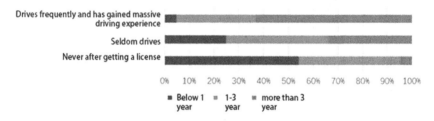

Fig. 3. Cross analysis of driving experience and getting license years.

3.2   Qualitative Research

Quantitative research confirms that the driving style of Chinese novices is mainly anxious driving style and divides driving behavior into various dimensions. Combining predicted driving behavior of novices and the reasons obtained in questionnaires. This paper put forward a 1 on 1 interview outline. Depending on the interview outline, interviewed selected participants. Through information comparison and supplement of the interviews between novices and experienced drivers, confirmed the characteristics of novices, found out pain points and user needs of novices. The results obtained in this part will assist in the next stage of this paper.

In this stage, interviewed 32 participants, and 31 effective participants were selected, including 14 females and 17 males. 10 novices and 21 experienced drivers. The number of novice drivers is lower than that of experienced drivers. Because novice drivers have less practical experience and have a relatively shallow view of human-vehicle interaction, the number of experienced drivers is increased to get more opinions.

According to the above, combining cognition and suggestions of novices and experienced drivers, it can find that the main concerns of novice drivers are driving awareness and driving behavior. Driving awareness includes safety awareness, attention awareness, pre-judgment awareness, logical thinking and planning awareness. Driving behavior includes practical practice, speed assessment, accompanying driving and attention. As showed in Fig. 4.

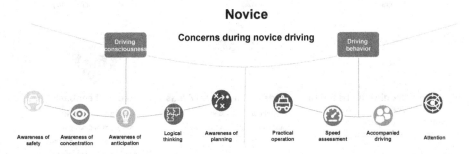

Fig. 4. Primary focus for novice drivers.

Depending on the above analysis results, this paper can get the driving pain points of novice drivers.

(1) In the early stage of driving, environmental changes of novice drivers pose a greater psychological challenge to novice drivers.
(2) Novice drivers are difficult to understand their driving situations in time.
(3) Novice drivers are often confused about their driving behaviors.

Based on the above pain points, it put forward opportunities for research.

(1) How to help novices choose the proper driving place at the early stage of driving?
(2) How to help novices knows the details of their driving in time?
(3) How to give time guidance/advice/helps to novices during driving?

3.3   Interaction Strategies for Novice Drivers to Increase Driving Confidence

Come up with Schemes. In view of the above research opportunities, through brainstorming, the scheme affinity diagram, classification and other design thinking methods. Eventually clustered same schemes and summarized and screened these schemes. The scheme after screening is presented in Fig. 5.

Interactive Strategy Journey Map. After screening, each scheme will be connected in series, and eventually form an interactive strategy scheme for novices to increase confidence. This strategy is convenient for drivers to practice, combined with self-efficacy factors affecting self-confidence, to cultivate driver self-confidence. Through this strategy, drivers are more likely to obtain a successful experience in the driving

Intelligent Route Planning

Exclude unsuitable locations、
Open roads and plann driving route
by grade

Chaperone Guide

Match guidance levels and
guidance staff based on
evaluation results

Intelligent Machine Evaluation

The onboard machine evaluate on
the basis of driving conditions
(number of mistakes, etc.)

Fixed Point Monitoring based on Trajectory

The driving track is recorded on the map
by GPS, and the feedback is unified.

Guidance In Certain Areas

Activate corresponding
guidance in the novice labeled
area

Record Feedback

Keep a record of driving
conditions and compared
standard conditions. Record
advice and comprehensive
opinions.

Fig. 5. Final solutions.

Li Mingxue: A novice who is not confident and has no driving experience after getting his driver'

Fig. 6. Interactive strategies -Journey map1.

driver's license.

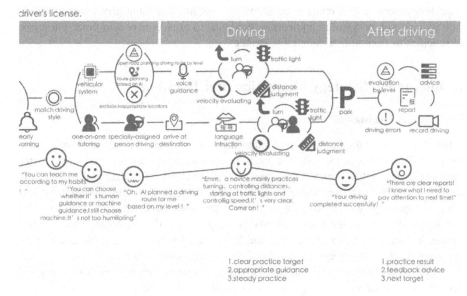

Fig. 7. Interactive strategies -Journey map2.

process and better predict difficulties to cope with. Both intelligent guidance and personal guidance can provide a good alternative experience for drivers, and help drivers absorb alternative experience. At the same time, with the assistance of guidance from all dimensions, drivers can keep a positive attitude. The interactive strategic scheme for novices who are not confident, and it is difficult for them to get on the road for the first time. It mainly combines six schemes: intelligent planning route, machine intelligent evaluation, personal accompanying guidance, trajectory fixed-point monitoring, specific area guidance and record feedback, it showed in Figs. 6 and 7.

Novices can use a mobile phone application to login in the system and choose rental vehicles or connect to their vehicle system. As novices, the system will evaluate their driving grade, at the same time they can choose the preference guidance mode in application, such as a comprehensive guide, key guidance or quiet companionship. You can also choose recording driving, early warning and emergency contact features. By measuring the grade and driving style, the application will be matched to the same driving style guidance. It has two modes of guidance. One is to match the corresponding experienced drivers as a special coach to guide; the other is to provide intelligent guidance by the vehicle system. The coach will drive the vehicle to a suitable area for practicing, and then the novice will conduct driving practice under guidance. Intelligent guidance of a system is to remove inappropriate locations according to driving grades of novices, and to plan a suitable route for novices to drive. This sub features mainly guides beginners through voice assistance. As the first practical driving for beginners, its main purpose is to adapt to the road driving environment based on general driving skills that learned from driving school. After driving, the driver can check his report, including the results of the grade evaluation and the record of his driving process, the mistakes in driving and related suggestions.

Trajectory monitoring is realized by recording feature, and intelligent planning guidance will give early warning and certain guidance to novice drivers in time. These are all schemes to accomplish interactive strategy.

4 Interaction Strategy Evaluation and Iteration

4.1 Expert Evaluation

In this paper, using the heuristic evaluation method in expert evaluation, three experts are invited to test and evaluate the usability of interactive strategy schemes. After listening to descriptions, expert assesses whether contents presentation, user journey, operation of the interactive strategy is reasonable, whether users can understand it and hands on quickly, and so on. Three experts the interactive strategy schemes. The interactive strategy scheme can effectively help novice drivers to increase driving confidence, let them drive in practice, and build a bridge between experienced drivers and novices, to help novices get guidance easier and drive better.

At the same time, experts put forward some pertinent suggestions. These suggestions mainly for easy, including the modes combination, evaluation objects and visualize interactions.

(1) Combine coach mode and intelligent mode. The system is separated from coach guidance and intelligent guidance.
(2) Evaluation should on both sides. Evaluation system provides evaluation to service providers on the one hand and encourages service providers on the other hand. Provide users with evaluation to stimulate users 'self-intuitive perception.
(3) Increase the interactive intuitive description or mode, so that novices can find their own location faster and seriously use the interactive feature.

4.2 Iteration

According to the evaluation contents put forward by experts, a scheme of automatically opening the intelligent guidance system when there is no special coach to give advice. Novice drivers can log on to the on-board interactive system according to their previous driving files. The system will set the driving route according to the information set up before, including the assessment area. After it, novice drivers can mark areas on the route that they think are difficult to drive (practice the novice's pre-judgment awareness, planning ability). When novice drivers to the marked area, the system will automatically turn on the guidance to assist novices to handle the driving situation at that time. In the process of novice driving, driving tracks and driving behaviors of novices will be recorded by GPS technology, which is convenient for later review and analysis. It also has the feature of collecting suggestions from other road users, and they can give corresponding suggestions. When the vehicle is driving the assessment area, the vehicle system will turn off the guidance function and turn on the recording function. If novices successfully pass the assessment area without emotional fluctuation, the system can consider upgrading the evaluation of novices. If there are large emotional fluctuations, help-seeking behavior or dangerous driving behavior, the guide feature will be automatically activated, and rescue signals will be sent to other road users around. In the process of driving, if the novice has dangerous driving behavior or detects danger in front of the driving, an early warning system will be opened to provide guidance according to the situation and novices driving rating.

5 Conclusion

At present, the rapid development of the Internet of vehicles aims at helping people connect easily and quickly to all parts of life. As a necessary stage for a driver, novice drivers not only have safety problems, but is also given a tremendous impact on driving behavior after learning session. Built on the study of novice drivers, this paper puts forward an interactive scheme that can help drivers to get through this stage better and can promote road traffic safety. Through this interactive program, novices can constantly correct their driving, develop safe driving habits, and gradually improve the driving skills. In the future research, it can further study and classify how to get the driving behavior of novice drivers easier and how to get the help of novice drivers in driving.

References

1. The National Bureau of Statistics of the People's Republic of China. Statistical communique of the People's Republic of China on national economic and social development in 2016. http://www.stats.gov.cn/tjsj/zxfb/201702/t20170228_1467424.html. Accessed 28 Feb 2017
2. Goel, A., Gruhn, V.: Integration of telematics for efficient management of carrier operations. Science **2005**, 1940–1943 (2005)
3. Sun, X.-H.: Research on key technologies and applications of car networking. Commun. Technol. **04**, 47–50 (2013)
4. Liu, Z.-W., Xu, K., Zhao, F.-Q.: Development status, bottlenecks and countermeasures of China's automobile networking industry. Sci. Technol. Manag. Res. **36**(4), 121–127 (2016)
5. Zhang, Q., Yang, P.-Z., Yan, C.-L., Fan, Q.-F.: Analysis of human factors in road traffic accidents in China. Autom. Pract. Technol. (6), 7–8 (2016)
6. Bian, N., Zhao, B.-H., Lai, F., Liu, J.-F., Chen, J., Zhou, J.-G.: Development and application of semi-automatic driving assistance system based on expressway. J. Auton. Saf. Energ. Conserv. **8**(2), 149–156 (2007)
7. Li, H.-N.: Multi-mode control of auto adaptive cruise system. Electron. World **16**, 131–132 (2017)
8. Sun, L., Chang, R.-S.: Research status and prospect of driving style. Hum. Ergon. **19**(4), 92–95 (2013)
9. Sun, L., Yang, C.-C., Chang, R.-S.: Revision and preliminary application of multidimensional driving style scale. Hum. Ergon. **20**(2), 6–9 (2014)
10. Liu, W.: Interaction Design. China Architecture & Building Press, Beijing (2013)
11. Zhan, G.-H.: Interactive Internet of Things. Tsinghua University Press, Beijing (2016)
12. Liu, J.: Application of human-computer interaction design in the technology products. Packag. Eng. **35**(18), 64–67 (2014)

13. Cross, N.: Engineering Design Methods: Strategies for Product Design. Wiley, Hoboken (2008)
14. Su, J., Wang, D., Zhang, F.-F.: Review of internet of vehicle technology. Technol. Internet Things **30**(16), 60–63 (2014)
15. Wang, J.-Q., Li, S.-W., Zeng, J.-W.: Research on develop model of Internet of Things. Technol. Dev. Comput. **12**(10), 34–37 (2011)

DUXU for Cultural Heritage

From the Museum-Temple to the Museum-Interface: A Case Study of the Virtual Museum Paço Das Artes

Priscila Arantes[(✉)]

Departament of Post-Graduation in Design,
University Anhembi Morumbi, São Paulo, Brazil
priscila.a.c.arantes@gmail.com

Abstract. The debate about the relationship between museum, exhibition and technology, as well as about the changes in the museum's operation, aiming a more effective engagement of the visiting public, is not recent. The *Crystal Palace*, a gigantic construction of iron and glass built in London, England, to host the Grand Exhibition of 1851, could be a starting point to the debates related to the modifications caused by the technology in the museum scope. It is interesting to approach the role of the museum from the closed and neutral space image contained in the expression "White Cube". On his essay "Inside the White Cube", published in the magazine *Artforum* in 1976, the artist Brian O'Doherty makes a strong critic to the modernist exhibition space, as it was instated for the Museum of Modern Art of New York, in the first half of the 20th century. Introspective and self-referential, the white cube is a space-temple, a sacred, aseptic and timeless place, remote from the reality of the world. It is exactly this asepsis and introspection that will be discussed by the contemporary museums that seek – using different strategies – to make the public experience increasingly attractive with the museum equipment. Digital museums, virtual museums, augmented reality, as well as social media, are some of the strategies that can be found nowadays. Finally, the project Virtual Museum Paço das Artes will be presented, a project being developed in the city of São Paulo, Brazil, product from a partnership among Paço das Artes, equipment from Estate's Secretary of Culture of São Paulo and the University Anhembi Morumbi.

Keywords: Digital museum · Museum-interface · Paço das Artes

1 Introduction

Transformations over this last century brought along deep changes in the field of culture and in public cultural policies. What can be perceived, in the specific case of Brazil, weakens the role of the state in the defense of cultural democratization, understood here not only as access to culture, but also as embracing of cultural diversity. However, we often identify a dismantling of the area of culture, especially in times of economic crisis, since it is generally considered by the state as a less important field when compared to others.

© Springer Nature Switzerland AG 2019
A. Marcus and W. Wang (Eds.): HCII 2019, LNCS 11585, pp. 183–194, 2019.
https://doi.org/10.1007/978-3-030-23538-3_14

Reflecting on the role of the museum within this context, taking into account that culture is a constitutional right (in the case of Brazil, implemented by the Citizen Constitution of 1988), is therefore extremely necessary.

The questioning of the institutional role is accompanied, especially in regard to the public sphere, by the perception of a mismatch between institutional practices—which are often directed exclusively at the development of spectacular proposals—and actions that can establish an effective dialogue and participation with the diversity of the public and the social space.

What is generally perceived is the development of contents unrelated to the heterogeneous subjectivities and to the different social classes that permeate the social sphere. Often, the roster of institutional actions hides a discourse that replicates existing models without genuinely proposing more expansive and cross-cutting alternatives.

In this context, two questions must be asked:

1. What are the possible strategies of museums today, especially considering spaces, such as Paço das Artes, with small budgets and which stand outside the great hegemonic centers of art production and circulation?
2. What is the place of art institutions that propose more experimental strategies, different from those produced by spaces aimed at the diffusion of spectacular proposals?

2   What Is the Contemporary?

Without intending to exhaust the subject, I would like to start with the essay What is the contemporary?, by the Italian philosopher Giorgio Agamben, written for the inaugural class of his Philosophy course, taught from 2006 to 2007 at the School of Art and Design, in Venice.

One of the first topics of this essay is the notion of untimely, developed by Nietzsche in his text The Birth of Tragedy. The contemporary, in this first perspective, is that which creates a mismatch, a disconnection in relation to its time. According to Agamben: "Those who coincide too well with the epoch, those who are perfectly tied to it in every respect, are not contemporaries, precisely because they do not manage to see it," says Agamben et al. (2009, p. 4).

We are interested, however, in the second meaning established by Agamben, who arrives at the definition of the contemporary as "he who firmly holds his gaze on his own time so as to perceive not its light, but rather its darkness" (2002, XIX). Thus, in the philosopher's definition, all times are, for those who experience contemporaneity, obscure.

But the dark does not represent here a privative concept; the simple absence of light, a non-vision, that is, something that would signal some form of inactivity or passivity of vision—on the contrary. Taking as a principle the notion from neurophysiology about the activities of the OFF cells—certain peripheral vision cells that come into activity by the absence of light—the author invites us to act in the dark. Agamben states:

[...] the contemporary is the person who perceives the darkness of his time as something that concerns him, as something that never ceases to engage him. Darkness is something that—more than any light—turns directly and singularly toward him. The contemporary is the one whose eyes are struck by the beam of darkness that comes from his own time.

Like the stars and galaxies, that project their light without ever reaching us, the contemporary continually escapes our grasp. Thus it is precisely through the recognition of the split with the time in which we are that we have the possibility of understanding what the contemporary is.

If the experience of contemporaneity requires, as Agamben says, courage to see in the dark, we might ask ourselves: What would it mean to be "contemporary" in the current context, taking into account museum strategies?

3 Decolonization of Museums: Collection and Power

This question has already been asked by a number of thinkers and theorists. Not surprisingly, we find the publication On the Museum's Ruins, appearing in the early 1990s, in which the American thinker Douglas Crimp declares the death of art institutions and, more specifically, of museums.

Establishing a dialogue with Hans Belting and Artur Danto, Crimp calls into question the modernist view of the museum or, more precisely, of a certain museological belief of representing art as a homogeneous system, supposedly universal, and art history as its ideal classification.

In part, this supposed universality was unmasked, either by the existence of cultures that are far from being identified as being part of the Euro-Western model, or because the traditional way of narrating history, through styles and characteristics that develop linearly, failed to encompass the plurality of artistic productions that emerged after the modernism in the field of the arts.

Not surprisingly, we have seen a series of discussions—whether in the field of the narrative of art history or in the actions of the museum field—that defend the process of decolonization of museums and the need to liberate the collections from the Euro-Western imperial and hegemonic perspective. Javier Rezzano, coordinator of Uruguay's National Museums System, for example, in a lecture at the 8th Ibero-American Museum Meeting (Lisbon, October 13–15, 2014), understands the term decolonization in a broad sense. Decolonizing, for him, meant necessarily making the museum more inclusive, bringing it closer to the community it serves.

Boris Groys, echoing this debate, innovatively discusses the relations between art and power. He addresses the recent art history in Russia, which was left out of the criteria of dominant evaluation and criticism precisely because it was linked to the propaganda of the Soviet regime—that is, it served other purposes than exclusively artistic ones, in the sense of what was considered "artistic and/or aesthetic" in the art circuit of the time.

Declaring the death of the museum has been a tradition maintained for more than a century now; we must recall the criticism of the futurists of the obsolete role of the museum. Curiously, however, this same century that has been continuously reasserting its death was also the one that witnessed its expansion more overwhelmingly. In São

Paulo alone, we can identify the Football Museum, opened in 2008, and the Museum of Sexual Diversity, inaugurated in 2012.

The question, however, is not of numbers, but especially of the fundamental role the museum plays, despite its alleged death sentences, for the circuit, circulation, nurturing, training and promotion of what is understood as art.

4   Beyond Specificity

If the process of decolonization of art history has been part of discussions surrounding the museum, we must call to mind, even if briefly, the debates related to the specificities of the means and the media—such as painting, sculpture etc.—advocated by the modernist critique championed by Clement Greenberg.

Such thinkers as Rosalind Krauss rightly advocate the shift from a purist vision to one that incorporates hybridization and contamination between languages. Indeed, such concepts as "expanded field," "extended field," "interfaced fields," among many others, seek to accommodate the pluralism of contemporary productions that no longer fit into rigid taxonomies, but which sprawl onto diverse areas, within of a cross-cutting view.

That is to say, contemporary language—often within the process of artistic dematerialization, the conceptual practices undertaken from the 1960s on and the hybridizations in the field of language—posed questions not only regarding the symbolic issues and the understanding we had about art, but also inquiries about customary museum-oriented and archival practices.

There is not only an art history crisis, but an accompanying institutional crisis that finds itself in an impasse in regard to the incorporation, in its collection, of contemporary art proposals which not rarely put into question valid premises for traditional institutions: instead of permanence, transience; instead of autonomy, contextualization; authorship shatters faced with the poetics of appropriation, and uniqueness is challenged by the technological reproducibility. Rigid classifications such as painting or sculpture, which until recently were considered commonplace, often cannot accommodate the pluralism and intersection of languages characteristic of contemporary poetics.

This expansion of the artistic field, combined with collaborative, participatory, ephemeral, mediatic artworks thus ushers in new ways of documenting, cataloging and preserving artworks. We should add to this brief account the digital works that often require emulation processes, due to their nature of works susceptible to "programmed" obsolescence of the technologies they employ.

Within this perspective, it is worth recalling the example used by Cristina Freire in her book Poéticas do Processo (1999). At one point in the book, when analyzing the official art narrative adopted by MoMA, centered on its permanent objects and aligned with a modernist view of artistic practices, the author points out the institution's difficulty in dealing with productions that break with traditional protocols. She says:

> Joseph Kosuth, one of the most important North American conceptual artists, presented at the MoMA in New York the work *One and three chairs* (1965), where he juxtaposed the royal chair to its representations (a dictionary definition of chair and a photograph of a chair). Although it was acquired by MoMA, this work was destroyed when it was incorporated into the

museum's collection, since the chair was sent to the Design department, the photo to the Photography department and the photocopy of the definition of chair to the Library! (Freire 1999, pp. 45–46).

5 The White Cube and the Museum-Temple

It is interesting to approach the role of the museum from the image of enclosed, neutral space contained in the expression "White Cube."

In his essay "Inside the White Cube" published in the Artforum magazine in 1976, the artist Brian O'Doherty presents a critique of the modernist exhibition space as established by the Museum of Modern Art in New York in the first half of the 20th century.

O'Doherty describes the space of the modernist gallery as "constructed along laws as rigorous as those for building a medieval church." The fundamental principle of this space is that the "outside world must not come in, so usually windows are sealed. Walls are painted white. The ceiling becomes the source of light," he claims.

Introspective and self-referential, the white cube is a space-temple, a sacralized, aseptic and timeless environment, far from the reality of the world. "In classical modernist galleries, as in churches, one does not speak in a normal voice; one does not laugh, eat, drink, lie down, or sleep," points out Thomas McEvilley in the introduction to O'Doherty's essay.

6 From the Museum-Temple to the Museum-Spectacle

Museums, as privileged grounds for the exhibition of cultural referents, have based their activities for centuries on an aura of historical and cultural authenticity of the objects they collected and exhibited. Such criteria as originality, language specificity, universal historical narrative, sacred exhibition spaces, were used for centuries to bestow the construction of narratives according to the cultural authority of modern museums.

The impact of the media, the establishment of digital culture, as well as the phenomenon of globalization, triggered profound changes in the field of culture and, consequently, in museums. The most pessimistic investigations of this new moment maintain the idea that the process of globalization, by radically removing culture from its spatial constraint, has promoted a process of cultural homogenization.

Economic globalization would, according to this view, be linked to the cultural globalization within a context in which culture would become a commodity produced and consumed on a global scale. From this perspective we would be experiencing a shifting process, from the museum-temple to the museum-spectacle.

In an interview to the newspaper Folha de São Paulo in the 1990s, the critic of postmodernity, Fredric Jameson, points out that the field of culture is one of the key foundations of what he calls late capitalism. He thus claims:

> It is an immense 'dedifferentiation,' in which the old frontiers between economic production and cultural life are disappearing. Culture is business and products are made for the market; (…) mass culture is no longer a set of radio comedies and Hollywood musicals and romances. It is a much more sophisticated production, made by talented people (…) in the logic of 'thingification,' the ultimate intention is to transform objects of all kinds into commodities. It doesn't matter if these objects are movie stars, feelings or political experience.

Jameson's "dedifferentiation" does not, however, limit itself to erasing the old frontiers between super and infrastructure, but it draws to mass consumption a set of manifestations hitherto labeled as elitist—such as art exhibitions, for instance—that are now projected on the mediatic agendas as mega-events. They occupy museums, cultural centers and outdoor spaces, attracting public financing and private sponsorship by taking advantage of tax incentive and tax exemption laws. Touring shows of artists the likes of Monet, Rodin, Cézanne and Picasso work as an attention-grabber for large-scale deals that start at the box office and sprawl onto the sale of catalogs, reproductions of paintings, videos, posters, calendars, t-shirts and other souvenirs.

Douglas Kellner, in Media Culture and the Triumph of the Spectacle, provides a very clarifying example of the spectacularization of culture in today's society:

> [...] Bringing the spectacle into the world of high art, the Guggenheim Museum's Thomas Krens organized a retrospective on Giorgio Armani, the Italian fashion designer. Earlier, Krens produced a Guggenheim show exhibiting motorcycles and plans to open a Guggenheim gallery in the Venetian Resort Hotel Casino in Las Vegas with a seven-story Guggenheim art museum next to it. (Kellner, in Moraes 2006, p. 132).

It is no coincidence that the German theorist Andreas Huyssen (1997, p. 223) claims that "the museum's role as site of an elitist conversation, a bastion of tradition and high culture gave way to the museum as mass medium, as a site of spectacular *mise-en-scène* and operatic exuberance."

This spectacularization is also seen through buildings often commissioned from star architects, such as the Guggennheim Museum Bilbao, designed by Frank Gehry, or the MAXXI museum in Rome, by Zaha Hadid.

Allied to the notion of cultural tourism, many of the museums that appeared after the 1990s incorporate major architectural projects that simultaneously reshape entire urban areas, such as Museu do Amanhã (Museum of Tomorrow), inaugurated in 2015 in Rio de Janeiro, and designed by Santiago Calatrava. Started in 2010, the conception of the work by the Spanish architect relates to the urban remodeling of the surroundings of Mauá Square, as well as to the overall urban upgrading project of the port region of Rio de Janeiro, from which the museum benefits, with open spaces resulting from the demolition of Perimetral.

In many cases, as Rosalind Krauss points out in her essay "The Cultural Logic of the Late Capitalism Museum" (published in the October magazine in the 1990s), the collection is not the central issue regarding the institution, but the acceptance of spectacular exhibition proposals that aim not only at giving visibility to the institution, but also attracting large sums in investment.

Many of these institutions tend to fit into a spectacular dynamic in which the number of visitors is one of the main indicators of success or failure of the venture. In São Paulo, for example, the exhibition Obsessão infinita (Infinite Obsession), by the Japanese artist Yayoi Kusama, held from May 22 to July 27, 2014, at the Tomie Oktake

Institute, was seen by 522,136 visitors, 43,000 of those alone during the exhibition's final weekend on view. Castelo Rá Tim Bum, held at Museu da Imagem e do Som, received more than 80,000 visitors during the two months it remained on view.

On the other hand, it is possible to notice, in many of these more recent shows, a completely different behavior of the public in relation to the exhibition space. Many people stood in front of the exhibited works, while cell phones or tablets recorded their presence at the show; presence that would gain prominence with the subsequent shares of those images on social networks, overspilling and imploding the notion of modernist white cube.

7 Experimental Museums and Radical Museology

It will be inaccurate from our part, however, to believe in the idea that this model of museum could be the only representative of the contemporary, even because the idea of contemporaneity points not toward a homogeneous view, but toward a heterogeneous and hybrid one.

From a different perspective, we can consider the museum less as a space of well-established definitions and narratives, and more as a kind of laboratory, territory for creating, experimenting with and producing knowledge. Not surprisingly, Walter Zanini, in his role as the director of MAC (Museum of Contemporary Art of the University of São Paulo), writes in the catalog of the 6th Contemporary Young Art Exhibition (JAC, or Exposição de Jovem Arte Contemporânea), held in 1972:

> (...) the directors of institutions have become absolutely aware of the impossibility of their entities remaining exclusively in the condition of technical organs of appropriation, preservation and exhibition of art objects, that is, of organs expectant of products destined for their contemplative exhibition rooms. (Zanini *apud* Freire 1999, p. 53).

The JACs, idealized by Walter Zanini in the late 1960s at MAC, can be seen not only as spaces to foster and legitimize the production of young Brazilian artists and to incorporate language production with new media and techniques in the museum space, but also as spaces to broaden discussions about the role of the contemporary art museum as forum and laboratory during the harsh years of military dictatorship in Brazil (1964–1985).

Without intending to exhaust the subject, I would like to allude to Claire Bishop's essay Radical Museology Or, What's 'Contemporary' in Museums of Contemporary Art? In this essay, Bishop departs from a critique of Rosalind Krauss's text The Cultural Logic of the Late Capitalism Museum, in which the American critic, in dialogue with Fredric Jameson's essay The Cultural Logic of Late Capitalism, points out that contemporary museums are the expression of a consumerist logic implemented in the field of culture in the present time.

In a first moment, Claire Bishop recognizes the difficulty in specifying what is contemporary, in addition to the impossibility of utilizing this notion within a universal and global perspective, not only in face of local particularities, but also of the different typologies of museums that exist today.

Bishop calls radical museology the experiences of museums that today can be called contemporary, and which somehow managed to distance themselves from the model of museum-spectacle. That is to say, they are an alternative to situate the institution museum in the 21st century.

These museums, somehow, would be those that can be considered, as Agamben would say, institutional spaces that are located in the dark and that occur beyond the usual spaces of the entertainment industry.

The author then cites three European museums that fall into this possible typology of Radical Museology: The Van Abbemuseum in Eindhoven; the Queen Sofía Museum in Spain; and the Sodobne Museum in Ljubljana. What they have in common is precisely the fact that they present projects that raise issues about the complexity of what it means to be contemporary and what is a museum in the contemporary world.

In the plans for the Van Abbemuseum, the collection, which is comprised of modern art, is continuously thought out from curatorial propositions. In the strategies adopted, it is worth mentioning the project "Time Machine: Museum Modules" (2009), which was an exhibition about exhibitions—that is, an exhibition addressing exhibition design, revealing that the exhibition formats are linked to certain curatorial visions. The exhibition thus shed light on the strategies devised by art institutions to exhibit works from their collection and the installation discourse that engendered them. The show, included, for example, in addition to works and furniture from MoMA's collection, the transparent displays designed by Lina Bo Bardi for MASP in 1969.

The Queen Sophia Museum, in turn, has been developing an exercise in revisiting history and art history. In recent years, the museum has adopted a self-critical stance regarding the Spanish representation of colonialism, positioning Spain and its history in a broader international context of revisions of history and art history. According to Bishop, what is at issue here is less the amount of people that will visit the institution, and much more how the audience will see the work.

The Sodobne Museum in Slovenia, founded in 2011, despite having no fixed headquarters and a very small budget, has become the epicenter of alternative culture in Ljubljana. One of the strategies adopted by the museum is not only reenacting exhibitions already held, expanding and broadening the original exhibition format, but also working with archival material, such as the "An Archive of Performance Art" project, which showed, in different ways, this type of practice through photographs, video, objects and re-performances.

The description of the cases studied by Bishop provides us with clues and tools to come up, at the present time, with alternatives to contemporary art museums.

8 Paço Das Artes: Museum-Access: Livro_Acervo, Mapa and Ex-Paço

Questioning traditional museographic patterns, creating more experimental curatorial devices, as well as making the collection more accessible, creating more active strategies of approach to the public have been some of the strategies put into practice by Paço das Artes. An institution linked to the Secretariat of the State of São Paulo and founded in the 1970s, Paço das Artes has created over the years a space focused on experimental art and young contemporary art, embracing the diversity of its languages.

Because it is not a museum in the strict sense of the word and, therefore, because it doesn't have a collection of works of art—and because it works in promoting and spreading the young contemporary Brazilian art—the work of registering and archiving becomes the fundamental axis of its "collection."

We could say that the actions of Paço das Artes make up a kind of Imaginary Museum, as defined by André Malraux: the collection of Paço das Artes comprises the artists, activities, curators, critics, educators and the public that have been in contact with the institution.

It was from this perspective—that of putting into debate and questioning the institutional "collection" of Paço das Artes, which is not exactly a museum in the strict sense of the term, but in that of being allocated within the museology sector of the State Secretariat of Culture, and of giving voice to other narratives, in this case, the young Brazilian art, that is, a type of production that is not widely recognized within the larger art circuits—that I conceived a curatorial series on archive and collection, with exhibitions whose objective was to give visibility and create a space for us to reflect on this issue. This is how Livro_Acervo (Book_Collection), MaPA, Arquivo Vivo (Living Archive) and Ex-Paço were conceived. Far from being independent curatorial projects, they can be seen as a work-in-progress, in which each curatorship and/or project expands and updates the discussion of previous projects.

9 Livro_Acervo

The first project, Livro_Acervo, was conceived by me in 2010 for the celebration of the 40th anniversary of Paço das Artes. The initial idea was to develop a "big" curatorial project that not only could revive the memory of Paço das Artes—the players and agents that were part of its history—but also offering viewers the possibility of accessing a curatorial project that would extend beyond the traditional exhibition space.

This perspective led to the idea of developing not only a curatorial project in the scope of the book—a kind of movable, touring curatorship—but also of developing a curatorship from the institution's "archive" and "collection," reviving one of its most important projects: the Project Season[1].

The project was comprised of three main parts[2]. In the first one, 30 artists who were selected for the Project Season were invited to develop an original work on paper sheets (such as the flip book Naufrágio [Sinking], developed by the artist Laura Belém). These works were printed for free distribution, together with the other items

---

[1] Paço das Artes's experimental vocation is confirmed mainly through the *Project Season*, which was created with the objective of giving opportunity for the production, promotion and spreading of the production by young artists. Conceived in 1996 by the technical director Ricardo Ribenboim and the then curator of the institution, Daniela Bousso, the *Project Season* had its first exhibition held in 1997 and became, over the years, a rich incubator for the young contemporary Brazilian art scene.

[2] Departing from the initial idea of the project, we invited the artists Artur Lescher and Lenora de Barros to develop and design the first curatorial project for *Livro_Acervo*.

that made up the project. In the same insert as the artists' notebooks there was the Enciclopédia (Encyclopaedia), the second part of the project, with information on each of the artists, curators and jury members that participated in the Project Season from its first edition. The third part consisted of a sound work of up to one minute, recorded on a CD-ROM, developed by the artists and curators who participated in the Project Season. It should be noted that the project (consisting of these three parts) took the form of a box/file, alluding exactly to the idea that this device contains a significant portion of Paço das Artes's history and part of the young contemporary Brazilian art.

10   Mapa

Moving forward with the Livro_Acervo project, in November 2014 we implemented MaPA: Memória Paço das Artes (Paço das Artes Memory), a digital platform for contemporary art that brought together all the artists, critics, curators and jury members that participated in the Project Season from its creation in 1996.

The platform is comprised of a database with more than 870 images of the works showcased in the Project Season, as well as nearly 270 critical texts and video interviews that have been especially developed for this project since 2014. Gathering more than 240 artists, 14 curatorial projects, 70 art critics and 43 jury members, the platform was built as a relational device and a work-in-progress, offering researchers the opportunity to access information from existing relationships in the Project Season.

At MaPA's home page, the public is presented, through a random system, to several names of artists, critics, curators, and jury members. By hovering the mouse cursor over any of these names/links, MaPA highlights, in bold, the other names involved in that edition of the Season. This is how a research on the MaPA platform begins: as a relational device that allows the public to get to know the trajectory of each artist together with the critic who evaluated them and the jury that selected them. The emphasis attributed to this "relational" history is explained in the dialogue with the proposal of the Project Season itself, which, by selecting artists, curators and critics at the beginning of their careers, ends up revealing talents in the art scene. This is why the organization and referencing to the information on the platform is made through the artists, curators and critics, valuing the trajectories and creative development of all involved in the production and in the contemporary art system.

Thus, MaPA can be seen not only as a device to revive part of Paço das Artes's trajectory and its "collection," but also as a fertile research device for all those interested in the directions of the young Brazilian contemporary art.

Last but not least, MaPA is a triggering instrument for the construction of other narratives in the history of the Brazilian art, of the young contemporary Brazilian art, which has rare opportunities of participating in or is altogether excluded from the discourses of the official art history.

11 Ex-Paço

As the last project of this trilogy, I would like to emphasize the work in development, Ex-Paço[3], conceived and idealized by me and Sérgio Nesteriuk after the change of headquarters of Paço das Artes, formerly located at the University of São Paulo.

Ex-Paço is a virtual, three-dimensional replica of Paço das Artes[4], with versions for computer (local and online), smartphone, cardboards and virtual reality glasses. Modeled in 3D from Paço das Artes's last headquarters, Ex-PAÇO is not only a memory space—in the sense that it recovers, in virtual reality, the former site/headquarters of the institution, and in this sense a political space, of resistance, if we may say so—but also a digital museum aimed at housing different curatorial projects and manifestations of contemporary art.

This new browsable space, suggestively allocated in the "outer space," is the starting point for us to think about new curatorial and exhibition dynamics enhanced by new technologies. These, therefore, aren't digital works shown in a museum or on a website, but rather the exhibition space itself becomes digital, virtual, thus opening up new creative possibilities within the exhibition field.

If in the Livro_Acervo and in the MaPA digital platform what was in focus were the strategies of access and information to Paço das Artes's collection—in the sense of contributing to the construction of the narrative of the young contemporary Brazilian art—in Ex-PAÇO, a project under development, what is at issue is not only the possibility of creating a digital museum, a museum without walls, for the development of online curatorial projects, but, especially, shedding light on the importance of Paço das Artes as a site for artistic creation and experimentation.

In this sense, it can be seen not just as a mobile space, but as a virtual political and critical site in relation to the history of the loss of Paço das Artes's headquarters, an outgrowth of issues regarding a specific moment of the institution.

12 Conclusion

It is in this sense that we understand this "museum," that I designate here as museum-interface, a museum that implodes the white cube and that presents museum-oriented and curatorial strategies that somehow give way to other voices that are not present in the traditional, spectacular sites.

The art institution is, in this sense, called for to reflect on its practice, especially the public institutions that, in principle, should exercise a democratic role and provide effective access to cultural assets. The issue here is thinking the museum as a

---

[3] Idealization and Conception by Priscila Arantes and Sérgio Nesteriuk. Undertaking: Memulab (Laboratory of Memory and Museum), Transmidialab, Group of Studies in Design, Art and Memory, and DEED – Research Group in Design, Entertainment and Education (UAM).

[4] In the late 2015, Paço das Artes had to leave the headquarters it occupied since the 1990s, at the district Cidade Universitária, inside the premises of the University of São Paulo. Created in the 1970s, Paço das Artes never had a definitive headquarters. Currently, the institution has a temporary headquarters located inside MIS (Museu da Imagem e do Som).

participatory, action-oriented device rather than a space enclosed in itself—as a white cube, in Brian O'doherty's expression.

The concept of interface here concerns thinking the museum not as a temple, nor as a space for entertainment, but as a medium that engenders a social interface, a museum that incorporates a more expanded and cross-cutting view of culture.

References

Agamben, G.: O que é o contemporâneo? E outros ensaios. E.Unichapecó, Chapeçó (2009)

Arantes, P.: Reescrituras da Arte Contemporânea: história, arquivo e mídia. Ed. Sulinas, Porto Alegre (2014)

Arantes, P.: Arte @ Mídia: perspectivas da estética digital. FAPESP/Editora Senac, São Paulo (2005)

Arantes, P.: Livro/Acervo. Org. Priscila Arantes. Imesp, São Paulo (2010)

Belting, H.: O fim da história da arte: uma revisão dez anos depois. Cosac Naify, São Paulo (2006)

Bishop, C.: Radical Museology. Koenig Books, London (2013)

Crimp, D.: Sobre as Ruínas do Museu. Martins Fontes, São Paulo (2005)

Danto, A.: Após o fim da arte: a arte contemporânea e os limites da história. Odysseus Editora, São Paulo (2006)

Freire, C., Longoni, A.: (ORG.) Conceitualismos do Sul/Sur. São Paulo: Annablume/EDUSP/MAC-AECID (2009)

Groys, B.: Art Power. The MIT Press/Cambridge Press, Massachusetts/London (2008)

Krauss, R.: The cultural logic of the late capitalism museum, October, Massachusetts, vol. 54, pp. 3–17 (1990). Disponível em: https://www.jstor.org/stable/778666?seq=1#page_scan_tab_contents. Acesso em: 03 Feb 2019

O' Doherty, B.: No interior do cubo branco: a ideologia do espaço da arte. Martins Fontes, São Paulo (2002)

Jameson, F.: "Falso Movimento". Entrevista a Marcelo Rezende. Folha de São Paulo, 19 September 1995

Kellner, D.: Cultura da Mídia e triunfo do espetáculo. In: de Moraes, D. (ORG.) Sociedade midiatizada. Mauad, Rio de Janeiro (2006)

Huyssen, A.: Memória do Modernismo. Editora da UFRJ, Rio de Janeiro (1997)

Zanini, W., Apud Freire, C.: Poéticas do processo: arte conceitual no Museu. MAC/ Universidade de São Paulo (1999)

Gamified Participatory Museum Experience for Future Museums

Hao He[1(✉)], Ziyang Li[2], Xiandong Cheng[2], and Jianjun Wu[3]

[1] Central Academy of Fine Arts, No. 8 Hua Jia Di Nan St., Chao Yang District,
Beijing, China
hehao@cafa.edu.cn
[2] Beijing City University, No. 269 Bei si Huan Zhong Lu, Hai Dian District,
Beijing, China
[3] School of Design, Jiangnan University, No. 1800, Lihu Avenue, Wu Xi,
Jiangsu, China

Abstract. Museums are cultural and educational institutions that collect, preserve, display and study their collections, and whose purpose is to represent nature and human beings, and provide knowledge and education to the public. Based on the participation and education of museums, this paper demonstrates how to enhance museum participatory and educational experience for visitors by means of gamified participatory experience. It systematically explains the concept of museum participatory experience for visitors. By trying to apply the new concept and method, we designed the "SPORTSWEAR EXHIBITION - Dress to Win" at Design Exchange Museum, Toronto, Canada. We studied the impact of gamified participatory experience and analyzed the effectiveness of using new technologies. Finally, we understand the importance of participatory experience in future museums.

Keywords: Museum · User centered design · Participatory experience ·
Participatory design · Gamified experience

1 Development for the Needs in Museums

Early museums emerged in the wealthy individuals as private collections. At the early days, collections were usually confined to the interpersonal circle of individuals and a few wealthy classes. Opening to the public is almost impossible. Even if it is open, it can only be seen and reached by a small group people at a specific time. Over time, the collection of museums was slowly opened to the public, and now more and more can be accessed by the public.

Now museums have evolved into places with multiple functions, including protecting, entertaining, learning, and education etc. According to the ICOM Statutes, adopted by the 22nd General Assembly in Vienna, Austria, on 24 August, 2007 "A museum is a non-profit, permanent institution in the service of society and its development, open to the public, which acquires, conserves, researches, communicates and exhibits the tangible and intangible heritage of humanity and its environment for the purposes of education, study and enjoyment" [1].

© Springer Nature Switzerland AG 2019
A. Marcus and W. Wang (Eds.): HCII 2019, LNCS 11585, pp. 195–208, 2019.
https://doi.org/10.1007/978-3-030-23538-3_15

People's understanding of museums and their exhibitions is constantly changing. Museologists and international museum associations have been modifying and refining the definition of museums. Nowadays, under the information age, experts and scholars are trying to present collections in a better way, which includes showing the value of the exhibition, and also contains sills to guide visitors. This requires the full participation of visitors. But how could museums build a good relationship with visitors in their context and understand the needs?

With the development of social economy, the increasing demand for the culture life of public, further study of museum and cognition development, museums are transforming from collection-based to visitor-oriented. In order to provide better exhibitions and education for visitors, museums have to open up their materials and invite people to participate, create and link to each other. For museums, their task is to make exhibitions more open and to better understand the needs of their visitors.

2 Museum Participatory Experience and Problems

In the participatory museum experience, we wish that visitors should be active participants rather than passive consumers. In museums, visitors should be able to create, share, and connect with each other through the contents of exhibitions. Create means that visitors can contribute their own ideas, objects, and creative expressions to museums and each other. Share means discussion among visitors that they can bring ideas home, integrate their new creativities then share it again. Connect means the social communication between museums and visitors, or special interests between museum employees and visitors. It is very important that the dialogue and innovation among visitors should be centered with museum theories, ideas, and collections.

The goal of museums nowadays is to encourage dialogue, express ideas, or share learning and working together. Every design process starts with some simple questions. The question here is, what tools and techniques can we use to create the need for participatory experience?

In the current museum experience design, Designers study visitors' experience in many ways, and design labels and contents for different visitors. Designers know what kind of interactions can stimulate visitors, and what can lead to deep thinking and exploration. But in many cases, they might be incorrect. Basically, designers are guided by experience. The quality of the decisions they make during design will determine whether they can successfully delivery their ideas or create a sound experience for visitors.

When museums want to develop participatory experiences, it is very important to consider how visitors can create, share, and connect each other's experiences through content. The biggest difference between traditional and participatory design is the way information flows between museums and visitors. In traditional exhibitions, museums provide content for visitors to consume. Designers focus on consistency and quality of content so that visitors can have a reliable and relatively good experience, no matter what background or interest they have.

In most cases, there will be a guide to lead visitors to museums. The guide is usually a staff member of museums. He or she presents the single voice of authorities (museums). The introduction will be prepared by museums and exhibitions and information are very well structured. This is the most common case. It is a one to more structure. This is a typical traditional and passive experience. Visitors are consumers that they can only passively consume the given information (Fig. 1).

Fig. 1. One to more

On the contrary, in participatory design exhibitions, museums need to support multi-directional experience of the content. Museums act as "platforms" that connect different visitors. Visitors will play the role as sharers, creators, observers, and collaborators of the content. Because visitors play different roles that means museums could not guarantee the consistency of their experience. Instead, museums provide opportunities for different visitors to create experiences together. Museums and visitors, visitors and visitors share and create content together. Every visitor should be a member or a part of create of meaning in museums (Fig. 2).

More to more is a new museum experience which is a new form. It requires visitors' participation and it encourages visitors to create meaning in museums. Our understandings of society are based on our personal experience and the explanations provided by others. If these understandings are only based on personal experience, then human consciousness may be very limited. Our knowledge is built on the communication between us and our surrounding environment. Museums, as research institutions, can play an important role in defining our physical world and personal identity.

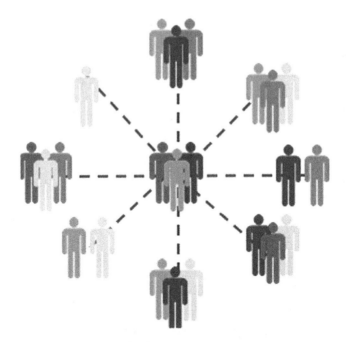

Fig. 2. More to more

3 How to Create Participatory Museum Experience

3.1 The Concept of User Centered Design

It would be a great help to design a participatory museum experience if we have a deep understanding of user-centered design. UCD emerged in the 1970 s due to the development of human-computer interaction. The principle of human-computer interaction is to copy or translate users' knowledge into principles or instructions that the designer can work on. According to Preece's study in 2002, in UCD, users are the center of information sources [2]. The aim of UCD is to find out a lot about the users and their tasks, and using this information to inform design. In UCD, during the process of the design cycle, designers should pay attention to what is being designed (products, interfaces, services, etc.) and looking for ways to meet users' needs [3].

The ultimate goal of UCD is to provide users with an optimized product, process, or system. UCD requires thinking from the users' perspective throughout the design process to understand the relevant cognitive level of users in order to achieve the goal. In addition, UCD requires to observe and think from the users' perspective from the beginning of the design. Users will be the core and fundamental part of the design process.

In 1977, a study by Nisbett and Wilson (Nisbett, R. E. and Wilson), they claim if users were given an active and central role in the design process that more useful and better ideas will emerge [4]. In addition, through the UCD approach, it is possible to eliminate the gap between the traditional systems actually works and the way users perceive and interact with it.

3.2 The Development of UCD

In 1999, UCD defined by the ISO (International Certification Standard). The standard number is 13407, which clarifies the UCD basis principles. "The goal of the standard is to ensure that the development and use of interactive systems take account of the needs of the user as well as the needs of the developer and owner to name but a few stakeholders [5]." ISO Standard 13407 was updated in the later development and was newly released as ISO9241-210 "Human-computer interaction and human-computer interaction ergonomics, Part 210. It presents a higher and broader overview of activities that suggested for UCD.

This standard includes 6 basic principles to ensure that real users are placed at the center of the design process. They are:

1. Design needs to be based on a clear understanding of users, tasks, environments and other factors.
2. As users, they will participate in the entire design and development process.
3. Design needs to be carried out, revised and refined by using UCD assessment.
4. The whole process needs to be interactive in real time.
5. Every design issue or question should be related to users' experience.
6. Design teams need to have interdisciplinary capabilities and perspectives.

By following the principle and process of UCD, the finished products will be easier for users to understand and use [5]. The six basic principles of UCD can be divided into four stages to execute (see Fig. 3).

- The first stage is the analysis: We need to know who are going to participate and what functions are going to use in what kind of context.
- The second stage is to refine: Identify users' requirements and goals.
- The third stage is design and prototyping: Design will be divided into several phases and provide solutions for each one. Develop the design from a rough concept to a real product.
- The fourth stage is the evaluation: The best way to get feedback is from user experience testing.

There are many uncertainties in the process of user-centered design. According to the specific needs of users, user-centered design can be done in different ways. In traditional user-centered design engineering projects, users are primarily involved in the phase of usability testing. But in new user-centric design requires users to be involved in every design stages from concept to prototyping.

3.3 Concept of Participatory Design

The idea of participatory design emerged in Scandinavia in the 1970s, partly because local unions promoted workers to have more democratic rights so that workers could better control their job changes [7]. Since then, in participatory design, user

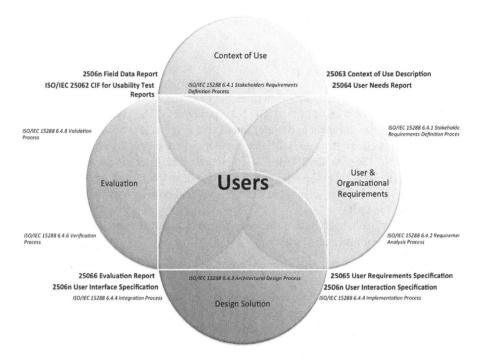

Fig. 3. User centered design process [6]

engagement has reached a deeper level: as users can participate more actively in the design process, it is more likely that they can become an important part of the entire design team [8, 9].

Sanders defines participatory design as a new attitude to design, which requires new ways of thinking and working. In addition, she introduced the concept of co-design that people can design together. In this way, people will have the opportunity to get better ideas and extend their ideas more effectively [3].

Nowadays, participatory design is defined as a set of theoretical and practical methods, which emphasizes that the role of the user should be fully involved in the whole design process. Basically, users are people who get involved in the design. Participatory design has increasingly mentioned and used as the first step in user-centered design.

3.4 Participatory and Gamified Design in Museums

Since the 1960s and 1970s, museums have begun to pay attention to the growth of their visitors and the economic potentials. They used new methods and methods to create a better experience for visitors. Museums and exhibition designers have gradually begun to pay more attention to the needs of visitors. Different participatory techniques and methods foresee how visitors will participate individually in different levels of participatory experience.

When visitors become active participants in the design process, the designer need to focus their concerns on visitors' needs and the motivations behind their actions. The greatest wealth of the museum is actually the creativity of their visitors. No matter what the topic of the exhibition is, visitors will have a lot of very interesting ideas, and no matter subject is, they also would like to share their opinions too. Especially younger visitors, who are more skilled at applying and mastering new technologies than older visitors, and using their abilities to express their ideas and opinions.

3.5   Techniques for Design with Visitors

In participatory design, every design partner (participants or design experts) should establish common goals and participate in design activities together. So far, we have a lot of ways to design with different participants.

In participatory design activities, we need to ensure that the results and contributions created by participants are taken seriously. In the participatory design process, no matter what impact participation may have, it should be able to go beyond the general procedure of traditional design, and truly support design to become meaningful and proactive activities.

In some design projects, participants have been able to get involved in all design stages. Experts and designers are responsible for analyzing participants' work and testing them as prototypes for applications. There will be two phases in participatory design projects. First, is to define the theme, then brainstorming. Second is to create the prototype. We can do a lot of interesting activities to help participants making prototypes.

In 2016, Alexandra's new book Resilience by Design (Advanced Sciences and Technologies for Security Applications) mentioned, if participants are able to actively participate in collaboration and integrate into the design process, they will have a sense of responsibility for the projects or tasks they are involved in [10].

3.6   Gamified Participation

Over years a lot of researchers have spent so much time on defining what a "game" is. In 2013, Adams defined the game as "a type of play activity, conducted in the context of a pretended reality, in which the participant(s) try to achieve at least one arbitrary, nontrivial goal by acting in accordance with rules" [11].

Game has become an important part of the "human cultures" in our life [12]. When people play games, they can have a positive influence. For example, games can promote a wide range of cognitive skills. Game can be an effective way to encourage and stimulate emotions. Games can develop social skills [13]. In 2015, Jane mentioned in her book Super Better that traditional video games are more complex and harder to master, and they require that the player learn a wider and more challenging range of skills and abilities [14].

In 2012, McClarty et al. described a theoretical and experimental evidence of games play. They claim that the use of games in education can provide the following advantages: 1. learning principle. 2. Engagement of the learner. 3. Personalized learning opportunities. 4. 21st-century modern learning skills. 5. Environment for authentic and relevant assessment [15].

Game is one of the most participatory activities. In 2001, Prensky's research shows that at first, games need to be as simple as possible at the beginning (simple is easy to participate). A game should be fun and engaging so that the player can reach an active state (interesting can increase engagement and encourage player continually to participate to reach active state). Moreover, it is very important that game has a defined structure with rules, and a good story to transfer emotions. And there are some more important elements. For example, results and feedback (players can have feedback information which will encourage them to keep participating and learning). Conflict, Challenge, and Competition (make players feel satisfied and constantly stimulate their adrenaline). Solutions (inspire the creativity of the participants) [16].

3.7   Encourage Gamification

Using gamified experience to encourage participation and learning through play is a very effective way. By using this theory as a way to make participation and educational activities more entertaining and engaging can make participation and learning more smooth and effective. Therefore, the use of gamified methods has recently appeared in different types of research and literature.

The broad definition of gamification is the process of defining the elements which comprise games, make games fun and motivate players to continue playing [17]. There are so many studies have shown that use game elements in a non-game environment (such as school and classroom) can influence behavior. These studies show that gamified products are not necessarily games. Instead, they use only some elements of game design to encourage people outside of a game context. The same mechanism can also be used to encourage collaborative and cooperative behavior [18].

Now we have a lot of researches on gamification. Games are a form of participation, interaction, or entertainment, and learning as a participatory process can benefit from adopting game concepts into it [11]. The gamification of education or the gamification of learning, especially, integrates game-like concepts into the learning process, so as to engage learners or participants in associate with their natural learning context [18]. The purpose of gamification learning is to "maximize enjoyment and engagement through capturing the interest of learners and inspiring them to continue learning" in their own context [19]. Gamification has the potential of "disruptive innovation" for institutions with traditional educational functions (museums are one of the typical sample), which changes the future in a positive way [20].

4   Design Practice: SPORTSWEAR EXHIBITION - Dressing to Win!

Sport is ubiquitous touching almost every aspect of our lives from health and wellbeing to fashion, culture, technology, design and architecture. "SPORTSWEAR EXHIBITION - dressing to win" was held at Design Exchange Museum, Toronto, Canada. The exhibition is about sportswear, which has a history a little more than a century. Its evolution has been rapid largely due to its strong association with technology. This exhibition is divided into four sections associated with ethnographics, nature, fashion, and performance. Although there are four different themes, but we hope to provide with a complete experience. Our target audience will be involved with different types of visitors, especially young ones. At the early stage of planning, in order to make the abstract concepts easier to understand, we drew them into maps. Based on these two maps, we could have better analysis and design (See Fig. 4).

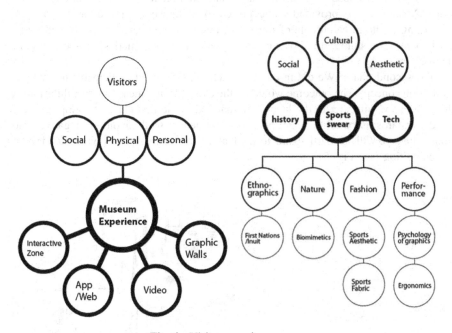

Fig. 4. Visitor experience maps

These two maps can be used for: 1, to show the physical space of exhibition, collections, and visitors' personal experience are all related to the museum experience. 2, the themes of the exhibition and the content and information need to be delivered to visitors. At the stage of research and the process of planning, we have been constantly comparing these to maps to verify the ideas and possibilities of encouraging visitors.

4.1 Two Phases for Gamified Participatory Design

The first phase: We invited five participants of different genders and ages to come together and design the museum exhibition, which can meet their own needs. We took them to visit the exhibitions in the Design Exchange Museum then gave them a small assignment to make a note during the visit. After the visit, they were required to develop a set of "good" and "bad" standards of the museum experience.

Then we introduced the basic exhibition ideas for the participants such as exhibition theme, content, objectives, etc. and gave them some green and red labels.

Participants were then asked to recall the good or bad experience in the exhibition and to write down the reason why they are good or bad. Good ones are on green labels and bad ones on red labels. After that, we categorized labels into groups. Participants will cross compare the experience of the exhibition with the content of the labels to discuss it.

After the discussion, most of the questions on the labels will be incorporated into the concept design process. Then participants will begin the second phase. The work of the first phase provided a good foundation and support for the later work of participants. Meanwhile, it provided some pieces of evidence for museums to evaluate. According to the research data of museums, many of the questions mentioned by the participants are similar to those in many evaluation summaries of the museums themselves.

The second phase: We did in the lab at school. We asked participants to create an exhibition concept. The outcome would be the concepts and ideas for the exhibition. At this phase, we will refer to the labels summarized in the first phase, to adopt as many good standards as possible to get positively influence, while avoiding negative emotions. Then we will ask participants to work along to construct their own basic ideas for the exhibition (see Fig. 5).

Fig. 5. Form for concepts and ideas (Form by Erin Lu, Storyboard by Paula Aguirre Gómez) Form finished by Erin Lou, Storyboard drawing by Paula Aguirre Gomez

We will guide participants to create stories and ideas for the exhibition and understand the needs of the visitors by asking them to fill out some design forms. In order to fill in this form with a better result, participants will use the method of sharing.

By answering some simple questions, for example: how does the exhibition begin? How are the collections of the exhibition presented? In what form? The role of collections in the exhibition and how could they encourage the visitor to participate? After answering these questions in the forms participants will transform the concept of the exhibition into a prototype. These forms will help participants and us to identify some relevant exhibition design elements, development, and specific methods for encouragement. Each participant should have his or her own prototype when all these works are done. All participants will share their prototype design together and they will refine or improve their design in terms of color, functions and goals. Finally, everyone will work on further details for the prototype.

In the following work, participants were asked to design different levels of participatory experience of the exhibition through other forms, and complete the core mechanism documents of the exhibition visit. The core mechanism documents were based on the previous concept document. Participants kept working on the core mechanism documents or the exhibition and built the level of participatory experience of visitors. Then participants will work on details of the exhibition design based on the progressive relationship between the levels (see Figs. 6 and 7).

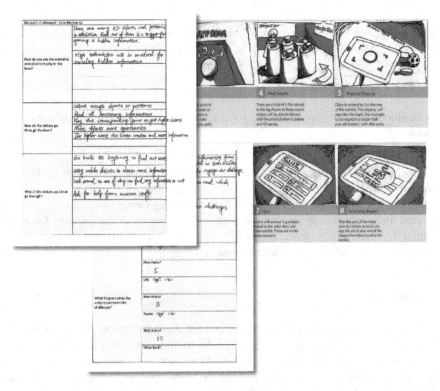

Fig. 6. Forms for core mechanism (Form by Erin Lu, Storyboard by Paula Aguirre Gómez) Form finished by Erin Lou, Storyboard drawing by Paula Aguirre Gomez

Fig. 7. Level passage conditions (Form by Erin Lu, Storyboard by Paula Aguirre Gómez) Form finished by Erin Lou, Storyboard drawing by Paula Aguirre Gomez

4.2 The Final Outcomes Are

- Conditions and conceptual design for transfer between different levels during the visit.
- A complete concept design of participatory museum experience.

Finally, we asked participants to show their design prototype of the design and demonstrate the interactions of participation and functions.

Participants would ask each other of their interest and write down their comments on cards. Participants will share these card and then write down answers for every question for each other. After answering questions, they will vote for everyone's prototype and choose the most favorite design.

5 Conclusion

In this gamified museum participatory experience design practice, we found that the quality of the final design results will be gradually improved over time. This demonstrates that participants shared ideas, improved concepts and learnt to work together by doing participatory design. Designers need to be engaged in the dialogue with participants all the time during the different design process and explain the museum exhibition design based on their professional knowledge. It can be very helpful for participants to improve their design results.

Gamified participatory experience can create collaboration and encourage visitors' participation. In gamified participatory experience process, cooperation means that participants work together to explore and learn together. Different participants working together can form some kind of heterogeneity, which can help museums receive more ideas. Gamified participatory experience can enhance visitors' sense of personal responsibility. Besides, there is an important value for a gamified participatory experience that can encourage face-to-face communication. Providing visitors more opportunities to participate means encouraging them to get involved in exhibition activities, and to promote positive emotions. Giving visitors more responsibilities means stimulating them to explore and express their ideas.

According to the research and practice prove that participatory design is positive and effective, and also shows that we should encourage visitors as the designer to participate in museum exhibition design. These findings from the practical research can provide professional and valuable references and guidance for future participatory exhibition design activities.

References

1. ICOM Statutes, adopted by the 22nd General Assembly, Vienna, Austria, 24 August 2007. http://icom.museum/the-vision/museum-definition/
2. Preece, J., Rogers, Y., Sharp, H.: Interaction Design, 1st edn. Wile, New York (2002)
3. Sanders, E.B.-N.: From user-centered to participatory design approaches. In: Design and Social Science (2002)
4. Nisbett, R.E., Wilson, T.D.: Telling more than we can know: verbal reports on mental processes. Psychol. Rev. **84**(3), 231–259 (1977)
5. ISO 9241-210: Ergonomics of human-system interaction human centred design for interactive systems, international standards organization (2010)
6. Furman, S., Theofanos, M., Wald, H.: Human engineering design criteria standards part 1: project introduction and existing standards DHS S&T TSD standards project, p. 78. National Institute of Standards and Technology, Patrick D. Gallagher, Under Secretary of Commerce for Standards and Technology and Director, April 2014
7. Ehn, P., Kyng, M.: The collective resource approach to systems design. In: Bjerknes, G., Ehn, P., Kyng, M. (eds.) Computers and Democracy - A Scandinavian Challenge, pp. 17–58. Avebury, Aldershot (1987)
8. Greenbaum, J., Kyng, M. (eds.): Design at Work: Cooperative Design of Computer Systems. L. Erlbaum Associates Inc., Hillsdale (1992)
9. Schuler, D., Namioka, A. (eds.): Participatory Design: Principles and Practices. L. Erlbaum Associates Inc., Hillsdale (1993)
10. Lee, A.J.: Resilience by Design. ASTSA. Springer, Cham (2016). https://doi.org/10.1007/978-3-319-30641-4
11. Adams, E.: Fundamentals of Game Design, 3rd edn. Pearson, Allyn and Bacon, Boston (2013)
12. Greenberg, B.S., Sherry, J., Lachlan, K., Lucas, K., Holmstrom, A.: Orientations to video games among gender and age groups. Simul. Gaming **41**(2), 238–259 (2010)
13. Granic, I., Lobel, A., Engels, R.C.M.E.: The benefits of playing video games. Am. Psychol. **69**(1), 66–78 (2014)

14. McGonigal, J.: SuperBetter: A Revolutionary Approach to Getting Stronger, Happier, Braver and More Resilient - Powered by the Science of Games. Penguin, London (2015)
15. McClarty, K., Orr, A., Frey, P., Dolan, R., Vassileva, V., McVay, A.: A literature review of gaming in education. Research report (2012)
16. Prensky, M.: Fun, play and games: what makes games engaging. In: Digital Game - Based Learning (2001)
17. Deterding, S., Sicart, M., Nacke, L., O'Hara, K., Dixon, D.: Gamification: using game-design elements in non-gaming contexts. In: CHI 2001 Extended Abstracts on Human Factors in Computing Systems, pp. 2425–2428. ACM, New York (2011)
18. Glover, I.: Play as you learn: gamification as a technique for motivating learners. In: World Conference on Educational Multimedia, Hypermedia and Telecommunications (2013)
19. Huang, W., Soman, D.: A practitioner's guide to gamification of education. Research Report Series Behavioural Economics in Action (2013)
20. Christensen, C.M., Raynor, M.E.: The Innovator's Solution: Creating and Sustaining Successful Growth. Harvard University Press, Cambridge (2003)

Design and Research of Museum Matching Digital Applicationlication Based on Exhibition Content and User Demand

Dai Luo$^{(\boxtimes)}$, Xiangcheng Wei⦿, and Le Chang

Beijing Forestry University, Beijing 100083, China
ed17878@hotmail.com, 187009006@qq.com,
1524461687@qq.com

Abstract. Achieving good communication between the theme of the exhibition and the psychology of the visitors is the value of digital technology in museum exhibitions. The purpose of this study is to make digital technology better serve museums and audiences. The innovation is to incorporate user needs into the design of museum digital applicationlications. This paper summarizes a museum digital applicationlication design process specification. Then develops a set of digital applicationLICATION to test it, which will help the perfect applicationlication of digital technology in the museum.

Keywords: Museum exhibition · User needs · Digital technology · Digital applicationlication · Design process

1 Introduction

Looking at the current situation of museums all over the world, it is obvious that the use of digital technology has injected sufficient impetus into their development. The digital construction of museums in various countries mainly includes the construction of Museum website, mobile applicationlication design, the development of in-library tour guide system, virtual reality tour and the applicationlication of holographic projection imaging technology. For example, the collections of the New York Museum of Science and Technology in the United States are presented on its official website through a clear and concise framework on the Internet, the mobile applicationlication *Le Louvre Museum*, which integrates the voice guide and works applicationreciation of the Louvre Museum, the British Museum applicationlication, which can plan the tour route in an easy and interesting way, and the Smithsonian Museum in the United States, which realizes the roaming function of virtual reality.

In China, the applicationlication of new media especially digital technology in Chinese museums has also greatly changed the way museums are displayed. However, nowadays, the development and utilization of digital technologies in museums is not completely suited with the exhibition itself, and the use of digital technology is relatively reluctant. The advantages of technology to the exhibition were not fully present, which obviously affected the missionary effect of the museum and the visitor experience. Visitors are the main target of museum exhibitions and the main users of museum

A. Marcus and W. Wang (Eds.): HCII 2019, LNCS 11585, pp. 209–220, 2019.
https://doi.org/10.1007/978-3-030-23538-3_16

digital technology. An in-depth analysis of the exhibition and visitors is the key to the success of digital technology in museum exhibitions.

The purpose of this study is to explore a digital applicationlication design process specification for museum exhibitions and user needs in order to make digitalization better applicationlicable to museum exhibitions. The main work includes: First, through the investigation and study of the digital applicationlication in the current use of Chinese museums, summed up a museum digital applicationlication design process based on the content of the exhibition and user needs. Second, based on the process, design and develop an applicationlication for a specific museum exhibition to test the rationality of the process.

2 Design Process Research

In order to develop a museum digital applicationlication design process specification for museum exhibitions and audiences' actual needs, the research group studied the applicationlication of digital technology in museums in the world's advanced countries, and also studied the use of digital technology in Chinese museums. Through the comparative analysis of domestic and foreign results, we found out the pain points and difficulties in the use of digital technology in Chinese museums at present. First, the degree of convergence between digital technology and museum exhibitions is low. Second, digital technology cannot satisfy the actual demands of audiences. Through the detailed analysis of the above pain points and difficulties, as well as study the successful experience of applicationlying digital technology to the construction of museum exhibitions at home and abroad, this paper innovatively proposes a digital applicationlication design process based on the museum exhibition content and audience needs (Fig. 1).

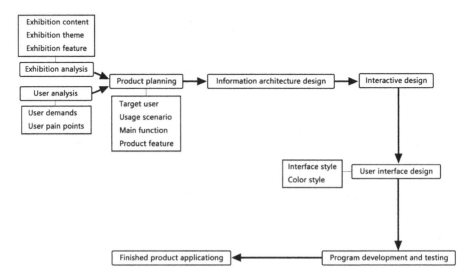

Fig. 1. Design progress

2.1 First of All, Deeply Understanding the Content, Themes and Features of the Exhibition, Meanwhile Conducting User Research, Grasp User Needs and Pain Points

The exhibition is one of the main functions of the museum and the root cause of the applicationlication of digital technology to the museum. Although digital technology has played an obvious and positive role in the development of museums, to be honest, digital technology is only an auxiliary means of museum exhibitions. The use of digital technology simply enhances the form of museum exhibitions and does not shake the core position of the exhibition content. Therefore, in order for digital technology to truly serve museum exhibitions, it is necessary to focus on the core of museum exhibitions, truly understand the main purpose of the exhibition, explore the exhibition content deeply, actively explore the characteristics of the exhibition, and firmly grasp the core of the exhibition content. In addition, in order to make the exhibition design more responsive to the audience's preferences and needs, conducting user research will provide the necessary assistance. User research will help planners better understand the audience's preferences, needs, habits and pain points in order to better plan and design the exhibition.

2.2 Secondly, Planning the Digital Applicationlication Integrally; Finding the Target Users, Usage Scenarios, Main Functions and Product Features

After fully grasping the content, the main theme, the characteristics of the museum exhibition, as well as understanding the needs and pain points of the audience, we can use these as basics for the overall planning of the digital applicationlication. The overall planning of the digital applicationlication includes the target user, usage scenarios, main functions and product features.

The target user is the main user of the product, that is, the audience most likely to use digital technology among the visitors who visit a particular museum exhibit. By analyzing the main audience of the exhibition, the main users of the digital applicationlication can be basically determined. By analyzing these people's living habits, behavioral characteristics, hobbies and interests, digital applicationlication can be designed to more in line with the interests of these people.

The usage scenario refers to the occasion where the digital applicationlication is used. From a macro perspective, the use of the digital applicationlication for museum exhibitions is the museum's exhibition venue, which is an enclosed or open indoor environment. From a microscopic point of view, digital applicationlication is applicationlied in fictional spaces that symbolize different time and space and different cultural backgrounds. The design style of applicationlication is best consistent with the style of the environment.

The main function is the core usage of the digital applicationlication, which is the core goal of designing and developing this applicationlication. Such as knowledge function, communication function, and so on.

Product features are unique to digital applicationlication for museum exhibits and audience needs. Each product is different from any other product, and its features are its most important valuable.

The target users, usage scenarios, main functions and product features are the necessary links for the overall planning of the digital applicationlication for museum exhibitions and audience needs. These four parts of the work have laid a solid foundation for the follow-up development of digital applicationlication.

2.3   Third, Designing Information Architecture and Making Overall Content Framework of the Applicationlication

After completing the overall planning of the digital applicationlication, the next work is to enter the detailed development of the application. The design of the information architecture has made the first step for the development of application. Information framework design refers to the content to be conveyed through the application structure. If the overall design builds the outline of the digital application, then the information architecture design is to build the skeleton of the digital application, so that the subsequent development would have a definite direction.

2.4   Fourth, Interactive Design, Listing the Interaction Process

Interaction design refers to the human-computer interaction design of digital application based on museum exhibitions and audience needs. Human-computer interaction is an important part of determining whether application content can be successfully delivered to users. A successful human-computer interaction can enhance the applicationeal of the application to the audience, increase the chance of the viewer encountering the application, and thus promote the application content to the audience. The detailed interaction design needs to take into account every step and every detail of the user's using process.

2.5   Fifth, User Interface Design, Determines the Page Style and Color Style of the Applicationlication

User interface design can be described as the cloak of the digital application. After the previous basic work has been completed, the user interface design is put on the agenda. Although the user interface design is only responsible for the applicationearance of the application, it is by no means an undesirable step. User interface design as part of the overall development of the digital application, in order to do well, it must be closely related to the content and framework of the application. Designers should do their best to find ways to let the user interface show the core concept of digital application, by designing the applicationropriate color, hue, interface style, let the content of application be better displayed through visual elements.

2.6 Sixth, Program Development and Testing, Timely Discovery of Problems and Continuous Improvement

Coding is the process of make the entire digital application come to live. Rigorous codes can make the digital application run more smoothly and flexibly. Thereby the applicationlication would be better accepted by the users. The development of the program is not a one-time process, in which various problems may show up and countless tests are required. After the program is developed, it is necessary to carry out the necessary tests, in order to find the shortcomings of the current program, then continually modify and improve should be done.

2.7 Finally, the Digital Application Is Officially Used for Museum Exhibitions

After the above series of processes, the digital application can finally come to the museum to meet with the audience. But that doesn't mean ending. In the process of applicationlying the digital application to the museum exhibition, it is necessary to carefully observe and record the operation status of the application, the use of the audience, and so on. This will accumulate valuable experience for the future upgrade of the application and the future development of other products.

3 Practice of Design Process

This article is based on the Beijing Science and Technology Commission's 2015 Social Solicitation Science Project "Beijing Forestry University Museum Comprehensive Exhibition Hall". The project cycle from January 2015 to December 2015, which has been successfully completed and passed the Beijing Municipal Science and Technology Commission Expert acceptance. The main content of this project is divided into two parts. The first is to build the *Hoh Xil* real ecological environment science exhibition area. The venue of the exhibition area is located in the comprehensive exhibition hall on the fourth floor of the Beijing Forestry University Museum. The exhibition area is 40.10 m^2. There are 9 kinds of animal specimens, including Tibetan antelope, yak, Tibetan wild ass, snow leopard, vulture, mountain scorpion, snow rabbit, rabbit scorpion and scorpion. There are as well as 3 plant specimens, including Androsace mariae, Arenaria gerzensis, Arenaria bryophylla; second, digital display system development. In combination with the characteristics of the *Hoh Xil* real-life exhibition area, we designed and developed a *Hoh Xil* digital applicationlication based on the mobile platform for the content of the real exhibition area.

The *Hoh Xil* science exhibition area adopts a different form from the traditional exhibition. It adopts the "scenario + theme" exhibition form, combined with the real landscape of the Hoh Xil, and reproduced the natural features and habitat characteristics of the Hoh Xil Nature Reserve by simulating the habitat of the biological species. At the same time, the exhibition uses the interactive means of digital applicationlication of mobile platform. Thus the form of exhibition is more diversified, and the immersion of the audience in the exhibition is enhanced. The audience can walk freely in the exhibition area, and observe the specimens and landform at a close distance. They are placed in the simulated landscape of Hoh Xil, and the exhibition area is comprehensive and multi-dimensional. At the same time, during the visit, you can use the tablet PC equipped in the exhibition area, use the *Hoh Xil* digital applicationlication which has been already installed on the tablet computer, and learn about relevant science knowledge about the exhibition and original nature environment. You can also use the jigsaw puzzle and knowledge quiz game in the application to learn science knowledge and enhance environmental awareness (Fig. 2).

Fig. 2. Exhibition area photograph

3.1 Digging into the Exhibition Content and Exploring the Audience's Needs

We designed a digital mobile applicationlication based on the Hoh Xil exhibition area of the Beijing Forestry University Museum. The exhibition area is intended to build a high-simulation exhibition environment through original habitat materials and broadcast ecological civilization. Target audiences are museum visitors of all ages and social groups. The audience who come to visit the museum are composed of adults, young children, and their identities can be divided into scholars, students, and the public. We can regard all visitors of different ages and different identities as one group. The main needs of them can be summarized as learning the knowledge of animal specimens, plant specimens, topography and others displayed in the exhibition area with the help of digital applicationlication. They will get a whole understanding of the geographical environment, biodiversity, and environmental protection of the exhibition area. This demand can be regarded as the primary rigid requirement of the digital applicationlication. Secondly, the youth group of visitors is more willing to watch pictures, videos, and listen to sounds instead of reading a lot of textual descriptions when learning knowledge. Through research, we learned the characteristics of the exhibition area were to promote ecological civilization through habitat display, and the desire of visitors were to understand knowledge content through digital technology. According to this, the corresponding product planning is given, that is, the knowledge of the exhibition area is conveyed by various media to enhance the participation and interest of the audience. We designed the information architecture of four modules: exhibition area overview, animal specimens, plant specimens, and game interaction. Text, images, audio and video present a wealth of knowledge of the exhibition area. Interactive games consolidate the knowledge gained through the form of entertaining and learning, and increase the fun of the exhibition process. In terms of interaction design, the first-level page and the second-level page adopt the form of radial navigation, and the content page adopts horizontal label design on both sides. We also choose a flat interface style and a low-purity color mode for the applicationlication. The simple structure and bright color matching perfectly enhance the knowledge content and bring users a pleasant experience. After several tests and polishing, the applicationlication was finally applicationlied to the exhibition area.

3.2   Overall Design

The *Hoh Xil* digital applicationlication is a museum science applicationlication based on the mobile platform. This applicationlication mainly uses digital means to integrate graphics, images, videos and audios. Information on the scientific knowledge of bio-logical specimens, plant specimens and ecological environment protection in the exhibition area of the Hoh Xil science exhibition will be introduced and displayed through the integration of texts, images, videos and audios. In terms of visual pre-sentation, based on the characteristic of youth user group, the applicationlication uses two-dimensional cartoon image, transform the professional and serious scientific knowledge into an easy-to-understand graphic image. Meanwhile, combining cartoon images with audio, video and other content to make sure the science knowledge spreading successfully. In the aspect of interaction design, the integration of jigsaw puzzles and knowledge quiz game design realizes the game function of the digital applicationlication. Optimized the fun and entertainment of the exhibition. Users can absorb the information and deepen the knowledge through the game in the applica-tionlication. In this way the purpose of education and fun has been truly achieved (Fig. 3).

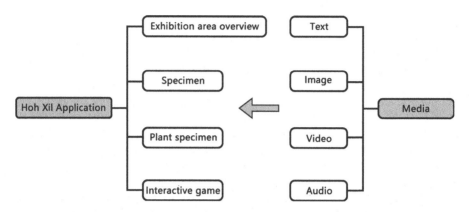

Fig. 3. *Hoh Xil* applicationlication information frame

3.3 Information Architecture Design, Building the Overall Content Framework of the Applicationlication

The *Hoh Xil* digital applicationlication is an interactive exhibit of the Hoh Xil Real Exhibition Area. Its purpose is to provide information display functions for the biological specimens and science knowledge in the exhibition area, so that the audience can understand the rich science knowledge in the exhibition area and the environmental background of the exhibition area. The application uses four media forms, such as text, image, video and audio. The applicationlication also designs four functional modules, which are animal specimens, plant specimens, exhibition area overview and game. The animal specimens module includes the introduction of animal specimens in the nine exhibition areas, which are displayed on the content unit pages of science knowledge and beautiful pictures. The plant specimens module includes introductions of plant specimens in the exhibition area, and are also displayed on the content unit pages of popular science knowledge and beautiful pictures. Interactive game module includes jigsaw puzzles and quiz games.

3.4 Interactive Design, Listing the Interaction Process of the Applicationlication

The home page layout of *Hoh Xil* digital applicationlication adopts the matrix layout mode of "central distribution". The four modules included in the applicationlication are clearly presented in front of the user, giving the user a central index. The user clicks on the category icon to go to the relevant details page, so that the main content can be quickly obtained. According to his or her interest, the user can determine which category to browse first. The first layout of each secondary page also continues the matrix tiling mode of "centralized distribution", showing that the content unit contains content with clear directivity.

The content page of the *Hoh Xil* digital applicationlication uses a vertical navigation layout combined with a sidebar Tab button layout mode. It sets the action class buttons, such as forward and backward, at the top of the page. This layout pattern combines the advantages of a vertical navigation layout with a tab navigation layout. First, the left vertical navigation layout lets the user view the details in a linear fashion. No matter where the user is in the applicationlication, he or she can clearly know which category of content unit he is in by clearly passing the status of the current column. This design quickly and easily navigates the user when the user gets lost. This design also allows the user to quickly return to the front page of this content unit or switch between different content units.

3.5 User Interface Design, Determining the Applicationlication's Page Style and Color Style

The user interface of the Hoh Xil digital applicationlication has a flat, translucent style. Icons are decorated with a card-shaped outline and a circular mask image. The colorful pictures matched with a dark bottom card-like shading. Icon button combine the image and text together. In particular, the picture of animals and plants in the icon increases the recognition feature. With a strong visual applicationeal, it is ideal for youth users. The animal display content of the animal specimen page is in the form of two-dimensional animation, which constitutes an interface style that is close to nature.

The *Hoh Xil* digital applicationlication uses a clear, cheerful low-purity, high-definition color style. The home page uses a high-definition background image to visualize the Hoh Xil area. The animal specimen module uses a two-dimensional cartoon illustration style to draw the image of the animal specimen. The visual style of cartoon style is easy to be accepted and loved by young users and it is easy to get closer to the group of young users. The game module page uses a wooden shading texture to distinguish it from the display part of the applicationlication. At the same time, the wooden texture can also build the natural and environmentally friendly visual communication.

3.6 Coding and Testing, Find Problems in Time and Keep Improving

Through code development, the functions of the *Hoh Xil* digital applicationlication are implemented. Through continuous correction of errors and vulnerabilities, to ensure that the system logic and interactive functions are implemented normally. The applicationlication is mainly published through the Android platform. It uses the Android native applicationlication for view control and interactive settings, uses the Surface view to play the video, uses the Media player for audio playback, uses the Image view to implement the image function and uses the View pager and Radio button to publish the interactive content of the knowledge quiz game. Finally, digital applicationlication *Hoh Xil* is officially used for museum exhibitions (Fig. 4).

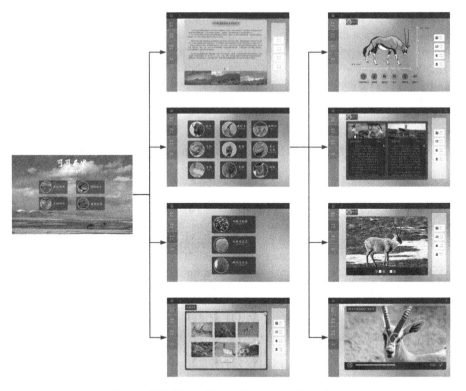

Fig. 4. *Hoh Xil* applicationlication interface design

4   Results

The research results mainly include the following aspects:

First, by analyzing the successful cases of digital technology applicationlied by museums at home and abroad, and systematically analyzing the shortcomings of Chinese museums in using digital technology to assist exhibitions, this paper proposes a systematic and comprehensive museum digital applicationlication design process based on exhibition content and user needs. This will provide a powerful help for the future Chinese museum to use digital technology to assist the exhibition.

Secondly, based on the above design process, the research group relies on the Beijing Science and Technology Commission's 2015 Social Solicitation Science Project "Beijing Forestry University Museum Comprehensive Exhibition Hall", with the exhibition requirements and user needs as the guidance, developed a digital applicationlication Hoh Xil. During the process of development, we carried out the user research, determined the target user group, scientifically and rationally analyzed user needs, met practical applicationlication products, designed and planned product functions and expression forms, and combine user research, interaction design, visual design, multimedia design, programming and other aspects of knowledge. The *Hoh Xil* digital applicationlication is designed from the whole to the local. With the integration of functions such as images, sounds, videos, games, etc., the information promotion function of the Hoh Xil real science exhibition area and exhibits knowledge is realized, and the purpose of displaying information is enriched, so that the audience can browse and understand a large amount of popular science knowledge through the applicationlication.

Third, designing game interactions in mobile applicationlications is a major innovation in this design. In the museum visit, in order to achieve the educational and entertaining style of the visit, combined with the cognitive characteristics of the low age of the visitors, the research team carried out the design and development of the interactive section of the applicationlication. We designed interactive games based on the content of the exhibition area. This enables the audience to re-cognize and re-learn the exhibition and exhibit knowledge in real-time interaction, which enhances the audience's interest in the exhibition, adds interest and entertainment to the exhibition process, and also broadcast science knowledge and public education.

Fourth, the Hoh Xil exhibition Area of Beijing Forestry University Museum is an indispensable part of the museum. On the one hand, it provides an indispensable platform of teaching, experimentation, and scientific research for many majors, such as the protection and utilization of wild animals and plants, soil and water conservation and desertification control, nature reserve construction and management, biodiversity conservation and utilization, The Eco-Cultural Research Center, etc. On the other hand, it provides a platform for industry and research for information technology and art design related majors. Students can conduct art practice and design in the exhibition area. The development of related digital products, as well as the development of simulation technology, promote the digital process of the museum. In addition, the school has established a platform for close contact with the experts, teachers, students, international academic exchanges and the public to understand the environmental conditions and ecological environment protection of the Hoh Xil Nature Reserve. It plays an invaluable role in promoting environmental protection, promoting the cherish of endangered species and popular science education.

5   Conclusion and Discussion

Based on the mobile platform development technology, this paper conducts in-depth research and exploration on mobile applicationlication interaction design principles, visual design style trends and interactive entertainment methods and studies the design of museum display applicationlication by theory and practice. To realize the diversification of information, visual stylization, interactive entertainment and common customs of the museum display system, the design principles of interactive exhibits based on mobile platforms and the value of public science education are summarized. The research results of this paper are as follows.

First, this paper combines the digital museum display design requirements for mobile platform applicationlication and user needs, gathers interactive design, visual design, game interactive design and other aspects of knowledge, to achieve the overall design of the *Hoh Xil* digital applicationlication. The work includes product requirements analysis, product function planning, product information architecture design, product prototyping, visual style design, UI interface design and game interaction design. The design ideas and methods of the museum exhibition mobile application-lication are comprehensively discussed, and the design process of the museum mobile applicationlication is summarized and refined.

Second, by the use of the digital applicationlication *Hoh Xil*, the functional characteristics of digital museum interactive entertainment and popular science communication education are realized. It has played a scientific publicity value in protecting biodiversity and environmental protection.

Through research analysis and practice testing, this paper proposes a method for digital applicationlication design of museums, which is of great value to the development of digitalization of Chinese museums and public education. Our research has the following shortcomings: The foreign language function area is not set in the digital applicationlication, which is not conducive to the development of the museum's external communication. In the future, the function and depth of the applicationlication should be further strengthened in this respect to better serve the audience and museum exhibitions.

References

1. Meng, Z.: Understanding and thinking of digital museums. Chin. Mus. **2**, 74–77 (2000)
2. Zhang, Y., Wang, C.: Wisdom museum, my museum - mobile application based museum audience experience system. Chin. Mus. **1**, 46–51 (2012)
3. Gong, H., Wang, Y., Hu, C., et al.: Comparing and commenting of the current situation of digital museum at domestic and abroad. J. Mod. Inf. **35**(4), 164–171 (2015)
4. Media Art History Homepage. http://www.mediaarthistory.org/wp-content/uploads/2017/12/Paul.pdf. Accessed 2004
5. Yang, Q., Du, H.: Education concept and practice of contemporary American university museums. Mod. Univ. Educ. **04**, 54–60 (2017)
6. Gong, L.: From social education to public service: Nanjing museum's practice in improving public service and some thoughts. Southeast Cult. **03**, 107–112+127–128 (2017)

Design of a Contextual Digital Wayfinding Environment

Isabel Morais[1], Manuel Condado[1], Ryan Quinn[2], Sahil Patel[2],
Patricia Morreale[1(✉)], Ed Johnston[2], and Elizabeth Hyde[3]

[1] School of Computer Science, Kean University, Union, NJ 07083, USA
{moraisis, condadom, pmorreal}@kean.edu
[2] Robert Busch School of Design, Kean University, Union, NJ 07083, USA
{quinryan, psahil, jedward}@kean.edu
[3] Department of History, Kean University, Union, NJ 07083, USA
ehyde@kean.edu

Abstract. The user experience presented here illustrates how a digital wayfinding experience was developed for a museum website, using both natural and historical context engagement. A general web site tour is supported for visitors to the museum website. In addition to this standard experience, a botanical and historical tour can be taken. For the botanical and historical layers depicted, the layered maps support differentiated experiences in a digital wayfinding environment, which is particularly important for users not able to be physically present at the site. The botanical layer of the website provides botanical information specific to the property. Using primary historical artifacts, a historical context is provided. Historical documents supporting the grounds layout, such as documents regarding the original plant orders, are presented alongside the landscape at that time. Both the physical and virtual experience of the site is enhanced, depending on the pathway selected by the user through the digital material presented. This digital wayfinding integrates user experience with historical fact, landscape architecture, and physical site information.

Contributions of this research include a methodology for digital wayfinding design at other physical locations and lessons learned regarding best practices in developing discrete information layers for traversal by differentiated user communities. Users reported increased interest in the differentiated general, botanical, and historical content when it was presented in context. Overall, interest in visiting the actual museum increased by fifteen percent after users completed the digital wayfinding experience.

Keywords: Digital wayfinding · Layered maps · Botanical · Historical · Museum

1 Introduction

Wayfinding is the way in which people orient themselves in physical space and navigate from place to place. People regularly use wayfinding tools, such as Google Maps or Waze, to help them navigate and reach destinations while driving. Wayfinding is not as popular when pedestrians navigate in an enclosed outside environment, such as an

© Springer Nature Switzerland AG 2019
A. Marcus and W. Wang (Eds.): HCII 2019, LNCS 11585, pp. 221–232, 2019.
https://doi.org/10.1007/978-3-030-23538-3_17

orchard. While it could be argued that wayfinding tools are not needed in an orchard or open space because everything to see is right in front of the visitor, this assumes that only the current physical layout is of interest. What if a person wanted to see what the space had looked like in the past?

Using layers to add onto maps, the research presented here created different experiences within one garden. Each layer represents a different way to interact with the garden's botanical environment or a different part of history. Each map holds unique information, making no two trips alike. Unlike other wayfinding systems, which have a user input a destination and a pre-set route is provided, this layered, intelligent wayfinding system is able to understand what the user wants to see and gives the user multiple paths he or she might find interesting. This places the user in control of the content and individual experience.

In this study, we created a wayfinding system for the grounds at Liberty Hall in Union, New Jersey, using layered maps that each convey a different user experience. These maps provide either general, botanical, or historical knowledge. Additionally, each map appeals to the different demographics that Liberty Hall Museum caters to, including senior citizens and K-12 students. Many senior citizens would like to know the historical information behind the herbs and trees planted in the garden or the overall history of the property. Science teachers may teach their students about the botany of the plants and trees in the orchard, while senior citizens and other students may only want a general knowledge of the property, not specific, and to observe nature. The layered mapping presented here provides a free, unrestricted experience.

Prior research that has been done about quick response (QR) codes, layered maps, and wayfinding systems in place was used in designing this experience. The hardships or challenges of promoting the visibility of an orchard [1, 2] were considered. We give insight into our methodology of each experience in the orchard and its layered maps. Finally, we discuss our conclusions, explain limitations, and suggest further research.

2 Prior Work

Global positioning systems (GPS) have been around for years as an alternative to physical maps as a wayfinding tool, yet they still lack the quality of physical maps. Physical maps for outdoor wayfinding have been found to increase the survey knowledge of users [3–6], thus helping the user become more spatially aware. In fact, spatial awareness is vital to a contextual understanding of an environment. However, in another study participants found that their smartphones provided them confidence with wayfinding tasks rather than hindering them, as some other literature suggests [7]. These two sides of the argument creates a level ground in which both can be improved upon.

Creating wayfinding systems in an outside environment, such as a garden or orchard, has proven to be difficult. The placement of trees and plants in an orchard are all carefully planned by the owner of the land or an arborist. The arborist wants visitors to become aware of the nature surrounding them when visitors are physically in the orchard [6]. This is done by placing the trees in certain areas, expressing different landscapes, and creating pathways for a visitor to experience nature as it is intended to be experienced. Gardeners are constantly looking for ways to help maintain the longevity of their land and a way to do that is to pair areas of the garden with appropriate historical content. However, it is hard to find documents that provide historical information pertaining to tree and plant placement because of ambiguous document keeping from the past. Gardeners frequently have to sift through documents, leaving out the "interesting but not relevant" parts [4].

Combining parts of a garden and historical documents is a way for visitors to connect with the garden itself. To accomplish this, the garden would need an interface for visitors to use so that they could get the information. One study proposed using QR codes to enhance the experience of government websites, such as the U.S. National Park Service (NPS) [5]. The study was able to create a waypoint system for visitors of the park to use while also creating park incentives through the website. This study found a way to combine the experience of the actual park with the information available on the park's website. Using QR codes greatly improved the visitor's knowledge of park activities and general information.

The original map for Liberty Hall (Fig. 1) did not provide sufficient detail on the general, botanical or historical aspects of the site. The presentation was basic, with shapes and color being the primary visual indicators. No informative or descriptive text was provided, only the identification of a street name which borders the property.

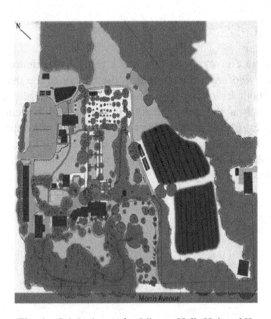

Fig. 1. Original map for Liberty Hall, Union, NJ.

3   Methodology

In the early phase of this project, a decision had to be made regarding how to develop the website for Liberty Hall Grounds (www.libertyhallgrounds.org). Given the length and intent of the project, it was not possible to hardcode the entire website. Additionally, the Liberty Hall staff are not familiar with programming, therefore making the idea unsustainable in the long-term. The Liberty Hall staff communicated that they needed to be able to easily update the museum website in the future. With this in mind, the Webflow platform was selected.

Webflow is a web-based drag-and-drop tool for building responsive websites. With Webflow, a user with no programming experience can create their own website, and if a user knows how to code, then the user can create a more sophisticated website. Webflow is useful for people with no programming skills both to create websites, and to update websites in the future as coding is not required to update content. This was a solution to a significant hurdle and the main reason Webflow was selected to create the website. Webflow gives the Liberty Hall museum staff the control to change the website at will without having to worry about not knowing how to program.

At the conclusion of the project, a decision was made regarding the site's hosting. Multiple hosting services were considered, however they all required us to export code from Webflow. This would defeat the purpose of using the platform in the first place because by exporting code, if Liberty Hall wanted to make changes, then the staff would have to know how to program. Ultimately, Webflow was selected to host the website, as Liberty Hall could keep their easy access.

4   General Map

The first experience to convey to visitors was a general experience. This experience caters to individuals who are not interested in the botany of the trees and plants and who do not care about historical significance. The resulting map (Fig. 2) contains points of interest, such as the trees, the formal garden, and Serpentine Path without focusing on the context of each object. The objective was to make sure that visitors did not feel pressured when looking at this map, that they felt free to do what they wanted and see what they pleased. The idea that visitors were free made a huge impact on the experience we wanted to convey.

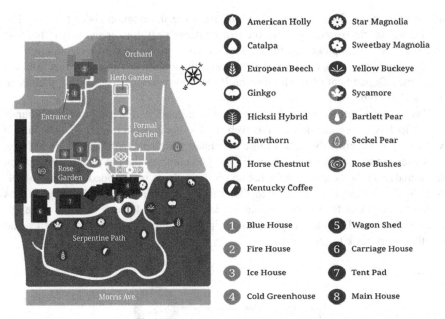

Fig. 2. New general map and guide for Liberty Hall, Kean University, Union, NJ., with botanical and site building detail.

5 Botanical

The second experience tackled was the botanical experience (Fig. 3). Before this project started, the orchard had no place for visitors to lookup botanical information on its champion trees. A website was created that contained each tree's picture, scientific

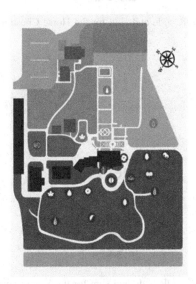

Fig. 3. Botanical map for Liberty Hall, Kean University, Union, NJ

and common name, background, and a link for more information about the tree. The website has fourteen trees, yet the orchard contains sixty-four trees, this is because these select few were picked by the orchard's arborist as the orchard's champion trees. Of these champion trees, certain tree sections on the website contain statistics from the New Jersey Department of Environmental Protection regarding records that the tree at Liberty Hall holds.

Having the information on the website was a good start, visitors to the grounds needed to have a connection to the website for botanical information. The user's experience on the grounds needed to be integrated with the experience of the website.

A user friendly and non-age restrictive way to combine the physical experience on the grounds and the botanical information on the website was needed. The use of QR codes allowed users easy linkage to the website with each QR code. A code was created for each tree for the visitors' convenience. Figures 4 and 5 show how the QR codes are integrated into the display, supporting the digital wayfinding experience and directing users back to the website.

Fig. 4. QR code and sign for the Horse Chestnut tree.

Fig. 5. QR code and sign for the Seckel Pear.

6   Historical

The final experience addressed was the historical experience. The grounds at Liberty Hall are rich with historical context, from the first Governor of New Jersey, William Livingston, owning this land to the structure of the garden itself, modeled after 18th century Europe. Using a layered map ideology, several maps were created from the main map. The first layer (Fig. 6) contained the original front of the house, which is the formal garden. This formal garden is modeled after French gardens in the 1700s. In a letter from Louis-Guillaume Otto, French consul in New York, to Charles-Claude de La Billarderie, who was in charge of France's royal gardens, wrote that, "gardening in America was in its infancy. Most Americans, in his opinion, were either indifferent to the amelioration of the garden arts, or too engaged in producing 'mauvais fruits et des légumes' for mere subsistence" [2]. William Livingston was one of the few in America who wanted to create a beautiful garden, because maintaining a garden meant that he was a gentleman. In our layered map, we wanted to convey how Livingston created his orchard from nothing to an elaborate, thought-out sanctuary. Detail from historical documents which include his orders for fruit trees (Figs. 10 and 11) are provided as well.

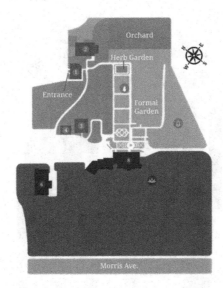

Fig. 6.   Layered, historical map for Liberty Hall showing Early Liberty Hall, pre-1770.

The second layer (Fig. 7) to the historical map takes place a few years after, when Livingston added to his orchard by working on the back of his house. There, he added the Serpentine Path, which took visitors around a new path and through his new trees. This layout was modeled after the English, which took on a more "free flowing" path. This second map combined the map of the front of the house and the new additions to the back of the house. With this, visitors could see how, when times changed, so did the

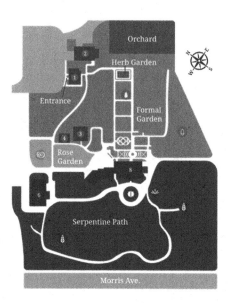

Fig. 7. Layered historical map 2, showing Liberty Hall's evolution from 1770–1788.

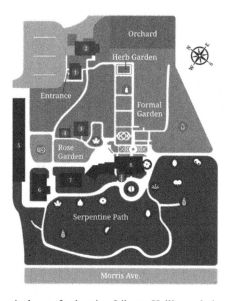

Fig. 8. Layered historical map 3, showing Liberty Hall's evolution from 1798–present.

garden. When the English garden style became prevalent, Livingston added it onto his property. Visitors are able to take a trip to the past and move forward, seeing the orchard's change.

The final layer (Fig. 8) to the historical maps included the same idea as the second layer. The difference being that, after the Serpentine Path was added, the orchard

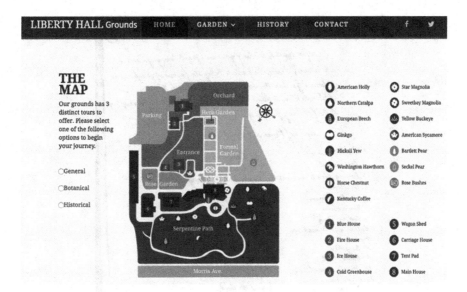

Fig. 9. Map presented, with the three experiences – general, botanical, and historical – visitors can select. www.libertyhallgrounds.org

Fig. 10. William Livingston's plum order in 1766.

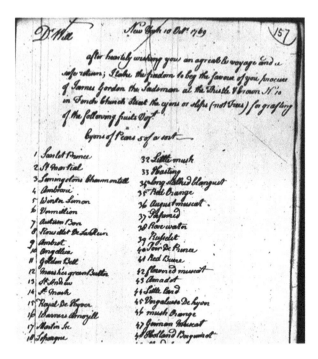

Fig. 11. William Livingston's order of pears in 1766.

expanded its tree collection, added a rose garden, and built a wagon shed around 1900. Visitors would be able to see how in the 1900, the wagon shed was built to store farm machinery because farming was very important during its time. The orchard also sees the addition of a rose garden, because roses started to become more prevalent in society.

Lastly, the final layer added tree icons to show visitors what trees were planted at what time periods. Considering Livingston died in 1790, visitors can then see what types of trees the new owners, such as the Kean family, planted. This content is very important to Liberty Hall because, by showing when trees were planted, it helps convey the importance of the champion trees and the records they break by being on the grounds. The purpose of these layered maps is to help each visitor experience the past as it were. By physically show the expansion in segments, users are able to fully understand the whole picture as it evolves.

The layered, historical maps (Fig. 9) can each be seen on the history's Land page of the website created (www.libertyhallgrounds.org). While walking throughout the orchard, visitors can follow along on the website to see how the maps progress. Meanwhile, information that may be confusing to comprehend by looking at the map is written below the maps. This is for users who are more verbal learners than visual.

7   Results

To test the user experience, a survey was conducted. To evaluate if the new botanical map was visually appealing, a five-point Likert Scale was used, which has the participant choose from five options varying from extremely appealing to extremely unappealing. Of the responses received (n = 41), all responded with either an extremely appealing or appealing answer. This is a significant difference compared to when participants were asked if the old map was visually appealing, in which all participants responded with either unappealing or extremely unappealing.

Users reported increased interest in the differentiated general, botanical, and historical content when it was presented in context. User perception of the features of the botanical, and historical maps was high (70–80%). Overall, interest in visiting the actual museum increased by 15% after users completed the virtual digital wayfinding experience. Integration of the physical wayfinding experience with the digital wayfinding environment has great potential to enhance the physical experience, while opening the environment to a larger community of users and visitors.

From these results of the survey, we can conclude that the general map needs more of a distinction that it is a general, all-purpose map. Even though participants saw that the general map had buildings numbered, as well as tree icons, almost half of the participants did not understand. A future map should prioritize user understanding. There should be additional testing done to identify how users can be encouraged to distinguish between different maps, such as a general map or a botanical map in this case.

Furthermore, the results showed that the new maps created were much more visually appealing than the older map. The new map provides color and appropriate icons that are easily distinguishable with the help of the map's legend. The old map did not contain a legend, so the ability for users to now know what they are looking at on the map is very beneficial.

8   Conclusion and Future Work

In conclusion, three new maps were created to show visitors different paths through the Liberty Hall Museum grounds which visitors can experience. First, there is the general map, which shows all of the points of interest, including buildings and trees. Next, there is the botanical map, which only shows users information about the champion trees on the grounds of Liberty Hall. Finally, there is the layered, historical maps which show how the Liberty Hall grounds have changed over time, from Governor William Livingston in 1770 to present time. These maps are accessible through the website specifically created for the grounds at Liberty Hall. This website can be reached by either typing out the website (www.libertyhallgrounds.org) in the browser manually or by using one of the multiple QR codes that are placed around Liberty Hall's grounds. Future work will continue to bring this historical environment to both visitors to the physical site and visitors to the virtual site on the web, extending the reach of the physical property while increasing access and understanding of the general, botanical, and historical information available through the digital wayfinding experience.

References

1. Martins, T., Machado, P., Rebelo, A.: The garden of virtual delights. In: ACM SIGGRAPH 2013 Posters on - SIGGRAPH 2013 (2013)
2. Auricchio, L., Cook, E., Pacini, G.: Invaluable Trees Cultures of Nature, 1660-1830, p. 186. Voltaire Foundation, Oxford (2012)
3. Bertel, S., Dressel, T., Kohlberg, T., von Jan, V.: Spatial knowledge acquired from pedestrian urban navigation systems. In: Proceedings of the 19th International Conference on Human-Computer Interaction with Mobile Devices and Services - MobileHCI 2017 (2017)
4. Gorichanaz, T.: A gardener's experience of document work at a historic landscape site. In: Proceedings of the Association for Information Science and Technology, vol. 53, no. 1, pp. 1–10 (2016)
5. Lorenzi, D., Shafiq, B., Vaidya, J., Nabi, G., Chun, S., Atluri, V.: Using QR codes for enhancing the scope of digital government services. In: Proceedings of the 13th Annual International Conference on Digital Government Research (2012)
6. Mima, Y., Kimura, K., Yanagi, H.: ThinkingGarden. In: Proceedings of the 20th ACM International Conference on Multimedia, MM 2012 (2012)
7. Ricker, B., Schuurman, N., Kessler, F.: Implications of smartphone usage on privacy and spatial cognition. GeoJournal **80**(5), 637–652 (2014)

Gamification in Local Intangible Cultural Heritage Museums for Children: A Case Design

Yuchen Weng, Tao Shen, Sihuang Chen, and Bing Xiao[⊠]

School of Design, Shanghai Jiao Tong University, Shanghai, China
shellyoveluna@163.com, stsjtu@126.com,
sihuangchen@hotmail.com, xbingdesign@163.com

Abstract. Nowadays, local intangible cultural heritage is in danger of disappearing. The museum is a good way to protect it but the current problem is that visitors are less willing to visit boring museums. Gamification in museums is a great solution, that includes the theory of museum information dissemination and the theory of gamification. The theory of museum information dissemination points out the change of design concept of interaction and the update of equipment and technology today. And the theory of gamification shifts the problem of intangible cultural heritage of museums to a motivation, including external rewards of BPL and internal motivation of parents' participation. Based on the theory and analysis above, this paper designed a museum exhibit for Fotiaoqiang (a kind of traditional Chinese dish), and an experimental test. This design aims to improve the effectiveness of information dissemination of Fotiaoqiang and children's absorption when visiting the museums, in order to reserve local intangible cultural heritage from generation to generation. The result of the experimental test indicated that the gamification in this design was positive, but the motivation was still controversial.

Keywords: Gamification · Museum · Design

1 Introduction

With the growth of industrialization in developed countries and the global cultural expansion [1], many intangible cultural heritages are in danger of dying out, because the environment in which they exist has changed significantly. Due to the popularity of various kinds of modern entertainments today, intangible cultural heritage is facing a grim situation that there will be no successors. Fewer and fewer generations are willing to pass on their own local tradition or even have an interest in it, which causes the fading of it, especially those with no entity. However, intangible cultural heritage that contains profound traditional culture is so significant that it's the basic identification mark of a nation. It's also a driving force in preventing the soul of a nation from being obliterated by foreign culture [1]. The importance of intangible cultural heritage has been valued by many governments, and several official organizations were established to prevent it from disappearing. According to the Convention for the Safeguarding of Intangible Cultural Heritage, a committee composed of the delegates of 24 contracting

© Springer Nature Switzerland AG 2019
A. Marcus and W. Wang (Eds.): HCII 2019, LNCS 11585, pp. 233–245, 2019.
https://doi.org/10.1007/978-3-030-23538-3_18

governments held a meeting annually to monitor the implementation of the 175 countries that have ratified this legal instrument and have incorporated the protection of intangible heritage into their national legislation. In spite of this, many intangible cultural heritages approved by UNESCO are still on the verge of extinction, which shows that the world still faces the problem of how to protect the intangible cultural heritage.

Building museums is a good way to remind residents of local intangible cultural heritage (ICH) [2]. Different from tangible cultural heritage, intangible cultural heritage is a kind of treasure that is passed down from generation to generation, which is very dependent on the individual. However, fewer and fewer people are willing to pass on these "outdated" cultures. For the protection and preservation of intangible cultural heritage, museums have their own special advantages. Firstly, museums have a scientific system for the protection and preservation of their heritage. Secondly, a great number of professionals work for museums to protect the heritage. Thirdly, it is the only permanent institution in the field of heritage protection, so it can be said that museums are irreplaceable institutions for scientific protection of intangible heritage and permanent collection. In fact, the museum world is extending its protection to the vast field of intangible heritage. According to International Council of Museums (ICOM), it's their central mission and responsibility to protect the relatively fragile intangible heritage. The theme of the 2004 Seoul International Exposition and Association Conference was "Museum and Intangible Heritage", which the further expresses the importance that ICOM attaches to the issue.

Although governments have highly valued the protection of their own intangible cultural heritages and the construction of museums, the current state of such local museum is that visitors are scarce. Contrary to the science museums with lots of interactive devices, local culture museums that are packed with excessive text boards tend to be too traditional, or in other words too boring for children to learn. As children are the next generation of museum-goers, they should be given priority in museum education. What's more, though most children visit with the company of their parents, the museum still lack of parental interaction to guide them. A survey entitled "Why You Don't Want to Go to a Museum", published by Oliver Smith in the Daily Mail Online, lists 21 reasons, most of which were related to boredom, such as: "You'd be happier doing something else", "Because this is considered museum-worthy", "The artefacts are boring", "The atmosphere is funereal", "You've no idea what you're looking at" [3]. Some scholars have pointed out the central problems: firstly, less attention is paid to museum-centric educational activities in museums; secondly, most museums are lack of interaction, not only between exhibits and visitors, but also between visitors themselves.

Faced with the difficulties in intangible cultural heritage protection and current problems of museums mentioned above, it is of great value to apply gamification to the design of intangible cultural heritage museums from the perspective of visitors' experience and focus on cultivating the interest of the next generation in intangible cultural heritage and a sense of responsibility for its protection. The specific research significance and value of this paper are as follows:

- With the arrival of the information age and the rise of various intelligent devices, museum display and information dissemination are also going digital, which provides more feasibility for gamified interactive modes.
- Nowadays, driven by the information age, museums have changed their ways of displaying and information dissemination. Compared to traditional way of display boards, gamification is more focused on the interaction between exhibits and visitors, or even between visitors themselves, which is more conducive to the efficient dissemination of museum information.
- The demands of museum experience, such as curiosity, confidence, challenge, control, play and communication [4], are perfectly matched with the "game elements" of gamification. Therefore, making gamification a suitable solution to the central problems around museums.
- Education, the most important purpose of museum for children, can play a better role and improve learning efficiency under the catalysis of gamification. Moreover, the fun brought by gamification is in line with the preferences of children, who are the target population of this study, therefore the concept should more easily accepted by children.

This paper designed a museum exhibit for Fotiaoqiang, a famous Chinese dish with a long history, through the theory of museum information dissemination and the theory of gamification, and an experimental test to prove the gamification to be positive. This design aims to improve the effectiveness of information dissemination of Fotiaoqiang and children's absorption when visiting the museums, in order to preserve local intangible cultural heritage from generation to generation. The gamification design is based on both extrinsic rewards and intrinsic motivation. For extrinsic rewards, the design uses badges, points and leaderboard (BPL) to attract children's attention and make them keep playing. For intrinsic motivation, the design tries to make parents to participate in children's learning by kinship and parents' emotional response and affection to their local tradition, which can help children immerse themselves in the experience. The experimental test was to confirm the effectiveness of extrinsic rewards and intrinsic motivation in this gamification design.

2 Museum Information Dissemination and Gamification

2.1 Museum Information Dissemination

The arrival of the information age had a great impact on museum display and information dissemination, including the change of design concept and the update of equipment and technology.

Change of Design Concept. Museums have begun to focus on interactive experience design guided by a user-centered concept. Since Norman put forward the user-centered design concept [4], more and more design-related studies have been focusing on the needs of users. Museum design has also begun to focus on user experience and the corresponding interactions according to its needs. At present, the design concept of museums has been undergone a huge transformation. The service object turns from objects to visitors, and the flow of information transforms from unidirection to interactional [5]. This people-oriented design concept points out that the interaction is not only between visitors and exhibits, but also between visitors themselves. The museum is no longer simply a warehouse for storing cultural relics, but should be based on the needs of visitors. It is education, entertainment and social needs that constitute the main demands of museum visitors. Among these needs, the educational needs of children visitors are paramount for the intangible cultural heritage museum, which is in urgent need of successors. And entertainment need and social need, which are instinctive for children, can be a boost to education needs. This is because that pleasure in entertainment needs, as well as friendship and kinship in social needs, are all in a child's nature.

Update of Equipment and Technology. Nowadays, the rise of various intelligent devices is making museum information dissemination to become digital, which provides more possibilities for interactive museum exhibits, such as interactive electronic display board, virtual museum on mobile devices, virtual reality (VR), augmented reality (AR) and etc. For the hyperactive children who are curious about the world, they would be more interested in interactive museum exhibits that they can be involved in.

2.2   Gamification

The definition of gamification is the use of game design elements in non-game contexts [6]. Studies have shown that memory is enhanced when learning is done in an interesting way [7]. The main function of the museum is to efficiently make visitors receive information in the shortest possible time. Therefore, gamification can help staid and boring intangible cultural heritage museums to effectively educate children. Moreover, gamified museum exhibits should be easily accepted by children, because the fun brought by gamification is in line with the preferences of children. The needs of museum experience match the game design element of gamification. According to the theoretical model of museum experience proposed by Perry in 1993, needs of a visit to museum include curiosity, confidence, challenge, control, play and communication [8], which are similar to what is needed in a game. So, gamification could be a good solution to this issue.

Motivation affordance [9] transfers the research method of gamification from observing behavior to the problem of motivation. The motivation of gamification can be divided into extrinsic motivation and intrinsic motivation. Some scholars believe that intrinsic motivation is the source of efforts and should be the core of the incentive mechanism, which is complementary to intrinsic and extrinsic motivation [10].

Extrinsic Rewards. A common but controversial implementation of gamification in education is BPL (referring to badges, leaderboards and points). On the one hand, BPL has been proven to be efficient through many usability tests [11]. On the other hand, BPL has also been proved by research that most extrinsic rewards could reduce internal motivation in education [12]. Once the extrinsic rewards are removed, the gamification won't work any longer [13]. However, the educational needs of gamification in museums do not need long-term motivation, as the average visit to museums is only a few hours and will not be repeated frequently. What is needed is to improve learning efficiency and interest in a limited time, so BPL is more suitable as the external reward for gamification in museums.

Intrinsic Motivation. Intrinsic motivation is a kind of activity or work motivation caused by the characteristics of the activity process itself or the individual's endogenous spiritual needs. The relevant influencing factors mainly involve individual needs and emotions, characteristics of work tasks, individual achievement goal setting, self-efficacy, organizational authorization and exchange, and extrinsic motivation, etc. The related theories of intrinsic motivation include self-determination theory (SDT) [14] and flow theory.

Self-Determination Theory (SDT). SDT points out that when a person actively chooses to take an activity rather than complete an external purpose, the same activity is more likely to make the person more stimulated and happier. Gamification driven by intrinsic motivation is considered meaningful gamification. Therefore, it will be more efficient to use gamified fun to attract children to learn relevant knowledge of intangible cultural heritage. Therefore, if museums can successfully use gamification design to attract children actively through the fun engaging activities, this will ensure an effective and efficient means of education. Moreover, if parents who are locals can participate together, their sense of belonging to the local intangible cultural heritage and affection for their children will also become part of the intrinsic motivation.

Mental Flow. The theory of mental flow was first proposed by Csikszentmihalyi, which referring to the mental state of a person who is absorbed in a certain behavior in psychology. According to this theory, players of high ability who engage in less challenging things are more easily bored, while players of low ability who do high-challenging things tend to become more anxious. It has been widely used in video game design to keep players hooked to a game by tying to balance users' ability with the difficulty of the game, or in other words keeping the players in a state of flow. In fact, the purpose of gamification design in museums is to engage children as if they are playing a video game. There have been several validated scales of mental flow such as E-flow Scale, FSS and DFS, which can be used as the feedback to measure the effectiveness of gamification in museums.

3   Design Process

In order to verify the effectiveness of gamification in the intangible cultural heritage museum and the influence of internal motivation and external rewards, this paper applied these theories to the museum exhibit design of Fotiaoqiang, a local intangible cultural heritage in China.

3.1   Background of Fotiaoqiang

Fotiaoqiang, a traditional Chinese dish, is a soup that contains many expensive ingredients such as abalone and sea cucumber. The typical recipe and cooking process of Fotiaoqiang is very complicated, and its history can be traced back hundreds of years in ancient China. It was approved by the State Council to be included in the second batch of national intangible cultural heritage list in 2008. However, most Chinese people's impression of Fotiaoqiang is limited to its high price, but they know nothing about the history and practice of this famous dish.

3.2 Design Goal

This design aims to improve the effectiveness of information dissemination of Fotiaoqiang for children in museums, in order to reserve this local intangible cultural heritage from generation to generation.

3.3 Technical Path

After collecting the relevant information of Fotiaoqiang the information was carefully arranged and summarized to three interesting key points: the place it comes from (as a basic knowledge of Chinese food), the origin of its strange name and its special way of cooking. In accordance with the museum information dissemination theory and gamification theory, the information was processed to a mock-up kitchen and an introduction was shown to children in a gamified manner on a touch screen and with the help of parents through hints from related application on a smart phone. The mock-up kitchen consists of plastic cooking utensils and ingredients with NFC, which can identify if the right ingredients are in the right utensils and show the corresponding cooking progress on the touch screen. The technical path is shown in Fig. 1.

3.4 Motivation Analysis

According to the gamification theory mentioned in the previous chapter, this museum exhibit design combined intrinsic motivation with extrinsic rewards. The extrinsic rewards mainly used BPL mechanism. Intrinsic motivation includes parents' sense of belonging to the local intangible cultural heritage and affection for their children through their participation. The following is a detailed description of the design based on the motivation classification:

Design of Extrinsic Rewards: BPL. Internal motivation in this design was triggered through BPL mechanism. Players go through three levels: birthplace, origin and traditional recipe (see Fig. 2). In each level, players can get 0 to 3 stars, depending on their response. If the wrong answer is selected, the system will provide the correct answer and explain it in detail. Players must complete one level to unlock the next level, and the difficulty is gradual. In the first and second level, players will be asked to answer illustrated multiple-choice questions on the touchpad, but will require more patience to hear the whole story of the origin of the name in the second level. Table 1 shows how the details of each level.

Design for Internal Motivation: Participation of Parents. Internal motivation in this design was triggered through participation of parents, including hints, mock-up kitchen and digital photo souvenir.

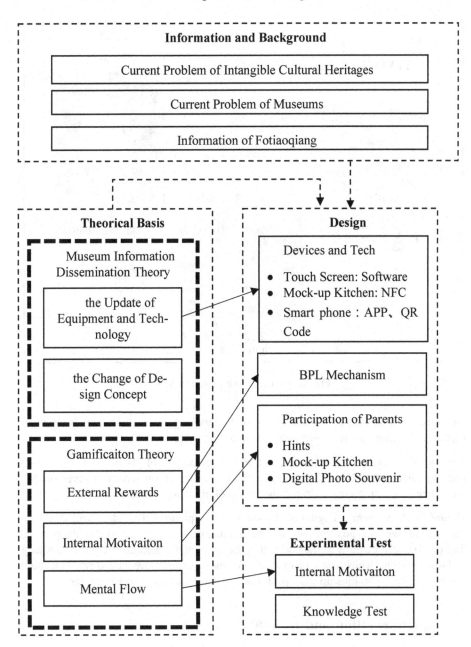

Fig. 1. A figure of the technical path

Hints. Hints are some implied text about the answer, which can be found by scanning the QR code in the corner of every page of questions or missions. To get higher scores, children will have to rely on their parents' smart phones to get the hint. For example,

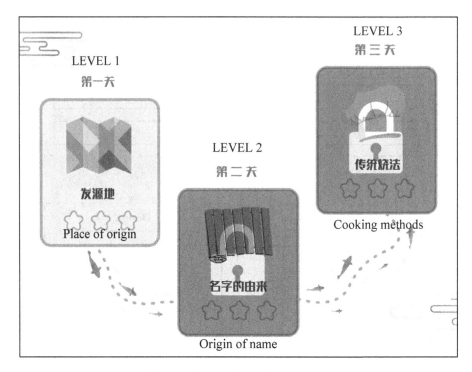

Fig. 2. User interface of three levels

the corresponding hint of the birthplace of Fotiaoqiang in the first level is south of China, which can narrow down a certain range of choices.

Mock-up Kitchen. Mock-up kitchen is a real space consist of plastic cooking utensils and ingredients with NFC. Compared with virtual kitchen on screen, it gives parents more space to help their children finish the cooking task together.

Digital Photo Souvenir. Digital photo souvenir is a photo that children will take with their parents when stage clear, and will be automatically sent to the APP of the parents. The photo is decorated with the badge they have got and illustration about Fotiaoqiang and this museum, which can be a unique souvenir to remind parents and children about this experience. The kinship may push parents and children to finish the task.

4   Experimentation and Results

4.1   Experimental Test

The experiment is to verify the effectiveness of gamification of different motivation in prototype of the design above. Limited by technology and equipment, parents' QR code hints were replaced by paper version, and the digital photo souvenir was processed afterwards. And the mockup-kitchen were replaced by similar toys with no

Table 1. Details of each level in the design.

Level	Content	Score
Level 1: birthplace	1. Which of the eight major cuisines does Fotiaoqiang belong to? (multiple choice)	Pass: 1 correct answer = 1 star 2 correct answers = 2 stars 3 correct answers = 3 stars Fail: 0 correct answer = 0 star, restart this level
	2. Which district did the Fotiaoqiang come from? (multiple choice)	
	3. Select the birthplace of Fotiaoqiang on the map of China	
Level 2: the origin of the name	1. Illustration story one (judge whether it is true or not): the original name Fushouquan (means healthy and well in Chinese), which sounds similar to Fotiaoqiang, was invented by an official to please Emperor Daoguang	Pass: 1 correct answer = 1 star 2 correct answers = 2 stars 3 correct answers = 3 stars Fail: 0 correct answer = 0 star, restart this level
	2. Illustration story two (judge whether it is true or not): A bride in Fujian tried to cook for her parents-in-law for the first time but forget the recipe, so she used lotus leaves to wrap 18 dishes brought from home and boiled them together	
	3. Illustration story three (judge whether it is true or not): A beggar cooked a pot of leftovers outside a temple. The dish smelled so delicious that a monk could not help jumping out of the temple wall to find it	
Level 3: traditional recipe	Mock-up Kitchen: Put 10 different ingredients into 10 different cooking utensils and cook them separately. After ingredients are cooked, place a lotus leaf on the bottom of each ingredient (agent) and boil them together in a jar	The progress bar for each pot and the total progress bar are displayed in the corner of the touch screen. If the step is wrong, restart this level. Fail = 0, get 3 stars $1 \leq$ Fail ≤ 3, get 2 stars Fail ≥ 4, get 1 star
Stage clear	A virtual badge will be awarded to the player based on his final score. Children can get a photo with their parents, on which decorated with the badge they got and illustration about Fotiaoqiang and this museum	0–3 stars = kitchen killer 4–6 stars = foodie 7–8 stars = gastronome 9 stars = god of kitchen

NFC, which was controlled by the guide of the experimenter. 30 pairs of volunteers were divided into three group, aged 10 to 12, all from local Chinese families. The average age of the children in each group was basically the same to ensure the fairness of the results in each group. There are two reasons to choose the age group of 10–12 years old as follows. Firstly, G1 requires a large amount of text reading ability, while Chinese children learn to read characters from the age of 6 and can 10 can read a lot at a rapid pace at about the age of 10. Secondly, the subjective assessment scale children need to fill is more suitable for older ones, because they can better understand the scale.

In the experiment, the children all learned the same content about Fotiaoqiang, but displayed in totally different ways:

- G1(Group one): Children were given traditional text-based display board.
- G2(Group two): Children were asked to experience the museum exhibitions described in the previous chapter on their own, which means no hint of QR code or any other participation of their parents. The parents were asked to wait in another room.
- G3(Group three): Children were asked to experience the museum exhibitions described in the previous chapter.

G1 stood for no gamification. G2 represented gamification with only extrinsic rewards. G3 stood for both intrinsic motivation and extrinsic rewards. Because internal motivation is beneficial in theory but difficult to implement with design, G2 was to verify the effectiveness of parents' participation as internal motivation. According to the theory and analysis above, the hypothesis was as follows:

- Assumption 1: If the G2 was better than the G1, the design for external rewards was proved to be effective.
- Assumption 2: If the G3 was better than the G2, the design for internal motivation was proved to be effective.

4.2   Measure

After the game, all the children were asked to do fulfill the Short Flow State Scale-2 (short FSS-2) immediately to measure their concentration and a knowledge test to exam their mastery of Fotiaoqiang a day later.

Knowledge Test. The knowledge test was designed to analyze the educational efficiency by measuring how much knowledge the subjects had remembered. The test consisted of seven multiple-choice questions about Fotiaoqiang, which were all mentioned in the design or the text-based display board. Each question has an option "I don't know" to prevent the subject from guessing the answer and disturb the results.

Short FSS-2. Flow state has been regarded as a positive outcome of gamification. The State Flow scale-2 (FSS-2) is one of the most commonly used methods of heart flow measurement, which is used to measure the flow state under specific conditions. Short FSS-2 is the abbreviated version of it. FFS-2 consists of 36 items, but too many items increase the burden on the subjects. Studies have shown that the average time to complete the Chinese version of FSS-2 is 20.4 min, while the average time to complete the Chinese version of short FSS-2 is only 4.7 min, saving more than 4 times [15]. The reduction of test time not only contributes to the recruitment of the test subjects, but also improves the reliability of their answers. Moreover, the subjects in this experiment were children, so it was difficult for them to complete the complex scale carefully. Moreover, the difficulty of understanding increases after it is translated into Chinese, which may cause greater reading burden on children. So, the abbreviated version was selected.

Short FSS-2 consists of 9items, with one item to represent each of the nine flow dimensions. It is rated on a 5-point Likert scale, ranging from "1" (strongly disagree) to "5" (strongly agree). The score is to sum the 9 items together and then divide by 9.

4.3   Result and Conclusion

The conclusion was that the gamification in this design was positive. The effectiveness of external rewards was obviously positive, while the effectiveness of internal motivation was positive but not very significant. The following is two conclusions corresponding to the two assumptions.

Conclusion 1. G2 was significantly better than G1 in both knowledge test and short FSS-2, which proved that the previous design for gamification of external rewards is positive.

Knowledge Test of G1 and G2. In knowledge test, G1 and G2 was significantly different after the t-test ($P = 0.002 < 0.05$). The children remembered more through the design for gamification of external rewards than no gamification (see Fig. 3).

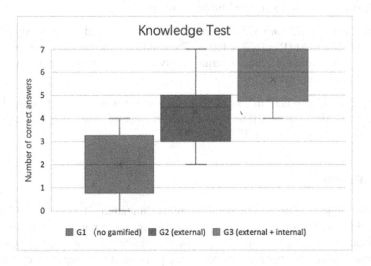

Fig. 3. A box plot of the Knowledge Test.

Short FSS-2 of G1 and G2. In short FSS-2, G1 and G2 was significantly different after the t-test ($P = 0.008 < 0.05$). The children were more absorbed through the design for gamification of external rewards than no gamification (see Fig. 4).

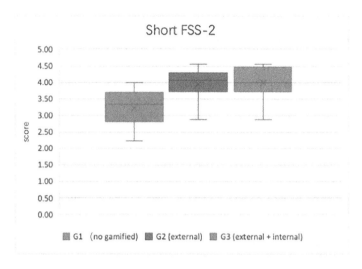

Fig. 4. A box plot of short FSS-2.

Conclusion 2. There was no significant difference between G3 and G2, But the average score of G3 is slightly higher than G2, which proves that the previous design for gamification of internal motivation is positive to some extent, but the difference was not particularly large and still need further research.

Knowledge Test of G2 and G3. In knowledge test, G1 and G2 was significantly different after the t-test ($P = 0.03 < 0.05$). The children remembered more through the design for gamification of both internal motivation and external rewards than no gamification (see Fig. 3).

Short FSS-2 of G2 and G3. In short FSS-2, G2 and G3 was not significantly different after the t-test ($P = 0.8 > 0.05$). The children's state of flow didn't change a lot between these two groups (see Fig. 4).

5 Discussion

As for the subjects, due to the reading ability limitation of G1 and difficulty of understanding the following test, the younger children were not involved. But in fact, the gamification of G3 is very suitable for younger children who are very dependent on their parents, as they are more interested in such games and their dependency will make them more willing to cooperate with parents.

From the results, the effectiveness of gamification in this experiment was obviously positive, but the motivation still needs further research. From the perspective of flow state, the design for internal motivation didn't matters. But in the measurements of knowledge mastery, the result is positive. Maybe it could be partly affected by children being afraid of parents' supervision instead of children's internal motivation.

References

1. Dongju, Z.: Interaction between museums and intangible cultural heritage. Guangxi Ethn. Stud. **2006**, 198–204 (2006)
2. Yoshida, K.: The museum and the intangible cultural heritage. Mus. Int. **56**, 108–112 (2010)
3. The Telegraph – Telegraph Online, 21 Reasons Why I Hate Museums. https://www.telegraph.co.uk/travel/lists/21-reasons-why-I-hate-museums/. Accessed 19 Aug 2014
4. Perry, D.L.: Beyond cognition and affect: the anatomy of a museum visit. In: Visitor Studies, vol. 6, pp. 43–47 (1993)
5. Norman, D.A., Draper, S.W.: User Centered System Design: New Perspectives on Human-Computer Interaction. Lawrence Erlbaum Associates, Hillsdale (1986)
6. Xin, H., Li, N.: The interactive design method in contemporary museum display. Decoration 104–105 (2011)
7. Deterding, S., Sicart, M., Nacke, L., O'Hara, K., Dan, D.: Gamification: using game-design elements in non-gaming contexts (2011)
8. Stuart Brown, L., Vaughan, C.: Play: How it Shapes the Brain, Opens the Imagination, and Invigorates the Soul. Avery, New York (2009)
9. Zhang, P.: Motivational affordances: fundamental reasons for ICT design and use. Commun. ACM **51**, 145–147 (2008)
10. Pu, Y., Zhao, G.: Intrinsic motivation and external incentives. Chin. Manag. Sci. 95–100 (2003)
11. Goehle, G.: Gamification and web-based homework. Primus **23**, 234–246 (2013)
12. Deci, E.L., Koestner, R., Ryan, R.M.: Extrinsic rewards and intrinsic motivation in education: reconsidered once again. Rev. Educ. Res. **71**, 1–27 (2001)
13. Zichermann, G., Cunningham, C.: Gamification by Design. Oreilly Vlg Gmbh & Co., Sebastopol (2011)
14. Csikszentmihalyi, M.: Flow: The Psychology of Optimal Experience. Harper & Row, New York (1990)
15. Jackson, S.A., Eklund, R.C.: Assessing flow in physical activity: the flow state scale-2 and dispositional flow scale-2. J. Sport. Exerc. Psychol. **24**, 133–150 (2002)
16. Procci, K., Singer, A.R., Levy, K.R., Bowers, C.: Measuring the flow experience of gamers: an evaluation of the DFS-2. Comput. Hum. Behav. **28**, 2306–2312 (2012)
17. Hamari, J., Koivisto, J.: Measuring flow in gamification: dispositional flow scale-2. Comput. Hum. Behav. **40**, 133–143 (2014)

Investigation on the Current Status of Qingdao's Li House and Countermeasures for the Reconstruction of Li House Area for Service Design

Wei Xiong[✉], Yun Yang, and Xiaoqing Yu

School of Design, South China University of Technology,
Guangzhou 510640, China
6788036@qq.com

Abstract. Starting from the architectural history, the architectural form and the architectural composition of Li House, through a year-long field research, the paper will thoroughly study the current situation of the existing Li House, explore the cultural connotation and characteristics of the Li House, combine the results of reconstruction of existing Li House, domestic similar cases and service design theory and finally try to propose a number of reconstruction measures in the Li House area. The paper is aimed at integrating the relevant resources of Qingdao Li House, coordinating the research results in various fields and permeating these into the reconstruction of Li House, cultural communication, developing tourism resources and other aspects by the form of service design, and then meet the needs of the cultural inheritance and development of Li House.

Keywords: Li House · Reconstruction measures · Service design

1 Introduction

Li House is a form of architecture formed in the 19th century in Qingdao. Its history is almost coincident with the history of Qingdao in the time span. It is a witness to the history of Qingdao. Qingdao Li House is the result of the collision and blend of colonial culture and local culture in history, but it is also extremely embarrassing existence under the impact of modern culture. For the indigenous people in Qingdao, it carries their memories of the traditional Qingdao culture and the Chinese traditional neighborhood culture. However, compared to the current living conditions and higher economic level, Li House with poor living conditions has gradually kept away from the prosperous age, and even became synonymous with "dirty" and "mess".

© Springer Nature Switzerland AG 2019
A. Marcus and W. Wang (Eds.): HCII 2019, LNCS 11585, pp. 246–263, 2019.
https://doi.org/10.1007/978-3-030-23538-3_19

2   Necessity and Feasibility of Research on Reconstruction of Qingdao Li House Area

2.1   The Destruction of the Li House Buildings Is Serious

The urbanization process has had a huge impact on the Li House buildings. The first is the abnormal population density that makes the Li House overloaded. According to records, the total population of Qingdao in 1933 was only 400,000, but it was close to 4.05 million in the early days of the founding of the People's Republic of China. In contrast, the actual number of the Li House buildings increased from 506 to 513 during the 17 years from 1933 to 1949 [1]. This has led to a reduction in the per capita area of the Li House, and the Li House facilities have been unable to meet the basic needs of modern life. In order to seek space, the crowded residents arbitrarily expanded in the Li House, which inevitably causes damage to the Li House buildings (see Fig. 1).

Fig. 1. Expansion of the Li House

The second is the damage caused by the construction of infrastructure to the Li House buildings. The building of the Li House was built in the late 18th and early 19th centuries. Due to the social conditions at that time, the original Li House was not energized, and one building was only one to four running water supplies according to its size. After the founding of New China, the water pipeline renovated several times, the buildings electrified and the road rebuilt. Each time the construction of infrastructure brought convenience to the local residents, it was also a destruction of the original structure of the Li House.

The fourth is the demolition of the Li House buildings. Due to the exclusion of Japanese architecture during the Japanese occupation of Qingdao, the buildings built at the time were the first to be demolished. Now, the renovation of the old city is still going on. The website of the Qingdao Urban Planning Bureaus shows that a large number of Li House buildings are facing the result of demolition or collection.

The last one is accidental disasters. Most of the Li House buildings are made of wood, and some have collapsed due to disrepair for years. Some of the Li House buildings are uninhabited, and weeds grow rapidly, that accelerating the corrosion and destruction of the buildings. The wooden structure is very prone to fires. The largest-scale Li House Guangxingli suffered a fire in September 2016, which directly caused nearly half of the building to be burned.

2.2   The Bad Image of Li House Is Harmful to the Image of Qingdao

Before China's reform and opening up, Li House was always the commercial center of Qingdao. But after China's reform and opening up, especially in the past two decades, the economic center moved eastward, the establishment of the Laoshan commercial district and the Huangdao development zone all dispersed the commercial functions of the Li House area. At the same time, Li House is located in the core area of Qingdao tourism, surrounded by famous scenic spots of Qingdao, which is in great contrast with the surrounding environment and other buildings (see Fig. 2). In today's Li House, population and construction problems coexist. The image of the Li House has become a tricky problem for the Qingdao government.

Fig. 2. The contrast between the Li House and its surrounding environment

2.3   Feasibility of Reconstruction in Li House Area

In the process of modernization, the importance of cultural heritage has become increasingly prominent, and it has become a symbol of national sovereignty and a basis for determining national identity. In the context of globalization, all countries in the world are concerned about localized heritage protection and renovation to adapt to the development of the times [2].

In order to gain a deeper understanding of the local residents' willingness and the government's intention to reconstruction, in a period of more than one year, our team visited 36 Li House, interviewed 21 households, visited the Zhongshan Road Street office in Qingdao, consulted relevant experts and scholars and issued 350 question-naires. Through interviews and questionnaire surveys, a large number of first-hand data on the history and current situation of the Li House was obtained. The data combined with the government's intentions and experts' views provide strong support for the research on the reconstruction of the Li House.

For the protection and reconstruction of regional cultural heritage, there have been many successful cases in China, which are analyzed in detail later. These provide support for feasibility the reconstruction of the Li House area and provide models and ideas that can be used for reference. In the Li House area, individuals and the government have tried to reconstruct, although the results are not ideal, but it proves that the reconstruction has certain social and economic value and provides ideas for the research on the reconstruction of the Li House.

3 Overview of the Basic Status of Qingdao Li House

3.1 Overview of the History of Li House

The first batch of Li House can be traced back to the Tapautau in the early 20th century. At that time, Qingdao was occupied by the Germans. The German government made a new urban plan in 1898: it was bounded by the Tapautau, the south was the area for white people, and the north was for Chinese [3]. As the demarcation point between Chinese area and European area, the unique geographical location makes the buildings in the Tapautau blend with the characteristics of Chinese and Western buildings. Guangxinli (see Fig. 3), the most well-preserved and largest-scale Li House, which was built in 1897, is a typical representative.

Fig. 3. Panorama of Guangxinli

As a young type of building, the Li House has always changed its architectural form. The external factors of the society drive the change in the Li House, which is reflected in the structure of the building, the structure of the residents, the way of their life, and the cultural. The history of the Li House can be summarized as the two modernizations of the Li House.

The first modernization was based on the beginning of the colonial history of Qingdao, with the emergence and rapid development of the Li House as result. At the end of the 19th century, Germany occupied Qingdao and devoted large amount of financial resources, which greatly promoted the modernization of Qingdao. In the 17 years of being colonized, Qingdao has become a famous port city in China from a fishing village. This has far-reaching implications for the emergence and rapid development of the Li House. In the process of urban planning and construction of the German colonists, the Li House was planned to be the main building of the Tapautau, a Chinese gathering area in the three major districts of Qingdao. The perfect infrastructure and commercial prosperity in the core area of the Tapautau have attracted a large number of people, that provided a population basis for the initial development of the Li House.

The second modernization of the Li House was accompanied by the beginning of the reform and opening up. After the reform and opening up, Qingdao has developed rapidly with its well-preserved economic base and strategic position as an important port city in the north. The modernization and urbanization have made the Li House fall behind the requirements of the times more and more serious. First, there are many problems in the Li House, such as old buildings and mixed residents. Second, the backward structure of the Li House has been unable to meet the increasing demand for the quality of life. More young people have left and driven the middle-aged and older people to leave the Li House. Third, the inhabitants of the migrant population, especially the bottom population, and the loss of the original population have changed the population structure of the Li House, which directly led to the loss of the multi-culture of the Li House. Under the pressure of this, in the government's urban planning for Qingdao, the Li House area was clearly listed as an old city and will be gradually reconstructed.

3.2 Distribution Status of Existing Li House

The Li House is located in the old city of Qingdao, namely the Shinan District and the Shibei District. In the two districts, the Li House is clustered. The Li House expanded on a street-by-street basis (see Fig. 4).

3.3 Architectural Form of the Li House

Li House was called the buildings "compromised Chinese style and foreign style" in the 1922 *Qingdao Outline* [4]. The design style of the Li House combines Chinese and Western architectural styles. First, it conforms to the layout of western modern urban planning ideas and it conforms to the internal structure of traditional Chinese courtyard. Second, it conforms to the stone building system that Western architectural features and it conforms to Chinese-style wooden corridors, doors and windows. It perfectly

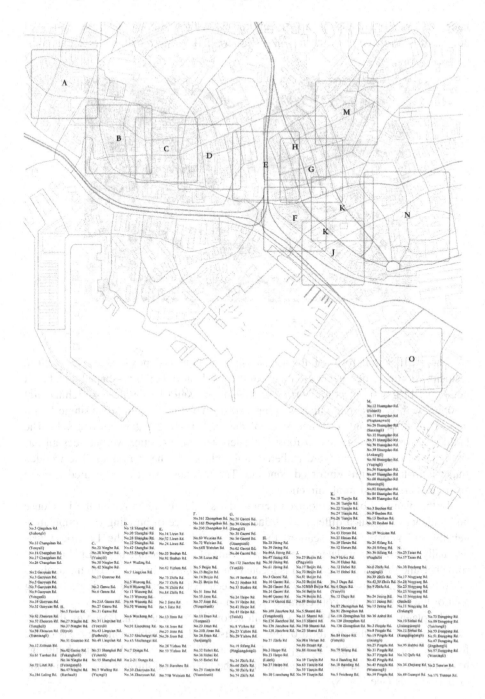

Fig. 4. Information map of distribution of the Li House

integrates western new-style apartment houses with traditional Chinese courtyard houses. It is a reflection of the fusion of Eastern and Western cultures (see Fig. 5).

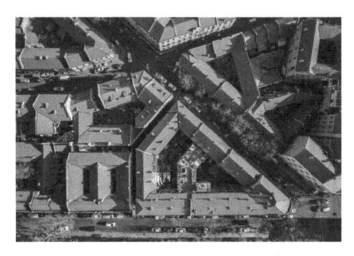

Fig. 5. Top view of Li House

The architectural form of the Li House is unique and novel (see Fig. 6). The residents of the older generation called the Li House the tube-shaped apartment buildings. In the architectural form, the Li House should be defined as architectural complex with courtyards, which is composed of two-story to four-story single buildings. The building unit has three sides of the wall, leaving a door on one side. The building units are connected to form a cluster. The three-section vertical design has skylights on the roof, courtyard gathered in the plane and the front door. The wooden frame is matched with reinforced concrete. The internal layout is structured and the corridor stairs extend in all directions.

In the planning of the colonized period, the single building area of the Li House buildings was not much different, but due to the influence of building use, population density and geographical location, the single building area of the Li House was gradually polarized in its later development. Some of them became larger Li House and some became tiny Li House which is located on the edge of the city. From the analysis of 46 typical Li House (see Fig. 7), it can be seen that the majority of single building area of the Li House are concentrated between 400 m^2 and 700 m^2.

The planning of the Li House was built according to the terrain. Based on the hilly terrain in Qingdao, the flat form of the Li House is also variable. On the basis of the four basic forms ("I" type, "L" type, "冂" type and "匚" type), the Li House buildings have formed a rich and varied planar form in the later period through the combination of basic forms (see Fig. 8).

Fig. 6. The architectural form of the Li House

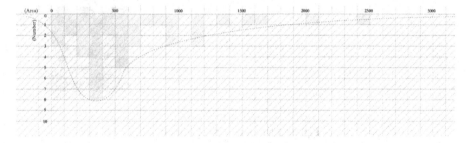

Fig. 7. Chart of the single building area of the Li House buildings

3.4 Cultural Connotation and Characteristics of Li House

Li House, as a representative of Qingdao, is closely related to Qingdao's history, humanities and residents' lifestyles. The culture of the Li House, which was born out, developed and even disappeared because of the influence of the buildings themselves and society.

Inclusiveness of Immigration Culture. As a colonized city, it decided Qingdao's early immigration culture. During the German occupation period, the immigrant population in Qingdao increased rapidly, and the Li House played an important role in carrying the immigrant population. The residence of the Li House was divided into three categories at that time: the business center of Zhongshan Road as a commercial center, the residents of Xizhen were handicraftsmen, and the Li House around customs were more engaged in railway and port related staff. In the Li House, people of all

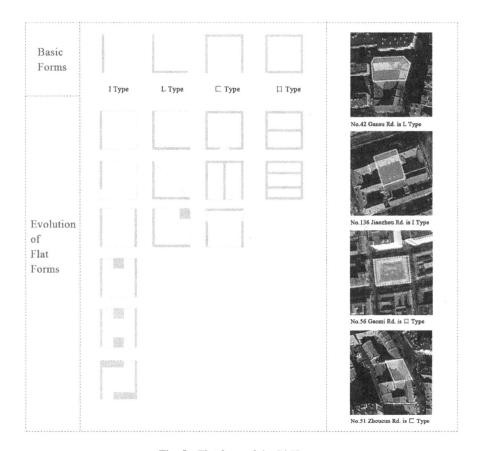

Fig. 8. Flat form of the Li House

social class and birthplace can find their place here. This inclusiveness of architecture constitutes a unique immigrant culture in the culture of the Li House.

Unique Neighborhood Culture. The unique structure of the Li House promotes the birth of a unique neighborhood culture. Compared with the characteristics of personal privacy and the pursuit of personal freedom in the Western architectural structure, the early residents of the Li House were influenced by the tough social environment and the traditional concept of "neighbors are better than distant relatives". They help each other and live in harmony. "One house is a small family and one courtyard is a big family." The residents in the Li House familiar with each other and help each other.

Commercial and Entertainment Center for Commercial and Residential Use. The special commercial and residential dual-use function, dense population and the core urban area of Qingdao make each Li House, especially the large Li House, play a rule of commercial and entertainment center which is similar to modern department before the reform and opening up. The role of the Li House forms the unique culture of the center of commercial and entertainment. According to records, before the founding of

China, the Li House was full of shops, and the service industries were also intertwined. For example, the largest existing Li House, Guangxingli, was used as a cinema; Pingkangwuli used to be the largest and most famous brothel in Qingdao; the Jiangning Hall in the Pichaiyuan was the most prosperous teahouse in Qingdao. The whole area only needs one kind of building that can meet commercial and residential needs. It can be rare in China to satisfy people's living and entertainment.

3.5 A Summary of the Living Conditions of Li House Residents

Population Structure of Li House. During the German occupation period, the Li House has become a place that people yearn for in Qingdao and its surrounding areas because of the commercial and residential use. During this period, the population structure of the Li House has three characteristics. First, in age composition, people aged 20–55 were dominant. The age of the population tended to be younger, that injected vitality into the economic and cultural development of the Li House. Second, the occupational composition was influenced by the immigrant culture of Qingdao. Most of the residents were immigrants and they were generally individual merchants. It was also the basis for the economic prosperity of the Li House. Third, in terms of population, the prosperity of the Li House has attracted more and more people. The population has increased rapidly during this period.

After the reform and opening up, the population structure of the Li House has undergone big changes. A large number of outsiders poured into Qingdao. A lot of original residents of the Li House moved out and sold or leased the house to migrant

Table 1. Demographic characteristics of Li House

Item	Index	Proportion (%)
Gender	Male	62.5
	Female	37.5
Age	Under 45	12.2
	45–50	36.5
	51–60	35.4
	Above 60	15.4
Population structure	Original residents	23.2
	Migrant workers	76.8
Educational level	Illiteracy	4.2
	Primary school	23.8
	Junior high school	50.9
	High school	16.3
	Specialty, undergraduate and above	4.8
Monthly income	Under 2500 yuan	8.0
	2501 yuan–4000 yuan	47.4
	4001 yuan–5500 yuan	32.2
	Above 5500 yuan	12.4

workers who pursued price and geographical advantage. The resident composition was transformed into migrant workers and original residents. According to our research in 2016 (see Table 1), there were only two or three families of original residents in each Li House, and the other residents were migrant workers. Due to the needs of urban construction planning, the government demolished some of the dilapidated Li House and residents were forced to leave. The population of the Li House is decreasing year by year.

Living Conditions of Residents in the Li House. The purpose of the reconstruction of the Li House is to protect the traditional buildings of the Li House, and on the other hand, to improve the lives of local residents. It is most meaningful to investigate and study the living conditions of the residents from the basic needs of their lives. Through this research on the state of living conditions, it is possible to bring different ideas to the protection and reconstruction of the Li House.

Cooking. Most families do not have a separate kitchen, they are cooking in a temporary kitchen of less than two square meters on an outdoor aisle. The health conditions in the Li House are extremely poor, and the conditions for cooking and eating are simple. Residents use natural gas, induction cookers, gas and a simple cooking pot to cook. A small number of residents eat outside.

Toilet. The majority of residents use public toilets inside the Li House. Some public toilets are unmanaged. The drainage system is seriously blocked. Excreta disposal is not timely, which causing stinky smell. Some residents in small Li House coordinate to clean toilets, so the toilets are better sanitary.

Sanitation Status. The resident population of Li House has decreased and the number of people renting has increased. No one is responsible for public areas, so sanitation is poor. There is not enough indoor storage space, and the aisles are full of debris, which appears to be very messy. Even some residents' daily garbage is thrown directly from the upper floor.

Property Security. The doors of the Li House are made of wood. In the past, residents used padlocks outside the door. It is known that there have been several incidents of property theft. After that, padlocks were changed to rim locks, but it still could not solve the theft problem fundamentally.

Fire Problem. The Li House buildings have a large number of wooden structures. And they have debris piles, small entrances and exits, no clear fire instructions and fire equipment. The residents lack basic fire awareness. There are serious safety hazards.

4   Research on the Countermeasures for the Reconstruction of Li House Area

4.1   Domestic Reconstruction Case Analysis

The Five Avenues. The Five Avenues in Tianjin is the most exclusive residential area in the British Concession in the early 20th century. For more than 100 years, it has retained its original streets and is currently the largest and most complete foreign concession in China. The reconstruction of The Five Avenues completely preserved the buildings at that time, avoiding the consequences of the destruction of the original historical features after the large-scale demolition of other cities in China. The Tianjin government has adopted a small-scale, gradual update model. The focus is on protecting the historical appearance of buildings of The Five Avenues and coordinating with the surrounding environment. It embedding the social functions required by some modern societies into the original buildings under the premise of not destroying the outlook of historical buildings.

Kulangsu. Kulangsu in Xiamen is be called "Architecture Expo". This is because Kulangsu was occupied by many countries in the early 20th century and built embassies. Xiamen attaches great importance to the historical identification and protection of embassies of various countries. At the same time of protection, tourism is introduced as a development factor. Local residents benefit from the tourism industry and cooperate with the development of the tourism industry to make other historical buildings fully used. After the tourism industry in Kulangsu was fully developed, the local government formulated laws to restrict tourists and required merchants to undertaking the responsibility of protecting historic buildings while develop their own business.

4.2   Existing Case of Li House Reconstruction

The existing case of reconstruction of the Li House is a single building reconstruction and reuse, but there is no research in the overall planning and reconstruction.

Pichaiyuan in Li House. Located in the commercial circle of Zhongshan Road in Qingdao, Pichaiyuan was once the food and entertainment center in the 1930s and 1940s. After the reform and opening up, the catering industry was still booming. However, after the 1990s, due to the eastward movement of the city center, the Zhongshan Road business district gradually declined. The Pichaiyuan became deserted and lost its original vitality.

Conditions Before and After the Reconstruction. Before the reconstruction in 2007, the Pichaiyuan was already ruined. The original old buildings inside the Pichaiyuan were mixed with illegal buildings. The living condition in the Pichaiyuan was also evil. Due to years of disrepair, the wooden stairs were corrupt, and the corridor and the walls were cracked.

In 2007, the Qingdao Municipal Government re-planned and reconstruct it. The Pichaiyuan finally restored its original features and the economy began to revive. Today's Pichaiyuan is a food street that is loved by local people and tourists in Qingdao.

Reconstruction Positioning. The area where the Pichaiyuan is located has a high density of buildings and an excellent location, which makes the Pichaiyuan no longer suitable for the original functional mode. Considering this situation, The Qingdao Municipal Government positioned its reconstruction as a commercial street of food that reflects the local culture of Qingdao.

Planning Layout of Reconstruction. Taking the Jiangning Road Cross Street as the axis, the Pichaiyuan is divided into a snack street and four functional areas (see Table 2).

Table 2. A snack street and four functional areas (Quoted from *Protection and Renovation of Qingdao Li House Buildings*)

Functional areas	Introduction
Jiangning Road Snack Street	Keep the street pattern and façade form of Jiangning Road unchanged. By re-division of indoor space and improvement of various infrastructures, the original snacks of original Pichaiyuan will be regrouped. The popularity of the entire Pichaiyuan will be driven by the snack street
Specialty dining area	Based on the new stage of No. 10 Li House on Jiangning Road, combined with small-scale performances and other activities, small and medium-sized restaurants with special features are developed
Folk inn area	After the reconstruction of No. 34 Li House of Jiangning Road, No. 5 and No. 11 Li House of Tianjin Road, they are used as a folk inn with the cultural of Li House
Recreation area	The area of No. 33 Li House of Hebei Road, No. 23 Li House of Jiangning Road and No. 5 Li House of Jiangning Road is transformed into a special industrial zone with entertainment as the mainstay and snacks as the supplement
Local snack area	Setting Qingdao's first snack block in the region by introduction of snacks with distinctive features from all over China. At the same time, build a temporary exhibition building where visitors can learn about the Pichaiyuan and culture of Qingdao

Lessons Learned. What can be learned: First, the implementer of the reconstruction is the Qingdao Municipal Government. While protecting the original features of the historical district, it also considers the tourism development and building protection in the area. Second, in the reconstruction of the Pichaiyuan, the means of functional replacement has been adopted, and while restoring its historical positioning, it has also brought about the economic recovery of the surrounding areas. Third, it has adopted a step-by-step reconstruction to protect the basic features of the Li House buildings as much as possible, highlighting the Li House culture.

Inadequacies: First, the investment is too large, and the rate of return is slow. Second, some buildings have been dismantled for new construction, which has destroyed their original features.

Li House Inn. Li House Inn is located at No. 10 Baoding Road, south of the west gate of Pichaiyuan, next to Zhongshan Road. The Li House Inn was originally a dilapidated Li House. It was transformed into a hotel by private investment. It was repaired on the basis of not destroying its original structure and combined with modern architecture and home design (see Fig. 9).

Fig. 9. Li House Inn (Color figure online)

Li House Inn has 35 separate rooms. Due to the characteristics of the Li House buildings, the structure of each room is different, and the decoration is different. It shows the unique structure of Li House. There is an open-air table in the courtyard for visitors to chat, so that guests can return to the time of "neighborhood harmony".

Architectural Environment Design for the Reconstruction of Li House Inn. In the reconstruction design process of the Li House Inn, the designer restores the original historical features as the main goal. Through the reconstruction of the existing Li House and the use of modern new materials and decorative styles, the combination of new and old is realized.

In order to continue the style of the historic buildings in the Li House, the Li House Inn did not change the original structure of the house, and retained and repaired the red wooden railings, red tiles, wooden stairs and other features of the Li House. In the details, the color of the building still uses the original color of the Li House, but with minor adjustments to create a retro but warm atmosphere.

On the Corridor of the Li House Inn, the contrast photos before and after the reconstruction of the Li House Inn were hanged to help visitors understand the structure of the Li House.

Lessons Learned. What can be learned: First, the Li House Inn has largely restored the historical architecture of the Li House. Second, the reconstruction of the Li House Inn is a fusion of tradition and modernity, enriching the image of the Li House; Third, it makes full use of the commercial value of the Li House.

Inadequacies: First, the implementation of the reconstruction is limited to individuals and small groups. Second, the scope of the reconstruction is small, not enough to be used as a model for the reconstruction of all the Li House.

Through the analysis of the above two cases of reconstruction of the Li House, it can be seen that the reconstruction of the Pichaiyuan is dominated by the government for the purpose of the revival of the old city and the economic and tourism development. The reconstruction of the Li House Inn is dominated by individuals and small groups in order to make full use of the new commercial value developed by the Li House. Although both of them have made different attempts to reform the Li House, the results are not ideal. The Li House has not fully played its role in the new era, and its influence is not great.

4.3   Research on the Reconstruction of the Li House Under the Service Design

The Combination of Li House Reconstruction and Service Design. From the analysis of many domestic cases, in the old city reconstruction based on the unique architectural form, highlighting its service function to people is the main trend. Li House is an old building form with the same history as Qingdao. The problems of architecture, society and population in its area are complex. To rebuild it, we must balance the relationships among architecture, economy, society and residents [5]. It is one of the feasible ways to explore the countermeasures for the reconstruction of Li House in combination with service design for the bottleneck encountered in the reconstruction of Li House at present.

In recent years, service design has gradually penetrated into all aspects of social production from the field of design specialty [6]. Service design is integrated into life, changing human's view of the world and human's way to life [7]. Service design is a comprehensive design that combines tangible products and intangible services [8]. Effective integration of service design into the reconstruction research of Li House can bring new concepts for protecting Li house buildings and inheriting Li house culture.

From the point of view of service design, it is meaningless to study architecture alone [9]. The change of architectural form is the result of adapting to the development of society. All architectural forms serve people's life. The residential function of the Li House is bound to be eliminated in the process of social and economic development. The decline and extinction of the Li House buildings are accompanied by the cultural heritage of Qingdao and the spiritual sustenance of the first generation of Qingdao people. However, the Li House only lost its actual habitability, and its social, cultural and economic value can still play its role through service design. The combination of architectural reconstruction and service design [10]. The Li House without residential function, after reasonable reconstruction, can provide people with more other services, and even better inheritance of cultural heritage.

Exploration of the Reconstruction of Li House

Based on the Development of Qingdao Tourism. From the successful cases of the reconstruction of Li House, the main line is the development of tourism and the reconstruction of Li House. Qingdao is a famous tourist city in China, and the Li House Cluster is located at the core of Qingdao tourist area, with a huge flow of people. Combining the tourism industry with the unique architectural form of Li House will revitalize the vitality of the old buildings, give tourism cultural new connotation, and even become a new feature of Qingdao tourism.

As a typical seasonal tourist city, Qingdao takes the seashore as its tourism characteristic, which is greatly influenced by the season. In the peak season, the scenic spots are crowded, while in the off season, tourists are scarce. If we develop tourism routes that do not depend on the coast, such as Li House, it will help to disperse the flow of tourists, improve the tourist experience, expand the tourism diversity of Qingdao and get rid of the current tourism pattern which is greatly affected by the season. With the development of tourism in coastal cities such as Yantai and Weihai nearby, Qingdao's tourism industry has been impacted. Qingdao urgently needs to develop other special tourism routes besides coastal tourism.

Overall Planning. To maximize the role of the Li House, it is impossible to achieve it only by the reconstruction of some Li House. Both the Pichaiyuan and the Li House Inn are attempts to do reconstruction in a single Li House. Although the actual habitability of the Li House has been transferred to the tourism industry, it has not had a great impact in China. The main reason is that there is no overall planning for the whole Li House area, the value of each part of the Li House area is not fully utilized, and the relationship between each part is not well coordinated.

Therefore, the best choice for the reconstruction of Li House is to make overall planning, so that the reconstruction of Li House not only serves the tourism industry, but also serves the architectural protection, cultural inheritance and the life of the residents of the Li House. While protecting the Li House buildings, the local residents can benefit from it, so that the residents may not move out, and the culture of Li House can be preserved and inherited.

Li House buildings is relatively centralized. The historic cities with centralization include Pingyao ancient city in Shanxi Province and Wuzhen in Jiaxing. Their development is to delimit a region as a tourist area, in which there are no manufacturers or other industries unrelated to tourism services. Therefore, the Li House area can be built as a tourism service area in entirety, encouraging and supporting the original residents transform into the service industry. Some old-fashioned catering businesses in Li House can also be retained to form Qingdao characteristic catering. The unique space structure of Li House buildings will give tourists different experience from other residential quarters. Therefore, some of the well-preserved Li House can also be transformed into characteristic residential quarters according to the original room pattern, in order to form an integrated tourism service system of entertainment, experience, catering and accommodation.

Make Full Use of the Unique Architectural Form of Li House. The unique architectural form of Li House is the biggest characteristic of Li House area. This unique architectural form provides a variety of possibilities for its reconstruction. The combination of Chinese quadrangle and Western apartments makes it unique in shape, reasonable in layout and large in capacity. It can be used for visiting or reconstructed into museums, showrooms, apartments and residential quarters. Commercial and residential building form can be transformed into shops, business districts, tourist streets, etc.

From the perspective of propaganda after reconstruction, the unique architectural form of Li House itself is a kind of propaganda material. During the research period, we met a crew who was filming in Pingkangwuli. After consulting the newspaper, the buildings in Li House area have attracted film and television crews to shoot many times. Some buildings with image shooting value can be repaired and restored. They can be planned to be small film bases that be used for tourists to visit and film crews to shoot. Film taken in the Li House can play a propaganda role for Li House.

Combining with Li House Culture and Qingdao Culture. Li House culture mentioned above is a unique culture based on Li House architecture. In the reconstruction of Li House area, it must be supported by Li House culture. First of all, in the process of reconstruction of Li House, we should not abandon the culture of Li House or only repair Li House buildings and make use of its economic value. Li House culture is a kind of inclusive culture. This inclusive spirit is embodied in the reconstruction of the old architectural form and the development of the new era. The reconstruction must combine Li House buildings with the development of the times. Second, we can make full use of Li House culture in the service function of Li House. The characteristics of neighborhood culture in Li House culture are missing in the contemporary era, so it can be transformed into a unique experience and integrated into the service of Li House, such as creating the atmosphere of neighborhood in Li House tourism service and enhancing the experience of "neighborhood harmony" that consumers desire.

In addition, Qingdao is rich in local folk culture which can be display and exhibition in Li House building. Some similar examples made success in China such as 798 Art Park in Beijing, Liangzhu Culture Village in Taiwan and Tianzifang in Shanghai. There are also Creative 100 Park in Qingdao, but Creative 100 Park is a purely creative industry, not combined with Qingdao characteristics. Therefore, the local folk culture and art of Qingdao can be introduced into Li House area to create an innovative Park combining artistic innovation with traditional architectural folklore. This is not only conducive to the spread of Qingdao folk culture, but also conducive to increasing the influence of Li House area.

5   Conclusion

In the process of urbanization in China, the phenomenon of "Same Imagine of the Cities" is serious. The historical heritage of many cities is covered by modernization. As a part of the cultural heritage of Qingdao and one of the main components of the texture of the old city, the Li House buildings are being destroyed more and more seriously, and they are no longer suitable for people to live in. At the same time, the culture of the Li House is also declining. Therefore, the protection of the Li House is urgent. The reconstruction of the Li House ought to be based on the characteristics of the Qingdao tourist city, combine with the unique architectural form of Li House, consider comprehensively the life of the residents and include the culture of Li House.

References

1. Chen, Q.: The Investigation of Reform and Reuse for Li House in Qingdao. Xi'an University of Architecture and Technology (2014)
2. He, C.J.: Beijing Traditional Courtyard Buildings to Protect and Re-utilization. Beijing Forestry University (2010)

3. Liu, Q.: Research on Protection and Utilization of Material Culture Heritage in Qingdao Area. Shandong University (2010)
4. Huang, B.Q.: Research on old architecture status of Zhongshan road in Qingdao City. Shanxi Archit. **40**(30), 8–10 (2014)
5. Li, C.: A research on service design based on the well-being and cultural demand of the elderly. Design (1), 162–164 (2014)
6. Shostack, G.L.: Designing services that deliver. Harvard Bus. Rev. **41**(1), 133–139 (1984)
7. Kimbell, L.: Designing for service as one way of designing services. Int. J. Des. **5**(2), 41–52 (2011)
8. Xin, X.Y., Cao, J.: Positioning service design. Packag. Eng. **39**(18), 43–49 (2018)
9. Han, B.X., He, S.: Research on urban vegetable market service design based on social innovation background. Design (23), 11–13 (2018)
10. Sangiorgi, D., Junginger, S.: Emerging issues in service design. Des. J. **18**(2), 165–170 (2015)

Reflection on Museum Service Design Based on a UX Foundation Course

Di Zhu, Wei Liu[(✉)], and Yaru Lv

Beijing Normal University, Beijing 100875, China
{di.zhu,wei.liu}@bnu.edu.cn, yaru.lv@mail.bnu.edu.cn

Abstract. This is a reflection paper, based on empirical experience that artic-ulates a new attitude towards the use of methods to stimulate creativity in first year UX master students. It describes reflections from UX Foundation, a project-based course of UX master program. A real project to enhance user experience of the Beijing Natural and History Museum. It was the first-time students teamed up and did a service design project. Based on previous two iterations of the course, teaching team carefully designed the curriculum, methodological logic and supplementary materials. This paper clustered series reflections which learned from a particular practical experience and feedback collected from teaching team and students. Benefits and improvements can help teaching team to improve the next iteration of the course.

Keywords: User experience · UX education · Service design · UX Foundation

1 Introduction

Beijing Normal University (BNU) is running China's first User eXperience (UX) master program in faculty of psychology. UX Foundation course is a basic course in curriculum that equips classical design thinking process and foster user centered perspective. Students will divide into several groups and work on a same project. Every year the course will introduce different project into class. This year, UX Foundation course had a collaboration with Beijing Natural and History Museum.

1.1 UX Master Program in China

In 2016, a new master program titled "User Experience" (UX) was founded at Beijing Normal University (BNU). A rising number of students with multi-disciplinary undergraduate degrees apply for the entrance exam each year. However, not more than seventy students are admitted (Beijing Normal University 2015). This first UX master in China has - for Chinese education tradition - an innovative approach: it is interactive, practice- oriented, module based and project-based. UX Master aims to support the design and development of new products, services and systems in the conceptual design phase, by developing innovative methods and techniques, foster user centered designers and leading multi-disciplinary projects. Our main research and education

© Springer Nature Switzerland AG 2019
A. Marcus and W. Wang (Eds.): HCII 2019, LNCS 11585, pp. 264–274, 2019.
https://doi.org/10.1007/978-3-030-23538-3_20

directions: User Research, Smart Living (Driving) and Working, Context and Concept, Interactive Technology, Embodied and Tangible Interaction, and Service Design. UX Master closely collaborates with both national and international innovation companies. And it focuses on user, context, emotion, interaction, technology and human factors, through practicing innovation design thinking (Sun and Teng 2017). Until the end of 2018, UX Master has collaborated over 20 companies which have different field.

1.2 UX Foundation Course

UX Foundation course is an integrated course in the first semester. Every year the course will combine with the latest research field and topic. It aims to equip students with UX theory while gaining practical experience in a real project setting. And it will invite experts to join in the project. This year, it was third iterations and collaborated with Beijing Museum of Natural History and topic was museum service design. This course promotes UX research and explore how psychology, design, technology, and business could integrate together. So, this course will combine four keywords together and help students to build a basic knowledge of user experience and give them a broad view of two years studies. Projects' topic comes from a real company and the course will use a real project setting that invites mentors to supervise each group and invites stakeholders to evaluate outcomes. And after this course, every group can provide designers, researcher, or developers at companies with first-hand data, insights, or mockups on new ways.

1.3 Beijing Museum of Natural History

Beijing Museum of Natural History grew out of the preparation department of National Central Museum of Natural History founded in 1951. Beijing Museum of Natural History was formally named in 1962 (Beijing Museum of Natural History 2018). Being the first large-scale museum of natural history founded on our own strength after new China was established, the museum bears three main functions: the specimen collection, the academic research and the science popularization of paleontology, zoology, botany. The permanent exhibitions in the Beijing Museum of Natural History are mainly arranged according to the evolutionary trend of organisms, showing the Biodiversity and its relationships with the environments and establishing a panorama of the emergence and development of life on Earth (Fig. 1).

1.4 Conclusion

It was the first collaboration with Beijing Museum of Natural History. The museum has small space rather than latest museums, and research found that interactive facilities are rarely used because of bad service design. So, the museum wanted to improve user experience of services.

Fig. 1. Front gate of Beijing Museum of Natural History

2   Setting

This course had 5 internal mentors who are teachers in UX master program and 5 external mentors who are from Beijing Museum of Natural History. And 68 students divided into 14 groups which worked on different target user groups and 3 design briefs during 1 and half months.

2.1   Mentors and Students

It had internal mentors who taught students user experience methodology and external mentors to critic solutions from stakeholders' perspective. Mentors are all from different background and have different expertise. Museum experts regularly joined the course, attended presentation sessions, and provided feedback, in order to make sure the end results can provide the museum with key designs and growth opportunities. 68 first-year students were divided into 14 groups, 4–5 students from different background worked together on a design brief assigned by museum.

As Fig. 2, showed, students are from various background: Science (45%), Engineering (26%), Management (12%), Literature (9%), Economics (3%), Law (3%), Art (1%) and Medicine (1%).

2.2   Design Brief and Resource

The Museum assigned 3 design briefs to 14 groups. Improve user experience of basic services, exhibitions hardware, educational activities. The project focused on service

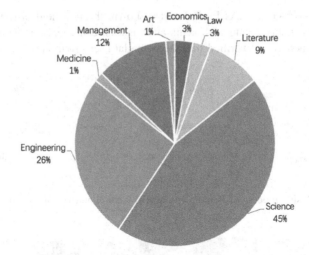

Fig. 2. Proportion of different majors during the undergraduate period

design. In the first topic, students should focus on general context in a service industry. In the second topic, students should concentrate more on hardware interaction includes text, layout, and embodied interaction. In the last topic, students should do a lot of research on existing educational activities. The museum designed exclusive identification to help students to interview participants. So, students had free entrance at any time to visit the museum and it was an official activity which authorized by the Museum. Teaching team set up review time for each group every week to make sure each group has a right direction and advised students.

2.3 Conclusion

Under guidance of internal and external mentors, each group started their first UX project and chose 1 or 2 topics. During these months, students worked hard to define target user groups and scenarios. The museum has good opinions on final outcome.

3 Design Process

To make this project more feasible, teaching team designed a whole process for students, as it was the first time they did a UX project. Research process can be divided into the following three design thinking phases: expropriation by interviewing and observing participants. Definition by connecting different kinds of user research results and prioritizing insights. And visualization by drawing storyboards, journey maps and shooting videos.

3.1 Exploration

In order to understand how museum services work, how visitors interact with exhibition (Folkmann 2010), so that students can generally understand this field and explore target user groups. As Figs. 3 and 4 shown, through field observing, experiencing products, interviewing with staffs and visitors, can deeply understand human-exhibition interaction and verified that the potential user group is researchable.

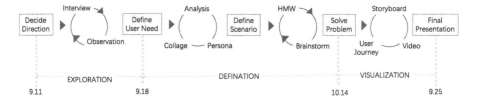

Fig. 3. Design process of Beijing Museum of Natural and History service design

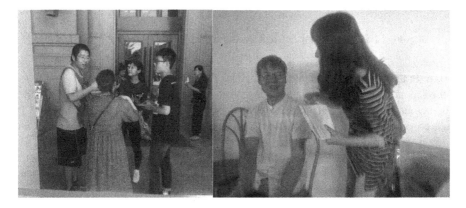

Fig. 4. Students interviewing visitors in the Museum

Every group iterated interview outlines twice to dig out further information of target user's pain points and user needs. For instance, in order to understand how users to approach the museum information, instead of asking that how do you know the information about Nature Museum, students asked what made you decide to visit the museum.

3.2 Definition

When students collected a large number of first-hand user research data. They combined all kinds of results together to analyze user needs. As Fig. 5 shown, it can help students to define for whom and for what problem or challenge they plan to design (Van Boeijen et al. 2014). Through previous understanding of target user group, divergent thinking and summarizing several key points of target user group. And then each group built a persona in order to help solve design questions. These personas need to be based on user research and can also be described in narrative form.

Fig. 5. Collage of a group

Based on persona to brainstorm potential scenarios and solutions. And according to feedback from mentors to prioritize solutions.

3.3 Visualization

Storytelling is increasingly used in user experience field today in order to use a vivid way to show ideas. This trend echoes the deeply rooted need of all humans to be entertained. Stories are illustrative, easily memorable and allow any firm to create stronger emotional bonds with the users (Hummels and Frens 2009). So, this course used user journey map, story board and video scenario to tell stories.

As shown in Fig. 6, story board is a graphic organizer in the form of illustrations or images displayed in sequence for the purpose of pre-visualizing a video and how to use main features.

Fig. 6. Story board of a group

4   Reflection of Mentors

It can conclude following reflection by interviewing both internal mentors and external mentors.

4.1   Highlight of UX Foundation Course

This course has several highlights. This project had 14 groups which focused on different user group to understand their needs. It covered users from 6–65 years old and supplied a gap of variety (Kann 2014). And the museum will have more options. This project can generate more social benefit rather than other projects in UX Foundation Course, because Beijing Museum of Natural History is a nonprofit organization which main feature is servicing all of people.

After deploying some solutions of 14 groups, citizens will get the real benefit of user experience improvements. Service design is a popular branch of user experience which concentrates on touch points in the whole service process. Sometimes it will be invisible in our daily life but do affect a lot. This course gave students a chance to expose themselves to new development. Design briefs came from real need of the museum. Students can approach high quality information that collected from real users within a long period. Based on these opportunities, students had more suitable context to learn user experience methods and practice skills in real project setting.

4.2   Opportunities of Involving Stakeholders

It is a tradition of UX master program to involve stakeholders into projects, by face to face meeting or online meeting. It can help teaching team to bridge the differences between an academic field and a industry field. This course invited many stakeholders who have rich museums management and services design experience and abundant working experience. Based on rich experience in the museum industry, they brought a lot of opportunities to the course.

They reviewed solutions from museum experts' perspective and give more well-directed and useful comments. Stakeholders built a bridge between the Museum and students. They helped students to contact more users include visitors and staffs. It helped research was conducted very well and saved time. Stakeholders provided a lot of professional resources according to different progress of groups. So, students can reach out more targets information instead of misleading information.

4.3   Balance of Academic Research and Real Project

In both developed and developing countries, a gap exists between universities and industry (Baumer et al. 2014). In developed and industrialized countries. Universities are in the process of forsaking their ivory towers and forging strong links with industry, mainly through sponsored research and continuing education (Zaky and Elfaham 1998). Collaboration always needs to gap between companies and universities.

In this course, the museum didn't mention limitations such as money, technology and target user group. So, students had more space to come up with more innovative ideas. When students working on a project, the teaching team encourages them to think about a real-world limitation, but don't want to limit their innovation (Xin et al. 2018). Teaching team should keep a good balance between academic and industrial.

4.4   Conclusion

This course has several highlights that involved stakeholders into project and kept good balance between academic research and real project.

5   Reflection of Students

After this project, teaching team collected reflection from each group, including feedback, experience and suggestions.

5.1   Opportunities and Challenges in Multi-disciplinary Team Work

Teams work better when the team members know everyone has a voice and can express their dissent and support openly without concerns of retaliation. Some students were afraid of speaking their ideas and comments in a group. It is nice to let them know every opinion should be valued. One benefit of teamwork is its ability to promote unity within an organization. Every team was cross-functional, bringing in individuals from several different background. Many teams are insightful and creative because they draw on a variety of backgrounds in terms of expertise and experience. For instance, a group has a psychology background student who is good at user research, an engineering student who understands how to make it come true, and a marketing student to help them to build a business mode. This diversity can lend itself to innovative ideas and cutting-edge solutions that would not be possible without the combined skills and experience of the team.

Communication among team members often is difficult. This might be especially true of teams that have not had much experience working together in the past. In this case, it was the first collaboration. As a result, many groups spent a lot of time on team work but it was not effective. They can set a deadline to keep it effective. And some students need a *translator* or facilitator to translate language on their own. It will take some time, but they have to adapt themselves into a different context.

5.2   Improvement of Professional Skills

After the final presentation of this project, students thought they can improve their professional skills in two years. They found that progress control skill is very important to make sure project into a right arrangement. In this project, some group stayed up late until midnight before deadline, because they overestimated their ability. Based on performance of the final presentation, many groups thought that they can do it better.

Professionals need to be capable of speaking to others clearly and presenting information effectively. Almost every course requires some public speaking.

To think critically, students should learn how to put aside any assumptions or judgments and merely analyze the information they receive. They need to be objective, evaluating ideas without bias, especially when listen to experts' comments, it doesn't mean you are wrong. It means you should think more carefully.

5.3   Benefits of Project and Module Based Learning

This course used a new teaching and learning approach-project and module-based teaching and learning (PMBTL). The PMBTL approach incorporates the merits of project/problem based and module-based learning methods, and overcomes the limitations of these methods (Hou 2014). It introduced a real-world design brief for the project, and students' attention was attracted by discussions and hands on sessions. Students benefited a lot from practice class tutor, and achieved better outcomes of using the designed practice materials in practice classes (De Vos et al. 2018). And teaching team provided students with examples, reference materials, templates and samples in the assignment design. It greatly helped students understand the assignment requirements and ensure their assignments are on the right track. Students really like assignment assessment that is designed not only for the teaching team to assess the quality of student assignment work, but also for students to get a guidance of doing the project properly and professionally.

UX Mater Program create a module-based curriculum. So, each course will last 2–3 months. As a foundation of 2 years study, it connects User Research, User Interface Design, Experimental Design and Technology in Psychology, etc. Students studied UX Foundation course on weekends under guidance of the teaching team. During week days, every group did a lot of field research.

5.4   Conclusion

As a result, students were motivated to study and apply their knowledge and skills comprehensively and professionally. With this teaching and learning method, students can get an overall picture of the user experience design rather than individual facts, understand the teaching and learning content better, know how to apply what they have learned, and learn how to use these methods to solve real problems.

6   Discussion

Although the course was for most of the students an introduction to design thinking and UX design, the underlying idea was to let students discover by themselves that they can be creative and understand the general process of UX design. Overall, the learning outcomes of the course were largely met, but there is still an opportunity to improve them as well as the flow of the course. UX research always requires a larger sample size to ensure a representative distribution of the population and to be considered representative of groups of people to whom results will be generalized or transferred. But because of lack of funding, students couldn't recruit participants from a wide range. Next year course should enhance observation and in-depth interview practice, so that students can dig more information from users. And select some desk research papers to students. Then they will know how to conduct a good literature review and it can help them to define their target user groups. Teaching team should set more time on reflection session, and assign an article to students to write down their feedback and reflections. Useful feedback can help teaching team to update the course setting. This course does not rely on any quantitative evidence or rigorous modeling, but on empirical knowledge. So, in the next iteration, the course can use some quantitative methods to combine qualitative research with quantitative research.

7 Conclusion

Based on the previous two iterations of the course, teaching team carefully designed the curriculum, methodological logic and supplementary materials. This project-based course had produced 14 schemes over 1 and half months. Beijing Museum of Natural History would implement several results. With an agile user experience design approach, the project is delivered via a series of iterations, continually evolving and improving, and delivering a robust, tried and tested solution that is fully-rounded and ready to present. And this course invited experts who have rich museums management and services design experience and abundant working experience. They brought a lot of opportunities to the course.

Acknowledgements. We thank all students for their enthusiasm and hard work. We thank Li Jianwen, Hongtao Zhao, Miao Jin, Yuhui Chai and Jing Liu for their knowledge. We thank Beijing Museum of Natural History for trust. We thank faculty of psychology at BNU for their support.

References

Baumer, E.P., Khovanskaya, V., Matthews, M., Reynolds, L., Schwanda Sosik, V., Gay, G.: Reviewing reflection: on the use of reflection in interactive system design. In: Proceedings of the 2014 Conference on Designing Interactive Systems, pp. 93–102. ACM, June 2014
Beijing Normal University: School of psychology holds ceremony for UX lab and user experience and human-computer interaction & professional postgraduate UX enrollment conference (2015). http://english.bnu.edu.cn/universitynews/79105.htm. Accessed 10 Dec 2018
Beijing Museum of Natural History. http://www.bmnh.org.cn/en/. Accessed 24 Dec 2018
Van Boeijen, A., Daalhuizen, J., van der Schoor, R., Zijlstra, J.: Delft Design Guide: Design Strategies and Methods (2014)
Hou, J.: Project and Module Based Teaching and Learning. Int. J. Soc. Behav. Educ. Econ. Bus. Ind. Eng. **8**(3), 791–796 (2014). World Academy of Science, Engineering and Technology
De Vos, E., Xin, X., Emmanouil, M., Liu, W.: Make the future visible today! A reflection on using design thinking and futures studies techniques to foster creativity. In: Proceedings of the Sixth International Symposium of Chinese CHI, pp. 31–38. ACM, April 2018

Folkmann, M.N.: Enabling creativity. Imagination in design processes. In: DS 66-2: Proceedings of the 1st International Conference on Design Creativity (ICDC 2010) (2010)

Hummels, C., Frens, J.: The reflective transformative design process. In: CHI 2009 Extended Abstracts on Human Factors in Computing Systems, pp. 2655–2658. ACM, April 2009

Kann, V.: Using reflections in a program integrating course. In: Proceedings of the 2014 Conference on Innovation & Technology in Computer Science Education, p. 350. ACM, June 2014

Sun, S., Teng, L.: Establishing China's first UX master program based on applied psychology perspective. In: Marcus, A., Wang, W. (eds.) DUXU 2017. LNCS, vol. 10288, pp. 767–775. Springer, Cham (2017). https://doi.org/10.1007/978-3-319-58634-2_55

Xin, X., Liu, W., Wu, M.: Reflecting on industrial partnered and project based master course of 'UX Foundation'. In: Marcus, A., Wang, W. (eds.) DUXU 2018. LNCS, vol. 10919, pp. 148–157. Springer, Cham (2018)

Zaky, A.A., Elfaham, M.M.: The university-industry gap and its effect on research and development in developing countries. In: Frontiers in Education Conference. IEEE (1998)

DUXU for Well-Being

Research on the Furniture Design Criteria for Children's Psychological Development in Home Environment

Linong Dai[1] and Boming Xu[2(✉)]

[1] School of Design, Shanghai Jiao Tong University, Shanghai, China
Lndai@126.com
[2] College of Furnishings and Industrial Design, Nanjing Forestry University,
Nanjing, China
phdboming@126.com

Abstract. The growth of birth rate and consumption upgrading have brought opportunities to China's children's furniture industry. However, Chinese children furniture design still remains at the level of meeting children's physiological needs, mainly focusing on the size, safety and health issues, and neglecting their needs of psychological development. This paper aims to examine the correlations between parenting styles and children's furniture preferences in regard to children's psychological development and mental health by studying a group of middle and high income families in Shanghai. The research used the ethnographic method to collect data of family daily life, hypothesis was formed following an in-depth analysis and verified through a questionnaire survey. The psychological factors of children's furniture design were extracted. Based on such psychological factors and the different types of family environment extracted, this paper proposes a differentiation model to understand children's furniture design as a medium favoring the development of children's psychological health.

Keywords: Children's furniture · Children's psychology · Family · Furniture design

1 Introduction

In 2016, China implemented the "two-child policy" in an all-round way, directly affecting the proportion of children in China. According to the National Bureau of Statistics, the birth rate in 2017 was 12.43%. Nowadays, more than 230 million Chinese children are aged 0–14, accounting for 16.8% of the total population. This proportion continues to increase. In addition, the children related consumption represents 1/4 to 1/3 of total household consumption in China, which is close or even equal to an adult's [1]. Because of the increasing penetration rate of children's furniture in household brought about by the continuous growth in purchase power and urbanization, that market may reach nearly CNY 100 billion by 2022 [2]. However, China's children's furniture design still stays at the level of safety, appropriate size and diversified look, little attention has been paid to its relations to children's psychological

© Springer Nature Switzerland AG 2019
A. Marcus and W. Wang (Eds.): HCII 2019, LNCS 11585, pp. 277–286, 2019.
https://doi.org/10.1007/978-3-030-23538-3_21

development. In fact, parents choose a furniture not just only for its most basic functions, but also to constitute a growth environment for children's mental health development. At present, children's furniture on the market is rarely designed to meet these needs. Hence comes the necessity to explore the psychological factors of furniture design to children's growth.

That is why we had conducted a research on a sample of 22 middle and high income Shanghai families with children, in order to better the correlations between parenting styles and psychological factors in choosing children's furniture. We chose Shanghai because it has a large population and its life style leads the rest of China. Furthermore, middle and high income families are the main consumers of children's furniture. The research findings would have a fair applicability in China's children's furniture market.

From a literature review of children's furniture design research, we can identify three main directions: (1) Children's physiology: the main purpose is to study the effects of physiology and security. (2) The influence on children's behavior and psychology: Holden [3] points out that the act of assembling furniture by children themselves or together with adults can help develop children's problem-solving abilities and creativity, which are critical in their adult life [3]. (3) Decision-making on furniture's purchase: According to Shen and Zhang [4], 43.1% of parents in China would spend CNY 5,000–8,000 on the children's room decoration. This shows the importance that parents attach to their children's growing environment [4]. A survey in 2015 found that parents make the main decision in choosing the style of their children's room in both developed and developing countries [7]. In a survey conducted by one author of this paper in 2017, only 10.6% of the households chose "children-oriented decision-making in purchasing children's furniture" [5]. Therefore, parents are the main decision makers and purchasers of children's furniture in China.

2   Method

2.1   Ethnography

Ethnography, including field work, has been applied in the collection of household data. The sample consisted of 22 middle and high-income families in Shanghai, covering a wide range of areas from urban to suburban, with a variety of parents' educational background, family structure, living environment and so on. Methods mainly include observation, shadowing, in-depth interview, Censydiam test, children's psychological drawing, physical (trace) document, and measurements (Figure 1).

2.2   Persona

Persona is the outline of the real characteristics of the end user group, and it creates the comprehensive prototype of real users. We study the goal, behavior and viewpoint of our end users, and abstract these elements into a set of descriptions of typical product users to identify the market segment of the product. Persona ensures that the user groups

Fig. 1. Ethnographic data collection and data entries

of children furniture can be obtained. This application allows other research methods of social sciences to be integrated into the design subject, in a comprehensive way.

2.3 Coding

Traditional persona analysis is relatively a "black box" process for data analysis. Although induction is used, it is not built on a logical and rigorous reasoning of the process. It relies more on researchers' experiences and existed theories. In this research, we carry out three steps of coding in light of the grounded theory: the first step is an open initial coding; the second step is an axial coding; and the third step is a core coding. Raw data are proceeded step by step until the conclusion is drawn.

2.4 Questionnaire Survey

In-depth qualitative research on a small sample leads us to draw hypothesis. However, the hypothesis still needs to be verified through a research of larger scale. A questionnaire survey has been conducted for this purpose. The questionnaire mainly aims at the statistical verification of the hypothetical correlationship between variables "parenting styles" and "children's furniture design factors". A total of 430 respondents in Shanghai and 939 in other Chinese provinces completed the survey by random sampling.

3 The Design Factors of Children's Furniture Based on the Development of Children's Mental Health

3.1 Design Factors of Children's Furniture

Through reviewing the studies on children's furniture design from various countries, 29 factors in children's furniture design were identified. From them, seventeen design factors for children were obtained by clustering, disassembling and regrouping. They are: stability, age appropriateness, learnability, environment friendliness, emotion experiencing and regulating, parent-child interactivity, adaptability, mobility, space saving, easy-cleaning, fault tolerance, self-support, interesting, intelligence-promoting, aesthetics/artistry, kids only, high-quality.

3.2   Constructing a Common Design Factor Model Based on Children's Psychological Development Law

There are two factors influencing children's mental health development: heredity and environment. The research on heredity is mainly built on the theory of psychological development, while the research on environment, on the theories of environmental behavior and those of influence of family environment on children's psychological development.

According to Professor Xu Boming's theory of "Scene, Person and Product" chain [6], in the household, "Persons" are family members, and the "Scene" is family environment. But the family environment here not only refers to the surrounding objects like furniture, but also includes the family culture composed of the life forms of family members. Research also shows that the objective surroundings in Chinese families are mainly set up by the parents. Therefore, since parents are the most important users of children's furniture and the most dominant purchase decision-maker in a family, they are the most important environmental factor to consider besides the needs of children as the first user. Parents' consideration of purchasing children's furniture can be divided into two aspects: commonness and difference. Among them, the common factor is that children's furniture must conform to the laws of children's physical and mental development; while the difference design factors are the specific needs of different types of families, that is, family user grouping.

The study of common factor is mainly based on Maria Montessori's theory of children's environmental development and Jean Piaget's theory of cognitive development. According to the laws and characteristics of psychological development of children of different genders in different age stages, the formula of common factor in children's furniture design can be summarized as follows:

$$CFD = f(CA, CG) \tag{2}$$

CFD-Common factor of children furniture designing; CA-Children age; CG-Children gender. CA and CG are independent variables.

3.3   Derivation of User Clustering and Differentiation Model Based on Persona

The differentiation factors in children's furniture design are derived theoretically from environmental behavior studies. The research adopts the family environment system theory, draws lessons from the parenting education model, and uses Censydiam's consumer motivation theory in order to analyze parents' purchase decision behavior. The construction of differentiation model comes from our field work and data analysis.

In the part of qualitative analysis, 12 categories are obtained by initial coding, such as "BR-2 bedroom or 3 bedroom", "CC-Child caring and education", "CN-Child need", "CP-Child and parent needs", "CS-Consume style", "EB-Education background", "FA-Family social activity", "FC-Furniture Choosing", "FE-Family education view", "FN-Family needs", "FS-Furniture style", "FT-Family structure", "FV-Family Value", "FW-Family working", "IL-Income level", "MC-Censydiam evaluation of members in Family" and "PN-Parent need".

Then, axial coding is applied to the results of initial coding to identify and summarize the relationship between categories. In this step of coding, causality, inclusion, semantics and sequential relationships are used to identify generic relationships between categories. The axial coding process results in four secondary categories as "FD-Family decision", "FL-Family level", "PS-Parenting style", "OE-Objective element". Among them, the first three are related to this research. Finally, after comparing and analyzing the interrelation strength of the three secondary categories, the "PS-Parenting style" is retained as the "core category" to be analyzed. This line of thinking leads to our hypothesis: "A Family, with a specific parenting style, by choosing children's furniture accordingly, can realize its expectations for children's future mental health growth." The following functional formula expresses the relationship between factors at all levels in family clustering for children furniture (FG is Family Grouping):

$$FG = f\begin{pmatrix} FD, \\ FL, \\ PS \end{pmatrix} = f\begin{pmatrix} g_1(FT, FW, CS), \\ g_2(EB, IL, FV, FN, FA), \\ g_3(FE, CC, MC) \end{pmatrix} \tag{2}$$

In the formula, among three independent variables such as "FD-Family decision", "FL-family level", "PS-parenting style", "PS-parenting style" is the most important factor.

Family persona grouping is constructed by means of core coding, which gives 4 types of "parenting style families", namely "trusteeship and self-achievement family", "elite, hierarchical family", "liberal-and-sociable-type family" and "liberal-and-intellectual family". The hypothesis of design differentiation factor model based on different types is deduced as follows (Table 1).

3.4   Hypothesis Validation and Conclusion Revised

The findings from qualitative research have been verified with a questionnaire survey. The correlation analysis can tell us which factors are strongly correlated, which factors are necessary attributes. Once clustered, these results help to comprehensively revise the conclusion of qualitative research.

The reliability of the questionnaire is tested twice, the Cronbach's Alpha and Cronbach s Alpha based on standardization items are respectively 0.629 and 0.828, so that the questionnaire is reliable. The KMO value of factor analysis is 0.782, which proves that the questionnaire has good structural validity.

The questionnaire was distributed to a random sample, with a response rate of 98%. From the Dendrogram Comparison of the national and Shanghai data (Fig. 2), we

Table 1. The primary model of 4 types of families for children's furniture design.

Family type	Parenting style	Child development tendency	Factors in children's furniture design	The influence of children on parents' furniture choice
Trusteeship and self-achievement family	Affirmation-belonging, high trust	Vitality with enjoyment	Stability, fault tolerance, easy-cleaning, space saving, interesting and adaptability	Very strong
Elite, hierarchical family	Belonging with low affirmation, high doubt	Control	Kids only, age appropriateness	Very weak
Liberal-and-sociable-type family	High belonging, trust	Belonging	Parent-child interactivity, aesthetics/artistry, emotion experiencing and regulating	Strong
Liberal-and-intellectual family	Affirmation, doubt	Recognition with power	Intelligence-promoting, high-quality, mobility and self-support	Weak

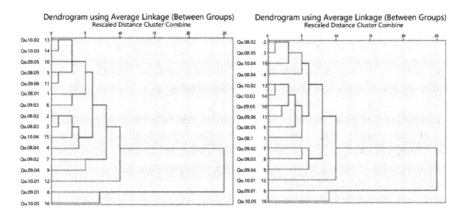

Fig. 2. Dendrogram comparison of Shanghai data (left) with the national data (right)

noticed the only difference is about the question of location, while the others are quite similar. Therefore, the results of in-depth research in Shanghai can be generalizable on the nationwide to a certain extent.

Was analyzed the correlation between Questions 4 and 7 about "Parenting style" and Questions 8–10 about "Children's Furniture Design Factor". All significant positive correlations (sig values < 0.05) are listed as follows (Table 2).

Table 2. Positive correlations between "Parenting style" and "Children's Furniture Design Factor"

Options for Qu. 4, Qu. 7	Options for Qu. 8–10	Chi-square test sig value
Qu. 4.2 (have the right to choose)	Qu. 8.3 (interesting)	0.043
	Qu. 9.4 (adaptability)	0.045
	Qu. 10.1 (emotion experiencing and regulating)	0.032
Qu. 4.4 (Independence and keep one's own opinions)	Qu. 9.1 (kids only)	0.033
Qu. 7.1 (everyone can use)	Qu. 8.4 (parent-child interactivity)	0.012
	Qu. 9.4 (adaptability)	0.007
	Qu. 9.5 (environment friendliness)	0.005
Qu. 7.3 (kids use furniture by their parents' rules)	Qu. 9.1 (kids only)	0.000
	Qu. 10.6 (age appropriateness)	0.002
Qu. 7.2 (kids only, with distinct personality of children)	Qu. 8.1 (self-support)	0.000
	Qu. 9.1 (kids only)	0.002
Qu. 7.4 (kids can use in any way they want)	Qu. 8.4 (parent-child interactivity)	0.001
	Qu. 10.1 (emotion experiencing and regulating)	0.003
	Qu. 10.4 (aesthetics/artistry)	0.032

The Questions 4 and 7 about "Parenting style" are negatively correlated with the Questions 8–10 about "Children's Furniture Design Factor" (sig < 0.05) as shown in Table 3.

Table 3. Negative correlations between "Parenting style" and "Children's Furniture Design Factor"

Options for Qu. 4, Qu. 7	Options for Qu. 8–10	Chi-square test sig value
Qu. 4.2 (have the right to choose)	Qu. 8.2 (intelligence-promoting)	0.002
	Qu. 9.1 (kids only)	0.04
Qu. 7.1 (everyone can use)	Qu. 8.1 (self-support)	0.000
	Qu. 8.3 (interesting)	0.004
	Qu. 9.1 (kids only)	0.027
Qu. 7.2 (kids only, with distinct personality of children)	Qu. 8.4 (parent-child interactivity)	0.000
	Qu. 9.4 (adaptability)	0.000
Qu. 7.3 (kids use furniture by their parents' rules)	Qu. 8.4 (parent-child interactivity)	0.000
	Qu. 9.3 (fault tolerance)	0.013
	Qu. 9.4 (adaptability)	0.000
	Qu. 10.1 (emotion experiencing and regulating)	0.026
Qu. 7.4 (kids can use in any way they want)	Qu. 9.1 (kids only)	0.000

By using Censydiam model to visualize above positive and negative correlations data (Fig. 3), we can see the correspondence between each design factor and family cluster intuitively. A = "Liberal-and-Intellectual Family" cluster, B = "Liberal-and-Sociable-Type Family" cluster, C = "Trusteeship and Self-Achievement Family" cluster and D = "Elite, Hierarchical Family". Their respective children's furniture design factors are shown below with Table 1.

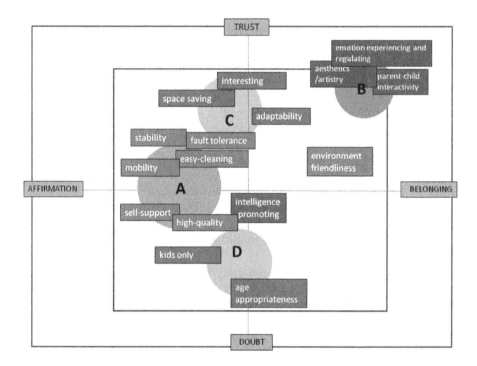

Fig. 3. Censydiam model of clustering and correlation analysis

4   Discussion

In this study, the qualitative and quantitative analysis yields a picture about the relationship between the family parenting style and parents' choice of children's furniture for children's psychological development. In particular, according to the data from our in-home investigation on the Shanghai families, it is found that families have certain regularity in choosing children's furniture design, dependent on their parenting style. This can help us to rethink children's furniture design criteria as reference for children's furniture enterprises and designers.

Parents from "trusteeship and self-achievement family" are more fond of their children and willing to meet their children's requests. Therefore, they prefer to choose interesting children's furniture which can be combined in many ways. Thus, the design of children's furniture for such families should focus more on furniture's interestingness and adaptability. Parents from Elite, hierarchical family like to personally take care of their children's education issues. They believe in "Striving to achieve life", pay attention to children's learning and ability training to build children to become elites in the future. Therefore, they tend to choose more professional look design, such as specific furniture for a specific age, a specific function and so on. Thus, the design of children's furniture for this kind of family should lay more emphasis on kids only and age appropriateness.

Both liberal-and-sociable-type and liberal-and-intellectual families strive to create a free and equal atmosphere. But liberal-and-sociable-type families also emphasize collectivism, love and communication, more sensibility, full understanding of children's emotions, and the cultivation of personality and talent. Generally speaking, they are sensitive to the style and artistry of furniture, prefer to choose furniture for parents and children using together. Therefore, the design of children's furniture for such families should favor parent-child interaction, aesthetics and emotion experiencing and regulating, such as a princess-style bed, so that children can read and imagine together with their mothers before going to bed. In contrast, liberal-and-intellectual families respect individuals more than liberal-and-sociable-type families. Parents also would be more rational, scientific and technological, will actively guide and cultivate children's technical expertise. So the children of those families are more independent. Therefore, the design of children's furniture for such families should favor more self-support and mobility, with new technology application if possible.

Rethinking the correlations between parenting style of four kinds of family parents and their preferences for children's furniture design, we believe that the value of "Scene, Person and Product" chain conception of design is fully supported. It is a contingent approach to design criteria that we can summarize as follows: the furniture is the media with which parents construct the scene (household as hard environment) and actualize their parenting (soft environment). Parents' choice of children furniture is contingent to their understanding of relatedness of furniture attributes to children's mental development expected.

5 Conclusion

The ethnographic investigation of 22 families in Shanghai and the questionnaire survey lead us to draw following conclusions:

(1) There are similarities and differences in the furniture design criteria for children's psychology. The commonness is mainly consisted of the physiological and psychological development law of children of different ages and genders, while the differentiation is mainly caused by many factors of family environment, notably parenting style.

(2) A family's criteria for children's furniture choice is correlated to their parenting style, family decision making and the living level. 4 family user personas are constructed among Shanghai-based middle-and-upper-income families.

(3) Based on these 4 family personas, we have identified 4 types of preferences for children's furniture. "Trusteeship and self-achievement families" have preferences

for children's furniture design factors such as interestingness, adaptability and space saving; "elite hierarchical families" pay more attention to learning furniture, and prefer the kids only and age appropriateness of children's furniture design; "liberal-and-sociable-type families" prefer to have more social functions, and like children's furniture with parent-child interactivity, aesthetics and emotion experiencing and regulating design; "liberal-and-intellectual families" prefer the self-support, high quality and mobility.

Because of the large span of children's age in sample, correspondingly, the age gap between parents of different families is large as well. With the rapid development of Chinese economy, intergenerational life styles and concepts have changed tremendously over the past 30 years. Therefore, we must be cautious that the conclusions of the study may have temporal characteristics, and not be applicable across time. In addition, although Shanghai leads China's first-tier city children's furniture market to a certain extent. However, due to regional and cultural varieties, we need a much more extensive research in order to truly understand the psychological factors for children's furniture design in China.

Acknowledgment. (1) This study is funded by the National Social Science Foundation of China, Art Project under agreement No. 17BG143.

(2) Part of the data in this paper come from the research projects completed by Shanghai Jiaotong University for HANSSEM Corporation (Korea) and Shanghai ForU Sleep Technology Co., Ltd. For details, one can refer to the author's doctoral dissertation "Design and Research on the Children Furniture of Shanghai Middle-and-upper Income Families Based on Persona". (Nanjing Forestry University, 2017).

(3) Thank Mr. Song Suchen and Mrs. Qian Yuxia for their proofreading.

References

1. A Survey Report on Consumer Behavior Habits of Chinese Parents and Children. http://www.wzaobao.com/p/g58k2D.html. Accessed 16 June 2015
2. Home Industry Series Report (5) Children's Furniture Industry: 100 billion New Blue Sea. http://finance.qq.com/a/20160926/016479.htm. Accessed 24 Sept 2016
3. Holden, A.M.: Creativity in children's furniture design. Dissertations & Theses - Gradworks (2013)
4. Shen, S., Zhang, Y.: A preliminary study on interior design of contemporary teenagers' rooms. Furnit. Inter. Decor. **12**, 56–57 (2011)
5. Dai, L.: Design and Research on the Children Furniture of Shanghai Middle-and-upper Income Families Based on Persona. Nanjing Forestry University (2017)
6. Xu, B.: Furniture Design, 2nd edn. China Light Industry Press, Beijing (2019)
7. Yalçin, M., Yildirim, K., Bozdayi, A.: Developmental implications of children bedroom in the interior environment and implementations of adults preferences. MEGARON **10**(3), 305–316 (2015)

"Thanks for Writing, But I'm Not Interested": A Qualitative Analysis of Men's Experiences of Online Dating

Chris Fullwood$^{(\boxtimes)}$ ⓘ, Emma Boultwood, and Darren Chadwick ⓘ

Department of Psychology, University of Wolverhampton, Wolverhampton, UK
{c.fullwood,D.Chadwick}@wlv.ac.uk,
emmaboultwood@yahoo.co.uk

Abstract. Research investigating the personal experiences of online daters is currently limited. Moreover, evidence implies that men are likely to experience online dating rather differently to their female counterparts and that this discrepancy warrants further investigation. Eight heterosexual adult males aged 18–60 were interviewed about their experiences of and attitudes to using online dating sites and apps. Data were analysed qualitatively using thematic analysis. A number of themes were identified from the data, including "necessary but effective online dating", reflecting the perceived utility of dating sites and their ability to enhance certainty and reduce rejection salience. "Negative impact on self" was revealed through participants' experiences of online interactions, with participants demonstrating various protective strategies to maintain self-integrity. "Clouded judgements", insofar as the intentions of other daters were often more difficult to judge accurately, and "frustration", relating to negative experiences with online dating platforms and the gendered norms within them, were also noted. The last theme was one of "resiliency" which was demonstrated throughout descriptions of participant experiences. Findings provide a rich narrative of the lived experiences of male online daters and the strategies they employ to reap rewards as well as the barriers to success that they incur.

Keywords: Online dating · Male perspective · User experience · Qualitative

1 Introduction

1.1 Online Dating Services

Personal relationships, as manifest in the attraction of an intimate partner, are considered a fundamental aspect of many peoples' human experience. Intimate partners can facilitate many key life achievements, e.g. having children, and intimate partners can also be a source of social standing and support [1]. We also know that there is a significant cost and toll to wellbeing related to pervasive loneliness [2]. Since the introduction of ICTs the inception and development of such relationships has, for many, moved online [3]. Online dating services (ODS), including dating sites and apps, principally function to assist people to initiate romantic relationships [4]. Some sites are free to join, whilst others charge a fee and claim to offer more bespoke services, for

© Springer Nature Switzerland AG 2019
A. Marcus and W. Wang (Eds.): HCII 2019, LNCS 11585, pp. 287–302, 2019.
https://doi.org/10.1007/978-3-030-23538-3_22

example match-making algorithms. These algorithms, used by sites such as Elite and eHarmony for instance, are a time-saving feature for the user and offer potential matches from the information that they and other daters provide. Other ODS (e.g. Match.com) use 'see and screen' methods. In other words, the user is able to select specific criteria based on their own preferences to search for other daters and then choose the individuals with whom they wish to interact. Some ODS, such as OKCupid, use a mixture of both methods [5]. ODS offer convenience, flexibility and the ability to tap into a vast pool of potential partners that one may be unlikely to meet in everyday life. It is easy to see why ODS have become such a popular method for finding love. Indeed, Smith and Anderson [6] noted that in 2015 15% of all American Internet users had used an online dating site or app. Additionally, they report that the social stigma around using ODS has significantly reduced in recent years, so we should expect ODS to continue to increase in acceptance and popularity. Although relationships flourish for many users following their interactions on ODS, approximately one third of all active online daters report having never progressed to a face-to-face date [6]. It is therefore important to explore the lived experiences of online daters to provide a deeper understanding of the barriers to success as well as how these obstacles to finding love might impact on the self.

1.2   Impression Management in Online Dating

Pivotal to online dating success is impression management, or the various ways in which we can influence the impressions that others form of us [7]. As online dating is about connecting with strangers and initially there is no physical interaction, employing strategic impression management tactics in order to be thought of positively by other daters is common practice [8]. ODS offer daters a great deal of flexibility in how they present themselves to others, for example they may choose a photo which has been edited or put through filters or exaggerate aspects of their appearance, personality or interests in written and visual descriptions to make themselves appear more attractive [9, 10]. Additionally, daters may accentuate more positive aspects of the self, whilst concealing more negative qualities in order to increase their chances of success [11] and to compete with other rivals on the site [12]. One potential ramification of selective and idealised self-presentation, however, is that this may lead some users to develop unrealistic expectations about what they think they are able achieve via ODS [13].

Despite the potential to refine certain aspects of one's online persona, this has to be balanced against the goal of meeting face-to-face. Indeed, online daters will need to walk a fine line between creating desirable yet truthful self-images, in the potential scenario that a face-to-face meeting occurs [14]. Profiles which are flagrantly unrealistic tend to be disregarded from the offset and judged as fake [15]. Moreover, although there is evidence to suggest that many daters intentionally misrepresent themselves [8], in many instances daters may also be subject to self-deception. Indeed, Ellison, Heino, and Gibbs [14] discuss the 'Foggy mirror', which highlights the discrepancy between how daters perceive themselves in comparison to how they are assessed by others. Part of the motivation for creating idealised self-images lies in the fact that online daters are acutely aware that physical attractiveness is an important quality in receiving positive attention from other users [16]. Males, however, place more value on physical attractiveness than females when evaluating others and in making decisions about whether or not to initiate contact [17].

1.3 Advantages and Disadvantages of Dating Online

One of the main perks for joining ODS is that they increase our chances of meeting individuals who may not be contactable in the offline world [18]. In traditional forms of dating, having to identify potential partners involves making an assessment of an individual's relationship status, which can be challenging. Hence, joining a ODS removes this ambiguity to a large degree. ODS are also advantageous in that they are a more convenient and accessible method for screening potential dates, which might be particularly helpful to those who live very busy lives as they have more control over the timing and pace of interactions [19]. Another component that makes ODS advantageous is that they can help to soften the blow of rejection, which is particularly beneficial to those who are more sensitive to rejection [20]. For some males, striking up a conversation with a female offline may be a source of angst, with any rejection potentially being played out in public and thus heightening their embarrassment. Conversing with strangers online helps to alleviate this fear as they do not have to face the online dater in public, thus reducing the potential for loss of face [21].

Many features of ODS may also result in disadvantages for some users. For example, some members may not know how best to sell themselves, and with abundant competition from other users this can be a daunting task. Indeed, males who were evaluated as cautious in their text were contacted less frequently [22]. Further, individuals with lower self-esteem may be less inclined to join dating sites for concerns over presenting themselves to multiple individuals simultaneously, therefore they engage in an avoidance strategy to protect their self-worth [23]. Research has also found that when fostering a relationship through CMC, conversations between potential daters may halt abruptly without any warning and this tends to be a predominately male experience [24]. Qualitative data from male online daters demonstrates a level of uncertainty around the reasons why communications sometimes cease, with some users indicating that they had already disclosed personal information and were under the impression that the conversation was going well [24]. Although abrupt endings to communications may come as a surprise to male users, females are more likely to receive messages more abundantly. Unlike males, who need to be proactive to initiate contact, females are able to be more discerning in who they interact with as they have more choice [24, 25]. Further, it could be argued that through being inundated with messages, some females may develop an exaggerated sense of value and perceived desirability from the attention garnered [21].

In contrast to face-to-face communication, where obvious or subtle body language cues (e.g. avoidance of eye contact) may signal disinterest, this is not always easy to gauge through CMC [10]. This can be elucidated by cues-filtered-out theory [26] which purports that this ambiguity may result in a more limited ability to interpret the meaning of behaviour due to the absence or attenuation of contextual cues and non-verbal signals [27]. As interactions take place with strangers, severing contact online can be done with very few repercussions to the individual. In contrast, in a face-to-face scenario this might be harder to do, as it may be perceived as breaking social etiquette, thought of as rude, and the person would likely be appraised negatively [24].

Relying on attributional cues, which are present in private messages and on daters' profiles, is the primary method for evaluating compatibility before meeting face-to-face. Because people can communicate online with less inhibition [28], this can lead to heightened self-disclosure and a swifter process for the revelation of personal and intimate information [29]. Ultimately, it is argued that may also result in some daters developing a false sense of intimacy [29], which may lead to unrealistic expectations of one other. In addition, misread cues, such as humour, which is postulated to be a predictor of intelligence and can play a pivotal role in fostering bonds that equate to dating success, may be exaggerated through CMC and not always translate to face-to-face communication [30]. Leary and Kowalski [31] propose that this occurs because what we are actually doing is interacting with the impression that we have formed of the person, rather than the person him or herself, per se. This may lead to discrepancies when meeting face-to-face and could result in disappointment with the date. As a consequence, often another date is not pursued, as judgement to suitability has been clouded, and in some cases the spark or chemistry that was present in CMC may not transpose to a face-to-face date. This can result in the whole process having to be repeated again and could lead to feelings of frustration, or people removing themselves from ODS altogether [24].

1.4 The Current Study

The literature reviewed suggests that heterosexual men and women experience online dating rather differently. It has been argued that females are at an advantage on online dating sites, having a far greater chance of meeting a potential romantic partner from the offset [22]. Males not only outnumber females, but they are more active on ODS and this is put forward as one of the contributing factors to why females receive significantly more messages than males; men are essentially competing with other men in an arena that is male-dominated [22, 32]. Males initiate more contacts [21] and need to send out on average 58 messages (compared to 13 for females in the same age bracket) in order to get a response [33]. Further, as men may experience a lack of feedback in ODS, encountering a void of communication, many will develop a fear of rejection and gain concerns that they are undesirable, and in frustration they may experiment with varying communication styles to see if they can excite responses [24]. Masden and Edwards [34] interviewed OkCupid and Tinder users and also found, in support of Zykto et al.'s [24] findings, that frustration was a central theme. They concluded that men receive considerably fewer messages than women, but did not provide a detailed evaluation of how this might impact on the self, and this study intends to build on this limitation.

Implications of the online dating experience for self-esteem will also be explored in this study. Impacts of rejection in the dating arena for male daters will be considered in relation to self-affirmation theory [35], which focuses on the manner in which people adapt to experiences or information which might threaten self-worth in order to maintain self-integrity. This current exploratory research study intends to build on and develop the research and theories discussed, and explore online dating from the male's perspective through the narrative of the male experience, by exploring the following research questions:

RQ1: How do men experience online dating and how does this compare to their experiences of more traditional dating?

RQ2: What are the perceived advantages and disadvantages of using online dating services from the viewpoint of men?

RQ3: How do men use online dating services to connect with others?

RQ4: Do men's experience with online dating services link to their self-evaluations and subjective well-being?

2   Method

2.1   Participants

A purposive, opportunity sample of 8 heterosexual males were recruited into the study. Inclusion criteria included being active on ODS within 2 years of participation and being at least 18 years of age. Participants' ages ranged from 18–60 with a mean age of 39.40 years. Participants were recruited through social media sites, such as Facebook and Twitter and via the University of Wolverhampton's participant pool.

2.2   Approach and Procedure

To address the research questions, an exploratory qualitative approach was utilised, underpinned by a post-positivist epistemology [36]. Specifically, we conducted interviews with 8 heterosexual males in order to gather insights into their attitudes to and experiences of using ODS. An interview approach was deemed more appropriate than focus groups given the private and personal nature of the topic. Interviews were expected therefore to elicit more candid and authentic responses.

Following ethical approval for the project being gained from The University of Wolverhampton Ethics Committee, interviews were conducted between December 2016 and February 2017 over the telephone (N = 3) or face-to-face (N = 5), depending on the participant's preference. In the first instance, an information sheet was given to the participant, detailing the aims of the study, and informed consent was sought. The interview followed a semi-structured format, asking opened-ended questions such as 'what in your opinion are the main advantages or disadvantages to using online dating sites?' and 'has online dating had an impact on how you evaluate yourself?' Probes were used to motivate participants to elaborate in more detail on their personal experiences. For example, for the question 'tell me about your experience of online dating', participants were probed with follow-up questions such as 'before using online dating sites what was your attitude or understanding of them?' and 'tell me a little about why you choose to use online dating sites?' At the end of the interview the participants were given the chance to feedback anything they thought relevant to their experience that had not been explored. All of the interviews were audio-recorded using a Dictaphone. Upon completion of the interview, participants were debriefed and provided with contact details of the research team should they have any questions or wish to withdraw from the study.

2.3   Data Analysis

Interviews lasted between 17:39 and 85:02 min (mean = 42:01 min; S.D = 22:51). The interviews were transcribed verbatim, imported into NVivo and analysed by a single member of the research team using Thematic Analysis. Participants were assigned pseudonyms to protect their identity. The analysis followed the process recommended by Braun and Clarke [37], which included: familiarisation with the data, generation of initial codes, searching for themes, reviewing themes, and defining and naming themes. An inductive approach was employed thereby allowing the data to structure the analysis through the interpretations of the researcher. To strengthen the trustworthiness of the findings, the themes developed by the principal coder were checked and verified by the other two members of the research team with any inconsistencies and themes identified refined through discussion. Also, a copy of the transcript of the interview was provided to two of the participants to feedback for accuracy. Both participants felt the transcripts accurately reflected the interview and their experiences of online dating. In addition, a member-checking process was implemented to enhance confirmability of the analysis. Three participants were offered a summary of the findings, and confirmed that the themes emerging from the analysis accurately represented and summarised their experiences. Two participants gave written feedback and one provided feedback verbally.

3   Results and Discussion

Analysis resulted in five central themes of 'Necessary but effective online dating' (including the subthemes 'utility of ODS', 'enhanced certainty' and 'reduced rejection salience'), 'Frustration' (including the sub-themes 'attitudes to dating sites' and 'gendered norms'), 'Clouded judgements' (including the subthemes 'initial investment' and 'physical and interpersonal incongruence'), 'Negative impact on self' (including the sub-theme 'strategies to protect the self') and 'Resiliency'. These themes will each be discussed in turn.

3.1   Necessary but Effective Online Dating

Speaking to the utility of ODS, all interviewees regarded online dating as a superior method for finding a potential partner, compared to more traditional ways of meeting. The more traditional route was roundly discounted by participants as not being a valid option to attain dating success.

> *"Without dating apps what other way is there?"* (Ben, 39)
> *"Everybody's online so you give it a go"* (David, 47)

The effectiveness of ODS was also considered in relation to being able to connect with a wider network of potential dates, whilst being able to search for individuals on the characteristics which were deemed important to the user.

> *"You know, it makes it really easy to sort of filter out a lot of people and even wider than your current circle"* (Charlie, 22)

Part of what made ODS effective was the numerous advantages that it offered to members. Largely, these advantages reflect what has already been discussed in the research literature [18–21]. For example, using dating sites/apps allows one to speak to numerous individuals simultaneously, therefore increasing the odds of finding a connection.

"Yeah, but, I mean - This is one thing I've found - I mean, I've spoken to probably thousands of people" (Charlie, 22)

ODS also allow users to interact with individuals who one would have been unlikely to meet in the offline world.

"Well, definitely wouldn't have met her in our day to day life because obviously, like we wouldn't have come in contact with each other" (Seb, 44)

ODS offered participants the flexibility to access other single people where and when they liked, and this convenience was seen as a major advantage, for example Tom (60) enjoyed the ability to *"dip in and out"* when it suited him.

The overriding motivation for using ODS was to make connections which could lead to dates and many participants indicated that they were not meeting single females in their offline lives, for example because they were too busy with work and family commitments.

"You're busy with work. I'm working full time, so it's like easy access to hundreds of people, that's why" (Lucas, 35).

Most had no desire to go to bars or pubs with the intent of seeking a partner.

"So it's trying to find something that fit in with my lifestyle rather than me hanging around in city bars" (Tom, 60)

Some of the males spoke of struggles establishing the relationship status of females in their offline lives and referred to this being a barrier to initiating contact offline. Using ODS therefore enhanced the certainty around the availability of the women they were seeking to make a connection with, at the same time ensuring that one's time was not wasted in the process of attempting to discover this information.

"Well, at least the people who were on that (ODS) are looking for a relationship. So that, you know...because people you meet in your daily life, you don't know if they're in a relationship or not" (Bertie, 50)

While some participants extended no adverse feelings towards ODS, for others there was some reluctance to participate, for example because it was considered a more *"impersonal"* (David, 47) method of interacting with potential dates, linking to cues-filtered-out theory [26] and the notion that it may be more difficult to express and interpret the emotional tone of messages in the absence of non-verbal communication cues. Despite this, all participants considered online dating sites as a necessary way to meet women in contemporary society.

Appropriate etiquette around approaching and seeking information about the relationship status of women in their offline lives was a concern for some participants, particularly those with professional careers. There was also some fear of embarrassment around having to interact again in the future with women who may have spurned their advances. Thus, using ODS was seen as removing this risk of embarrassment or public rejection. For instance, Tom (60) indicated that it was easier to talk to women on ODS as there were some assurances of them being single and this was preferable to *"doing things in a big, um, sort of public social arena."* In comparison to face-to-face communication, ODS therefore offer a reduced sense of risk of rejection, including a reduction in the emotional impact of rejection. Rejecting or being rejected was also considered to be easier on ODS in comparison to face-to-face contexts, not just because the rejection wouldn't be played out publicly, but because it decreases any consequences of dealing with the rejecter/rejected in one's offline life.

3.2   Frustration

All participants spoke of their frustrations around using dating sites and apps and this accords with the research of Zykto et al. [24] and Masden and Edwards [34] which also uncovered frustration as central theme in the male online dating experience. One area of contention which aroused anger and a sense of inequity centred on feelings that men were being coerced into paying for the full functions of dating sites, whereas women were not.

> *"From a male's perspective, from my perspective, it's hard enough trying to get people to respond to you at the best of times, let alone being limited to only talking to five people a day and then only being able to message those that you match with. And it makes you feel like you've got to pay. It's like, I'm not paying to speak to people."* (Charlie, 22)

Some sites, such as Match.com, encourage men to pay for add-ons that allow them to contact all users (including members who do not have a paid subscription). Men far outnumber women on dating sites [32], and may feel obliged to pay because the assumption would be that other males will do the same. Women on the other hand may feel less obliged to pay for subscriptions under the assumption that men will make every effort to initiate contact with them [21]. This predicament was summed up by Ben (39):

> *"Match.com, uh, well I registered myself probably in August last year, and it's free. But it's quite easy to fall into its, of uh, paying a subscription."*

An additional facet to this experience is that sites which restrict users' choices and ask for payment, often give the notion that paying will result in greater success (e.g. as they are not competing against males that do not pay). Hence, this may give the potentially false impression that they are reducing the competitive field [38], which may account to why some males self-select to pay such a premium. This unfavourable treatment revealed a feeling of frustration for participants. This was supported and furthered by David (47) who felt that through his experience of Elite singles, where he paid a premium to get the complete bespoke service that he deemed as *"absolutely hopeless"*, and considered no better than the free sites he was also using. Moreover, he also voiced suspicion at this site, expressing mistrust in their motivation to make money.

> *"So, they gonna do everything they can and I don't just trust them really"*

This account also hints at the notion of a level of entitlement, in other words the expectation of results based on payment for a service.

Frustration was also expressed concerning how men and women were assigned to unspoken gender norms and roles, which resonates with a very traditional idea of dating offline, deriving from and supporting the evolutionary perspective [39]. Although the Internet should be a great leveller and a socially liberating environment in which to contest stereotypical gender norms, the experiences of these male participants suggests otherwise. When it came to initiating contact, instigating dates, and in some cases paying for all of the dates, participants considered that this was the 'expected' role of the man. Nearly all of the participants spoke of frustration with regard to how the onus appears always to be on the male to approach females.

"Like, you know, the typical way it works is that men will send out tonnes of messages to women. Women will then choose and pick the ones that they want to respond to" (Charlie, 22)

Corroborating prior literature [34], two participants had never experienced a female ever initiating contact with them. For example Bertie (50) indicated:

"Yeah, well I don't think anyone ever even initiated a single conversation with me"

Two other participants found that it was a rare occurrence to be contacted by women on ODS. For example, Lucas (35) noted:

"No very rare, it's always the man, not the woman"

The lack of females initiating contact had, as a consequence, left many of the males at a loss as to why this was happening and participants realised quite quickly that if they were going to have any success that they needed to be proactive in creating this for themselves.

"This is the 21st century and women can chase too. But, uh, there are women out there who actually are so old-fashioned - that they expect the man to come forth, to chat them up and do everything and it's really frustrating to gauge whether the woman is interested or not" (Ben, 39).

Moreover, participants expressed a level of frustration with initiating countless communications, but rarely receiving a response. Even when responses were forth-coming, they were often generic pre-selected messages. Nonetheless, these replies were still appreciated, because at the very least they inferred some sort of acknowledgement that the message had been received, therefore reducing uncertainty around whether or not someone was actually at the other end of the profile.

"Most of them you wouldn't strike up a conversation, but every now and then one would reply and say, 'Thanks for writing but I'm not interested,' which is nice because 9 out of 10 weren't doing that" (Bertie, 50).

3.3 Clouded Judgments

Participants noted that some of the cues on ODS, for example photographs or char-acteristics of the online daters they were interested in, were clouded by the medium of the Internet. Hence, this affected the outcome of their interactions impacting on dating success, as judgements about potential compatibility of dates were sometimes difficult to ascertain correctly. Moreover, when meeting face-to-face, this often resulted in disappointment. Lucas (35) recounted one such experience:

"I didn't get on with her at all. And she wasn't anything like um, what I thought she was going to be. And then I had to do the awkward um, 'No I'm just gonna to go home,' [laughs]".

Inferring accurate impressions of other daters is pivotal to successful use of ODS. Participants had to make informed decisions about who they were going to try to strike up a dialogue with from a vast array of potential choices. All participants spoke about a dialogue being built up, sometimes *"for weeks"* (Seb, 44), before the face-to-face meeting took place, therefore an initial investment was built up, leading to increased frustration when they didn't hit it off in the flesh.

"Already, I could tell she doesn't look like her pictures but I stopped for a moment I double backed and see if I go through with it. I am a gentleman. I say I haven't done that yet. I will go on a date, take her for a drink see how it goes" (Ben, 39)

The rapport that was fostered online did not always transfer to the initial first date. For example, Ben (39) discussed one particular incident:

"This woman for me to be able to go on a date with, uh, we must have had common ground. There must have been something funny about her. We just had a dialogue going. But it just didn't click to see her in the flesh and the way she acted."

These experiences resonate with previous work suggesting that online communications can sometimes lead to a false sense of intimacy, perhaps because the disinhibited nature of cyberspace results in the swifter revelation of more intimate and personal disclosures, yet the level of mutual trust and knowledge might not have been built up to sustain the relationship at that level of intimacy [29].

The physical and interpersonal incongruence of how daters are perceived online versus offline might also be accounted for with reference to impression management theory. For instance, one has the potential to polish one's online persona and create optimal self-presentations because of the idiosyncratic features of cyberspace. For example, with reference to Walther's hyperpersonal theory of CMC [40], users can create a more favourable presence due to editability (e.g. the ability to choose which photos frame the person in the most attractive light) and asynchronicity (e.g. the ability to edit messages to perfection because communication does not take place in real time). Thus, some daters may be presenting an idealised self, or being strategic in their self-presentation, but meeting face-to-face violates expectations and the connection made through CMC might be regarded as contrived.

In particular, participants considered the photograph to be highly valued in terms of making judgements as to whether to make an initial contact with daters. All participants placed importance on the photograph, as they all felt that physical attraction was part of the decision-making for whether or not they contacted someone.

"You want someone that you're attracted to. I think that's been my dating factor that the first point is, someone that you're attracted to" (Lucas, 35)

What emerged as one of the most contentious issues for participants was the notion that many of them had experienced dates with individuals who did not look like their images online. David (47) for instance noted:

"I mean, I had one date last year and her photograph was about ten years old"

This topic induced an array of responses from participants: annoyance, confusion, humour, and concern that they would not recognise individuals on a first date. The participants quickly understood through their experiences that self-enhancement was a common occurrence in the online dating world.

"Only a woman can do it as well as they do. Uh, it's so deceptive. You meet them in the flesh and sometimes you say, oh, jeez you don't look like your pictures" (Ben, 39)

For the most part participants did not think that these daters were intentionally trying to deceive, but rather were trying to present their 'ideal' self rather than their 'actual' self. For instance, Bertie (50) indicated:

"Yeah, but I'm not saying that they are being deliberately, you know, deliberately misleading. I just think they have just chosen perhaps a– because you're on there trying to sell yourself and choose a flattering photo, and it might be a couple of years older."

Although it has been argued that employing self-enhancement tactics needs to be mitigated by the goal of meeting face-to-face [14], this does not necessarily reflect the experiences of the participants in this study, who reported abundant self misrepresentations of others. Consequently, instead of treating the date like a 'date', it was more often used as a continuation of the initial impression formation process and could feel like starting from scratch.

"It's like I have to start again, whether I have- okay, I have already made up my mind whether I like the look of you, but here I am, I have to make that decision again" (Ben, 39)

3.4 Negative Impact on Self

The theme of 'negative impact on self' was salient for the majority of the participants and included the sub-theme 'strategies to protect the self'. Throughout the participants' narratives, detailed encounters of numerous situations were provided where threats to the self were mentioned. These threats ranged in depth and prevalence, but what was clear is that being an active member of an ODS makes users vulnerable to a variety of different adverse behaviours. For example, many participants indicated that messages they had sent had been deleted without being read, others noted that they had gone for long periods of time without receiving replies, while some recounted personal stories of communications ceasing suddenly and with no explanation. For example, Lucas (35) noted:

"You might be messaging someone and you think it's going really well, and you think the conversation's going well, and they just disappear. I guess they didn't think the same"

The need to belong is a fundamental human drive [41], so it is not surprising that encounters such as this might negatively impact on one's self-concept. Indeed, Lucas (35) further noted that fears of being appraised negatively would sometimes lead to him deactivating the app to remove the threat source.

"Yeah, definitely, there's been a few times where I deleted it because I thought I just needed a break away from it"

When discussing their experiences, participants highlighted how such encounters could undermine their confidence in themselves and their interpersonal interactions online.

"So it kind of knocks your confidence" (Charlie, 22)
"You just come over in some way as being somebody who is um, not- not of personal interest or undesirable I suppose, in that respect" (David, 47)

Participant accounts spoke of the dehumanising effect of receiving limited interest from others and the damaging impact this could have on one's self-esteem. For instance, Ben (39) noted:

"I don't have many matches on Tinder basically. I was thinking, okay, why are things drying up, now that people, other women are recognising my face? They're fed up of seeing it? And not bothered by it and oh 'it's him again' and thinking that this is why they swipe left. Are they thinking that my bio is no good?"

Despite the negative ramifications for the self, participants also rationalised the behaviour of others as a coping strategy to minimise the negative attributional implications for the self. David (47) for example shifted the blame on to the technology itself:

"I think the Internet enables rudeness in a way that you don't get in the real life"

Indeed, previous research has argued that there are few ramifications for the individual who is ceasing communications online because the individual they are cutting contact with is unlikely to be known to them in the offline world [22]. It may be easier to distance ourselves emotionally from someone who is on the other side of a screen because their physical reactions, including their sense of disappointment, are essentially invisible to us, making it easier to see them as *less* human [28].

Protective strategies were evident throughout participants' narratives. Drawing on self-affirmation theory [35], it was clear that many participants attempted to reframe rejection in such a way as to maintain self-integrity. David (47) for example, bolstered his own self-worth by implying that he wasn't like all of the other men on the site.

"Um, I think that um – I think it's had a positive impact in as much as I am quite pleased that I am not the kind of person who, as a man – I am quite pleased, as I see it, I am not a typical man on a dating site".

Self-affirmations occurred through participants looking at these experiences in a broader sense. Subsequently, they were able to distance themselves from the situation by taking value from their own personal characteristics and strengths, making healthy adjustments when faced with setbacks. Nate (18) for instance stated:

"So, if something happened like that, I'm just, I will just sort of get over it real quick and just carry on with what I'm doing"

Therefore, this indicates that behavioural adjustments had taken place, thereby reducing investments and expectations of future contact.

Some participants also expressed personal growth through adversity, improving personal outcomes, bolstering their sense of self-worth and strengthening their identity. For instance, Ben (39) discussed the following example:

"If I hadn't been as, if I hadn't been as shit online dating as I am - then I wouldn't have been as, as confident the way I've, er, um, pitched myself. You know, if I just found the first woman that came along and just clicked immediately - just settled, but I would've been the same all old Ben as before".

3.5 Resiliency

All of the males interviewed were not only at different stages in the lifespan, but at different cycles in their online dating journey. Two were in relationships with individuals they had met on online dating sites, and one was currently single and debating whether or not to re-join. Emerging from this narrative was a central theme of 'resiliency' that was prevalent throughout the discourse.

Psychological resiliency is a complex and multifaceted characteristic that promotes positive adaption when presented with adversity and stress [42]. The participants in this study had very different life experiences, for example some had gone through a divorce or a relationship break-up. In addition, there were individual differences in protective factors such as personal, familial and social safe guards, although participants were united in their goal of seeking dates and potential partners. In trying to achieve this goal, all of the participants experienced some degree of adversity, such as dates that went badly or being ignored by others on the sites they were using. Often they were left to ponder why they were not having the dating experience they desired, experiencing a negative impact on self-evaluations.

"I was feeling a little bit down beat you see" (Ben, 39)
"There's been a few times where I deleted it because I thought I just needed a break away from it. And if you're sending messages to people and you get no reply you start to think 'huh, well why?'" (Lucas, 35)

Although most of the participants experienced some degree of success, adversity was the prevailing theme. While recounting their negative experiences, this aroused humour and laughter from many of the participants. Thus, positive emotions were present alongside negative emotions. This was true for David (47) who out of all the males interviewed appeared to find the experience the most unpleasant, but did not let the experience define him:

"I don't have a high opinion of them and I don't have a good experience but I don't think it's affected me in my view of who I am"

All participants utilised positive adaptive coping strategies, being flexible, remaining optimistic, and displaying competence in their beliefs [43].

"And so, you know, there are successes to be had" (Bertie, 50).

They remained motivated, exhibiting stamina and tenacity rather than maladaptive strategies, garnering resilience throughout their ODS experience rather than ruminating over the rejection. For example, Charlie (22) noted:

"For me, if someone is not interested no, I've learned over my periods on that. If someone is not interested, that's it. Move on"

3.6   Conclusions and Future Directions

This exploratory and novel study has provided rich insights into the lived experiences of heterosexual male online daters. The five central themes which emerged from participants' narratives have elucidated on the bifurcation which is said to exist in how the sexes experience online dating. The participants in this study provided accounts suggesting that men are likely to encounter frequent disadvantages in their quest to seek love online, with numerous barriers to their successful use of these sites. Moreover, these barriers have also been described as sources of frustration, potentially impacting on the dater's self-perceptions. However, what was also clear is that ODS offered opportunities to meet a partner that were simply not available to them offline, making ODS an enticing and compelling option regardless of the negative ramifications of site membership. Inaccuracies in self presentation identified when online relationships move offline may serve to undermine initial benefits of ODS and lead to frustrations. Despite the negative connotations however, there was also evidence of resiliency, personal growth and tenacity among the participants enabling them to stay true to themselves and persist with online dating, despite the obvious challenges of 'playing the game'.

Future research may wish to delve further into the psychological impacts of the online dating experience for heterosexual men. Much of the research which has been conducted to date has utilised cross-sectional survey designs. Gathering data from users over the course of their online dating journey should permit insights into which specific parts of the dating cycle are likely to cause the most distress and threats to self-worth. For example, although fledgling members may be characterised by a sense of optimism, experience of multiple rejections may impact negatively on the individual's psychological wellbeing. It may also be interesting to investigate potential relationships between male misogyny and persistent experiences of being ignored and rejected on dating sites. Dating sites should also consider addressing the inequity in subscription fees between the sexes. Those which encourage men to purchase add-ons are likely to be met with dissatisfaction from their male demographic. Moreover, there may be some utility in offering online daters opportunities to verify the accuracy of the online personas of other daters prior to arranging a meeting (e.g. via video chat facilities) to ameliorate a smoother transition from online to offline. ODS may also consider taking a leaf out of the book of Bumble, a dating site which encourages women to make the first move. Although this research has prioritised the heterosexual male experience, there is both the scope and need to look at the experiences of heterosexual females and online daters from the LGBTQ community, who might experience online dating very differently.

References

1. Sedikides, C., Oliver, M.B., Campbell, W.K.: Perceived benefits and costs of romantic relationships for women and men: implications for exchange theory. Pers. Relat. **1**(1), 5–21 (1994)
2. Mellor, D., Stokes, M., Firth, L., Hayashi, Y., Cummins, R.: Need for belonging, relationship satisfaction, loneliness, and life satisfaction. Pers. Individ. Differ. **45**(3), 213–218 (2008)
3. Attrill, A.: Cyberpsychology. Oxford University Press, Oxford (2015)

4. Finkel, E.J., Eastwick, P.W., Karney, B.R., Reis, H.T., Sprecher, S.: Dating in a digital world. Sci. Am. **25**, 104–111 (2016)
5. D'Angelo, J.D., Toma, C.L.: There are plenty of fish in the sea: the effects of choice overload and reversibility on online daters' satisfaction with selected partners. Behav. Brain Sci. **12**(01), 1–14 (2016)
6. Smith, A., Anderson, M.: 5 facts about online dating. Pew Research Center 29 (2016)
7. Chester, A., Bretherton, D.: Impression management and identity online. In: McKenna, K., Joinson, A.N., Reips, U.D., Postmes, T. (eds.) The Oxford Handbook of Internet Psychology, pp. 223–236. Oxford University Press, Oxford (2007)
8. Hancock, J.T., Toma, C.L.: Putting your best face forward: the accuracy of online dating photographs. J. Commun. **59**(2), 367–386 (2009)
9. Ellison, N.B., Hancock, J.T., Toma, C.L.: Profile as promise: a framework for conceptualizing veracity in online dating self-presentations. New Media Soc. **14**(1), 45–62 (2012)
10. Fullwood, C.: The role of personality in online self-presentation. In: Attrill, A. (ed.) Cyberpsychology, pp. 89–110. Oxford University Press, Oxford (2015)
11. Uski, S., Lampinen, A.: Social norms and self-presentation on social network sites: profile work in action. New Media Soc. **18**(3), 447–464 (2016)
12. Lo, S.K., Hsieh, A.Y., Chiu, Y.P.: Contradictory deceptive behavior in online dating. Comput. Hum. Behav. **29**(4), 1755–1762 (2013)
13. Fullwood, C., Attrill-Smith, A.: Up-dating: ratings of perceived dating success are better online than offline. Cyberpsychol. Behav. Soc. Network. **21**(1), 11–15 (2018)
14. Ellison, N., Heino, R., Gibbs, J.: Managing impressions online: self-presentation processes in the online dating environment. J. Comput.-Mediated Commun. **11**(2), 415–441 (2006)
15. Whitty, M.T.: Revealing the 'real' me, searching for the 'actual' you: presentations of self on an internet dating site. Comput. Hum. Behav. **24**(4), 1707–1723 (2008)
16. Hitsch, G.J., Hortaçsu, A., Ariely, D.: What makes you click?—mate preferences in online dating. Quant. Mark. Econ. **8**(4), 393–427 (2010)
17. Fiore, A.T., Taylor, L.S., Mendelsohn, G.A., Hearst, M.: Assessing attractiveness in online dating profiles. In: Proceedings of the SIGCHI Conference on Human Factors in Computing Systems, pp. 797–806. ACM, New York (2008)
18. Rosenfeld, M.J., Thomas, R.J.: Searching for a mate: the rise of the Internet as a social intermediary. Am. Sociol. Rev. **77**(4), 523–547 (2012)
19. Henry-Waring, M., Barraket, J.: Dating & intimacy in the 21st century: the use of online dating sites in Australia. Int. J. Emerg. Technol. Soc. **6**(1) (2008)
20. Blackhart, G.C., Fitzpatrick, J., Williamson, J.: Dispositional factors predicting use of online dating sites and behaviors related to online dating. Comput. Hum. Behav. **33**, 113–118 (2014)
21. Kreager, D.A., Cavanagh, S.E., Yen, J., Yu, M.: "Where have all the good men gone?" Gendered interactions in online dating. J. Marriage Fam. **76**(2), 387–410 (2014)
22. Fiore, A.T., Taylor, L.S., Zhong, X., Mendelsohn, G.A., Cheshire, C.: Who's right and who writes: people, profiles, contacts, and replies in online dating. In: 2010 43rd Hawaii International Conference on System Sciences (HICSS), pp. 1–10. IEEE, New York (2010)
23. Kim, M., Kwon, K.N., Lee, M.: Psychological characteristics of Internet dating service users: the effect of self-esteem, involvement, and sociability on the use of Internet dating services. CyberPsychol. Soc. Network. Behav. **12**(4), 445–449 (2009)
24. Zytko, D., Grandhi, S.A., Jones, Q.: Impression management struggles in online dating. In: Proceedings of the 18th International Conference on Supporting Group Work, pp. 53–62. ACM, New York (2014)
25. Heino, R.D., Ellison, N.B., Gibbs, J.L.: Relationshopping: investigating the market metaphor in online dating. J. Soc. Pers. Relat. **27**(4), 427–447 (2010)

26. Kiesler, S., Siegel, J., McGuire, T.W.: Social psychological aspects of computer-mediated communication. Am. Psychol. **39**(10), 1123 (1984)
27. Kim, J.Y.: Social interaction in computer-mediated communication. Bull. Am. Soc. Inf. Sci. Technol. **26**(3), 15–17 (2000)
28. Suler, J.: The online disinhibition effect. Cyberpsychol. Soc. Network. Behav. **7**(3), 321–326 (2004)
29. Cooper, A., Sportolari, L.: Romance in cyberspace: understanding online attraction. J. Sex Educ. Ther. **22**(1), 7–14 (1997)
30. Greengross, G., Miller, G.: Humor ability reveals intelligence, predicts mating success, and is higher in males. Intelligence **39**(4), 188–192 (2011)
31. Leary, M.R., Kowalski, R.M.: Impression management: a literature review and two-component model. Psychol. Bull. **107**(1), 34 (1990)
32. Abramova, O., Baumann, A., Krasnova, H., Buxmann, P.: Gender differences in online dating: what do we know so far? A systematic literature review. In: 2016 49th Hawaii International Conference on System Sciences (HICSS), pp. 3858–3867. IEEE, New York (2016)
33. Hickey, W.: Here's how many messages men have to send to women on a dating site to be sure of getting a response. Business Insider, 17 July 2013. https://www.businessinsider.com/online-dating-message-statistics-2013-7?r=US&IR=T. Accessed 15 Feb 2019
34. Masden, C., Edwards, W.K.: Understanding the role of community in online dating. In: Proceedings of the 33rd Annual ACM Conference on Human Factors in Computing Systems, pp. 535–544. ACM, New York (2015)
35. Steele, C.M.: The psychology of self-affirmation: sustaining the integrity of the self. Adv. Exp. Soc. Psychol. **21**, 261–302 (1988)
36. Denzin, N.K., Lincoln, Y.S.: The Landscape of Qualitative Research, 3rd edn. Sage, Los Angeles (2008)
37. Braun, V., Clarke, V.: Using thematic analysis in psychology. Qual. Res. Psychol. **3**(2), 77–101 (2006)
38. Halaburda, H., Jan Piskorski, M., Yıldırım, P.: Competing by restricting choice: the case of matching platforms. Manag. Sci. **64**(8), 3574–3594 (2017)
39. Buss, D.M.: Sex differences in human mate preferences: evolutionary hypotheses tested in 37 cultures. Behav. Brain Sci. **12**(01), 1–14 (1989)
40. Walther, J.B.: Selective self-presentation in computer-mediated communication: hyperpersonal dimensions of technology, language, and cognition. Comput. Hum. Behav. **23**(5), 2538–2557 (2007)
41. Leary, M.R., Baumeister, R.F.: The nature and function of self-esteem: sociometer theory. Adv. Exp. Soc. Psychol. **32**, 1–62 (2000)
42. Yu, X., Zhang, J.: Factor analysis and psychometric evaluation of the Connor-Davidson Resilience Scale (CD-RISC) with Chinese people. Soc. Behav. Pers.: Int. J. **35**(1), 19–30 (2007)
43. Windle, G.: What is resilience? A review and concept analysis. Rev. Clin. Gerontol. **21**(02), 152–169 (2011)

Gamification of a Stress Management App: Results of a User Study

Alexandra Hoffmann[✉], Corinna A. Faust-Christmann,
Gregor Zolynski, and Gabriele Bleser

Junior Research Group wearHEALTH, Technische Universität Kaiserslautern,
Kaiserslautern, Germany
hoffmann@cs.uni-kl.de

Abstract. The use of gamification in the context of mHealth has been suggested to positively influence both usage behavior and user experience. Nonetheless, the integration of gamification in the context of stress management is a critically discussed topic. So far, little is known about the users' perceived quality of gamified stress management apps. This study therefore, investigated the quality of the gamified stress management app "Stress-Mentor" in a user study. For this purpose 19 participants tested Stress-Mentor's full version for a period of 4 weeks. Afterwards participants rated the app's quality, in a semi-structured interview, using uMARS. The results were then compared to those of a previous study investigating the quality of the app's first version (minimal viable product, MVP). This aimed at determining improvements of the app as a result of its iterative development process. The results revealed a trend of improvement for Stress-Mentor's full version compared to the MVP. In fact, the app's ratings increased in the categories engagement, aesthetics, information, and perceived engagement. Functionality scores remained at a high level. The users made positive comments regarding the app's concept. They also found Stress-Mentor to be fun and engaging. As a reason for this they mentioned gamification. This demonstrates that the combination of stress management methods with gamification was well received by the users. The results therefore, support the importance of including gamification in stress management apps. Furthermore, this study shows that the iterative development involving the user can lead to an increase of a mHealth product's overall quality.

Keywords: mHealth · Stress management · Gamification · Agile methods · User study · App quality

1 Introduction

1.1 Background

Chronic stress and its negative impact on health are a growing problem in today's society [1]. A solution for this problem that is met with increasing approval is the use of health-promoting smartphone applications (mHealth). "Ovia", "Mevi", "DeStressify" and "myCompass" are only some of the available stress management apps. First

© Springer Nature Switzerland AG 2019
A. Marcus and W. Wang (Eds.): HCII 2019, LNCS 11585, pp. 303–313, 2019.
https://doi.org/10.1007/978-3-030-23538-3_23

evidence that the use of such apps can have positive impact on a person's stress level has already been published [2–4].

To ensure their effectivity, stress management apps should integrate evidence-based content. This includes well-established coping and relaxation methods, as well as behavior change techniques [5–7]. However, current app reviews show that only few of the available stress management apps include a broad range of established methods [8, 9]. Notwithstanding the importance of appropriate content, these methods alone have been suggested as insufficient to promote long-term behavior change through apps [10]. The integration of gamification in mHealth products has been proposed as a possible solution to this problem.

1.2   Gamification in Health Apps

Gamification is defined as the use of game elements in non-game contexts [11]. It can have positive effects on user experience [12] and usability [13], as well as on the user's motivation and engagement [14]. Moreover, the implementation of gamification can improve usage consistency and thus result in a greater exposure to the content of mHealth products [10]. Nevertheless, it is critically discussed whether gamification should be used in stress management applications. So far, studies report positive as well as negative or neutral effects with respect to behavioral and cognitive aspects. In addition, the effects of gamification are often dependent on the context and aim of the application [12]. For example, a study in the context of smoking cessation suggests that the combination of game elements and behavior change techniques can be well received by users [15]. On the other hand, the developers of the stress management app "Ovia" report that users do not wish for an integration of game elements in this context. This shows that users might not accept game elements in the context of stress management. Users are clearly reluctant towards linking stress management with gamification [2]. This might be one reason why, despite its great potential, gamification is hardly found in current stress management applications [16]. Notwithstanding, the users' reluctance toward the hypothetical use of gamification in stress management apps, little is known about how game elements are actually perceived in this context.

1.3   Stress-Mentor

To close the identified gaps we developed a first prototype of the stress management app "Stress-Mentor". This MVP (minimal viable product, [17]) combined the self-monitoring of stress-relevant behaviors and events through a diary [18] with vicarious reinforcement through the appearance of an avatar. The MVP's general quality was then assessed in a longitudinal study. The MVP was tested by 26 participants over a period of 4 weeks [18]. After the 4-week trial period the participants rated the MVP's quality with the user version of the mobile application rating scale for health apps (uMARS) [19]. The uMARS was applied as a semi-structured interview in order to receive suggestions for improvement. The results of this first study showed that linking the self-monitoring of stress-relevant behaviors with vicarious reinforcement through an avatar was well received by users. However, the study also revealed that the inclusion of more game elements might be needed to improve the usage behavior [18].

Including the user into the development process in this manner is an important tool to ensure the functionality of health technologies. Thus, as is recommended in iterative app development [20], the user feedback from this first study was used to create an extended app concept.

Based on the feedback additional stress management, behavior change and gamification features were incorporated in Stress-Mentor's full version. For example, in addition to self-monitoring through a diary and its long-term visualization [21], the full version includes daily stress management exercises (i.e., breathing, progressive muscle relaxation, meditation, visualization, euthymic methods, physical exercises, cognitive aspects, time management, setting priorities, and planning social support and change). Moreover, the full version links these stress management aspects with a number of game elements. Besides the avatar, the full version includes an agent that guides the user through the app by explaining new functions and providing tips on stress and stress management. When using the app for the first time, the agent hands over the responsibility of raising the avatar to the user through a behavioral contract, which provides a narrative context. This means in addition to reflecting the user's diary entries through its appearance, the user's progress is visualized through the avatar's growth in the full version. The user can capture this progress in a photobook. The avatars pictures can also be shared with others. This provides a social component. Additionally, the user's progress is visualized through progress bars. The full version also supports goal setting by providing the stress management exercises in "tasks of the day" and "tasks of the week". Here the user can chose one out of three suggested exercises he or she wants to accomplish each day. The app's consistent usage is rewarded through badges. Another reward system is the points the user receives for every task and diary entry. These points can be exchanged for items for the user's avatar in a shop. The addition of new gamification aspects over time is aimed at upholding the user's curiosity. This is further supported through random sales in the app's shop, randomly provided motivating quotes of famous persons and the randomly provided option to take pictures of the avatar.

The resulting full version of Stress-Mentor thus, combines an extended gamification framework with evidence-based stress management methods and behavior change techniques. For more information regarding Stress-Mentor's concept see Christmann et al. [22]. Screenshots and content of both the MVP and the full version are displayed in Fig. 1.

The full version's general quality was again evaluated in a 4-week user study using uMARS. The aim of this study was to assess Stress-Mentor's quality and to reveal improvements compared to the MVP.

> ### Stress Management:
>
> **self-monitoring through a diary**, breathing, progressive muscle relaxation, meditation, visualization, euthymic methods, physical exercises, cognitive aspects, time management, setting priorities, plan social support and change

Gamification:

appearance of the avatar depends on the user's diary entries; feedback regarding diary entries through traffic light coloring of entries; progress visualization through the growth of the avatar, photo book and progress bars; agent that guides the user though the app, explains new functions and provides tips regarding stress and stress management; badges for regular usage; points for tasks and diary entries; narrative context; economy through item shop; goal setting through tasks

Fig. 1. Screenshots and content of the stress management app's first test version (minimal viable product, MVP, left screenshot) and its full version (right screenshot). The app combines evidence-based stress management techniques with gamification. The content already included in the MVP is highlighted in bold print.

2   Methods

2.1   Participants

Participant recruitment was carried out via an e-mail distribution list of the Technische Universität Kaiserslautern and associated research institutes, as well as an article in a local newspaper. All participants gave written consent to participate in accordance with the declaration of Helsinki.

In 2016 the MVP was tested by 27 participants (mean age = 23.38 years, SD = 3.01, 11 female, 16 male) in a first user study [18]. Of these participants 6 were in employment and 22 were university students.

In 2018 Stress-Mentor's full version was again tested in a user study with 20 participants. However, one participant did not return for the final study appointment. This resulted in a total of 19 participants (mean age = 33.6 years, SD = 8.8 years, 10 female, 9 male) that were included in the analysis. Of these participants 12 were in employment and 7 were university students.

To ensure that the testing conditions were as realistic as possible the app was installed on the users' own smartphone (Android version 4.4 or higher) and then used for 4-weeks in both studies. Therefore, the regular use (at least once a day) of a smartphone or tablet was a prerequisite for participation. In addition, participation in both studies required a minimum age of 18 years and fluency in German (all app instructions are only available in German).

2.2 Procedure

At the beginning of the study, each participant was informed about the course and aim of the study, as well as about the collected data. Each participant gave his or her written consent to participate. Subsequently, the participant's demographic data was collected and the lead investigator installed the full version of the stress management app on the participant's smartphone or tablet. After the installation, a brief introduction was given by the lead investigator. First the participant had to adjust the settings to his or her gender and age, as well as his or her preferences (tracking of alcohol and coffee consumption, reminder, color schemes and text size). Then he or she made an entry in the app's health diary (sleep duration and quality, duration and intensity of sport, positive and negative events, general degree of stress, prevailing mood, consumption of water, vegetables and fruit, caffeinated drinks and alcohol). This was followed by a 4-week usage period, during which participants should use the app daily.

The study was completed with a second meeting that took place at least one day and a maximum of 14 days after the end of the 4-week usage period. As was done with the MVP, the participants then again rated the full version's quality using uMARS [19].

2.3 App Quality

The user version of the mobile application rating scale (uMARS) [19] was applied to assess the quality of both the MVP and the app's full version. uMARS was specifically designed to assess the quality of health apps from the user perspective [19].

Participants rated each of the questionnaire's items on a 5-point likert-scale (from 1 inadequate to 5 excellent). uMARS was applied as a semi-structured interview. This means after each rating, participants had the opportunity to explain their answer and provide feedback and suggestions for changes in the app (open response format). Presenting questionnaires as semi-structured interviews provides deeper insight into the reasoning for the ratings, as well as suggestions for possible improvements (e.g., [23]).

A total of three questions were removed from the questionnaire. One question from the category information (16. "Does the app come from a credible source?") was removed because the participants were informed of the app's source in detail prior to participation. Furthermore, two questions from the category subjective quality were removed: 18. "How many times do you think you would use this app in the next 12 months if it was relevant to you?" because this question was not included in the MVP questionnaire due to a shorter targeted usage period and 19. "Would you pay for this app?" because it is planned to make the app available for free. The term health behavior in the questions of the app specific section was replaced with stress management.

2.4   Analysis

In order to check whether the addition of established stress management methods and other gamification techniques (see Fig. 1) had a positive effect on the perceived quality of the app, the results from both studies were tested for mean differences. T-tests were calculated to identify differences in mean uMARS ratings of the full version and the MVP. Bonferroni correction was used to adjust the t-test results for an accumulation of alpha errors.

3   Results

The analysis revealed significantly higher ratings for the full version (M = 4.514, SD = 0.327) compared to the MVP (M = 3.992, SD = 0.346) regarding the app's general quality; t(44) = 5,198, p < .001, d = 1.541. In detail, improvements in the full version (M = 4.221, SD = 0.503) compared to the MVP (M = 2.926, SD = 0.738) could be observed for the category engagement; t(44) = 7.076, p < .001, d = 1.985. Moreover, higher ratings were observed in all questions of this category (i.e., entertainment, interest, customization, interactivity and target group). With regard to aesthetics, the full version (M = 4.667, SD = 0.314) also received better ratings than the MVP (M = 4.235, SD = 0.451); t(44) = 3.600, p = .001, d = 1.078. However, here only the question visual appeal showed a significant improvement, while no difference could be found between the rating regarding Stress-Mentor's layout and graphics. An improvement of the app's full version (M = 4.456, SD = 0.590) in comparison with the MVP (M = 4.000, SD = 0.686) could also be detected regarding the category information, t(44) = 2.413, p = .020, d = 0.704. The ratings for both the quality and quantity of the included information increased. No difference between MVP and full version was identified regarding the app's visual information. Even though the app is now much more complex and has a lot more features, ratings for the app's functionality did not decrease and its functionality was assessed as excellent for both the MVP (M = 4.806, SD = 0.244) and full version (M = 4.711, SD = 0.315); t(44) = −1.104, p = .278, d = 0.346. This is also reflected in the rating of each of the questions regarding the app's functionality (i.e., performance, ease of use, navigation and gestural design). There is no difference between MVP and full version with respect to these aspects. In contrast, MVP (M = 2.648, SD = 1.040) and full version (M = 3.763, SD = 0.865) differed with respect to their perceived impact; t(44) = 3.956, p < .001, d = 1.147. The app's full version received higher ratings for all questions in this category (i.e., awareness, knowledge, attitudes, intention to change, help seeking and behavior change). In addition the full version (M = 4.210, SD = 0.164) received a better overall star rating than the MVP (M = 3.333, SD = 0.207); t(44) = 3.327, p = .002, d = 4.602. Also, participants were more likely to recommend the full version (M = 4.315, SD = 0.217) of Stress-Mentor to others in comparison to the MVP (M = 2.888, SD = 0.235); t(44) = 4.464, p < .001, d = 6.264. The corresponding means and standard errors for the rating of the uMARS questions of both studies are displayed in Fig. 2.

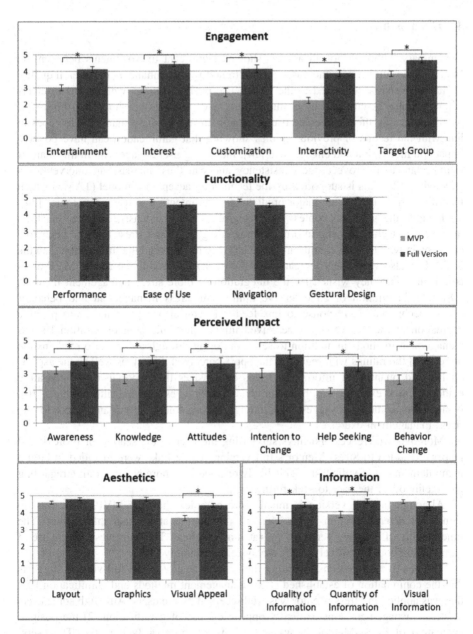

Fig. 2. uMARS (user mobile application rating scale) ratings of the MVP (minimal viable product) and the full version of Stress-Mentor are displayed. Depicted are means and standard errors. Significant differences between the groups are marked with an asterisk (*).

4 Discussion

In summary, although not all aspects showed significant improvements between the MVP and the full version, there is a general trend towards enhancing the overall quality of the full version compared to the MVP. The positive ratings with regard to entertainment, interest, customization, interactivity and target group show that the use of gamification can affect perceived user engagement in a positive manner. This goes in line with the results of previous studies showing that gamification can have positive impact on motivation and engagement [14]. Increasing user engagement in this manner is important to improve usage consistency and can thus, increase an intervention's effectivity [12]. This is supported by the technology acceptance model (TAM3) which identified joy of use as one major predictor for the intention to use technologies [24].

Besides the gamified context, the integration of an extensive number of stress management techniques and information regarding stress and stress relevant behaviors can explain why the participants are more likely to recommend the full version than the MVP. It is also very likely the cause for the improved overall star rating. MVP users commented that they wished for the integration of more stress management methods [18]. The integration of an extensive number of stress management and behavior change techniques in response to this feedback, can also explain the more positive evaluation of the full version's perceived impact. The inclusion of additional stress management methods in addition to self-monitoring through a diary also explains the increase of the ratings with regard to the app's perceived impact, as well as the aspects quality and quantity of information. This emphasizes the importance of integrating evidence-based exercises and behavior change techniques into mHealth products [10]. Nonetheless, some users suggested including more graphics, pictures and videos for the stress management exercises.

Moreover, references and links supporting the user in the search for professional help were added to Stress-Mentor's full version. These links were included in both a menu item and in specific tasks. This likely resulted in a more positive rating regarding the likelihood of the user to seek further help.

Although the full version is much more complex than the MVP, there was no significant deterioration in Stress-Mentor's navigation and visual information. The functionality of both app versions was rated as excellent. This indicates that the use of gamification could positively affect the system's usability [13].

The positive evaluations regarding the general quality of the full version suggests that the combination of established stress management methods and gamification [22] that was applied in Stress-Mentor was well received by the users. Although some users of stress management apps explicitly oppose the use of gamification [2] the positive evaluation of Stress-Mentor shows that this is not necessarily the case. The users' comments emphasized that the embedding of stress-related aspects into a gamified context was perceived in an overall positive way. In fact, the participants found the app interesting to use and enjoyed exploring its contents. This goes in line with previous results that indicate that the combination of gamification with evidence-based content from stress management and behavior change could have positive effects on the user's engagement and thus, potentially make health apps more effective [15].

However, it is apparent that users are not aware of the effect of gamification [25]. Some of the participants said that the gamification concept would not have been necessary in their opinion. However, they also described that they tried to adjust their behavior so that they could make positive entries in their diary in order to make their avatar look healthier. This observation coincides with previous results on the effectiveness of vicarious reinforcement through avatars (e.g., [26]). It further underpins the potential usefulness of gamification in the context of stress management.

This demonstrates that it is not sufficient to ask potential users whether gamification is desired in a particular context. Rather, studies must examine if the implementation of game elements in a specific context appeals to the user and how their use influences the effectiveness of the product [27, 28]. When integrating gamification, the context and goal of the app should therefore always be taken into account [12]. The positive response to combining gamification with stress management in Stress-Mentor is probably due to the fact that the integrated gamification elements support the actual goal of the app, namely the learning of stress management methods through daily and weekly tasks. Nonetheless, the effect of gamification on actual usage behavior is still unknown. This aspect is the focus of our next study, where we are comparing the usage behavior of a gamified version of Stress-Mentor with a non-gamified version of the app.

5 Conclusion

In summary, an overall trend of improvement could be observed for Stress-Mentor's full version. The positive ratings confirm that Stress-Mentor is of good general quality, speaking for the app's successful, iterative development. This study therefore, shows that an iterative development process involving the user can lead to an improvement in the product's overall quality.

Even though some users of stress management apps were opposed to the use of gamification [2], this study demonstrates that the combination of stress management methods with gamification was, in fact, well received. This highlights the potential usefulness of gamification in the context of stress management.

Acknowledgements. The junior research group wearHEALTH is funded by the Federal Ministry of Education and Research (Bundesministerium für Bildung und Forschung, BMBF, reference number: 16SV7115).

References

1. Wiegner, L., Hange, D., Björkelund, C., Ahlborg, G.: Prevalence of perceived stress and associations to symptoms of exhaustion, depression and anxiety in a working age population seeking primary care - an observational study. BMC Fam. Pract. **16**(1), 78 (2015). https://doi.org/10.1186/s12875-015-0252-7
2. Ahtinen, A., et al.: Mobile mental wellness training for stress management: feasibility and design implications based on a one-month field study. JMIR Mhealth Uhealth **1**(2), e11 (2013). PMID:25100683

3. Economides, M., Martman, J., Bell, M.J., Sanderson, B.: Improvements in stress, affect, and irritability following brief use of a mindfulness-based smartphone app: a randomized controlled trial. Mindfulness 49(1–2), 55 (2018). https://doi.org/10.1007/s12671-018-0905-4

4. Lee, R.A., Jung, M.E.: Evaluation of an mHealth app (DeStressify) on university students' mental health: pilot trial. JMIR Ment. Health 5(1), e2 (2018). PMID:29362209

5. Chittaro, L., Sioni, R.: Evaluating mobile apps for breathing training: the effectiveness of visualization. Comput. Hum. Behav. 40, 56–63 (2014). https://doi.org/10.1016/j.chb.2014.07.049

6. Harrison, V., Proudfoot, J., Wee, P.P., Parker, G., Pavlovic, D.H., Manicavasagar, V.: Mobile mental health: review of the emerging field and proof of concept study. J. Ment. Health 20(6), 509–524 (2011). https://doi.org/10.3109/09638237.2011.608746

7. Morris, M.E., et al.: Mobile therapy: case study evaluations of a cell phone application for emotional self-awareness. J Med. Internet Res. 12(2), e10 (2010). https://doi.org/10.2196/jmir.1371

8. Coulon, S.M., Monroe, C.M., West, D.S.: A systematic, multi-domain review of mobile smartphone apps for evidence-based stress management. Am. J. Prev. Med. (2016). https://doi.org/10.1016/j.amepre.2016.01.026

9. Christmann, C.A., Hoffmann, A., Bleser, G.: Stress management apps with regard to emotion-focused coping and behavior change techniques: a content analysis. JMIR Mhealth Uhealth 5(2), e22 (2017). PMID:28232299

10. Vandelanotte, C., Spathonis, K.M., Eakin, E.G., Owen, N.: Website-delivered physical activity interventions. Am. J. Prev. Med. 33(1), 54–64 (2007). https://doi.org/10.1016/j.amepre.2007.02.041

11. Deterding, S., Khaled, R., Nacke, L.E., Dixon, D.: Gamification: toward a definition. In: Proceedings of the 2011 Annual Conference Extended Abstracts on Human Factors in Computing Systems. ACM, New York (2011). ISBN: 978-1-4503-0268-5

12. Johnson, D., Deterding, S., Kuhn, K.-A., Staneva, A., Stoyanov, S., Hides, L.: Gamification for health and wellbeing: a systematic review of the literature. Internet Interventions 6, 89–106 (2016). https://doi.org/10.1016/j.invent.2016.10.002

13. Zagel, C., Bodendorf, F.: Gamification: Auswirkungen auf Usability, Datenqualität und Motivation. In: Koch, M., Butz, A., Schlichter, J. (eds.) Tagungsband: Mensch und Computer: Oldenbourg Wissenschaftsverlag, pp. 15–24 (2014)

14. Hamari, J.: Transforming homo economicus into homo ludens: a field experiment on gamification in a utilitarian peer-to-peer trading service. Electron. Commer. Res. Appl. 12(4), 236–245 (2013). https://doi.org/10.1016/j.elerap.2013.01.004

15. Edwards, E.A., et al.: Creating a theoretically grounded, gamified health app: lessons from developing the cigbreak smoking cessation mobile phone game. JMIR Serious Games 6(4), e10252 (2018). PMID:30497994

16. Hoffmann, A., Christmann, C.A., Bleser, G.: Gamification in stress management apps: a critical app review. JMIR Serious Games 5(2), e13 (2017). PMID:28592397

17. Lenarduzzi, V., Taibi, D.: MVP explained: a systematic mapping study on the definitions of minimal viable product. In: SEAA 42nd Euromicro Conference on Software Engineering and Advanced Applications, Limassol, Cyprus, pp. 112–119. IEEE, Piscataway, 31 August–2 September 2016. ISBN: 978-1-5090-2820-7

18. Christmann, C.A., Zolynski, G., Hoffmann, A., Bleser, G.: Towards more interactive stress-related self-monitoring tools to improve quality of life. In: Bagnara, S., Tartaglia, R., Albolino, S., Alexander, T., Fujita, Y. (eds.) IEA 2018. AISC, vol. 818, pp. 121–130. Springer, Cham (2019). https://doi.org/10.1007/978-3-319-96098-2_17

19. Stoyanov, S.R., Hides, L., Kavanagh, D.J., Wilson, H.: Development and validation of the user version of the mobile application rating scale (uMARS). JMIR Mhealth Uhealth 4(2), e72 (2016). PMID:27287964

20. Stinson, J., et al.: Usability testing of an online self-management program for adolescents with juvenile idiopathic arthritis. J. Med. Internet Res. **12**(3), e30 (2010). PMID:20675293
21. Christmann, C.A., Zolynski, G., Hoffmann, A., Bleser, G.: Effective visualization of long term health data to support behavior change. In: Duffy, V.G. (ed.) DHM 2017. LNCS, vol. 10287, pp. 237–247. Springer, Cham (2017). https://doi.org/10.1007/978-3-319-58466-9_22
22. Christmann, C.A., Hoffmann, A., Zolynski, G., Bleser, G.: Stress-Mentor: linking gamification and behavior change theory in a stress management application. In: Stephanidis, C. (ed.) HCI 2018. CCIS, vol. 851, pp. 387–393. Springer, Cham (2018). https://doi.org/10.1007/978-3-319-92279-9_52
23. Anderson, K., Burford, O., Emmerton, L.: App chronic disease checklist: protocol to evaluate mobile apps for chronic disease self-management. JMIR Res. Protoc. **5**(4), e204 (2016). PMID:27815233
24. Venkatesh, V., Bala, H.: Technology acceptance model 3 and a research agenda on interventions. Decis. Sci. **39**(2), 273–315 (2008). https://doi.org/10.1111/j.1540-5915.2008.00192.x
25. Thorpe, A.S., Roper, S.: The ethics of gamification in a marketing context. J. Bus. Ethics **23**(9), 123 (2017). https://doi.org/10.1007/s10551-017-3501-y
26. Fox, J., Bailenson, J.N.: Virtual self-modeling: the effects of vicarious reinforcement and identification on exercise behaviors. Media Psychol. **12**(1), 1–25 (2009). https://doi.org/10.1080/15213260802669474
27. Cafazzo, J.A., Casselman, M., Hamming, N., Katzman, D.K., Palmert, M.R.: Design of an mHealth app for the self-management of adolescent type 1 diabetes: a pilot study. J. Med. Internet Res. **14**(3), e70 (2012). PMID:22564332
28. González, C.S., et al.: Learning healthy lifestyles through active videogames, motor games and the gamification of educational activities. Comput. Hum. Behav. **55**, 529–551 (2016). https://doi.org/10.1016/j.chb.2015.08.052

A Prototype System for Saving
and Representing Personal Moments

Fei Jiang[1,2(✉)]

[1] MIT Media Lab, Cambridge, USA
[2] Shanghai Academy of Fine Arts, Shanghai, China
pcboy0309@sina.com

Abstract. This study is the first stage of the ongoing research called *Moments* which is divided into three stages: *Reproduction, Enhancement* and *Evolution*. The first stage *Reproduction* is designed to create a way for user to save a special moment and to experience that moment in a user-friendly way in the future. Firstly, a multi-sensor equipment is designed to collect environment data in user's daily life. Secondly, the data integration system can collect relevant information based on user data from open data platform. At last, an immersive virtual reality environment is provided for user to explore his/her past experiences.

Keywords: Multi-senor · User-friendly · Virtual reality · Virtual reproduction · Personal data

1 Introduction

Reproduction is an ongoing research project between Shanghai Academy of Fine Arts and MIT Media Lab, introducing a user-friendly system which can save and reproduce special moments for individuals in their daily life. According to statistics, there are more than 1 trillion selfies taken on social networks each year. There is an increasing tendency for people to photograph and post their photos on social platforms, those pictures including work, life, travel, food and pets. Among others, the convenience of taking photos by mobile phone is crucial to the fashion trend, more importantly, the merit of this phenomenon has reflected that people are blithe to record the moments at a particular time, at a specific place, or with a special person. It is highly memorable to look at the scene stored in the photo in a special day in the future. It has been around two hundred years since the camera was invented. Irrespective of black or color pictures, and dynamic photos to panoramic photos in different imaging effect, there is no remarkable difference in nature. While it is valuable to look through the taken pictures and recall memories for users. An obvious flaw in the picture is that only limited image information can be gained from a piece of photo. With the passage of time, it is most likely to forget the time, place, climate or accompanying people in the photo, even no memory of the experience. The overarching purpose of the study is to collect more environmental information through current technologies operated easily like taking photos, and to have better experience methods to look through these information for users.

A. Marcus and W. Wang (Eds.): HCII 2019, LNCS 11585, pp. 314–322, 2019.
https://doi.org/10.1007/978-3-030-23538-3_24

The research takes into consideration the final outcome based on the needs of users. What kind of browsing environment can help users find memories of the past? The answer is to maximize the restoration of the original experience of the environment so as to wake up the user's sense of space and existence at a particular time. A review of history, from the *Sala delle Prospettive* created by Baldassarre Peruzzi in the early 16th century, to the panorama of the 18th century, to the virtual reality that emerged at the end of the 20th century, has presented a situation that the creators have devoted themselves to using 360-degree image space to surround the audience in a closed environment which can create an impression in the image so that the audience will generate a sense of space and a sense of existence. As Wolfgang Kemp described it, panorama is "a space of existence", the essence of which is to make participants feel trapped in the illusion of a real scene. With the popularity of 360 cameras in recent years, it has become more convenient to take 360 photos than to take ordinary photos, because they do not have to focus or composition, on the contrary, users only need to press the shoot button for recording the whole scene including themselves. In addition, it is convenient for users to immerse themselves in 360-degree panoramic space, browse the scene at any angle and have a good experience with the support of VR headsets. Therefore, the research takes 360 shooting and virtual reality as the main input and output modes.

2 Related Work

Over past the years, research in Wearable Device mainly centres on human health. Research in Spatial Augmented Reality has found innovative ways to include the physical home environment for entertainment and remote collaboration to create a more immersive experience. Another expansion of this research field is into accommodating further sensory modalities, e.g. mechanical, haptic or even olfactory manipulation.

3 Data Collection

When it comes to data collection, it mainly consist of environmental data and user data. The former refers to collect photos and environmental sound, because photography is the most direct way to record environmental features, and sound is a very important factor in scene reconstruction. In order to realize the environmental data collection conveniently and comprehensively, the equipment used for execution mainly includes a 360 camera and an ambisonic audio recorder, which can record the visual and auditory materials of the current environment quickly. On the other aspect, user data means the collection of heartbeat rate of users when they take photos. After collecting these basic data, more useful data will generate online to reconstruct the current environment for users by connecting some open data platforms in the later period. The 360 camera used this time is Ricoh Theta S. It can get GPS information by using a connected cell phone, so the metadata of the photos collected contains geographic information. After extracting geographic and temporal information, more environmental data can be obtained through an open data platform, including temperature, wind direction, humidity and local headlines (Fig. 1).

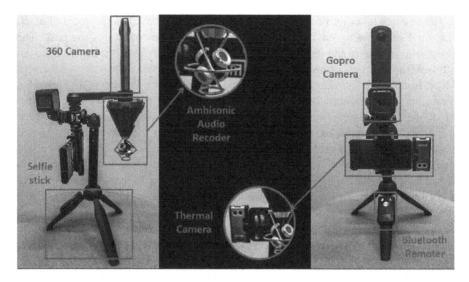

Fig. 1. The apparatus of data collection.

The ambisonic audio recorder harnessed to collect the environmental sound is ZOOM H3-VR, which integrates four ambisonic microphones to record the VR sound of four channels in real time. It is beneficial to locate the sound source in the virtual environment.

The 360 camera and the ambisonic audio recorder are fixed on a portable selfie stick, and the recording direction of the microphone must be consistent with the direction of the camera in the 360 camera to match the direction of the image and the sound source. Apart from the mentioned two equipment, the selfie stick also has a user-controlled and sound-recording phone, a thermal camera on the phone, a Gopro camera and a bluetooth camera switch.

The thermal camera is positive to the user, used to take selfies and record the temperature of the user and the surrounding environment. Due to the limitation that the open data platform can only get the outdoor temperature, the user can obtain the temperature data of the surrounding environment through the device in indoor environment. The direction of the Gopro camera which is in line with the user's view is used to catch what the user sees. Going forward, users can tap the bluetooth camera switch to trigger the built-in application program for the collection work of all data in one-step via controlling the mobile phone.

The project requires users to wear a wearable device that records heartbeats when shooting 360 photos. Considering the phone used in the study is iPhone, out of the compatibility, the device used to record heartbeat data is Apple Watch.

The experiment to collect data is almost similar to take selfie with a selfie stick. The user can only point the front camera of the 360 camera at what they see in their eyes, because other devices have been installed in the right direction according to the position of the 360 camera. All equipment will be triggered after setting up all information in App, what users need to do is to press bluetooth camera switch for obtaining all data.

The information obtained from a recording process is as follows: A 360 view photo with time and location information, a five-second VR audio file, a thermal imaging selfie with user temperature information, a 5-s high-definition video file and the user's heartbeats (Fig. 2).

Fig. 2. The way of using the apparatus.

4 Virtual Scene

The images, sounds and related data collected will be applied to create virtual reality scenes. The hardware used in this project is Oculus Go virtual reality glasses for its relatively cheap price and the characteristics of single-machine operation, so it is more suitable for ordinary consumers.

The purpose of creating a virtual scene is to recreate the moment saved by user and to visually, audibly and psychologically help user to reshape his/her previous experiences. The interactive scene of the user is set in a three-dimensional space. When the user wears the Oculus Go headsets, he/she can choose to view the thumbnail of the scene through a controller, which is very similar to the process of browsing photos on the computer. When the user selects the scene, the entire virtual scene will be surrounded by a 360 photos. The interactive process is very intuitive and users can freely change their views and look through the details of the environment in their own scenes. At the same time, you can also hear the sound coming from all directions of the scene, because the recorded sound matches the direction of the scene, so the sound heard by both ears will change when the user turns his head, genuinely reconstructing the original auditory feelings. All in all, The user can open the environment information menu through the controller. The menu includes the following six functions:

(1) Weather Conditions (2) Heartbeats (3) Breathing (4) Geographical Location (5) News Headlines (6) Scene Restoration.

4.1   Weather Conditions

Weather conditions: obtain the weather information on the day of shooting on the open data platform according to the time and location of 360 photo. The information includes temperature, weather conditions, wind direction, wind speed and humidity. If the users are indoor, they can choose to view thermal photos to get indoor temperature.

4.2   Heartbeats

Heartbeats: user's heartbeats is displayed several times per minute next to a heart-shaped button. When the user clicks on the button, the sound of the heartbeat appears in the scene, which is generated in real time in consistence with the heartbeats rate, and the whole scene will flash last for 5 s.

4.3   Breathing

Breathing: this is the breathing sound (breathing = heartbeat number/4) which is simulated according to the number of heartbeats. Although the frequency is not accurate, it plays a certain role in setting off the atmosphere.

4.4   Geographical Location

Geographical location: based on the GPS information of the 360 photo, the user can adjust the size of the display area by using the satellite view of the shooting place obtained by Google Map API.

4.5   News Headlines

News headlines: get local headlines on public platforms in light of the time and location of 360 photos. When the user clicks on the headline picture, there is a voice-over news profile.

4.6   Scene Restoration

Scene restoration: this is a function of mixing all the information, images, sounds, video images, and all the relevant data in this scene are deconstructed to produce a random effects of about 10 s, mainly including mingling of various sound sources, and changes in the light and shade of the scene, etc. (Fig. 3).

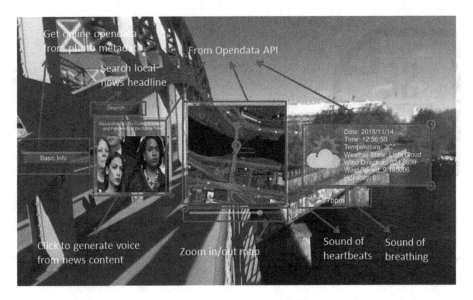

Fig. 3. The main scene in VR.

5 Archive Data

There are three options of saving and loading user file: 1. Open a standard 1 by 2 360 photo which contains GPS data information. 2. Open a SE(Shared Environments) file on use's disk. 3. Make an archive SE-file based on user data. The software extracts key elements which mainly affect human's feeling from raw data and then fuses them with

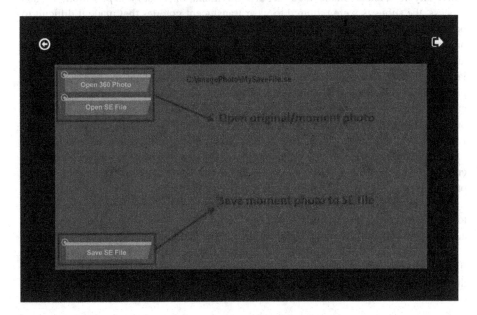

Fig. 4. The menu for saving and loading file.

Achive
(Compression file, e.g. *.rar, *.zip)

- 360 Picture   Seeing
- Ambient Sound (Environment, Users, Medias) Hearing
- Temperature (Environment, Objects, Users)   Touching
- Heart Beats   Feeling
- Location   ⎤
                   ⎬ Remembering
- Data and Time ⎦

Fig. 5. SE archive file

open data to generate a personal SE file which stores information-rich data for future applications to represent user's past monments (Figs. 4 and 5).

6   Limitations and Future Work

Sensory is the response of the human brain to the individual attributes of things that directly impact the sensory organs. The five main human sensations are visual, auditory, tactile, taste and olfactory, the first three of which are the top priority in human-machine interaction. Sensory plays a bridge role helping people to feel and recognize all kinds of attributes of external objects. Back in 1954, psychologists at McGill University in Canada made their debut experiment of *sensory deprivation*. In this process, the subjects were required to wear translucent goggles that made it difficult to produce vision; a monotonous sound emitted by an air conditioner was to limit its hearing; tactile sensation was limited through wearing paper sleeves and gloves on arms and securing legs and feet with splints. The subjects were left alone in the laboratory, and a few days later they appeared a series of many pathophysiological phenomena: delusional hallucinations, distracted attention, slow thinking, tension, anxiety, fear, etc. It is found that the development of the brain and their sophisticated degree are developed on the basis of extensive contact with the external environment. Living in the environment free from stimulation for a long time will weaken all aspects of the human organs. In this connection, it is an effective way to full explore their creativity with the help of a moderate stimulus to human perception. The VR devices at present used in the study are only limited to the ranges of visual and auditory stimulus to users, and in the future, more considerations will be taken into, for example, sensors to data acquisition and tactile and olfactory feedback equipment to output devices are added both. This can be more likely to restore the scenes saved by users.

In addition, an online platform will be built for users to upload and download SE files through their mobile devices or computers. On this platform, mobile applications that allow users to reedit their moments and share SE files with others. Once a user download a SE file, he/she can use the application to experience the representation of moments in Virtual Reality (Figs. 6 and 7).

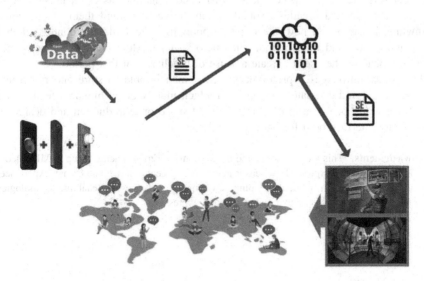

Fig. 6. SE online platform.

Fig. 7. Development process.

7 Conclusion

When entering the virtual space, the weather conditions help users recall their body feelings, heartbeat and breathing sound is conductive to remind them of emotions. Meanwhile, location and news headlines support users to build the context of that particular location and time period. The audio-visual mixture created by the scene-restoration benefits the user to create a sense of familiarity of that period.

This study introduces a prototype system which is able to store and represents user's moments and evaluates the key data which mainly affect human's feeling and fused them with open data to generate a virtual space of reproduction and designs a user-friendly interface both for hardware and software.

Acknowledgments. This work is supported by Responsive Environments group at MIT Media Lab. This group mainly explores how sensor networks augment and mediate human experience, interaction, and perception, while developing new sensing modalities and enabling technologies that create new forms of interactive experience and expression.

The Potential Role of Digital Nudging in the Digital Transformation of the Healthcare Industry

Christian Meske[1,2(✉)], Ireti Amojo[1,2], Akira-Sebastian Poncette[2,3], and Felix Balzer[2,3]

[1] Freie Universität Berlin, Garystr. 21, 14195 Berlin, Germany
c.meske@fu-berlin.de
[2] Einstein Center Digital Future, Wilhelmstraße 67, 10117 Berlin, Germany
[3] Department of Anesthesiology and Intensive Care Medicine,
Charité – Universitätsmedizin Berlin
(Corporate Member of Freie Universität Berlin, Humboldt-Universität zu Berlin,
and Berlin Institute of Health), Berlin, Germany

Abstract. New information technology has led to an ongoing transformation of the healthcare industry, supporting caregivers and caretakers. In some cases, such technologies may not be used in practice as intended by those who designed or implemented them. In other cases, the full potential of such technologies in terms of guiding user behavior has not been exhausted to the fullest. This is where "digital nudging" can help to overcome according issues. Nudging was invented in behavioral economics and aims at eliciting behavior that is beneficial for the individual, at the same time respecting the individual's own preferences and freedom of choice. *Digital* nudging can therefore help to guide user behavior in information systems. In this work, we investigate the potentials of this concept in hospitals. We come to the conclusion that digital nudging in hospitals can positively influence the use of technology, new value creation, the change of structures and consequently financial dimensions of digital transformation, supporting not only caregivers but also caretakers.

Keywords: Digital nudging · Healthcare · Hospital · User behavior · Adoption

1 Introduction

The digital transformation of life and work in western societies as well as their economies is omnipresent [1, 2]. Despite the lack of a generally held definition for the digital transformation, current literature mentions many different descriptions of the phenomenon providing a well-rounded understanding of what digital transformation processes are. Therefore, we understand that digital transformation processes include: (1) any integration of technologies into formerly held analogous processes [3], (2) a restructuring of the organizations culture and behavior [4], or (3) a transformation from partly digitized into fully digitized business models [5]. While the integration of new technologies into organizational processes (e.g. a new project management software) describes interorganizational transformation processes on the micro-level, the transformation of an

© Springer Nature Switzerland AG 2019
A. Marcus and W. Wang (Eds.): HCII 2019, LNCS 11585, pp. 323–336, 2019.
https://doi.org/10.1007/978-3-030-23538-3_25

organizations' business model due to new products or ways of work describes the macro perspective of digital transformation processes. As both aspects of transformation also take place in this works' research area of interest, we will provide relevant distinctions when assessing possibilities and future potentials for the digital transformation of the *healthcare industry*. Moreover, the different stakeholders involved are also not to be neglected when speaking of digital transformation processes in hospitals. For that reason, we chose to take a dual perspective including both, caregivers and caretakers, as relevant players in the digital transformation of the healthcare industry.

Due to the fast-paced life with ever changing innovations and growing consumer needs dictating the free market, the digital transformation has become one of the key strategies for businesses [6]. The healthcare industry too feels pressure to adapt to the status quo and demands of its patients as its digitization processes often lag behind other industries (e.g. retail or automotive industries) [7, 8]. As described in literature, this lacking behind other industries dictates the changes that are anticipated in the healthcare industry. Accordingly, researchers expect many strategic changes of the current service- and healthcare-delivery-driven business models, for instance in hospitals, to become more customer-(patient)-centric in the future [9, 10]. Researchers further anticipate, that the mentioned business model transformation could increase and improve the access to patient care.

One particular phenomenon that emerged in a variety of different fields of application is the concept of *nudging*. Originally developed as a concept to assist and improve customer decision-making in the offline world [11], nudging has especially been given renewed attention as a concept of user assistance or guidance in digital environments (see e.g. [12–14]). Thaler and Sunstein [11], the founding fathers of nudging, first conceptualized it as a form of overt and predictable behavior change. They state that nudging methods, such as encouraging prosocial behavior in 'nudgees' (individuals who are nudged), can be effective, all the while being libertarian, in that the nudgees' freedom of choice remains untampered with. More specifically, this is guaranteed by not excluding any possible choice, or not introducing (financial) incentives to extrinsically alter behavior [11].

Introducing the concept of nudging into digital healthcare services can therefore bring benefits to the stakeholders of both sides of the equation. That being said, one of the nudging examples in digital environments involves the simplification of user interfaces (e.g. color codes to assist navigation and highlight preferential choices). That way, caregivers can implement elements of assistance and guidance in new patient-centric technologies to improve their services. Similarly, the same nudging measures can be implemented to assist caretakers' decision-making processes while using computerized software to fill out prescriptions for instance.

In this paper we will discuss current possibilities for implementation and future potentials for digital nudging in the healthcare industry, especially in hospitals. In a first step we will provide the background on digital transformation and according dimensions. On the basis thereof, we will assess potentials of digital nudging in hospitals in a second step. In the next step, we will discuss the overall findings and provide implications for science and practice. The paper ends with a conclusion and outlook to further research.

2 Digital Transformation

Most literature revolving around the digital transformation in organizations is preoccupied with research efforts on how new (digital) technologies can be implemented on the micro-level to advance overall business performances and consequent competitive advantages [10, 15]. Research further states that the implementation of new technologies and the strategic changes involved in these processes are so fundamental that organizational cultures may change as well. Further, and most importantly it has also been pointed out that the value created by digital transformation processes can bring both, tangible as well as intangible benefits [10].

Building on the Digital Transformation framework as developed by Hess et al. [16], and more recent research efforts to transfer the framework into the healthcare context by Ghosh et al. [8], we will consider four different dimensions when reflecting on digital transformation processes in the healthcare industry. This includes (1) use of technologies, (2) changes in value creation, (3) structural changes, and (4) financial attributes as the four pivotal dimensions in our work. Said dimensions will be shortly introduced in the following and are important to consider in the assessment of possible nudging implementations in the digital health sector.

The first dimension, use of technology, deals with the way institutions either build on existing technologies or the degree to which institutions may choose to integrate new technologies as part of the strategic goal alignment in their organizational infrastructures on the micro-level. Given the rise of electronic health (eHealth) startups working to make useful contributions in the industry, we can find some possibilities to implement nudges. These include nudges to support the digital transformation process of either expanding existent or adopting new technologies in the health sector. Here, caregivers can be nudged to more easily adopt and accept new technologies in their work environments. Meanwhile, caretakers can also be nudged to adopt to new technological innovations implemented in the patient care.

The second dimension, considering the changes in value creation, is closely connected to the former. Here, research describes a digital transformation process in which both, micro- as well as macro-level innovations can bring about new ways of creating value for the organization [10, 16–18]. In the healthcare industry, micro-level innovations may include technologies that allow a new way of interacting with patients or slimming down patient care processes to improve healthcare services [19]. On a macro-level transformation process, value creation may imply expanding healthcare services into new markets, which could be realized by providing wearables for better preventative care of outpatients for instance.

Meanwhile, the third dimension, structural changes, is often a direct consequence of the former dimension. This level of transformation can be realized in an institution where macro-level value creation processes have been nudged already. In this dimension, technologies enable the organization to undergo internal transformation processes in form of e.g. less hierarchical communication structures (e.g. [20, 21]), acquiring new skills or introducing agile business processes [10]. Nevertheless, some institutions, such as hospitals, keep transformational processes mostly separate from their core business. Here structural changes can be viewed more as a form of transformation integrated within existing technologies [10]. Therefore, a nudge would be implemented as a form of an add-on to support or improve existing technology functionalities.

Lastly, the fourth dimension concerning financial attributes of the digital transformation, is most important and distinctive for the level of integration of all other dimensions [10]. While this dimension mainly influences the possible degree of change in most industries, financial attributes are not the only driving factor in the healthcare industry. Here, other factors such as patient safety [22], or patient satisfaction [23] can often be equally as important [10]. Nevertheless, as hospitals too face budget shortages, and tight competition amongst one another, nudging measures can be implemented especially in the work environments of caregivers. When implemented in already existing technologies, nudges could steer caregivers towards making more cost-effective decisions when prescribing medicine for instance. As demonstrated above, there are several possibilities to integrate nudging into what is understood as digital transformation processes in the healthcare industry. In the following we will elaborate on the concept of nudging in more detail to highlight relevant aspects. Further this will help us distinguish nudging from the explicit manipulation of decision-making processes, which should have no standing in the healthcare industry.

3   Digital Nudging

3.1   Background and Definitions

It is important to get a thorough understanding of nudging in its original context of behavioral economics before applying it to digital or health contexts. The concept of nudging was first introduced by Thaler and Sunstein in 2009 [11]. They proposed a way of influencing human decision-making based on social-psychological and cognitive theories. Accordingly, they defined nudging as *"(...) any aspect of the choice architecture that alters people's behavior in a predictable way without forbidding any options or significantly changing their economic incentives"* [11, p. 6]. Thereby nudging applies to cognitive thinking processes that guide human decision-making. A choice architecture, also simply referred to as a set of choices people may choose from, is thereby arranged in a more simplified or preferential way to assist and guide decision-making processes. Further, in distinction to manipulation and persuasion, Thaler and Sunstein [11] argued that nudging introduces a way of influence according to the affected person's own preferences. In literature, this aspect of nudging is also often simply referred to as a liberty preserving form of paternalism. More recently, nudging is frequently introduced in the Information Systems (IS) research field, applying the concept to digital contexts including the healthcare industry.

The IS research field focuses its research efforts on challenges and problems with information technologies applied in organizational contexts. That is why many of the epistemological perspectives and theories introduced in the discipline are based on sociotechnical paradigms entailing the analysis of human and technical factors in enterprise settings [24]. Therefore, the sociotechnical paradigm is a core piece and also establishes its legitimization among other research fields, such as computer sciences [25] and HCI. Digital nudging refers to *"a subtle form of using design, information and interaction elements to guide user behavior in digital environments, without restricting the individual's freedom of choice"* [13, p. 3]. Simply put, nudging and its extended implementation in the digital environment follow the same basic principles. The fundamental difference lies in the greater versatility and opportunities for constructions of choice architectures in the virtual world. Namely because virtual environments have a much more dynamic character, often demanding users to process and comprehend large amounts of information. Therefore, the decision-making in digital environments is based on automation processes and simple heuristics, which simplify decision-making but also lead to poor decisions [26]. As digital interfaces are human-made and therefore follow a certain purpose and consequent choice architecture, we understand digital (user) interfaces as the environment which influences decisions [27] in the healthcare industry. Accordingly, the choice architecture of digital interfaces and their consequent influence on both, caregivers as well as caretakers in hospital contexts will be at the core of our research agenda in this work.

3.2   Rationalities of Nudging

Due to its rather novel introduction to IS research and the multifaceted applicability in many different research fields, nudging is a controversially discussed topic. Therefore, there are some aspects that have to be considered especially when introducing the concept into the healthcare industry. Some researchers criticize the broad definition of nudging, leaving several questions unanswered and too much leeway for interpretation. The researchers Nys and Engelen [28] criticize for instance, that the current definition of nudging neither defines roles and responsibilities in nudging situations nor does it specify the boundaries of libertarian paternalism. They claim that a nudge does not necessarily have to be designed towards the nudgees own interests but can also be working towards the interest of the nudgers, as long as they are not paternalistic [28]. Another often criticized aspect of the broadly defined nudging concept is its similarity to persuasion. Previous research even suggests that both nudging and persuasion are comparable as they aim to influence people towards a specific behavior [29].

In computer science, the concepts of persuasion and persuasive technologies mainly evolved around the ideas introduced by Fogg [30]. According to Fogg [30], persuasion can be defined as *"an attempt to change attitudes or behaviors or both (without using coercion or deception)"* (p. 15). By strongly distinguishing persuasion from manipulative characteristics such as coercion and deception, similarities between nudging and persuasion become apparent. However, the most fundamental difference between both concepts prevails that both, nudging and persuasion have been developed in different disciplines with partially different goals for implementation. As pointed out before, nudging was developed in economics and aims to preserve the liberty of the nudgee to choose freely. Persuasion on the other hand allows a more freely interpreted level of technically enabled influences. Nevertheless, despite this fundamental difference, research by Meske and Potthoff [13] focused on the similarities between nudging and persuasion in the attempt to provide a valuable contribution by borrowing from both concepts. Amongst other things, the researchers derived an overview of integrative digital nudging components they believed to be important to operationalize behavioral change [13]. Accordingly, the researchers' integrative overview will provide the key components we can transfer to digital nudging in the healthcare industry as well. All in all, the researchers Meske and Potthoff [13] were able to show that (digital) nudging and persuasion, two related concepts with separate bounded rationalities stemming from distinct research streams, entail important elements that can be integrated to expand the complexity of design components in digital environments. The resulting nudging components are illustrated and shortly explained below in Table 1. The illustrated components in Table 1 are applicable, for instance, in hospital affiliated decision situations, which e.g. include user interfaces in computer software [12].

Table 1. Nudging elements [13]

Nudging elements	Related to nudging	Related to persuasion
Anchoring *(providing pieces of information, e.g. numbers as anchors for decision-making)*	[11, 31, 32]	
Customized information (Tailoring) *(personalized information to provide a better environment-individual fit)*	[33]	[34, 35]
Decision staging (Tunneling) *(highlighting preferential options but including all possible options)*	[33]	[35]
Default setting *(normative information or adjusted settings according to individuals' preferences)*	[31, 36–40]	
Framing *(a change in environment or wording when presenting information)*	[32, 36, 41–44]	
Informing *(distribution of (personalized) information)*	[31, 32, 45–49]	
Limited time window *(providing limited time windows for certain choices)*	[33]	
Praise and reward (Gamification) *(subtle form of reinforcement to increase motivation)*		[50, 51]
Pre-commitment strategy *(seeking commitment and preferential choice set to reinforce target behaviour)*	[11, 42, 48]	
Priming *(using implicit memory effects through subtle exposure to information)*	[48, 52]	
Reminders *(e.g. notification to help people counteract undesired behaviour)*	[48]	[35, 53]
Simplification (Reduction) *(reduced information to prevent overload and yet still provide the entire choice set)*	[32, 33, 41, 52]	[53]

(continued)

Table 1. (*continued*)

Nudging elements	Related to nudging	Related to persuasion
Social influence (Social comparison) *(providing information about others to influence alignment with social norms)*	[11, 31, 44]	[35, 50]
Warning *(signaling risks to provoke natural instincts)*	[11, 32, 48, 52]	

4 Potential Use Cases for Digital Nudging in Hospitals

As pointed out above, there are four relevant digital transformation dimensions that we consider for the implementation of digital nudging components in hospitals. In the following we will attend to each dimension by providing possible use case examples.

4.1 Opportunities for Digital Nudging to Increase and Support *the Use of Technology*

The use of technology dimension of the digital transformation in the context of hospitals describes the institution's ability as well as its willingness to make use of new digital technologies [16] on the micro-level. There are several opportunities to make use of nudging components, which have been tested in other contexts outside of the healthcare industry (e.g. [27, 54]) and anticipate that nudging components can also help caregivers as well as caretakers to adopt new digital environments in hospitals. Several theories model the user adoption of new technologies; however, two theories have become widely accepted for the prediction of user adoption of new technologies [55]. The technology acceptance model (TAM) [56] and the unified theory of acceptance and use of technology (UTAUT) [57] explain the rationale behind users' adoption behavior and assess individuals' behavior when deciding to adopt an innovation. UTAUT for instance describes social influence, performance expectancy, effort expectancy and facilitating conditions as predictors of technology adoption and use. As a consequence thereof, we assume, that nudging components could apply to exert e.g. social influence by providing information (e.g. pop-up windows, banners) of how many other colleagues use the new technology in the hospital or department. The mechanism at play is, that caregivers (e.g. doctors) could feel encouraged to use a new technology (e.g. a new system to monitor patients) if they are under the impression that doing so has become an institutional (social) norm. Meanwhile, caretakers (e.g. diabetes patients) could also be nudged to use new technologies to help control the disease in and outside of hospitals if nudging components such as simplifications, decision staging or default settings based on patient information and preferences could help increase the performance expectancy and hence perceived usefulness of the technology.

4.2 Opportunities for Digital Nudging in Providing *New Value Creation*

Meanwhile, the second dimension of digital transformation in the context of hospitals describes the influences and changes new technologies (e.g. new products, markets or services) have on the institution's value creation [16]. Based on the success and acceptance of the first digital transformation dimension in a hospital, new forms of value can be created on the macro-level.

There are already a few examples of how wearables or mobile applications help patients manage their chronical diseases or stay ahead of their preventative checkups. This is where the implementation of such technologies can be seen as both, a primary example of the digitization in form of the introduction and use of new technologies on the micro-level (dimension one) as well as in terms of new value creation for the hospital (dimension two) on the macro-level. Creating new value in terms of extended patient care and new health products beyond the dismissal of the patient from the hospital is part of a hospitals' patient centered or value centered outcome approach. One aspect distinctive of this healthcare approach is that hospitals continue to monitor vital signs of patients with pacemakers, in order to inform them of cardiac fibrillations when necessary. Nowadays, contacting the affected patient is still done by hospital personnel via the telephone. However, due to the digitization efforts, there are some new possibilities to introduce technologies or services, which undertake contacting the patients. Accordingly, hospitals have the opportunity to introduce new products and thereby tap into new markets by partnering with research institutions or health service providers (e.g. fitness trackers) to improve preventative medical care. There are many opportunities to implement nudges within the technological infrastructures for the prolonged care of outpatients. Here, caretakers could be nudged to arrange their regular preventative check-ups on time (e.g. via reminders, informing). In general, the entire list of integrative nudging components can be implemented as preventative measures in wearables, to not only trigger, remind, or motivate patients to reach their average goal of steps per day but also integrate praise and reward nudges or anchoring to nudge a healthier diet or a more frequent checkups at the doctors.

In terms of value creation through providing new services, there are already digitization efforts in the telemedicine such as the tele intensive care unit or the digital diabetes ambulance. These are digital services offering medical care to caretakers independent of time and space. Here, caretakers have remote access to caregivers who offer virtual medical care. These services are distinctive of the increasing diversification of medical care made possible through the digital transformation. Nudging components can play an important role in motivating or encouraging caretakers in remote areas to make use of the services. This can be done through simplification nudges on mobile applications or website interfaces to encourage the technology use as well as informing nudges by providing statistical information on the expected benefits of using the telemedicine services in acute emergencies, increasing the usage of according technology and hence increasing the added value for the hospital.

4.3 Opportunities for Digital Nudging in Eliciting and Guiding *Structural Changes*

The structural changes dimension of the digital transformation in the context of hospitals describes the institution's efforts to introduce or manage new organizational structures, work processes or skills in order to make efficient and effective use of the new technologies [16]. As macro-level value creation brings about structural changes in the institutions, macro-level nudging components also have a continued effect on the intra-institutional level. Hereby, it is important to point out that technologies, which bring about structural change do not just re-structure patient care processes as described above but also have an influence on the way caregivers work in general. Large parts of the caregivers' work not directly done on the patient involves computers and therefore provides many different opportunities for nudging. That is why managers and researchers (e.g. in research hospitals) have taken a particular interest in the analysis of the large amounts of data for evidence-based quality management to improve internal processes or statistical analyses of trends in diagnoses and suggested treatments to improve the patient care. However, because of traditional routines, caregivers prefer using free text, which they can type in to document diagnoses, rather than using structured data entries. This creates a big pain point for evidence-based management and research, as only structured data are valuable for quantitative analyses. In this context, nudging components could be used to trigger and encourage caregivers to invest the extra time to choose the pre-formulated data entries. Another possibility to use nudging components during the caregivers' decision-making process concerns the treatment of the patients. Here, nudging components could entail statistical decision staging mechanisms, which nudge caretakers to reflect on planned treatments and hence the planned process of caregiving. In both cases, nudging could be implemented in the context of changes processes and may lead to improved medical decisions.

Also, on the micro-level, where caregivers and caretakers are already within physical proximity, nudging mechanisms may be used to slim down administrative processes or improve services. For instance, the admission processes of new patients often leave long paper trails. Therefore, hospitals are already working on digital substitutes, which not only regulate the initial admission of new patients but also track new information of re-admissions in form of a digital patient diary. Here again, nudging components (e.g. signaling, decision staging) can be implemented to remind patients to thoroughly fill out admission forms. Upon continued hospital visits, different nudging components can become effective to make admission processes more effective. Nudging patients to revise outdated information about their physical conditions is one way of increased effectivity, potentially leading to new or changed processes and hence structures. Thereby, digital nudging could encourage patients to inform their caregivers of new symptoms ahead of or after their new physical examinations for instance. Another use case could regard the coordination of caretaker appointments and examinations. Here, through GPS tracking of the caretakers' whereabouts in the hospital, e.g. informing nudges could be used coordinate capacities of waiting rooms or hallways by suggesting patients to take a walk or visit the cafeteria in-between appointments.

4.4   Opportunities for Digital Nudging in *Providing Financial Gains*

The financial dimension of the digital transformation in the context of hospitals describes competitive pressure between institutions as well as the availability of required resources to fund the transformation [16]. Even though the treatment of patients and providing care are at the core of the business, staying profitable and competitive in the industry remain important business aspects of hospitals. Therefore, digital transformation processes are inevitable and mandatory for the continued success of hospitals given the overall digitization of the healthcare industry. We determine, that financial gains through nudging can be realized on both, the micro- and macro-level of digital transformation processes. Overall, we argue, that the financial dimension and hence potential, external funding of transformational endeavors is indirectly supported through the successful implementation of nudges in the other three domains of technology use, value creation and structural changes.

5   Discussion

On the basis of existing conceptualizations of digital transformation dimensions and the body of knowledge on nudging in digital environments, we conclude that digital nudging has a rightful place in the healthcare industry. Altogether, there are four digital transformation dimensions, which we regarded more closely and used as reference for the implementation of possible nudging components. Taking the different dimensions into consideration allowed us to reflect on possible micro- or macro-level nudging implications in hospitals from multiple angles.

Even though structural change and financial attributes are important dimensions of the digital transformation on the macro-level, we want to point out to the importance of influences of nudging on micro-level technology use and value creation dimensions. This being the case, the caregiver-caretaker perspective was in the focus of this work. On the caregiver side we recognize that nudging components primarily assist the hospital personnel in creating value by offering new services as well as making daily work routines more time and cost effective. Digital nudges can also primarily be used to encourage technology use in the first place or assist the technology adoption processes.

Meanwhile, caretakers experience value creation more directly in terms of technology use and thereby save time during initial hospital admissions as well as reoccurring admission processes. Digitizing the admission process in hospitals is a popular digital transformation topic that does not yet involve nudging components. Here nudging could play a central role in easing the caretakers into the technology use in hospitals. At the same time nudging components such as reminders or customized information could assist caretakers to revisit and update their patient information when filling out digital questionnaires. Nudging caretakers to keep their patient history up to date in turn could help provide the necessary paper work and gather important information about the progression of the sickness or the appearance of new symptoms to help prepare the caregiver before the actual patient-care.

Finally, nudging components applied on the macro-level dimensions are equally as useful, as structural changes and financial attributes on the institutional-level eventually also have an influence on the transformation processes on the micro-level. Nudging may apply and contribute in every dimension of digital transformation process in hospitals. It is a relatively easy and inexpensive implementation into already existing technological infrastructures, which, if implemented correctly and hence also respecting the freedom of the users' choice, can have a significant impact on the development, acceptance and continued use of technologies in hospitals for both sides, caregivers as well as caretakers.

6 Conclusion

In this work, we show that digital nudging can be a useful instrument to support digital transformation in the healthcare industry by discussing hospital context specific case examples in which nudging components can find an immediate implementation within existing technological infrastructures. Additionally, we also provide case examples of how nudging could find seamless implementation in future digital technologies and processes in the hospital context. In general, we highlight several nudging potentials in hospitals in order to lay out the possible future and necessity for nudging in the healthcare industry. Future research may empirically investigate the effectiveness of different nudges in varying settings from the caregivers' as well as caretakers' point of view. It should also be analyzed, how an important principle of nudging, respecting the individuals' preferences and freedom of choice, can be achieved in domains such as the healthcare industry.

References

1. vom Brocke, J.: The networked society. Bus. Inf. Syst. Eng. **58**(3), 159–160 (2016)
2. Meske, C., Kissmer, T., Stieglitz, S.: Global adoption of unified communication technologies as part of digital transformation in organizations: a cross-cultural perspective. In: Proceedings of the 10th Multikonferenz Wirtschaftsinformatik (MKWI), pp. 133–144 (2018)
3. Liu, D., Chen, S., Chou, T.: Resource fit in digital transformation: lessons learned from the CBC Bank global e-banking project. Manag. Decis. **49**(10), 1728–1742 (2011)
4. Moreton, R.: Transforming the organization: the contribution of the information systems function. J. Strateg. Inf. Syst. **4**(2), 149–163 (1995)
5. Riedl, R., Benlian, A., Hess, T., Stelzer, D., Sikora, H.: On the relationship between information management and digitalization. Bus. Inf. Syst. Eng. **59**(6), 475–482 (2017)
6. Dery, K., Sebastian, I., van der Meulen, N.: The digital workplace is key to digital innovation. MIS Q. Executive **16**(2), 135–152 (2017)
7. Gupta, M.: Digital Transformation in Healthcare: 5 Areas of Immediate Growth. https://www.visioncritical.com/digital-transformation-health-care/. Accessed 12 Dec 2018
8. Ghosh, K., Dohan, M., Veldandi, H.: Digital transformation strategies for healthcare providers: perspectives from senior leadership. In: 24th Americas Conference on Information Systems, ERF (2018)
9. Ghosh, K., Khuntia, J., Chawla, S., Deng, X.: Media reinforcement for psychological empowerment in chronic disease management. Commun. Assoc. Inf. Syst. **34**(22), 419–438 (2014)
10. Yang, Y., Kankanhalli, A., Chandran, S.: Evolution of information technology in healthcare. In: Pacific Asia Conference on Information Systems (PACIS), p. 215 (2014)

11. Thaler, R.H., Sunstein, C.R.: Nudge. Int'l. Penguin Books, London (2009)
12. Weinmann, M., Schneider, C., vom Brocke, J.: Digital nudging. Bus. Inf. Syst. Eng. **58**(6), 1–9 (2016)
13. Meske, C., Potthoff, T.: The DINU model – a process model for the design of nudges. In: Proceedings of the 23rd European Conference on Information Systems (ECIS), pp. 2587–2597 (2017)
14. Schneider, C., Weinmann, M., vom Brocke, J.: Digital nudging: guiding online user choices through interface design. Commun. ACM **61**(7), 67–73 (2018)
15. Bharadwaj, A., El Sawy, O.A., Pavlou, P.A., Venkatraman, N.V.: Digital business strategy: toward a next generation of insights. MIS Q. **37**, 471–482 (2013)
16. Hess, T., Matt, C., Benlian, A., Wiesböck, F.: Options for formulating a digital transformation strategy. Manag. Inf. Syst. Q. Executive **15**(2), 123–139 (2016)
17. Wilms, K., et al.: Digital transformation in higher education – new cohorts, new requirements? In: Proceedings of the 23rd Americas Conference on Information Systems (AMCIS), pp. 1–10 (2017)
18. Matt, C., Hess, T., Benlian, A.: Digital Transformation Strategies. Bus. Inf. Syst. Eng. **57**(5), 339–343 (2015)
19. Wilson, E.V.: Patient Centered E-Health. IGI Global, Hershey (2008)
20. Riemer, K., Stieglitz, S., Meske, C.: From top to bottom: investigating the changing role of hierarchy in enterprise social networks. Bus. Inf. Syst. Eng. (BISE) **57**(3), 197–212 (2015)
21. Stieglitz, S., Riemer, K., Meske, C.: Hierarchy or activity? The role of formal and informal influence in eliciting responses from enterprise social networks. In: Proceedings of the 22nd European Conference on Information Systems (ECIS), Track 07, Paper 12 (2014)
22. Kaushal, R., Barker, K., Bates, D.W.: How can information technology improve patient safety and reduce medication errors in children's health care? Arch. Pediatr. Adolesc. Med. **155**(9), 1002–1007 (2001)
23. Or, K., Karsh, B.T.: A systematic review of patient acceptance of consumer health information technology. J. Am. Med. Inform. Assoc. **16**(4), 550–560 (2009)
24. Sarker, S., Chatterjee, S., Xiao, X.: How 'sociotechnical' is our IS research? An assessment and possible ways forward. In: ICIS 2013 Proceedings, pp. 1–24 (2013)
25. Benbasat, I., Zmud, R.W.: The identity crisis within the IS discipline: defining and communicating the discipline's core properties. MIS Q. **27**(2), 183–194 (2003)
26. Mirsch, T., Lehrer, C., Reinhard, J.: Making digital nudging applicable: the digital nudge design method. In: International Conference on Information Systems, Paper 5 (2018)
27. Schneider, D., Lins, S., Grupp, T., Benlian, A., Sunyaev, A.: Nudging users into online verification: the case of carsharing platforms. In: Proceedings of the International Conference on Information Systems, Paper 11 (2017)
28. Nys, T.R., Engelen, B.: Judging nudging: answering the manipulation objection. Polit. Stud. **65**(1), 199–214 (2017)
29. Oinas-Kukkonen, H.: A foundation for the study of behavior change support systems. Pers. Ubiquit. Comput. **17**(6), 1223–1235 (2013)
30. Fogg, B.J.: Persuasive Technology: Using Computers to Change What We Think and Do. Morgan Kaufmann Publishers, San Francisco (2003)
31. French, J.: Why nudging is not enough. J. Soc. Mark. **1**(2), 154–162 (2011)
32. Oullier, O., Cialdini, R., Thaler, R.H., Mullainathan, S.: Improving public health prevention with a nudge. In: Oullier, O., Sauneron, S. (eds.) Improving Public Health Prevention with Behavioural, Cognitive and Neuroscience, Centre for Strategic Analysis, Paris, France, pp. 38–46 (2010)
33. Johnson, E.J., et al.: Beyond nudges: tools of a choice architecture. Mark. Lett. **23**(2), 487–504 (2012)

34. Consolvo, S., Everitt, K., Smith, I., Landay, J.A.: Design requirements for technologies that encourage physical activity. In: CHI 2006 Extended Abstracts on Human Factors in Computing Systems - CHI EA 2006, p. 457. ACM Press, New York (2006)
35. Oinas-Kukkonen, H., Harjumaa, M.: Persuasive systems design: key issues, process model, and system features. Commun. AIS **24**, 485–500 (2009)
36. Acquisti, A.: Nudging privacy: the behavioral economics of personal information. Secur. Priv. Econ. **7**(6), 72–75 (2009)
37. Grüne-Yanoff, T., Hertwig, R.: Nudge versus boost: how coherent are policy and theory? Mind. Mach. **26**(1–2), 149–183 (2016)
38. Knijnenburg, B.P., Kobsa, A.: Increasing sharing tendency without reducing satisfaction: finding the best privacy-settings user interface for social networks. In: ICIS 2014 Proceedings, pp. 1–21 (2014)
39. Marteau, T.M., Ogilvie, D., Roland, M., Suhrcke, M., Kelly, M.P.: Judging nudging: can nudging improve population health? BMJ **342**, d228 (2011)
40. Sunstein, C.R.: Nudges and Public Policy (2014)
41. Lehner, M., Mont, O., Heiskanen, E.: Nudging – a promising tool for sustainable consumption behaviour? J. Clean. Prod. **134**, 166–177 (2016)
42. Luoto, J., Levine, D., Albert, J., Luby, S.: Nudging to use: achieving safe water behaviors in Kenya and Bangladesh. J. Dev. Econ. **110**, 13–21 (2014)
43. Thomas, A.M., Parkinson, J., Moore, P., Goodman, A., Xhafa, F., Barolli, L.: Nudging through technology: choice architectures and the mobile information revolution. In: Proceedings of 8th International Conference on P2P, Parallel, Grid, Cloud and Internet Computing, 3PGCIC 2013, pp. 255–261 (2013)
44. Zhang, B., Xu, H.: Privacy nudges for mobile applications: effects on the creepiness emotion and privacy attitudes. In: Proceedings of the 19th ACM Conference on Computer Supported Cooperative Work & Social Computing - CSCW 2016, pp. 1674–1688. ACM Press (2016)
45. Blitstein, J.L., et al.: Adding a social marketing campaign to a school-based nutrition education program improves children's dietary intake: a quasi-experimental study. J. Acad. Nutr. Diet. **116**(8), 1285–1294 (2016)
46. Evans, W.D., Pattanayak, S.K., Young, S., Buszin, J., Rai, S., Bihm, J.W.: Social marketing of water and sanitation products: a systematic review of peer-reviewed literature. Soc. Sci. Med. **110**, 18–25 (2014)
47. Newell, R.G., Siikamäki, J.V.: Nudging energy efficiency behavior: the role of information labels. In: NBER Working Paper Series, vol. 1, no. 19224, p. 43 (2013)
48. Sunstein, C.R.: Nudging: a very short guide. J. Consum. Policy **37**, 583–588 (2014)
49. Wilkinson, T.M.: Nudging and manipulation. Polit. Stud. **61**(2), 341–355 (2013)
50. Sohn, M., Lee, J.: UP health: ubiquitously persuasive health promotion with an instant messaging system. In: CHI 2007 Extended Abstracts on Human Factors in Computing Systems - CHI 2007, p. 2663. ACM Press, New York (2007)
51. Toscos, T., Faber, A., An, S., Gandhi, M.P.: Chick clique: persuasive technology to motivate teenage girls to exercise. In: CHI 2006 Extended Abstracts on Human Factors in Computing Systems - CHI EA 2006, vol. 31, p. 1873. ACM Press, New York (2006)
52. Balebako, R., Cranor, L.: Improving app privacy: nudging app developers to protect user privacy. IEEE Secur. Priv. **12**(4), 55–58 (2014)
53. Lee, G., Tsai, C., Griswold, W.G., Raab, F., Patrick, K.: PmEB: a mobile phone application for monitoring caloric balance. In: CHI 2006 Extended Abstracts on Human Factors in Computing Systems - CHI EA 2006, p. 1013. ACM Press, New York (2006)
54. Kissmer, T., Potthoff, T., Stieglitz, S.: Enterprise Digital Nudging: between adoption gain and unintended rejection. In: Proceedings of the 24th Americas Conference on Information Systems (2018)

55. Venkatesh, V., Thong, J.Y.L., Xu, X.: Unified theory of acceptance and use of technology: a synthesis and the road ahead. J. Assoc. Inf. Syst. **17**(5), Article no. 1 (2016)
56. Davis, F.D., Bagozzi, R.P., Warshaw, P.R.: User acceptance of computer technology: a comparison of two theoretical models. Manag. Sci. **35**(8), 982–1003 (1989)
57. Venkatesh, V., Morris, M.G., Davis, G.B., Davis, F.D., Smith, R.H., Walton, S.M.: User acceptance of information technology: toward a unified view. MIS Q. **27**(3), 425–478 (2003)

Development and Usability Evaluation of a Nutrition and Lifestyle Guidance Application for People Living with and Beyond Cancer

Gareth Veale[1], Huseyin Dogan[1(✉)], and Jane Murphy[2]

[1] Faculty of Science and Technology, Bournemouth University, Poole, UK
{i7765155,hdogan}@bournemouth.ac.uk
[2] Faculty of Health and Social Sciences, Bournemouth University, Poole, UK
jmurphy@bournemouth.ac.uk

Abstract. There is a need to provide accessible information for health care professionals and for people living beyond treatment. Mobile and digital health technologies provide an ideal platform to access diet and nutrition guidance that is both trusted and evidence-based and so that people know how to alter and monitor eating patterns and behaviours to improve the quality of life. Participatory design and usability evaluation approaches have been utilised to develop a nutrition and lifestyle guidance smartphone application for both people living with and beyond cancer, and for health care professionals involved in advising such patients. The challenges centred on the design, development and evaluation of the first version of a new mobile application named 'Life Beyond' are presented. This proof of concept application aims to centralise evidence-based nutrition and lifestyle guidance for those living beyond cancer. It enables users to obtain guidance and information, create and track nutrition and activity related goals and track their progress in the completion of these goals. Consistent feedback from participatory design and usability evaluations drove this research and helped to create an initial solution that met the user expectations. The System Usability Scale (SUS) score of 67.69 denotes an 'average' usability and hence further development. More research of extensive end user engagement is needed before an optimal solution is disseminated.

Keywords: Nutrition · Lifestyle · Digital health · Cancer ·
Participatory design · Usability

1 Introduction

The number of people living beyond a cancer diagnosis in the UK has doubled in the past 40 years due to earlier detection and improved treatments [1]. People living with and beyond a diagnosis of cancer are all at increased risk of cancer recurrence as well as other chronic conditions such as diabetes, osteoporosis and cardiovascular disease [2]. Nutrition is an important modifiable factor that could reduce these risks, thereby promoting long-term health. Dietary change may also impact quality of life, particularly those diagnosed with prostate, breast and colorectal cancers [3]. The World

© Springer Nature Switzerland AG 2019
A. Marcus and W. Wang (Eds.): HCII 2019, LNCS 11585, pp. 337–347, 2019.
https://doi.org/10.1007/978-3-030-23538-3_26

Cancer Research Fund (WCRF) has a Continuous Update Project that provides an analysis of International research on diet, nutrition and physical activity and weight in relation to cancer risk and survival. In 2018 the WCRF provided an update of their recommendations for a healthy population to be a healthy weight, be physically active, eat a diet rich in wholegrains, vegetables, fruit and beans, limit the consumption of 'fast foods' and other processed foods high in fat, starches and sugars, red and processed meat, sugar sweetened drinks, alcohol consumption and not to use supplements [4]. Currently, it is recommended that people living after a cancer diagnosis should follow these, whenever possible, unless advised otherwise by a qualified health professional. Following a cancer diagnosis, people become strongly motivated to modify their diet behaviours to increase well-being, maintain health and prevent recurrence [5–7]. Yet, studies have shown that they have received unsatisfactory experiences of nutritional care from health professionals and received very little, or confusing advice on how best to approach nutrition for their cancer and for the different stages of their treatment journey [8–10]. They are more likely to seek and obtain dietary information from unreliable sources often via the internet that might be unsafe or explore complementary and alternative medicine including nutritional therapies despite the absence of scientific evidence from controlled clinical trials to support their claims [11, 12]. In 2015, a patient survey undertaken by the NIHR Cancer and Nutrition collaboration showed that patients were not receiving the advice and support they want. Patients reported needing "clear, uncomplicated information"; needing mechanisms to "overcome conflicting advice and tailored, cancer-specific advice that is fact-based" and to be "given information, rather than needing to conduct their own research" [13].

Health care professionals are not trained to provide dietary advice or are not aware of the relevant guidelines that exist. They want further support in areas such as: dietary advice for specific cancers and cancer stage, assessment of nutritional status, alternative dietary approaches, and use of dietary supplements in cancer [14].

There is a need to provide accessible information for health care professionals and for people living beyond treatment [10, 13]. Mobile digital health technologies provide an ideal platform to access diet and nutrition guidance that is both trusted and evidence-based and so that people know how to alter and monitor eating patterns and behaviours to improve quality of life and potentially reduce the risk of cancer recurrence. The popularity of smartphones and the increasing adoption rates of M-Health applications reinforced the need to utilise such platforms for nutrition and lifestyle guidance. Existing nutritional applications are also reviewed in this paper to understand whether they promote behaviour change.

This paper presents the challenges faced when designing, developing and evaluating the first version of a new mobile application named 'Life Beyond'. This includes the feedback from the pilot studies, participatory design study and usability evaluation of the first version of the application with health care professionals. The paper also presents the limitations of existing nutritional applications to produce a system in line with end user requirements. 'Life Beyond' aims to centralise evidence-based nutrition and lifestyle guidance for those living beyond cancer and debunk the nutrition myths in an accessible format. It enables users to obtain guidance and information, create and track nutrition and activity related goals and track their progress in the completion of these goals. The section in the paper are as follows: existing nutrition applications are covered in section two; the method utilised including participatory design and usability evaluations are described in section three; the results including the SuS score are presented in section four; discussions centred on the solution and its limitations are covered in section five; and the final section is the conclusion where the shift toward a recommender system app based on user profiling is highlighted as future work.

2   Nutrition and Mobile Health

Mobile health applications offer an incredible opportunity to increase the accessibility of healthcare. Remote medical diagnoses are an example of an area being developed heavily in order to reduce healthcare costs and decrease face to face communications between health care professionals and patients [15]. A variety of nutritional applications have become popular, helping users track their daily food consumption and monitor their progress in achieving fitness related goals. Example of these are reviewed below in an attempt to infer the strengths and limitations of each.

MyFitnessPal [15] is an application that enables users to track eating habits on a daily basis. This is offered through a feature that enables users to create a food diary. Subsequently, energy (calorie) intake and consumption of micro and macronutrients are automatically calculated. Users have the ability to personalise dietary goals and track fitness related progress through weight monitoring. This application incorporates goal setting and an extensive progress tracking feature, both important behavioural change techniques. However, as the name suggests, this application is targeted towards the fitness industry. Though it may be applied to monitor dietary behaviours and patterns, it is in no way specific to cancer.

Daily Dozen [16] has been built to serve as a companion to the book 'How Not to Die' authored by Dr Michael Greger M. D. Users are shown a list of foods that, if consumed as part of a healthy lifestyle, can help to prevent major chronic diseases. Users have the option to select each item to obtain additional information around serving sizes and foods that fall under each category. Though this application is very simple it offers an extremely useful tool for ensuring important food groups are consumed on a daily basis. The daily progress feature provides users with an incentive to consume each of recommended foods and can be categorised as goal setting. Again, this application is not cancer specific and it does not offer information related to cancer and cancer related nutrition. Medscape [17] is an application aimed at health care professionals, it provides a myriad of information ranging from prescriptions to operating procedures. This application does not promote behaviour change and is not aimed at those living beyond cancer. However, it offers an example of how evidence-based and academic research can be presented to users in a user-friendly and positive format. Patient specific data has also been incorporated into other areas for nutrition consultation and benefit demonstrated to support self-monitoring for weight loss and measure dietary intake [18, 19] and glucose monitoring in type 1 diabetes [20].

Researchers have also developed and tested a mobile phone app to reduce the risk of breast cancer through healthy behaviours by recording dietary intakes and activity levels and connectivity with commercially available products for monitoring and tracking physical activity and intake [21]. Moreover, a pilot study [22] has explored the feasibility and applicability of a mobile phone app to assess dietary behaviours in oncology patients who needed to increase dietary intake following cancer diagnosis and treatment. By tracking daily dietary behaviours, the participants were more likely to reach their nutritional goals.

Goal setting, monitoring indicators and tracking features have been documented to drive successful M-health apps [22]. Thus personalised guidance and information can create a more intimate experience likely to be incorporated into a user's lifestyle. However there remains no smartphone application that has been specifically designed to provide nutrition and lifestyle guidance for both people living with and beyond cancer, and for health care professionals to help advise their patients.

Time should be spent understanding consumer requirements and expectations, using this data to inform design decisions and to encourage self-monitoring to meet this gap [23, 24]. Consequently, the following section provides an overview of the methods used to involve users in the development process of the Life Beyond application.

3   Method

3.1   Participatory Design Supporting the Implementation

Creating an excellent User Experience (UX) can be defined as 'the designing of applications that a person of average ability and experience can figure out how to use the thing to accomplish something without it being more trouble than it's worth' [25]. UX is important in capturing the attention of users and if done poorly can force users to look elsewhere. Participatory Design (PD) is an approach committed to directly involving end users in the design of new technologies [26]. PD is receiving attention in the behavioural change research. For example, PD is used to develop a digital toolkit to promote quality of life of people with multiple sclerosis through using cognitive behavioural therapy [27]. Although we used PD with two Health Care Professionals due to limited resources and time, it was still invaluable in designing the features for the Life Beyond application.

Agile has been used as the software development methodology for the implementation. There are many variations of agile, two of the most popular, Scrum and Extreme Programming (XP) were considered. Scrum is a methodology that leverages a concept known as sprints. These sprints are fixed lengths of work cadences – typically one or two weeks - where development takes place and iterations are produced. Since agile underpins this software model, focus is placed on the users and assumes an empirical approach, adapting to dynamic requirements and accepting that the project cannot be fully defined from the outset [28]. Scrum has been selected for its suitability to small and medium sized projects. Since the development of this application involves a single developer, the scalable nature of Scrum fits well. Holistic sprints encompass requirements capture, development, testing and evaluation; this produces a user focused product, in line with expectations [28].

3.2   Usability Evaluation

There are a number of usability evaluation techniques including the think aloud protocol and cognitive walkthrough. Think aloud involves participants verbalising their thought processes whilst engaging and moving through the user interface [29]. Cognitive walkthrough offers insight into a system's learnability and ease of use by simulating user problems [30]. The System Usability Scale was used together with semi-structured interview to elicit an overall usability score with more detailed feedback on the various aspects of the application.

System Usability Scale (SUS) is a simple, easy to use approach for measuring the usability of a product or service. The approach consists of a ten-item questionnaire, and five response options ranging from strongly agree to strongly disagree. In order to calculate the system usability score, each question has a rating scale with a value from one to five. The answers to the odd questions are subtracted by one, the answers to odd questions are subtracted from five. The total is then multiplied by 2.5, giving a result out of 100 [31]. SuS results were compared from 500 studies and resolved anything above 68 is considered to be above average [31].

Semi-structured interviews were conducted to gather requirements from end users and evaluate all aspects of the application. Interviews are a convenient data collection technique enabling the engagement of end-users and key stakeholders, and offer an opportunity collaboratively define the problem in depth. Outputs provide reliable, comparable and qualitative data and although they can be time consuming and resource intensive, this data proved vital throughout.

4   Results

4.1   Procedure and Participant Profiles

Weekly review meetings were conducted involving: the primary developer, a Human Computer Interaction (HCI) expert, and a nutrition and diet expert with experience in offering cancer related guidance. These sessions together with expert guidance helped to establish the design of the application and drove continued iterations in the development and identified improvements to be completed prior to evaluations. Throughout the design, development and evaluation process the project nutritional expert coordinated continued engagement with relevant health care professionals that care for those living with and beyond cancer. The health care professionals (n = 13) included dietitians (n = 9) and general practitioners (n = 2) and an oncologist (n = 1) with experience in offering cancer related guidance. All participants obtained a qualification including an undergraduate degree (n = 7), postgraduate diploma (n = 1) and postgraduate degree (n = 5). Further details about participant profiles are shown in Table 1.

These engagements helped drive content and feature design, improvements and evaluation. Each HCP participated in a semi-structured interview and completed the SUS evaluation. Only two health care professionals contributed to Participatory Design sessions due to time limitations.

Table 1. Health care professional profiles.

						Health Care Professionals					
ID	Gender	Age	Job	Work in Cancer/ Oncology	Highest Education	Source of info on nutrition	Source details	Training on nutritional care for cancer patients	Phone usage	O/S	Regular device owned
#1	Female	36-45	Dietitian	No	Post-graduate degree	Early influences (family and/or school)	Training undertaken from employment / Colleagues/friends / Academic journals / Degree in dietics	Yes / Cancer survivorship / PHD	Samsung A3	Android	Smartphone / Tablet
#2	Female	36-45	Dietitian	Yes	Degree	Courses on diet and nutrition		Yes	iPhone	iOS	Smartphone / Tablet / Laptop
#3	Female	26-35	Dietitian	No	Post-graduate degree	Courses on diet and nutrition / Early influences (family and/or school)	Training undertaken from employment	Yes	iPhone	iOS / iOS	Smartphone / Tablet
#4	Female	18-25	Dietitian	Yes	Degree	Courses on diet and nutrition	Training undertaken from employment	Yes	iPhone	iOS	Smartphone
#5	Female	26-35	Dietitian	Yes	Post-graduate degree	Courses on diet and nutrition	Training undertaken from employment	Yes	iPhone	iOS	Smartphone
#6	Female	36-45	Dietitian	Yes	Degree	Early influences (family and/or school)	Training undertaken from employment	Yes	Note 2	Android	Smartphone
#7	Female	36-45	Dietitian	Yes	Degree	Courses on diet and nutrition	Training undertaken from employment	Yes	iPhone	iOS	Smartphone
#8	Female	26-35	Dietitian	Yes	Diploma	Courses on diet and nutrition	Training undertaken from employment	Yes	iPhone	iOS	Smartphone
#9	Female	26-35	Dietitian	Yes	Degree	Early influences (family and/or school)	Training undertaken from employment	Yes	iPhone	iOS	Smartphone
#10	Female	46-55	Oncologist	Yes	Degree	Courses on diet and nutrition	Training undertaken from employment	Yes	iPhone	iOS	Smartphone
#11	Female	36-45	Dietitian	Yes	Degree	Early influences (family and/or school)	Training undertaken from employment	Yes	iPhone	iOS	Smartphone
#12	Female	36-45	GP	No	Post-graduate degree	Courses on diet and nutrition	Academic journals	Yes	iPhone	iOS	Smartphone
#13	Male	26-35	GP	No	Post-graduate degree	Early influences (family and/or school)	Training undertaken from employment	Yes	Samsung S8	Android	Smartphone

4.2 Design Iterations

The PD design iterations included creating a sitemap that presents the basic navigational structure of the application. Since mobile development requires a more simplistic hierarchy, a top level holistic tab navigation is used, directing users to the main navigation (Fig. 1). Feature mapping, signposting and wireframe designs were other outputs of the PD sessions. Sample resources were used for the signposting.

Fig. 1. Life beyond application user interfaces.

The PD design iterations resulted in designing the key features of the application as shown in Table 2.

Table 2. Key features of the application.

Feature	Description	Rationale
Signposted information	A collection of evidence-based guidance, a short description of the information within and a link to the site of origin	The primary offering of the application according to the client's requirements will be to provide a centralised store of information for users
Slideshow	A slideshow of images and links to highlight the key, recent research related to cancer and nutrition/lifestyle choices	Slideshows offer a visual method of highlighting key and important news to users and have been used to effect in existing M-health apps
Food intake tracking	A feature that offers users the ability to track a fully customizable list of foods to be consumed on a daily basis	The application must promote behavior change through a number of features, as required by the client. This feature offers users the ability to create a list of foods to consume on a daily basis and incorporate the guidance (signposted to) into their daily lives
Daily tracking	A feature that offers users the ability to track a fully customizable list of daily activities to be completed on a daily basis	The application must promote behavior change through a number of features as required by the client. This feature offers users the ability to create a list of activities to complete on a daily basis and incorporate the guidance (signposted to) into their daily lives
Goal setting	A feature that enables users to set a list of custom goals related to food consumption and daily activities	Such features promote sustained completion of goals and help to shape new behaviors into habits
Progress tracking	A feature that enables users to track their progress in completing their customized goals, displaying the number of goals completed and the number of successful days etc.	Offering a progress tracking feature enables users to sustain completion of goals and helps to promote continued motivation
Sharing feature	A feature that enables users to share the application to their friends, family and network	Social features and sharing capabilities in behavior change applications are found to be some of the most important and successful features

4.3 System Usability Score (SuS) and Interview Results

The participants (n = 13) were asked to complete a number of tasks within the app without guidance. This formed the task-based analysis of the evaluation and participants were asked to speak aloud their thought process, giving the authors indication to the various limitations of the application. Following the analysis, participants were asked to answer questions relating to the System Usability Scale (SuS) scoring. This usability evaluation technique is used to metricise the usability of a system, technology or otherwise. The answers to the questions are calculated and used to determine an overall usability (or system usability) score and can be seen below. Following is a list of tasks that participants completed.

- Find the list of nutrition information
- Find the list of exercise information
- Find the list of charitable organisations
- Find the food track behaviour change feature
- Add a new food to track
- Complete one of the tracked foods
- Find the list of daily activities to be tracked
- Add a new daily activity
- Complete one of the activities
- Find the progress screen

The average SuS score came to a total of 67.69. This represents an average system in regard to usability, with improvements to be made. That said, this application was merely a proof of concept, designed to elicit feedback and conduct initial evaluations.

Semi-structured interviews formed the final phase of each evaluation. Participants were asked a number of qualitative questions, designed to elicit more detailed feedback on the various aspects of the system. The comments received here vary in subject, however some topics highlight a number of trends. Most participants felt the application to be easy to use, colourful and conceptually, a very strong idea. However, feedback highlighted the application must be more cancer specific, accounting for specific needs of those living with and beyond cancer. Additionally, participants felt the application should be structured with less text and more pictures, giving users an aesthetically pleasing, and removing the need to trawl through large amounts of information.

5 Discussion

This proof of concept of paper has, for the first time provide an application to centralize evidence-based nutrition and lifestyle guidance for health and care professionals and for people living beyond cancer. It has enabled users to obtain guidance and information create and track nutrition and activity related goals and track their progress in the completion of these goals. The findings from feedback of participatory design and usability evaluation have informed a preliminary solution that has met user expectations.

The advantages for the management of other lifestyle conditions such as diabetes, hypertension and obesity have already been demonstrated [19, 20, 32] and for the prevention of breast cancer [22] and to increase dietary intake and provide nutritional support for cancer patients [21]. However the smartphone app intervention developed and tested in this study is innovative. No other studies have provided a solution for those living with and beyond cancer treatment and who would require support and monitoring to follow healthy lifestyles to meet current WCRF recommendations [4]. However a limitation is that the app was not designed to focus on a particular type of cancer but appropriate support and guidance is enabled and signposted. What also emerged were the requirements for health care professionals that differed with those of people living with and beyond cancer in terms of the user engagement and presentation of information. As such it is important that further work considers nutrition and life-style information presented not only in appropriate format but also at an appropriate reading level for all individuals including those with marginal literacy skills.

6 Conclusions and Future Work

This study has demonstrated the potential to provide a new digital health care platform for health care professionals and people living with and beyond cancer to access nutrition and lifestyle guidance and meet lifestyle goals by changing behaviours and improve nutritional wellbeing and quality of life. Further research and extensive end user engagement is needed to confirm these initial findings and test the feasibility and applicability on a larger scale to inform an optimal solution.

Acknowledgements. The authors acknowledge the contribution of all the participants in the study and the support offered by the NIHR Cancer and Nutrition Collaboration.

References

1. Maddams, J., Utley, M., Møller, H.: Projections of cancer prevalence in the United Kingdom, 2010–2040. Br. J. Cancer **107**, 1195–1202 (2012)
2. Travis, L.B., Rabkin, C.S., Brown, L.M., et al.: Cancer survivorship–genetic susceptibility and second primary cancers: research strategies and recommendations. J. Natl. Cancer Inst. **98**, 15–25 (2006)
3. Kassianos, A.P., Raats, M.M., Gage, H., Peacock, M.: Quality of life and dietary changes among cancer patients: a systematic review. Qual. Life Res. **24**, 705–719 (2015)
4. World Cancer Research Fund/American Institute for Cancer Research (2018). Diet, Nutrition, Physical Activity and Cancer: a Global Perspective. Continuous Update Project expert Report. https://www.wcrf.org/dietandcancer
5. Maskarinec, G., Murphy, S., Shumay, D.M., Kakai, H.: Dietary changes among cancer survivors. Eur. J. Cancer Care **10**, 12–20 (2001)
6. van Weert, E., et al.: A multidimensional cancer rehabilitation program for cancer survivors – effectiveness on health related quality of life. J. Psychosom. Res. **58**, 485–496 (2005)
7. Demark-Wahnefried, W., Jones, L.W.: Promoting a healthy lifestyle among cancer survivors. Hematol. – Oncol. Clin. North Am. **22**, 319–342 (2008)
8. McBride, C.M., Ostroff, J.S.: Teachable moments for promoting smoking cessation: the context of cancer care and survivorship. Cancer Control: J. Moffitt Cancer Center **10**, 325–333 (2003)
9. Anderson, A., Caswell, S., Wells, M., Steele, R.J.C.: Obesity and lifestyle advice in colorectal cancer survivors—how well are clinicians prepared? Colorectal Dis. **15**, 949–957 (2013)

10. Beeken, R.J., Williams, K., Wardle, J., Croker, H.: "What about diet?" A qualitative study of cancer survivors' views on diet and cancer and their sources of information. Eur. J. Cancer Care (Engl.) **25**(5), 774–783 (2016)
11. Jones, L.W., Demark-Wahnefried, W.: Diet, exercise, and complementary therapies after primary treatment for cancer. Lancet Oncol. **7**, 1017–1026 (2006)
12. Van Tonder, E., Herselman, M.G., Visser, J.: The prevalence of dietary related complementary and alternative therapies and their perceived usefulness among cancer patients. J. Hum. Nutr. Diet. **22**, 528–535 (2009)
13. Cancer and Nutrition NIHR infrastructure Collaboration – Summary of Phase one July 2015. http://cancerandnutrition.nihr.ac.uk/
14. Corfe, B.M., Murphy, J.L., Davey, F.P., et al.: Nutritional screening, assessment and provision of advice for people living with and beyond cancer - a UK survey of clinicians. Proc. Nutr. Soc. **77**(OCE1), E25 (2018)
15. MyFitnessPal Inc.: MyFitnessPal (Version 18.11.5) [Mobile application software] (2018). https://www.apple.com/uk/ios/app-store/
16. NutritionFacts.org: Daily Dozen (Version 2.0) [Mobile application software] (2018). https://www.apple.com/uk/ios/app-store/
17. WebMD, LLC.: Medscape (Version 5.13) [Mobile application software] (2017). https://www.apple.com/uk/ios/app-store/
18. Burke, L.E., Conroy, M.B., Sereika, S.M., Elci, O.U., Styn, M.A., Acharya, S.D., et al.: The effect of electronic self-monitoring on weight loss and dietary intake: a randomized behavioral weight loss trial. Obes. (Silver Spring) **19**(2), 338–344 (2011). https://doi.org/10.1038/oby.2010.208
19. Finkelstein, J., Bedra, M., Li, X., Wood, J., Ouyang, P.: Mobile app to reduce inactivity in sedentary overweight women. Study Health Technol. Inform. **216**, 89–92 (2015)
20. Ryan, E.A., Holland, J., Stroulia, E., Bazelli, B., Babwik, S.A., Li, H., et al.: Improved A1C levels in type 1 diabetes with smartphone app use. Can. J. Diabetes **41**(1), 33–40 (2017). https://doi.org/10.1016/j.jcjd.2016.06.001
21. Coughlin, S.S., Besenyi, G.M., Bowen, D., De Leo, G.: Development of the Physical activity and Your Nutrition for Cancer (PYNC) smartphone app for preventing breast cancer in women. Mhealth **3**, 5 (2017). https://doi.org/10.21037/mhealth.2017.02.02
22. Orleman, T., et al.: A novel mobile phone app (OncoFood) to record and optimize the dietary behavior of oncologic patients: pilot study. JMIR Cancer **4**(2) (2018). https://doi.org/10.2196/10703
23. Peng, W., Kanthawala, S., Yuan, S., Hussain, S.: A qualitative study of user perceptions of mobile health apps. BMC Public Health **16**(1), 1–11 (2016)
24. Anderson, K., Burford, O., Emmerton, L.: Mobile health apps to facilitate self-care: a qualitative study of user experiences. PLoS ONE **11**(5), e0156164 (2016)
25. Krug, S.: Don't Make Me Think, Revisited. New Riders, Berkeley (2014)
26. Muller, M.J.: Participatory design: the third space in HCI. Hum.-Comput. Interact.: Dev. Process **4235**(2003), 165–185 (2003)
27. Fairbanks, B., et al.: Creating a FACETS digital toolkit to promote quality of life of people with multiple sclerosis through Participatory Design. In: 2nd Workshop on Human Centred Design for Intelligent Environments (HCD4IE). The 32nd Human Computer Interaction Conference (British HCI 2018), Belfast, 3 July 2018 (2018)
28. Agile PrepCast: Comparison of Agile Methods by The Agile PrepCast [online]. Project Management Prepcast (2015)
29. Nielsen, J.: Thinking Aloud: The #1 Usability Tool. Nielsen Norman Group (2012). https://www.nngroup.com/articles/thinking-aloud-the-1-usability-tool/

30. Spencer, R.: The streamlined cognitive walkthrough method, working around social constraints encountered in a software development company. In: Proceedings from ACM CHI 2000: Conference on Human Factors in Computing Systems. ACM Press, New York (2000)
31. MeasuringU: Measuring Usability with the System Usability Scale (SUS) [online]. MeasuringU (2011). https://measuringu.com/sus/. Accessed 1 Mar 2018
32. Kang, H., Park, H.: A mobile app for hypertension management based on clinical practice guidelines: development and deployment. JMIR Mhealth Uhealth 4(1), e12 (2016). https://doi.org/10.2196/mhealth.4966

An Interaction Design Approach
of Fitness APP

Jun-Qi Wang[1(✉)], Jing-chen Cong[2], Zhi-yuan Zheng[3], Yang Meng[4],
and Chao Liu[5]

[1] School of Arts, Tianjin University of Commerce, Tianjin 300134, China
2767458713@qq.com
[2] School of Mechanical Engineering, Tianjin University, Tianjin 300350, China
[3] School of Design and Arts, Beijing Institute of Technology,
Beijing 100081, China
[4] Lian Xian Education of Tianjin, China, Tianjin, China
[5] Baidu, Beijing, China

Abstract. At present, the number of App users in China is soaring, but it still faces the problem of low user stickiness. The interactive design approach of fitness App is proposed to improve the App and motive users to form the habit of permanent use of fitness App, and ultimately achieve the goal of increasing the fitness App's stickiness. The ideal fitness App lifecycle can be divided into three stages: the initial trial stage, the habit-forming stage, and the habit-keeping stage. It is proposed that fitness App should improve user experience in three stages of the ideal lifecycle by improving interaction design at the three levels of "instinct level, behavior level and reflective level". The specific interaction design approach at the instinct level, behavior level and reflective level are also put forward.

Keywords: Motivation theories · Fitness apps · Interaction design

1 Introduction

Fitness App is a kind of sports assistant tool which provides users with fitness knowledge, formulates fitness plans, shows exercise courses and recommends recipes according to different physique. It attracts a large number of users for its advantages, such as unlimited time and space, customizable courses and detailed records of sports data.

Nowadays fitness is becoming more and more popular in China. The number of people who often take physical exercise in China is increasing year by year. By 2020, the sports population in China is expected to reach 435 million [1]. However, with the growth of national fitness demand, the limited national public sports resources and high gymnasium fees have limited the national fitness aspirations. Therefore, fitness App has gained a large number of users with its advantage of being unrestricted by the venue. The user scale, average daily use time and average daily use frequency are all in a steady growth trend. By June 2018, the industry penetration rate of fitness App was 9.5%, and the number of users reached 104 million. The average daily use time per user

© Springer Nature Switzerland AG 2019
A. Marcus and W. Wang (Eds.): HCII 2019, LNCS 11585, pp. 348–358, 2019.
https://doi.org/10.1007/978-3-030-23538-3_27

lasted up to 20.17 min, rose by 30.8% year-on-year. The average daily use frequency per user was 3.05 times, rose by 20.08% year-on-year [2].

At present, the research on fitness App mainly concentrates on the realization of fitness function and fitness technology process. The single research on fitness App users mainly focuses on sports education and physical & mental health of teenagers, including the use of fitness App for college students [3, 4], and the physical activity [5] motivation of fitness App for students and young people [6]. While in China, the fitness habits of the nationals are developed late, so fitness App face the problem of how to help users develop fitness habits. The core problem that needs to be solved in the interactive design of fitness App is how to motivate users to generate fitness behaviors and keep on doing fitness by the continuous usage of App.

2 Motivation Theories in Fitness App

The word "Motivation" comes from the Latin word "Movere", which original meaning is promotion or participation in an activity. According to Atkinson, motivation refers to the impact of the direction, intensity and sustainability of the action at this moment [7]. Motivation model is the application of motivation theory. Researchers extract and classify the motivation elements of motivation theory, and establish motivation model for practical application. It includes a theory of intrinsically motivating instruction [8] proposed by Malone, Fogg Behavior Model (FBM) [9] proposed by Fogg, and the ARCS model proposed by Keller etc. In which ARCS, referring to the four elements of Attention, Relevance, Confidence and Satisfaction, it emphasizes that to realize the function of motivating learners to learn, the motivation to inspire learners must be combined with the application of these four elements [10]. Combined with the theme of fitness, ARCS motivation model is applied to fitness: (1) Attention. Inspire interest and maintain attention through colorful presentation and novel tasks. (2) Relevance. Connect training content with reality, which is to help users understand which skills can be improved through training, and what does it mean for real life. (3) Confidence. Help users build confidence and believe that they have the ability to achieve fitness goals. (4) Satisfaction. Give positive feedback and encouragement to users' fitness achievements. Fitness App need to motivate users to have fitness through the App and cultivate their long-term fitness habits. The core of cultivating habits is to establish a relationship between "pay" and "reward", and the key to establishing a relationship lies in the appropriate motivation mechanism.

3 The Relationship Between Ideal Lifecycle and Interactive Design on Fitness App

Fitness App cultivates users' habit of using the App to assist fitness through the way of motivation, thereby reducing users' withdrawal and abandonment due to fatigue and laziness, and strives to develop the user's continuous fitness behavior into regular App use for fitness in the process of repeated use. The ideal fitness App lifecycle can be divided into three stages: the initial trial stage, the habit-forming stage, and the habit-keeping stage. The initial trial stage is the process of gathering users' information to the willingness to perform or having completed the first workout. After the initial fitness behavior, users continue to use App to assist in fitness. With the increase of fitness frequency and satisfaction, the user enters the habit-forming stage. With the accumulation of user fitness data, the user stickiness of the system will also exhibit nonlinear enhancement. Users regard App as a regular fitness aids, gradually develop lifelong fitness habits, and enter the habit-keeping stage.

It is mentioned that in this article, the system motivates users to use App to assist in fitness by enhancing interactive design. Donald Arthur Norman put forward three levels of design: instinct level, behavior level, reflective level [11]. This study proposes that fitness App should improve the user experience in the three stages of "initial trial stage, habit-forming stage, and habit-keeping stage" by refining the interaction design at the three levels of "instinct level, behavior level and reflective level".

The initial trial stage corresponds to the instinct level of interaction design, which is very strong in the sensory stimulation, to meet the basic requirements of users for their survival needs, so as to inspire users' interest at the beginning of contacting fitness App. At this stage, interaction design should pay more attention to the system content. Continuous use stage corresponds to the behavior level of interaction design, which reflects the user's behavior when using the product. It is the level of user's perception from physiology to psychology. At this stage, interaction design should focus on the design related to practical function and good service. Permanent use stage corresponds to the reflective level of interaction design, which pays more attention to personal emotions. The interaction design of this stage pays more attention to users' social needs, respect needs, self-fulfillment needs, and makes the users generate the emotional resonance, and establish a permanent relationship with the system naturally.

4 Interactive Design Approach of Fitness App Based on Motivation Theories

Interaction design is a new subject separated and developed from the field of human-computer interaction [12]. Shneiderman puts forward the interaction design approach for most interactive systems [13]. On this basis, this study proposes that fitness App can be designed to motivate users at different stages by following the principles of inter-action design at different levels, as shown in Fig. 1.

4.1 Interaction Design Approach at the Initial Trial Stage

1. Ensuring that the content and functionality meet the basic needs of users. Health factors belong to the most basic physiological and safety needs of Maslow's hierarchy of needs [14]. Adhering to physical fitness to maintain good health has become the most basic user demand of using fitness App. Fitness App should provide professional and detailed fitness records, scientific and standardized fitness guidance and detailed fitness data to help users know the physical activity every time and better achieve fitness goals. Take Keep as an example, Keep provides a

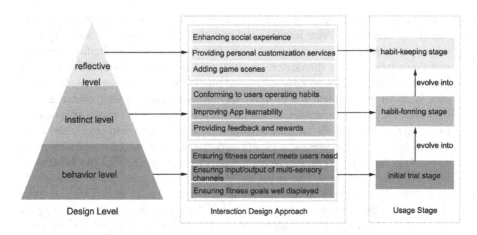

Fig. 1. The interaction design approach of fitting app

novice entry area for first time users of the App, including knowledge and information about fitness, diet and basic introductory training courses for novice. It also provides entrance for fitness ability test and physical data collection, as shown in Fig. 2. And formulates fitness training plan according to the user's gender, age and fitness needs, to help novice quickly complete the Entry stage of fitness.

Fig. 2. Fitting plan content page (Picture Source: Keep App)

2. Ensuring the input and output of multi-sensory channels. Fitness App should adopt visual, auditory and tactile senses to transmit information more effectively. Meanwhile, it should expand the channels for system to receive information. Visual feedback is still the most important form of feedback. But when exercising, mobile devices are often worn on the wrist or tied to the arm. To ensure the fluency and safety of the exercise, auditory and tactile feedback will be better than visual feedback. "Lemon Running" is a fitting App which mainly provides running services. When

users use the App, the intelligent devices are usually worn on the arms. It is inconvenient to check the device interface to know the running progress. So every time when users complete the running mileage of one kilometer, the vibration reminder and voice broadcast of the device can transmit the information of the completed mileage and the moving speed to users, and provide voice encouragement when the user is about to complete the process, so that users can get their own real-time information without having to read the interface and get a better sports experience.

3. Ensuring the fitness goals are clearly displayed. It is necessary to clearly show the goal of fitness, so that users can clearly understand the effect of completing exercises. App can quantify the movement data to make people feel the benefits of exercise more intuitively. The target difficulty should be matched with the user's own skills, or be slightly difficult, and long-term goals should be divided into some short-term goals, to motivate users to complete the challenge step by step, and gain a sense of achievement and satisfaction in the process of approaching the goal. According to the whole fitness cycle of the user, Hot Fitness App displays the daily fitness training consumption and diet guide in the form of progress bar, as shown in Fig. 3. Users will know their current fitness process in real time and get the fitness results in advance, further more have a better understanding of the entire fitness plan framework. All in all it will help users build confidence and inspire motivation to implement their own fitness programs, and make users believe that they have the ability to achieve the fitting goals.

Fig. 3. Fitting plan content page (Picture Source: Hot Fitting)

4.2 Interactive Design Approach at the Habit-Forming Stage

1. Conforming to users' operating habits. Fitness App should conform to users' operating habits, and the final interactive interface should match the user's mental model of the system. In the sports scene, users hope to understand the main

functions and operation modes of the App quickly, and put into training as soon as possible. App fits for matching narrow and shallow navigation design, with simple and easy-to-use operation process, and well-known interactive gestures to reduce learning cost. As shown in Fig. 4, in the running module of Mi Sports App, a reasonable interactive gesture can avoid the users' misoperation during the operation of pause and termination, so that users can clearly check their own fitting process in running time, and enhance the immersion of users.

Fig. 4. Running content page (Picture Source: Mi Sports App)

2. Improving App learnability. The system can improve the App learnability by novice guidance video, primary and secondary interface design, fitting data visualization to make the system more transparent to users. The interface information levels is clearly divided, and the fonts, icons and buttons designed are unified and coordinated, which can improve the App learnability and enable users to learn the use of the App more quickly. The App will help users understand fitness actions through fitness guidance video, and help monitor the users' body by using smart connected open architecture product [16]. When fitness action is not up to standard, smart connected open architecture product will remind users or assist users to meet the standard.

3. Providing feedback and rewards. The system should provide feedback on users' fitness results at an appropriate time to avoid users' dull and bored moods. Regular rewards will inspire users' expectations, and irregular rewards will attract users' addiction. When the user is in fitness, a random reward to the user whose fitness time reaches a certain amount will bring surprise. Similarly, when the fitting plan is interrupted, the system can assist users to find the reasons, such as busy time, physical discomfort, or high goals etc., and provide corresponding solutions, something like the time extension, and the fitting plans or goals adjustment. Taking Joy Run App as an example, in order to encourage users to open App more often and run more, the App

has designed a medal award system, as shown in Fig. 5. The system is divided into six categories: Joy Run Guru, online marathon, brilliance, music life, challenging action, and invincibility. These medals cover activities, constellations, solar terms, geographical location and some other aspects. When users complete the running mileage and off-line marathon, they will be awarded medals accordingly. By collecting medals, the self-fulfilment psychology can be satisfied.

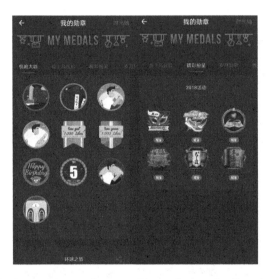

Fig. 5. Medals award system (Picture Source: Joy Run App)

4.3   Interaction Design Approach at the Habit-Keeping Stage

1. Enhancing social experience. Fitness App sets up a social network for fitness communication, which can help users get a sense of participation and belonging in social communication, and provide users with spiritual strength. The App can also show the number of training and the training results of other people in the course detailed page, to motivate fitting continuously by group psychology. Taking Rejoice Sport as an example, as shown in Fig. 6, in the circle module of the App, users can set up or join the circles they're interested, participate in interesting topics, give dynamical Likes or comments to friends, and follow users nearby. In the circles that users join, the App will rank according to the number of training minutes, the number of likes and the number of selection of every user in the circle, and list training lists, popularity lists and contribution lists, as shown in Fig. 7. On the one hand, it will provide a circle talents reference for novice users, and on the other hand, it will motivate users to have fitting actively and enhance their communication of fitness experience.

Fig. 6. Circle topic discussion page (Picture Source: Rejoice Sport App)

Fig. 7. Circle ranking list page (Picture Source: Rejoice Sport App)

2. Providing personal customization services. Fitness App can use artificial intelligence technology to formulate personalized fitting programs when setting fitting goals and plans for users. And at the same time give users the right to modify programs. It can consider the individual's learning progress and thinking changes.

Users' physical condition and training objectives will change in the process of using App to assist fitness, and the system should change and improve accordingly to help users achieve new goals at all times. As shown in Fig. 8, try - Fitness and Weight Loss App, it analyzes the recorded data according to the user's health goals, and formulates personalized programs for users to help them cultivate healthy habits

Fig. 8. Dietary calorie data record page (Picture Source: Try- Fitness and Weight Loss App)

3. Adding game scenes. Fitness App can design a game scene and create a relaxed atmosphere. This way can not only reduce the boredom of fitness, but also motivate users' interest to maintain their attention. Designers can apply the thinking and mechanism of gaming to the design of fitness App. As shown in Fig. 9, WALKUP drives the whole game by recording the number of users' steps, combined with fitting records and world travel. The App records the users' number of steps every day through the mobile device's step-counting function, converts the steps into the energy to travel around the world, and brings users with the experience of exploring cities around the world. During the trip, the App prepares a variety of interesting events and scenarios. Users can compete with their friends in the number of steps, or get rewards by completing the mission. All of these will help users enjoy the fun of fitting and games in the world travel.

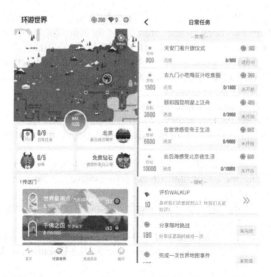

Fig. 9. Game mission content page (Picture Source: Walkup App)

5   Conclusion

Starting from the lifecycle of fitness App, this article divides the ideal lifecycle of fitness App into three stages, and summarizes the interaction design approach corresponding to each stage, by combining with the three levels of interaction design. The interactive design approach of fitness App proposed in this article lays a theoretical foundation for the spread of interactive design work. Compliance with this approach, interactive design can effectively enhance users' willingness to use the system. This study is still limited to the consideration of the Chinese market. In the future work, the range of study will be broadened, and will be focused on the interactive design of global fitness App.

References

1. Analysys Co., Ltd.: China Mobile Sports Fitness Market Special Analysis (2017) [EB/OL]. http://www.199it.com/archives/623777.html
2. Jiguang Co., Ltd., Jiguang Insight: Fitness APP users are over 100 million [EB/OL]. https://mp.weixin.qq.com/s/8_DcmiIMy16EMN7jp14CPA
3. Gowin, M., Cheney, M., Gwin, S., et al.: Health and fitness app use in college students: a qualitative study. Am. J. Health Educ. **46**(4), 223–230 (2015)
4. Cho, J., Lee, H.E., Kim, S.J., et al.: Effects of body image on college students' attitudes toward diet/fitness apps on smartphones. Cyberpsychol. Behav. Soc. Netw. **18**(1), 41–45 (2015)
5. Martin, M.R., Melnyk, J., Zimmerman, R.: Fitness apps: motivating students to move. J. Phys. Educ. Recreation Dance **86**(6), 50–54 (2015)

6. Direito, A., Jiang, Y., Whittaker, R., et al.: Smartphone apps to improve fitness and increase physical activity among young people: protocol of the Apps for Improving Fitness (aim fit) randomized controlled trial. BMC Public Health 15(1), 635 (2015)
7. Atkinson, J.W.: An Introduction to Motivation. UT Back-in-Print Service (1964)
8. Malone, T.W.: Toward a theory of intrinsically motivating instruction. Cogn. Sci. 5(4), 333–369 (1981)
9. Fogg, B.J.: A behavior model for persuasive design. In: Proceedings of the 4th International Conference on Persuasive Technology (2009)
10. Keller, J.M.: Development and use of the ARCS model of instructional design. J. Instr. Dev. 10(3), 2 (1987)
11. Norman, D.A.: Emotional Design. China CITIC Press, Beijing (2015)
12. Saffer, D.: Designing for Interaction: Creating Innovative Applications and Devices. New Riders Publishing (2009)
13. Shneiderman, B.: Designing the user interface: strategies for effective human-computer interaction. J. Assoc. Inf. Sci. Technol. 39(1), 603–604 (1988)
14. Maslow, A.H.: Motivation and Personality. Harper & Brothers, New York (1954)
15. Cooper, A., Reimann, R., Cronin, D.: About Face 3: The Essentials of Interaction Design. Wiley, Hoboken (2007)
16. Pai, Z., Yuan, L., et al.: Smart, connected open architecture product: an IT-driven co-creation paradigm with lifecycle personalization concerns. Int. J. Prod. Res. 57, 2571–2584 (2018)

Design of an Anti-domestic Violence Product Based on Emotion Regulation

Yinxiao Yan[1](✉) and Xuyang Liu[2]

[1] School of Design, Shanghai Jiaotong University,
800 Dongchuan RD. Minghang District, Shanghai, China
346707719@qq.com
[2] Communication Design, Pratt Institute, 200 Willoughby Ave, Brooklyn,
NY 11205, USA
xliu35@pratt.edu

Abstract. Domestic violence, as an act of serious violation of human rights, has indeed the very potential to render familial harmony as well as social stability in peril. Taking the current situation of domestic violence against women into consideration, this paper offers not only a comprehensive study on the users from the perspectives of their characteristics, requirements and relevant usage scenarios, but also a comparison of the existing products against domestic violence. On such basis, this paper attempts to put forward a design of anti-domestic violence product through the means of regulating emotions. Secondly, based on the detailed research of environmental psychology and the related theories of emotion regulation, three cost-effective emotion influencing elements are applied to the very design of a mood-soothing lamp which functions to prevent domestic violence from the perspective of the perpetrators.

Keywords: Anti-domestic violence · Emotion regulation · Mood-influencing elements

1 Introduction

On a global scale, the majority of victims of domestic violence are women. Compared with their male counterparts, women often suffer from more severe forms of violence incurred by gender inequality as well as outmoded social conventions. According to the statistics offered by the United Nations, the number of those women who have ever suffered physical or sexual violence accounts for one third of the entire female population worldwide, and the dominant portion of the very perpetrators who commit domestic violence against women are no other than their intimate sexual partners or spouses. In China, the incidence of domestic violence approaches 29.7%–35.7%, of which 90% of the victims are women [1].

In some countries, domestic violence is even justified in some way or another, and thus is not considered to be a crime. One of the most important factors that fuels the proliferation of domestic violence in those regions is the prevalent notion that it is justifiable to abuse a woman both verbally and physically. Relevant studies indicate that many women are reluctant to admit that they have ever been victims of domestic

A. Marcus and W. Wang (Eds.): HCII 2019, LNCS 11585, pp. 359–369, 2019.
https://doi.org/10.1007/978-3-030-23538-3_28

violence: less than 40% of those women who have suffered domestic violence try to seek for help from others, and less than 10% of them resort to legal intervention or protection. Although, many male violence-doers are overwhelmed by guilt and shame after their committing of domestic violence, they still cannot effectively control their emotions when another conflict or confrontation occurs. In this way, a vicious cycle is in gear: tragedy repeats itself again and again.

Therefore, if domestic violence is to be completely eradicated, it is essential that a tool which can interfere with the act of violence when the perpetrators lose self-control and then help them to ease their negative emotions should be contrived. On such basis, the purpose of this paper is to design an anti-domestic violence product that deploys emotion regulation as a means to prevent the occurrence of domestic violence and to establish a harmonious spousal relationship.

2 Investigation and Research

2.1 A Big Data Analysis of the Current Status of Domestic Violence

Male-to-female violence within intimate relationships (especially the spousal relationship) has already become a cross-cultural prevalence in the modern era (Fig. 1). As is indicated by the multinational study conducted by the World Health Organization on women's health and domestic violence that 15% to 71% of women in 10 countries reveal that they have ever suffered physical or sexual abuse inflicted by their intimate partners [2].

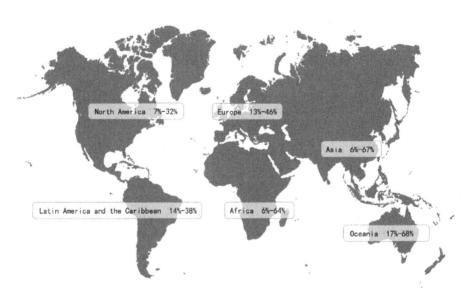

Fig. 1. The percentage of women who have experienced intimate partner violence.

The Supreme People's Court of China released a set of data in the "Special Report on the Divorce Dispute Judicial Big Data" which shows that during 2016–2017, among all the cases of divorce disputes involving domestic violence, 91.43% of them entail male-to-female domestic violence. To put it in a more readily perceptive way, given that there are altogether 430 million families in China, that is to say, every 7.4 s there is one woman suffering from domestic violence in China. It is worth noting that, the females who have been subjected to domestic violence are by no means limited merely to those married women, teenagers, even children are also on the bloody list of victims. As for the perpetrators, not only partners or spouses but also non-partners are potential abusers. For example, ex-boyfriends, ex-husbands and other family members may also transform into the perpetrators who impose all sorts of violence upon women. Therefore, being a kind of gender violence, domestic violence is never merely a private matter but rather a public nuisance to which due social attention must be paid.

2.2   User Research

The Characteristics and Behavioral Patterns of Domestic Violence Perpetrators. Most of the perpetrator are inclined to have one or more of the following defining characteristics:

- They are, more often than not, rather radical, impulsive, and own poor emotional control.
- Their volatile temperament bears indispensable and direct relationship with the traumatized experience that they have endured in their original families. Freud believes that childhood experiences have a great impact on the psychological development of individuals, including ones' mental growth and the formation of their unique personality. That is to say, the direct exposure to domestic violence may cause an inerasable negative impact on children. And children who have been raised up in such family environment are more likely to commit domestic violence against their partners in the future. It is because that, on the one hand, the children who have once witnessed the scene of domestic violence tend to follow suit and observe the same behavioral patterns when they form their own familial bond later in the future; On the other hand, children will absorb subtly and spontaneously that violence is the most efficient way to solve all problems or conflicts, and such notion will receive its enforcement as the times of their exposure to domestic violence increase [3]. In this way, children with similar traumatized experience are very likely to become a new gear of the vicious cycle of the domestic violence.
- They tend to suffer from greater mental stress, such as the pressure on financial management, children's education, property dispute, estrangement in spousal relationship, etc.
- Most of them have bad habits, such as alcoholism, drug abuse, cigarette obsession, etc.
- They have internalized the belief in male superiority and deep-ingrained gender biases.
- They have an overwhelming desire to hold all things as well as all people in control. One case in point is that more than a half of males believe that they must occupy the dominant status in family and should be endowed with the power to have the final say in making all important decisions; Another pertinent case is that nearly half of males believe that more strict restrictions should be placed on woman's clothing.

In a nutshell, based on the above user research, this study finds that many perpetrators of domestic violence do not intentionally carry out violent acts. Most of the cases of domestic violence occur only when those perpetrators could no longer materialize a valid control over their own emotions under certain highly provocative circumstances, and a dominant portion of them would confess their mistakes and feel guilty after their reason and ration having been restored.

The Characteristics of the Victims. The United Nations has once conducted a survey on violence and abuse against Chinese women which discloses that about 39% of Chinese females admit to having experienced violence and abuse imposed by their partners, and nearly 52% of males acknowledge that they have abused their female partners. The disparity between these two percentages is loaded with profound implications which reveal the fact that many women in China are reluctant or refuse to admit that they are actually victims of domestic violence. Although the current campaigns fighting against domestic violence reaches its climax on a worldwide scale, influenced by the traditional yet biased concepts such as "Don't wash one's dirty linen in public" [3], seeking for legal intervention remains the last choice for Chinese females who suffer from domestic violence. Instead, nearly 40% of them are more willing to ask for help from their other intimate family members rather than resort to proper legal intervention or protection.

Moreover, sexism and gender discrimination still remain widespread and deeply-rooted in some parts of China, in particular those economically underdeveloped rural regions. Surveys show repeatedly that women are not equally aware of the significance of attaining gender equality as their male counterparts. This always leads to the tragedy that a forced and illusive family integrity or harmony is established at the very expense of women's welfare: woman, the prescribed care-giver according to the traditional gender role, becomes the sacrifice for the consolidation of patriarchal hierarchy to which she falls an easy prey. In most cases, women have no other choice but to forgive those violence doers. Given their financial dependence, women are so helplessly compelled to reach a compromise with males and nearly impossible to break loose from the infinite cycle of domestic violence (Fig. 2). Ironic enough, only 59% females regard domestic violence to be a crime, and most of them believe that it is futile to call the police when they are subjected to domestic violence, because, as they believe, such act would only further enrage the perpetrators and thus beget other unexpected catastrophic consequences.

Fig. 2. The cycle of domestic violence.

User Requirements. After analyzing the characteristics and behavioral patterns of the perpetrators of domestic violence, it finds that most of them do not intentionally resort to violent means to dissolve domestic confrontations and conflicts, because, afterwards, they will always be carried away by a sense of remorse and self-blame. So this paper believes that a sort of emotion regulating device that can release their negative feelings at the first stage before the act of domestic violence truly takes place is in urgent need. In other words, such a tool should serve as a reminder to warn those people who are approaching the verge of losing self-control that their current behavior is not appropriate. And as for the requirements of victims, on the one hand, they want to ensure their own safety and avoid domestic violence; While on the other hand, they also hope that the embarrassing situation that they have been subjected to will remain confidential to the public.

2.3   Usage Scenario

Domestic violence usually occurs in relatively private and enclosed occasions such as the living spaces (Fig. 3). The typical scene can be described as that, for some reasons, verbal disputes arise between a couple. Then, as the contradictions gradually intensify, the perpetrator loses totally his control and thus carries out violence against the one who occupies the disadvantaged position.

Fig. 3.   Usage scenario.

2.4   An Overview of the Existing Domestic Violence Prevention Products

It is strikingly obvious that there are scant products that have been contrived to prevent domestic violence. It is true that there is indeed a small amount of products circulating in the market which aim at preventing domestic violence, nevertheless, most of them are designed for the victims, the product that takes the perpetrators as its central user group is in a crying need on a global scale.

Products that fall into the former category are listed as follows: Echo Dot (Fig. 4), a hands-free voice control device, can send digital messages to the nearby police station immediately when its user speaks out the pre-set codes such as "Call the Police"; PFO Shield bracelet is a wearable device that functions to send the detailed location information of its user and a distress signal by pulling the bracelet when its user confronts with a dangerous situation, allowing rescue teams to locate quickly and accurately his/her location and then to perform prompt and proper rescue operations. Although, both of the two products are designed to ensure personal safety, in the process of sending a distress signal to the rescuers, victims may face the very danger of further enraging the perpetrators, and a great challenge is posed to the timeliness and validness of the rescue operations. Different from the above two devices, the Emotional Remote Control is a product designed for the perpetrator. It deploys different colors of light to regulate its users' emotions and guide their behavior, but the carrying out of its proper function requires a rigid temporal and spacial conditions: it can not be fully functional during the daytime or when the user is exposed to a circumstance where the light is too strong.

Echo Dot   PFO Shiled Bracelet   Emotional remote control

Fig. 4. Existing anti-domestic violence products.

3   Relevant Theoretical Research

3.1   Environmental Psychology

Environmental psychology is a branch of applied social psychology that studies the relationship between the environment and human psychology as well as behavior [4]. Its major research issue consists in the adaptability of human beings to various environmental factors. Therefore, environmental psychology is very concerned about the impact of the environment on human behavior, emotions and decision-makings.

The environment can indeed play a decisive role in changing people's mental and emotional states. The landscape, shape, color and other elements of the environment will instantly stimulate people's visual senses and evoke a certain visual psychological reaction accordingly. A full consideration of the proper deployment of environmental psychology can reduce, to a certain extent, the occurrence of domestic violence even if one is situated in an environment prone to provoke domestic violence.

Grieder and Chanmugam ([5], 22(4):365–378) once applied environmental psychology to the shelter of domestic violence to reduce the occurrence of domestic violence by increasing residents' happiness, especially by adopting design strategies of an increasing sense of control, social support and reducing environmental pressure [5].

3.2   Mood-Influencing Elements

It is widely accepted that individuals' emotions fluctuate around multitudinous internal and external factors. Among all of them, the following five elements can exert a tremendous impact on human emotions which offers inexhaustible inspirations as well as a solid theoretical foundation for the design of domestic violence prevention products.

Color. Compared with the form or shape, the color of an object or an environment is a more direct and intense stimulation of human vision. The colors with different hue, brightness and saturation will have different effects, both positive and negative, on individuals' mood and mental state. Studies have shown that people, even if in an irritable mood previously, would become much more tranquil and concentrated in an environment where blue is the background color [6]. People are more likely to foster a calmer temperament if they submerge themselves in such environment for a long term. Therefore, the design of anti-domestic violence products can make full use of the psychological influences on human beings brought about by different colors, and deploy the correct color to achieve the goal of regulating emotions.

Light. Both theoretical and clinical studies have proved that photo-therapy is an effective way to cure emotional disorders. Gheorghita et al. ([7], 71(1)) believe that the perception of light and its effect on humans is subjective. Lighting determines the appreciation and influences people's behavior: how they feel in a place, how they perceive it, behave in it, and how they use the place [7]. The change of lighting or illumination is closely related to the visual perception and physiological changes of the human body. Appropriate lighting will make users feel comfortable and at ease both physically and mentally.

Sound. Researches suggest that not only people's blood pressure does decrease when certain melody and rhythm are heard, but also the speed of breathing and the rate of basic metabolism will accordingly slow down which together lead to a milder physiological response toward distress and pressure. Sound actually plays a special role and has a significant function in regulating people's emotions. It affects people's feelings, physiology as well as behaviors through the process of resonance, infection, resonance, coordination, etc.

Pulsed Electromagnetic Field. The pulsed electromagnetic field (PEMF) is a kind of high-energy non-ionizing radiation which is highly sensitive to the electromagnetic field of a certain frequency. When the human body is stimulated by such pulsed electromagnetic field, it can generate curative effect through activating the hypothalamic-adrenal system: it has regulatory functions on cortical bioelectricity, endocrine and even the whole human body. Therefore, as a therapeutic method that can regulate emotions and tranquilize anxieties, the pulsed electromagnetic field can be used as an accessory treatment to cure a variety of psychologist and psychiatric diseases [8].

Brain Implant Chip. In 1950, the first human brain chip appeared. Husse Dirkado was the pioneer who experimented persistently to implant such chip into human brains in order to regulate people's emotions by stimulating slightly a certain targeted part of the human brain. According to an article published in the journey Nature, a research team subsidized by the Defense Advanced Research Projects Agency (DARPA) has designed a brain chip controlled by AI (Artificial Intelligence) that can detect the brain activity of the implanter. When an emotional disorder occurs, the chip will send an electrical pulse through an algorithm to stimulate the specific areas of the brain to regulate or even "control" human emotions and behaviors, restoring the brain to a healthy, normal state.

4   Comparative Analysis and Conclusions

Based on the previous theoretical research, this paper endeavors to make a comparative analysis of the five mood-influencing elements (light, color, sound, pulsed electromagnetic field and brain implant chip) from following three aspects: they are namely effect, cost and safety (Fig. 5).

As is shown by the figure that though the pulsed electromagnetic field and the brain implanted chip can indeed exert more significant influences on people's emotion, their cost is higher than that of required by the other three elements, and users' safety cannot be fully guaranteed if these two high-tech devices are to be applied. Given that victims who suffer from domestic violence always locate in a disadvantaged financial position which is directly caused by their underprivileged physical and social status, it is obvious that few of them can afford a high price. While light, sound, and color therapy are comparatively much safer, user-friendly and also more cost-effective, and all of them indeed have satisfying conditioning effects on emotions. Therefore, light, sound and color are more suitable mood-influencing elements for the design of anti-domestic violence products.

Fig. 5. A comparison of the five emotional elements.

5   Design of an Anti-domestic Violence Product

Based on the preliminary research on the status quo of domestic violence, the existing anti-domestic violence products as well as the related theories, this paper proposes to design a product targeted at the potential perpetrators of domestic violence which contributes to reduce their violent inclination to the minimum: to restore a peaceful environment and to re-establish a harmonious relationship by adjusting and regulating the emotions of those potential perpetrators when quarrels or conflicts break out or are going to break out. Incorporating the three aforementioned constitutive mood-influencing elements of light, sound and color, the product is a mood-soothing lamp (Fig. 6) which functions as a vent to release ones' negative emotions. The entire structure of the product can be divided into four parts: cover, speaker, monitor and lampshade (Fig. 7).

The whole operating mechanism is divided into three procedures: information-receiving, information-processing, and information-feedback. The monitor is responsible for receiving and processing the information, and the information is fed back by the speaker and the lamp (Fig. 9).

Fig. 6. Design sketch.

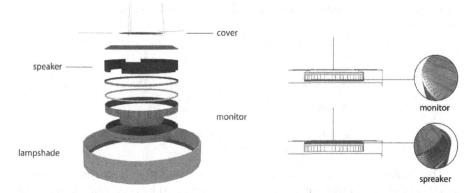

Fig. 7. Structure diagram of mood-soothing lamp.   **Fig. 8.** Operating mechanism.

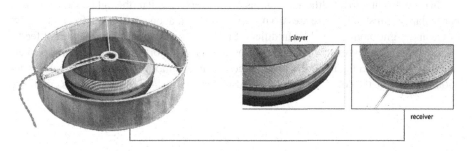

Fig. 9. Operating mechanism.

The monitor is installed at the bottom of the mood-soothing lamp and has a number of small holes in its surface for receiving information (Fig. 8). During the process of information received, the notion "emotional prosody", which is characterized as an individual's tone of voice in the speech that is conveyed through changes in pitch, loudness, timbre, speech rate, and pauses, will be deployed to detect even the slightest fluctuation of an individual's emotion. In the design of mood-soothing lamp, the emotional prosody is divided into five categories to detect whether there is domestic violence taking place in the room (Fig. 10): anger (produced with a lower pitch, higher intensity, more energy (500 Hz) across the vocalization); hot anger (produced with a higher, more varied pitch, and even greater energy (2000 Hz)); disgust (produced with a lower, downward directed pitch, with energy (500 Hz), lower first formant, and fast attack times similar to anger); Fear (have a higher pitch, little variation, lower energy, and a faster speech rate With more pauses) and sadness (produced with a higher pitch, less intensity but more vocal energy (2000 Hz)). Due to the fact that most cases of domestic violence are caused by quarrels, the built-in vocal monitor of the lamp will stay constantly alert and detect for keywords or phrases that are regarded as assaulting in domestic context from the verbal exchanges between the potential victim and the perpetrator. Besides, the monitor is also sensitive in detecting subtle changes of the volume, pitch and rhythm of the human voice: it can distinguish between different voice frequencies and analyze them in real time. Once an abnormality is detected, immediate feedback will be made.

anger   hot anger   dishust   fear   sadness

Fig. 10. The classification of emotional prosody.

The speaker installed at the top of the mood-soothing lamp functions as an audio out-put unit that plays soothing sounds once it is instructed by the digital message sent by the monitor (Fig. 8). Lamp bulbs are placed around the main body and the lamp-shade and will change their color according to the monitor's instruction (Fig. 6).

In order to cater to the different options of the users as well as the light conditions of a particular circumstance, there are two modes available that one can switch freely: the day mode and night mode (Fig. 11). In different modes, this lamp will make different feed-backs: during the daytime, when the monitor detects an abnormality, the built-in speaker will play some soothing melodies to ease ones' strained emotion. At night, except for the soothing sounds, the color of the light will also change into blue to pacify one's emotion.

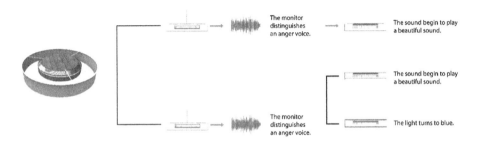

Fig. 11. Two different modes.

6 Evaluation Plan

This product has not yet been put into large-scale production and is still in the testing stage of its physical model. But the satisfying outcome of series of practical experiments, the generally positive public reception as well as the result of the market survey all indicates that such product owns a promising prospect. Experiments show that while placed in a specific environment where equipped with this mood-soothing lamp, most of the subjects state that after hearing the sounds let out by the lamp, their mood becomes more tranquil and pacified. And some state that after seeing the change of the color of the light, there is a sort of psychological suggestion would be produced in their mind reminding that they should hold their temper in control.

In the next phase, experiments will be conducted around several families with domestic violence problems in order to assess the effectiveness of the product and to collect actual data in real domestic context. However, based on the previous tests, the author believes firmly that the mood-soothing lamp can prevent domestic violence to a great extent, because that in physiological sense its functions can adjust the emotions of the perpetrators; and in psychological sense, it serves as a psychological hint which can remind the perpetrators to pay attention to their remarks and behaviors.

7 Discussion

The effect of this anti-domestic violence product is positive, but its scope of application is still controversial. The disadvantages of this product are as follows: First of all, it can only avoid the occurrence of domestic violence to a certain extent, it is more targeted at those who can not control their emotions. Second, its scope of application is limited to indoors.

References

1. Qingran, W.: Analysis of issues related to anti-domestic violence legislation. In: Legal Expo, pp. 145–146 (2018)
2. Akhter, R., Wilson, J.K.: Using an ecological framework to understand men's reasons for spousal abuse: an investigation of the Bangladesh demographic and health survey 2007. J. Fam. Violence 31, 1–12 (2016)
3. Youhua, C., Li, E.: Domestic violence: social work intervention and sociological reflections. J. Yangzhou Univ. (Humanit. Soc. Sci. Ed.) 22, 14–22 (2018)
4. Xin, S.: The application of environmental psychology in interior design—taking the rural library as an example. J. Jilin Province Coll. Educ. 34, 13–18 (2018)
5. Grieder, M.A., Chanmugam, A.: Applying environmental psychology in the design of domestic violence shelters. J. Aggress. Maltreat. Trauma 22, 365–378 (2013)
6. Bei, X.: Talking about the application of architectural psychology in architectural design. Smart City 4, 33–34 (2018)
7. GheorghiţĂ, C.C., Grigorovschi, M., Ciolacumiron, D.E.: Light and emotion: achieving emotions in landscape architecture by using light. Bull. Univ. Agric. Sci. Vet. Med. Cluj-Napoca Hortic. 71 (2014)
8. Hong, W., Jianqing, G., Wenquan, L., Guifen, Z.: Experimental study and application of pulsed electromagnetic field. Chin. J. Phys. Med. Rehabil. 23, 182–183 (2001)

The Potential Impact of Depression User Spatial Experience on Emotional Management: A Case of High School in Greater Bay Area, China

Chang Yang[1] and Zhen Liu[2(✉)]

[1] Guangzhou Ulink College, Guangzhou 510000, People's Republic of China
[2] School of Design, South China University of Technology, Guangzhou 510006,
People's Republic of China
liuzjames@scut.edu.cn

Abstract. Depression is the most common mental illness in the world. People shape architecture, and architecture also develops people. There is a few studies look into the phenomenon between spatial/architectural experience and emotional management, such as depression. Hence, this paper mainly studies the potential impact of spatial user experience on emotion within two international high schools, in Shenzhen and Guangzhou of Greater Bay Area, China, and discusses how to optimize contemporary feelings of the high school students by improving the existing space environment. Questionnaire and follow-up interview were employed for this study. The results reveal that architecture does affect the psychological and emotional management of users. The deemed areas of the schools have the most negative impact on students emotion are the teaching area and living area. Girls are more likely to have psychological and emotional management problems than boys, because girls are more delicate than boys and have more intimate activities and more emotional thinking. Students with psychological and emotional management problems are mostly between 16 and 18 years old. This may be related to the pressure of adulthood and academic strength. The psychological problems of domestic high school students have indeed become an urgent problem, and its seriousness needs the attention of all sectors of society.

Keywords: User experience · Spatial experience · Emotional management · Architecture · Mental illness · Depression · High school student · Greater Bay Area

1 Introduction

1.1 Significance of the Study

Social psychological problems accompany the development of human society. Depression is the most common mental illness in the world, and it is the leading cause of suicide in mental illness. With depression as the example. From 2005 to 2015, there was an 18-percent increase in the number of depression patients [1]. By 2015, the number of depression patients with depression alone reached 322 million [1], accounting for more than 4% of the global population. The incidence of depression was 23.8% higher in Chinese school students [2], and the detection rate of depressive symptoms in middle school students was 23.7%–54.4%, among which the detection rate of severe depressive symptoms was 3.3%–9.68%. The burden of mental illness continues to increase in all countries of the world, with significant health implications and significant social, human and economic consequences. And the existing health systems in present society are limited. As a result, scarcity has appeared, there is a great contradiction between the need for treatment and the limited supply of health systems. In developing countries, only 15%–24% of people with depression receive treatment of health systems [3]. However, in developed countries, 50%–65% of people with depression are in the same situation [3]. Are there any ways can help depressed people beside health care services? People spend almost 3/4 of their lives indoors. Can we improve people's emotions by enhancing the use of space of architecture? Why can architecture affect people's feelings? What kinds of design interventions can be made to help us to eliminate the sad emotions of daily life?

People shape architecture, and architecture also develops people. We're always told what's on the inside that counts. However, as architects, our responsibility is making a personal connection - not only people with the physical environment but also how it triggers people's emotional responses. If we can use architecture space to solve psychology problems, we will balance these serious issues about limited medical resources and people with mental disorders provision alongside the social. We also will satisfy the needs of spiritual and emotional of people in daily life.

1.2 The Range of the Study

This paper mainly studies the potential impact of spatial user experience on emotion within two high schools, i.e., one international school in Shenzhen and one international school in Guangzhou, Greater Bay Area, China, and discusses how to optimize contemporary feelings of the high school students by improving the existing space environment. And mainly combines developmental psychology with actual data from the cognitive perspective of architectural designers, from the standpoint of the perception of architectural users, and from the perspective of environmental space to human psychology, to explore the chaos of human space versus vision and even subconscious.

Architectural Psychology. Architectural psychology is a marginal subject that studies the interaction between the internal and external environment of a building and human psychology [4]. It is an interdisciplinary subject between psychology and architecture. The concepts and scientific knowledge provided by psychology about psychological phenomena, spiritual needs, and behavioral psychology help to build an architectural environment that meets people's needs. It is a relevant field where findings reveal how we can design buildings better for occupants. By understanding more about how occupants experience built form and take on a more occupant-centered approach.

1.3 The Current Situation of the Study

In today's academic world, scholars generally believe that the built environment can have a particular impact on the user's psychological and self-emotional management. The architect Robert venturi thinks that the complexity and contradiction of architecture is a reflection of human psychology, complexity, and inconsistency in the real world [5]. Andreas Meyer-Lindenberg at the University of Heidelberg has shown that good design of architecture can change brain biology in some people, resulting in reduced gray matter in the right dorsolateral prefrontal cortex and the perigenual anterior cingulate cortex, two areas where changes have previously linked to early -life stressful experiences [6]. However, some scholars believe that emotional management and psychological state are determined by the internal state of the person, and have nothing to do with external factors such as the built environment [7]. Psychologist Li Hongfu believes that the leading cause of mental illness and emotional management confusion is the patient's unhealthy psychology [8]. Many environmental problems that are considered important by patients may be just a representation of the patient, a point of projection, perhaps without this problem, and another. There is a few studies look into the phenomenon between spatial/architectural experience and emotional management, such as depression. Hence, this study focus on investigating the phenomenon in a case of high schools in Greater Bay Area, China.

2 Research Methods

2.1 Literature Review

Analytical tests are qualitative research methods that are common in research. The literature review method refers to the analysis method of the research object by analyzing the collected literature materials to find out the nature and condition of the research object. The researchers borrow books, newspapers, and periodicals from the library, and accesses news, self-media information, and videos from the highly trusted educational websites to collect information such as "architectural psychology," "the status of depressed patients in high school students," and "space and emotion management." In the process, the author understands merely and selects the content of the literature through the abstract, and then effectively reads or intensively reads the novel, excerpts the keywords and phrases during reading, and summarizes the reading content. Finally, the researchers summarizes the literature review and sorts the cost times.

2.2 Questionnaire

The authors uses the questionnaire because it has many significant advantages: the results of the survey are easy to conduct statistics and analysis; the questionnaire survey is the fastest and most effective way to collect data (under the premise that the investigator can accurately understand the questions in the questionnaire); Appropriate wording and an excellent overall sense in the questionnaire allow the respondents to be free from negative emotions when filling out the questionnaire, and the credibility is increased; The written form can be spread more widely and widely, thus expanding the sample size and diversity; Questionnaires in writing can better protect the privacy of investigators [9].

The researchers distributed a questionnaire to a total of 1,250 high school students aged 15 to 19 years old in three high schools as experimental samples. The questionnaire is divided into two phases. The first phase aims to screen out subjects with depression and depression. In the second stage, the researchers designed a questionnaire about "Have them ever had negative emotions because of space in the school." In further step, the researchers will use five senses graph devised by Lee [10]. Along the y-axis, it has a scale from 0 to 10, 10 is high intensity, 0 is no intensity. Along the x-axis, it has the five senses. Senses include sound, touch, sight, smell, taste. On this basis, the researchers devised six emotions graph, use six emotions instead of five senses along the x-axis. The feelings are happiness, sadness, fear, disgust, anger, and surprise, as shown in Fig. 4. And the researchers will ask students to record their user experiment in different school quarters on five senses graph and six emotions graph. Finally, the researchers collected the data and made the average s senses graph and normal six feelings.

2.3   Follow-up Interview

The follow-up interviews are in the form of one-on-one meetings. In a limited time and space, the researcher conducts a purposeful and natural conversational interview with high school students with depression and tendency. Through interviews, the researcher wants to understand their needs and the current state of the school and the sense of campus space experience. The researchers' language ability, social ability, and improvisation ability need to be excellent. All respondents volunteered to participate in the focus interview and expressed great interest in the subject of this study. The researcher first sorts and summarizes the subjective views in the questionnaires of the participants, to list the interview outlines and interview questions. By analyzing the psychological characteristics of each subject, the researcher prepared a response strategy for emergencies.

After the focus interview, the researcher collects the data, organizes it into a form of the manuscript, classifies the respondents' answers, captures the key points in the interview process, and makes a text report.

3   Results

3.1   Questionnaire

Shenzhen Mesa College. In the high school of Shenzhen Mesa college, a total of 377 students participated in the questionnaire survey, including 198 male students and 179 female students. A total of 72 students, or 19%, as shown in Fig. 1, were either depressed or at risk of depression. Among them, 34 boys, accounting for 17% of the total number of boys, 38 girls, accounting for 21% of the total number of girls.

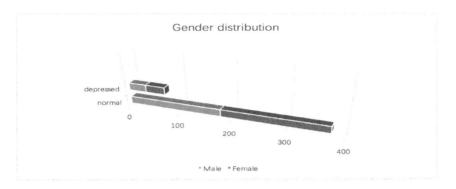

Fig. 1. Current depressed or at risk of depression students in terms of gender in Shenzhen Mesa College.

Regarding age distribution, the 18-year-old high school student has the highest number of people with or with depression, up to 38, accounting for 44% of the total, as shown in Fig. 2. There are 21 people at the age of 17, accounting for 19% of the total number of people in that age group. Twelve people aged 16 years, accounting for 11% of the total number of people in that age group. Four people aged 15 years, accounting for 6% of the total number of people in this age group. There is one person at the age of 19, accounting for 50% of the total number of people in that age group.

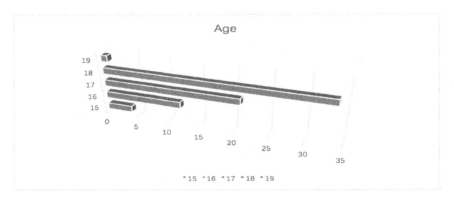

Fig. 2. Current depressed or at risk of depression students in terms of age in Shenzhen Mesa College.

Of the 72 people, 66 have had negative emotions in the existing campus environment. Among them, 48 people have attended regular junior high schools in China and 18 people have attended international junior high school, as shown in Fig. 3.

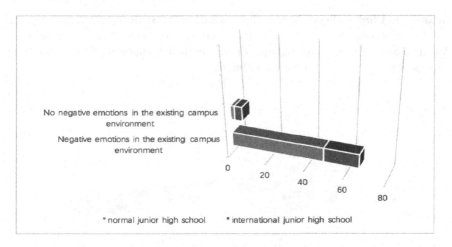

Fig. 3. Students' emotions in the existing campus environment in Shenzhen Mesa College.

Regarding different spatial and emotional intensity of the campus, the results are compared with the ideal state. The living area has the most significant adverse impact on the user's emotions, followed by the teaching area, as shown in Fig. 4. The aversion index of these two areas is as high as 6. In the multi-purpose zone, the joy index reached a relatively high of 7. Relative to other regions, the outdoor activity zone has a corresponding average of 2.5, but its fear index has reached a relatively high of 4. The landscape area has two relative highest values, the sadness index and the surprise index, which deserve research attention.

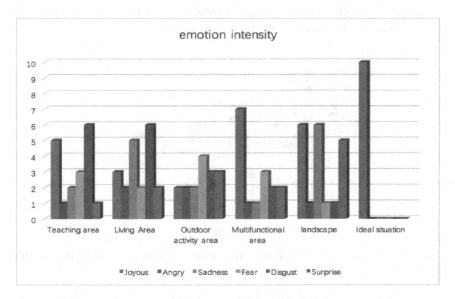

Fig. 4. Students' emotional intensity to spatial areas in the existing campus environment in Shenzhen Mesa College.

Guangzhou Ulink College. In this school, a total of 103 students have or tend towards depression, accounting for 23% of the total number of participants, as shown in Fig. 5. Among them, 47 are boys, accounting for 19% of the total number of boys, and 56 are girls, accounting for 28% of the total number of girls.

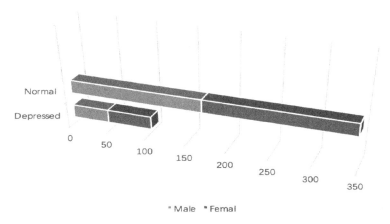

Fig. 5. Current depressed or at risk of depression students in terms of gender in Guangzhou Ulink College.

Regarding age distribution, 9 people aged 19, accounting for 27% of the total number of people in that age group. 20 people aged 18, accounting for 25% of the total number of people in this age group. 31 people aged 17 accounted for 22% of the total number of people in that age group. 27 people aged 16 years, accounting for 21% of the total number of people in this age group. 16 people aged 15 years, accounting for 23% of the total number of people in that age group, as shown in Fig. 6.

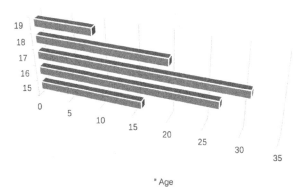

Fig. 6. Current depressed or at risk of depression students in terms of age in Guangzhou Ulink College.

Of the 103 people, a total of 87 people have had negative emotions in the existing campus environment, of which 68 have attended regular junior high schools, and 19 have attended international junior high schools, as shown in Fig. 7. Sixteen people did not have negative emotions in the existing campus environment. Three of them had participated in regular junior high school, and 13 had participated in international junior high school.

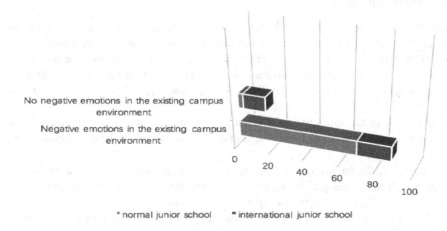

Fig. 7. Students' emotions in the existing campus environment in Guangzhou Ulink College.

Regarding different campus spaces and emotional intensity, the school's teaching area has the most negative impact on students, and the fear index have reached the maximum relative value of this figure, as shown in Fig. 8. The living area is the second

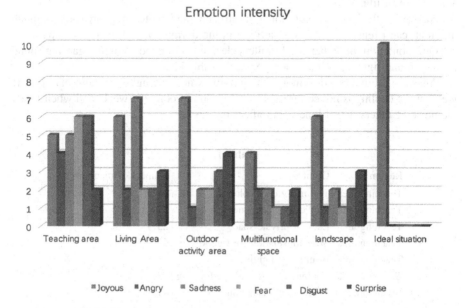

Fig. 8. Students' emotional intensity to spatial areas in the existing campus environment in Guangzhou Ulink College.

most serious area, and its sadness index is as high as 7, which is the relative highest value in the figure. The index of the outdoor activity area and landscape area of the school is relatively similar to the ideal situation.

3.2   Follow-up Interview

From the six emotions graph, it is indicates that the negative impacts of the living areas and teaching areas of the two schools on the user's emotions are relatively obvious, so the researchers decided to focus on the subject in the focus interview. The researcher streamlined and compiled the interviews of the two schools into a form. The content of the meeting is divided according to different functional areas of the campus, as shown in Table 1.

Question: In the subjective answer part of the questionnaire, you mentioned that you want to use warm colors in the teaching area. Why, how does the use of cool colors affect your mood?

Answer: ...the interior of the teaching building is monotonous, with a lot of cold tones, which makes people depressed... The large white wall in the stairwell is desperate... the color of the light is crisp white and desperate...

Question: Have you mentioned that the public space in the teaching area is too narrow, which has a negative impact on your emotions. Is it convenient to explain it in detail?

Answer: ...the corridor is too narrow, the lighting is insufficient, and it will be scared at night... The stairs are narrow...the traffic is heavy, crowded, and irritating... The teacher's office area is away from student activities...the area is too close and constrained...

Question: You think that the design of the living area is very dull and lacks the atmosphere of life. Why?

Answer: ...the lack of decoration...the structure and the teaching area are not much different, can't relax...there is no partition in the dormitory, lack of private space...

Question: You think that the dormitory design is not good enough regarding sound insulation and lighting. What made you feel of this idea?

Answer: ...I live in a dormitory facing north, where the lighting is abysmal, people feel that the cooling is not comfortable... The soundproofing is weak, and when I hear the noise of others, I feel lonely and affect my rest...

Table 1.

Region	Opinions	Number of mentions
Teaching area	Too many cool colors	31
Teaching area	Public space crowded	27
Teaching area	Lack of private space	23
Teaching area	Sound insulation isn't good	17
Teaching area	Insufficient lighting	13
Teaching area	Campus culture isn't performing	3
Living area	Poor sound insulation	41

(*continued*)

(*continued*)

Region	Opinions	Number of mentions
Living area	Poor lighting	32
Living area	Lack of private space	18
Living area	Lack of decoration	12
Living area	Inconvenient daily life	5
Living area	Too long corridor	1

4   Discussion

By comparing the data, the students' depression rates in the two international schools were 19.1% and 22.8%, respectively, which were higher than the 18.9% of the depression rate index of ordinary high school students in Guangdong Province announced by the Guangdong Provincial Education Bureau [11]. Why is the depression rate in international schools higher than that in regular junior high schools? This may be related to the type of school the school student was previously attending. According to data from two international schools, an average of 84.3% of students who have depression and have negative emotions due to the existing environment on campus have attended regular junior high school and started high school in high school. It is well known that there are vast differences between international schools and private teaching systems and methods. Hence, the process from a private junior high school to international high school may lead to emotion management problems.

The percentage of female students with the same psychological and emotional management problems is higher than that of male students in both international schools. In the personal answers to follow-up interviews and questionnaires, it indicates that girls' responses are more emotional and emotional than boys. Therefore, in international schools in the Greater Bay Area, China, girls are more likely to have psychological and emotional management problems than boys, because girls are more delicate than boys and have more intimate activities and more emotional thinking. Regarding age distribution, students with psychological and emotional management problems are mostly between 16 and 18 years old. This may be related to the pressure of adulthood and academic strength.

From the results of the follow-up interviews, the students' demand for the existing campus is mainly concentrated on the visual and auditory environment design. Vision plays the most fundamental and direct role in the student campus experience. Therefore, the arrangement of the light in the environment, the lighting arrangement, and the color arrangement will have a series of psychological effects on the user. Combined with the number of times the user mentioned in the interview, color and light are the most active factors for the user's visual experience. The essential thing is often what the user cares about the most.

5   Conclusion

5.1   Contribution of This Study

After the above research results, which reveals that architecture does affect the psychological and emotional management of users. At the same time, the negative impact of the environment on user sentiment can be reduced by improving the existing building space. The psychological problems of domestic high school students have indeed become an urgent problem, and its seriousness needs the attention of all sectors of society.

The results of this study can be used as a sample for comparison with data from other schools. If the data is similar or the student experience is identical, it can indicate that there is a problem with the existing space environment of the school.

5.2   Introspection and Future of Study

Some errors and prejudices will inevitably appear in conclusion. This may include the objectivity caused by the researchers personal experience, and the end of the survey will be affected by the bias of the survey data. Some interference factors are inevitable, but there are many ways to reduce its impact. To reduce the results of the method of solving procrastination only in specific populations, in the next phase of the study, the researchers will extract people of different ages and backgrounds to test and ensure that the methods suitable for them are improved. To reduce the impact of data on the results, the researchers will expand the number of samples, generalized areas and so on. Use this method to cut some of the factors that affect the outcome. The limitations of the subjective and objective conditions, the accuracy of the investigation methods such as overcoming the method questionnaire are another limiting condition that should be considered. As everyone knows, many people will fill in the survey volume when they fill out the survey volume, but the researchers are also well prepared to deal with these restrictions. After the investigation, the above reasons are mainly due to external interference and objective factors such as time and mood. The solution is first to ensure the patience and professionalism of the attitude, to provide respondents with a relatively comfortable answer environment.

Acknowledgements. The authors wish to thank all the people who provided their time and efforts for the investigation.

References

1. World health organization. https://www.who.int/mental_health/management/depression/prevalence_global_health_estimates/en/. Accessed 30 Jan 2019
2. Sohu education news. http://www.sohu.com/a/283638675_100214791. Accessed 30 Jan 2019
3. Clarke, J.L., Skoufalos, A., Medalia, A., Fendrick, A.M.: Improving health outcomes for patients with depression: a population health imperative. Report on an expert panel meeting. Popul. Health Manag. **19**(Suppl. 2), S1–S12 (2016)

4. Pol, E., Robson, C.: Environmental Psychology in Europe: From Architectural Psychology to Green Psychology. Avebury, Aldershot (1993)
5. Venturi, R.: Complexity and Contradiction in Architecture. The Museum of Modern Art Press, New York (1966)
6. Bond, M.: http://www.bbc.com/future/story/20170605-the-psychology-behind-your-citys-design. Accessed 30 Jan 2019
7. Oosterwijk, S., Lindquist, K.A., Anderson, E., Dautoff, R., Moriguchi, Y., Barrett, L.F.: States of mind: emotions, body feelings, and thoughts share distributed neural networks. NeuroImage **62**(3), 2110–2128 (2012)
8. Liu, C., Liu, Y.: On the application of architectural psychology in architectural design. Shanxi Sci. Technol. **31**(4), 143–145 (2016)
9. Lu, Q., Shi, D.: The application of gestalt psychology in school architecture design. China Real Estate Ind. (2), 87 (2017)
10. Lee, J.: https://www.ted.com/talks/jinsop_lee_design_for_all_5_senses. Accessed 30 Jan 2019
11. Gao, Y., Li, L.P., Kim, J.H., Congdon, N., Lau, J., Griffiths, S.: The impact of parental migration on health status and health behaviours among left behind adolescent school children in China. BMC Public Health **10**(1), 87 (2010)

Intelligent Service System Design of Food Therapy Experience into Chronic Disease

Yan Zhang[1]([✉]), Jun Wu[1]([✉]), Chen Xu[2]([✉]), and Ming Zhou[3]([✉])

[1] Jiangsu Vocational College of Information Technology, Huishan Area,
Wuxi 214000, China
516114027@qq.com, 11979516@qq.com
[2] Wuxi No. 2 Chinese Medicine Hospital, Binhu Area, Wuxi 214000, China
iloveorange@qq.com
[3] Yushanfang Early Bird, Liangxi Area, Wuxi 214000, China
785965743@qq.com

Abstract. Chronic disease is a global health problem. According to the WHO, 71% of the world's deaths are caused by chronic non-communicable diseases and it is recognized as the world's biggest killer. In 2017, the sub-healthy Chinese population reached 75% of the total population. The top five chronic diseases were: hypertension, fatty liver, dyslipidemia, diabetes, and chronic gastritis or gastric ulcer. According to the theory of Chinese medicine, the disease comes from the mouth. In fact, many problems are caused by eating. In this context, the main goal of this study was to develop an intelligent feedback interaction system based on food therapy as a way to combat chronic disease. Based on the strategic combination of service design and artificial intelligence, this study proposes a new model. Our goal is to create a new food therapy experience service system to meet the demands of our customers. In this paper, a new food therapy service system based on chronic disease is proposed in order to improve food therapy experience and to mine innovative points of people with chronic diseases.

Keywords: Food therapy · Chronic disease · User experience · Service design · Artificial intelligence (AI) · Design innovation

1 Introduction

Chronic disease is a global health problem. People often ignore their lethality because they are not so painful nor require hospitalization. According to the WHO, 71% of deaths originate from chronic non-communicable diseases and are recognized as the world's biggest killer. According to the World Health Organization, 388 million people will die of chronic diseases in the next 10 years. About 300 million people in China suffer from chronic diseases, and China's chronic disease mortality rate ranks 80th in the world. On the other hand, the first sentence of the newsletter on the Medicalx-press website puts the United Kingdom, the United States and China together, and believes that the three countries can not match the prevention and control of chronic diseases in Italy, France, South Korea and Australia. As we foresee, the proportion of chronic disease deaths will increase. The control and resolution of chronic diseases is a real challenge for all countries; although we have made many efforts to treat chronic diseases, chronic diseases continue to threaten people's well-being and social development. In this context, the main goal of this study was to develop a service model based on food therapy. This service model includes monitoring of food treatment effects, experience feedback and food treatment recommendations. The service model we designed is an interactive prototype based on service design and artificial intelligence. The purpose is to avoid the uncertainty of food treatment and ensure the treatment effect of food on chronic diseases.

2 Chronic Diseases and Food Therapy in China

Chronic diseases are defined broadly as conditions that last 1 year or more and require ongoing medical attention or limit activities of daily living or both. Chronic diseases such as heart disease, cancer, and diabetes are the leading causes of death and disability in China. According to the official statistics, 75% of people in China have chronic diseases. If we don't treat chronic diseases, we may get more serious diseases.

On April 10, 2015, the National Health and Family Planning Commission released a report on the progress of China's disease prevention and control (2015), which was reviewed and summarized with a large amount of detailed data in disease prevention and control in China over the years since the founding of the People's Republic, especially the last 10 years. According to the report, although we are trying to prevent and control chronic diseases, the situation is still serious. Chronic diseases such as cerebrovascular diseases and malignant tumors have become the main causes of death. The number of deaths caused by chronic diseases has accounted for 86.6% of the total deaths in China, and the disease burden accounts for nearly 70% of the total disease burden. It is predicted that the total number of deaths caused by infectious diseases, maternal and perinatal diseases and nutritional deficiencies will decline by 3% in the next 10 years, while the number of chronic disease deaths will increase by 17% in the same period. Although chronic disease develops slowly, it can cause an acute attack or death. The harm of chronic diseases is mainly the damage of important organs such as brain, heart and kidney, which is easy to cause disability, affecting labor ability and quality of life, and the medical expenses are extremely expensive, which increases the economic burden of society and family.

Most chronic diseases are caused by a short list of risk behaviors: Tobacco use and exposure to secondhand smoke; Poor nutrition, including diets low in fruits and vegetables and high in sodium and saturated fats; Lack of physical activity; Excessive alcohol use. Now many people in cities have chronic diseases, such as hypertension, high blood sugar, qi deficiency, heavy humidity, obesity and so on. According to the theory of traditional Chinese medicine, diseases start from the mouth, and many chronic diseases are caused by the fact that we often eat take-out food, don't go to the farmers' market, but go to the supermarket to buy food of any origin and season, etc., which leads to the fact that we can't get enough of the most seasonal food at the best time and achieve the best physical conditioning, as the traditional Chinese medicine food therapy and health maintenance says.

Food therapy is a method that uses the characteristics of food under the guidance of the theory of traditional Chinese medicine to regulate the function of the body so that it can obtain health or cure diseases. It is generally believed that food is an edible substance that provides various nutrients for human growth, development and healthy survival. In other words, the most important function of food is nutrition. We believe that one way to control chronic diseases is through food therapy. As Zhang Xichun, a modern doctor, pointed out in "Shenxi Lu in the heart of medicine", food "can not only cure diseases but also satisfy hunger when taken by patients". Chronic diseases are usually mild diseases. People can treat chronic diseases slowly through the natural "prescription" of food to recuperate their bodies, change their eating habits and life-style. This is not only to treat a chronic disease, but also to stay healthy for a long time.

The process of food therapy should constantly obtain feedback information and update the food menu according to different physical conditions and recovery conditions. There are some official TCM institutions that support food therapy, but this is still an area of opportunity for China. As we can see from the above information, the prevention and treatment of chronic diseases is not only a current problem, but also a future problem. That's why we decide to develop a service model based on traditional Chinese medicine food therapy. This service model includes the monitoring of thera-peutic effect, experience feedback and dietary advice. To accomplish this task, it is necessary to explore service design tools; In particular, we chose the method from Jurgen Tanghe, and we found that it is more suitable for use in the context of food therapy in China.

Service design is the design for the system, including stakeholders, touchpoints, service offering and process. In fact, service design is very life-oriented. We cannot live without service in all aspects of clothing, food, housing and transportation, and we also need the intervention of service design to provide better services. For example, the whole process of didi's car rental service includes a series of contacts such as online booking, car pick-up, car return, etc. Through scientific design methods, car users, staff and car rental companies can easily, efficiently and happily complete the whole pro-cess. The participation of users makes the service system form a closed loop. It is one of the important principles of service design to take users as the center, gain insight into users' needs and optimize the overall service experience.

Jurgen Tanghe's service design tool is based on four stages: scale, Discovering and Learning, Analysis Framework and Implementation. They are developed through a multidisciplinary process in which business model, UX, TECH, product and other fields are integrated and communicated. The implementation of the service requires an easy-to-apply process, so we chose Leavitt's Diamond method. In addition, in order to support the real realization of dietary therapy, we have also chosen The transtheoretical model (TTM) of behavioral change, developed by psychologists Carlo DiClemente and James Prochaska, which can support decision makers to choose their own most important tasks in each product application stage.

3   Methodology

We consider that a combination of practical tools: Service Design and Change manage-ment, which could contribute significantly to the strategic fulfillment of service innova-tions, whether are management pitch, service blueprint or a (working, functioning) prototype. For the purpose of this research, we departed from both approaches and developed a Methodology we called as: Service Design for Change Management.

This methodology is composed by 4 stages (Fig. 1):

(1) Scaling
   We can't invite the whole organization to join our service, we need to help the organizations to confirm the target users.
(2) Discovering and Learning
   While many claim that people hate change, the truth is more complex. We can't change people, we need to set up the context for change instead. To get the biggest chances of success, first we start with unwillingness; second we find the condition of food therapy; third we need to know the motivation.
(3) Analysis Framework: Elements of Change
   Its goal is to draw up the circumstances and context that give people the biggest chance of changing their behavior in a way that is beneficial for the service.
(4) Implementation
   In this final step application of the service becomes a reality; the transtheoretical model (TTM) specify how to make the change after we establish the need for change and a minimal level of motivation.

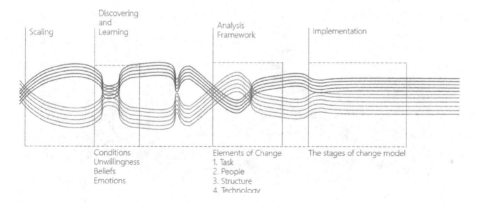

Fig. 1. Service design process for change management.

4 Application

4.1 Scaling

It seems that all patients with chronic diseases need food therapy, but in fact, there are many ways to treat chronic diseases, such as medicine, injection, acupuncture, physical therapy, massage, sports and food therapy. According to their lifestyle and conditions, only a small number of people can accept food therapy. We scaled target users through questionnaire survey.

150 questionnaires were sent through WeChat, and 126 valid questionnaires were returned. The summary data is as follows (Fig. 2).

After investigation, we found that white-collar patients suffer from chronic diseases, but they do not want to take medicine or injections for a lifetime. Compared with blue-collar workers, white-collar workers want more food for health. The old man thought it was easy to take the medicine anyway, and he could buy a medicine box to remind himself that he was taking drugs, which was not easy to forget. And many old people do not want to trouble young people, do not want to let their children follow their own to eat some kind of food, so do not want to eat therapy. But the elderly know a lot about food therapy, so they know a lot about it but they don't like the memory or the purchasing power. The family is relieved. Young people don't cook much themselves, so fast food and pills are the most convenient way to live. Patients with chronic diseases in the short term feel that taking medicine can cure them faster. Women are more emotional, they feel that this gentle way of food therapy is more in line with the needs of the body.

Therefore, our scaling results showed that female white-collar patients aged 30 to 45 years old with long-term chronic diseases were more likely to prefer food therapy.

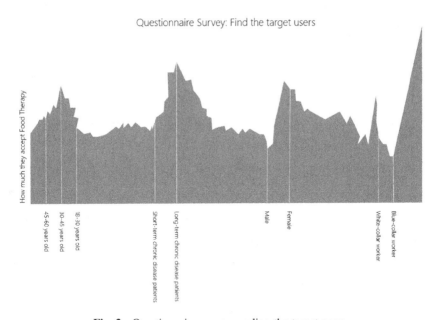

Fig. 2. Questionnaire survey: scaling the target users.

4.2   Discovering and Learning

What is the current state of food therapy? Why is food therapy acceptable to people, and why is food therapy unacceptable to some people? How can people receive food therapy? Why do people accept change? We first analyze the characteristics of food therapy objectively. And then to find out what are the points that food therapy and people's current lifestyle fit into, what are the points that conflict with each other.

Status. The current status of food therapy is as follows:

Mild without irritation;
Less side effects;
You can take it at any time and you don't have to follow a set schedule of medications;
Check information to buy ingredients for cooking;
Not bitter;
No Pain;
You don't get poisoned if you eat too much;
You don't have to face a doctor (acupuncture is done by a professional).

Unwillingness. Through Participation and co-creation, I can identify reasons why people don't like food therapy:

Food therapy effect is slow;
Eating certain foods for a long time;
Do not know how long to eat before the effect;
It is quite possible to eat something for a long time only to find that it has no effect;
In case it takes a long time to have no effect, it will delay the course of treatment;
I don't know how long it will take to have an effect;
Don't know how much to eat to have an effect;
Do not know when to eat to be able to take effect and make corresponding adjustment according to convalescence condition. (don't know how much to eat to stop or reduce or increase);
Can't cook food anytime, anywhere;
Can't eat food anywhere at any time, there are requirements for the dining environment;
There is no expert advice on what to eat and how much to eat is best for you.

Start with Motivation. Chances of success are biggest if we can start with motivation. For a long time we thought that the key to getting people to change was answering the question "How can I do this? How can I be good at this? Most of the steps are related to the belief that you are able to make the change.

First, we use the same empathy to get the beliefs as follow:
We want to treat chronic diseases effectively;
Visualization of efficacy progress;
Anytime, anywhere;
Know how much and what kind to eat;
Don't take it as a pill, don't take it as a task.

Second, we need to remember the power of emotions. Emotions are the biggest driver of behavior. That is where the energy comes from and that is where action starts. It can be very hard, or nearly impossible to convince people to take action or change based on pure rational arguments. One of the strengths of designers and design thinkers is being in contact with the emotions of people in an organization. And the strength should be utilized in change management efforts.

We use a human-centered approach to get the emotions from food therapy users. We find that food therapy lovers love food therapy because they have the following feelings about food:

advanced;
Keeping in good health;
Making people live forever;
Side effect free;
Light luxury;
Organic;
The filial piety;
Caring.

4.3   Analysis Framework: Elements of Change

Task. What's the staff expected to do? This paper aims at developing a new system based on experience and service demands, through analyzing unmet demands in food therapy service experience and new opportunities brought by artificial intelligence, thereby a new service system of food therapy experience can be obtained which contains data collection by user participation, OBO (blended online/offline) touch-point, food therapy service experience scene and experience feedback. In this manner, the uncertainty of food therapy can be avoided and the food therapy's effect of People with chronic diseases can be guaranteed.

What is the job of each of the roles in the organization? Analysis stakeholder's organizational positions and establish a relationship with a group of people accustomed to that behavior (Fig. 3).

Farmers provide fresh quality ingredients.
Food identification experts identify ingredients to ensure quality.
The courier is responsible for the fresh-keeping delivery of the ingredients. The courier ensures that the nutrients and moisture of all ingredients are minimally lost, equipped with a standard-standard refrigerator (0–4 °C) and a freezer (−18 °C). The logistics personnel are separately stored according to the unique fresh-keeping needs of each product, and the whole-chain cold chain distribution is provided for more than 8 h.
Nutrition experts analyze body data and provide recommendations for diet menus.
R&D and production of medical wearable devices for the research and design of wearable devices for various chronic diseases.
System operators continue to update the system design.
Food manufacturers and chefs design food packages for chronically ill patients.

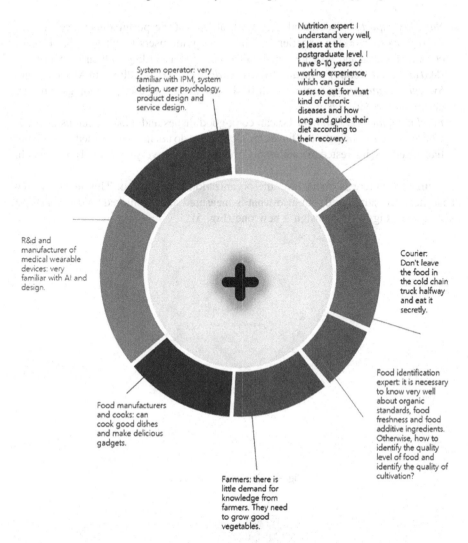

Fig. 3. A figure caption is always placed below the illustration. Short captions are centered, while long ones are justified. The macro button chooses the correct format automatically.

People. Think about the people we need in our organization. Analysis the knowledge and skills do they need, and make sure if they require any formal training or education (Fig. 3).

Farmers: there is little demand for knowledge from farmers. They need to grow good vegetables.

Food identification expert: it is necessary to know very well about organic standards, food freshness and food additive ingredients. Otherwise, how to identify the quality level of food and identify the quality of cultivation?

Courier: They don't leave the food in the cold chain truck halfway and eat it secretly.

Nutrition expert: I understand very well, at least at the postgraduate level. I have 8–10 years of working experience, which can guide users to eat for what kind of chronic diseases and how long and guide their diet according to their recovery.
R&d and manufacturer of medical wearable devices: very familiar with AI and design.
System operator: very familiar with IPM, system design, user psychology, product design and service design.
Food manufacturers and cooks: can cook good dishes and make delicious gadgets.
Chronic disease patients: can have chronic disease, do not like to take medicine, do not like injections, interested in traditional Chinese medicine, very concerned about health.

Structure. Structure is about how the organization is organized. This includes how departments are structured, but also what is measured and monitored. We can analyze existing one (Fig. 4) and design a new one (Fig. 5).

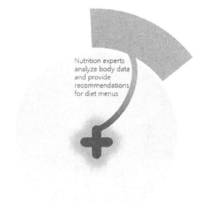

Fig. 4. Current system map

Fig. 5. New system map.

Technology. Medical equipment monitoring technology, artificial intelligence, such as: wisdom gene detection, AI images, medical and health management, hospital management, intelligent monitoring and testing, blood pressure monitor, blood glucose meter, infant abdominal movement monitor, intelligent sleep alarm clock, a food allergy source detector, the micro spectrometer (detect the fruit is fresh, food calories, whether you need the tire cheer, recently did meat), etc.

4.4   Implementation

Based on the analysis, we design the prototype and testing. We design a simple model of the stages of change based on the Transtheoretical model (TTM) of behavioral change as it follows.

Behavioral change contains 6 parts: Chronic disease detection, food list recommendations (from dietitian), custom convenience packs (from chefs and manufacturers), eating, sensory experiences, emotional experiences, body detection, new food list recommendations, and new meal packages. Behavioral change is in this circle (Fig. 6)

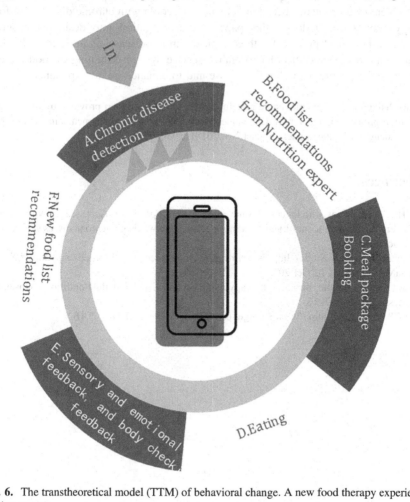

Fig. 6. The transtheoretical model (TTM) of behavioral change. A new food therapy experience service system.

5   Conclusion

In this paper, a new food therapy service system based on chronic disease is proposed in order to improve food therapy experience and to mine innovative points of people with chronic diseases. User experience is the key to verify the market and the service. However, food nutrition is always concerned while user's sensory experience, emotional experience and food treatment effect feedback are ignored.

A food therapy service system prototype is established by extracting food therapy interaction mode through the difference table of user's experiencing process, which is obtained by comparing food experiencing and body feedback process from people with different chronic disease. The implicit demands based on their experience process can be transformed into knowledge elements of system designing by establishing the mapping relationships between service design tool and the special experience of people with chronic disease. The service design tool can be used to guide food therapy experience system and product design innovation. Upon this point of view, an innovative system design prototype based on service design is proposed in order to solve the problem of mismatches between demands of people with chronic disease and food therapy experience mode. In this paper, an investigation into designing progress focused on treatment process for three typical chronic diseases is performed. Implicit demands are discovered in order to realize service system designing of food therapy experience for people with chronic disease and to enhance users' experience.

Acknowledgement. The authors are grateful for the financial support provided by the research innovation project funding for College students' innovation and entrepreneurship training program in Jiangsu Province under Contact No. 201813108049T.

References

1. WHO. https://www.who.int/chp/chronic_disease_report/part1/en/. Accessed 21 Nov 2015
2. Centers for Disease Control and Prevention. https://www.cdc.gov/chronicdisease/. Accessed 12 Oct 2018
3. AnnaFoodTherapy Studio. http://www.healthy-chinese-recipe.com/foodtherapy.html#.XBs3o zgzaM8. Accessed 12 Oct 2018
4. Food therapy Online. http://foodtherapyonline.com/services/individual-nutrition-counseling/. Accessed 21 Nov 2016
5. LNCS Homepage. http://www.springer.com/lncs. Accessed 21 Nov 2016

DUXU for Learning

Improving Mobile News Reading Experience for Chinese Users: An User Interview and Eye Tracking Study

Chenyi He[(✉)], Nan Chen, Minjuan Zhou, Hui Li, Kecheng Chen,
and Daisong Guan

Content Ecosystem User Experience Department, Baidu, Beijing, China
hechenyi@baidu.com

Abstract. In recent years, mobile news apps, featuring personalized recommendation based on AI algorithm, have been widely popular among Chinese netizens. Study on the reading experience of news detail pages is the key to optimize the using experience of mobile news apps. Study I focused on critical factors that affect users' reading experience in news detail pages, in which we invited 54 users to participate in the interview. The results show that the body text and headlines typesetting and information in the description section are the critical factors affecting users' preference. The demands of users include a comfortable and clear body text typesetting, an eye-catching and bold headline typesetting, as well as abundant and authentic information in the description section. Based on Study I's result, Study II, with the 4 (font size) × 5(line spacing) between-subject design, explored effects of body text typesetting on the reading experience of news detail pages, including reading fatigue, reading efficiency, along with subjective satisfaction, through eye tracking methodology together with users' rating. Sixty participants were invited in the experiment to be grouped by font size. The TOBII X60 eye tracker was used to record the eye movements when participants were reading five articles with different line spacing. The results show that: (1) font size has a marginally significant effect on Saccade amplitude and Saccade amplitude in font 57px was significantly less than that in 51px; (2) line spacing has a significant effect on subjective overall satisfaction indicating that larger line spacing had higher overall satisfaction.

Keywords: Mobile news · Reading experience · Typography ·
Eye tracking methodology · User interviews

1 Introduction

In the era of mobile Internet, mobile news apps, based on AI algorithms, becomes an essential source for users to obtain information. They currently rank fourth in the mobile internet industry in China regarding app session, second only to instant message, long video, and short video apps [1]. Continuous optimization of the news reading experience on mobile phones is one of the critical factors to improve sessions of news apps.

© Springer Nature Switzerland AG 2019
A. Marcus and W. Wang (Eds.): HCII 2019, LNCS 11585, pp. 395–412, 2019.
https://doi.org/10.1007/978-3-030-23538-3_31

At present, researches on reading at domestic and foreign mainly focus on reading on computers or in print with materials such as textbooks, novels, and Chinese exam papers, and students selected as samples. However, due to the differences between mobile phones and computer screens in size, between news and texts, and between other wider range of users and students, existing research conclusions have limited guidance on optimizing the reading experience of mobile news apps.

Therefore, this study focuses on the news reading experience on mobile phones and conducts researches in two stages. Study I explored critical factors that influence the users' mobile news reading experience. While Study II, based on findings of Study I, focuses on how to optimize the body text typesetting, one of the key factors, to improve the reading experience. The research results guide the optimization of the reading detail pages of mobile new apps.

2   Literature Review

Current domestic and foreign researches on reading and mobile new apps are mainly divided into three categories: (1) researches on reading fatigue, mainly to explore effects of factors such as task difficulty, mental load and text typesetting; (2) researches on reading efficiency, mainly to explore the effects of text typesetting, contrast, reading material difficulty and other factors; and (3) researches on users' experience of mobile new apps, mainly to explore the effects of factors including information and navigation structure.

2.1   Researches on Reading Fatigue

Research methods to judge subjects' levels of reading fatigue can be divided into three categories: (1) from characteristics of subjects, their physiological parameters are obtained by eye tracking/electroencephalogram/Galvanic skin response monitoring devices; (2) based on the subjective feelings of subjects, they are asked about to subjective feelings after completing the task; and (3) from the task performance, performances of subjects in a specific task are evaluated.

Chi and Lin compared seven indicators of measuring fatigue, including pupil diameter, accommodation power, visual acuity, critical fusion frequency (CFF), eye movement velocity, subjective rating of visual fatigue, and task performance, and found that pupil diameter, eye movement velocity, and subjective rating of visual fatigue were connected to visual fatigue [2]. When studying visual fatigue caused by visual display terminals (VDTs) tasks, Chi et al. found that as tasks were being performed, blink frequency of subjects would increase, and the growth tended to diminish and eventually stabilizes after 30 min [3]. Researches done by Yong and others showed that fatigue would cause an increased pupil diameter while increased mental load would cause a deceased pupil diameter [4], which was consistent with previous findings of Loewenstein and Loewenfeld [5]. When exploring effects of font size on the laptop screen on reading fatigue, Mingchuan found that Song typeface would cause the lowest level of reading fatigue and the smallest change in pupil diameter under the same time of reading [6].

2.2 Researches on Reading Efficiency

In early studies on English reading, Legge et al. measured the reading rate as a function of the contrast (0.90, 0.30, 0.10 and 0.03) and character size (0.25°, 1°, and 1.2°) of text for subjects with normal vision with the method of gliding leading format, and found that reading speed sharply dropped regardless of the font size when the contrast was 0.1 [7]. However, results of studies on Chinese reading were different. Lian and others adopted RSVP to study the effects of font size, stroke and contrast on Chinese text reading on a 19-in. LCD screen. They found that the more the stroke was, the slower the reading speed was and that the higher the contrast was, the faster the reading speed was. The font size had an effect of "critical font size." When the font size was smaller than the critical font size, the reading speed increased as the font size increased; when the font size was larger than the critical font size, the reading speed was substantially the same [8]. Liying studied the effects of font size, font type, word spacing and line spacing on the reading speed and accuracy of individuals with the macular disease when reading print materials, and found that font size, font type, and line spacing affected their speed and accuracy. Among them, results on font size were consistent with Lian's theory of "critical font size"; the reading speed and accuracy in line spacing 1.0 were significantly higher than those in 1.0, but when line spacing 3.0 failed to be appropriate to reading habits of subjects, it would distract subjects and lower their reading speed and accuracy [9]. Rayner's research found that increases difficulties of articles would lead to shorter saccade amplitude [10]. Philips and Edelman found that saccade amplitude accounted for much more of the variability and improvement in performance than did fixation duration in visual search tasks [11]. Therefore, saccade amplitude can also be regarded as an indicator of reading efficiency and difficulty of recognition.

2.3 Researches on Mobile News Apps

Huayu explored the information architecture design and navigation layout design principles of mobile news apps from the perspective of users' cognition. He believed that the design of mobile news apps needed to reduce the cost in searching, cognition, and learning of users, improve their reading efficiency, and create an immersive experience [12]. Ting and Wenjun, based on favorite news apps in the Chinese market, discussed eye movement in visual browsing and visual search of three basic graphic layout structures, i.e., the picture left and text right type, the text left and picture right type, and the text above and picture below type. They found that the text above and picture below type had the highest visual search efficiency [13]. Nevertheless, researches on detail pages of mobile news apps are hardly available now.

By reviewing previous studies, we find that there is much research experience on the key factors and measurement methods that affect reading efficiency and reading fatigue, but limitations also exist. (1) Existing studies are mainly about the large-size screen on PCs, and only a few studies are on mobile phones; (2) independent variables have limited numbers but too large value range; and (3) there are no studies on news detail pages. Therefore, existing research results can hardly directly guide the design of detail pages of news apps.

Given limitations above and the broad application of mobile news apps among Chinese netizens, it is necessary to conduct in-depth research on factors affecting the reading experience and specific design principles of mobile news detail pages, so as to guide the optimization of the detail pages of news apps and enhance their reading experience. To this end, this paper is divided into two parts to study factors mattering the experience of reading news detail pages and body text typesetting of news detail pages respectively.

3 Study I: On Factors Mattering the Experience of Reading News Detail Pages

This study focuses on the detail pages of mobile news apps and explores factors affecting the reading experience of Chinese users.

3.1 Research Focus and Methodology

During the one-on-one interview, users were invited to read three designs of news detail pages, and rank them with reasons given. We would explore critical factors affecting Chinese users' reading experience of news detail pages by analyzing those reasons.

The three design schemes of news detail pages for comparison were from the three mobile apps with the highest DAU in the Chinese market in January 2018, which were numbered by A, B, and C respectively. To avoid effects of users' degrees of interest and the number of pictures, every subject in the experiment was asked to read one piece of social news and one piece of entertainment news that was most interesting for and read by Chinese users. Social news represented news with few pictures while entertainment represented news with many pictures. To balance the sequence effects, the order of presentation of different schemes was grouped and randomized before the interview, and then the grouping of users was also randomized. After users read the three different designs, researchers would have interviews with them about their ranking and reasons given.

All users were required to finish two tasks:
Task I:

A. Users randomly read the three design schemes, A, B, and C, of the same piece of social news.
B. Users compared the three design schemes of detail pages, and ranked them according to their reading experience.
C. Users explained their reasons for ranking in the interview sessions.

Task II:

A. Users randomly read the three design schemes, A, B, and C, of the same piece of entertainment news
B. Users compared the three design schemes of detail pages, and ranked them according to their reading experience
C. Users explained their reasons for ranking in the interview sessions.

3.2 Participants

Given that young workers were primary users of mobile news, 54 participants (27 males and 27 females) were all workers aged between 18–34 years old who used mobile news apps more than 4 times a week. They received a reward for their participation after the interview.

3.3 Design of Materials

Materials were designed according to three principles: to reproduce the real conditions of products, to avoid effects of content, and to avoid effects of brands.

Therefore, news content shared by three products was chosen for the experiment. Materials had the same headlines, body text, pictures and author names, but were typeset according to design specifications of products A, B, and C respectively (see Table 1, original designs of title, text font, font size, line spacing, spacing between paragraphs, margins on both sides, and other elements, were kept). Brand information (such as brand names, brand colors, special operation icon) was also removed (see Fig. 1). Besides, because of the effects of background color and contrast [14] on the reading experience, all materials had a white background color and were presented with the same screen brightness on mobile phones.

Table 1. Material design specification

	A	B	C
Font	PingFang	PingFang	PingFang
Font size of headlines	72px	72px	69px
Font color of headlines	#000000	#222222	#222222
Font size of body text	54px	54px	51px
Line spacing of body text	1.5	1.5	2.0
Space between paragraphs of body text	1.7	1.6	2.3
Word space of body text	Default	1px	1px
Margins	51px	45px	45px
Background color	White	White	White

Fig. 1. Typography designs A, B, and C of Social and Entertainment News

3.4   Results

Based on the ranking of social news and entertainment news, the results about users' reading experience of the three new detail pages are as follows (Table 2):

Table 2. Rank of design schemes of news detail pages.

	A	B	C
1st	40%	35%	25%
2nd	30%	45%	25%
3rd	30%	20%	50%

In the case of removed brand information (without brand logo, brand color, or special operation icon), A was most liked by users, followed by B, and finally C.

By analyzing reasons given by users for their favorite products, we found that the body text typesetting, headline typesetting and information in the description section were the critical factors affecting users' reading experience.

(1) Body text typesetting. 57% of users emphasized the font size and line spacing, and preferred clear and recognizable text and obvious line spacing. In terms of specific schemes, most users preferred both A and C.

"The font size in scheme A is the best. Bigger font size makes me feel the text is not that cramped." – User 17, female, 19 years old

"I like scheme C. Its line spacing is large, but its font size a little small." – User 50, male, 33 years old

(2) Information in the description section. The description section is shown in the red box below (see Fig. 2), including the author's name and profile photo, release time, comments, and followers. 46% of users emphasized the news source, release time, and profile photo of the author and hoped that such information was authentic, abundant and complete. In terms of specific schemes, most users believed that A was the best, better than B and C.

"In scheme A, there is information about the source and release time, which I pay more attention to in news to judge its truthfulness/reliability." – User 23, female, age 28 years old

"I prefer the author's profile photo in scheme A program. Words in the profile photo of scheme B are too small to recognize." – User 13, male, 22 years old

(3) Headline typesetting. 24% of users emphasized the color and font size of headlines, and expected large and bold headlines that were eye-catching and easy to read. In terms of specific schemes, most users believed that A was the best, better than the other two.

"The headline in scheme A program is large and clear in a bold and eye-catching color." – User 43, male, 29 years old

"The color of headline in scheme A is darker and bolder than scheme C, and is more appropriate for headlines." – User 33, male, 32 years old

3.5 Discussion

From reasons given by users, critical factors mattering the reading experience include:

(1) Clear body text that is easy to read. Users demanded proper font size and line spacing, recognizable font and clear line breaks that do not lead to crowded or cramped text.

(2) Authentic, abundant and complete information in the description section. Users demanded complete and true information about the news source/author, release time, originality, and profile photo of the author.

Fig. 2. Description sections of Social and Entertainment News

(3) Bold and eye-catching headlines. Users demanded bold and eye-catching font of headlines, and the large font size and dark font color in scheme A were preferred by users.

Among the three factors, typesetting of the body text was the most important, which occupied the essential position of the entire page. There was no definitive conclusion or standard about the favorite combination of font size and line spacing of body text. Some users preferred scheme C (font size: 51px, line spacing: 2.0), and believed that larger line spacing created better reading experience while some users preferred schemes A and B (font size: 54px, line spacing: 1.5), and thought that the font size was large and the font clear which made the text easy to read. Therefore, it is necessary to conduct further researches on the font size and line spacing of the body text of news detail pages to explore their effects on users' reading experience.

4   Study II: On Body Text Typesetting of News Detail Pages

This study focuses on the body text typesetting of news detail pages and explores effects of different font sizes and line spacing on users' reading experience.

4.1   Research Framework

In previous studies, factors such as font type, font size, line spacing, word spacing, word boundaries, background color [14], and contrast influence users' reading experience. Reading fatigue and reading efficiency are mainly used to assess users' reading experience. Common indicators of visual fatigue include blinking frequency, pupil diameter, CFF, LF/HF, and subjective level of fatigue, while those of reading efficiency include reading speed, reading accuracy, vertical saccade, saccade amplitude, fixation duration, number of fixations, regression count and so on.

Study I shows that the body text typesetting is one of the critical factors affecting users' preference for news detail pages and that users have different opinions on better font size and line spacing. Therefore, it is necessary to continue to explore the effects of different font sizes and line spacing on reading fatigue and reading efficiency. The research framework of Study II is as follows (see Fig. 3).

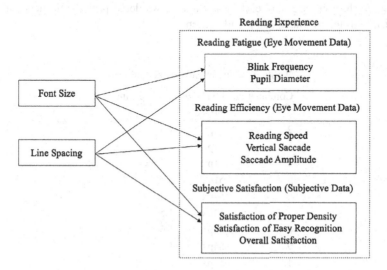

Fig. 3. Research framework

4.2 Experimental Hypotheses

Effect of Font Size and Line Spacing on Reading Fatigue.
H1: Font size affects users' reading fatigue.
H2: Line spacing affects users' reading fatigue.

Effect of Font Size and Line Spacing on Reading Efficiency.
H3: Font size affects users' reading efficiency.
H4: Line spacing affects users' reading efficiency.

Effect of Font Size and Line Spacing on Subjective Satisfaction.
H5: Font size affects users' subjective satisfaction.
H6: Line spacing affects users' subjective satisfaction.

4.3 Methodology

Participants. 60 users, including 30 male and 30 female workers, participated in the experiment. They were aged between 23 and 35 with a university degree or above, and used mobile news apps more than 4 times a week. Their vision or corrected visual acuity was normal. They received a reward for their participation.

Experimental Design. The 4×5 between-subject design was adopted for the experiment. Variable 1 was font size at four levels, i.e. 51px, 54px, 57px, and 60px, while variable 2 was line spacing at five levels, i.e. 1.4, 1.5, 1.6, 1.7, and 2.0. The value range of font size and line spacing was based on the design of the top six news apps with the highest DAU in the Chinese market in January 2018. The experiment included 20 typography schemes (see Table 3), and users were randomly divided into 4 groups according to the font size, and each group read news detail pages with the same font size but five different line spacing and content.

Table 3. Experimental combinations.

Combination	Font size	Line spacing
1	51px	1.4
2	51px	1.5
3	51px	1.6
4	51px	1.7
5	51px	2.0
6	54px	1.4
7	54px	1.5
8	54px	1.6
9	54px	1.7
10	54px	2.0

(*continued*)

Table 3. (*continued*)

Combination	Font size	Line spacing
11	57px	1.4
12	57px	1.5
13	57px	1.6
14	57px	1.7
15	57px	2.0
16	60px	1.4
17	60px	1.5
18	60px	1.6
19	60px	1.7
20	60px	2.0

Three dependent variables were measured in the experiment: (1) visual fatigue, including blink frequency and pupil diameter. A higher blink frequency and a smaller pupil diameter indicate a higher level of mental load of the user; (2) reading efficiency, including reading speed, vertical saccade and saccade amplitude. A higher reading speed indicates higher reading efficiency. A smaller vertical saccade indicates fewer reading errors and higher reading efficiency. A larger saccade amplitude indicates getting more information before saccade and higher reading efficiency. (3) subjective satisfaction, including proper density, easy recognition and, overall satisfaction.

The questionnaire for subjective satisfaction is as follows:

Please rate the satisfaction of the following three items separately and give reasons. *(The score is from one to five, of which one is very dissatisfied, three is neutral, and five is very satisfactory)*

	1.4	1.5	1.6	1.7	2.0
Proper density that is comfortable for reading					
Proper font size that is easy to identify					
Overall satisfaction					

Materials. Six pieces of social news articles were chosen from news apps, one of which was for the pilot and the other five of which were for the formal experiment. With 700–800 words, all news read smoothly and was free from mistakes such as syntactic, semantic or word-boundary ambiguities. Each article was evaluated for its difficulty, and simple words accounted for around 70% of its total words. The difference in the proportion of simple words among the five articles was less than 5% to control the difficulty of articles.

To avoid the effect of content on users, 20 scheme designs were produced for the five articles, and a total of 100 materials were produced for the formal experiment (Fig. 4).

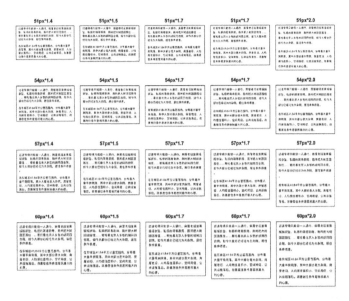

Fig. 4. Twenty schemes of one article

Apparatus and Conditions. The experimental equipment included 2 TOBIIX60 eye trackers, 2 sets of handheld equipment operation tables for placing mobile phones and eye trackers (the user is 60–65 cm away from the eye tracker), 2 laptops, 2 Logitech cameras, 12 iPhone 6plus (screen size: 5.5 in., resolution: 1920 × 1080, one of the most popular screen sizes on the market), two of which were used for eye movement experiments and the other ten of which were divided into two groups for scheme comparisons. The screen brightness of each iPhone 6plus remained the same. The experiment was carried out in a closed conference room with fluorescent lamps.

Procedures. H5 links specially developed for this experiment was used in the whole process, and opened on iPhone 6plus with the same browser app for reading.

(1) Before the experiment, participants were told about the entire experimental procedures in detail.
(2) Eye tracker calibration. Users sit down in front of the eye tracker for calibration.
(3) Pilot. Users were instructed to get familiar with the experimental procedures. They read the news article for the pilot according to their own habits, and scored their satisfaction of the design of the article.
(4) Formal experiment. Participants were asked to read five news detail pages with different content and designs. Each time when they finished reading one detail page, they scored their satisfaction from three aspects, including proper density, easy recognition, and overall satisfaction.

(5) Then participants were given five mobile phones that displayed one article but with five different typography (the same font size but 5 different line spacing), and asked to score the subjective satisfaction according to their own preferences and explain the reasons.

To avoid sequence effects, Materials in each group were made for H5 links in advance based on the Latin square design, ensuring that the probability of each article and each design appearing in the first, second, third, fourth, and fifth place was the same.

Data Analysis. All data were analyzed by repeated measures ANOVA using SPSS20 software package. $p < 0.05$ was considered significant.

4.4   Results

Effect of Font Size and Line Spacing on Reading Fatigue

The effect of font size on blink frequency was not significant ($F(3,59) = 0.37$, $p > 0.05$); the effect of font size on pupil diameter was not significant ($F(3,59) = 1.314$, $p > 0.05$). Therefore, H1 hypothesis is not correct (Tables 4 and 5).

Table 4. Blink frequency and pupil diameter influenced by font size only ($n = 60$).

	Blink frequency		Pupil diameter (mm)	
	M	SD	M	SD
51px	311.58	36.92	4.20	0.29
54px	288.45	35.82	4.03	0.28
57px	256.72	38.13	3.89	0.30
60px	293.20	38.13	4.67	0.30

Table 5. Blink frequency and pupil diameter influenced by line spacing only ($n = 60$).

	Blink frequency		Pupil diameter (mm)	
	M	SD	M	SD
1.4	291.08	26.05	4.12	0.17
1.5	249.63	22.32	4.33	0.16
1.6	291.86	29.94	4.12	0.17
1.7	295.52	28.71	4.23	0.16
2.0	309.34	27.59	4.19	0.14

The effect of line spacing on blink frequency was not significant ($F(4,59) = 1.11$, $p > 0.05$); the effect of line spacing on pupil diameter was not significant ($F(4,59) = 1.51$, $p > 0.05$). Therefore, H1 hypothesis is not correct.

Effect of Font Size and Line Spacing on Reading Efficiency

The effect of font size on reading speed was not significant ($F(3,59) = 0.46$, $p > 0.05$); the effect of font size on vertical saccade was not significant ($F(3,59) = 1.49$, $p > 0.05$); the effect of font size on saccade amplitude was marginally significant ($F(3,59) = 2.18$, $p < 0.1$), and saccade amplitude in font size 57px was significantly higher than that in 51px in pairwise comparisons. Therefore, H3 hypothesis is partially correct.

The effect of line spacing on reading speed was not significant ($F(4,59) = 0.90$, $p > 0.05$); the effect of line spacing on vertical saccade was not significant ($F(4,59) = 1.24$, $p > 0.05$); the effect of line spacing on saccade amplitude was not significant ($F(4,59) = 1.09$, $p > 0.05$). Therefore, H4 hypothesis is not correct (Tables 6 and 7).

Table 6. Reading speed, vertical saccade and saccade amplitude influenced by font size only ($n = 60$).

	Reading speed (words/s)		Vertical saccade		Saccade amplitude (px)	
	M	SD	M	SD	M	SD
51px	9.99	0.84	81.70	10.38	42.81	2.08
54px	9.29	0.81	67.43	10.38	46.25	2.02
57px	10.48	0.86	52.15	10.72	50.43	2.15
60px	10.46	0.84	58.61	10.38	45.80	2.15

Table 7. Reading speed, vertical saccade and saccade amplitude influenced by line spacing only ($n = 60$).

	Reading speed (words/s)		Vertical saccade		Saccade amplitude (px)	
	M	SD	M	SD	M	SD
1.4	9.75	0.45	69.06	9.43	48.49	2.77
1.5	10.16	0.50	68.89	8.24	46.56	1.63
1.6	10.34	0.57	64.18	5.43	45.28	1.16
1.7	10.07	0.46	61.06	3.91	44.65	0.92
2.0	9.94	0.501	61.67	3.76	46.62	1.10

Effect of Font Size and Line Spacing on Subjective Satisfaction.

The effect of font size on satisfaction of proper density was not significant ($F(3, 59) = 0.68$, $p > 0.05$); the effect of font size on satisfaction of easy recognition was not significant ($F(3, 59) = 1.55$, $p > 0.05$); the effect of font size on overall satisfaction was not significant ($F(3, 59) = 1.85$, $p > 0.05$). Therefore, H5 hypothesis is not correct.

The effect of line spacing on satisfaction of proper density was not significant ($F(4,59) = 1.42$, $p > 0.05$); the effect of line spacing on satisfaction of easy recognition was not significant ($F(4,59) = 0.53$, $p > 0.05$; the effect of line spacing on overall satisfaction was significant ($F(4,59) = 4.87$, $p < 0.05$), and overall satisfaction in line spacing 2.0 was significantly higher than that in 1.4($p < 0.01$), 1.5($p < 0.01$) and 1.6 ($p < 0.05$), and overall satisfaction in line spacing 1.7 was significantly higher than that in 1.4($p < 0.05$) and 1.5($p < 0.05$) in pairwise comparisons. Therefore, H6 hypothesis is partially correct (Tables 8 and 9).

Table 8. Subjective satisfaction influenced by font size only ($n = 60$)

	Proper density		Easy recognition		Overall satisfaction	
	M	SD	M	SD	M	SD
51px	4.09	0.20	4.09	0.18	3.81	0.21
54px	4.20	0.19	4.28	0.18	4.18	0.20
57px	4.47	0.20	4.64	0.19	4.37	0.22
60px	4.16	0.20	4.26	0.18	3.79	0.21

Table 9. Subjective satisfaction influenced by line spacing only ($n = 60$)

	Proper density		Easy recognition		Overall satisfaction	
	M	SD	M	SD	M	SD
1.4	4.13	0.13	4.27	0.11	3.91	0.13
1.5	4.13	0.13	4.27	0.11	3.91	0.13
1.6	4.25	0.12	4.33	0.10	3.99	0.12
1.7	4.27	0.12	4.37	0.11	4.14	0.12
2.0	4.37	0.11	4.35	0.10	4.24	0.11

4.5   Discussion

(1) Effect of Font Size and Line Spacing on Reading Fatigue

Effects of font size and line spacing on blink frequency and pupil diameter were not significant. The value range of independent variables was based on the six most popular products in the market, and existing differences in their designs were not enough to cause differences in reading fatigue.

(2) Effect of Font Size and Line Spacing on Reading Efficiency

Effects of line spacing on reading speed, vertical saccade and saccade amplitude were not significant. Effects of font size on reading speed and vertical saccade were not significant, but its effect on saccade amplitude was marginally significant. Saccade amplitude in font size 57px was significantly less than that in 51px, which indicates that users had higher efficiency when reading materials with a larger font size of 57px.

(3) Effect of Font Size and Line Spacing on Subjective Satisfaction

Effects of font size on proper density, easy recognition, and overall satisfaction were not significant. The difference in overall satisfaction between different line spacing was significant. Pairwise comparisons showed that satisfaction in 2.0 was significantly higher than that in 1.4, 1.5 and 1.6, overall satisfaction in 1.7 was significantly higher than that in 1.4 and 1.5, and different in satisfaction between 2.0 and 1.7 was not significant. It indicates that larger line spacing had higher satisfaction. One user commented, "when the line spacing was small, the content presented on one page was too much and difficult to read. I don't like such typesetting."

(4) Interrelation and Difference between Subjective Satisfaction and Eye Movement Indicators

The difference in subjective satisfaction between different font sizes was not significant but the difference in saccade amplitude between font sizes 51px and 57px was significant. It shows that the users could not distinguish the advantages and disadvantages of 9px in their subjective feeing, and font size designs of mainstream mobile news apps on the market were subjectively acceptable for users. However, the eye tracker could still capture even a slight difference between different font sizes.

Difference between different line spacing in reading fatigue and reading efficiency was not significant but in subjective satisfaction was significant. Satisfaction in line spacing 1.7 and 2.0 was significantly higher than that in 1.4 and 1.5. In other words, a larger line spacing would cause a higher satisfaction. By reviewing reasons given by users for their scores of subjective satisfactions, we found that one user commented, "too small line spacing (such as 1.4 or 1.5) would make me feel there was too much content. I was pressured and could not believe I could finish it. I felt as if I was reading something formal such as academic papers or government announcements. A larger line spacing (such as 1.7, or 2.0) was more relaxing for casual news reading." In other words, when scoring their subjective satisfaction, users took into accounts more conditions of daily life than reading experience in the experiment, which led to inconsistencies between subjective and objective indicators.

5   Conclusion

Critical factors mattering the reading experience of news detail pages include body text and headline typesetting and information in the description section.

When the detail pages of mobile news apps are designed, the following principles can be referred to:

- A comfortable and clear body text typesetting. Choose 57px font size because saccade amplitude in 57px is significantly larger than that in 51px, and the reading efficiency is also better. Avoid line spacing 1.4 and 1.5 which make the text too crowded and have significantly lower overall satisfaction than line spacing 1.7 and 2.0.
- An eye-catching and bold headline typesetting. The font size needs to be large, and the font color be dark. 72px and darker colors such as #222222 are good choices.
- Authentic, abundant and complete information in the description section. The author's profile photo should be true, and the release time be detailed to the moment.

6 Limitations and Future Studies

This research program, mainly studying detail pages of the mobile news apps, focuses on effects of the font size and line spacing of body text typesetting on the reading experience. Its approach is based on current mainstream designs, with specific and limited choices in the value range of independent variables, user groups, and mobile devices. Its results proved to exist within certain limits.

There are extensive researches on Chinese reading in the field of psychology. However, a few studies in China are about reading Chinese on mobile phones. We propose that future studies will, based on the experience in this paper, first expand the value range of independent variables, especially font size to enrich the experimental results. The range of line spacing should also be supplemented and expanded to explore continuous changes. Secondly, the scope of ages and educational background of subjects will be broadened for comparisons of different user groups. Thirdly, mobile devices of different sizes can also be included. Their distance with users when being used are different, which will cause different reading experience. Such more comprehensive experimental results have a wide range of application to design mobile news apps.

References

1. Autumn report on China's mobile internet. http://www.questmobile.com.cn/research/report-new/46 Accessed 31 Dec 2018
2. Chi, C.F., Lin, F.T.: A comparison of seven visual fatigue assessment techniques in three data - acquisition VDT tasks. Hum. Factors 40(4), 577–590 (1998). https://doi.org/10.1518/001872098779649247
3. Lee, E.C., Park, K.R., Whang, M., et al.: Measuring the degree of eyestrain caused by watching LCD and PDP devices. Int. J. Ind. Ergon. 39(5), 798–806 (2009). https://doi.org/10.1016/j.ergon.2009.02.008
4. Yong, L., Guoen, Y., Yanli, C.: Effects of fatigue and mental load on pupil diameter in reading. Stud. Psychol. Behav. 2(3), 545–548 (2004)
5. Loewenstein, O., Loewenfeld, I.E.: The sleep-waking cycle and pupillary activity. Ann. NY Acad. Sci. 117, 142–156 (1964). https://doi.org/10.1111/j.1749-6632.1964.tb48169.x
6. Mingchuan, H.: A research on effects of font size on visual fatigue in electronic reading. Beijing University of Posts and Telecommunications, Beijing, China (2015)
7. Legge, G.E., Rubin, G.S., Luebker, A.: Psychophysics of reading—V. The role of contrast in normal vision. Vis. Res. 27(7), 1165–1177 (1987). https://doi.org/10.1016/0042-6989(87)90028-9
8. Lian, Z., Chenxiao, W., Jicang, H., et al.: The effects of font, stoke and contrast on the reading speed of Chinese characters. Chin. J. Optom. Ophthalmol. 10(2), 96–99 (2008)
9. Liying, L.: The effect of font size, font type and text spacing on reading performance of individuals with macular disease. Jilin University, Jilin, China (2015)
10. Rayner, K.: Eye movements in reading and information processing: 20 years of research. Psychol. Bull. 124, 372–422 (1998). https://doi.org/10.1037/0033-2909.124.3.372
11. Phillips, M.H., Edelman, J.A.: The dependence of visual scanning performance on saccade, fixation, and perceptual metrics. Vis. Res. 48(7), 926–936 (2008). https://doi.org/10.1016/j.visres.2008.06.025

12. Huayu, W.: The research of navigation design of mobile news client based on cognitive psychology. Jiangnan University, Nanjing, China (2015)
13. Ting, L., Wenjun, H.: Graphic layout design study of mobile news app based on visual behavior. J. Beijing Univ. Post Telecommun. (Soc. Sci. Ed.) **18**(3), 6–13 (2016)
14. Jiang, Z., et al.: The effects of electronic text contrast polarities and color combination patterns on reader's visual fatigue. Psychol. Explor. **35**, 18–23 (2015)

Research on Chinese Traditional Handicraft Education Expansion Model Based on STEAM

Yi Ji, Yutong Liu$^{(\boxtimes)}$, Xiaohong Sun, Peng Tan, Tieming Fu,
and Kaiping Feng

School of Design Arts, Guangdong University of Technology,
729, Dongfeng Street, Guangzhou 510000, Guangdong, China
jiyi001@hotmail.com, 236160939@qq.com

Abstract. Nowadays China has some problems with the application of STEAM education. STEAM education in China have its limitations: A(Art) is always detached from STEAM, falling into a secondary position, which does certainly adverse to the exploration of creativity and the improvement of comprehensive ability. Besides, since Chinese traditional handicrafts have profound humanistic heritage and cultural connotations, they could be used as high-quality teaching resources, but lack the educational forms and teaching contents that meet the demands of the era and are easily accepted by the public. Especially for traditional handicraft teaching, due to the one-sidedness of teaching content, the passive nature of teaching methods and the conventional non-cooperative teaching form, participants can only experience the production process in a short period, but lack awareness of the history and diversity of traditional crafts. We put forward the research and practice of the STEAM class extended curriculum with the theme of traditional handicrafts based on the STEAM education framework. From the four dimensions of knowledge, ability, thinking and innovation, the participants' ability to innovate and apply traditional handicrafts are significantly enhanced, thereby we could gradually improve the participants' individualized perception of traditional handicrafts. provide time-oriented and cultural teaching contents for STEAM extended curriculum in China, new development ideas, and models for current traditional handicraft teaching. This paper takes Cantonese Porcelain as an example to explore the STEAM extended curriculum. We designed and organized the intelligent handicraft innovation workshop, and systematically discussed how to design the teaching content and education practice based on the multi-level extended education model of STEAM education framework.

Keywords: STEAM · Traditional handicraft · Cantonese porcelain · Education model

1 Introduction

With the advancement of modern science and technology, STEM education has been difficult to meet the needs of diverse talents in modern society [1], which gave birth to a comprehensive quality education concept: STEAM. To a certain extent, STEAM education has achieved some accomplishments in China, but it has a few critical

A. Marcus and W. Wang (Eds.): HCII 2019, LNCS 11585, pp. 413–427, 2019.
https://doi.org/10.1007/978-3-030-23538-3_32

problems: Teaching content requirements become more diversified while the current teaching contents are still homogenized, lacking interest, diversity, pertinence, as well as the STEAM research and practice for traditional handicraft education.

Because of the late start of steam education in China, most of the teaching practice takes the education of developed countries of the west as the template [2], and the teaching content has the tendency of convergence, lack of innovation, ignoring the importance of education localization. The workshops and tutoring classes organized by most of China's training institutions are usually only labeled with STEAM [3], and they do not achieve the teaching effect of discipline integration. Generally, courses focusing on rational thinking, such as programming education and robot production. In the future research and educational practice, how to develop the STEAM education system and teaching content with Chinese characteristics is the goal and direction of our research.

At present, traditional handicraft workshops mainly focus on short-term practical teaching, so that the students could understand the knowledge about traditional handicraft, learn the cultural background of traditional handicrafts, and practice the production process [4]. As a result, the participants' creative practice is only counterfeit of traditional form, which cannot make them truly understand the cultural connotation of traditional handicrafts, and it is difficult to stimulate the imagination and creativity of them.

Therefore, we use STEAM education methodology to provide scientific and effective solutions to the problems existing in traditional handicraft teaching, and use traditional handicrafts as a high-quality teaching resource to enrich the teaching content of STEAM. Based on the STEAM education framework, we integrate interdisciplinary integrated teaching content, project-oriented teamwork teaching forms, and self-inquiring teaching methods and refine the teaching level by dividing the participants' cognitive depth of traditional handicrafts: knowledge (creating knowledge connections), competence (thematic embedding), thinking (multidisciplinary integration), innovation (interdisciplinary application), and value (personalized cognition). This results in a multi-level, multi-dimensional traditional handicraft extended education model. Based on this, the teaching content of traditional handicrafts was re-planned, and a scientific teaching process was constructed to gradually improve participants' cognitive depth of traditional handicrafts, thereby enhancing participants' ability to innovate and integrate traditional handicrafts.

2 Development Status of STEAM Education in China

STEM is a course for American students who have gradually lost interest in science and engineering knowledge. It aims to cultivate technology-oriented talents through the comprehensive teaching curriculum design of science, technology, engineering and mathematics [5]. However, due to the rapid development of social economy in recent years, along with the continuous generation of diversified talents, technical talents can no longer meet the demands of the new age [6]. Empirical studies have shown that art education can improve students' creativity, critical thinking, collaboration and interpersonal communication skills, in addition to improving cognitive ability, spatial reasoning, abstract thinking, divergent thinking [7]. Therefore, in the development of STEM education practice research, art courses have been added. Since then, the STEAM education concept has been popular in the United States, South Korea, the United Kingdom and other countries and areas [8].

Until 2016, STEAM Education was mentioned in the "Thirteenth Five-Year Plan for Education Informationization" in China, and it was valued and supported by the development of science and technology education; The 2017 Compulsory Education Primary School Science Curriculum Standard advocates the interdisciplinary learning approach of STEM education; In 2018, the China Academy of Educational Sciences released the "China STEM Education 2029 Action Plan". The Ministry of Education has issued a curriculum standard for various subjects in the general high school (2017 edition), and similar educational concepts to STEAM appear in the curriculum standards of multiple subjects. Provincial and municipal education in Shanghai, Jiangsu, Shenzhen and other regions have included STEAM education in local education priorities [9].

It can be seen that China's implementation standards for STEAM education are constantly being refined and specified, and the implementation strategies, application scope and practice forms are gradually improving and moving toward a systematic and standardized path. In contrast, China is not paying enough attention to STEAM education. It only appears in the relevant regulations of science and technology education [10], but has not been included in the relevant policies of national development. STEAM education lacks artistic integration in the practice of China, with STEM as the main teaching content, which taking the imitating the teaching practice of western developed countries as the main source of the subject and ignoring the importance of localization of education.

3   The Status of Traditional Chinese Handicraft Education Model

With the development of history, traditional handicrafts have been inherited and developed. It are not only practical in daily life, carrying crystallization of laborers' wisdom, but also have good artistic quality [11]. It has formed a unique cultural connotation through the precipitation of years, and is a precious cultural heritage and a quality teaching resource. However, the following problems exist in its teaching (Fig. 1):

Teaching content: Through practicing in the short-term workshop, the students can get a preliminary understanding of the traditional crafts and experience the production process. Teaching method: Using the traditional teaching method, the passive knowledge input model leads to low knowledge conversion rate and poor learning effect. Teaching form: The main form of craftsman teaching and public participation in learning practice [12], which emphasizes the teaching method of individual learning and lack of communication with others and collaborative project learning experience.

From the perspective of the participants: most of the teaching focus of the workshop is on technical training and creative practice [13], which pays insufficient attention to the students' cultural literacy, theoretical speculation and innovation ability. It does

Fig. 1. The scene of traditional craft teaching

not meet the demands of talents in modern society, so it is difficult to mobilize the interest and motivation of participants for long-term learning. From the organizer's point of view: this procedural [14], stereotypical teaching method is difficult to mobilize the interest and learning motivation of contemporary young people. It lacks initiative and inquiry to learn traditional handicrafts, so it is difficult to achieve the original intention of promoting the traditional handicraft culture.

4   Multi-level Teaching Method Based on STEAM Education Frameworks

On the one hand, China's STEAM education urgently needs to explore the content of Chinese traditional culture and cultivate innovation application talents with scientific and humanistic literacy [15]. On the other hand, traditional handicrafts need to combine the advanced teaching concepts in the modern context, explore innovative education models to improve students' participation degree, creativity and the ability to solve problems, and students' knowledge of traditional handicrafts.

With the widespread application of STEAM teaching philosophy in teaching practice [16], it provides a new direction for traditional handicraft education model. STEAM education aims to cultivate innovative talents with interdisciplinary thinking skills. It has the characteristics of problem-oriented, interdisciplinary learning and group collaboration [17], which makes up for the gap between traditional handicraft teaching and modern talent demand. Moreover, based on the STEAM education framework to build a multi-level education model, this model gradually improves the cognition of traditional handicrafts in multidisciplinary integration and interdisciplinary applications.

According to relevant literature research, the current domestic STEAM education is still in its infancy, so it is necessary to make full use of valuable traditional Chinese cultural resources to explore more high-quality teaching content and extended courses.

In the training of students' thinking model and the edification of Chinese traditional excellent culture, students' scientific thinking is developed to promote the development of students' comprehensive ability [18]. Therefore, this expansion model mainly solves the following problems:

(1) Exploring the content of STEAM's focusing on Chinese localization characteristics and strengthening the influence of traditional culture, improve the use of participants' humanistic literacy and comprehensive ability.

(2) Based on the STEAM education framework, we expand and innovate the traditional handicraft education model, and use STEAM comprehensive learning content, team-based teaching forms and independent inquiry learning methods to improve curriculum participation, knowledge conversion rate and learning efficiency, thereby enhancing the cognitive depth of traditional handicrafts.

4.1 STEAM Education Framework

(1) The Education target level: guided by lifelong learning, is a holistic and long-term educational goal. The constantly changing social development process makes education not limited to imparting specific subject knowledge and application methods, but through the training of learning thinking, the ability and awareness of lifelong learning should be cultivated to adapt to the evolving social needs [19].

(2) The integrative level aims to encourage participants to apply interdisciplinary and interdisciplinary knowledge comprehensively to solve problems encountered in projects through practical project-oriented teamwork practices, thereby improving the ability of problem solving and overall application.

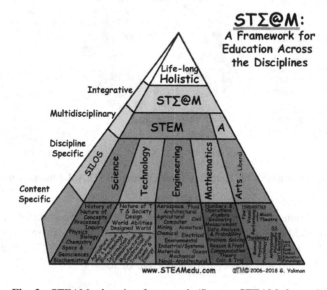

Fig. 2. STEAM education framework (Source: STEAMedu.com)

(3) Multidisciplinary level (Meaning of the Art not only refers to narrow concepts such as aesthetics and crafts, but also includes music, humanities, language arts, etc.): It is the application of multidisciplinary knowledge. Organize the study of two or more subject areas by surrounding the same subject, but maintain their independence between disciplines [20]. In the collaborative design of teamwork, the enjoyment/ interestingness of the classroom is improved, and the teamwork ability, communication skills and comprehensive application ability of the participants are cultivated.

(4) Discipline Specific level: Enrich the teaching of other subjects with the theme of a certain subject. This theme should have rich connotations, diverse forms and era value.

(5) The specific content level is the design of the specific content of the teaching activities, aiming at how to create knowledge links between disciplines (Fig. 2).

4.2   The Construction of Traditional Handicraft Education Model Based on STEAM Education Framework

Based on the STEAM education framework, the teaching of other disciplines is enriched with traditional handicrafts. Due to the artistry, practicality and complexity of traditional handicrafts, based on the cognitive depth of traditional handicrafts, the teaching content is divided into five levels (Fig. 3):

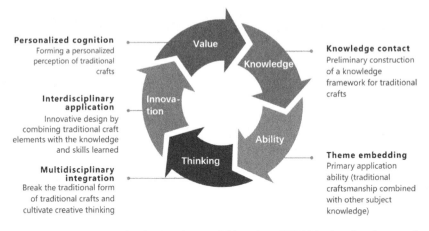

Fig. 3.   Traditional handicraft education model based on STEAM education framework

(1) Specific content level- knowledge: The analysis of the complex and lengthy information of traditional handicrafts is organized into several categories to help participants build a knowledge framework of traditional handicrafts, so that they can adequately understand and master the knowledge of it.

(2) Discipline Specific level- ability: In the embedded teaching of traditional handicrafts and other subjects, the content and technology of other disciplines are used to increase the learning and application forms of traditional handicraft content.

(3) Multidisciplinary level- thinking: Integrate traditional craftsmanship with teaching content in multiple disciplines to create connections between different disciplines. Breaking the traditional form of traditional crafts, participants can be aware of the connection between traditional crafts and multidisciplinary knowledge, and cultivate participants' dynamic, flexible and creative thinking.

(4) The integrative level- Innovation: Participants flexibly use traditional craft elements and creatively design by combining traditional craftsmanship elements with the knowledge and skills they have learned, which gives the traditional handicrafts a new form of creation that adapts to the needs of the age.

(5) Education target level - value: Through step-by-step teaching content, participants can learn by doing and think by learning, grasping knowledge in practice to form a personalized cognition of traditional handicrafts.

Such a multi-level expansion model of traditional crafts bases on the STEAM education framework. It combines constructivism, problem-based Learning, and student-centered self-inquiring teaching methods. Therefore, the participants gradually improve the cognitive depth of traditional handicrafts in a diverse, compelling and dynamic learning environment.

5   A Preliminary Study on the Extended Education Model with Cantonese Porcelain

Combining geographical advantages, resource advantages, and team expertise, we launched a four-week (32 class hours) workshop on smart handicraft innovation, With the theme of Cantonese Porcelain (Cantonese Porcelain is an prominent representative of traditional Chinese handicraft and is listed as the second batch of intangible cultural heritage), in Nov. 2018. The project is widely supported by the school, the Guangzhou Municipal Government and folk artists in the Guangzhou Social Science Planning Project (2018GZMZYB17).

There have 28 students from undergraduate and graduate students of different majors at the Guangdong University of Technology.

5.1   Set Teaching Objectives

This smart handicraft innovation workshop combines Cantonese Porcelain and smart technology to enable participants to improve the cognitive depth of Cantonese Porcelain and cultivate the comprehensive ability of the students through integrative learning methods and featured teaching content in the intelligent interactive lamp design project with Cantonese Porcelain as the element (Fig. 4).

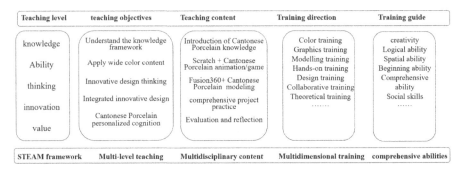

Teaching level	teaching objectives	Teaching content	Training direction	Training guide
knowledge	Understand the knowledge framework	Introduction of Cantonese Porcelain knowledge	Color training Graphics training	creativity Logical ability
Ability	Apply wide color content	Scratch + Cantonese Porcelain animation/game	Modelling training Hands-on training	Spatial ability Beginning ability
thinking	Innovative design thinking	Fusion360+ Cantonese Porcelain modeling	Design training Collaborative training	Comprehensive ability
innovation	Integrated innovative design	comprehensive project practice	Theoretical training …….	Social skills ……
value	Cantonese Porcelain personalized cognition	Evaluation and reflection		
STEAM framework	**Multi-level teaching**	**Multidisciplinary content**	**Multidimensional training**	**comprehensive abilities**

The highest goal: gradually realize the personalized cognition of Cantonese Porcelain

Fig. 4. Teaching system diagram based on traditional craftsmanship multi-level education model

5.2 Course Design Based on Multi-level Education Model

Based on the STEAM education framework, the traditional handicraft multi-level extended education model builds a teaching process from basic knowledge, professional skills learning, and practice linkage and reasonably planned the teaching content of Cantonese Porcelain, thereby gradually increasing the participants' cognitive depth of Cantonese Porcelain and improving the level of comprehensive application of participants in practice (Fig. 5).

Course structure of multi-level extended teaching mode			
	Knowledge	Preliminary introduction of Cantonese Porcelain knowledge	Preliminary establishment of Cantonese Porcelain knowledge system
		Scratch interface introduction and software operation	
		Trace the colorful pattern with scratch	
	Ability	In-depth study of Cantonese Porcelain knowledge	Use constructivist learning theory to deeply understand and master the knowledge of Cantonese Porcelain
		Scratch professional skills operation	
		Create a colorful animation/game with Scratch	
	Thinking	Cantonese Porcelain's element application, familiar with fusion360 interface	With the support of creative tools, break the traditional design thinking and establish creative thinking
		Fusion360 professional skills	
		Lighting design with wide color theme	
	Innovation	Cantonese Porcelain's element application	Adopt project-oriented teamwork to enhance the cognitive depth and comprehensive ability of Cantonese Porcelain
		3D printing, ceramic printing, laser engraving and other molding techniques	
		Lamp model making, intelligent interactive mode design, product improvement	
	Value	The formation of Cantonese Porcelain's personalized cognitive system	Form a personalized perception of Cantonese Porcelain in teacher evaluation, student mutual evaluation, and self-evaluation
		The formation of a personalized evaluation system for project works	
		Report project results (self-assessment / mutual evaluation)	

Fig. 5. Intelligent craftsmanship innovation workshop multi-level education model course structure

Knowledge Level

According to the content of Cantonese Porcelain, it creates links with other disciplines, enriches the content and form of teaching, and provides students with a variety of optional learning contents to enhance their participation and interest in learning.

We systematically organized and summarized the information of Cantonese Porcelain, which was finally summarized into six aspects: history, crafts, tools, patterns, colors, and modeling. Moreover, each part of the brief introduction and representative pictures made into teaching cards, which is convenient for students to intuitively and efficiently grasp the knowledge structure of Cantonese Porcelain. In addition, students can also get more information about the part by scanning the QR code on the teaching card (Fig. 6).

Fig. 6. Students use the teaching card to learn the colorful knowledge in class

Lesson 1–2: In classroom teaching, teachers will guide the students to use the education cards distributed before class to learn more about Cantonese Porcelain. In addition to studying in class, students can also use their spare time to study online. Lesson 3–4: After introducing the interface and basic operation of a programming software Scratch, the students were asked to draw a Cantonese Porcelain pattern as a class-exercise. When using programming software to draw, students need to arrange and plan the pattern drawing and generation methods reasonably.

By creating a knowledge link between Cantonese Porcelain and Scratch programming, students can also exercise their logical, mathematical, and reasoning skills while creating art.

Ability Level

After having the most basic understanding of Cantonese Porcelain, we will enrich the content of other disciplines with the theme of it, so that students can deepen their understanding of Cantonese Porcelain while learning technical skills.

In this stage of instructional design, we chose Scratch visualization programming software, which can be operated by beginners without the foundation of computer language, so that students can quickly familiarize themselves with the operation and create programming works in short term. Research has proved the importance of visual programming language to instructional design, which is very helpful for logic ability, mathematical thinking, artistic creation and understanding of history [21].

Lesson 5–8: The teachers encouraged the students to use the elements of Cantonese Porcelain to create animations and games using Scratch. In the elaborately design of the animation, students can only design the background, soundtrack, lines, characters, etc. after extensive research on Cantonese Porcelain. The content of 9-10 lessons is the study report of the above-mentioned exploratory projects, which are mainly divided into four parts: design concept, design process, design display, design self-evaluation and reflection. During the period, the teacher will evaluate from multiple dimensions, such as the work of the students, the production process, and the thinking process.

Compared with the traditional education model, the basic knowledge of Cantonese Porcelain is usually based on the teaching method, which is difficult to attract students' interest in learning. We combined Cantonese Porcelain with visual programming, and students independently explored its knowledge to make animations/games. Therefore, transforming passive indoctrination learning into active exploratory constructivist learning can improve learning interest and learning efficiency. During the reporting process, students communicate with each other to improve the breadth and depth of understanding of Cantonese Porcelain in the collision of ideas.

Thinking Level

According to the artistic characteristics of Cantonese Porcelain, combined with the display form and manufacturing technology of modern technology, students are encouraged to break through the traditional forms and use creative thinking to innovate the expression of it.

Fusion360 supports top-down parametric modeling technology, which can adapt to frequent modification of products, and applies to the conceptual design stage of products, providing technical support for the creative implementation of the students. Fusion360 combines multidisciplinary knowledge such as mathematics, technology, and art to train students' logical thinking, spatial thinking, and creative thinking. In addition, it can improve the ability of cognition(knowledge), emotion (attitude), and psychomotor (skill) [22].

The teaching content of the 11–16 class is the skill learning of Fusion360. After the students can master the 3D modeling technology, the teacher asks the students to design the lighting modeling. Lesson 17–18: The teacher will answer questions for the students, check the team's project progress, suggest appropriate perspectives, and guide the problem -solving direction. The content of the 19–20 class is to report the final design plan and project implementation plan. The teacher will advise on the aesthetics, achievability and rationality of the project model.

As a guide for learning, not a decision maker, the teacher will give the students room to think and explore. As the leader of the project, the students will estimate and arrange the project's design orientation, strategic goals, implementation plan, and project results, so as to cultivate students' integral and systematic thinking.

Innovation Level

In the design of intelligent interactive lamps, each group is required to flexibly use the Cantonese Porcelain elements to combine the knowledge and skills learned to carry out innovative design.

As a rapid prototyping technology, 3D printing is a personalized creation tool with "design thinking", expanding more shapeable modellings, giving students a broader space for creation and imagination [23], which is an indispensable technical support for application innovation.

Lesson 25–28: Students try to use a variety of molding techniques to create a similar lamp model, after 3D model modification, determining molding technology, material selection, component printing, assembly completion, model improvement. Lesson 29–30: Students combine the product's styling and design concepts to design the intelligent interaction mode of the lamp.

Due to the different conditions and environment, the theoretical knowledge accumulated by the students and the actual application exists a gap. Therefore, there may be many problems in the project, whether the shape can be realized by using existing molding technology, whether the model material is appropriately selected, whether the structural design is stable, and whether the wiring design is reasonable etc. This requires students to communicate with each other in the team, weigh the pros and cons to get the best solution to improve the students' ability to solve problems and comprehensive application.

Value Level

In the project design, through the in-depth teaching content guidance and project-oriented team practice, the understanding of Cantonese Porcelain is gradually deepened, so that the students can achieve personalized cognition of Cantonese Porcelain.

The content of 31–32 class hours is the summary report of the design of Cantonese Porcelain intelligent interactive lamps. Rethinking the process and results of the project, through the teacher evaluation, student mutual evaluation and self-evaluation, the students establish a personalized evaluation system for the works in the exchange of ideas, thus forming a personalized cognition of Cantonese Porcelain.

6   Results

In the workshop, students are required to use their imagination and creativity, apply their knowledge and skills, and carry out innovative design with the theme of Cantonese Porcelain.

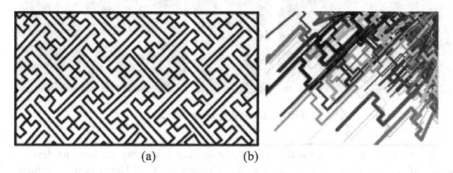

(a)   (b)

Fig. 7. (a) Wanzi Jin (original pattern of Cantonese Porcelain), (b) Creative graphic

Figure 7(a) is the Scratch creative graphic re-artified by the students, based on the Wanzi Jin. What can be seen from the comparison in Fig. 7 is that through the change of the form, reconstruction of organizational methods, and the reorganization of units have made Wanzi Jin modern and contemporary.

This exercise will transform the intuitive learning method into a rational composition analysis, which will enable the students to more accurately understand the composition of the Cantonese Porcelain pattern in the programming of the reproduction pattern, and it is easier to grasp the constituent elements and connotations of the pattern in essence.

Fig. 8. Screenshot of the student game works

After a preliminary understanding of Cantonese Porcelain, the teacher asked the students to make games or animations with the theme of it. Each team selects projects based on their interests: a one-minute animation showing the history of Cantonese Porcelain, an educational game according to the production process of Cantonese Porcelain, a program to customize the mobile phone case.

Shown in Fig. 8 is the game created by the students. Game makers needed to think about how to turn the production process into a complete and interesting game experience through arranging reasonably so that players can learn from playing: through every level of the game, they can know the tools and production process of Cantonese Porcelain (Fig. 9).

Fig. 9. Student lighting works

In the practice of integrated projects, the teacher asked the students to design a smart interactive lamp with the theme of Cantonese Porcelain. The students completed the entire design process in the form of a group: basic skills learning, determining the theme, program design, program screening, model making, lamp interaction pattern design, product display and reflection. In the process, the students' ability to solve problems and the depth of cognition of Cantonese Porcelain are enhanced.

Compared with the traditional education model, the workshop's lighting works are more diverse, more expressive, more creative and expressive (Table 1).

Table 1. Comparison of traditional model and multi-level education model

	Traditional teaching model	Multi-level expansion teaching model
Teaching content	Experience the production process	Combining the content of multidisciplinary knowledge with the theme of Cantonese Porcelain
Teaching process	Master explanation, practical operation, comment exchange	Create knowledge connections, topic embedding, multidisciplinary integration, interdisciplinary applications, personalized cognition
Teaching form	Teaching form	Self-inquiry form
Work form	Counterfeit of traditional Cantonese Porcelain styles, such as porcelain plates	Combine the diverse forms of modem technology, such as computer programming images, games, animation, smart lighting
Teaching achievement	Hands-on ability, color ability, creative ability	Hands-on practical ability, color ability, creative ability, Logical thinking, spatial thinking, problem- solving ability, Comprehensive ability, etc.

Conduct targeted interviews with classmates after each class: We conduct research on interest, mastery, and satisfaction regarding teaching content, teaching style, and teaching methods. In addition, research on the use of teaching tools and opinions on teaching arrangements can be summarized. The results of the interviews can be summarized as:

83% of the students agreed with the teaching content of Cantonese Porcelain combined with Scratch, Fusion360 and smart interactive lamp design and considered very interesting and novel; 91% of the students said that the group-cooperative teaching form helps to communicate with each other to learn and solve problems; 75% of the students agreed with the student-centered independent inquiry learning in the workshop; 83% of the students said that they have their own opinions and evaluation criteria for the evaluation of Cantonese Porcelain works; 75% of the students said that they had a new understanding of Cantonese Porcelain after studying in the workshop.

7   Conclusion

Based on the comparison of the traditional education model with the extended course education model and the post-class interviews and the observer's records of the class indicate: In the practice of the project with the theme of Cantonese Porcelain, this model can provide students with rich learning content and learning forms. It can enhance the students' interest and enthusiasm for learning, improve the learning experience and learning efficiency, and be recognized and loved by the students. Through interdisciplinary teaching content and cross-disciplinary learning experience, participants can flexibly use the colorful elements to carry out innovative design and integrated project practice to develop participants' ability to comprehensively apply knowledge in various fields to solve problems and deepen their understanding and cognition of Cantonese Porcelain.

This paper introduces in detail the teaching practice process of the intelligent handicraft innovation workshop with the theme of Cantonese Porcelain, and provides a reference path for the development of STEAM extended curriculum with Chinese characteristics, which provides a practical reference for the teaching of traditional handicrafts. However, there is still no authoritative evaluation standard for the teaching results of this workshop. It is difficult to prove that this model is conducive to improving students' ability to solve problems and comprehensive ability.

References

1. He, K., Wang, Z., Ling, W.: The development of thematic curriculum under the STEAM educational concept—Taking "Science in Chinese traditional architecture" as an example. Digit. Teach. Prim. Second. Sch. (07), 66–68.1 (2018)
2. Anderson, D., Jiao, J.: From STEM education to STEAM education—A dialogue between David Anderson and Ji Jiao on museum education. J. East China Norm. Univ. (Educ. Sci. Ed.) 35(4), 122–129 (2017)
3. China Future Family STEAM Education Trend Research Report 2018. iResearch Series Research Report (No. 12, 2018), p. 53. Shanghai Ai Rui Market Consulting Co., Ltd. (2018)
4. Ji, Y., Tan, P.: Exploring personalized learning pattern for studying Chinese traditional handicraft. In: Proceedings of the Sixth International Symposium of Chinese CHI. ACM (2018)
5. Perignat, E., Katz-Buonincontro, J.: STEAM in practice and research: an integrative literature review. Think. Ski. Creat. 31, 31–43 (2018)
6. Kim, P.W.: The wheel model of STEAM education based on traditional Korean scientific contents. EURASIA J. Math. Sci. Technol. Educ. 12(10) (2016)
7. Perignat, E., Katz-Buonincontro, J.: STEAM in practice and research: an integrative literature review. Think. Ski. Creat. 31, 31–43 (2019)
8. Kim, S.W., Chung, Y.L., Woo, A.J., et al.: Development of a theoretical model for STEAM education. J. Korean Assoc. Sci. Educ. 32(2), 388–401 (2012)
9. Fan, J., Li, Z.: The development of STEM education in China. China Natl. Educ. (Z1), 13–15 (2018)
10. Boy, G.A.: From STEM to STEAM: toward a human-centered education. In: European Conference on Cognitive Ergonomics (2013)
11. Zhang, M.: An overview of Chinese traditional folk paper-cut art. Lit. Life Wenhai Yiyuan, (3), 165 (2015)
12. Ji, Y., Tan, P., Duh, H.B.-L.: Research on personalized learning pattern in traditional handicraft using augmented reality: a case study of cantonese porcelain. In: Kurosu, M. (ed.) HCI 2018. LNCS, vol. 10902, pp. 304–316. Springer, Cham (2018). https://doi.org/10.1007/978-3-319-91244-8_25

13. Kang, Z.: Discussion on the art education model of workshops, workshops and studios in handicrafts. Des. Art Res. **2**(06), 31–34 (2012)
14. Wu, Z.: Study on the practice and exploration of primary school STEAM education based on Chinese excellent traditional culture—Taking the development of textbooks for primary school science textbooks as an example. Educ. Equip. Res. **34**(09), 19–22 (2018)
15. Kim, Y., Park, N.: The effect of STEAM education on elementary school student's creativity improvement. In: Kim, T., et al. (eds.) SecTech 2012. CCIS, vol. 339, pp. 115–121. Springer, Heidelberg (2012). https://doi.org/10.1007/978-3-642-35264-5_16
16. Zhong, J.: Research on design and application of STEAM teaching activities. East China Normal University (2018)
17. Wei, F., Wang, X.: When the customer encounters STEAM education. Mod. Educ. Technol. **24**(10), 37–42 (2014)
18. Henriksen, D.: Full STEAM ahead: creativity in excellent STEM teaching practices. Steam J. **1**(2), 1–9 (2014)
19. Wei, X., Yu, B., Yu, H.: The framework, characteristics and enlightenment of American STEAM education. J. East China Normal Univ. (Educ. Sci. Ed.) **35**(04), 40–46+134–135 (2017)
20. Zhao, H., Zhou, Y., Li, Y., Liu, Y., Wen, J.: The training strategy of "Artisan" innovative talents in interdisciplinary perspective—Based on the design of American STEAM educational activity design. J. Distance Educ. **35**(01), 94–101 (2017)
21. Sáez-López, J.M., Román-González, M., Vázquez-Cano, E.: Visual programming languages integrated across the curriculum in elementary school: a two year case study using "Scratch" in five schools. Comput. Educ. **97**, 129–141 (2016)
22. Suhada, R.T., Ariyanti, S., Fajar, A.V., et al.: Training Autodesk fusion 360 for teenage of senior high school graduates in improving ability in disasters. In: ICCD 2018, vol. 1, no. 1, pp. 285–289 (2018)
23. Sun, J., Wu, Y., Ren, Y.: Innovation in 3D printing education: maker space, innovation lab and STEAM. Mod. Distance Educ. Res. (4) (2015)

Application Experience of Human-Computer Interaction in Educational Management at Colleges and Universities

Tongtong Li[✉]

Jinan University, West Nanxinzhuang Road 336, Jinan, Shandong, China
947385677@qq.com

Abstract. After more than half a century of development, human-computer interaction has become a very important composition of computer science research. Global diversification has pushed the gradual filtration of human-computer interaction into all fields of society; yet its great progress has been made along with the rapid development of science and technology. This technology has undergone three stages of development: command-line interface, graphical user interface, and natural human-computer interaction. As an achievement of social progress, human-computer interaction launched the era of intelligence: its emergence and development have improved greatly work-life balance, i.e. it liberates people from clutter for a much more relaxing life. In our age of intelligence, human-computer interaction applies in all aspects of life, from cloud computer to smart phones, from planes in the sky to vehicles on the ground, from spaceships and detectors in space to daily drones for entertainment... The more increasing material and cultural needs people require, the more dependent they remain upon intelligent machines, which are expected, in place of manpower, to complete tasks efficiently and accurately in accordance with human's instructions, based on further implementing and expanding permissions via human-computer interaction. Therefore, the relation between mankind and computer becomes increasingly close and inseparable. In the educational field, human-computer interaction has unique predominance compared with old educational models: the wide application has improved educational quality as well as teaching effects. Especially it plays an extremely important role in educational management: instead of former management models, it improves a better balance between manpower and technology not only to liberate staff from heavy workload but to increase workplace productivity as well as managing effectiveness, which has gained massive positive responses from educational management professionals. Considering educational management practices, the paper focuses on the application of human-computer interaction in the educational management at colleges and universities, in compliance with its working patterns and features, to analyze advantages and challenges, on the basis of which, the research continues upon basic principles and experience improvement as well as application prospects human-computer interaction in educational management at colleges and universities.

Keywords: Human-computer interaction · Educational management · Application experience

© Springer Nature Switzerland AG 2019
A. Marcus and W. Wang (Eds.): HCII 2019, LNCS 11585, pp. 428–443, 2019.
https://doi.org/10.1007/978-3-030-23538-3_33

1   Introduction

Human-Computer Interaction (HCI) refers to research on the interaction between humans and computers, guided by the theoretical knowledge of various disciplines such as computer science, cognitive science, psychology, behavioral science, and sociology. This pioneering technology aims to realize the completion of human-computer interaction and system communication in a convenient and efficient way (Fig. 1).

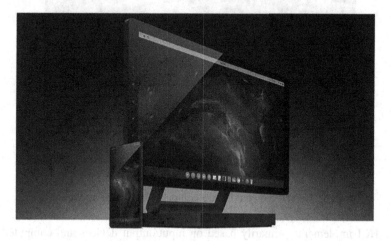

Fig. 1. HCI

The development of human-computer interaction, in short, is a discourse from people's adaption to computer to computer's gradual adaption to human beings. It has experienced several stages of development, i.e. the early manual operation phase, the job control language and the interactive command language phase, the graphical user interface (GUI) phase, network user interface phase, and multi-channel, multimedia intelligent human-computer interaction phase (Fig. 2).

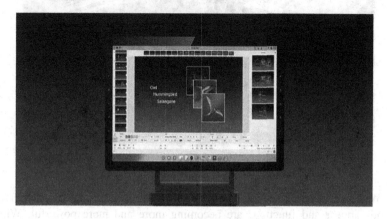

Fig. 2. HCI interface

Since the late 1990s, with the rapid development and popularization of high-speed processing chips as well as multimedia technology and Internet Web technologies, HCI research has focused on the intelligent and multi-modal (multi-channel) interaction, such as multimedia interaction, virtual interaction and human-computer interaction, which means its orientation to human-centered human-computer interaction technology (Fig. 3).

Fig. 3. Human-centered human-computer interaction technology

The HCI implements primarily based on input/output devices and computer software, whose main function is to control the operation of the related devices and executive various commands and requirements. The devices include mostly a keyboard display, a mouse, various pattern recognition machines and so on; yet the corresponding software, the operating system, plays an important part in the HCI function (Fig. 4).

Fig. 4. HCI peripherals

As With the development of computer technology, more and more operational commands appear and functions are becoming more and more powerful. With the development of input devices for pattern recognition such as speech recognition and Chinese character recognition, it is possible for HCI to perform at a syntactic level like natural language or restricted natural language, which signifies the continuous rapid progress toward intelligent HCI (Fig. 5).

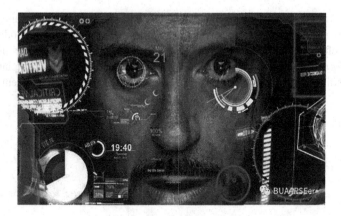

Fig. 5. Artificial intelligence

Fig. 6. Artificial intelligence

At present, human-computer interaction technology has been involved and applied in various fields, constantly affecting the rhythm and mode of our work and life. Meanwhile, people are also keen to have human-computer interaction technology emerged in all aspects of our work and life, not only to form a good partner interaction model, but also to apply human-computer interaction technology as a tool for us to save time and energy, improve efficiency, and ensure quality, so that people can be freed from heavy work and life load and win more time to think and do more meaningful things. The application of human-computer interaction technology in the teaching management of colleges and universities fully demonstrates its importance and positive significance in current times, and it will have a profound impact on the teaching management mode of colleges and universities (Fig. 6).

2   The Positive Application of HCI in Educational Management

Compared with the traditional teaching management, HCI educational management is more efficient: the forms are more various, the range much wider, and the modality more flexible and effective. In the educational management of colleges and universities, HCI is mainly performed, through the applicable system software or information platform, for the purpose of the integration and standardization of educational management (Fig. 7).

Fig. 7. Educational administration management information platform

2.1   System Management

The system management module is the information center of the entire educational management platform, whose main function is to authorize user's availability to the system for the related fundamental data. The ordinary uses except the administrator don't obtain the access. Therefore, the system management module is a general commander in control of the planning and coordination of all teaching management programs, that is, the access and authority granted to the teaching management personnel. The HCI between the administrative staff and the system management module maximizes the rigor and uniqueness of permission distribution against the possibility of human-induced errors (Fig. 8).

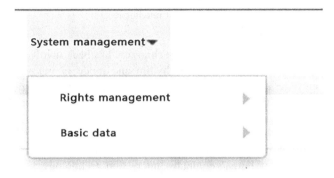

Fig. 8. System management

2.2   Student Status Management

The student status management module, used to monitor the student status in the college, can roughly be divided into several parts: class information management, student information management, query class information by term, minor registration management, and student changes major. The system can manage all-around school roll, based on the integration of students' identity verification and information collection, review targetedly and analyze specifically for varied issues in order to keep better track of student status and dynamic condition (Fig. 9).

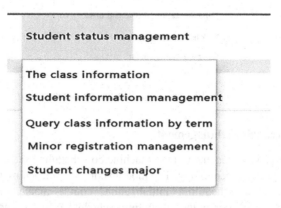

Student status management

The class information

Student information management

Query class information by term

Minor registration management

Student changes major

Fig. 9. Student status management

In this way, the educational management staff, with the help of HCI, just clicks the right buttons to give clear instructions for the student status rather than the offline tediousness of collecting, organizing and registering data. Therefore, the system provides the exact and comprehensive data via assembling information at the first time, which facilitates the staff in managing the student status.

2.3   Teaching Plan Management

As the system interactive channel for arranging teaching programs, the teaching program schedule management module mainly includes course library management, curriculum replacement management, training program management, teaching implementation plan, implementation of teaching tasks, task implementation query and calendar management. It is designed to carry out the course arrangement in a step-by-step manner. Each step is very clear and easy to operate. The teaching schedule management is top priority for the educational management. The related staff needs to put 200% of their energy whenever they deal with it, as this complicated work is involved in many interlocking processes. There is little leeway if anything goes wrong: one wrong step may even affect student's regular graduation in the future. By means of HCI, the educational management staff clarifies the process, follows the displayed interfaces to schedule and double-check the courses orderly, which realizes the human-machine teaching program scheduling in an efficient and orderly way (Fig. 10).

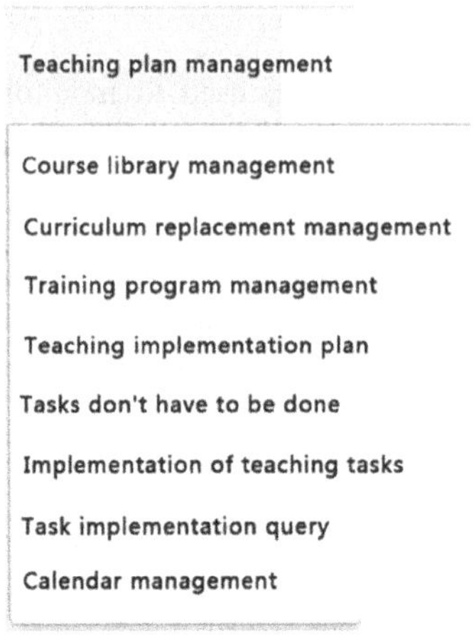

Teaching plan management

Course library management

Curriculum replacement management

Training program management

Teaching implementation plan

Tasks don't have to be done

Implementation of teaching tasks

Task implementation query

Calendar management

Fig. 10. Teaching plan management

2.4   Course Arranging Management

The Course arranging management, man-machine co-scheduling the curriculum, is the fullest realization of HCI technology. The module consists of teaching site information, task scheduling, class scheduling initialization, course management, interactive scheduling, other human-computer scheduling, schedule to print, and class situation enquiry. This function is a follow-up work after the teaching plan management function. The former manual curriculum scheduling modality is time-consuming and inefficient, especially considering the high confliction between class schedule and teachers' availability, which leads to repeated modifications on a basis of the continuously tedious work

Courses arranging management

Teaching site information

Task scheduling

Class scheduling initialization

Course management

Interactive scheduling

other human-computer scheduling

Schedule to print

Class status enquiry

Fig. 11. Course arranging management

of educational management staff. The application of the scheduling management module will promptly display the interface for reminding conflicts during the curriculum scheduling course; moreover, it will prohibit operators from continuing the conflict scheduling. Therefore, it successes to avoid the risk that the teaching management staff have no awareness of having arranged the conflicted schedule. In this way, HCI obviously improves efficiency and increases accuracy rather than lots of work in vain (Fig. 11).

2.5 Course Management

The course selection management module aims to help students elect, recover, and retake courses of different types and natures, so as to realize course selection query and credit charging. It is mainly divided into the following sub-items: teaching registration management, course selection task setting, course selection list adjustment, course selection queries, rebuild management, management of course credit collection. Although students are able to freely select courses by instructions of their own course selection system, sometimes it needs the involvement of educational management staff in such circumstances as individual's failure in selecting within deadline and individual's unavailability without access due to schooling suspension. With their help, students in special situations are able to select courses, attend classes, take exams, gain credits, and then graduate smoothly. For students, HCI application in course selection management, to a great extent, guarantees the initiativity and fairness of course selection, i.e. who selects first, who gets first; besides, it is free and convenient to adjust their choices within deadline. Meanwhile, regarding the educational management staff, it avoids the potential confliction on scheduling and ensures the accuracy of course selection (Fig. 12).

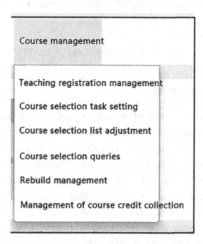

Fig. 12. Course management

2.6   Performance Management

The performance management module, composed of record setting management, results the query, grade and credit recognition management, statistical analysis of performance and students performance ranking statistics, offers grade input channel to teachers. It protects privacy of grade input process, that is, the system generates, in response to each teacher and each course, different codes which can be exported. In addition, the educational management staff can monitor student performance via HCI as well, especially engaged in the credit recognition for students with particular situations. They make a statistical analysis on performance data with reference to a class or a major, in order that they are able to get the big picture of student performance status based on the grade distribution for the necessary academic early warning to remind the related students to complete their studies on time (Fig. 13).

Fig. 13. Performance management

2.7   Examination Management

Examination management module plays an important part in the educational management as well. Nothing can go wrong in the interlocking processes: from the exam hall organization, basic data setting, to release of exam tasks, examination and Invigilation arrangements, and then to exam information inquiry. The following items are involved: examination room information setting, basic examination data, test task management, make-up examination management, security management, centralized test scheduling management, decentralized test scheduling management, arrange test list management, and examination information query. Concerning the past manual examination arrangement, operated by the educational management staff, it is inevitable to omit examination arrangement in response to certain courses and overlapped schedules of invigilators. It is barely ensured to avoid mistakes despite of double check. The current HCI examination management system manages to improve the accuracy of examination management thanks to the mutual cooperation and supervision between manpower and computer. Once the inconsistency appears, the operator is alarmed promptly for the immediate rectification. Moreover, the functional development of examination information inquiry means that the educational management staff do not have to manually fill in the exam admission ticket and registration form of exam circumstance; instead, both students and invigilators can query online the information needed in respective systems. Therefore, the HCI facilitates not only the educational management staff, but also teachers and students (Fig. 14).

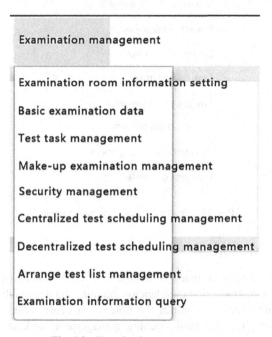

Fig. 14. Examination management

2.8   Graduation Project (Thesis) Management

The graduation project (thesis) management module, for the consistency of managing students' graduation projects, is sectioned in graduation project control, supervisor management, project management, subject to monitor, task management, process management, defense management, performance management and excellent graduation thesis. It is designed for educational management staff to timely monitor the entire graduation process step by step, in the way that students, under the instruction of tutors, follow up with all the requirements, meet the credit standards, and finally gained the graduation qualification. The HCI successfully replaces the former modality, in which educational management staff needs to load so tedious work during the graduation period as offline thorough investigation, continuous tracking and consistent reminding. Therefore, it improves actual effect and mechanism so as to proceed the graduation smoothly with high standards (Fig. 15).

Fig. 15. Graduation project management

2.9   Graduation Management

The graduation management module divided into three functions: academic early warning management, graduation qualification examination and result printing, aims to master the learning situation, confirm the graduation qualification and final performance presentation. It is the final teaching management work at the end of each semester. Through the HCI system, the teaching management staff can conduct data surveys on the students' academic completion status based on semester or academic year, and then figure out and alert the students whose grades are not qualified. Early warning enables students to pay attention to learning without missing exams needed to be retaken or courses needed to be restudied in case of graduation unqualification. After verification, the educational management staff filtrate students without graduation qualification, who, off-campus, are notified to apply for completion or extension with the procedure and return to retake the examination in the next semester for the supplementary graduation certificate and bachelor's degree with the qualified transcript. Therefore, for educational management staff, the HCI initiates the intelligent modality of credit calculation, instead of the former way to audit manually each undergraduate's transcript with the print version. It hence improves the standardization and operability of graduation process for the smooth implementation (Fig. 16).

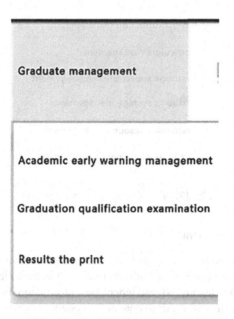

Fig. 16. Graduation management

2.10 Teaching Material Management

The teaching material management module, as the name implies, is the uniform subscription and management of the textbooks used by teachers and students. It is divided into basic information management, curriculum material management, textbook subscription management, textbook storage management, textbook stock-out management and textbook settlement management. The HCI in this module has greatly improved the qualification of subscription for the final selection of the most suitable teaching materials. Compared with the former modality to find out the accordance with the course content only after the usage of textbook, the intelligent system manages to filtrate a collection of good teaching materials appropriate to both teachers and students. Teaching management staff can interact with the system and select certain suitable teaching materials for the teachers to preview first, until they find the most satisfactory version, and then recommend them to students. In this way, it not only saves a lot of invalid expenses, but optimizes the approach on the subscription, which favors any party and ensures teaching quality for the good teaching effectiveness (Fig. 17).

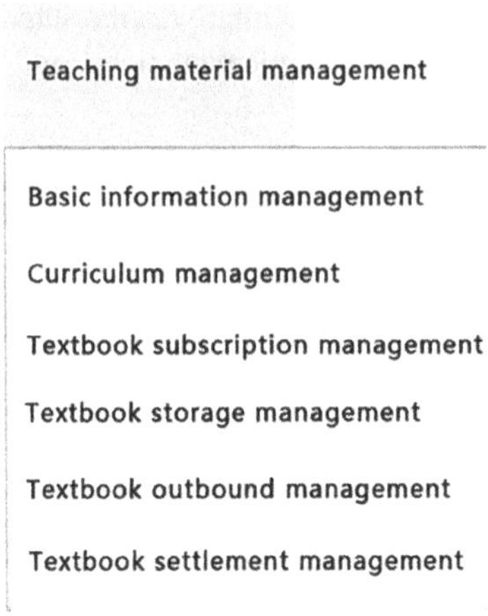

Teaching material management

Basic information management

Curriculum management

Textbook subscription management

Textbook storage management

Textbook outbound management

Textbook settlement management

Fig. 17. Teaching material management

2.11   Teacher Management

Teacher management module functions mainly for routine maintenance management in terms of teacher resources and related information, such as their identity, title, employee ID number, affiliate they belongs to, and other basic information. For retired teachers, the educational management staff needs to note in the system as "retired" without access any longer to the system assigned by administrators. For newly recruited teachers, the operator should promptly enter all the basic information in the system in order to facilitate the follow-up teaching work. As for educational management staff, the HCI approach thus greatly improves the operating mode to acquire and monitor the specific status relating to the teachers, which conducts data storage and extraction conveniently, quickly and efficiently, and fully guarantees the integrity and accuracy of the teacher information.

The application of HCI has prevailed in the educational management at colleges and universities because of those advantages as stated above. It is a good opportunity for colleges and universities to develop rapidly their educational management. On the basis of the HCI platform, they can consistently realize more satisfactory effects in accordance

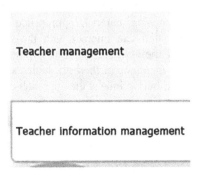

Fig. 18. Teacher management

with user requirements by means of more command and instructions, and consequently make educational management more systematic, and effective reduce teaching costs, improve teaching quality for the better service of education and management (Fig. 18).

3 The Deficiency of HCI Application in the Educational Management

Despite the fact that the HCI application in the educational management at colleges and universities has achieved remarkable results in good trends, there are also certain deficiencies in the actual operating experience. These incompleteness more or less affects the effectiveness of HCI. The restraint and even confusion occur occasionally when the staff give operating instructions, which obviously impacts work and application experience.

3.1 The Instability of HCI System

In actual use, the educational management staff encounter some stability issues of HCI system, which limits the access and further work of progress. Sometimes they are even forced to shut down the work in process and delay it behind schedule. For example, they often experience the access control problems: they need to constantly change various input channels with uncertain outcome, which costs lots of time and causes their mental stress. Even if they enter the system, they have got to receive passively the different access in compliance with different input address, i.e. in terms of the same module, it functions with this address, yet it fails with another one; consequently they have to repeatedly change addresses and consistently log in and out for the same module. It brings a lot of trouble and leads to the daily work time-consuming and inefficiency. In addition, the educational management staff also confront the confusing situation that when double check, they find the input data has changed automatically after the assignment; they somehow have got to delete the wrong data and re-enter them, however, the re-entry is not guaranteed to be absolutely correct after submission. In this case, it brings the staff lots of efforts in vain and much inconvenience.

3.2 Uncertainty of HCI System

Meanwhile, the staff find some uncertainties of the HCI system in the actual use as well, which make them too puzzles to confirm the accuracy of the work. For example, when engaged in reviewing student performance and credits, the educational management staff fell overwhelmed by varied sets of data because various data are scatted in different modules or sections, and different sets of data displays in correspondence with diverse output modes of the modules or sections. In the end, the only way to resolve is the mutual check of data between the educational management system and student's own system for the final confirmation. However, here comes the new problem: the data presentation relating to teaching programs in student system is inconsistent with that of staff's system, which causes eventually the unavailability to check mutually. As for the educational management staff, these uncertainties have brought great inconvenience to the performance review and credit review, which has increased a lot of work in vain ineffective, without eventual certainty of the accurate and satisfactory results.

3.3   Disnormativity of HCI System

The disnormativity of HCI system consists in the actual use as well, which leads to inconvenience and work delay. Take the humanized dysfunction of the module for instance. The failure in exporting data and displaying for sequence causes the staff to search the required data in a disorderly manner. Even if the data could be automatically sorted in the system, the exported data is still arranged in a mixed manner without any rule. In the end, the staff need to manually sort the data to review the relevant data clearly. Furthermore, the disnormativity of the system also lies in the unavailability to operate and modify data in terms of certain special case or segment. The data has to be submitted, returned, or deleted as a unit, thus altering a datum means to change the entire data as the system requires. The educational management staff, therefore, have to bear heavy workload. The disnormativity of design module in the system reflects the limitation of designer's concept of the HCI system with little experience, which brings such troubles to the educational management, that the staff fail to experience the comprehensiveness and meticulousness of the application modules against the application experience.

4   The Fundamental Principles and New Requirements of Application Experience of HCI Needed to be Followed in the Educational Management

For the good future of HCI technology in the educational management at universities over against the current inadequateness, it should bear human-centered design concept and practical operation for the user-friendly and available experience as the fundamental design principles.

Humanization of the HCI system plays a crucial role in the friendliness and availability of computer system. In compliance with ergonomic philosophy, the system engineers should focus on the human-centered compatibility between human and computer, otherwise it is hard to reach the satisfactory human-computer interactive results for the comfortable application experience. Meanwhile, we must also take into account that ergonomics does not negate training, although it is the desire of teaching management workers to avoid training. However, whether it can be fully realized is not determined by our subjective will. The purpose, characteristics, occasions and implementation cost of the management task determine the natural procedures that HCI human-computer interaction should achieve. This is the true meaning of being human-centered and it will enhances the practical operability of the interactive system.

Therefore, the "people-centered" design concept is the basis and premise for enhancing the friendliness and usability of the computer system. Only with the humanized design can the function of the computer system be optimized, and its operational function can be more practical, producing perfect interaction effect with half the effort. This is a new problem facing university teaching management personnel in the HCI human-computer interaction technology experience.

5 The Promising Prospects of HCI Technology in the Educational Management

Although HCI technology is still in a stage of gradual development, and there is large space for improvement, its development prospects are still very encouraging. The ideal HCI mode is "user freedom", which means the computer is mainly directly manipulated and partially controlled by command language, especially natural language. Therefore, HCI technology still has a very broad development space and a good development potential in the teaching management application of colleges and universities. University administrators can take "user freedom" as the next development goal, gradually realize the upgrade function of each module in the system, and finally achieve the independence and intelligence of the entire system, so that the teaching management staff can liberate their hands and command by voice, which saves time, effort and management costs. Thereby, the teaching management work will be more standardized, systematic and efficient.

Playing a key role in the teaching management of colleges and universities the HCI system forms a tight connection with the teaching management workers as a partner and as well as a comrade-in-arms. They undertake the teaching management work cooperatively and overcome the difficulties together, which created an unbreakable friendship between human and computers. There is enough reason to believe that HCI technology will surely be more comprehensive, powerful and perfect in cooperating with people's daily life, and enter into the era of intelligence with broader development space and the fastest speed.

References

1. Qiu, M.: Research on the usability principle of information inquiry system supporting interaction. Libr. Sci. Res. **2**, 7–8 (2018)
2. Chai, J.: Research and construction of the teaching agent mental model in human-emotional interaction system. Mod. Educ. Technol. **17**(1), 55–57 (2007)

The Application of Student Participation in the Design of Virtual Reality Educational Products

Ziyang Li$^{1(\boxtimes)}$, Xiandong Cheng^1, Limin Wang^1, Hao He^2,
and Bin Liang^1

^{1} Beijing City University, No. 269 Bei si huan Zhong lu, Hai dian District,
Beijing, China
li.ziyang@bcu.edu.cn
^{2} China Central Academy of Fine Arts, No. 8 Hua Jia Di Nan St.,
Chao yang District, Beijing, China

Abstract. With the development of computer hardware and human interface devices, Virtual Reality (VR) has become a commonly adopted educational tool. In recent years, changes have taken place in technological innovation, with principles of user-centered design and human-computer interaction behavior receiving more attention. This paper presents the application of student participation in the design of VR educational products. By analyzing the data on students who use VR educational products, this paper investigates the relationship between educational objectives and the audiovisual experience, usability, exploratory nature, direction and feedback, and enjoyability. A method for involving students in the design of VR educational products is proposed and subsequently adopted in the development of VR teaching on Beijing Subway maintenance. Hence, the significance of VR educational products is demonstrated.

Keywords: Design thinking · Participation design · Virtual reality · Interactive design · Educational application

1 Introduction

The ultimate goal of educational applications is to enable users to acquire knowledge or skills more intuitively. This is termed the educational objective [1]. Therefore, creating an immersive experience and imparting knowledge are the two most crucial considerations. Advances in computer hardware have widened the use of digital technologies in education, especially in recent years when connected cellphones have become a necessity in daily life, allowing individuals to download educational applications in order to study math, foreign languages, history and physics among other subjects. In the 1990s, various educational software packages were sold in large bookstores throughout China. The software consisted of 2D animations and aroused users' interest in learning through vivid images. Consequently, users could seek out knowledge and thus gain pleasure. With recent and rapid development in digital technology, numerous individuals are no longer content with the passive impartment of knowledge, instead

© Springer Nature Switzerland AG 2019
A. Marcus and W. Wang (Eds.): HCII 2019, LNCS 11585, pp. 444–456, 2019.
https://doi.org/10.1007/978-3-030-23538-3_34

wanting virtualized and dramatized knowledge with which they can interact with computers and simultaneously improve their problem solving skills. However, creating a qualified human-computer experience which integrates education remains a significant challenge. Moreover, the best means of converting the enjoyability of digital entertainment into education also merits investigation [2].

The design of educational applications differs from that of ordinary entertainment games. Instead of perfect visual effects, strong tactile feedback and complex scenarios, educational applications must be able to balance entertainment and educational objectives. No unnecessary objects need be preserved, as proper feedback with well created plots centered on key knowledge can help students to better realize their educational goals. Application developers alone cannot complete the whole design process. If they can neither blend in and communicate with service objects (teachers or students) nor offer clear educational objectives, they will be unable to produce qualified educational products. Hence, application developers as well as service objects (teachers or students) should be involved in the design of educational products. The design process extends beyond system development, encompassing communication between individuals with different perspectives and values. The aim is to identify a method for accomplishing educational objectives that can satisfy all parties [3].

In this study, students are required to use several VR educational applications and evaluate their audiovisual experience, usability, exploratory nature, direction and feedback, and enjoyability. These evaluations are quantified in order to determine the relationship with educational objectives and thus construct a participatory design method. This method is used to conduct participatory design evaluations with service objects (teachers or students) who are jointly developing the beta version of the Beijing Subway Maintenance Teaching System VR (BSMTS VR).

2   Student Participatory Design

Participatory design began in Scandinavia during the 1970s–1980s, when trade union movements forced through new laws which gave employees new rights and a say in working environment change [4]. Moreover, manufacturers also noticed the limitation in product development, with design revolution especially important. Bela H. Banathy, a famous system design expert from the US, identified the four generations of design in human activity systems. The first generation, Design by Dictate, is deeply affected by the Systems Engineering Approach and often implemented from top to bottom through legislation. The second generation is known as Designing for, according to which experts and consultants are invited to investigate a specific system problem, conduct demand analysis and provide solutions to decision-makers. The third generation is called Designing with/Designer Guided, according to which design is produced following the discussion between designers and decision-makers. The fourth generation is called Designing Within, which proposes that human activity systems must be jointly designed by those within the system, those using the system and those the system serves [5]. This paper believes that the fourth generation method can serve as the fundamental basis for participatory design. This method differs from the first three generations in that communication, cooperation and sharing are required, with user participation playing a role from the very beginning of the design. Users become an integral component of the entire design team through active participation [6, 7]. Therefore, everyone involved is both a designer and a user, thus exerting direct influence on the ultimate product quality.

According to participatory design, students, as the service objects in educational applications, should participate in app design and development so as to improve app quality and the extent to which students' demands are satisfied.

3   VR Educational Applications

VR creates a virtual space accessible through the use of computers and sensors. Users can sense and operate virtual objects with the help of various sensors and participate in virtual events. Participants can immerse themselves in the vivid environment created. In short, VR constitutes a virtual world similar to the real one where people can interact through watching, listening, touching and feeling, thereby engendering vivid interactions.

VR educational applications differ from ordinary educational applications in that the latter imparts knowledge in a simple and straightforward manner, while the former advocates student-centered design and guides students in actively acquiring and understanding knowledge while simultaneously formulating a knowledge network. This is part of Constructivism. The role of educational applications is to promote and guide students in developing their own knowledge network, rather than simply imparting knowledge [8]. Therefore, the situation, activity and interaction in constructivism-based learning environments can constantly challenge the students' experience, so as to promote the development of new knowledge [9].

VR technologies can vividly fill 3D space, thus providing students with the opportunity to directly interact with objects and experience a stronger sense of involvement. Multi-dimensional VR learning environments can offer students direct and efficient means of acquiring knowledge and skills. Therefore, thanks to its many advantages, VR is often utilized in special education, simulation experiments and specialty training. Here, special education refers to dangerous or difficult education for which direct student involvement is rarely required in reality, such as learning to drive. In this scenario, new drivers typically receive extensive theoretical training before actually driving on the road. Furthermore, theoretical training is rather limited compared to actually driving. Therefore, VR can be adopted in order to enable new drivers to experience real on-the-road driving at an earlier stage. Moreover, virtual high-risk driving is made possible through VR. Consequently, data concerning how new drivers handle high-risk incidents can be collected and analyzed in order to improve their ability to anticipate and thus reduce risk [10].

The BSMTS VR case is another example. Given the danger associated with subway maintenance, VR adoption in training could greatly reduce risk in real-life scenarios.

However, applying VR in education up until now has focused more on technology, such as improving simulation vividness and the interactive experience from a hardware perspective. This paper believes that, when designing VR educational applications, users can be better assisted in achieving their objectives by adopting a user experience perspective rather than a technological perspective. Operation should be made as easy as possible, with training offered to teachers and students. Expansibility should be available so that users can themselves edit and adjust the application to some extent, thus allowing them to better adjust to and recognize the virtual environment and enhance their interest in learning.

4   Participatory Design of VR Educational Applications

Participatory design emphasizes user participation. Kuhn & wino-grad suggest that the participation degree can be evaluated from four dimensions: participation mode, time, scope and control [11]. He stresses that designers should fully consider user demands when designing a teaching system. In VR application design, such factors must also be taken into account. In previous teaching, student problems encountered while using VR educational applications included short participation time and a lack of understanding of interaction behavior, which directly impacted their accomplishments. Therefore, it is hoped that students can participate in the design and development of VR educational applications, by researching and analyzing the audiovisual experience, usability, exploratory nature, direction and feedback, and enjoyability. Subsequently, how these factors relate to educational objectives can be determined.

- Audiovisual experience: How users evaluate the images and sounds encountered when using the application.
- Usability: The extent to which using the application is perceived as difficult by users.
- Exploratory nature: How users evaluate the participation process and their time when using the application.
- Direction and feedback: How users evaluate operation directions and proper feedback when using the application.
- Enjoyability: To the extent to which users enjoy using the application.
- Accomplishments: The extent to which users have mastered relevant knowledge after using the application.

Before designing BSMTS VR using the participatory design method, existing educational applications were investigated and analyzed. Two existing VR applications of science popularization were selected: THE BODY VR and Seismic VR. Then, user research was conducted vis-à-vis the five variables (see Fig. 1). THE BODY VR [12] is a VR game where players use VR devices to explore the microscopic world of human bodies. Users can travel through the organs and learn how they work. This application is more than a game, it is a biology teaching software. Seismic VR simulates a seismic event and guides users in properly escaping. In addition to explaining what should be done when seismic activity is detected, the application also emphasizes practice and action. Both applications are distinctive. THE BODY VR focuses on imparting knowledge, while Seismic VR has practical value. Data from 11 THE BODY VR users and 10 Seismic VR users were analyzed. All users are college students without professional knowledge in biology or disaster mitigation. However, they have all studied biology and participated in live seismic exercises at middle school. Hence, they have some basic knowledge. Students evaluated the applications with regard to the five variables after using them, as well as their own accomplishments. Then, other students or experts questioned the students in order to test their real accomplishments.

Fig. 1. THE BODY VR and Seismic VR user research

According to the data (see Figs. 2 and 3), the two applications barely differ in terms of the audiovisual experience, usability, exploratory nature, direction and feedback, and enjoyability. Both applications are well rated by students. However, the accomplishments of THE BODY VR are rated lower than those of Seismic VR in both self-evaluation and the teacher's test. Two potential reasons were identified following discussion with students and teachers. First, students unanimously believe that, in terms of visual effects and enjoyability, THE BODY VR is superior to Seismic VR. However, during use, the interaction is more concerned with creating interesting cells, which do not complement the background voice imparting cell knowledge. In this case, the visual effects may even distract students. In addition, the teachers found that students paid more attention to observing the shape and motion of objects within cells but cared little about the background knowledge.

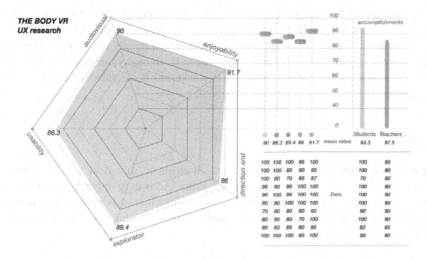

Fig. 2. THE BODY VR UX research data

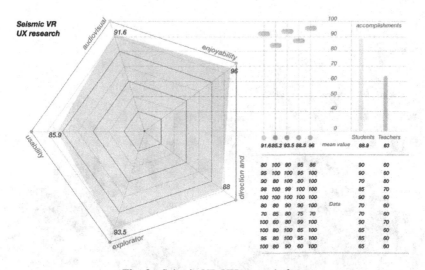

Fig. 3. Seismic VR UX research data

According to the evaluations of both students and teachers, THE BODY VR is a theory-based VR application, which allows users to do something that is not possible in real life - entering cells. However, in THE BODY VR, interaction is not closely related to the knowledge, meanings students are still passively imparted knowledge, but with more attractive images. Seismic VR requires students to practice their theoretical knowledge and thus improve their understanding. Hence, Seismic VR is an operation-based application. All operations are related to the knowledge, thus solidifying students' understanding and enhancing their accomplishments.

In summary, VR-based education suits operation or practice-based activities, which requires students to get involved in each step in person in order to solidify their foundational knowledge. For traditional activities which mainly impart knowledge, VR can enhance engagement and interest compared to traditional video teaching. However, the impact on students' accomplishments is weaker, as is the case in the BSMTS VR application.

5 BSMTS VR

Subway maintenance is highly dangerous. Students in this field require extensive practice before they can master the relevant skills. According to teachers in this field, new students are at a greater risk than old ones. Therefore, it is necessary to design a VR teaching application for subway maintenance, so that students can acquire knowledge with minimal risk.

Fig. 4. Participatory design process with students

The first stage in this VR application is cleaning locomotive screws, which is jointly developed with the participation of seven students majoring in subway maintenance. This paper details the four versions of the participatory design process, analyzing student usage data in the design process (see Figs. 4 and 5). The four versions are as follows:

- BSMTS VR version 1 (video explanation): Explains the process and risks associated with cleaning subway locomotive screws through the medium of video.
- BSMTS VR version 2 (VR): Explains the process and risks associated with cleaning subway locomotive screws using VR.
- BSMTS VR version 3 (VR direction and hint): Incorporates text directions and feedback based on Version 2.
- BSMTS VR version 4 (voice hint and a score mechanism): Incorporates voice directions and a score mechanism based on Version 3

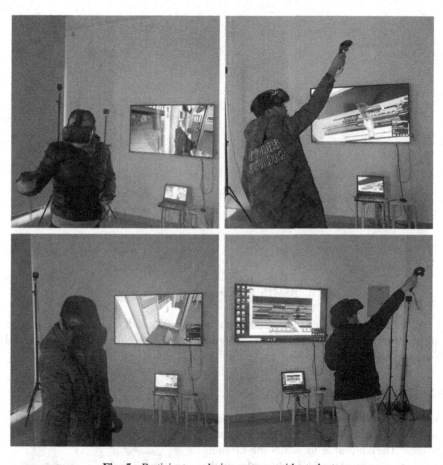

Fig. 5. Participatory design process with students

5.1   BSMTS VR Version 1

This version explains the process and risks associated with cleaning subway locomotive screws through the traditional medium of video. The students are asked to watch and evaluate the video using the participatory design method. The results are as follows (see Fig. 6):

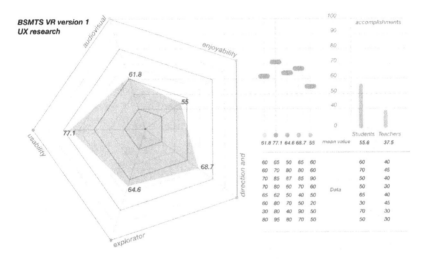

Fig. 6. BSMTS VR Version1 UX research data

According to the results, the students are not satisfied with the overall performance except for its usability. Moreover, the accomplishments are poor and the method fails to arouse their interest (see Fig. 6).

5.2   BSMTS VR Version 2

Compared to Version 1, in Version 2, students can wear a VR helmet and enter a virtual subway carriage. They are able to watch the cleaning process in the virtual world, freely exploring the carriage and interacting in a simple manner without directions or educational objectives. Students simply observe the carriage. Students experience and evaluate this version in turn using the participatory design method. It is hoped that they can offer suggestions. The results are as follows (see Fig. 7):

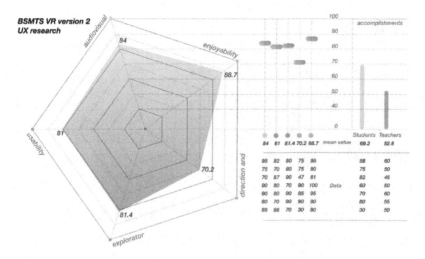

Fig. 7. BSMTS VR Version2 UX research data

The results show that students' evaluations of the audiovisual experience, exploratory nature and enjoyability increase significantly, while their accomplishments improve only mildly. However, no significant improvements are visible in usability and direction and feedback (see Fig. 7). The students believe that the VR technology enables them to personally experience and involve themselves in the cleaning process, arousing their interest in a short time. However, merely watching and interacting superficially do not allow students to understand and remember all operations. It would be better if someone were present in order to guide them through real operations at this point in time.

5.3 BSMTS VR Version 3

In BSMTS VR Version 3, a blackboard with operation procedures is placed next to the coach door. All the necessary objects are labeled with their names above them. Students can follow the procedure in order to learn operations step by step. The students are also required to evaluate this version. The results are as follows (see Fig. 8):

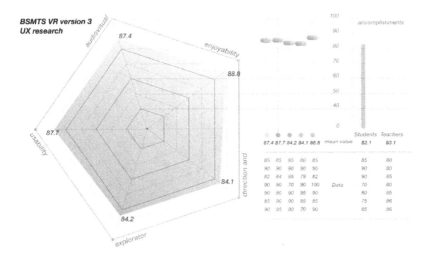

Fig. 8. BSMTS VR Version3 UX research data

The results reveal a significant improvement in usability, direction and feedback, as well as accomplishments (see Fig. 8). In the students' view, the procedures and added names are of great help because they allow students to follow the procedure for cleaning the screws step by step. Compared to passively watching as in Version 2, the practical operation element in Version 3 can better help students to acquire and retain the relevant knowledge.

5.4   BSMTS VR Version 4

In the discussion on Version 3, students express the belief that the time could be limited to 100 s, with a reward and punishment system added. Therefore, both voice directions and a score mechanism are included in Version 4. After each step, voice directions are given for the next step. The overall operation time is calculated after each student completes the task. Then, their

performance speeds are ranked against one another. The students are again required to evaluate this version. The results are as follows (see Fig. 9):

The results demonstrate significant improvements in the audiovisual experience, usability, enjoyability and accomplishments. According to the students, the improvement in the audiovisual experience and usability can be attributed to the voice directions, but these do not produce a significant improvement in direction and feedback (see Fig. 9).

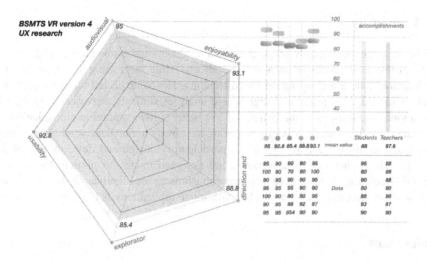

Fig. 9. BSMTS VR Version4 UX research data

The results for all the four versions are presented together in a single graph (see Fig. 10). The results show that using the participatory design method facilitates the development of the BSMTS VR. Students evaluate the current version in terms of the audiovisual experience, usability, exploratory nature, direction and feedback, and enjoyability. Moreover, they also offer suggestions for future versions. In the development and evolution of previous versions, accomplishments improved significantly. The same method will be adopted in the development of future versions in order to further optimize the participatory design method.

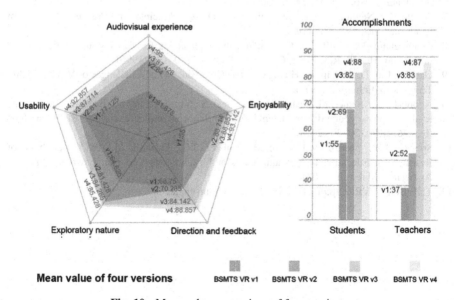

Fig. 10. Mean value comparison of four versions

6   Conclusion

VR has become a commonly adopted method in educational applications, but designers and developers typically emphasize the effects while neglecting the technology's participatory nature and operation-based teaching. Hence, expected teaching goals are rarely achieved. This paper investigates and analyzes students' experiences using VR educational applications in the belief that VR better suits operation and practice-based teaching activities. Finally, students majoring in subway maintenance and management are invited to involve themselves in the participatory design and development of the BSMTS VR application. Four versions are designed using the participatory design method. According to tests, students' accomplishments are significantly improved and the use of participatory design in VR educational applications is efficient.

References

1. Bloom, B.S. (ed.): Taxonomy of Educational Objectives: The Classification of Educational Goals: Handbook I, Cognitive Domain. Longmans, Green, New York (1956)
2. Kiili, K., de Freitas, S., Arnab, S., Lainema, T.: The design principles for flow experience in educational games. Procedia Comput. Sci. **15**, 78–91 (2012)
3. Qin, C., Mo, Y.: Participatory design: connotation, philosophical foundation and practice purport. E-educ. Res. **2010**(12), 9–11
4. Weinhery, J.B.: Participatory Design in a Human-Computer Interaction Course: Teaching. ACM Digital Library (2002)
5. Banathy, B.H.: Comprehensive systems design in education-who should be the designers? Educ. Technol. **31**(9), 49–51 (1991)
6. Greenbaum, J., Kyng, M. (eds.): Design at Work: Cooperative Design of Computer Systems. L. Erlbaum Associates Inc., Hillsdale (1992)
7. Schuler, D., Namioka, A. (eds.): Participatory Design: Principles and Practices. L. Erlbaum Associates Inc., Hillsdale (1993)
8. Cunningham, D., Duffy, T.: Constructivism: implications for the design and delivery of instruction. Handb. Res. Educ. Commun. Technol. 170–198 (1996)
9. Gao, Y., Liu, D., Huang, Z., Huang, R.: The Core Factors and Challenges of Virtual Reality Technology Enhanced Learning
10. Agrawal, R., Knodler, M., Fisher, D.L., Samuel, S.: Virtual reality headset training: can it be used to improve young drivers' latent hazard anticipation and mitigation skills. Transp. Res. Rec. **2672**(33), 20–30 (2018)
11. Spector, J.M., Merrill, M.D., van Merrienboer, J.G., Driscoll, M. (eds.): Handbook of Research on Educational Communications and Technology, 3rd edn. Lawrence Erlbaum Associates, Mahwah (2008)
12. THE BODY VR. http://thebodyvr.com/journey-inside-a-cell

Design and Application of University Intelligent Learning Environment Centered on Improving User Experience

Guang Liu[1], Zejiang Liu[1], Fang Lu[1], Qinmei Ye[1], and Zhen Liu[2(✉)]

[1] Educational Technology Center, Academic Affairs Office,
South China University of Technology, Guangzhou 510006,
People's Republic of China
[2] School of Design, South China University of Technology, Guangzhou 510006,
People's Republic of China
liuzjames@scut.edu.cn

Abstract. With the emergence of new technologies, such as the Internet of things (IoT), big data, cloud computing and mobile communication, smart education has gradually become a new driving force for national education development. China's Ministry of Education called for the in-depth promotion of "Internet + higher education", breaking the time-space boundaries and school walls of traditional education. Currently, China's reconstruction of the intelligent learning environment is mainly focused on the design of smart learning spaces. The difference between the stage of wisdom education and other stages of informationization development is to emphasize the cultivation of learners' creativity. This directly becomes the main starting point for the design of a new generation of learning spaces. Therefore, the intelligent learning environment will combine the combination of creativity and digital as the key to innovation. However, there is currently a lack of innovation in the improvement of the user experience in an intelligent learning environment. Therefore, this paper focuses on the analysis of the main problems of the current Chinese university learning environment, such as teaching-centered classroom setting unsuitable for classroom interaction, public learning space with low user experience, and lack of teaching decisions supported by big data analysis and learning behavior analysis, and then achieves the best student learning effect through the reconstruction of the smart learning environment centered on improving the use experience, including physical and virtual environments. The use experience-centered smart learning environment ultimately has been evaluated in a case study, which indicates that the environment can effectively improve students' self-learning and problem-solving abilities.

Keywords: Intelligent learning environment · User experience ·
Learning environment innovation · University students · Learning space ·
Interactive learning · Learning behavior · Learning-centered furniture design ·
Space interaction

© Springer Nature Switzerland AG 2019
A. Marcus and W. Wang (Eds.): HCII 2019, LNCS 11585, pp. 457–471, 2019.
https://doi.org/10.1007/978-3-030-23538-3_35

1 Introduction

At present, with information technology developing, technological change on people's lives have a huge impact. With the emergence of new technologies, such as the Internet of things (IoT), big data, cloud computing and mobile communication, smart education has gradually become a new driving force for national education development [1].

In 2018, China's Ministry of Education called for the in-depth promotion of "Internet + higher education", breaking the time-space boundaries and school walls of traditional education, and promoting the rapid development of higher education with profound changes in the mode of education and teaching. It requires to vigorously promote the application of modern information technology, build smart classrooms, smart LABS, and smart campuses, which needs to explore and implement networked, digital, intelligent, and personalized education, reshaping education and teaching patterns [2].

Currently, China's reconstruction of the intelligent learning environment is mainly focused on the design of smart learning spaces. The difference between the stage of wisdom education and other stages of informationization development is to emphasize the cultivation of learners' creativity. This directly becomes the main starting point for the design of a new generation of learning spaces. Therefore, the smart learning environment will combine the combination of creativity and digital as the key to innovation. However, there is currently a lack of innovation in the improvement of the user experience in a intelligent learning environment. Therefore, this paper focuses on the analysis of the main problems of the current Chinese university learning environment, and then achieves the best student learning effect through the reconstruction of the smart learning environment centered on improving the use experience, including physical and virtual environments.

2 The Main Problems on the Learning Environment in Universities in China

2.1 Teaching-Centered Classroom Setting Unsuitable for Classroom Interaction

In general, the traditional teaching-centered or teacher-centered classroom is not conducive to teacher-student interaction, and is not conducive to brainstorming and association creation. From the perspective of physical environment, it is difficult to maintain efficient group discussion, group collaboration and effective classroom interaction with fixed tables and chairs and little discussion writing space. Raised platform, is not conducive to the teacher down the platform, the platform position also pull far the distance between the teacher and the students. From the perspective of equipment, a single multimedia device cannot show and evaluate students' achievements in real time. The power supply and wireless network in the classroom have weak support for students' own device, i.e. bring your own device (BYOD).

2.2   Public Learning Space with Low User Experience

In the early point of view, the public learning space in the teaching buildings of universities is more concerned with the economy and safety of public space and other factors, and it is not recommended to gather people freely. Closed Spaces and corridor are more used, and students cannot enter without permission. In an interview with the Colombian newspaper EL Tiempo, Frank Locker, a professor at harvard's school of education/school of architectural design, even called the learning space a prison, arguing that schools should have a sense of community. At present, the public learning space of most universities, from the spatial structure and the size of the venue to the indoor and outdoor supporting facilities, is basically constructed from the perspective of "educator" teaching, giving priority to the convenience of teachers and facilitating managers [3]. In addition, the shortage of classrooms and library seats is a common problem in universities. The public spaces such as school corridor and lobby are mostly standardized design of traffic space, and the ecology is not friendly enough, resulting in relatively low user experience. Lack of connectivity to the surrounding classroom learning environment and social features are not conducive to creating a learning atmosphere of interactive communication and collision of wisdom.

2.3   Lack of Teaching Decisions Supported by Big Data Analysis and Learning Behavior Analysis

Since the form of the class teaching system of Comenius "The Great Didactic" has been established, the same or similar age characteristics and cognitive level are the basic premise of the traditional school placement teaching. The formulation and adjustment of teaching decision such as teaching objectives, teaching activities, and teaching evaluation in the teaching process of teachers are standardized behaviors at the expense of individualized needs of students. At the same time, due to the large number of students, the traditional classroom teaching observation method is difficult to obtain the behavior data of all students. It is difficult for teachers to comprehensively observe and record the learner's learning situation. It is difficult for managers to accurately quantify the teacher's teaching behavior and student learning behavior in classroom teaching, students are difficult to fully express themselves, the evaluation of teaching and learning is difficult to be scientific and precise, the optimization and improvement of teaching and learning lacks the support of data.

At present, most universities do not have an information-based classroom interaction system, such as the handheld feedback system. Even if equipped with a small number, it is difficult to benefit all classes. Due to the lack of appropriate auxiliary tools for classroom interaction, it is difficult for teachers to grasp the design of the form, time and content of classroom interaction and the control of the interaction process [4].

Such a learning environment affects students' performance in the classroom more or less, the students' participation in the classroom is low, and the teacher-student interaction is less. In addition, limited by class time and the number of students, teach-led/fronted closed questions only require students to show specific facts, which makes it difficult to complete the initiation-response-feedback IRF interaction cycle [4]. Hence, "Class questions" is ineffective.

3 The Overall Design Idea of University Intelligent Learning Environment Centered on Improving User Experience

The learning environment is the place and foundation for effective learning. The learning environment renovation is the premise of education and teaching reform. The learning environment with good user experience will make the dialogue happen more naturally. The "Redesign Learning Space" has been mentioned in the Horizon Report (Higher Education) for the past three years. In the 2018 report, it has changed from the "mid-term trend" in 2017 to the "short-term trend". Redesigning the learning space will be the focus of higher education. The purpose of redesigning the learning space is to design a variety of physics teaching spaces under the support of digital technology to help individuals and groups find a more appropriate learning style [5], so that the environment can inject new impetus into the growth of learners. It can be seen that the design of the learning environment mainly starts from two aspects: physical space and virtual space [6].

After researching the learning environment of Nanyang Technological University, Sichuan University, Peking University and Shanghai Jiaotong University, this research starts with the human-oriented physical learning environment design and the smart learning environment supported by digital technology, and analyzes the design concept of a smart learning environment centered on improving user experience and its application practice in South China University of Technology.

4 Design Concept and Practical Case of Physical Learning Environment Centered on Improving User Experience

4.1 Learning-Centered Furniture Design on the Comfort Level of Students

The use of free combination of mobile tables and chairs, focus on the combination and application of teaching furniture, highlighting the comfort, flexibility and harmony, and requirements to meet the needs of different course scenes. As shown in Fig. 1, different classroom layouts can arrange different learning activities and educational practices. Flexible indoor layouts and seats are convenient for students to participate in classroom teaching activities. Bright modern office facilities are conducive to mobilizing students' excitement and sense of professionalism. The seats are ergonomic in design, and the tables and chairs are flexible, movable and can be combined as needed. Students sit together in groups of three or five. Even with their backs to the teacher, mobile learning devices and screens on multiple walls can ensure all-angle classroom interaction to meet the needs of different teaching and group discussion. The splicing of the desk adopts strong magnetic tape and clasp to achieve double fixation and overall uniformity. The wiring hidden in the floor can be used with the application of BYOD mobile terminals such as tablet and notebook.

Fig. 1. Learning-centered furniture design for intelligent learning environment to enhance user experience.

The space layout is flexible and the desks and chairs are ergonomic. Depending on the area, each classroom provides 1–3 all-in-one machines. Each wall is covered with a glass whiteboard or coated with nano wall. Different learning groups can be freely combined according to different teaching needs, and carry out group learning with the corresponding wall display screen or writing board.

4.2 The Wall-Centered Space Design for Assisting Students' Creativity and Achievements

According to the school's funds, around the wall, deploy a blackboard, whiteboard, glass magnetic whiteboard, or paint a writable paint such as rewritable nano wall paint on the wall. At least two "walls" in each classroom can be used by students to write, and become a brainstorming, discussion, and learning achievement display area, as shown in Fig. 2. Through the change of the space environment, the students actively participate in, interact, explore and contribute to the learning behavior, and stimulate teachers to have more interest and willingness in the innovation and exploration of the teaching form. Committed to designing an open learning space that allows teachers and students to work together and interact more.

Fig. 2. The wall-centered space design to assist students' creativity and achievements in terms of user experience.

Deploy a fixed or mobile all-in-one machine, display screen, etc. in the classroom, and use the split-screen display technology and multi-screen interactive technology to support the interaction between teachers and students, and give full play to the role of students' own devices. Media with memory functions such as electronic blackboards can extend the brain function of learners, making it easy for teachers and students to remember at any time. Inside and outside the classroom, teachers can interact with students' handwriting, image interaction and video interaction. The student terminal can interact with the group discussion screen, the teaching dual screen and the group discussion screen, and the group discussion screen. Rich interactive means deepen the level of interaction and enhance students' sense of learning achievement and self-efficacy.

4.3 Renovation of the University Public Learning Space to Create a Learning Environment Concept - Study Everywhere

In the renovation of public learning space, the concept of service education and intensive integration is adopted. Natural energy is utilized to strengthen space greening design. Different learning spaces are provided according to different learning forms to attract and guide students to study, research, communicate or relax in the public learning space, as shown in Fig. 3.

Fig. 3. Renovation of the university public learning space.

Moreover, the first phase of learning space renovation was carried out in the Boxue building of South China University of Technology, giving full play to the public learning space as a demand for learning, exhibition, social contact and rest. According to the adult reading distance of 3.75–8 m, set up the creative reading area, provide the network and power interface, equipped with books, media resources and so on; renovate the patio to learn the garden; in the overhead floor, corridors and corners, public spaces, corners and bumps In the area, there are small leisure tables and chairs with a variety of tones combined with each other; through moving furniture, green plants, bookshelves and other movable building components, the space is enclosed, and a relatively independent and quiet immersive learning space is established.

Furthermore, China is in the era of mass innovation and mass entrepreneurship, universities pay great attention to the cultivation of students' awareness of entrepreneurship and innovation and innovators' ability. In the public learning space, the theme corridor will be built, and the theme display panels and other publicity materials will be built to superimpose the demand on the function of learning needs, so as to satisfy the display of student innovators and practical works. The informal learning space can be seen everywhere, and it becomes a complex space for various functions such as traffic evacuation, communication activities, and display, creating a learning environment of "study everywhere" and a learning atmosphere of "everyone learning".

5   Case Study on the Design and Application of Intelligent Learning Environment in University to Enhance User Experience

On June 21, 2018, the ministry of education held a new era national conference on undergraduate education in institutions of higher learning. At the conference, 150 colleges and universities jointly issued the declaration on first-class undergraduate education, proposing to cultivate first-class talents and build first-class undergraduate education. There are ten articles in the declaration on first-class undergraduate education, among which Article 5 proposes to promote the classroom revolution and turn the silent and one-way classroom into an interactive place for collision of thoughts and enlightenment of wisdom. Article 7 proposes to vigorously promote the application of modern information technology, build smart classrooms, smart laboratories and smart campuses, explore and implement networked, digital, intelligent and personalized education, and reshape education and teaching forms [2]. In order to reconstruct learning, it is necessary to reconstruct the classroom, get through the physical space and virtual space, and avoid 'High Technology Low Learning'. Therefore, with the hardware renovation, highlighting the advantages of the new generation of information technology represented by the IoT, cloud computing, and big data, the teaching quality analysis supervision can be controlled, and provide data and decision-making assistance for the optimization of teaching and learning. Learning analysis, IoT technology, and mobile internet technology supported by big data can better realize the informationization and intelligence of teaching and management processes, and create a smart learning environment with high user experience.

5.1   Use Existing Equipment to Renovate and Optimize Resource Allocation

Make full use of the original equipment in the classroom for low-cost renovation, pay attention to diversification, multi-function, and re-usability. For example: using standardized monitoring equipment to achieve normalized recording, online supervision, cross-campus interactive live classroom. The existing classrooms are classified and renovated, and the large classrooms are used for the large class teaching of famous teachers, so as to make full use of the resources of famous teachers, and the small classrooms are used for the personalized and discussion-based small class teaching, so as to achieve the optimal allocation of classroom resources.

5.2 Intelligent Management and Operation of Learning Environment

As students study in the classroom for a long time, classroom illumination and air quality not only greatly affect the students' physical health, but also play an important role in the students' learning quality and efficiency. Studies have shown that working or learning efficiency decreases by 4% at warmer temperatures and 6% at cooler temperatures [7]. Therefore, the classroom, based on the IoT and Internet technology, combines new technologies, such as big data, cloud computing and artificial intelligence to automatically monitor and adjust environmental data such as temperature, humidity, illumination and carbon dioxide content in the learning environment and public space, as shown in Fig. 4. According to different teaching scenes and standards, automatic start and adjustment of air conditioning, fresh air system and other environmental equipment are carried out to enable students to study in a healthy and comfortable environment with high efficiency. In terms of operation and maintenance, equipment assets in the learning environment are managed and operated in the whole life cycle to improve the quality and efficiency of equipment use and greatly reduce failure rate through early warning. At the same time, indoor and outdoor visual system and all-in-one machine that are unified with the campus image system are deployed at the main entrance and exit of the corridor. In combination with the electronic class board and other information release terminals at the entrance of the classroom, efficient campus information dissemination can be realized with the help of cloud technology and network technology.

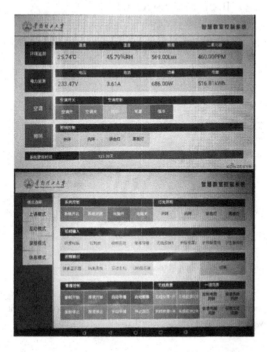

Fig. 4. Intelligent classroom control system of South China University of Technology.

5.3   Intelligent Analysis of Teaching and Learning Behavior

The collection and analysis system of learning behavior based on classroom big data, real recording classroom scenes through the recording and broadcasting system, collecting multi-modal data of learning behaviors such as language, expressions and actions of students, providing multi-dimensional intelligence analysis information such as students' concentration curve, number of interactions between teachers and students and multimedia use, S - T behavior curve, head-up rate, and head-down rate, provide big data analysis results for teaching supervision, teachers' improvement of teaching methods and students' improvement of learning methods, support teaching method innovation, and provide personalized teaching resources and activity design; Through procedural quantitative assessment, timely warnings help teachers find learning underachiever, provide big data support for teaching and learning scientific decision-making, improve the objectivity and standardization of teaching effect evaluation.

As shown in Fig. 5, the system recorded the number of times that students visited the courseware of the "digital learning" course in the first semester of the 2017–2018 academic year. The system automatically records the students' answers to questions in a class, and displays the scores and time of all students' answers in real time in the mobile terminal of the teacher, and shows an early warning for students with low accuracy and high time consumption, as shown in Fig. 6.

Fig. 5. A example of mobile learning system automatically counting the number of people watching the courseware.

Fig. 6. A example of mobile learning system automatically recording the score and time spent in answering questions.

5.4 Use of Interactive Classroom Teaching System for Intelligent Classroom Teaching

This study takes "digital learning" in the first semester of 2017–2018 academic year as an example to carry out flipped classroom teaching in an intelligent learning environment. Using the student group high viscosity of mobile devices, smart phones and mobile applications, to carry out the teaching reform of mixed learning modes such as flipping classrooms, enhance the learning effect, and solve the individualization of students with different cognitive levels and information literacy skills to a certain extent. The released class time is used to develop high-level thinking skills such as collaborative task solving. Before class, teachers send notices, micro video and other teaching resources and assignments to students' mobile phones, encouraging students to use fragmented time for personalized learning at their own pace. In class, the teacher's PowerPoint file is pushed to the student's mobile phone synchronously, and the student can check it in time during the course of listening, as shown in Fig. 7. Use mobile phones to organize teaching activities such as check-ins, votes/questionnaires, question answers, as shown in Fig. 8, in-class quizzes, bullet screens, snap answers, random roll call answers, designated student answers, discussion groups, etc., so as to improve the participation rate of students in class, continuously bring about a small climax in class teaching and hold students' attention. If students do not understand a certain slide, they can click the "do not understand" button on the page or make comments. The teacher can see which slide the student does not understand in real time on the mobile phone, as shown in Fig. 9, after the class, they are specifically explained by voice or text. The data are analyzed according to the learning behavior, and the consolidated learning resources are pushed out after class. To some extent, classroom reform realizes "discovering differences, improving capabilities and developing personality".

Fig. 7. Slides played by the lecturer can be seen by the students synchronously and asynchronously in the interactive classroom teaching system.

Fig. 8. Students' responses to the objective questions in class teaching.

Fig. 9. Students' feedback for the teaching.

6 Results

After a semester trial, the mean value of the students' experience in the five courses are all above 4.8, where the full score is 5 points, which is highly praised by the students. The scores of the students are 10% before the general education class, and the quality of the undergraduate classroom teaching is excellent. The students interviewed believe that the use of mobile apps as interactive tools in class can improve their concentration in class, enable them to actively think and participate in class, and help them get to know their learning partners in class through interaction, so that they have a strong sense of learning achievement. The questionnaire survey of 128 students shows that all students think that the physical environment of the smart classroom and learning space is better than the traditional physical environment, and they like it very much, and the user experience is very high [8]. According to the data analysis of learning behavior analysis, the sleeping rate in class is almost zero. Students say that in this kind of class, the attention of teachers and the dominant position of students in the classroom are not easy and they are embarrassed to doze off. This study adopts the self-learning quantization table and problem-solving ability quantization table, which are verified by credibility and validity. Respectively in the first week of the semester and the last week of the student to carry on the preliminary test and post test, the use of SPSS 11.5 for data statistics and independent sample t-test, Sig. (bilateral) = 0.000 < 0.01, that is, there are significant differences between the pre-test and post-test scores, and the post-test scores are significantly higher than the pre-test scores, indicating that the environment can effectively improve students' self-learning ability and problem-solving ability.

7 Conclusion

In an increasingly people-oriented smart society, universities as an important training base for talents, are more focused on building a smart learning environment centered on enhancing user experience. To promote the innovation of teaching content, teaching method, learning method and school organization with the innovation of learning environment, and improve the quality of innovative talents.

Acknowledgements. This research is supported by 2018 Guangdong Higher Education Teaching Reform Project - "Empirical Research on the Application Mode of Smart Internet Supporting Environment Based on Mobile Internet", 2018 Higher Education Research Fund Project, South China University of Technology - "The Construction, Application, Intelligent Operation and Maintenance Research on College Wisdom Classroom from the Perspective of International Campus", and 2018 University Teaching and Research Teaching Reform Project, South China University of Technology - "The Current Situation, Problems and Countermeasures of the School's Inverted Classroom".

References

1. Ding, C., Wang, Y.: Smart learning space: from knowledge sharing to knowledge creation. Modern Educ. Technol. **8**, 40–46 (2017)
2. First-class undergraduate education declaration. http://www.moe.gov.cn/jyb_xwfb/xw_fbh/moe_2069/xwfbh_2018n/xwfb_20180622/sfcl/201806/t20180622_340649.html. Accessed 21 Jan 2019
3. Locker, F.: El papel del profesor es ser la guía para la exploración. In: EL TIMEPO, pp. 1–16 (2017)
4. Lu, F., Liu, Z., Liu, Z.: Smart phone endowed intelligent teaching for university general education curriculum in China. In: 2018 IEEE International Conference on Teaching, Assessment, and Learning for Engineering (TALE), pp. 690–695 (2018)
5. Johnson, L., Becker, S.A., Cummins, M., Estrada, V., Freeman, A., Hall, C.: Contribution title. NMC horizon report: 2016 higher education edition. The New Media Consortium, Austin (2016)
6. Wang, Z.: Recurring teaching space reconstruction. China Educ. Netw. 11–12 (2018)
7. Lan, L., Wargocki, P., Wyon, D.P., Lian, Z.: Effects of thermal discomfort in an office on perceived air quality, SBS symptoms, physiological responses, and human performance. Indoor Air **21**(5), 376–390 (2011)
8. Lu, F.: University flipping classroom teaching in mobile internet environment. High. Eng. Educ. Res. **4**, 158–167 (2018)

Universal Quadrant Model (UQM): Enhancing Usability of a Collaborative Cloud Tool for Sharing Best Practices Among Novice Users

Justus N. Nyagwencha[1]($\boxtimes$) and Cheryl D. Seals[2]($\boxtimes$)

[1] United States International University-Africa, P.O. Box 14634-00800,
Nairobi, Kenya
justus.nyagwencha@hamptonu.edu
[2] Auburn University, 2703 Shelby Center, Auburn, AL 36832, USA
sealscd@auburn.edu

Abstract. This paper proposes and simulates an innovative approach to hierarchical group management model, the Universal Quadrant Model (UQM); a recursive, nondeterministic and backtracking generic algorithm. The model is as a result of For Youth For Life (FYFL) cloud tool research that was tasked to identify a unique solution to a problem of identifying an easy to use, scalable, cost effective, and fault tolerant collaborative system or tool for members of communities of practice to share best practices in line with Computer Supportive Collaborative Work (CSCW) field. The research was conducted in 4 phases; Phase I dealt with requirements gathering, Phase II was prototyping the system, Phase III was testing and comprehensive evaluation and Phase IV was to solve the Group Management Problem. Phase I - III problems were deciphered following the software engineering principles solutions, however, we could not find a proper documented method for managing groups spread across a spatial locality i.e. 4-H members (study group) which then necessitated the design of UQM. We consider UQM a computational framework that manages self-purporting and emerging groups and provides a mechanism that limits fictitious accounts within an online community. It estimates the number of quadrants to represent spatial locality of groups relying on population density as its main input factor. UQM is designed to cope with issues of adaptability, scalability, effectiveness, and efficiency in managing groups within a community of practice and is used for moderating users, navigation, locating and distribution of resources within an online system. The model provides a user friendly and efficient method for moderating a high number of users within groups by automating group formation. It also addresses the membership anonymity problem, and perpetuates self-purporting and sustaining groups within a spatial locality i.e. (a community of practice group). In terms of performance compared to the initial non-recursive method of group creation and management, UQM is recursive, segmenting and self-managing with a $O(n\log_4 n)$ run time. Therefore, implementing UQM presents highly significant run time theoretical gain compared to the initial solution's $O(n)$ performance.

Keywords: Programming · User interface · Usability ·
WebOS (web operating system) · Communities of practice ·
Computer collaborative work · Secure · Access information · Technophobia ·
Online collaboration · For Youth For Life (FYFL) · Cloud

© Springer Nature Switzerland AG 2019
A. Marcus and W. Wang (Eds.): HCII 2019, LNCS 11585, pp. 472–482, 2019.
https://doi.org/10.1007/978-3-030-23538-3_36

1 Introduction

Engaging community of practice members especially a broad youth audience across this country and internationally is a tremendous challenge in today's online environment. Current and developing communication technologies offer fast paced online environments through which they can engage in entertainment, online games, social networking, knowledge searches, and other experiences.

The online learning environment is largely informal in nature in that the user explores at their initiative in a self-directed manner. It can also be formal in nature as a more deliberately directed experience with established objectives generally related to obtaining certification of some sort or a degree. Another approach combines aspects of informal and formal learning in what is known as non-formal learning with some crossover. Non-formal learning, which also includes experiential learning, for youth is the predominate form of learning in organizations such as 4-H Youth Development, scouting, and other venues that target a youth audience. Many internet sites provide learning for youth through one approach or the other.

This research explores how to provide content to the public in formal, informal, and non-formal methods through a collaborative online tool that is easy to use and learn. The research is in line with CSCW (computer supportive collaborative work) the mission of land grant universities and the U.S. Department of Agriculture (USDA). The exploration and its success is pegged on a more recent concept of e-extension that seeks for a means of extending knowledge and information in a more focused manner from the land grant university system (LGU), the Cooperative Extension Service (CES), and to some degree the U.S. Department of Agriculture (USDA) to the American public through a common online means. By engaging Communities of Practice (CoPs) online, content to its clientele or communities can be provided in a secure and user friendly manner.

This paper is organized follows: Sect. 2 gives the literature review. Section 3 outlines the approach to the Research and the basis of our research. Section 4 outlines the experiment, experimental results and analysis. Section 5 concludes and discusses several extensions.

2 Literature Review

A lot of research is focused in the area of CSCW (computer supportive collaborative work) after researchers from various academic disciplines realized that computers should be designed according to the user's needs and that various technological designs and efforts can greatly benefit from the input of others in the areas of cognitive science and humanities. This has led to a new theory and branch of computer science CSCW and user centered design.

The usage of the term CSCW inside various academic fields and fortiori across the fields is wide [3]. Beside the wide range of usage of the term, this research will focus and include specific tasks which will require member participants to converge to a shared understanding of CSCW among members of communities of practice for the purposes of collecting data, analyzing, and evaluating it to ascertain the impact on subjects. The study chooses to utilize a cloud based tool to support communities of practice in a method that is user friendly, secure, efficient, effective, and ease of use compared to most social CSCW networks systems. This work is inspired by the appeal of Facebook and its ease of use. The motivation is to create an environment that will support a large community of practice in virtual space. The environment will encourage K-12 teachers and 4-H members to share and re-use best practices in the initial phase.

CSWC is an area of study with numerous unexplored benefits for a cross section of the population groups [2, 3]. For example, through CSWC K-12 teachers can be encouraged to share and re-use best practices as a community of practice (to emulate) the business industry which has highly benefited from sharing best practices through collaboration (e.g. the software development industry that successfully utilizes code-re-use during software development through collaboration). This project aims at evaluating and validating a tool or framework that can be used to encourage sharing of best practices within a community of practice to steadily benefit and enhance member's career aspirations through CSCW as witnessed in the code-re-use within the software development industry [5]. The research will validate the need to incorporate a tool to support virtual communities to share and re-use of best practices and take advantage of the numerous benefits offered by the CSCW tools. This work will be validated through surveys about the FYFL cloud and a virtual community that has been developed in our HCI lab in collaboration with the Alabama e-extension department. The research findings are aimed at highlighting the following benefits of collaborating through the secure CSWC tools verses traditional methods. These benefits include:

1. Possibility to Communicate Effectively
   There is a high a possibility for members of a community of practice to learn how to communicate effectively, by reaching out to each other and building trust and understanding through friendships by seeking common ground [5, 6].
2. Motivation to Collaborate
   Members of community of practice groups will build a sense of responsibility by feeling obligated to the group and will take responsibility for the group. In due course they will learn to be responsible and become team players with the skills necessary to succeed in today's world [5, 6].
3. Secure and Efficient Access to Information
   Members of community of practice will access information and other resources easily without the restriction of time and place, unlike the prevalent face-to-face collaboration system. In addition the permanency of records on shared practices, the independence of time and place to access information will allow members (e.g. students, teachers, and 4-H members) to learn and complete the tasks at hand remotely. This will also eliminate the fear of starting from scratch when the need for a practice arises and encourage members to focus on the task at hand [5, 6].

In this research, a CSCW cloud tool was used and evaluated by authors as an effective secure online tool for sharing best practices. The study investigated and focused on usability and security issues that affect online environments. The evaluation was to ensure that the tool met minimum online usability standards and had robust security to safeguard member privacy. The process utilized HCI techniques and design guidelines gathered feedback on how to improve the initial system from usability experts, K-12 teachers, 4-H members who were nominated as the initial user test population. The survey responses provided valuable input for re-designing user interfaces and re-affirmed security concerns as a major issue among novice computer users. However, issues concerning security and how it relates to HCI will not be addressed in detail in this research.

The main goals of this research were to examine the issue of providing a collaborative tool to support communities of practice members engaged in informal learning online and propose a group management model for emerging groups by combing an informal learning and spatial locality theories. We relied on CSCW usability evaluation acceptance test approach necessary to effectively provide an environment feasible to accommodate and support novice users. The work resulted into a FYFL cloud tool to support communities and a model to foster and manage emerging groups relying on literature reviews on collaborative theory and online group principals. Our recommendation is a first attempt supported by empirical usability and acceptance tests data from focus groups on online collaboration and information learning.

Thus, the research utilizes a cloud tool (FYFL) and focus groups to validate a CSCW tool in relation to (1) sharing and re-use of best practices, (2) justify the usability of the selected collaborative tool (FYFL) and the effects on novice users.

3   The Approach to the Research

This study has identified K-12 teachers and 4-H club members as the initial subgroups. The main criterion for choosing members to participate in the study is a voluntarily acceptance of teachers and schools to participate by willingly subscribing to use the FYFL cloud tool to collaborate and share best practices. Participants provided a feedback on its usability, efficiency and suitability for collaboration purposes.

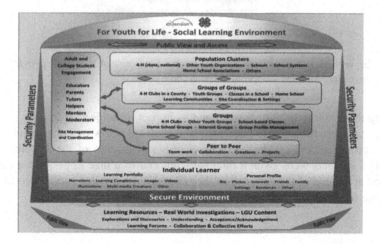

Fig. 1. The Initial For Youth, For Life theory – The Envisioned Secure Social Learning Environment Copyright. © 2009 Auburn University, Alabama Cooperative Extension System.

The 5 main goals of the study are:

1. Select an appropriate secure tool for CoP to share best practice for available utilizing an expert inspection and feedback report.
2. Configure the secure tool to accommodate the user group in accordance to software engineering principles.
3. Come up with a minimalist tutorial for the redesigned tool.
4. Conduct a usability and acceptance test with the test group before deploying the tool.
5. Design a usability management model for group formation and perpetuation.

Thus the study aims to encourage and promote the informal learning through a new environment for collaboration among groups of CoP. We hope to accomplish this goal by focusing on the usability of the tool because a previous survey conducted among the K-12 teacher population in the initial stages of this study, concluded that teachers will utilize the prototype tool only with improved usability. To ascertain the usability of the selected tool, a broad array of questions to be answered by the experimental participants were created to gather data for the research through a survey. The survey required a user to identify themselves as a novice or having advanced computer skills for the purpose of

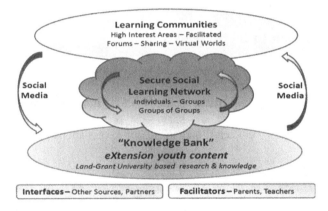

Fig. 2. The revised and improved Social Learning Environment theory Copyright © 2010 Auburn University, Alabama Cooperative Extension System

assessing the usability level of the tool and its impact on subjects (Fig. 1).

The study was broken into three phases as outlined below to gather requirements, create a prototype and conduct a comprehensive evaluation of the system. During evaluation, subjects were given a minimalist tutorial to utilize to perform a series of tasks and at the end of the list of tasks they completed a detailed survey questionnaire to provide feedback on their experiences with the system.

3.1   Phase I: Requirements

Requirements were gathered in phase I of the study to assemble the building blocks for the system. A thorough scenario based usability, security inspection and analysis approach ensued on the existing tools/software to identify the best suited tool to support the gathered requirements.

3.2   Phase II: Prototyping

Guided by the requirements, the team selected two suitable tools and modified them for evaluation. The resulting tool received a prototype step through scenario based usability, security inspection and analysis from the experts group. The modifications were necessary before testing with the potential users in line with CSCW guidelines. The requirements served as foundation for an iterative design and development work for the desirable community of practice tool in Phase III.

3.3   Phase III: Testing and Comprehensive Evaluation

A comprehensive analytical and empirical analysis gauges the success of the collaborative tool to support informal learning among CoP groups. The process included a comparative expert security and usability inspection of the selected and modified tool, usability and acceptance survey test of the FYFL by potential users, and a detailed qualitative and quantitative analysis of results from study. The expert evaluation stages were meant to produce results leading to the answers to the research questions while potential user's data served as a guideline for measures to be taken to improve the overall usability and acceptance of the cloud tool.

Thus, the study adopted a cloud environment to leverage existing tendencies of human social nature and utilized it to enhance a collaborative environment based on the expert recommendation after reviewing more than a dozen tools. We anticipated that the participants of this work will have improved efficacy of their computer literacy, improved educational performance and more intrinsic motivation to spend more time concentrated on efforts that promote scientific content materials at the end of the study. In the second phase of the study, participants will work together as teams in a community of practice (e.g. student and teacher teams) that will utilize and contribute to this sharing and learning environment [1]. The usability and acceptability results of this study support the creation of an environment that supports communities of practice in creating and sharing more content materials in a virtual community in a cloud environment as outlined in Fig. 2. Our hope was that this method of resource presentation will increase the usage of educational materials and applications among community of practice members in line with HCI and CSCW research. The environment will support improved use of materials within the virtual community leveraging the ease of use and popularity of other social networking environment such as Facebook with enhanced security.

3.4   Phase IV: Group Management Problem

Managing 4-H members spread across wide region i.e. a state is challenging and poses an insider threat problem for users. To alleviate this problem, a formal model to manage this complexity is required to allow administrators to effectively navigate and locate resources within the system. For example, it is easy for an individual to moderate 100 members in a group, but intractable to navigate if the groups grows and surpasses 10,000 members within a spatial locality. To moderate a topic or a discussion among thousands of members by a single administrator is not solved through the currently available method. The model is effective in managing registered members through an appointed group leader. But, it is overwhelming for one administrator if the member's population exceeds a certain threshold (P), since the current system doesn't focus on monitoring and moderation of members activities in case there is an influx of member subscription.

Our analysis on the current solution reveals that it is intractable, static and lists all members in a single list without associating them to groups automatically. The model is 100% dependent on the administrator to create and assign registered members to specific groups/various groups manually. This method is recommended for possible for managing groups with a small number of users i.e. $N \leq 1000$ but is intractable and inefficient for a bigger N (i.e. $N > 10000$). Thus, the existing model does not support self-purporting and sustaining groups important for the success a collaborative tool to foster informal education among members of communities of practice.

4   The Universal Quadrant Model and Simulation Results

To overcome the $N > 10000$ limitation imposed on our earlier solution, we initially suggested solution for managing groups of groups. The solution involves listing/creating regions based on the political boundaries and alignments in the United States. The four regions (North East, South, Midwest and West), being the cornerstone and further delaminate the rest into states followed by counties. This is a practical solution, however it has it has it discrepancies. For example, some counties may not have clubs and will lead to dummy clubs without members and could affect the search process when N- is greater. Thus, it makes it an inefficient solution for a group problem. On the other hand, the formation of groups and management of posts is entirely depended on an administrator who should assign then manually an impractical task for an $N > 10000$ especially even considering having many administrators. Doing business this way, will slow the group formation process as well limit sharing of information on the cloud forum. Therefore, this is not an optimal solution for the group problem. It has a color coded interface; but doesn't automate the process or aid in the process of creating self-purporting and sustaining groups. It is an intractable solution

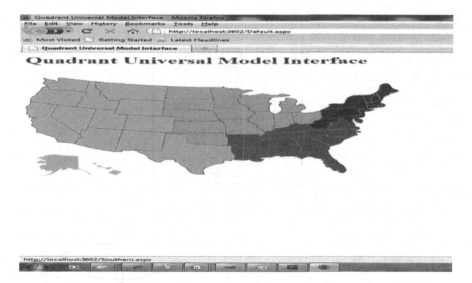

Fig. 3. Conceptual prototype for color coded regions

with an influx with members joining various groups. The solution's prototype is illustrated in Fig. 3. A conceptual prototype of the existing membership and group model supported by a data structure list with O(n) run time is represented by Fig. 3.

Our solution the UQM (universal Quadrant Model) improves the current model by providing a way to alleviating the fictitious membership's problem and promoting self-purporting and sustaining groups. The model allows vetting of memberships by associating applicants with spatial locality groups as well provides a graphical interface for easy management of those groups.

We propose a Quadrant Universal Model algorithm to address the problem. The algorithm will in addition address the membership anonymity problem, perpetuate new manageable groups within a spatial locality and associate it with the original group once a certain membership threshold is reached within a specific quadrant or region.

Managing individuals, groups, and groups of groups geographically (globally) in a less costly, manageable, predictable manner is NP-complete problem without an exact solution. However, the proposed set theory quadrant universal model (QUM) simplifies the management of individuals, groups, and groups of groups spatially and overcomes overlapping of memberships within groups.

QUM is a recursive, nondeterministic, backtracking algorithm that finds all solutions to number of quadrants needed to be represented by spatial locality groups based on the population. The goal is to select a subset of the quadrants and classify them based on geographical location and population density or count. This is meant to ease moderation and elicit training alerts of moderators when need arises (Fig. 4).

Compared to the initial method, UQM is recursive, segmenting and self-managing with $O(n\log_4 n)$ run time compared to the initial solution's $O(n)$ run time. Thus, implementing UQM presents highly significantly run time gain theoretically (Table 1).

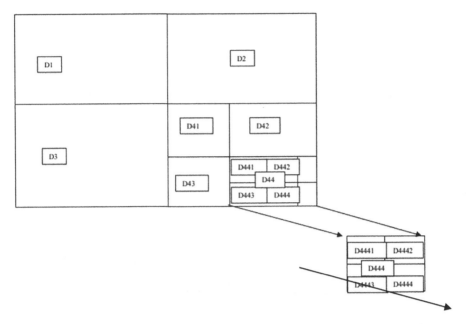

Fig. 4. This is an illustration of the UQM creating new groups recursively.

Table 1. Proposed UQM algorithm is a Tree structure with O(nlog$_4$n) run time.

Algorithm UQM functions as follows:
1. If the quadrant Q is empty, the problem is solved; terminate successfully.
2. Otherwise choose a quadrant (Q) NW, SW, NE or NW (deterministically).
3. Read P, total 4H members P, P-4H members population
4. IF P < threshold
5. Include quadrant in the partial solution.
6. For each quadrant such that P > threshold,
Divide quadrant into NWi, SWi, NEi, SEii = 1
6. Repeat recursively on the reduced quadrant Q.

The extended Universal Quadrant Model implements and defines a user interface for group creation and group management. The simulation which is an extension of the theoretical model provides a login user interface, a color coded group interface for users and managers to visually locate, view, monitor membership group status and determine those ready to split. Having such information at a glance will aid in the process of identifying a leader for the newly created groups. We believe that the color coded user instances, is an improvement on the previous solution which did not have a means of issuing a warning to managers on the size of groups in question.

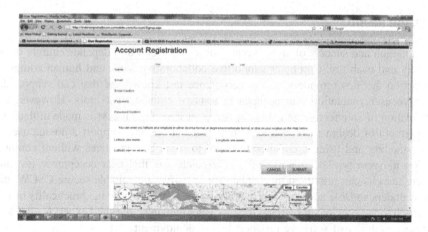

Fig. 5. UQM prototype account registration page

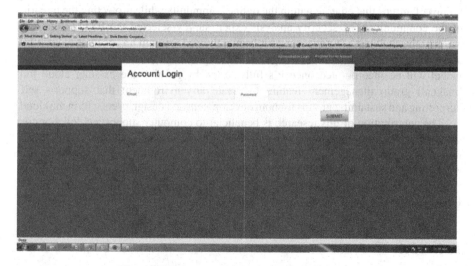

Fig. 6. UQM prototype account registration page

Figure 5, the account registration page uses Google maps for users to sign up and identify themselves in relation to a spatial locality of individuals by entering the latitude and longitude coordinates in the database of the current address and club.

The Information is fundamental in determining which group to be assigned. The process is automated and helps in creating groups as well as maintains accuracy for members since potential members will be vetted by an existing member of their local club limiting the number of false accounts significantly (Fig. 6).

The UQM supports the Table-Insert and Table-Delete. The Table-Insert inserts onto the table an item that occupies a single slot space for one item. Table delete can be thought of as a removing an item from the table.

5 Conclusion

The adoption and success of an informal educational cloud tool depends entirely on its security and usability. Computer supportive collaborative work and human computer interaction theories provide usability acceptance test knowledge that can support the effective user evaluation and acceptance tests of collaborative tools. However, the formulation of an effective and efficient acceptance testing process is made difficult by the plethora of design theories and models that outline how support a novice user in understanding and using a collaborative tool to share best practices without compromising its security. The premise of this research was that user acceptance test and expert analysis can provide a mechanism for identifying a suitable secure CSCW tool that is understandable and easy to use for a novice user. We base the practicality of this approach to the previous research efforts in using human studies and expert feedback to test the suitability of software products before deployment.

Initially our efforts were focused on identifying a viable tool for communities of practice to share best practices but later ventured into defining a model to aid in managing groups of groups that emerge within the online community while protecting the integrity of the community. The security analysis expert survey selected the FYFL cloud tool among other potential candidates and it been validated through an acceptance usability survey data from potential users. On group of group management, the universal quadrant model will be incorporated once it's fully tested by refining the existing cloud tool (manual) group management feature to create an environment that supports self-purporting and sustaining groups for both development and design users within the cloud.

The contribution of this research is beneficial to computer supportive collaborative work (CSCW) design, human computer interaction research, online group theory research, green computing and informal learning research, and usability studies research. Our major contribution is we also the proposed group management model "universal quadrant model (UQM)" aimed at mitigating insider threat within virtual groups and is validated through a simulation.

References

1. Cain, C.: Social networking teaching tools: a computer supported collaborative interactive learning social networking environment for K-12. Maters thesis, Auburn University, Auburn, AL (2010)
2. Diaz, D.P., Cartnal, R.B.: Comparing student learning styles in an online distance learning class and an equivalent on-campus class. Coll. Teach. **47**(4), 130–135 (1999)
3. Dieterle, E.: Handheld devices for ubiquitous learning. In: ISTE Conference. ISTE, Portland (2005)
4. http://link.wits.ac.za/papers/e-index-tanzania.pdf
5. Fahræus, E.R.: Collaborative learning through forum systems – problems and opportunities. Electrum 230, S-164 40 KISTA, Sweden (2000)
6. http://www.answers.com/topic/semiotics
7. Rosson, M.B., Carroll, J.M.: Usability Engineering. Morgan Kuafmann, San Ndiego (2002)
8. Dillenbourg, P.: What Do You Mean by Collaborative Learning: Cognitive and Computation Approaches, pp. 1–19. Elsevier, Geneva/Oxford (1999)

Interaction Testing on Using an E-Book Authoring Tool: A Case Study of the SaiteBooker (UNA-SUS/UFMA, Brazil)

Carla G. Spinillo[1(✉)], Edilson T. S. Reis[1], Ana Emília F. de Oliveira[2],
Dilson Rabelo Júnior[2], Camila S. de C. e Lima[2],
and Katherine M. de Assis[2]

[1] Federal University of Paraná, Curitiba, Brazil
cgspin@gmail.com, edilson.sreis@gmail.com
[2] Federal University of Maranhão, São Luís, Brazil
oliveira.anaemilia@gmail.com,
dilsonrabelo.unasus@gmail.com,
camilasclima@gmail.com, kathmarjorie@gmail.com

Abstract. In Brazil, the use of e-books has grown in the continuing education of health professionals. To facilitate the production of e-books, the Open University of the Unified Health System of the Federal University of Maranhão (UNA-SUS/UFMA) developed the SaiteBooker, a collaborative and open-source authoring tool. An interaction testing was conducted with 39 participants/healthcare professionals in Brazil. The results showed that, in general, the SaiteBooker authoring tool reached satisfactory results on usability and interaction. However, participants had difficulties in performing the task of adding images and videos, coping and pasting content from external links, editing text, and returning to pages. Based upon the results, improvements were made in the SaiteBooker, and recommendations were proposed to the design of graphic interfaces of authoring tools for e-books.

Keywords: Authoring tool · Usability · Information design

1 Introduction

The evaluation of digital artifacts and systems with users is fundamental to guarantee their effectiveness and efficiency not only in terms of usability but also in the user experience (UX) during the interaction. The literature provides a range of assessment methods/techniques with users that can vary in approach (qualitative and quantitative) and nature (behavioral and attitudinal) [1]. Methods/techniques with a quantitative approach evaluate users' attitudes and/or behavior in the interaction with artifacts and systems in an indirect, usually remote, way. On the other hand, those with a qualitative approach directly evaluate possible attitudes and/or behavior of the users when using/interacting with digital artifacts/systems. This may occur in laboratory condition (e.g., interaction testing, interviews) or in real context of use (e.g., ethnographic field studies; diary/camera studies). One of the advantages of the qualitative approach is to

© Springer Nature Switzerland AG 2019
A. Marcus and W. Wang (Eds.): HCII 2019, LNCS 11585, pp. 483–494, 2019.
https://doi.org/10.1007/978-3-030-23538-3_37

enable more in-depth verification of limitations and shortcomings of digital artifacts and systems with users.

Among the qualitative techniques, the interaction test is highlighted in this article because it allows the direct observation of the use of digital artifacts and systems through key tasks selected to be performed by the users. The selection of these tasks is usually based upon previous evaluations with experts, such as heuristic evaluation and technical inspection. The results of expert evaluation make it possible to foreseen difficulties that users may have when using digital artifacts and systems which should be verified in the interaction test.

Aspects of the graphic interface design may jeopardize the use of digital artifacts when they do not either meet design principles or promote a pleasant UX. This is particularly relevant in the health education field, given the need to train health professionals through digital artifacts, such as e-books. Considering this, the present article shows the results of an interaction test of the SaiteBooker authoring tool for e-books, which was developed by the Open University of the Unified Health System (UNA-SUS) of the Federal University of Maranhão, Brazil.

1.1 Interaction Design and Graphic Interface of Digital Artifacts

A good interaction design of digital artifacts and systems led them to be usable, effective and easy to learn, so as to provide users with a pleasant experience. A good interaction design prevents negative aspects of user experience (UX), such as frustration and annoyance, while at the same time, may promote positive attitudes/behavior, such as enjoyment and engagement [2]. For that, the graphic interface should be a facilitator of the interaction in the use of digital artifacts/systems. In this sense, the design of icons, the composition and visualization of interface elements should ease interaction. A good interaction design is only possible with a good graphic interface design.

When developing a graphic interface, some design principles must be taken into account to achieve effectiveness in usability and UX in the use of digital artifacts. Among the principles of interface design the following are highlighted here: visibility, action feedback, constraints to delimit interaction, interface consistency, and social signifier [2, 3]. The former principle regards the interface elements that must be visible to be easily perceived by users. In this sense, graphic aspects such as color, size, simplicity of form, organization and hierarchy of the elements are paramount to promote visualization of icons, buttons and menus in the interface. The more visible the elements of the graphic interface are, the more users will know how to interact with them, using their functions. The principle of action feedback assures users that the action was actually performed, allowing them to proceed in using the artifact/system. The principle of constraints aims at preventing interactions that may lead users to unwanted paths/actions during the interaction. In this sense, it predicts errors in the interaction. Thus, it establishes the forms of interaction which are beneficial to users. The principle of consistency ensures that there is no variation in the way the interface presents its elements and their functions. Finally, the principle of social signifier refers to elements of the interface design that 'give clues' to users about the functions they convey, i.e., what they are for (e.g., icons and buttons).

The principles abovementioned are in alignment with the literature on heuristics for digital artifacts and systems [3–7]. Among them, it is worth mentioning the heuristics for interface design proposed by Nielsen in the 1990's [8], but still in use since they aim at the design of intuitive graphic interfaces and systems. The author emphasizes that the system should employ words/language and concepts from users' repertoire to facilitate interaction (Match between system and the real world); users should have control and freedom in interacting with the graphic interface as for instance undo/redo an action (User control and freedom). The graphic interface should also present elements easily recognizable by users (Recognition rather than recall), and the system must be flexible and efficient to accommodate the demands of both experienced and novice users (Flexibility and efficiency of use).

Therefore, heuristics and design principles aim for an optimal user experience (UX) when they interact with digital artifacts and systems. In this sense, it is worth mentioning the well-known UX Honeycomb diagram proposed by Morville [9], which is composed of seven key-qualities of digital artifacts/systems: to be useful, usable, desirable, accessible, credible, findable and valuable (Fig. 1). Some of these qualities are extrinsic to users, i.e., refer to the artifact/system itself, whereas others are intrinsic to users. These are related to users' emotions and expectations which must be fulfilled by the artifact/system. In this sense, usable, useful, accessible and findable can be considered as extrinsic or objective qualities since they are in the domain of the artifact/system. On the other hand, desirable, credible and valuable would be the intrinsic or subjective qualities as they are in the domain of the users. Accordingly, for an optimal UX, an artifact/system should have a good usability (usable); provide the conditions to be used by people with disabilities (accessible); display easy-to-find elements/functionalities in the graphic interface (findable), make it possible to users to perform the intended tasks (useful), meet the aesthetic expectations of users (desirable), and promote trust and credibility (credible). As a result, the users will value the digital artifact/system (valuable). In this sense, it is possible to say that an artifact/system will be desirable, credible and valuable as long as it is useful, usable, accessible and (its elements are) findable.

Considering that UX aspects are related to how users behave when interacting with artifacts and systems, it is important to understand users' information behavior. Among the types of information behavior acknowledged in the literature, the information seek, information search and information use are highlighted here, as they are pertinent to users' experience with digital artifacts/systems [5, 10]. Information seek regards satisfying users' need to reach a goal, such as creating an e-book in a health topic. Information search regards the resources used to achieve a goal, such as looking for an authoring tool to create e-books. Finally, information use regards the physical and mental acts to utilize the acquired information, incorporating individual's existing knowledge, such as employing previous experience with digital artifacts/systems to use an e-book authoring tool.

The seek and search behaviors are related to the need for cognition. Individuals aim at finding order and meaning in the environment, that is expressed as a need to know and a desire to be informed [10]. Users receive and shape information from their cognitive perspective, aligned to their needs and motivation. They also seek to engage and enjoy agile information processing when interacting with digital artifacts/systems [5].

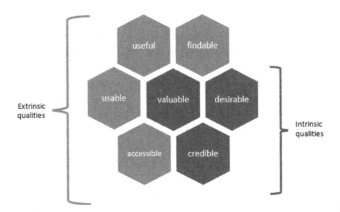

Fig. 1. UX Honeycomb diagram by Morville [9] with indication of the intrinsic and extrinsic qualities proposed here.

Based on users' information behavior, Lonsdale, Lonsdale and Lim [5] propose the Online Information Processing Model (Fig. 2) which considers three stages: (1) information need; (2) information seeking (users start a task, users continue the tasks and users find and extract information) and (3) information use. According to this model, users employ reading and navigation strategies when starting the task, and their task performance is influenced by factors the amount, quality, complexity and accessibility of information, and the time available to read the information. These factors may result in negative consequences, such as cognitive overload and strain, poor engagement, attention, retention and recall.

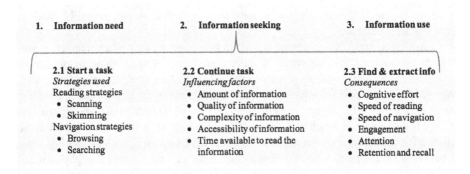

Fig. 2. The online information processing model based on Lonsdale, Lonsdale and Lim [5].

However, these undesirable results can be minimized, or even prevented, by employing information design principles and good practices [5, 6] to promote a positive UX. For example, grouping content units in the graphic interface; limiting typographic fonts and colors; balancing texts and images may decrease users' cognitive overload when interacting with digital artifacts/systems [5, 12]. Thus, graphic interface as well as interaction design are keys to an optimal UX. This is particularly important in the use of e-book authoring tools in the health field, since some content can be complex, requiring the inclusion of various educational resources (e.g., videos, animations about medical procedures). The following sessions briefly present the authoring tool for e-books in the health field, and the interaction test that evaluated its effectiveness in Brazil.

1.2 SaiteBooker: An Authoring Tool for E-Books

Several studies have investigated the efficacy of e-books in communicating content, pointing out their advantages and disadvantages, as well as readers' preference for printed books or e-books [7, 10, 13–20]. Among the advantages of e-books, the literature points: their flexibility in the inclusion and updating of content; the possibility of adding hypermedia resources, videos and animations; and the financial and environmental gains. These regards the cost of producing an e-book that is lesser than of a printed book, and the fact that its production does not generate paper and ink consumption [17].

However, some disadvantages are mentioned in the literature regarding possible discomforts in reading on screen, problems in the use of e-books caused by drawbacks in the interface design, in navigation and interaction design [21]. In order to improve the development of e-books, recommendations have been made, such as the inclusion of hyperlinks in the topics of the table of contents, adjustment of font size to meet individual's preferences/needs, and the inclusion of search resources [10]. Moreover, the employment of visual metaphors from the printed book (e.g., turn page) are suggested to facilitate readers' acceptance of e-books [10].

In Brazil, the use of e-books has grown in the continuing education of health professionals with the creation of the Open University of the Unified Health System (UNA-SUS) in 2008. It is a network of 36 public universities that has offered more than 60 e-courses to 1,097,330 medical professionals. To ease the production of e-books on health education, the UNA-SUS of the Federal University of Maranhão (UFMA) developed the SaiteBooker, a collaborative and open-source authoring tool for e-books. The tool is structured in five main areas:

1. *The project* area to enter general information about the e-books project;
2. *The theme area* to create the layout features of the e-book (e.g., color, font size, line spacing) and/or to choose from a range of themes available (layout default);
3. *The Media area* to upload, store and add images to an ongoing project;
4. *The Canvas area* to typeset the e-book pages and;
5. *The Export area* to upload the created e-book.

To verify the effectiveness of the SaiteBooker, studies have been conducted with experts on technology and information design in Brazil, being: (a) a technical inspection followed by heuristic evaluation and FIP technique (frequency, impact and persistence) to hierarchize problems according to degree of severity attributed to them; and (b) hands-on workshops with developers and healthcare professionals. The results of each evaluation enabled adjustments in the authoring tool, generating improved versions for testing. The last stage of evaluation was the interaction test with healthcare professionals, which is described next.

2 Interaction Test of the SaiteBooker Authoring Tool

The interaction test was carried out to verify the usability and interactivity of the SaiteBooker authoring tool through 19 tasks to be performed by the participants. The tasks were selected based on the results of previous evaluations, and they regard: login and register users; create and rename an e-book project; create and edit pages and texts; copy and paste content; add images and videos; preview the e-book project in different screen sizes (laptop, cell phone and tablet); browse the e-book pages (forward/backwards); unpack files and share the project link.

A simultaneous interview with the interaction test was conducted, followed by a satisfaction questionnaire. The interview made it possible to learn about participants' attitudes when performing the tasks; and to gather their opinions and suggestions to improve the tool. The research dimensions and metrics considered in the interaction testing are shown in Table 1.

Table 1. Dimensions and metrics used for the interaction test.

Dimensions	Metrics
Efficacy	Completion of the tasks
Ease of sue	Expression of doubts
Apparent usability	Activating non-clickable elements
Agreeability	Response to open question
Motivation	Response to open question
Satisfaction	Response to five-point scale
Utility	Response to five-point scale and recommendation to third parties

The results were analyzed qualitatively, however figures were considered in order to identify possible trends in the results.

2.1 Participants, Material and Procedures

A total of 39 health professionals voluntarily took part in the interaction test. The material used were laptops presenting the SaiteBooker authoring tool, printed protocols in A4 sheet for the interview, satisfaction questionnaire and the Free and Informed Consent Term to be signed by the participants. The interaction test was performed individually and in isolation by each participant. While carrying on the 19 tasks, participants were asked questions regarding the tasks in the simultaneous interview. After the interaction test/interview, a satisfaction questionnaire was delivered to the participants. Their responses and reactions were recorded in writing.

3 Results and Discussion

Most participants were female (N = 31), and the main characteristics of their profile (occurrences of responses) were: age range of 26 to 35 years (N = 17); expertise in the field of psychology (N = 10), and experience in the area of health between 5 and 15 years (N = 14).

The results of the task performance indicate that the majority of participants (N = 34) completed the 19 tasks satisfactorily (N = 548 out of 704 completions). In general, the interface of the SaiteBooker tool was positively assessed on the organization and size of its graphic elements, hierarchy, color and simplicity of the layout. Incorrect actions have not occurred during the test, since the system prevented interactions that could lead participants to unwanted paths/actions while performing the tasks. Most of the icons and buttons were easily located on the interface, and their functions were in most cases understood.

As for satisfaction with the SaiteBooker tool, participants' responses were positive about the organization and aesthetic aspects of its graphic interface (N = 20). They also considered the tool interesting (N = 21) and visually enjoyable (N = 20). In general, participants declared themselves very satisfied with the tool, and would recommend the SaiteBooker to other health professionals (N = 19).

However, problems were detected regarding interaction and navigation. A total of 106 attempts to activate non-clickable elements of the interface occurred during interaction with the tool. Doubts about how to carry on some tasks led participants to interrupt the task for not knowing how to proceed (N = 158 task interruptions). As a consequence of these problems, several participants requested the researcher's help to complete the tasks (N = 145 requests). The most difficult tasks were adding images and videos to the pages of the e-book project; copy and paste content from external links; editing text; and return to pages to insert content into the e-book project. The results lead to consider the following aspects as the main causes of the problems found by the participants:

- Excess of actions to use a function
- Inappropriate labels (wording) for icons
- Lack of feedback regarding action completion
- Poor differentiation between clickable and non-clickable elements
- Use of non-familiar graphic representation for icons
- Lack of visibility of functions to edit texts (hidden menu)

An example of the excess of actions to use functions of the tool is the insertion of texts (e.g., headings, captions). For that, participants should click on an icon of the menu and drag it to the editable area of the screen (Fig. 3). These actions were not easily inferred by the participants, and therefore they found inserting texts difficult during the interaction test. The actions of clicking and dragging the icons to add text in a page may have required a greater cognitive effort of the participants. This may be due to inserting text in other text editors (e.g., Word) can be done by just positioning the cursor on the editable area and then click. Moreover, participants could not promptly find the icons for adding and/or editing headings/titles. This was because participants were not acquainted with icons with the letter 'H' to convey these concepts. Thus, they had to search for the labels of the icons to be able to perform the task, what may have required a greater cognitive effort.

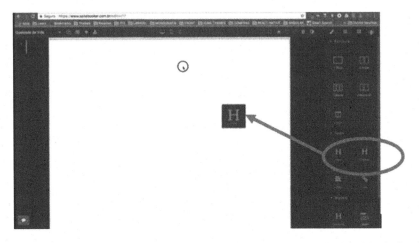

Fig. 3. Inclusion of headings in the page of an e-book by clicking and dragging the icons

Another example of drawbacks in the interaction test of the SaiteBooker regards the lack of visibility of the text editing functions (e.g., alignment, type size) which were in a hidden menu (Fig. 4). To view this menu, participants should pass the mouse over the area next to the inserted text. This was also not easily inferred by the participants, making finding the menu difficult. A possible reason for that could be it is not common for text editing features to be in hidden menus.

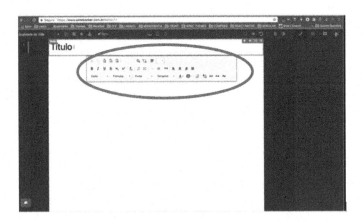

Fig. 4. Hidden menu with text editing features.

Regarding the lack of feedback in action completion, this has particularly affected the task of inserting images and videos in the pages of the e-book project. Participants expressed their doubts about the completion of this task during the interviews, leading to an insecure behavior.

Analyzing the results in light of the literature, the SaiteBooker authoring tool is in line with some principles and recommendations of the literature, but in dissonance with others. The tool met the following principles: constraints to delimit interaction; user control and freedom in interaction and flexibility of use [8]. It is also possible to say that the graphic interface of the SaiteBooker met users' aesthetic expectations and goals, thus, possessing the qualities of being desirable and useful [9]. Nevertheless, the results also indicate that the SaiteBooker tool has not fully met the following principles: visibility (hidden menu), action feedback (insert images/videos), interface consistency (clickable elements) and social signifiers (clues to infer actions) [3, 4]. This may have affected UX regarding the ease of finding the elements of the interface (findable) and the tool usability (usable).

With respect to the online information processing model [5], the results allow to infer that the stages of information need, information seeking (users start a task and users continue the tasks) and information use occurred satisfactorily during the inter-action test. However, with regard 'find and extract information' at the stage of information seeking, cognitive overload and strain may have occurred in the use of the SaiteBooker tool. This seems to be due to the tool's system and interface design have not fully taken into account participants' previous experience with other digital artifacts/systems regarding certain tasks (e.g., text inclusion and editing). This is in dissonance with the principle of 'Match between system and the real world' [8], in which language and concepts of users' repertoire must be employed in the design of digital artifacts and systems.

4 Conclusions and Final Considerations

Although the qualitative nature of the interaction test does not allow generalizations, some conclusions can be drawn based on the results. Overall, the healthcare professionals were satisfied with the SaiteBooker authoring tool and had use it adequately, since the difficulties they encountered regarded certain tasks only. Similarly, in the scope of human information behavior, most participants seem to have processed information satisfactorily, although problems were found at the stage of information seeking.

In terms of UX, the SaiteBooker tool was useful and desirable, despite not fully possessing the extrinsic UX qualities of usable and findable. Since the SaiteBooker was developed by the UNA-SUS/UFMA (Ministry of Health of Brazil), it is possible to conclude that the healthcare professionals would consider it a credible and valuable tool.

The problems identified in the interaction test made it possible to improve the SaiteBooker authoring tool and to propose requirements for future digital projects of UNA-SUS/UFMA. An example of the improvements made is shown in Fig. 5 regarding editing and adding texts in the title page, for that, now users just have to position the cursor directly on the marked fields.

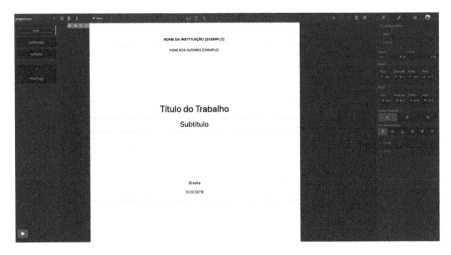

Fig. 5. Improvements made in the graphic interface of the SaiteBooker based upon the outcomes of the interaction testing.

The results of the interaction test aligned with the literature [1, 3, 6, 9, 20] also made it possible to propose recommendations for the design of the graphic interface of authoring tools. Those referring to clickable elements and presentation of the information are shown below:

Recommendations for clickable elements of the interface

1. Clearly identify clickable elements/areas;
2. Signal the links that have just been activated;
3. The icons should be self-explanatory in relation to their function;
4. Maintain consistency in icons/buttons (same icon, same purpose);
5. Use unambiguous terms for icons/buttons' labels;
6. Use icons and buttons familiar to users;
7. Display menus, icons and buttons in the same location.

Recommendations for presenting information

1. Present amount of information adequate to memory retention.
2. Position information logically on the screen, following the order of tasks to be performed.
3. Related information should appear on the same screen and not on different screens connected by links.
4. Present the information on the screen in a concise and graphically simple way.
5. Maintain consistency in the presentation of information.
6. Displays error messages in a different way from the other contents.
7. Present messages of confirmation (feedback) in a different way from the other contents.

Acknowledgement. Thanks are due to the health professionals who voluntarily participated in this study, and to the agencies FAPEMA (Foundation for Research Support and Scientific and Technological Development of Maranhão) and CNPq (National Council for Scientific and Technological Development - Ministry of Science and Technology of Brazil) for funding this research. Special thanks are due to Tiago Serra, Rodrigo Tubelo, Eduardo Zanatta and Patrícia Dias for their valuable contribution in the data collection of the interaction test, which made this article possible.

References

1. Rohrer, C.: When to use which user-experience research methods (2014). https://www.nngroup.com/articles/which-ux-research-methods/
2. Norman, A.D.: Signifiers, not affordances. Interactions **15**(16), 18–19 (2008). https://doi.org/10.1145/1409040.1409044
3. Preece, J., Rogers, Y., Sharp, H.: Design de interação: além da interação humano-computador, 3rd edn. Bookman, Porto Alegre (2013)
4. Gomes, F.C., Varanis, H.H.B., Giusepin, L.M., Oliveira, E.T.: Elementos que influenciam a Experiência do usuário na utilização de web sites. In: Intercom – Sociedade Brasileira de Estudos Interdisciplinares da Comunicação, 38, Rio de Janeiro. Anais, Rio de Janeiro, INTERCOM 2015 (2015). http://docplayer.com.br/2345336-Elementos-que-influenciam-a-experiencia-do-usuario-na-utilizacao-de-web-sites-1.html. Accessed 26 Feb 2019
5. Lonsdale, M.S., Lonsdale, D., Lim, H.W.: The impact of neglecting user-centered information design principles when delivering online information. Cyber security awareness websites as a case study. Inf. Des. J. **24**(2), 151–177 (2018)
6. Pettersson, R.: Research in information design. In: 3rd Information Design International Conference, Curitiba (2007)
7. Huang, J.: How interface elements for page turning in ebooks affect reader preference. Unpublished Master dissertation, The University of Waikato (2017)
8. Nielsen, J.: Enhancing the explanatory power of usability heuristics. In: Proceedings of the ACM CHI 1994 Conference, Boston, MA, 24–28 April, pp. 152–158 (1994)
9. Morville, P.: User experience honeycomb. Intertwingled (2016). https://intertwingled.org/user-experience-honeycomb/. Accessed 26 Feb 2019
10. Wilson, R.: Ebook readers in higher education. Educ. Technol. Soc. **6**(4), 8–17 (2003). ifets.ieee.org/periodical/6_4/3.pdf
11. Cacioppo, J.T., Petty, R.E.: The need for cognition. J. Pers. Soc. Psychol. **42**(1), 116–131 (1982). https://doi.org/10.1037/0022-3514.42.1.116
12. Tetlan, W. L., Marschalek, D.: How Humans process visual information: a focused primer for designing information. Visible Lang. J. (2016). Fall 2016
13. Martin, C., Aitken, J.: Evolving definitions of authorship in Ebook design. Inf. Serv. Use **31**(3–4), 139–146 (2011)
14. Rojeski, M.: User perceptions of ebooks versus print books for class reserves in an academic library. Ref. Serv. Rev. **40**(2), 228–241 (2012). https://doi.org/10.1108/00907321211228291
15. González, J.C., Guzmán, J.L, Dormido, S., Berengel, M.: Development of interactive books for control education. In: Proceedings of the 10th IFAC Symposium Advances in Control Education. The International Federation of Automatic Control, pp. 150–155 (2013)
16. Fojtik, R.: Ebooks and mobile devices in education. Procedia – Soc. Behav. Sci. **182**, 742–745 (2015)

17. Bidarra, J., Natálio, C., Figueiredo, M.: Designing ebook interaction for mobile and contextual learning (2015). researchgate.net/publication/268446567_Designing_eBook_Interaction_for_Mobile_and_Contextual_Learning. Accessed 20 Feb 2019
18. Yalman, M.: Preservice teachers' views about e-book and their levels of use of e-books. Procedia – Soc. Behav. Sci. **176**, 255–262 (2015)
19. Spinillo, C.G., Padovani, S., Smythe, K.C.A.S., Bueno, J., Figueiredo de Oliveira, A.E.: The open university of the unified health system in Brazil (UNA-SUS/UFMA): identification and hierarchization of problems in distance learning courses. In: Marcus, A., Wang, W. (eds.) DUXU 2017. LNCS, vol. 10290, pp. 724–739. Springer, Cham (2017). https://doi.org/10.1007/978-3-319-58640-3_52
20. Marshall, C., Bly, S.: Turning the page on navigation. In: Proceedings of the 5th ACM/IEEE-CS Joint Conference on Digital Libraries, pp. 225–234. ACM (2005)

Digital vs. Hard Copy? A Preliminary Study of Reading Style in Children Using Touch Screen and Paper Books

Maria Uther[1]([✉]), Kirsty Ross[2], Jordan Randell[2], and Rachel Pye[3]

[1] Department of Psychology, University of Wolverhampton, Wulfruna St., Wolverhampton WV1 1LY, UK
m.uther@wlv.ac.uk
[2] Department of Psychology, University of Winchester, Sparkford Rd., Winchester SO22 4NR, UK
[3] Department of Psychology, University of Reading, Educity, Iskandar Puteri, Johor, Malaysia

Abstract. The use of touch screen storybooks for children allows reading to be transformed into an interactive multimedia experience, in which text is augmented by animations, sound effects, and games. The present study is a follow-up to an earlier study [1] which found that touch screen storybooks negatively affected child readers' comprehension but resulted in more emotional engagement. Ross et al.'s earlier study used visual observations to determine the level of emotional engagement. The current study extends those findings to examine the acoustic and prosodic indices of speech whilst children are reading. It was hypothesized that if touch screens were more emotionally engaging, this may express itself in greater pitch variability in the read speech. Also, if reading were more task-focused, then this might express in more careful (and hence more disfluent) paper-based material. Very preliminary analysis on a small selection of speech samples from 5 participants aged 6–7 years in the Ross et al. [1] study show greater pitch range variability with paper-based storybooks as compared to touch-screen interactive versions. On the other hand, there appeared to be less variation in speech and articulation rate in the paper-based books compared to touch screen books. This was also coupled by a tendency for greater overall phonation rate and an increased speech and articulation rate in the paper-based condition, which may reflect a more fluid style for paper-based book reading. Discussion of these preliminary findings focuses on the future lines of enquiry and reflections on children's reading style using different mediums.

Keywords: Reading · Touch screen · Developing readers · Emotional engagement · E-books

1 Introduction

The development of digital technologies has transformed reading practices in current society, with a proliferation of mobile devices (especially tablets) used by children for reading. Of course, e-books offer novel features that paper-based books don't (e.g. facility to include multimedia elements, narration, hyperlinks, etc.). Although these

© Springer Nature Switzerland AG 2019
A. Marcus and W. Wang (Eds.): HCII 2019, LNCS 11585, pp. 495–502, 2019.
https://doi.org/10.1007/978-3-030-23538-3_38

features are potentially useful (e.g. they may deliver content in a way that might embed content in memory more effectively for the user), these features may also at the same time be distracting, particularly for younger users [2].

In essence, research has broadly focused on examining the pros and cons of using e-books in children for reading. Several studies have looked at a range of areas including: word learning/comprehension [3–5], fatigue [6], efficacy with children with disabilities [7], awareness of print/phonological awareness [8, 9], attention and engagement [10], parent interaction [1, 11, 12]. At this point in time, there is no clear consensus on the benefit of e-books vs traditional paper-based books. Indeed, the question is in all likelihood, not a simple one. It is likely that the answers vary on what measures are being examined, what age range the users are, as well as the reading context (e.g. with others or alone) (see [13] for a review of key research questions in the field).

This paper explores one key area that is often overlooked in the field of e-books – that of actual reading fluency and emotional expression in speech when children are reading aloud from different mediums. Much of the research comparing e-books and traditional books has looked at measures of comprehension and recall to examine how children's understanding of story content varies by medium- with e-books that are usually of a passive rather than interactive nature. However, there is still much to learn about how children attend to and engage with stories from different mediums. This can be achieved through microanalysis of children's behaviours and speech. Analysis of speech has been particularly neglected because in many previous studies, the children did not read aloud – they were read to by a researcher (or occasionally their mother), read silently or listened to audio narration.

Examining children's speech whilst reading aloud from different book mediums will tell us much about their engagement with reading material. We know that for example that the pitch range in speech articulated within the English language is critical for marking prosody, which in turn cues the speaker's intent or affect. As an example, within English, a question is often indicated by rising intonation at the end of a sentence. Similarly, emotionally-rich talk from mothers to their infants is marked by exaggerated pitch contours and a larger pitch range compared to talk directed at other speakers (e.g. [14]). Disfluencies (marked by slower speaking or articulation rate) may also be an indicator of whether the speech is more deliberate, and thereby less emotionally engaging and hence more task-oriented. Both of these areas are useful to explore within the context of developing readers, to determine whether their usage of different media is having a demonstrable impact on their reading style which in turn may reflect the level of engagement with the material.

Here we present a preliminary exploration of whether there would be differences in speech/articulation rate as well as pitch range in speech samples read by children from different media. On the issue of engagement, our previous data from video observations [1] and other research [10] would suggest that children engage more with touch-screen books (an interactive variant of the generic e-book). Hence, we expected that there was more pitch variation in our touch screen than paper book reading with children. On the issue of speech/articulation rate, previous research [10, 15] would suggest that e-books are read more slowly compared to paper-books. On this basis, we may also expect that there would be slower rate within the touch-screen version of the books.

2   Methods

The speech samples used in this paper were a subset of the audio clips extracted from video files used in [1]. We have initially only used 5 participants from this sample (all female and aged between 6 and 7 years of age). The scenario of usage and data collection is well described in [1] but in summary, the situation was one of child reading the books with their mother. It should be noted that within this sample, two children were using a highly interactive touch-screen book (The Fantastic Flying Books of Mr. Morris Lessmore) whereas three of the children were using a less interactive touch-screen book (The Prince's Bedtime).

2.1   Speech Editing

The audio stream from the video samples provided from the Ross et al. [1] study were extracted from the video files using an ffmpeg command line utility. Short samples (around 5 s) were chosen semi-randomly with the following constraints: (1) that the sample could not be within the first 20 s of the recording; (2) that the sample was free of background noise or overlapping utterance from the parent and (3) that it contained a complete sentence or phrase. The editing into smaller samples was completed using Audacity software.

2.2   Speech Analysis

The shorter speech utterances were analysed using Praat software. The utterances were transcribed into syllables using Praat TextGrids. Total phonation time was computed by subtracting pauses from total utterance time. Articulation rate was measured using number of syllables/total phonation (in seconds). Similarly, speech rate was measured using number of syllables/total utterance time (in seconds). Pitch range was measured over the entire sample, using recommended pitch settings for children Praat (150–600 Hz).

3   Results

As there was a very small subset of the total sample of the data, results are very preliminary and only trends can be noted at this point, rather than be subject to any statistical analyses. Given the small number in this sample, box plots were deemed the most appropriate to explore data rather than mean graphs which would be more susceptible to outliers. We collapsed across the different book titles due to the small sample size. Within the data below, there are some interesting trends to note.

3.1   Pitch Range

Pitch range was measured over the entire sample. In general, there was a trend for the paper-based book to be more variable in pitch range over the sample compared to the touch-screen medium, although overall pitch range medians were not that disparate (Fig. 1).

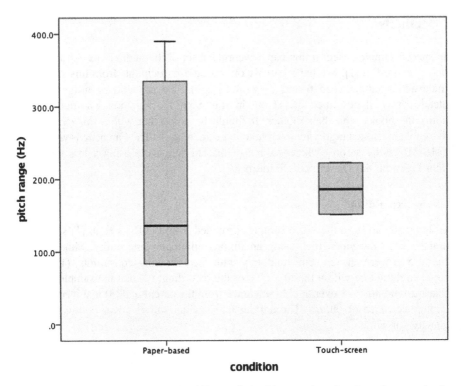

Fig. 1. Pitch range for child speech whilst reading with paper-based and touch-screen books

3.2   Articulation Rate

Articulation rate was measured over the entire sample. There seemed to be a slight increase in overall rates of articulation for paper-based vs touch screen books, although the touch screen book articulation seemed to be more variable (Fig. 2).

3.3   Speech Rate

Speech rate was measured over the entire sample. As for articulation rate, there seemed to be a slight increase in median speech rate for the paper-based books compared to touch-screen, but this was coupled by the observation that the touch screen book speech rate was possibly more variable (Fig. 3).

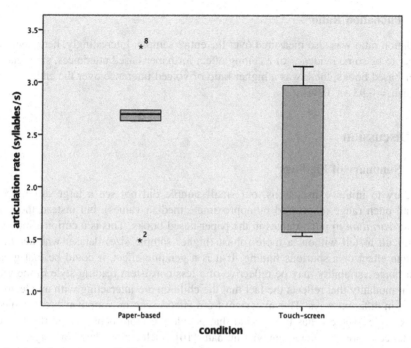

Fig. 2. Articulation rate (syllables per second for phonated utterance) for child speech whilst reading with paper-based and touch-screen books

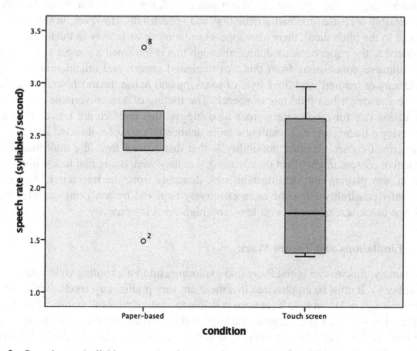

Fig. 3. Speech rate (syllables per second over entire utterance) for child speech whilst reading with paper-based and touch-screen book formats

3.4   Phonation Ratio

Phonation ratio was also measured over the entire sample. Interestingly, here, there did appear to be some evidence of a ceiling effect for paper-based utterances, such that for paper-based books, there was a higher ratio of voiced utterance over the entire sample (median = 0.93 vs. 0.84).

4   Discussion

4.1   Summary of Findings

Contrary to initial expectations, our small sample did not see a large difference in overall pitch range (expressed by approximate median values), but instead there was greater *variation* in pitch ranges in the paper-based books. This is a curious finding. It is difficult to tell without a more robust (higher sample size) dataset whether this a genuine effect or a spurious finding. If it is a genuine effect, it could be that greater pitch range variability may be reflective of a less consistent reading style in the touch screen modality that reflects the fact that the children are interacting with an electronic device in different ways. This may stem from effects seen in computer-directed speech for example, where it has been found that people are more deliberate in their speech register compared to interaction with humans [16]. Such a more deliberate style may be employed by some children and not others, but more robust analysis would be needed to determine whether this is the source of this effect.

Interestingly, when looking at speech and articulation rate, it also looks like there was possibly increased median articulation and speech rate. However, in this case (in contrast to the pitch data), there also appears to be more variability in the touch screen compared to the paper book mediums, although this is too small a sample size to make any definitive conclusions from this. An increased speech and articulation rate may reflect a more 'natural' and fluid style of speaking and hence the touch screen medium may be showing a less fluid rate of speech. The finding of a more variable speech and articulation rate for touch screens may also suggest that children are less consistently employing a fluent style as a result of a more deliberate, computer-directed speech style as described earlier. Another possibility is that distractions from the multimedia and interactive content might affect their reading (i.e. they were doing that task while video content was playing and dealing with task demands from the interactive 'buttons'). This latter possibility might be more effectively explored by analyzing samples from different touch-screen books with low- and high-level interactivity.

4.2   Limitations and Future Work

In summary, this was an initial foray into exploring children's reading style with touch-screenbooks. It must be emphasized that these are very preliminary results, with a small sample size (n = 5) that hasn't yet been possible to analyse with full statistical analyses. Future work will need to be done on the larger dataset to determine whether these trends will hold. It should also be acknowledged that this initial analysis was done on a small selection of short speech samples (5 s approximately) and a more robust approach would include either longer speech samples or a further selection of other utterances from the same speaker at different time points. It should also be noted that our measure of affective engagement here (pitch range) is a rather crude one and that there may be more fruitful avenues of enquiry to look at affect expressed through pitch (e.g. analyzing pitch contours themselves which may be classified by shape as more undulating or flat). Finally, we would need to conduct analyses on a much larger sample size to determine whether there were any differences in the less and highly interactive touchscreen books (the low N in this sample did not allow for any meaningful analysis in this respect). Nonetheless, this is a useful first exploration of the data that encourages us further to explore the vocal indices of reading style within different medium for children.

References

1. Ross, K.M., Pye, R.E., Randell, J.: Reading touch screen storybooks with mothers negatively affects 7-year-old readers' comprehension but enriches emotional engagement. Front. Psychol. **7**, 1728 (2016)
2. Troseth, G.L., Strouse, G.A.: Designing and using digital books for learning: the informative case of young children and video. Int. J. Child-Comput. Interact. **12**, 3–7 (2017)
3. O'Toole, K.J., Kannass, K.N.: Emergent literacy in print and electronic contexts: the influence of book type, narration source, and attention. J. Exp. Child Psychol. **173**, 100–115 (2018)
4. Valentini, A., Ricketts, J., Pye, R.E., Houston-Price, C.: Listening while reading promotes word learning from stories. J. Exp. Child Psychol. **167**, 10–31 (2018)
5. Dore, R.A., et al.: The parent advantage in fostering children's e-book comprehension. Early Child. Res. Q. **44**, 24–33 (2018)
6. Kang, Y.Y., Wang, M.J.J., Lin, R.: Usability evaluation of E-books. Displays **30**(2), 49–52 (2009)
7. Dural, R., Ünal-Logacev, Ö.: Comparison of the computer-aided articulation therapy application with printed material in children with speech sound disorders. Int. J. Pediatr. Otorhinolaryngol. **109**, 89–95 (2018)
8. Shamir, A., Shlafer, I.: E-books effectiveness in promoting phonological awareness and concept about print: a comparison between children at risk for learning disabilities and typically developing kindergarteners. Comput. Educ. **57**, 1989–1997 (2011)
9. Ihmeideh, F.M.: The effect of electronic books on enhancing emergent literacy skills of pre-school children. Comput. Educ. **79**, 40–48 (2014)
10. Richter, A., Courage, M.L.: Comparing electronic and paper storybooks for preschoolers: attention, engagement, and recall. J. Appl. Dev. Psychol. **48**, 92–102 (2017)
11. Krcmar, M., Cingel, D.P.: Parent-child joint reading in traditional and electronic formats. Media Psychol. **17**(3), 262–281 (2014)
12. Rees, K., Nadig, A., Rvachew, S.: Story-related discourse by parent–child dyads: a comparison of typically developing children and children with language impairments. Int. J. Child-Comput. Interact. **12**, 16–23 (2017)
13. Jamshidifarsani, H., Garbaya, S., Lim, T., Blazevic, P., Ritchie, J.M.: Technology-based reading intervention programs for elementary grades: an analytical review. Comput. Educ. **128**, 427–451 (2019)

14. Fernald, A., Simon, T.: Expanded intonation contours in mothers' speech to newborns. Dev. Psychol. **20**(1), 104–113 (1984)
15. Lin, P.-H., Su, Y.-N., Huang, Y.-M.: Evaluating reading fluency behavior via reading rates of elementary school students reading e-books. Comput. Human Behav. 1 (2018)
16. Oviatt, S., MacEachern, M., Levow, G.-A.: Predicting hyperarticulate speech during human-computer error resolution. Speech Commun. **24**(2), 87–110 (1998)

Design for Teaching Surroundings Based on Human-Computer Interaction Techniques

Wei Feng[(⊠)]

Shandong College of Tourism and Hospitality, 3556, East Jingshi Road, Jinan,
Shandong, China
13964076217@163.com

Abstract. Wisdom is far away, whereas Human-Computer Interaction (HCI) is
very close. The thesis derives from the big vision of a vocational teacher.
Education is a great system, and interaction appears here and there all the time,
like Human-Human Interaction and Human-Computer Interaction. With the help
of techniques like H5 Interactive media courseware, Multi-device cross-screen
interaction, 3D sensing human brain recognition technology, Interactive AI
teacher and VR immersion teaching VR, students do not need to enter set
classrooms. A simulated teaching place will do the job. Teachers will gather all
the teaching resources and it helps to break their limitation. It is possible for us
to build up harmonious and efficient teaching surroundings by using advanced
techniques based on Human-Computer Interaction Technique. One teacher can
do little by him/herself, while he/she can expand the way, and share with others
so that everyone has a chance to stand on the shoulders of giants and do the job
better. HCI Technique is just like the giant who offers his shoulder.

Keywords: Human-computer interaction · Design for teaching surroundings ·
Intelligent education

1 Introduction

At the time artificial intelligence (AI) started to be popular, many teachers began to be
anxious for the possibility that AI will take their place. How to break through the
current situation of dull lectures and old teaching methods? How to bring new vigor to
education? As a matter of fact, it is not only crisis of teachers, but also of education.
Traditional teaching mode and staying pat is getting farther from the need of social
development and students' progress. With more active ideas, wider outlook, modern
teachers are serving more qualified students with better digital literacy. Artificial
intelligence does not necessarily replace the teachers' job, but teachers who are skilled
in artificial intelligence can replace those who are not.

The original version of this chapter was revised: The author name was corrected. The correction to
this chapter is available at https://doi.org/10.1007/978-3-030-23538-3_42

© Springer Nature Switzerland AG 2019
A. Marcus and W. Wang (Eds.): HCII 2019, LNCS 11585, pp. 503–513, 2019.
https://doi.org/10.1007/978-3-030-23538-3_39

2   The Necessity of Teaching Environment Design Based on Human-Computer Interaction Technology

Everyone has experienced a good lecture that makes time flies and a bad lecture that kills time. It is a teacher's responsibility to make his/her lecture interesting, no matter how difficult it is. To make education effective and efficient, teachers must face their barrier and make good use all the resources. Only in this way can they get teaching achievements and make their students more concentrated and potential.

Albert Bandura, the famous American contemporary psychologist, has mentioned in his Reciprocal Determinism that behavior, human factors, and environmental factors actually act as determinants of interconnection and interaction.

2.1   Effective Teaching Principles of Teachers

Effective teaching refers to the establishment of a learning collaboration team under the guidance of teachers, allowing students to learn, to explore and to study independently, so as to improve learning effectiveness in a fixed period of time, to complete the established learning objectives of the curriculum, and to promote the overall development of students and the professional growth of teachers. Effective teaching is not only a process of achieving teaching, but also a process of high-qualified and high-efficient learning. It is the sustainable development of both teachers and students. The goal of effective teaching is to develop students' creative thinking. A large number of studies have shown that independent and exploratory learning is effective for developing students' creative thinking. In the process of effective teaching, teachers guide students to change from passive learning to diligent thinking, and gradually learn to cooperate and explore independently. It is necessary to use scientific methods to study the development of teaching. The only indicator to measure effective teaching is the progress of students.

According to Gary D. Borich, a professor at the University of Texas School of Education, of the seven elements of effective teaching, learning atmosphere and classroom activity are related to the teaching environment. Effective classroom teaching, which is one of the most important components of effective teaching, has limited effective teaching in time and space by full preparation, effective organization and scientific training to improve the practical utility, which mainly depends on a good teaching environment. Human-computer interaction technology is currently the best aid for building up a good teaching environment.

2.2   The Impact of Teaching Environment on Students

According to a survey conducted by MyCOS, the overall attendance rate of college students is less than 90%. Even in class, students who watch mobile phones, chat, sleep, and read books also account for a considerable proportion. Inadequate attention in class and initiative in learning have become a problem that must be solved in classroom teaching today. The investigation also shows that more than a half of the students use mobile phones in the classroom, and the proportion of students who regularly use mobile phones in class is higher than 30%. It makes it very difficult for teachers to carry out effective teaching. But when teachers play videos and practice object teaching, the situation will be significantly changed and more students began to focus on the class. The traditional teaching model is obviously difficult to adapt to the needs of the development of the times. In fact, it is not an easy task to rely solely on the student's own willpower to persist in learning. Various factors of the external environment often directly affect the efficiency of student learning. Constructivism Theory Emphasizes the Influence of Learning Environment on Learners' Knowledge Construction. The role of teachers has changed from the traditional transfer of knowledge to the guidance of students' learning. Teachers create situations and interactions between teachers-students and students-students. Developing useful teaching situations is the most important aspect in teaching design. Traditional teachers occupy the dominant position and control the teaching environment. In modern class, students play the major role of creating more active and free learning environment. At the same time, students can make use of various information resources in the environment (such as multimedia courseware, rich materials, literature from multiple sources of information, etc.) and auxiliary tools to achieve their learning goals. In this process, teachers' help and guidance, together with the collaboration and mutual support between students work and complement each other. Teachers should provide students with as comprehensive and rich information resources as possible (including various types of teaching courseware, teaching media and teaching materials), which are mainly used to support students' self-learning and team cooperation exploration.

2.3   A Good Teaching Environment Is a Powerful Guarantee for Effective Teaching

The teaching environment is usually divided into the physical environment of teaching and the psychological environment of teaching. The development of the times makes us pay more attention to the information environment of teaching. Contemporary students grow up in the digital age, and the environment in which they are exposed in is the digital environment. They are more likely to receive digital information than traditional teaching information. Education informatization refers to the use of advanced information technology to improve the quality and efficiency of education in the process of education, and to form a new educational model that meets the requirements of information society. Compared with traditional teaching, the digital teaching environment has richer teaching content, more active teaching process and better learning method. The informatization teaching mode is a self-exploration and interactive teaching mode, students play as the main body and teachers as the assistant. The classroom is the most direct interaction between teachers and students with thoughtful design and better experience, and it helps to grasp the heart of the students and achieve the best teaching result.

3 Human-Computer Interaction Technology and Education

Human-computer interaction technology has wide applications in somatosensory, artificial intelligence, simulation environment and so on. The purpose is to "make the machine know you better" and a better user experience. Traditional teachers-oriented classroom has obvious limitations like fixed teaching methods and teaching content that are not flexible enough to adapt to the changes of the times, the result is students lack practical and exploratory learning situations, which is not conducive to the creative thinking of students. Human-computer interaction technology can make up for these defects well.

At present, smart cities, smart homes, and unmanned vehicles have become the hotspots in the field of human-computer interaction, while it is rarely seen in integrated application to the education industry. As an important factor to the development of a country, education should share and participate in the wave of technology by making the students completely realize the power of high technology. Although not everyone has the ability to develop technology, you can use current digital technology to use AI as a powerful tool for learning and work growth. In fact, education is a better field of human-computer interaction learning and application than other industries. From Pearson to DuoLingo, we can see they are trying to use adaptive learning to design personalized learning services for students. Many companies in the education industry have begun to use this technology. These companies have helped us redefine "learning" and spread more advanced ideas whether for human beings or machines.

The essence of human-computer interaction technology is to improve the quality of life and serve the people, the core feature is user-centric that is committed to improving the "user experience"; the essence of education is people-oriented, the purpose is to obtain ability to promote personal development; modern education is based on students, teachers' job is to guide students to learn independently, and to cultivate individualized talents needed in the society. The idea of human-computer interaction technology is completely consistent with the concept of "cultivation" of education. To do something well, it is necessary to use good tools and techniques. Rational application of human-computer interaction technology in the field of education can improve the quality of education for effective teaching, extending unlimited teaching possibilities in a limited educational environment and making education more advanced, more efficient, and rejuvenating. Human-computer interaction technology and intelligent education are very suitable combinations.

China AI industry research report (2018) indicates that artificial intelligence has been integrated in education of teaching, learning and evaluation. It covers multiple artificial intelligence technologies such as self-adaption, voice recognition, computer vision, natural language processing, translating machine, learning machine, etc. and multi-function like class scheduling, scoring, evaluation and so on. Artificial intelligence is creating a smarter and more efficient and personalized learning environment that serves lifelong learning.

4 Design for Teaching Environment Based on Human-Computer Interaction Technology

The purpose of teaching environment design is to enable the students/end-users to obtain a better learning experience and stimulate learning initiative in teaching process, the purpose of which is to improve learning efficiency and fulfill the established learning objectives. Facing a new generation of learners and "network aborigines" who are surrounded by information technology and are more active in thinking and possess a broader vision, ways like comprehensive usage of a variety of human-computer interaction technologies, the development of a new teaching model based on human-computer interaction technology in the Internet era and design a teaching environment more in line with the characteristics of contemporary students can better solve the problems of education and teaching under the impact of artificial intelligence.

4.1 Principles of Designing Teaching Environment Based on Human-Computer Interaction Technology

The design of interactive teaching environment should be simple, well-arranged, clear-oriented, and easy to implement. Here are some principles to follow.

Combination of Physical Environment and Psychological Environment. The teaching environment is usually divided into the physical environment of teaching and the psychological environment of teaching. Physical environment is the external cause of students' learning motivation, while psychological environment is the internal cause of students' learning motivation. They complement each other and work together. If physical environment is regarded as the interface of human-computer interaction and interaction between people in the teaching process, teachers and students will be regarded as users. The user-friendly interface is good, and the viscosity is high, which directly affects the effects of teaching process. Well-designed physical environment will virtually relieve the external pressure of teachers, the result is more energy can be used to pay attention to the student's reaction and guidance/correction and greater help will be obtained in creating a harmonious teaching psychological environment.

Combination of Theoretical Teaching and Situational Teaching. Multi-subjects knowledge systems are divided into two parts: theoretical knowledge and practical operation, the proportions they account for in the system are different. Therefore, both should be considered when designing the teaching environment, that is to say, designers should not only pay attention to the study of theoretical knowledge, but also the situational design of practical teaching. Extinct immersive experience technologies, such as VR and AR, are ideal match to environmental design in practical teaching.

Combination of Traditional Teaching with Modern Teaching. Traditional teaching is systematic and rigorous, teachers act as the main body; modern teaching pays more attention to information-based teaching, which is more flexible and takes students as the main body. Both have their own advantages and cannot simply negate or support either side. In the design of the teaching environment, the proportion should be rationally distributed according to the characteristics and stages of the curriculum and make the best of both worlds.

4.2 Design Conception of Teaching Environment for Human-Computer Interaction Technology

For a long time, or even until today, teachers and students communicate through traditional blackboards, PPT and verbal language. Some universities in China, the United States, South Korea and Japan made some surveys recently and found there is basically no intelligent teaching that is applied systematically. Some schools implement mobile terminal applications such as attendance check and classroom evaluation, all of which need independent app or web platform account login methods. The functions are relatively simple and not related to each other, the truth is, multiple functions did not form a systematic application. The new technology cannot be systematically and timely applied in and promote to teaching in schools. Main reasons are: the technology is not mature enough, the support is not ideal, and the cost is high; conservative teachers are afraid to face new technologies and great changes in teaching, multiple functions are not properly designed and integrated, all these reasons lead to difficulties in wide application.

At present, 5G network technology, with wider coverage and faster transmission speed than the current 4G network, has matured and gradually taken into commercial use. Larger connection applications such as VR/AR, smart city and smart home become possible. The human-computer interaction technology is developing increasingly, the cost is reduced in a large scale, the technology and the use environment are improved, and the relevant application interfaces developed are friendly and easy to use. All of these lead to a result that wider and easier human-computer interaction technology will be put into use soon. A well-designed, well-planned, and integrated AI technology can be set into the teaching system and create a scientific teaching environment. The communication between teachers and students will be changed from traditional verbal languages, blackboards and PPT to human-computer interaction technology. The artificial intelligence will be transited with human-computer interaction as the core aspect and wisdom teaching will be realized (Fig. 1).

Lecture Preparation, Rhythm Control of Class, and Student-Oriented Teaching Activities. Teachers create class models, input student information and make related tools like PPTs, teaching videos, tests, questionnaires and other related teaching resources based on mobile terminals, and upload an interactive teaching platform database for students to review in advance, all these are supposed to be finished on Html5, the interactive media platform. With teachers' invitation, students are allowed to enter the corresponding online classroom. Hence a basic human-computer interactive teaching environment is built. Students log in to the classroom through the mobile terminal or PC and use face recognition technology to pass teachers' license certification to achieve attendance and effectively avoid absenteeism. At the same time, the attendance data is automatically put in the background database to complete the attendance module data collection, and relevant reports can be generated for teachers to refer to. In the process of teaching, multi-screen interactive technology is used to

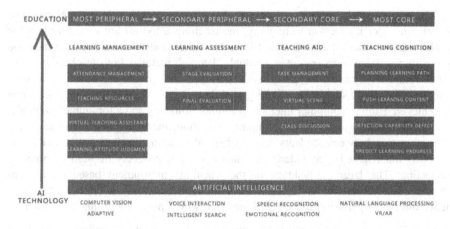

Fig. 1. Education and AI applications (Source: iResearch)

realize the three-screen display of mobile terminals, PCs and teaching large screens. The interactive teaching platform uses the forms of discussion, voting, and classroom testing to guide the teaching process and activate the classroom atmosphere. The results of the mission are publicly displayed on the spot to promote students' thinking. Virtual teaching assistants will answer questions and communicate with students after class. The virtual teaching assistants are online all the time and can communicate in a chat mode, or chat with the help of voice recognition. They can also learn and self-educated through interacting with the students and even perfect their own knowledge base, even more, they collect and analyze the highly frequent feedback of the students, and help the teachers to perfect the teaching system and realize the in-depth teaching (Fig. 2).

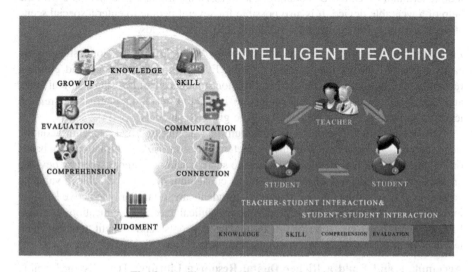

Fig. 2. Intelligent teaching (Source: Author)

The essence of the teaching process is also a serving process. In the application of human-computer interaction technology, the teaching activities are specialized. If the teaching environment is regarded as a large human-computer interaction interface, the user will not be an independent individual. "People" includes both teachers and students. With friendly interface, good user experience, and smooth and effective teaching activities, the user's stickiness will be greatly improved and good teaching results can be achieved. Human-computer interaction should ultimately serve for human-to-human interaction. While using human-computer interaction, the interaction between people (the interaction between students and teachers, the interaction between students and students) must also be considered to ensure smooth progress of human-computer interaction. The largest advantage of the teaching environment based on human-computer interaction technology is interactive experience, and the effect of the experience directly depends on the level of teachers, which needs more qualified teachers.

Human-Computer Interaction Technology to Create Realistic Teaching Scenes. Most real facilities and equipment used in practical teaching are expensive, not flexible, and hard to be updated in a timely manner. If VR and other technologies are used to construct virtual reality scenes for practical teaching, human-computer interaction can realize the interaction between people and the environment, and the situation is similar to that in real working place, which can greatly save money and integrate with reality.

Technologies like VR and AR are currently mainly used in the area of movies and television shows, games, architectures, etc., and are not widely used in teaching practice. In fact, VR and AR technology and many other teaching practice scenarios like mechanical manufacturing, environmental art, architectural design and tourism-related simulation hotels, simulated attractions, simulated aircraft cabins, etc. can be very well matched with real training situation. It is not difficult to publish to a PC or mobile terminal by Unity3D modeling, and to assist the immersive experience with the help of a wearable device. It is also possible for several people to enter a special scene at the same time. Related equipment surely needs some funds.

Pay Attention to Learning Status and Promote Active Learning. Some students are easily distracted during the learning process. Eye tracking technology and emotion recognition technology can be used to monitor students' learning status in real time, and give feedback to teachers through the interactive teaching platform to remind teachers so that reasonable guidance will be given to students.

Try to make good use of AI as a medium of teaching and make teaching context richer and more diversified. With the characteristics of massive information data based on AI, teachers can use the cloud platform to share teaching methods, thereby develop and perfect more contexts of teaching, adjust curriculum design, and achieve valuable education of both rationality and sensibility. Students are led not only to active learning knowledge in the process of advanced and technical means of education, but also broaden their horizons, develop ideas, update concepts, and benefit together with teachers from the advanced technologies and tools.

Accumulate and Build a Richer Digital Resource Library. The existing learning resources lack in-depth analysis of students and the design of learning content is dull.

There is no targeted knowledge sharing or sharing platform. Students are not interested which lead to poor learning results. To establish and enrich the library of teaching resources, we do need an abundant supply of teaching resources, and also, the resources from users/students are also needed. Students are both learners of knowledge and creators and promoters of knowledge. In the teaching process, teachers should guide them to master the knowledge and innovate, and update the learning resources in real time. In the process of teacher-student interaction and student-student interaction, Try to form a digital teaching resource library that is growing and suitable for students. There are several measures to take, like constantly improving the knowledge system, establishing a valuable relationship system between teaching objectives, teaching content and teaching environment.... The first step is to build and optimize the learning content model. Try to establish a knowledge model so that students can find the content that suits them more conveniently and accurately. The second step is to achieve adaptive learning. Utilize human-computer interaction technology to collect data through the students' daily learning process, intelligently derive their future performance, recommend the most needed learning content for them, and finally improve the learning effect efficiently and clearly. By data analysis, the system recommends appropriate learning methods and learning content for students, long-term learning information are provided, and a personalized growth model for students are established to help students achieve lifelong learning.

Improve Comprehensive Assessment and Improve Learning Initiative. Assessment is the last part of the learning process. It is not only testing the level of students, but also testing the teaching effect of teachers. Tests are usually divided into process testing, final testing of the discipline, and comprehensive proficiency testing according to the stage of study. The way of testing can be divided into objective test and subjective test. For teachers, it is a very difficult task, heavy and cumbersome. Objective testing of knowledge is the most difficult one. Testing is repetitive work that is boring and consumes a lot of teachers' energy.

At present, machine review has already been used in objective testing, such as multi-disciplinary computer test system. Teachers can use the H5 interactive media platform to collect data for process testing and final test design. Students can not only test their mastery of subject knowledge at any time, but the system can also automatically create a student's wrong question base based on the test results, and strengthen the practice of error-prone knowledge points. Teachers can also use human-computer interaction related technologies to interact with students, to test, collect and analyze results in real time, and activate classroom atmosphere. The system records each student's assessment each time. At the end of the semester, individualized test papers will be automatically generated for each student's learning situation, and assessed separately to break the unscientific situation of the same test papers.

It is difficult to achieve automatic review by technology in subjective testing because of the creative and personalized content. However, speech recognition and semantic analysis technology make machine scoring possible. For uncomplicated semantic statements, the machine can automatically identify and judge, and even assist the teacher to propose revisions, which will greatly reduce the burden on teachers and improve the teaching efficiency of teachers.

Knowledge learning has a life cycle from analyzing the key points and difficulties of the course to establishing a personalized learning model for each student, and, to the testing and final testing process in the study, and then, the consolidating the knowledge completion course, in which the teacher is in a guiding position. Teachers can make full use of students' dependence on smart mobile terminals to design learning activities such as upgrading and customs clearance, just like playing games. There are personal efforts and teamwork in the learning activities, the whole process has success and disappointment, rewards and punishment. Learning assessment covers the entire learning process.

4.3   Do What You Can and Build a Throughout Personalized Model

With advanced technologies such as cloud computing, big data and human-computer interaction, the system will create a growth file for each student, from the time of admission to the student's entire learning process. Try to establish a student's growth big data based on student's learning experience, each test score and each activity record in the school. Through systematic scientific analysis, students' interactive growth models are formed and every data about the student is clear, like the advantages and disadvantages of students' knowledge, ability, personality, and subject preferences, etc. The purpose is to provide the students with guiding advice to help students develop their advantages, avoid disadvantages, and further improve teaching and learning. The individualization, precision and effectiveness of learning make students realize that future can be expected, and it will stimulate students' internal motivation, constantly improve themselves to grow up into a valuable person (Fig. 3).

Fig. 3. Build personalized model (Source: Author)

In the construction of an interactive teaching environment should be done according to the situation of the school. Technology is getting more and more mature and the cost is falling. The way of adding economic pressure on students is not advisable.

5 Conclusion

In the era of smooth network access and human-computer interaction technology, it is not difficult to over the education crisis. As a development designer and guide for teaching activities, teachers are acting irreplaceable social attributes. As long as the scientific teaching methods and modern educational techniques are used reasonably and effectively, the teaching environment is designed reasonably, and the teaching process is scientifically guided, students can truly become the main body of learning and master the initiative of learning and benefit from it.

Mei Yiqi, former president of Tsinghua University once mentioned: A university is famous and successful not because of high buildings, it is because of great masters. Now we can say a good university is based on both high buildings and great masters, this is because high building represents the hardware and techniques we need to provide HCI, smart classroom and smart campus, the result is students can learn in a smarter way.

In the end, Human-computer Interaction would grow and turn into no interaction. The best user experience is no experience.

References

1. Ye, C.: Interactive study of future classrooms. China Inf. Techn. Educ. **11**, 80–84 (2012)
2. Sweet little life: what is the core of effective teaching? [EB/OL]. https://baijiahao.baidu.com/s?id=15777821163197146. Accessed 06 Sept 2017
3. Wang, Y.: How to improve the efficiency of classroom teaching. Educ. Art **01**, 42 (2014)
4. Yang, X.: The connotation of classroom teaching environment from the perspective of ecological philosophy. Teach. Manag. **03**, 6–9 (2012)
5. Wang, Z.: Theoretical Study on Constructivism Teaching Model and College Students' Innovative Ability. Xi'an Technological University, Xi'an (2006)
6. CCW: 2018 China artificial intelligence industry research report [EB/OL]. http://www.ccw.com.cn/tank/2018-06-19/2266.html. Accessed 19 June 2018
7. Sohu: 2018 education industry blue book [EB/OL]. http://www.sohu.com/a/277953114_660587. Accessed 26 Nov 2018
8. Deng, T., Fu, W.: Design of project teaching network collaborative platform based on "witkey model". Educ. Teach. Forum **03**, 97–98 (2014)
9. Li, H.: Research on Interactive Platform Construction of Teacher's Wisdom Learning. Southwest University, Chongqing (2016)

Research on the Influence of Situational Teaching Mode on Online Learning Experience

Yimeng Xu and Linong Dai[✉]

School of Design, Shanghai Jiao Tong University, Shanghai, China
eamon_xu@163.com, Lndai@126.com

Abstract. With the development of economy and technology, acquiring knowledge through online learning platforms has become the main choice of more and more users. But the popularity of online learning has gradually highlighted the problem of the poor online learning experience. However, many successful teaching models of traditional offline education such as situational teaching provide a reference basis for improving the online learning experience. In this paper, the comparative experiment method is adopted to conclude that the situational teaching model has a positive impact on online learning experience, and the factor analysis method is adopted to analyze the influence of situational teaching model on the factors of the online learning experience.

Keywords: Online education · Situational teaching · User experience · Factor analysis

1 Background

In the current digital age, the structure of people's developmental needs and the way they acquire knowledge have changed greatly. With the rapid growth of per capita disposable income, the structure of residents' needs has changed. The proportion of basic demand for basic survival needs such as eating and wearing has decreased, while the proportion of development-oriented needs, such as education, culture, and entertainment, has increased significantly. In 2018, the added value of cultural industries in the United States and some other developed countries accounted for more than 10% of GDP.

In addition, the way of acquiring knowledge is also changing from offline to online gradually. Obtaining information through online education has become an important way to acquire knowledge. And the usage rate of the online education platform for Chinese Internet users reached 19.2% in 2017 [1]. The data shows that 55.7% of the current users of online education platforms are workplace newbie (18–25 years old), and only 2.5% are students under 18 years old [2]. It can be seen that online education is not the exclusive way of higher education. More and more users choose to study through online education platforms, among which users aged 18 to 25 are the main users. In the era of information explosion, people's absorption of information increases dramatically, but in the face of such a large amount of information, the human mindset

A. Marcus and W. Wang (Eds.): HCII 2019, LNCS 11585, pp. 514–527, 2019.
https://doi.org/10.1007/978-3-030-23538-3_40

is far from being able to adapt in time, resulting in a series of self-compulsion and tension, which is easy to produce knowledge anxiety.

As an industry with such rapid development momentum, the user experience of online education platform is worrying nowadays. According to the 38th national statistical report on Internet development released by China Internet network information center, only 38% of users think that the current experience of online education platform is satisfactory [3]. Therefore, it is of great significance to explore multiple education models to improve the learning experience and learning effect of online education platform.

Traditional offline education has many successful models and can be the source of online education attempts, such as situational education model. As early as 1989, Allan Collins and Paul Duguid published a famous paper " Situated cognition and the culture of learning", which systematically discussed the theory of situational cognition and learning theory [4].

2 Literature Review

2.1 Situational Theory Research

Definition of Situational. From 1930s to 1960s, situational teaching model was established and developed by British applied linguists [5]. In 1983, Van Dijk proposed the concept of situational model. The idea is that when people have enough time and sufficient motivation to learn, a three-layer representation structure will be formed in their brain: surface code based on text words, text-based representation and situational model. Surface code is the analysis of text, and text-based representation is the semantic relationship between words and phrases. The situational model is the psychological micro world formed by the interaction between the basic representation of the text and the background knowledge of the reader [6]. However, most of the online learning materials or teaching materials are texts woven by words and symbols [7]. The addition of situational teaching can better help users deepen their understanding of knowledge and improve the learning emotional experience.

Situation Building. Situational teaching is a teaching method that, on the basis of traditional learning materials, purposefully introduces or creates vivid and specific scenes with certain emotional colors and images as the subject, so as to arouse students' subjective participation, thus helping students understand the textbook and developing students' psychological functions [8].

The core way of situational teaching is to develop the content of teaching by simulating the actual environment. Its core is to construct the situation. If you classify from the perspective of creating situational factors in teaching, the situations that trigger feelings, including vision and hearing, are regarded to be situational teaching. The purpose is to arouse students' experiential cognition of specific knowledge.

Situational Offline Teaching Mode. Situational education has been widely used in traditional higher education and offline education in various disciplines and fields.

Taking language learning as an example, PACE teaching model is a new foreign language teaching model proposed by American scholars Adair-Hauck and Donato in 2002 when they studied French teaching [9, 10]. This teaching method that focuses on both rules and meanings is called "story-based teaching method". The core of its implementation is to integrate knowledge points into the story context, and the learning materials must be interesting, situational and practical [11].

Interesting: it can attract learners' attention and interest in learning. Under the guidance of interesting language materials, learners can actively create vivid and familiar language situations so as to meaningfully construct their own knowledge.

Situational: it can help to stimulate the learner's imagination with certain plots and provide certain scenarios so that they can still recall the content of the material for a long time after contact.

Practical: include core knowledge, highlight key points, and make it easy to understand. Learning materials can be situational stories or poems.

2.2 Theoretical Research on Online Learning Experience

Meaning of Online Learning Experiences. Online learning experience includes learning effect and learner satisfaction. Eom et al. [12] found that learner satisfaction is an important predictor of learning outcomes in the study of structural equation model learning of an online course by 397 American learners [12]. Therefore, improving learners' satisfaction is of great significance for improving online learning experience.

Professor Wilson, Prosser, and Trigwell have empirically analyzed the relationship between learning environment and students' learning style. There are two learning styles for students: shallow learning style and deep learning style. The research shows that the better the students' perception is, the deep learning mode is used by the students; otherwise, the shallow learning mode is adopted by the students. Deep learning has been described by Prosser and Trigwell (1999) as a way to truly stimulating students' curiosity for knowledge and enable them to achieve better learning outcomes.

Measurement of Online Learning Experience. In measuring the learning experience of students, the CEQ questionnaire of Australia is the most authoritative and credible one. Since its inception, CEQ questionnaire has been applied to the research on the quality of higher education in many western countries such as Australia, Canada and Ireland. The Australian government uses CEQ test results to evaluate the teaching quality of universities and takes it as an important basis for university ranking [13–15]. However, Gu Zhixin found in his 2018 study that this questionnaire can also be used to test the experience of online learning and is included in 8 dimensions [16]. According to the ranking of the influence weight from big to small on online learning experience, they are "basic skills", "learning resources", "clear goals", "learning tasks and assessments", "quality teaching", "inspiring intelligence", "student learning support" and "learning community".

In addition, emotion is a better measure of learning perception. In Han Yusi's research, it is found that positive emotions can positively predict learning perception, while negative emotions can negatively predict learning perception. In the process of learning, users with positive emotions will take positive actions to actively cooperate with teaching activities, while users with negative emotions are prone to passive resistance, and it is easy to form a vicious circle of negative attitudes. Users with a negative attitude will think negatively about the problem. When they think they will fail, they will form a self-abandoned attitude and even give up before making any attempt [17]. Therefore, it is of great significance to enhance positive emotions and reduce negative emotions in the process of learning to improve learning perception.

The PANAS scale of positive and negative emotions is the most widely used method for measuring positive and negative emotions [18]. PANAS is a psychological measurement scale proposed by David Watson, Lee Anna Clark and Auke Tellegen in 1988. The scale is based on two systems in which positive emotions and negative emotions are relatively independent, and it has 20 5-point questions [19]. They are: Interested, Distressed, Excited, Upset, Strong, Guilty, Scared, Hostile, Enthusiastic, Proud, Irritable, Alert, crazy, Inspired, Nervous, Attentive, Jittery, Active, and Afraid.

3   Research Methods

3.1   Research Purposes

By simulating the comparative experiment of situational online education, the user's learning perception and learning effects are evaluated to explore the impact of situational teaching mode on the online learning experience. In addition, a questionnaire on learning experience factors was issued to obtain the influence degree of situational teaching mode on various factors of online learning experience. Finally, according to the conclusion of the influence of situational teaching mode on online learning experience, optimization suggestions and development opinions for future online education products are put forward.

3.2   Research Significance

Theoretical Significance. For the education industry, the online education model is conducive to balancing educational resources, lowering the threshold of access to education and improving the education link. The introduction of situational teaching can help improve the user experience of online learning. The research on the weight of each influence factor is helpful to guide the application mode of situational teaching method in online education.

Practical Significance. Situational teaching mode is more likely to arouse learners' emotional engagement and improve their understanding of knowledge and application scenarios. While maintaining the flexibility of time and space of online education, it also improves the learning experience of users.

3.3   Research Hypothesis

- Hypothesis 1: Online learning with the situational teaching mode is beneficial to alleviate negative emotions in the learning process;

- Hypothesis 2: Online learning with the situational teaching mode is conducive to improving positive emotions in the learning process;
- Hypothesis 3: Online learning with the situational teaching mode is conducive to the mastery of learning tasks;
- Hypothesis 4: Online learning with the situational teaching mode is conducive to improving learning experience;

3.4   Research Process

The research process is shown in Fig. 1, which is divided into two stages. In the first phase, a comparative experiment was used to verify that situational education mode was conducive to improving online learning experience, and in the second phase, factor analysis method was used to analyze the influence weight of situational education mode on various influencing factors of online learning experience by issuing questionnaires.

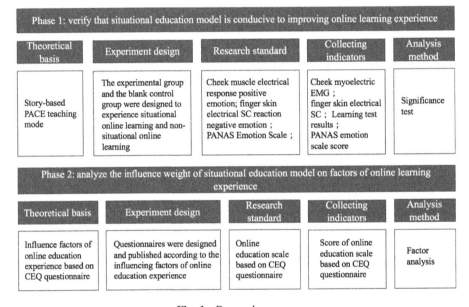

Fig. 1.   Research process

3.5   Experimental Design

Phase 1 Experimental Design. As the experiment in the first phase is a control experiment, it is necessary to exclude the influence of users' own knowledge, so German words are selected as the learning content of the experiment. It is only necessary to ensure that the user has no relevant learning experience to eliminate the impact of the user's own knowledge reserve. In the setting experiment, the story-based PACE teaching mode is the theoretical basis, which is a commonly used one in situational teaching. The variable is whether to add a fun and life-story background to the knowledge point. The experimental example is shown in Table 1. The cases in the table are in English and the German version is used in the actual experiment.

Table 1. Phase 1 experimental example

	Learning content	Example
Experimental group	one word + one related story	Audlt+One out of every seven German adults carries a plush toy with them when they travel.
Blank group	one word	Audlt

Phase 2 Experimental Design. The experiment in the second phase is questionnaire survey and factor analysis, which is used to get the influence weight of "general online education" and " situational online education" on each influence factor of online learning experience. According to the CEQ online learning version, the Likert scale questionnaire is set and issued. The specific filling logic is to first let users feel two different forms of online education modes, the experimental group and the control group. The specific experience content is the same as that in the phase I experiment, and then fill in the scale as shown in Table 2 (take the "basic skills" factor as an example in the table).

Table 2. Phase 2 experimental example

Factor	Question	Scale				
Basic skills	Exercised my ability to solve problems	1	2	3	4	5
	Enable me to solve unfamiliar problems	1	2	3	4	5
	Exercised my practical operation ability	1	2	3	4	5
	Exercised my ability to analyze problems	1	2	3	4	5

Instruction for scale filling: option 1 indicates that the learning model of the control group is more consistent with the description, and option 5 indicates that the learning model of the experimental group is more consistent with the description

3.6   Experimental Tools and Processes

Experiment Equipment. A Psytech-10 multi-channel physiological instrument, myoelectric sensor, skin electrical sensor, BioTrace+ software.

Measurement Standard. Positive/negative emotion index: the positive/negative emotion index is calculated according to the score of positive/negative emotion in the PANAS scale. According to the design principles of the scale, questions 1, 3, 5, 9, 10, 12, 14, 16, 17 and 19 are entitled positive emotion system, and the rest are negative emotion system.

Positive/negative emotion index: the positive/negative emotion index is calculated according to the score of positive/negative emotion in the PANAS scale. According to the design principles of the scale, questions 1, 3, 5, 9, 10, 12, 14, 16, 17 and 19 are entitled positive emotion system, and the rest are negative emotion system.

EMG index: EMG value of the myoelectric is often used to measure positive emotions. When positive emotions rise, the corresponding EMG value of cheeks will rise.

Paired sample T-test: T-test is a commonly used test method to determine whether there are significant differences between two samples. In this experiment, paired sample T-test is used to determine whether there are significant differences between samples since the data of the experimental group and the control group were obtained by the same user. When P is less than 0.05, there is a significant difference between the two paired samples.

Accuracy of German test: after learning a group of German words in the experiment, the user will complete the German word test and select the corresponding Chinese definition according to the given word. The accuracy of German test can be obtained according to the user's choice.

Reliability analysis: Reliability analysis is an analytical method for judging whether the quality of research data is credible. This experiment uses the Cronbach α reliability coefficient; if the value is higher than 0.8, the reliability is high; if the value is between 0.7 and 0.8, the reliability is good; if the value is between 0.6 and 0.7, then The reliability is acceptable; if the value is less than 0.6, the reliability is not good.

Validity analysis: validity analysis is a method used to analyze the design rationality of quantitative data (especially attitude scale questions). KMO value was used as the analysis index in this experiment. If the value is higher than 0.8, the validity is high. If the value is between 0.7 and 0.8, the validity is good. If the value is between 0.6 and 0.7, the validity is acceptable; if the value is less than 0.6, the validity is poor.

Factor analysis: factor analysis is an analysis method to extract common factors from variables. In this study, eight factors affecting online learning experience have been obtained according to CEQ online learning version scale, and the influence of situational teaching mode on each factor can be judged by factor analysis.

Experiment Process. The experimental process is shown in Fig. 2.

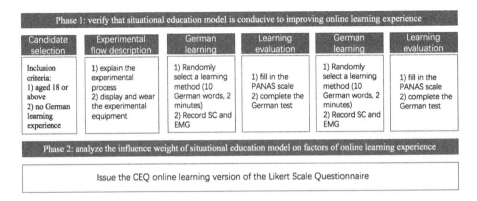

Fig. 2. Experimental process

4 Research Conclusions

4.1 Experimental Overview

In the phase 1 experiment, a total of 26 effective subjects participated in the experiment and completed the German learning, word test and emotion scale. The participants included 13 males and 13 females, aged 18–25 years, met the major user groups of online education at the current stage. The Cronbach α value of the PANAS scale was 0.823 > 0.8, and the KMO value was 0.777 > 0.7. Therefore, the reliability and efficiency of the PANAS emotional scale were good, which could be used for further analysis.

In the phase 2 experiment, a total of 78 valid users filled out the CEQ online learning version questionnaire. There were 38 women and 40 men, aged 18–25 years, which met the main user groups of online education at this stage. The reliability coefficient Cronbach α value of the scale is 0.955 > 0.8, and the KMO value is 0.883 > 0.8. Therefore, the reliability and validity of this questionnaire survey are extremely high and can be used for further analysis.

4.2 Experimental Conclusions

- In the process of online learning, negative emotions gradually decline while positive emotions are relatively stable with upward fluctuations.

In the German learning process of the phase I experiment, SC indexes in both the experimental group and the control group showed a declining trend with the increase of learning time. The cheek EMG index, which represents positive emotion, is relatively stable and accompanied by upward fluctuation, as shown in Fig. 3.

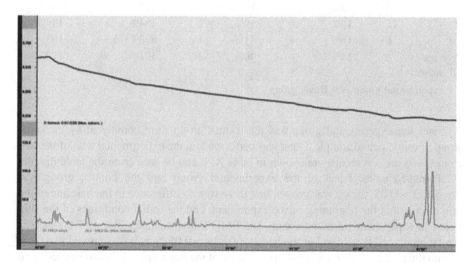

Fig. 3. Trend diagram of SC and EMG in the experiment (the top is the SC, and the bottom is the EMG)

- Online learning in a situational teaching model is conducive to improving the online learning experience, which has a significant impact on reducing negative emotions.

The previous 10 sample data are shown in Table 3. The calculation of the skin electrical decline is the reduction of the skin electrical mean value during the experimental period compared with the baseline value of the skin electrical at the beginning of the experiment. The increase in myoelectric was calculated as the increase in the mean value of myoelectric during the experiment compared to the baseline value of myoelectric at the beginning of the experiment. As can be seen from the table, in the process of learning, both the experimental group and the control group showed a decrease in skin electrical and an increase in myoelectric. However, the decrease of skin electrical in the experimental group was greater than that in the control group, and the increase of cheek myoelectric in the experimental group was greater than that in the control group. It can be seen that situational teaching mode is conducive to reducing negative emotions and improving positive emotions in the process of online learning. Therefore, situational teaching model is conducive to improving online learning experience.

Table 3. Experimental data of SC and EMG

Number	E-SC baseline	E-SC reduction	B-SC baseline	B-SC reduction	E-EMG baseline	E-EMG growth	B-EMG baseline	B-EMG growth
1	5	9%	4	5%	3	124%	3	70%
2	3	14%	3	7%	1	72%	1	103%
3	4	13%	5	16%	2	186%	3	87%
4	10	17%	7	17%	2	150%	2	326%
5	13	10%	15	11%	3	73%	2	94%
6	2	5%	2	7%	3	822%	2	724%
7	5	16%	5	14%	3	105%	3	249%
8	17	13%	13	14%	2	137%	1	124%
9	16	13%	18	19%	2	154%	2	189%
10	6	16%	4	1%	4	838%	3	103%
Average of all samples	6	14%	6	10%	3	191%	3	172%

E = experimental group B = Blank group

Since the experimental group and the control group were completed by the same group of users, paired sample T-test was performed on the experimental data of the two groups, and the test results are shown in table X. It can be seen from the table that the SC Paired-Samples T-test of the experimental group and the control group had $P = 0.673 > 0.05$, thus it was proved that there was no difference in the baseline of the skin electrical at the beginning of the experiment, and the initial conditions of the skin electrical experiment were consistent; The EMG Paired-Samples T-test of the experimental group and the control group had $P = 0.879 > 0.05$, thus it was proved that there was no difference in the baseline of myoelectric at the beginning of the experiment, and the initial conditions of the myoelectric experiment were consistent;

In the test of skin electrical decline and myoelectric increase, the skin electrical decline had P = 0.005 < 0.05, and the myoelectric increase had P = 0.629 > 0.05. Therefore, there was a significant difference in the reduction of the SC between the two groups during the learning process, but no significant difference in the increase of cheek EMG (see Table 4). Thus, it can be concluded that online learning under the situational teaching mode has a significant impact on reducing negative emotions in the learning process.

Table 4. Paired-Samples T-test results of SC and EMG

Paired-Samples T-test results			
Project	Pairing (mean ± standard deviation)		
	Pair 1	Pair 2	P
E-SC baseline pair B-SC baseline	6.00 ± 4.37	5.87 ± 4.45	0.673
E-SC reduction pair B-SC reduction	0.14 ± 0.09	0.10 ± 0.06	0.005*
E-EMG baseline pair B-EMG baseline	2.71 ± 1.36	2.69 ± 1.62	0.879
E-EMG growth pair B-EMG growth	1.91 ± 2.07	1.72 ± 1.50	0.629

* p < 0.05 E = experimental group B = Blank group

In order to verify the above conclusions, the PANAS scale filled by users in the two groups of experiments was analyzed in the same way. The first 10 data samples are also selected as examples, as shown in Table 5. As can be seen from the table, after the completion of online learning, the positive emotion index of the experimental group was higher than that of the control group, while the negative emotion index of the experimental group was lower than that of the control group, which was consistent with the experimental data. It also indicates that situational teaching mode is conducive to improving online learning experience.

Table 5. PANAS scale score

Number	B-Positive emotion score	E-Positive emotion score	B-Negative emotion score	E-Negative emotion score
1	24	29	32	14
2	25	26	22	16
3	25	27	18	16
4	30	32	19	11
5	23	25	12	11
6	24	31	15	16
7	21	30	22	17
8	34	32	21	15
9	29	41	20	15
10	39	33	18	13
Average of all samples	30.88	32.52	22.4	15.76

E = experimental group B = Blank group

Paired-samples T-test was also conducted on the positive emotion index and negative emotion index of users in PANAS scale (see Table 6). It can be seen from the table that the positive emotion index P = 0.242 > 0.05 and the negative emotion index P = 0.000 < 0.05 in the two groups. Therefore, it is also proved that online learning under the situational teaching mode has a significant impact on reducing negative emotions in the learning process.

Table 6. Paired-Samples T-test results of PANAS scale score

Paired-Samples T-test results			
Project	Pairing (mean ± standard deviation)		
	Pair 1	Pair 2	P
E-Positive emotion score pair B-Positive emotion score	30.88 ± 5.61	32.52 ± 7.50	0.242
E-Negative emotion score pair B-Negative emotion score	22.40 ± 7.66	15.76 ± 4.77	0.000*

* p < 0.05 E = experimental group B = Blank group

- There is no significant effect of online learning in the situational teaching mode on the mastery of learning tasks.

For the two groups of users, German word test was conducted after learning, as shown in Table 7. As can be seen from the table, the accuracy of the experimental group was higher than that of the control group, but P = 0.233 > 0.05. Therefore, online learning in the context teaching mode had no significant influence on the mastery of learning tasks.

Table 7. Accuracy of German test

	Blank group correct rate	Experimental group correct rate
Average correct rate of all samples	88%	93%
pairT	0.233 > 0.05	

- The situational teaching model improves the online learning experience in five dimensions: "learning community", "quality teaching", "learning tasks and assessment", "basic skills" and "inspiring intelligence".

After allowing users to try the online education of traditional mode and situational mode, they fill in the online education version scale of CEQ and choose which learning mode they prefer. The factor ordering obtained is shown in Table 8. The greater the variance contribution rate is, the greater the difference in user experience between the traditional mode and the situational mode under the factor dimension will be. When the average value is greater than 3, the user experience advantage under this factor is situational teaching. When the average value is less than 3, the user experience advantage under this factor is traditional teaching.

The overall mean value of the scale is greater than 3, indicating that the online learning experience of situational teaching mode is better than that of traditional teaching mode. In addition, situational teaching mode in the "learning community" "quality education", "learning tasks and assessments" "basic skills" and "inspiring intelligence" compared with the traditional teaching mode in five dimensions, improving the online learning experience, the degree of ascension from big to small, and in the "clear goals", "student learning support" and "learning resources" three dimensions of learning experience is not as good as the traditional teaching mode.

Table 8. Factor contribution rate of questionnaire

Factor contribution rate				
Factor ordering	Factor name	Factor contribution rate%	Mean	Advantage side
1	Clear goals (Clearly understand the direction and purpose of learning)	17.407	2.404	Traditional teaching
2	Learning community (Convenient communication with others during study)	14.801	3.321	Situational teaching
3	Quality teaching (Teaching content is clear and interesting, motivating learning)	14.439	3.162	Situational teaching
4	Student learning support (Easy access to learning resources)	13.434	2.654	Traditional teaching
5	Learning tasks and assessments (Easy to understand and master learning content)	12.627	3.444	Situational teaching
6	Basic skills (Improve problem-solving skills)	12.248	3.058	Situational teaching
7	Inspiring intelligence (Teaching content stimulates interest and enlightens intelligence)	10.822	3.436	Situational teaching
8	Learning resources (Rich and clear learning content)	4.222	2.872	Traditional teaching

5 Discussion

Good learning perception can improve learning effect, while good learning perception includes the weakening of negative emotions and the enhancement of positive emotions. In the experiment, it was found that the situational teaching model had significant significance in weakening negative emotions, but had no significant significance in improving positive emotions and learning outcomes, which might be related to the sample size of the experiment and the difficulty of learning tasks. However, from the perspective of overall impact, situational teaching mode has a positive impact on the experience of online learning.

In the existing theoretical research mentioned above, it is known that "basic skills", "learning resources", "clear objectives", "learning tasks and assessment", "quality teaching", " inspiring intelligence", "student learning support" and "learning community" are the eight factors that affect the user's online learning experience and the degree of influence is from large to small. Among them, the second, third and seventh influencing factors are the poor performance of situational teaching mode. If situational online teaching mode needs to be developed, it needs to be optimized for the online educational environment in these three dimensions.

6   Conclusion

Online learning under the situational teaching mode is beneficial to enhance the learning experience under the five dimensions of "learning community", "quality teaching", "learning tasks and assessments", "basic skills" and "inspiring intelligence"; So situational teaching mode in the "Convenient communication with others during study". "Teaching content is clear and interesting, motivating learning" "Easy to understand and master learning content" "Improve problem solving skills" and "Teaching content stimulates interest and enlightens intelligence" five aspects compared with traditional teaching mode can give online education better user experience.

In addition, compared with traditional teaching mode, online learning under situational teaching mode can significantly weaken negative emotions in the learning process, which is conducive to improving learning experience. However, the situational model has an impact on the improvement of positive emotions in the learning process and the mastery of learning tasks, but has no significance.

References

1. Wu, S.: Online education has made its mark in China. Chin. Bus. **z1**, 26–28 (2017)
2. User Behavior Study Online Education Sector. http://www.sohu.com/a/199875090_386633. Accessed 24 Oct 2017
3. Yang, Y.L.: Inspiring new posture of "Knowledge Crossing the Year". Xinjiang Daily **007**, 01–04 (2018)
4. Brown, J.S., Collins, A., Duguid, P.: Situated cognition and the culture of learning. Educ. Res. **18**, 32–42 (1989)
5. Shan, L.: Application of scene teaching in art teaching in junior high school. Emot. Read. **12**, 24 (2017)
6. Van Dijk, T.A., Kintsch, W.: Strategies of Discourse Comprehension. Academic Press, New York (1983)
7. Wu, G.: On the development of situational education in China and its theoretical implications. Educ. Res. **39**(07), 31–40 (2018)
8. Li, Z.Z.: Inspiring thoughts with emotion and environment. Chin. Teach. Res. **8**, 69 (2018)

9. Adair-Hauck, B., Donato, R.: The PACE model: a story-based approach to meaning and form for standards-based language learning. French Rev. **76**(2), 265–276 (2002)
10. Adair-Hauck, B., Donato, R.: The PACE model-actualizing the standards through storytelling: "Le Bras, la Jambe et le Ventre". French Rev. **76**(2), 278–296 (2002)
11. Zhu, T.Y.: Exploration of High School English Reading Teaching Based on PACE Teaching Model – A Case Study of Reading Teaching in Oxford High School English Module 5 Unit 1. Reference for Middle School Teaching, Yilin, Jiangsu Province (2017)
12. Eom, S.B., Wen, H.J., Ashill, N.: The determinants of students' perceived learning outcomes and satisfaction in university online education: an empirical investigation. Decis. Sci. J. Innov. Educ. **4**(2), 215–235 (2006)
13. Hirschberg, J., Lye, J.: The influence of student experiences on post-graduation surveys. Assess. Eval. High. Educ. **41**(2), 265–285 (2016)
14. Kreber, C.: The relationship between students' course perception and their approaches to studying in undergraduate science courses: a Canadian experience. High. Educ. Res. Dev. **22**(1), 57–75 (2003)
15. Byrne, M., Flood, B.: Assessing the teaching quality of accounting programmes: an evaluation of the course experience questionnaire. Assess. Eval. High. Educ. **28**(2), 135–145 (2003)
16. Gu, Z.X.: Study on the learning experience of online open courses for higher vocational students based on CEQ Questionnaire—Taking Nanjing Tourism Vocational College as an Example. Dist. Educ. China 1–10 (2018)
17. Zhao, H.: Reflections and countermeasures on negative attitudes of English learning in higher vocational students. J. Huaibei Vocat.Tech. Coll. 5 (2017)
18. Gong, S.Y., Han, Y.S., Wang, L.X., Gao, L., Xiong, J.M.: Relationship between task value and academic emotion and network learning satisfaction. J. Electrotech. Educ. **37**(03), 72–77 (2016)
19. Watson, D., Clark, L.A., Tellegen, A.: Development and validation of brief measures of positive and negative affect: the PANAS scales. J. Pers. Soc. Psychol. **54**(6), 1063–1070 (1988)

Designing an Artificial Intelligence Platform to Assist Undergraduate in Art and Design to Develop a Personal Learning Plans

DanDan Yu[✉], MuRong Ding, WenJing Li, Limin Wang,
and Bin Liang

Art and Design Academy, Beijing City University, Beijing, China
diane_yu@139.com

Abstract. This paper presents the initiative design research for developing a platform based on artificial intelligence technology. Though the platform, the students can be assisted to develop a personal learning plan and register for the courses they need. Follow the blooming of information technology; Artificial Intelligence begins to intervene deeply into different industries in China. Change people's life and work in considerable ways. In order to cultivate talents that adapt to the new type of social structure, the university continues to reform and innovative in the cultivation and teaching mode. In this paper, we put the emphasis on the introduction of personalized learning plan development and the learning information service system. The information service model will create new learning mode and opportunities to constructing students' knowledge structure. We design a learning information service platform for undergraduate. Though the platform, the student can be assisted to develop own learning plan based on own interest and career path. The AI system will recommend courses plan and schedule. In addition, the system can estimate the knowledge points required and time spent by different learning routes. The learning information service platform based on AI system and the new learning mode is showed as examples, and hope to provide a new framework for the further innovation in higher education model.

Keywords: Information service platform · Learning mode · Artificial intelligence · Higher education model

1 Introduction

Revolution of education goes together with technology development and the transformation of production relations, and is always motivated by promoting Teaching & Learning Intelligent Recognition Technology, Learner Tracing Technology, as well as Artificial Intelligence Technologies based on individualized learning process. In recent years, the prosperity of the new generation Artificial Intelligence and the application of 'Artificial-Intelligence Plus' teaching method have revealed an upcoming area for education that features individualized learning experience, visualized learning process, integrated learning assessment, and socially-oriented study, in which new personnel

A. Marcus and W. Wang (Eds.): HCII 2019, LNCS 11585, pp. 528–538, 2019.
https://doi.org/10.1007/978-3-030-23538-3_41

training model and frame can be developed on the strength of big-data technology and education big-data analysis.

As suggested by Design Education in 2013, until November 2012 a total of 1,917 institutions of higher education in 31 provinces, cities and autonomous regions of China had offered design-related education and over 574,000 students got enrolled, among whom over 303,000 were undergraduates. According to the latest statistics, in 2018 the number of institutions has risen to 1,928 where 8,208 relevant majors are available among which 4,670 are opened in general undergraduate colleges and universities. As the number of students majoring in art and design has boosted dramatically, it is expectable that more occupations are needed for those graduates, although not all of them will engage in major-related jobs. 'The essence of education is not teaching fact, theories or principles... not even to turn students into professionals. It is rather to broaden students' horizon and inspire and enlighten them even by overturning stereotypes', said Robert M Hutchins, the former principal of the University of Chicago. Therefore, the undergraduate Art Design education, whether its management or teaching mode, should focus on how to present students with a 'bigger picture', a diversified and flexible learning platform, open and tolerant environment, thus to contribute to their sustainable and overall development. As a result, the current uniform training mode can no longer work any more. The students should choose their own learning path according to their personal career development plan.

The Artificial Intelligence Market in the US Education Sector 2017-2021 report suggests that experts expect AI in education to grow by '47.50% during the period 2017–2021.' This program is aimed to establish a platform with artificial intelligence and big-data analysis where study guides are accessible for Art Design students— learning statistics extracted from individuals are analyzed so as to provide study suggestions in accordance with students' future career plan by which certain qualities are demanded, thereby to minimize the barriers between different fields and help students make their own study plans from a more general perspective.

2 Research Context and Concepts

While the fruit of information era, information technological revolution is changing people's production mode and life style in a profound manner. During the 40-year information age, we told computers what to do. With advances in artificial intelligence, particularly machine learning, and faster processing chips we can feed computers giant data sets and they can draw some inferences on their own. The rise of code that learns marks the beginning of a new era of augmented intelligence. It's a great opportunity for us to expand access to a great education and for students to make a big contribution. Individualized training towards Art Design students has become both a great challenge and a requirement for institutions of higher education that are eager to keep pace with the times.

2.1   Current Art Design Education in China

Nowadays in China, it is possible to study Art Design in approximately 2,000 colleges and universities where generations of smart and creative designers have been cultivated, which is somewhat reflective of the burgeoning design education. While the traditional Bauhaus teaching mode is obviously impossible to adopt any more considering the annual increase of the number of Art Design students, volume and uniform training can be more detrimental to the future development of individuals, in which sense it is in the long run both urgent and beneficial to inspect and make adjustment to the current education mode.

2.2   Current Training Mode

In China, the traditional way to training Art Design students was mainly derived from the Bauhaus teaching system—students, whether majoring in Design or not, have to take courses in conformity to the training program already fixed. In recent years however, institutions of higher education have done some change to allow free choice of courses in the first year regardless of any barriers, so that students can choose what they are really interest in as their major in the second year when the real professional training begins. Provided undergraduate Art Design education is however not only to cultivate applied talents proficient in craftsmanship, which is somewhat less than satisfactory, but to breed creative talents with broader view, the secret of success at this stage is then to encourage philosophic thinking, self-enrichment, and self-exploration rather than to impart knowledge. Even for those who do not engage in design after graduation, which will benefit them for the whole life.

2.3   Problems with Student Training

Among 638 graduates chosen randomly from those of applied universities and colleges majoring in Art Design, 45.6% engaged in professional counterparts; even for them only 19.1% appeared interested in their occupations but showed a proportion of 95.2% satisfaction towards the training given in universities. For those whose job is neither relevant to their major nor attractive for themselves, the satisfaction rate reached 61.8% [1]. As a result, the learning objectives of and enthusiasm about undergraduate education can exert a direct impact on study quality and result, although the undergraduate education mode in China has not achieved a combination between major with interest, or career planning with teaching.

Therefore, to decide where to go in the future, one has to take overall development, interest, and industry development into account, hereby to make study plans and reasonable arrange for the course order and study direction of each step (Fig. 1).

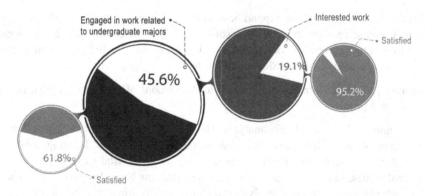

Fig. 1. Student satisfaction survey

3 Design Framework and Process

To re-understand what part education plays at every stage of one's life is of great importance in this Artificial Intelligence era. Education is never just about knowledge accumulation, but is to encourage self-recognition and world-exploration, thus to inspire students to positively, automatically and consistently acquire knowledge, to make decisions and solve problems innovatively when encountered with them, and to keep their taste, view, and thought in pace with the time. That is just the direction in which undergraduates should be cultivated.

Based on Artificial Intelligence technology, big data and perceptive technology, our Undergraduate Learning Platform is aimed to present new teaching method for individuals whose information has gone through full analysis. While the relationship between students, teachers and education administrators get redefined, the whole education process, a service provision system in other words, can be knowledgeable, visible and controllable, which should do help to students who want to know their capacities, strengths and shortcomings, and desire an individualized teaching plan and unique learning experience after learning about what they really want in the future.

We efforts to meet individual students' needs. Students' learning objectives, pace, and content are likely to vary to a greater extent. The idea behind AI platform is that personalized instructional approaches and strategies will improve student outcomes in the short term (e.g., stronger rates of growth in achievement) and in the long term (e.g., successful completion of a postsecondary degree or successful transition into a career).

3.1 Personalize Educational Path for Students

AI platform can deliver slightly different versions of the curriculum based on data that has been collected from their past performance on tests, quizzes, and other school work. A study conducted by Rand Corporation confirms that such personalized learning indeed improves the individual performance. Students, who followed custom lessons plans performed by 3 percentile points above the median in maths and reading, when compared to peers who were taught based on standard curriculum.

Of course, this concept can expand beyond the classroom. Artificial intelligence can even help create recommendations for students as they select classes, even choose universities. The personalization of the learning experience is indeed the first great ongoing transformation of the educational system.

1. Learner profiles maintain a rich and up-to-date record of student strengths, needs, goals, and progress.

Highlight student's academic analysis. Thanks to big data, it has become possible for universities and colleges to collect information about students' learning condition from multiple channels and various perspectives, which is vital to develop positive vocational values. In that way, teachers can know students better by tracing the history left of web platform (can be reflective of students' study attitude, professionality, and interest) or via the interaction between the two parties, so as to realize the shortcomings of students more accurately and adjust teaching methods, or exercise intervention and surveillance.

2. Personal learning paths provide appropriate and meaningful choices of course for each student to work on, with the necessary teacher supports.

Highlight individual experience. Career planning education based on big data can present students with an objective and just assessment and analysis of subjective and objective conditions, and of the balance between strengths and drawbacks, which should guide them to set feasible career goals suitable in this era and further arrange their learning path.

3. Competency-based progression enables these personalized paths to run their natural course.

By conducting a comparative analysis over personal capacity and goal competence, students' concentration can be directed to where lies their interest, so as to naturalize their learning path.

4. Flexible learning environments enable schools to allocate resources in new ways to best support these processes.

Highlight individualized teaching. Development of students' professionality and individualized teaching mode, rather than to impart knowledge, is the core to talent cultivation. Besides, the application of Internet has freed education from the limits imposed by time and space. Hence, online teaching platform is increasingly helpful to both teachers and students by providing massive teaching resources and rendering it possible to analyze students' performance, which is the basis for doing individualized teaching.

3.2   Learning Model

We hope that in the future students will have an AI lifelong learning companion. Essentially, this next generation of students will grow up with an AI companion that knows their personal history and school history. Therefore, it will know each student's individual strengths and weaknesses.

Our learning model is mainly comprised of three parts [2].

1. Students' personal information.

A student's online learning history can be reflective of his/her knowledge base, capacity indicators, interest and hobbies, as well as study habit.

2. Career information.

To analyze those engaging in a certain design-related field with big data, including their ability distribution, character strengths, social groups, learning path, and career planning.

3. Course platform.

To analyze the nature, knowledge objectives and ability goals of those courses in universities and colleges, besides which previous teaching content and practice, key and difficult points thereof as well as students' evaluation and comments are also accessible.

It is for students to set their own career goals based on what they like or what they want to fight for in the future. At the next stage the features of relevant occupation can be contrasted with personal information to present an overall analysis of knowledge structure and ability structure, and be matched with university courses to calculate a learning path. During the whole period of undergraduate study, students are allowed to adjust their learning path according to the changes of their interest or experience.

About the AI learning service Platform, the set of expectations and standards that students, teachers and staff follow in school.

- Motivated: students are self-driven, goal-oriented, exceeding expectations.
- Accountable: students are accountable for their own behaviors and actions.
- Knowledgeable: students learn and collaborate with peers and teachers.
- Encouraging: students inspire others through discussion and collaborative work.
- Respectful: students respect staff, community partners, peers and learning spaces.

Artificial Intelligence Learning Platform may clarify students' ability and characteristics, thus advice them about future career requirement, adjustment to expectation, and how to make learning path. By doing so, it would be easier for them to adapt to the society, face challenge, and make appropriate choice about their future plans (Fig. 2).

3.3 Design Touch-Point of AI Learning Service Platform

Our platform [3] is centered on students and their stakeholders. Information about students' learning process that is designed by 5 touchpoints contributes to the set of career goal and making of learning path at the next stage, hereby to enhance study efficiency, and present an individualized, flexible, and enjoyable learning experience. Those five touchpoints are as follows (Fig. 3):

1. Self-understanding [4]: Students via the platform can learn about their ability and habit. Before the professional undergraduate training, the system will conduct a full analysis about the student's sociability, expression ability, logic, imaginary thinking ability, practical competence, management competence, hobbies and skills based on all

Fig. 2. The information service model

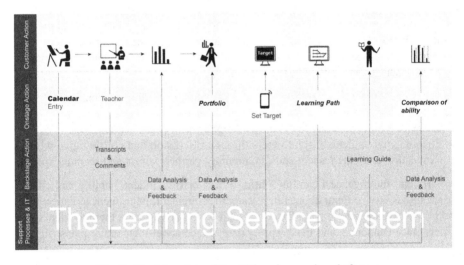

Fig. 3. The blueprints of the AI learning service platform

their training record and transcript, such as the drawing training, chess training, the scores of his/her mathematics and physics examinations in high school, all the prizes in contests, comments from teachers and so on. As comprehends as it is, students can form a better understanding about themselves. During the whole period of undergraduate study, our system will analyze students' professional competence according to their performance in the exams, such as basic modeling ability, design theory application and critical thinking, drawing performance, software application, design expression, design innovation, group communication, and project organization competence. In addition, the system will get students' learning style based on date for homework submission, an duration to complete the homework, and how to search materials and the scope of searching (Fig. 4).

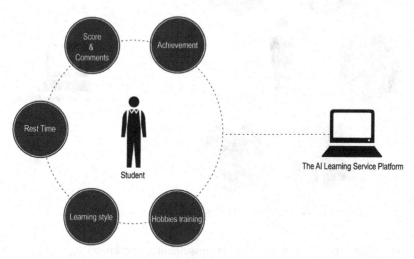

Fig. 4. The data collection model of students

2. Self-planning: A scientific and feasible career planning is the first step to success, which is the reason why a large number of institutions of higher education are opening relevant courses or holding public lectures about it; even so, the majority of Art Design undergraduates have not, however, got aware of what career planning really means. In that sense, our platform may deal partly with that problem by analyzing the competence of those engaging in that field and forming up their career development path. To take Design for Digital Media BA for instance, students can get a full understanding about that major by extracting the result from the platform. Good visual designers are usually between 22 to 28 years old, for whom what really matters is basic modeling ability, software application capability and design expression competence. Differently, product managers between 26 and 35, excellent in group communication, design innovation, and project organization are more likely to get highly recognized. Further, there generally exist two career development paths for product managers, which are visual designer—interaction designer—product manager, or web-developer—project manager —product manager. To summarize users are allowed to choose their own career goals or plan career development path based on their interest and enough information [5] (Fig. 5).

3. Self-learning: By making comparison between students' personal ability and their career goals [6], our platform will further propose suggestions about how to perfect the knowledge structure and practice structure, how to adjust directions and the meaning of each competence indicator. Moreover, the database will, taking into account the content, competence structure, and teachers of each course in that semester, recommend several learning paths for students. Every path has its own features, and

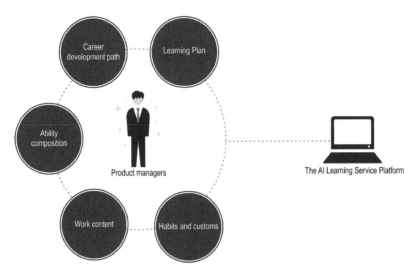

Fig. 5. The data collection model of target position

may differs with the other in duration, professionality, and knowledge scope, so that students may feel free to choose. When it comes to a clash between course arrangement, or a particular course is inaccessible due to special reasons, out-university courses or even E-courses may work to supplement knowledge gap and practice, thus to guarantee the completion of undergraduate study roughly in conformity with the learning path [7] (Fig. 6).

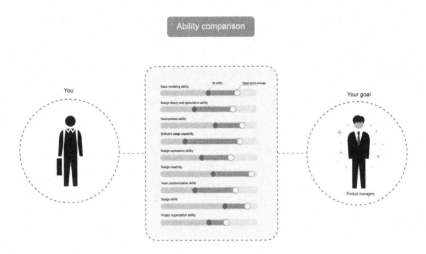

Fig. 6. The UI of ability comparison

4. Study guide: If you ask our students what classes they are taking and the meaning of taking those course, they might be confused, even for those who are about

to graduate. Generally speaking, to understand the position and importance of each course before putting our hands on it is of great significance, for that will improve study efficiency and enthusiasm, as well as inspire targeted learning. On that point, our platform not only points out the objectives and position of each course, but also assist to figure out the key and difficult points according to the individual learning path, thus to help students with finding out their targets. Students' performance can also get reflected on the score distribution. The accumulation of score will visualize the intangible competence indicators, hereby making it possible to observe one's progress and get a sense of achievement (Fig. 7).

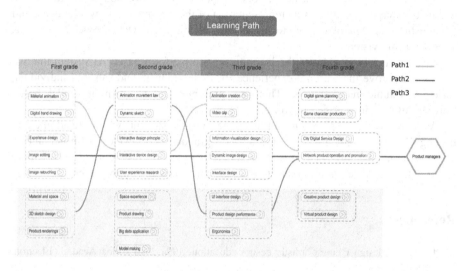

Fig. 7. The UI of the learning path

5. Teaching Aids: Big Data technology can play a role in supporting the complexity of the personalization process. When properly supported by teachers, it can help students learn independently and work at their own pace. Technology can also enable educators to take a more personalized approach in their teaching efforts and other activities they undertake to support student learning and development.

Artificial Intelligence era is an era when students' personal will gets fully respected, especially their free right to choose. Although the automatic request of students is predominant, teachers' guidance and help is still necessary. 'To let go students in this world saturated with information is never the best way; teachers are obliged to lead the way, tell them how to learn, and be supportive', said Tony Comper, the CEO of the Bank of Montreal. If teachers familiarize themselves with the situation of students before class, they would be able to adjust the teaching plan and reset the key and difficult points. Of course, individualized suggestion and support can also be achieved in that way.

4   Conclusion and Future Work

To change the passive talent cultivation mode in China is, in light of the long periodicity to breed talents, not only to reform the way in which higher education is conducted, but also to reform from a comprehensive perspective how the recipients live– from infancy and preschool period to undergraduate study period and even their whole life—a delicate and detailed design is all the way needed. Art Design needs education, and education needs design more.

AI can reshape education with its potential to impact educational policy on local, national, and international scale. In our proposed work, we sought to identify a framework that is complete in its representation of the information flow, elements, and relationships and generic enough to support to education. The Data Service Model was a result of this vision.

And we shortly introduced the learning service platform based AI system that we design to improve the learning experience for undergraduate and satisfied individual, variety, dynamic requirements. Then we presented future learning model based learning information service platform.

As future work, our plan is to follow up the study on students who were admitted to Beijing City University in 2018, and also on graduates to develop a further understanding about the influence of undergraduate learning on different stages of future career. Their feedback is important to plan the directions for improvements.

References

1. Li, W.: Redesign Chinese artistic design education. 1994-2018 China Acad. J. Electron. Publ. House
2. Xu, Y.: Path exploration from "artificial intelligence education" to "education artificial intelligence". Intell. Lead Wisdom Educ. **383** (2018)
3. Li, H., Wang, W.: Intelligent adaptive learning model supported by artificial intelligence. Intell. Lead Wisdom Educ. (2018)
4. Liang, S., Lai, J.H.: Exploration of university discipline construction in the period of AI + education. Mod. Comput. (12), 25 (2018)
5. Yu, S.Q.: The future roles of AI teacher. Open Educ. Res. **24**(1) (2018)
6. Chu, J.L., Krzyżak, A.: Analysis of feature maps selection in supervised learning using convolutional neural networks. In: Sokolova, M., van Beek, P. (eds.) AI 2014. LNCS (LNAI), vol. 8436, pp. 59–70. Springer, Cham (2014). https://doi.org/10.1007/978-3-319-06483-3_6
7. Zhou, H., Zhang, H., Zhou, Y., Wang, X., Li, W.: An online multi-agent competitive platform for AI education. In: Proceedings of the 23rd Annual ACM Conference on Innovation and Technology in Computer Science Education, July 2018
8. Neller, T.W.: AI education: open-access education resources on AI. AI Matters, **3**(1) (2017)
9. Wu, J.: ArtilectEra. China CITIC Press, August 2016
10. Tegmark, M.: Life 3.0: being human in the age of artificial intelligence. Penguin, July 2018

Correction to: Design for Teaching Surroundings Based on Human-Computer Interaction Techniques

Wei Feng

Correction to:
Chapter "Design for Teaching Surroundings Based
on Human-Computer Interaction Techniques"
in: A. Marcus and W. Wang (Eds.):
Design, User Experience, and Usability, **LNCS 11585,**
https://doi.org/10.1007/978-3-030-23538-3_39

The book was inadvertently published with an incorrect version of an author's name in Chapter 39 as "Feng Wei" whereas it should have been "Wei Feng". This has been corrected in the corresponding chapter accordingly.

The updated version of this chapter can be found at
https://doi.org/10.1007/978-3-030-23538-3_39

© Springer Nature Switzerland AG 2019
A. Marcus and W. Wang (Eds.): HCII 2019, LNCS 11585, p. C1, 2019.
https://doi.org/10.1007/978-3-030-23538-3_42

Author Index

Printed in the United States
By Bookmasters